NELSON EDITION

SCIENCE PROBE 8

British Columbia is perhaps the most varied of the Canadian provinces. Climate ranges from the relatively mild, even weather of the coastal islands to the extremes of the northern interior. The land rises from the sea to the mountains, and the environment ranges from rain forest to desert. All of this provides homes for the huge range of animals and plants that live in B.C. The cover shows a small, related part of that range: some of the organisms that share B.C.'s mountains.

On the cover is a bighorn sheep ram (Wendy Shattil/Bob Rozinski/ Tom Stack & Associates). In the small inset is a mountain flower (Jim Brandenburg/Minden Pictures). The background is an alpine meadow (The Stock Library).

SI Metric

NELSON EDITION

SCIENCE PROBE 8

Author Team
Frank Baumann
Jean Bullard
Donna Deschner
Nancy Flood
Gordon Gore
Eric S. Grace
Alan J. Hirsch
Barry McCammon
Gerry Sieben
W. A. Vliegenthart
Mary Kay Winter

Pedagogical Consultant
Sandy M. Wohl

Nelson Canada

I(T)P An International Thomson Publishing Company

Toronto • Albany • Bonn • Boston • Cincinnati • Detroit • London • Madrid • Melbourne • Mexico City • New York
Pacific Grove • Paris • San Francisco • Singapore • Tokyo • Washington

Science Probe 8 Project Team

Nelson Edition

Executive Editor: David Steele

Project Coordinator: Colin Bisset

Supervising Editor: Cecilia Chan

Proofreaders: Kate Baltais, Harold Otto

Art Director: Liz Nyman

Designer: Katharine Lapins

Assistant Designers: Suzanne Peden, Arlene Edgar, Gail Ng-A-Kien

Illustrators: Helen Marioncu, Sara Jane English, Kathryn Adams, Kam Yu, Visutronx, Helen Fox, Donna Guilfoyle/Art Plus Limited, Dorothy Siemens, Jane Whitney, Selwyn Simon

Photo Researchers: Vicki Hunter, Ann Ludbrook

Contributing Writer: Rosemary Tanner

Safety Consultant: Margaret Redway, Fraser Science Awareness Incorporated

Second Edition

Project Manager: Nancy Flight

Developmental Editors: Nancy Flight, Anne Norman, John F. Ricker, Barbara Tomlin, Yvonne Van Ruskenveld

Consulting Editor: Wilson Durward

Copy Editors: Anne Norman, Claudette Reed Upton

Proofreaders: Anne Norman, Barbara Tomlin

Indexer: Claudette Reed Upton

Contributing Writers: Vivien Bowers, Wilson Durward

I(T)P™
International Thomson Publishing
The ITP logo is a trademark under licence

Published in 1995 by
Nelson Canada
A division of Thomson Canada Limited
1120 Birchmount Rd., Scarborough, Ont. M1K 5G4

This book is printed on acid-free paper, approved under Environment Canada's "Environmental Choice Program." The choice of paper reflects Nelson Canada's goal of using, within the publishing process, the available resources, technology, and suppliers that are as environment friendly as possible.

Canadian Cataloguing in Publication Data

Main entry under title:

Science probe 8

Includes index.
ISBN 0-17-604715-8

1. Science - Juvenile literature. I. Baumann, Frank, 1947–

Q 161.2.S35 1994 500 C94-931686-5

All student activities in this textbook have been designed to be as safe as possible, and have been reviewed by professionals specifically for that purpose. As well, appropriate warnings concerning potential safety hazards are included where applicable to particular activities. However, responsibility for safety remains with the student, the classroom teacher, the school principal, and the school board.

Printed and bound in Canada by Interglobe Printing

9 0 ITIB 4 3 2 1

ACKNOWLEDGEMENTS

Science Probe 8, Nelson Edition, is the result of the efforts of a great many people. The publisher would like to thank those who assisted in the development of this learning resource.

Focus Group Members
Anand Atal, Burnaby South Secondary; Patricia Dairon, Delta Secondary; Dr. Gaalen Erickson, University of British Columbia; Lloyd Esralson, Burnaby North Secondary; Roger Fox, Premier's Advisory Council on Science and Technology; Lon Mandrake, Seaquam Secondary; Tony Williams, Dr. Charles Best Junior Secondary; Sandy Wohl, Hugh Boyd Junior Secondary

Teacher Reviewers
Norm Aitchison, J. N. Burnett Junior Secondary (Unit VI); Alan Campbell, Norkam Secondary (Unit II); Steve Cardwell, Delta School District (Unit I); Wayne Carlaw, West Whalley Junior Secondary (Unit I); Douglas Cunnian, Central Okanagan School District (Unit IV); Steve Fera, Tsawwassen Junior Secondary (Unit V); Utta Gagel, Len Sheppard Junior Secondary (Unit III); Albert Haynes, Sands Junior Secondary (Unit IV and Unit VI); Lois Hollett, District Incentive Program, Richmond (Chapter 1); Herb Johnston, University of British Columbia (Unit II); Dyan Kliman, Semiahmoo Secondary (Unit II); Jan Kroeker (Unit V); Wendy Lim, Richmond School District (Chapter 1 and Unit I); Douglas Mann, Central Junior Secondary (Unit III); John Maschak, Burnsview Junior Secondary (Unit I); Jane McFadyen, J. N. Burnett Junior Secondary (Unit III); R. H. Plowright, Hatzic Secondary (Unit V); Darrel Scodellaro, Seaquam Secondary (Unit II); Gerry Sieben (Unit II and Unit III); Dennis Siemens (Unit III); Bob Simpson, Quesnel Secondary (Unit VI)

Content Reviewers
Dr. Phil Comeau, B.C. Ministry of Forests (Unit VI); Dr. William Corrigall, Addiction Research Foundation (Chapter 4); Dr. Tom Dickinson, University College of the Cariboo (Unit VI); Carlo Giovanella, University of British Columbia (Unit V); Dr. Mel Heit, Simon Fraser University (Unit II); Dr. Peter Matthews, University of British Columbia (Unit III); Dr. Nancy Ricker, Capilano College (Unit I); Dr. James Rising, University of Toronto (Chapter 16); Dr. J. B. Tatum, University of Victoria (Unit IV)

We would also like to thank those people who provided information or reviewed portions of this book in manuscript form:

Leslie Anderton (Unit V), Kerry Babcock (Unit V), Peter Booth (Unit I), David Dodge (Unit IV), W. E. Dumont (Unit VI), Jean Game (Unit V), Malcolm Gray (Unit V), Guujaaw (Unit VI), Bonnie Hamilton (Unit I), Herb Hammond (Unit VI), Julie Hicks (Unit I), Sheila Hill (Unit I), Dr. Michael Hoebel (Unit VI), Bonni Hrycyk (Unit V), Maureen Krohman (Unit V), Judi Lalonde, Alcohol-Drug Education Service (Chapter 4), Patti Leigh (Unit II and Unit VI), Robie Liscomb (Unit III), Thomas J. Little (Unit I), Dave Malloly (Unit V), Don McIntyre (Unit II), Mustang Industries (Unit III), Ron Newport (Unit III), Karl Osmers (Unit VI), Deanna Wilson (Unit I), Dale Zunke (Unit III)

We would also like to thank Christine Austin for the Chinese lettering on page 7.

We would especially like to thank the staff and students of Burnaby South Secondary in Burnaby for taking part in photograph sessions.

Finally, we would like to thank Alcohol-Drug Education Service for permission to use the Making Decisions program as a basis for Activities 4A, 4E, and 4G in Chapter 4.

TABLE OF CONTENTS

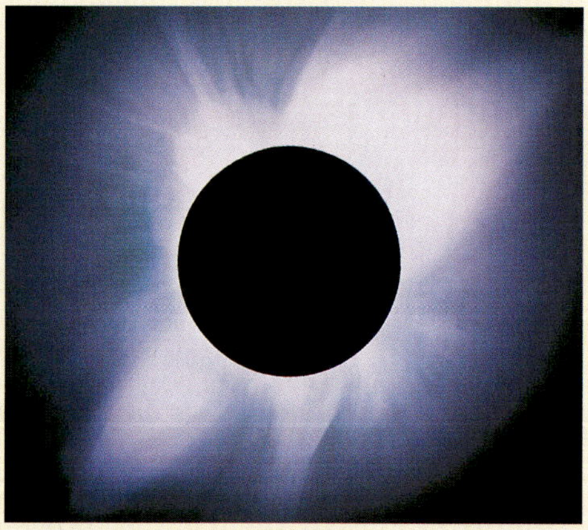

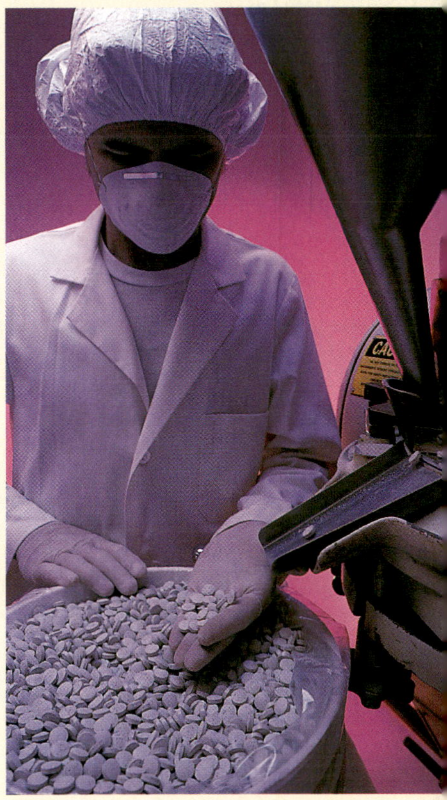

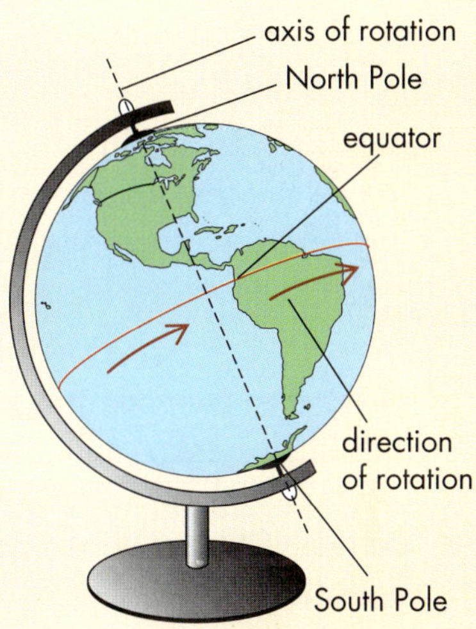
axis of rotation
North Pole
equator
direction of rotation
South Pole

FEATURES OF SCIENCE PROBE 8

■ *Science Probe 8* has an introductory chapter about the nature of science followed by six units, each representing a major area of science. These units can be studied in any sequence.

■ The text includes a variety of activities designed to foster the development of thinking skills and the processes and skills of investigation. The diverse formats include step-by-step experiments, reading activities, informal discussions, and student-designed investigations. All activities are designated by the same type of heading. The first activity in each chapter is designed to help students consider what they already know about the topic of the chapter and what they may want to find out.

■ Activities that are strong examples of the use of collaborative learning are marked with a Group Activity icon. (In addition to the activities that specifically require collaboration, many of the other activities, which are not marked with icons, can be conducted in pairs or in larger groups, as the teacher chooses.) Similarly, activities that require students to integrate other subject areas with science learning are marked with a Cross-Curricular icon.

■ Within an activity, the word CAUTION! followed by a few words or sentences indicates that the activity contains potentially dangerous procedures or materials. More information on safety can be found in *Safety Rules* on page ix.

■ Enrichment activities in the margin under the heading *Extension* are intended to challenge students or to reinforce new concepts. Under the heading *Did You Know?* are interesting facts and scientific discoveries.

■ Special features, *Profile*, *Career*, *Computer Application*, and *Science in Our World*, examine topics related to the chapter.

■ Terms considered essential for understanding new concepts are printed in **boldface**, defined in the text, included in the *Vocabulary* at the end of the chapter, and listed in the *Glossary*.

■ At the end of each numbered section, questions are listed under the heading *Review*. These questions allow students to check their understanding of content as they progress through the chapter.

■ Each chapter concludes with a five-part chapter review. *Key Ideas* lists the main ideas of the chapter. *Vocabulary* lists the boldface words and suggests two activities using these key terms. *Connections* require skills such as comparison, evaluation, prediction, and problem solving. *Explorations* suggest projects, research, and group activities. *Reflections* allow students to consider how the chapter has changed their ideas and to reflect on what they have learned.

■ The *Glossary* includes definitions of all boldface terms, along with other important scientific terms.

■ The *Appendices* provide information of general use and technical material related to Unit I.

■ The *Index* helps students to locate important topics and to find connections between units.

■ The *Science Probe 8 Teacher's Resource Guide* provides teaching strategies, lesson plans, practical tips, answers to questions, additional questions and activities, sample tests, blackline masters (some for overhead projection, some for student use), and other useful information for planning and teaching each unit.

■ The Test Item Bank provides a variety of questions and tests on disk in LXR software, both for Macintosh computers and those using Windows.

SAFETY RULES

Your school laboratory, like your kitchen, need not be dangerous. In both places, understanding how to use materials and equipment and following proper procedures will help you avoid accidents.

The activities in this textbook have been tested and are safe, as long as they are done with proper care. Take special note of the instructions accompanying the word CAUTION! whenever it appears in an activity.

Follow the safety rules listed below. Your teacher will give you specific information about other safety rules for your classroom. You will also be told about the location and proper use of all safety equipment.

1. Give your teacher your complete attention when listening to instructions.
2. Learn the location and proper use of the safety equipment available to you, such as safety goggles, protective aprons, heat-resistant gloves, fire extinguishers, fire blankets, the nearest fire alarm, eyewash fountains, and showers.
3. Inform your teacher of any allergies, medical conditions, or other physical problems you may have. Tell your teacher if you wear contact lenses.
4. Read through the entire activity before you start. Before beginning any step, make sure you understand what to do. If there is anything you do not understand, ask your teacher to explain.
5. Do not begin an activity until you are instructed to do so.
6. If you are designing your own experiment, obtain your teacher's approval before carrying out the experiment.
7. Clear the laboratory bench of all materials except those you are using in the activity.
8. Follow your teacher's instructions regarding the No Crowding Zone.
9. Wear protective clothing (a lab apron or a lab coat) and closed shoes during activities involving equipment or material. Long hair should be tied back.
10. Wear safety goggles when using hazardous or unidentified materials and when heating materials.
11. Do not taste or touch any materials unless you are asked to do so by your teacher.
12. Do not chew gum, eat, or drink in the laboratory.
13. Do not rock or lean on lab stools.
14. Do not run or play games in the laboratory.
15. Do not throw any objects.
16. Carry lab equipment, containers of chemicals, and glassware carefully.
17. Make sure you understand all safety labels.
18. Label all containers.
19. When taking something from a bottle or other container, double-check the label to be sure you are taking exactly what you need.
20. If any part of your body comes in contact with a chemical or specimen, wash the area immediately and thoroughly with water. If your eyes are affected, do not touch them but wash them immediately and continuously for at least 15 minutes and inform your teacher.

21. Handle all chemicals carefully. When you are instructed to smell a chemical in the laboratory, follow the procedure shown here. Never put a chemical close to your nose.

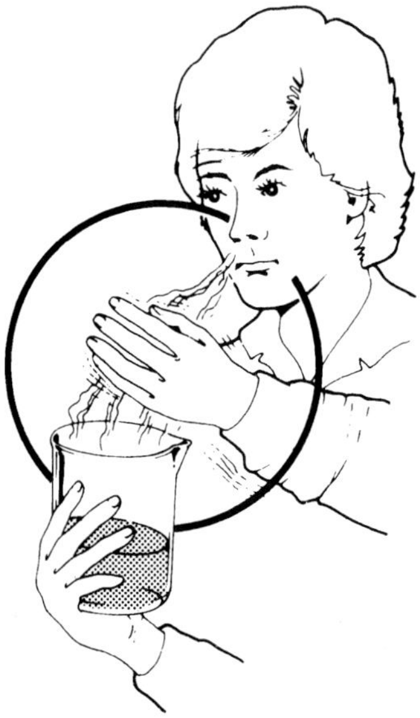

22. Hold the container(s) away from your face when pouring liquids.

23. Place test tubes in a rack before pouring liquids into them. If you must hold the test tube, tilt it away from you before pouring liquids in.

24. Clean up any spilled water, chemicals, or other materials immediately, following instructions given by your teacher.

25. Do not return unused chemicals to original containers. Do not pour them down the drain. Dispose of chemicals and waste materials as instructed by your teacher.

26. Whenever possible, use electric hotplates for heating materials. Use flames only when instructed to do so.

27. When heating materials, always wear safety goggles and use hand protection if required.

28. When heating glass containers, make sure you use clean Pyrex or Kimax. Do not use broken or cracked glassware. Always keep the open end pointed away from yourself and others. Never allow a container to boil dry.

29. When heating a test tube over a flame, use a test tube holder. Holding the test tube at an angle facing away from anyone, move it gently through the flame so that the heat is distributed evenly.

30. Handle hot objects carefully. Hotplates can take up to 60 minutes to cool off completely. Hot and cold hotplate burners can look the same. If you burn yourself, immediately apply cold water or ice.

31. Keep water and wet hands away from electrical cords, plugs, and sockets.

32. Always unplug electrical cords by pulling on the plug, not the cord. Report any frayed cords or damaged outlets to your teacher.

33. Make sure electrical cords are not placed where anyone can trip over them.

34. When cutting with a knife or razor blade, always cut away from yourself and away from others.

35. When walking with a pair of scissors or any pointed object, keep the pointed surface facing the floor, away from yourself, and away from others.

36. Watch for sharp or jagged edges on all equipment.

37. Place broken or waste glass only in specially marked containers.

38. Report to your teacher all accidents (no matter how minor), broken equipment, damaged or defective facilities, and suspicious-looking chemicals.

39. Be sure all equipment is shut off when not in use. Be ready to shut off equipment quickly if it breaks down or if an accident occurs.

40. Put away all equipment and chemicals after use.

41. Clean all equipment before putting it away.

42. Wash your hands thoroughly using soap and warm water after working in the science laboratory. This practice is especially important when you handle chemicals, biological specimens, or micro-organisms.

43. Do not take any equipment, materials, or chemicals out of the laboratory.

44. Do not practise laboratory experiments at home unless directed to do so.

45. If a Bunsen burner is used in your science classroom, make sure you follow the procedures listed below. (Note: Hotplates should be used in preference to Bunsen burners whenever possible.)

- Do not wear scarves or ties, long necklaces, or earphones suspended around your neck. Tie back long hair and roll back or secure loose sleeves before you light a Bunsen burner.
- Obtain instructions from your teacher on the proper method of lighting and using the Bunsen burner.
- Do not heat a flammable material (for example, alcohol) over a Bunsen burner.
- Be sure there are no flammable materials nearby before you light a Bunsen burner.
- Do not leave a lighted Bunsen burner unattended.
- Always turn off the gas at the valve, not at the base of the Bunsen burner.

46. If a fire occurs, make sure you follow the procedures listed below.

- Do not panic. Remain calm.
- Notify your teacher immediately. Act quickly to provide help in an emergency.
- Shut off all gas supplies at the desk valves if it is safe to do so.
- Pull the fire alarm.
- Follow your teacher's instructions if your assistance is required.
- If your clothing is on fire, roll on the floor to smother the flames. If another student's clothing is on fire, use a fire blanket to smother the flames.
- Avoid breathing fumes.
- Do not throw water on a chemical fire.
- If the fire is not quickly and easily put out, leave the building in a calm manner.

47. Become familiar with the warning symbols that are placed on containers of potentially dangerous materials. You should be able to identify and understand each of the labels shown here. Pay careful attention to any warning symbols on the products or materials that you handle.

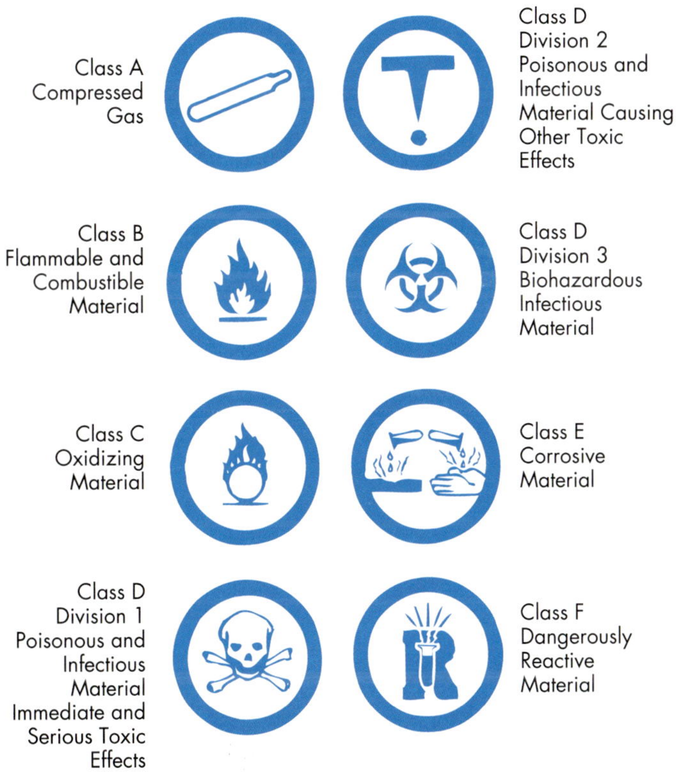

Workplace Hazardous Material Information System (WHMIS) Symbols

ACTIVITY A / SAFETY IN THE SCIENCE CLASSROOM

GROUP ACTIVITY

This activity will help you become familiar with some science safety rules.

PROCEDURE

1. Read the 47 safety rules listed in this section. Draw a table in your notebook like Table A, then classify the safety rules by using the following category codes:

- F for safety rules about fire
- B for safety rules about behaviour
- C for safety rules about chemicals
- D for other safety rules

2. After you have categorized the safety rules, choose 10 rules you believe are very important. Assign a priority number of 1 to the most important, 2 to the next most important and so on, up to 10. Use your table to record your priority numbers.

3. Work in groups to compare your priority numbers.

4. Discuss reasons for following safety rules. Choose three rules and consider what might happen if they were not followed. ❖

TABLE A ▶
Sample Data Table for Activity A

Safety rule number	Category code (F, B, C, or D)	Priority number (1 to 10)
1		

TO THE STUDENT

This book is about science in your world. You will find information here on how your nervous system works, how products like toothpaste are tested, what sound "waves" are, what causes erosion, why forests are important, and much, much more. In addition, this book contains activities and other suggestions to help you learn and understand science. A few of the many things you might do during science classes are described below.

Consider What You Already Know

At the beginning of each chapter in this book, you will find an activity that helps you consider what you already know about a particular topic. For instance, Activity 3A in Chapter 3 asks you to consider what you already know about your nervous system. As you read Chapter 3, you may find that you want to change or add to some of your original ideas. You may also find that you know a lot more about the subject than you thought you did.

Write in Your Learning Journal

Throughout this book, you will find references to "your learning journal." A learning journal is a notebook where you write your ideas and comments about your learning as you read and investigate. Writing down your ideas will help make them clear to you and to others, should you choose to share your writing. As well as helping you think, your learning journal will be a record of your learning in science.

Read Actively

Some of the activities in this book ask you to do something as you read. For instance, in Activity 15J in Chapter 15, you are asked to consider three questions while you are reading about glaciers. There are also reading activities that ask you to complete a task while you read. For example, you might be asked to fill in a table, make a flow chart, or draw diagrams. These reading activities will help you learn by allowing you to organize the ideas in a useful way.

Find out how glaciers grow and move in Chapter 15.

Make a Mind Map

In school, at home, and in the workplace, you use your ability to think. There are many ways you can record your thinking, including learning journals, illustrations, flow charts, poems, and stories. Another way to record your thinking is by using a mind map.

A mind map is drawn like a spider's web. You start a mind map by printing an idea in the centre of a page. Next, you think of other ideas that have something to do with the main idea in the centre. You print these ideas around the main idea and connect them to the main idea with lines. On the lines, you then print a few words that describe why or how these ideas are connected to the main idea.

Here is the beginning of a mind map that a grade 8 student drew about animals.

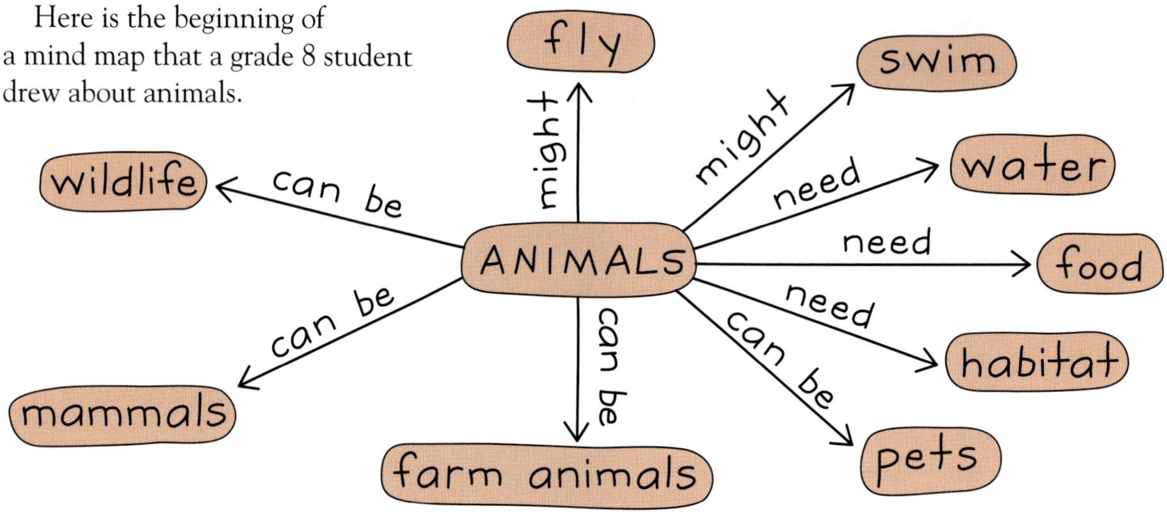

Here is the same mind map about animals with more details added.

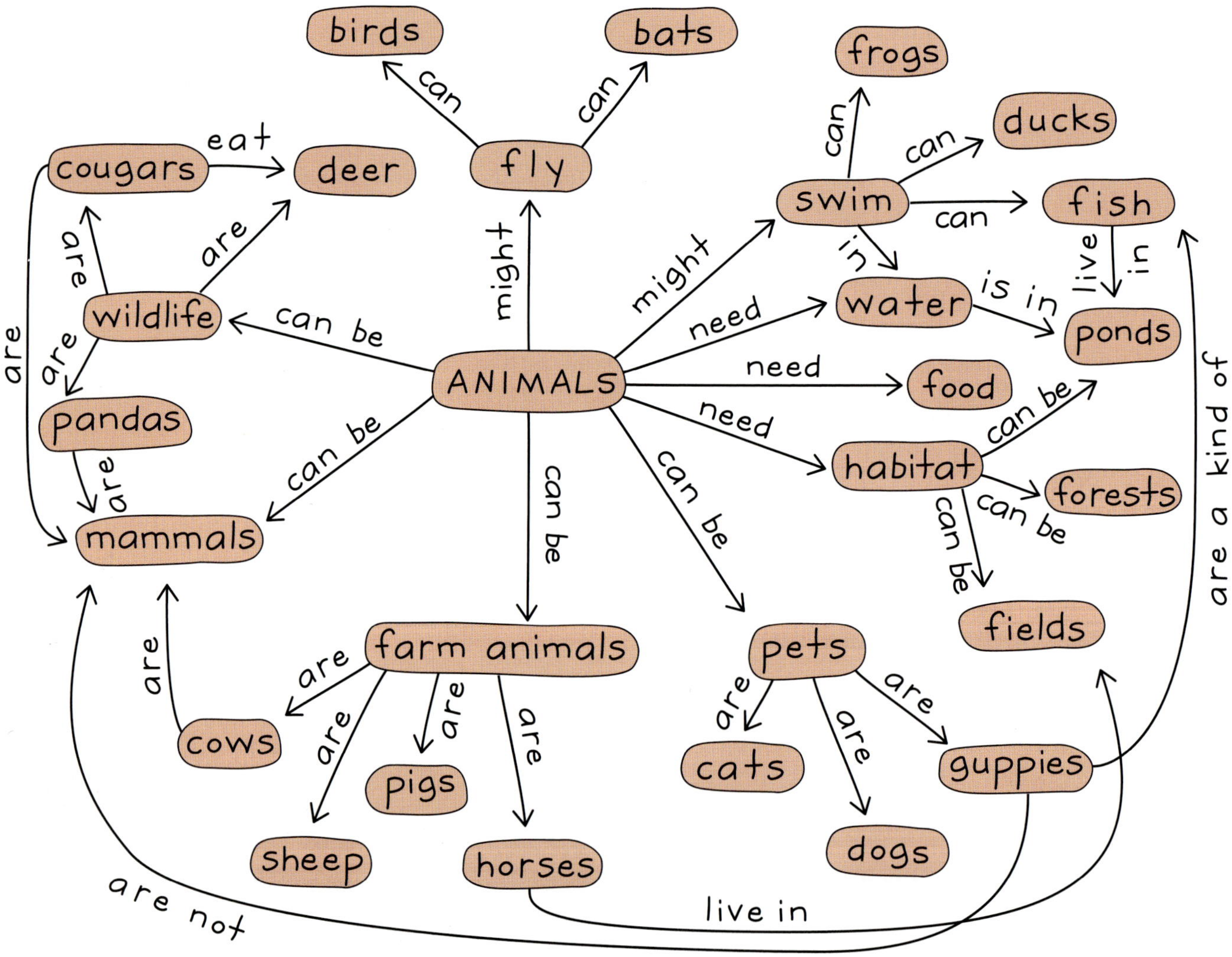

You can see that the student has provided more description for each of the new ideas by printing other ideas around them and connecting the ideas with lines and a few describing words.

Mind mapping is a good way to "brainstorm." You can quickly transfer many ideas from your brain to your paper. When you find an idea that appears in more than one location on your mind map, you can connect it with a line. By the time you have finished mapping, you usually have a giant spider web of ideas and lines. You might use colours and different styles of printing for the different levels of a mind map. You might also add your own drawings and designs to make your mind map attractive.

In this book, you will have many opportunities to practise mind mapping. In fact, at the beginning of several chapters in this book, you will be asked to draw a mind map of the things you already know about a certain topic. At the end of every chapter, you will be asked to draw a mind map of your new ideas. Making a mind map will help you sort information into categories and see relationships between ideas. The ideas that you include in your mind maps may come from your classroom learning, from reading books, magazines, or newspapers, and from experiences you have had.

Try making a mind map now. In your notebook, print the word "science" as the main idea for a mind map. Follow the suggestions in this section and your teacher's directions to create a spider web of your ideas about science. Share your ideas with your classmates. Were the same ideas about science recorded by several students in your class?

A mind map is like a spider's web.

Look Back at Your Learning

This book provides many opportunities to review and reconsider your learning and your thinking. The *Reflections* section at the end of each chapter contains questions that ask you to think about what you have learned or to add to your own ideas. For example, in Chapter 18 you are asked: "What did you think you could do to help the environment before studying this chapter? What do you think now?"

Share Your Ideas

In many of the activities in this book, you are asked to share your ideas with others, to express what you think you know, and to hear other ideas in return. For example, Activity 9A in Chapter 9 asks you to work with three other students to design and create a poster about energy. You are then asked to share your poster with the rest of the class. If you are afraid to do this because you might be "wrong," then you will miss the opportunity to see whether or not you can explain your thinking to others. So share your ideas. Then listen to the responses and the ideas of others and compare them with your own. You will not only learn more about science, you will also learn how to learn. You will develop skills that will help you long after you have finished this science course.

CHAPTER 1

SCIENCE AND YOU

What is science? Why is science important? What do scientists do? Do they have the right answers? Why do I need to study science? If you have asked yourself any of these kinds of questions, then you have made an important start in learning more about science.

Science has a lot to do with asking questions. Whenever you have wondered about something — why the sky looks blue, what happens when food cooks, or how your bicycle works — you have been asking scientific questions. Do you have ideas about what kind of food you need to eat to stay healthy? Have you ever expressed an opinion about how humans change the environment? If you have, you have probably been using science to help you form your opinions. Science is about asking questions and then looking for answers in an organized way.

In this chapter, you will investigate science: what it is, how it influences your life, what special words are used to talk about it, and which skills help you learn more about it. You may find that you know a lot more about science than you thought you did.

ACTIVITY 1A / WHAT DOES SCIENCE MEAN TO ME?

GROUP ACTIVITY

This activity will help you think about the meaning of the word "science."

PROCEDURE

1. In a small group, brainstorm at least 20 words or phrases that are linked to the word "science" in some way. Make a list of these words in your learning journal.
2. Use your list of words to construct a mind map. Write the word "science" in the middle of a sheet of paper. Look at your word list and decide which words have the strongest connection to "science" for you. Write these words around "science" and connect each word to "science" with a single line. Write a connecting word on each line. Continue to build your mind map out towards the edges of the page. You may use words from your word list or any other words.
3. When all the members of the class have finished their mind maps, display them around the classroom.

FIGURE 1.1
Hmmm...but is it science?

DISCUSSION

1. Describe what the word "science" means to you (Figure 1.1).
2. How are your ideas about science similar to those of other people in your class? How are your ideas different?
3. Suggest at least four examples of how science is important to you in your daily life. ❖

DID YOU KNOW

■ "Science" comes from the Latin word for "knowledge," *scientia*.

■ 1.1 WHAT IS SCIENCE?

People have been looking for answers to all kinds of questions for thousands of years. This search for knowledge has helped scientists find out why the sky looks blue, what happens when food is cooked, and how to make a bicycle. To gain this knowledge, scientists have asked questions, predicted possible answers, performed experiments, and examined the results to look for causes and effects. In this way, **science** is both a body of knowledge and a process for gaining more knowledge about the world in which we live.

Science may be divided into many branches. Some of these branches are shown in Figure 1.2.

FIGURE 1.2
Like a tree, science has many branches.

ACTIVITY 1B / THE BRANCHES OF SCIENCE

GROUP ACTIVITY

PROCEDURE

1. In your notebook, write down the names of all the branches of science shown in Figure 1.2. Use a dictionary to help you find out what is studied in each branch, and write that down too.
2. Find advertisements for three products that have been developed by scientists working in three different branches of science. You may use advertisements seen in a magazine or newspaper or on television.
3. Compare what you have written down and the advertisements you found with those of your classmates.

DISCUSSION

1. Did any of the advertisements you or your classmates chose involve more than one branch of science?
2. (a) Were any of the products in the advertisements connected in some way to activities that might be done in leisure or recreational time?
   (b) Do you think that a knowledge of science is important for recreational activities? Explain why or why not.
3. Explain why you agree or disagree with this statement: "A knowledge of science is important in studying all other subjects in school."
4. Can you think of any other branches of science to add to Figure 1.2? ❖

SCIENCE IS ALWAYS CHANGING

Scientists working in all branches of science try to understand the world around them and explain what they see. Scientists' explanations may seem to be true for a long time. But scientists keep investigating, thinking, and sharing ideas. Quite often the result is a change in an old explanation, or a new explanation to replace the older one. What scientists know today may turn out to be incomplete or incorrect in the future (Figure 1.3).

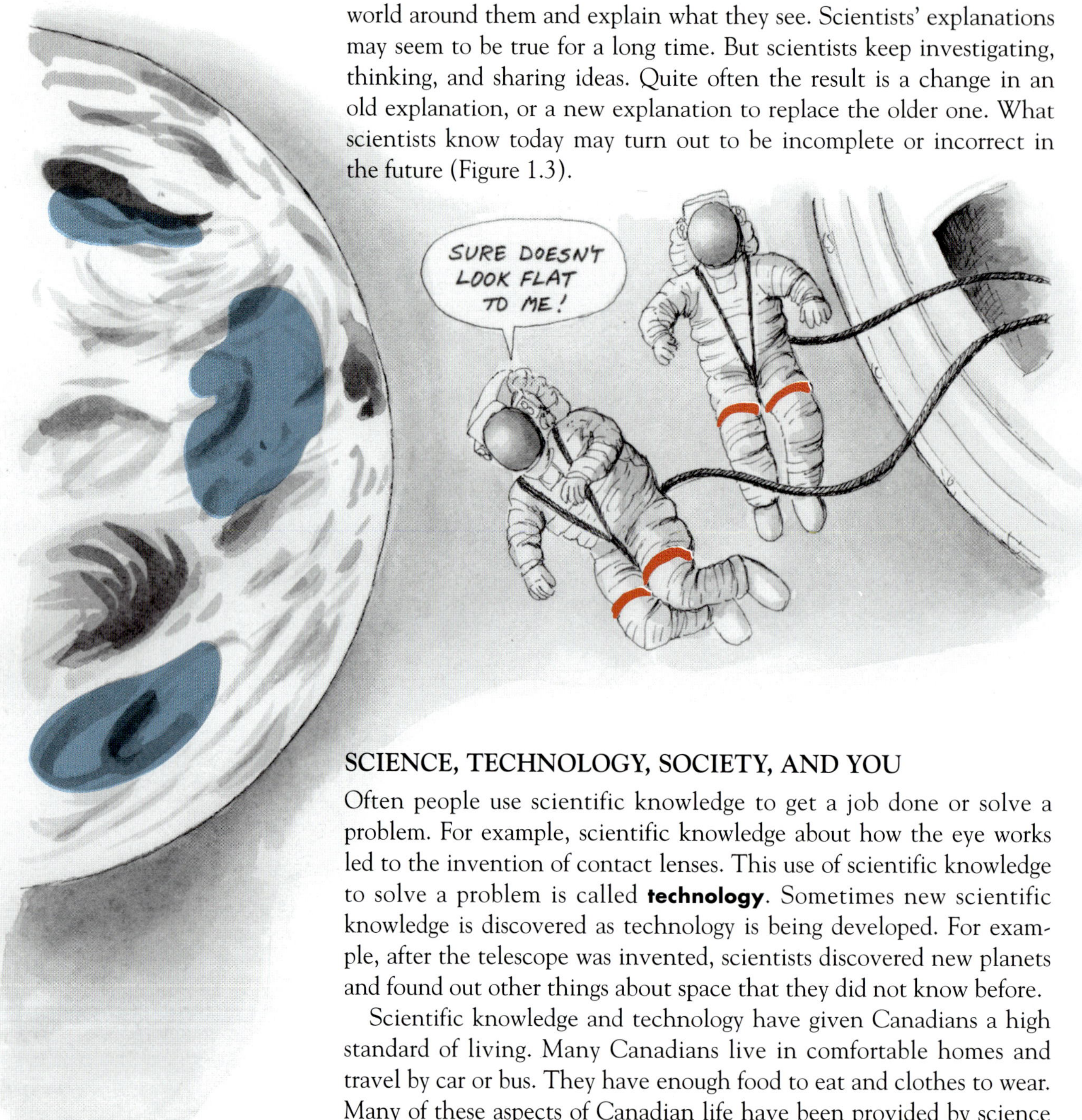

FIGURE 1.3
At one time, most people believed that the Earth was flat. What led them to this conclusion?

SCIENCE, TECHNOLOGY, SOCIETY, AND YOU

Often people use scientific knowledge to get a job done or solve a problem. For example, scientific knowledge about how the eye works led to the invention of contact lenses. This use of scientific knowledge to solve a problem is called **technology**. Sometimes new scientific knowledge is discovered as technology is being developed. For example, after the telescope was invented, scientists discovered new planets and found out other things about space that they did not know before.

Scientific knowledge and technology have given Canadians a high standard of living. Many Canadians live in comfortable homes and travel by car or bus. They have enough food to eat and clothes to wear. Many of these aspects of Canadian life have been provided by science and technology.

But science and technology have also caused problems in Canada and the rest of the world. For example, the car enables people to get around quickly and easily, but it also pollutes our air. Today one of the major problems we face is damage to our environment. Many people are worried about Earth's air, water, and soil, and the health of Earth's plants and animals. To protect the health of the Earth and all its inhabitants, we must change some of the ways we use science and technology.

All over the world, scientists are worried about the environment. They know that our environment can be hurt or helped by developing new technology. Many other people are also worried about the environment and are taking responsibility for what happens to it. Our **society** is made up of many individuals who must work together. The concerned members of any society take responsibility for looking after our world. Being a responsible citizen starts with thinking about your own actions. Should you ask your parents to drive you somewhere, or can you ride the bus or walk? What kind of containers should you pack your lunch in? What is best for the environment?

You can only make good decisions if you have the knowledge to help you make those decisions. As our society depends more and more on science and technology, it becomes everyone's responsibility to understand as much as possible about science and the use of technology in the world around us. As you use this book, you will have many opportunities to think about science, technology, and society.

DID YOU KNOW

■ In just one generation, scientists have developed kidney and heart transplants, space travel, nuclear weapons, microwave cooking, computers, plastics, and television. How would your life be different without these things?

ACTIVITY 1C / HOW RESPONSIBLE AM I ABOUT THE ENVIRONMENT?

GROUP ACTIVITY

In this activity, you will complete a checklist about you and the environment. Answer the questions in the checklist honestly. There are no right or wrong answers.

MATERIALS

a copy of "My Personal Environmental Awareness Checklist"

PROCEDURE

1. Carefully read the instructions for each part of the inventory.
2. Answer the questions honestly. Usually the first answer you think of is the most honest one.
3. When you have finished the checklist, prepare your reasons for answering the way you did. You don't have to show anyone your responses, but you should have opinions to share during a small group or class discussion.

DISCUSSION

1. Discuss your responses to the general statements about the world in Part I. It is not important to agree or disagree, but it is important to begin to think about your role in society as a responsible citizen.
2. Part II asks you to make decisions about your lifestyle. Are some choices harder to make than others? Why do you think that is?
3. You are asked to what degree you agree with opposing positions in Part III. As you are discussing where you stand on each issue, think about how you feel about the extreme opinions on the left and the right. Is an extreme position always good or bad? Where did most individuals in your group stand — at the extremes or somewhere in the middle? ❖

VOLUNTEERING AT SCIENCE WORLD

Have you ever visited Science World in Vancouver? If so, you may have met one of the student volunteers who help visitors enjoy the sights, sounds, and sensations of Science World.

Science World in Vancouver

In addition to the paid staff, 190 volunteers work at Science World. At least 40 are high school students. Volunteers must be at least 15 years old, friendly, enthusiastic, and responsible. They must also enjoy working with the public. Although there are no academic requirements, volunteers must have a keen interest in science.

Student volunteers work a minimum of 100 hours over six months, mainly during the summer break or on weekends. They answer questions about the exhibits in the five theme galleries and help with video production, workshops, and camp-ins. They also help visitors in the reception area and the gift shop, among other duties.

Louise Au Yeung, Andrew Lobley, Melissa Wingham, and Benji Simons are four teenagers who volunteer at Science World. Melissa enjoys working in the illusions gallery, which shows how our eyes play tricks on us. "I like working with little kids because they really get excited by the exhibits," she says.

One of Andrew's favourite activities is helping with Friday night camp-ins, where three hundred 6-to-12-year-olds sleep over at Science World after exploring the galleries or viewing special shows. Louise works in the search gallery, which has life science exhibits. "There's always something happening," she says. "People are asking questions, tadpoles are changing into frogs — it's never dull!"

Adult visitors to Science World are the biggest challenge for the students. Benji says that "in the beginning it was difficult to become the teacher." But when he and the others realized that the visitors were listening to what they had to say, they felt good about themselves. "My social skills have really improved," says Andrew. "I now have a lot of confidence in myself. It has been a very positive experience."

Working as volunteers has helped the students enjoy science more. "Science is fun!" they agree. They have also learned more about science. Although Andrew used to receive average grades in science, he now gets top marks.

"Science is all around you — when you sleep, when you eat, in everything you do," says Benji.

"You can't escape it, it's part of you," adds Louise.

Make a list of at least 15 activities you do after you wake up in the morning. Beside each activity, write down one or more ways that you think science is involved in that activity.

▶ REVIEW 1.1

1. Define "science."

2. Define "technology."

3. (a) List two examples of how science and technology have had a positive effect on Canadian society.
(b) List two examples of a negative effect of science and technology.

4. Explain how learning about science will help you become a responsible citizen.

■ 1.2 THE LANGUAGE OF SCIENCE

The people shown in Figure 1.4 are frustrated because they do not share the same language. Long ago, scientists realized that they needed a shared language to help them describe what they were doing. During the years 1100–1500, scientists living in the area now known as Europe used Latin as their common language. Latin was chosen because it was understood by all educated people in Europe, no matter what country they lived in.

You will find many scientific words in this textbook. Many of the words come from Latin and Greek. Some come from other non-English languages. Some of these words will be familiar to you from other subjects. Others may be completely unfamiliar to you. Whether familiar or not, a new scientific word can be seen as a puzzle to solve (Figure 1.5). Solving each new word puzzle will be easier if you learn more about how scientific words are made.

FIGURE 1.5
Solving the puzzle of a new scientific word.

FIGURE 1.4 ◀
It is difficult to communicate without a shared language.

You probably already know that words are made up of parts. Some sample word parts and their meanings are shown in Table 1.1 and Table 1.2. The three basic word parts shown in these tables are prefixes, roots, and suffixes.

A prefix is a syllable or word part attached to the beginning of a word to change its meaning or form a new word. A suffix is a syllable or word part attached to the end of a word to form a new word. A root is the main part of a word. Adding another root, a prefix, or a suffix makes a new word.

If you know what each part of a new word means, you can decode or figure out the meaning of the new word. Information from Table 1.1 and Table 1.2 makes it easy to decode words like "biology" or "kilometre."

TABLE 1.1
Word Parts and Their Meanings

Prefix	Meaning	Example
a	not; without	atypical (not typical)
de	do the opposite of	defrost
hemi	half	hemisphere
re	again; once more	redo
semi	half	semicircle
tele	over, from, or to a long distance	telephone
trans	across	trans-Atlantic
Root	**Meaning**	**Example**
astro	star, space	astronaut
auto	by itself	automobile
bio	life; living things	biosphere
cardio	heart	cardiogram
chemo	involving chemical reactions	chemist
eco	house; home; having to do with the environment	ecosystem
geo	earth; ground	geologist
hydro	water; watery	hydroelectricity
logy	the science of	ecology
meter	a device for measuring	voltmeter
metre	a unit of measurement	centimetre
micro	small	micro-organism
opti	see; vision	optical
phono	sound; voice	phonograph
photo	light	photograph
poly	many	polygon
thermo	heat	thermometer

Suffix	Meaning	Example
er	a device used for	circuit breaker
ist	a person who knows about	scientist
itis	inflammation; infection	tonsillitis
ize	to make	crystallize
oid	resembles; looks like	asteroid

TABLE 1.2 ***Number Prefixes and Their Meanings***

Number Prefix	Meaning	Example
mono	one	monotone
uni	one	unicycle
bi	two	bicycle
di	two	dioxide
tri	three	tripod
tetra	four	tetrahedron
quad	four	quadriplegic
penta	five	pentagon
quin	five	quintuplet
hexa	six	hexagon
hepta	seven	heptagon
octo	eight	octave
deca	ten	decade
kilo	one thousand	kilogram
mega	one million	megawatt
centi	one-hundredth (1/100)	centimetre
milli	one-thousandth (1/1000)	millilitre

Table 1.1 shows that "bio" means "life" and "logy" means "the science of." Thus, "biology" means "the science of life." Table 1.2 shows that "kilo" means "one thousand," and Table 1.1 shows that "metre" is a unit of measurement. Thus, a "kilometre" is "a unit measuring a thousand metres." By learning the meanings of some word parts and using a dictionary, you can decode many words used in science.

CROSS · CURRICULAR

ACTIVITY 1D / DECODING SCIENCE WORDS

MATERIALS

scientific journals
news magazines
a dictionary

PROCEDURE

1. In your notebook, draw a two-column chart with the headings "Word part" and "Word examples."
2. Write "bio" under the heading "Word part" on the first line of your chart.
3. Under the heading "Word examples," write two examples of science words that begin with "bio." You may already know two examples and can write them down immediately. If you do not, you can look in this textbook, a scientific journal, or the science section of a news magazine to find more examples. Spell these words carefully. If you do not know the meaning of a word, look it up in the dictionary.
4. Complete your chart by finding at least 2 words made from 10 other word parts listed in Table 1.1 or 1.2. Again, if you do not know what a word means, look it up in the dictionary. Do not use words already shown in the tables.
5. Compare your completed chart with a classmate's chart.
6. Choose five words from your chart or a classmate's chart and write them in your notebook along with their meanings. Try to use each word in a conversation or written assignment during the next few days.

DISCUSSION

1. (a) How many words in your "Word examples" column were new to you?
   (b) Where did you find most of the new words?
2. Which word part from your chart do you think you will see most often?
3. Select at least two or three words from your "Word examples" column and use them in a poem. You may wish to illustrate your poem. ❖

► REVIEW 1.2

1. Explain why a shared scientific language is important to scientists around the world.
2. Choose any five word examples in this section that were new to you. Use each word in a sentence to show its meaning. For example, a sentence using "thermometer" might read: "Ling put on a warmer jacket after checking the thermometer." ➡

3. Use a dictionary to discover the meaning and the origin of each of the following words. An example has been done for you.

Word	Meaning and origin
bacteria	single-celled micro-organisms, some of which cause disease (from the Greek word meaning "little stick")
carnivore	
electrolysis	
quantum	
chemotherapy	

1.3 USING SCIENCE SKILLS

You have learned that science is a process as well as a body of knowledge. A process is a set of actions done in a special order. In the process of doing science, scientists use many skills. These skills are sometimes known as **process skills**, or thinking skills. These skills are used by people besides scientists, too. Using process skills will help you find answers to questions as you study science and other subjects. The pages that follow describe some of these skills in more detail.

OBSERVING

To **observe** means to watch or examine carefully. Observing, however, does not always mean using your eyes (Figure 1.6). In science class, you observe things by using your senses of sight, hearing, touch, and smell. Under certain circumstances, you use the sense of taste also. It is important to record your observations as you make them. If you were asked to observe a burning match, which senses would you use?

FIGURE 1.6

CLASSIFYING

You **classify** objects or living things by grouping together those that are alike in some way. You can group objects or living things in many ways: by size, colour, shape, or other characteristics. The groups are called categories. In your notebook, divide your page into at least four group headings and then put the name of each article in Figure 1.7 into one of those categories. Why do you suppose scientists find this skill useful?

FIGURE 1.7
How does your classification system compare with those of other students? Is there a correct classification system?

ESTIMATING

To **estimate** means to roughly determine the measurement or nature of something. When you swing a bat at a ball, you estimate the speed of the ball and judge the moment you should swing your bat (Figure 1.8). You learn to estimate many things—time, distance, and speed are just a few. Your ability to estimate improves with practice. Estimates are often used in science when exact measurements cannot be obtained. For instance, we cannot measure the exact mass of the Earth, but we can estimate it.

FIGURE 1.8

MEASURING

To **measure** is to give exact information about characteristics such as height, length, or temperature. Scientist try to use exact words and careful measurements whenever possible (Figure 1.9). Imagine what could happen if exact measurements were not used when a pharmacist was mixing a medicine. Can you think of other examples where measuring is very important? (Chapter 5 contains more about measurement.)

FIGURE 1.9 ▶
Scientists prefer to use exact measurements to avoid situations like this.

PREDICTING

When you **predict**, you are describing what you think might happen. You use observations made in the past to make a prediction. Your observations and experience will then allow you to give reasons for your prediction. In Figure 1.10, the young skater predicted that the ice would be good for skating tomorrow. What observations and experience were used to make this prediction? You can test your predictions by doing experiments.

FIGURE 1.10 ▶
What experiments can these skaters perform to test their prediction?

MAKING INFERENCES

An **inference** is an explanation that results from an observation. An observer will infer that an event occurred for a particular reason, as illustrated in Figure 1.11. Sometimes you can make more than one inference from a single observation. If you saw a bird pecking the ground, you might infer that it was seeking food, signalling to other birds, or pulling up nesting material. You can test some inferences by doing experiments.

FIGURE 1.11
You observe that the dog is wet. You may infer that the dog has been swimming in the lake. What else could you infer?

STATING A HYPOTHESIS

A **hypothesis** (plural: hypotheses) is a possible explanation for something that happens. Scientists use observations and experience to make a hypothesis. Suggest why the hypothesis in Figure 1.12 was a poor one.

A scientist tests his or her hypothesis by carrying out many experiments. Other scientists repeat the experiments. If all the results of the experiments support the hypothesis, and none have shown it to be false, then scientists accept the hypothesis and call it a **theory**.

FIGURE 1.12

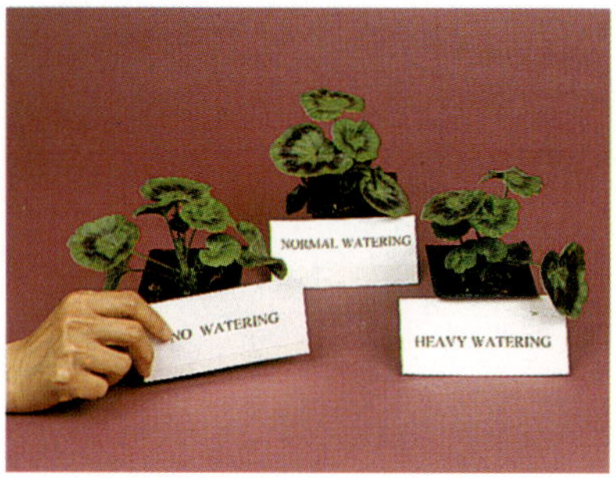

FIGURE 1.13
Which plant is the control plant? What variable is being tested? How could you improve this experiment?

DOING EXPERIMENTS

When you do an **experiment**, you plan and carry out a series of activities that help you solve a problem or find an answer to a question. Predictions, inferences, and hypotheses may all be tested by doing experiments. Experiments can involve some or all of the process skills described in this chapter.

Suppose that a home gardener is growing several geraniums indoors for transplanting in the spring. The plants are beginning to wither and die. One member of the family suggests that the geraniums are receiving too much water; another member thinks they are receiving too little. To discover which is the case, if either, the gardener performs a controlled experiment (Figure 1.13).

In a **controlled experiment**, only one factor, or **variable**, is changed at a time, while all the other possible variables remain constant, or the same. In the geranium example, the variable changed is the amount of water supplied to the plants. Other possible variables, such as the amount of sunlight, room temperature, and the amount of fertilizer added, are kept constant. One geranium plant, the **control**, continues to receive the same amount of water as before. The other plants receive more or less water. All plants are labelled, and observations are recorded for each plant.

If, after several weeks, the plant that received the least amount of water is the healthiest, then the gardener can conclude that the amount of water given to the plants should be reduced. If, however, the plants all appear to be in the same condition, then the gardener would have to try to test other variables, one at a time.

USING MODELS

Do you understand a problem more easily if it is presented in a diagram? Many people do. For some problems, you need to have either a picture in your mind or a picture on paper. Pictures and diagrams are both types of **models**. A model is an object, a design, or an idea that helps you to understand something that you cannot observe. For example, engineers and architects often make models, or small copies, of the structures (bridges, office towers, and so on) they intend to build (Figure 1.14). They then use these models to see if what they plan to build will work. Will the bridge be wide enough for rush-hour traffic? Will there be too many windows in the office tower? In this example, a model is being used to test the plan, which was developed by using process skills.

Models are also useful for showing things that are either extremely small (Figure 1.15) or extremely large (Figure 1.16).

Models do not have to look like the thing or idea they represent. For example, Figure 1.16 shows a model of the five inner planets of our

FIGURE 1.14
A model of downtown Vancouver. Models can help engineers and architects test their ideas.

solar system. This model helps us visualize the relative sizes and positions of the planets as they orbit the sun. The model is not exactly like the real thing. The scale used to show the size of the planets is 2000 times larger than the scale used to show the size of the orbits. (If the same scale were used for both planets and orbits, either the planets would be too small to see, or the model would be too large to fit into a football stadium!) The sun is also not shown to scale. (The diameter of the sun is about 10 times the diameter of Jupiter.) In spite of these problems, the model helps us to understand and compare the relative sizes and positions of the planets as they orbit the sun.

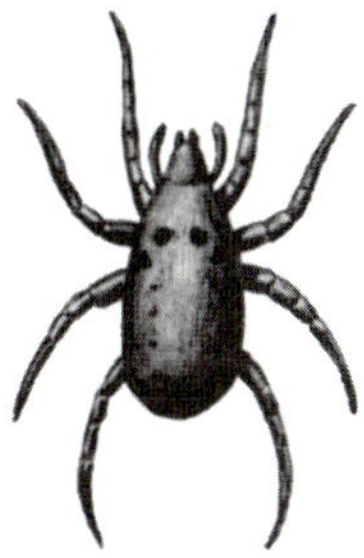

FIGURE 1.15
Even to the sharpest eye, a real spider mite looks like a dot. A model can be revealing.

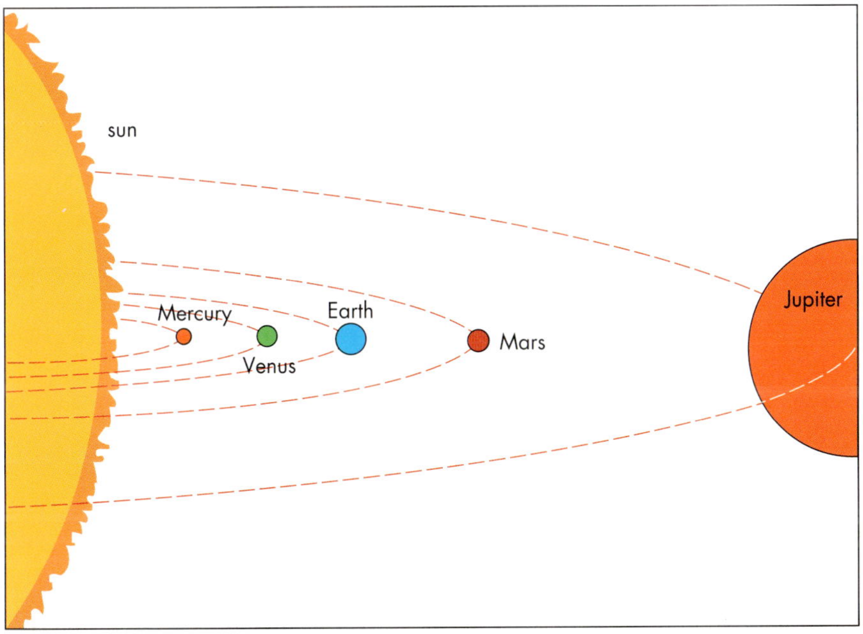

FIGURE 1.16
A model of the sun and five planets in our solar system.

FIGURE 1.17
What type of data is best suited to each method of recording?

RECORDING INFORMATION

As you use *Science Probe 8*, you will be recording a great deal of information, or **data**. You will be recording observations and measurements you make during activities, hypotheses you want to test, and some ideas of your own (Figure 1.17). Some of the ways you can record information include:

- notes
- tables
- graphs
- sketches
- reports of experiments
- mind maps

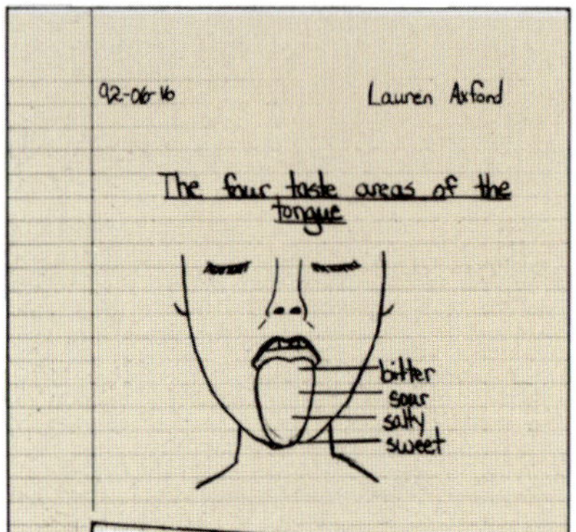

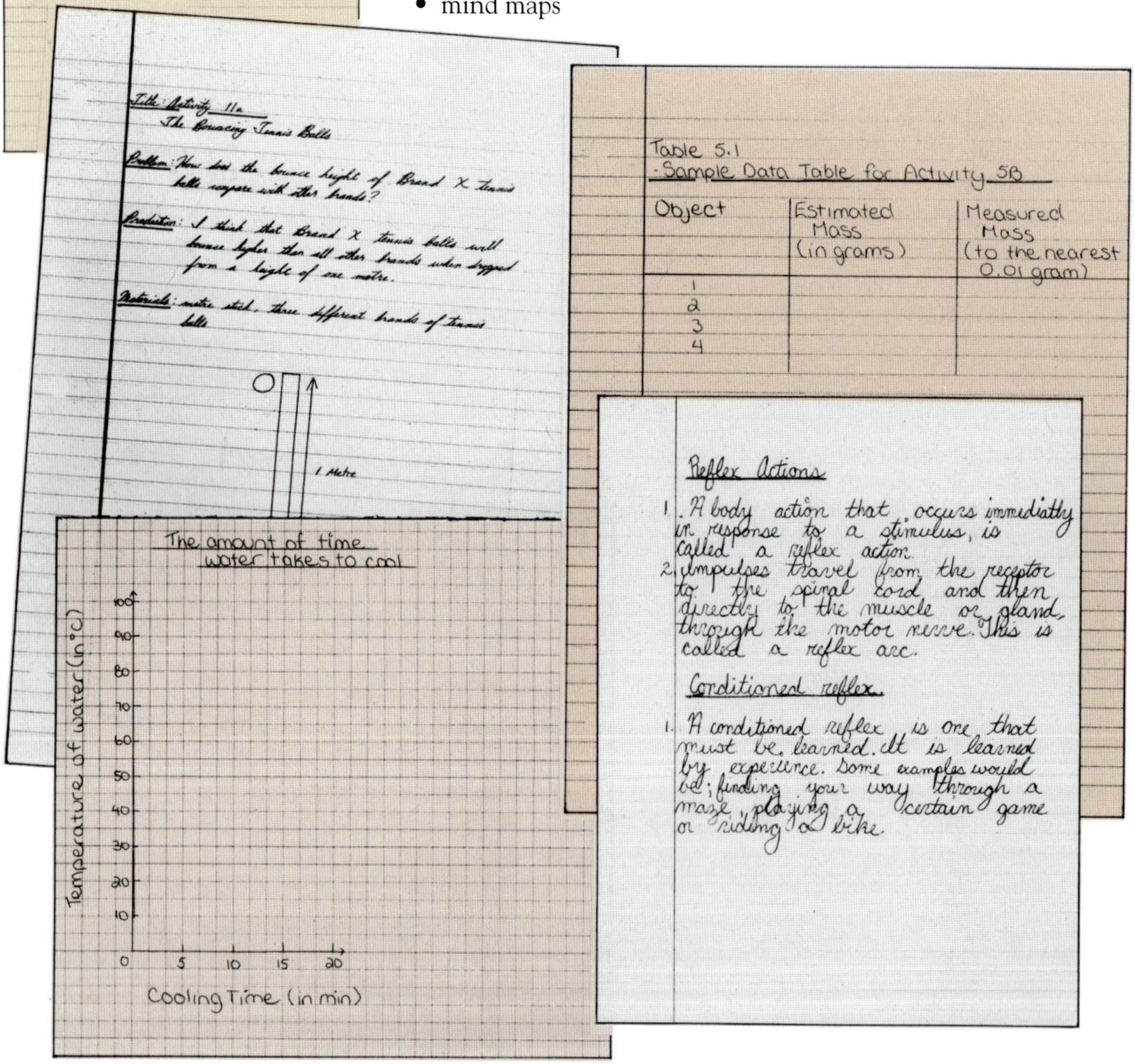

ANALYSING, INTERPRETING, AND ORGANIZING DATA

As you use *Science Probe* 8, you will also find that you need to look carefully at the data that you obtain from experiments. This examining, or **analysing**, of information allows you to find out whether there are patterns in the data. The patterns may help you understand your results. Making tables or graphs will often help you see patterns too.

You will also need to analyse some of the many problems or **issues** being discussed today. One such issue is our environment and what must be done to repair the damage caused by human activities. Different solutions are presented by people with different points of view. These ideas must be analysed.

As well as analysing possible solutions and data, you will need to explain the meaning of anything you have observed. This explaining, or **interpreting**, of data and observations is the last step in many activities.

Whenever you plan and carry out the experiments and investigations in this book, you will also be asked to organize your ideas and the information you gather. **Organizing** involves putting observations and data together so that they can be discussed with others and more easily understood. Whether you are doing an experiment (Figure 1.18), making a model (Figure 1.19), or investigating an issue (Figure 1.20), it helps to follow certain steps.

FIGURE 1.18
If you want to design a science experiment, here are some steps you could follow.

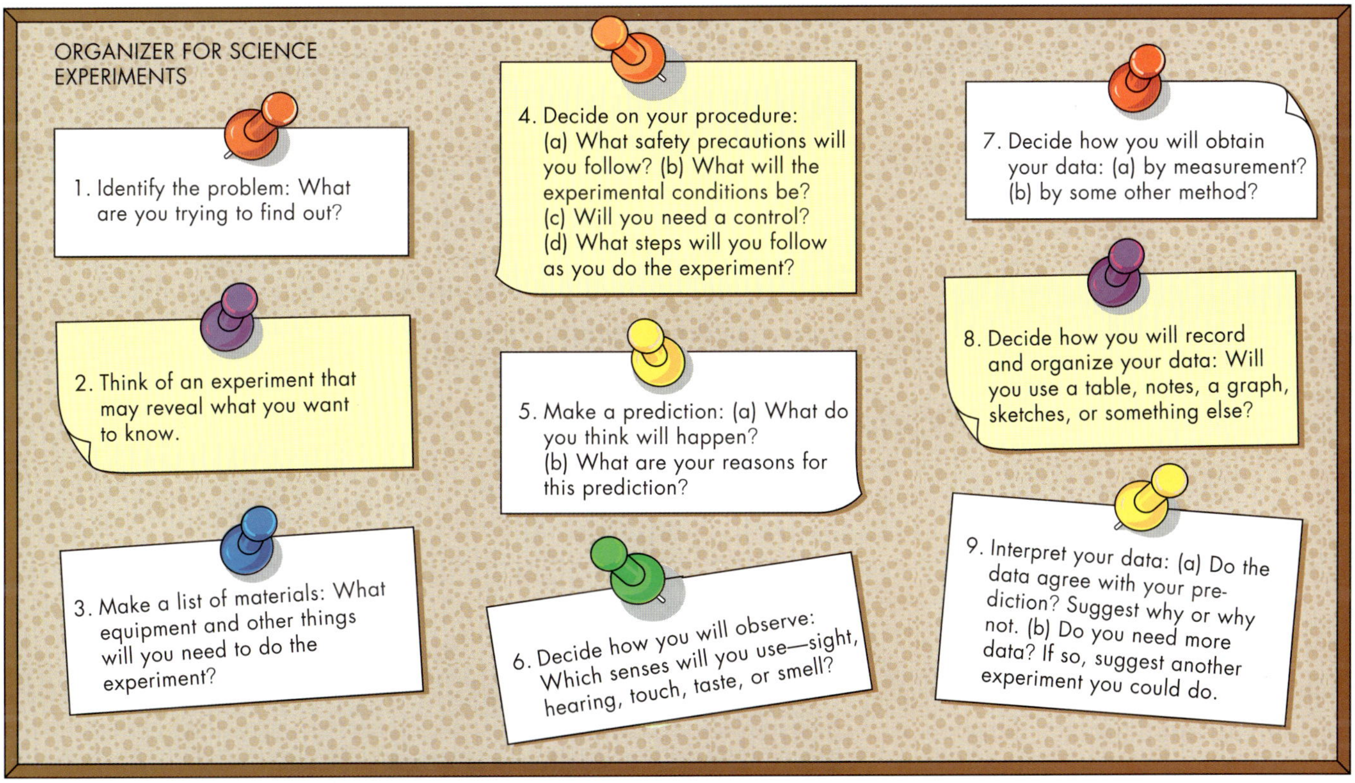

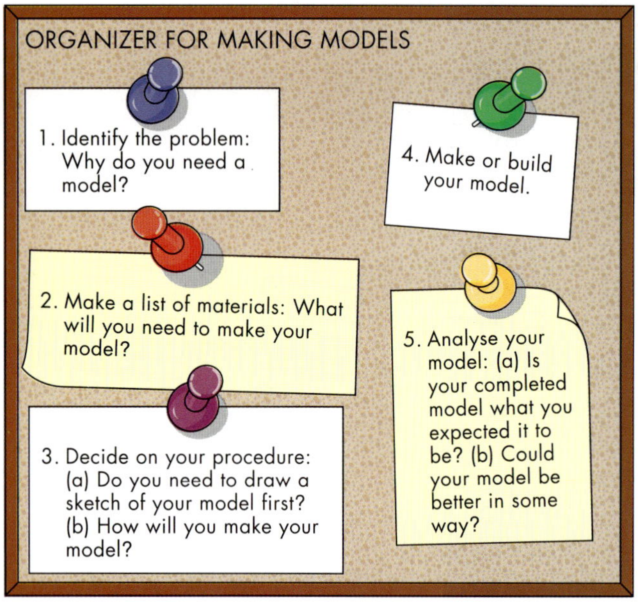

FIGURE 1.19
If you want to solve a practical problem by inventing or designing and building a model, you might want to follow these steps.

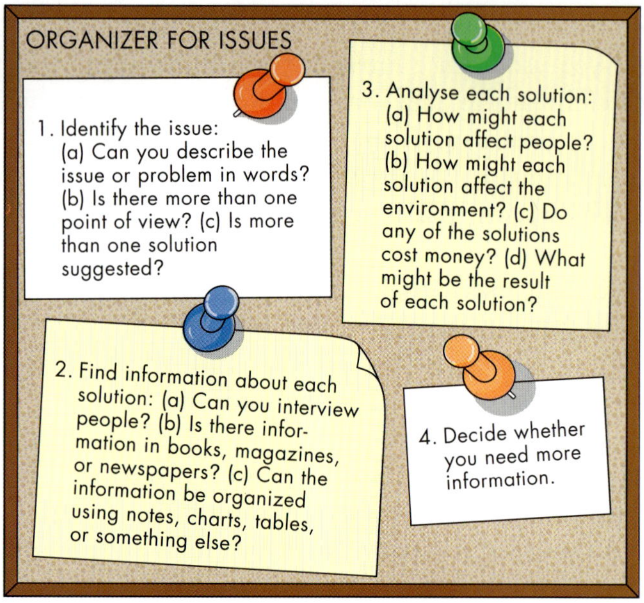

FIGURE 1.20
If you want to investigate an issue that affects people, think about following these steps.

ACTIVITY 1E / PRACTISING PROCESS SKILLS

GROUP ACTIVITY

Process skills are important tools that help you find answers to questions in science and other subjects. In this activity, you are asked to identify which process skill is being used in each of the statements below. If you are unclear about any skill, read the section describing that skill again.

PROCEDURE

1. Number your page from 1 to 20.
2. Read statement 1. Think carefully about it and decide which process skill or skills from the list are being used in that statement. Write the name of the process skill or skills beside number 1 on your page.
3. Now complete statements 2 through 20 in the same way. This should take you about 10 min.

PROCESS SKILL

Observing
Classifying
Estimating
Measuring
Predicting
Making inferences
Stating a hypothesis
Doing experiments
Using models

STATEMENT

1. I put all the red articles together.
2. I put one plant in the dark and left the other in the sun.
3. From my observations, it seems that plants grow better in direct sunlight.

4. I smelled sulphur after I struck the match.
5. The door was about 5 cm wider than the length of my arm.
6. The container of marbles had a mass of 1.2 kg.
7. Since my grandmother's tomato plants always produce lots of tomatoes, and she plants them in a very sunny area of her garden, I believe tomato plants grow best in direct sunlight.
8. When I bent the piece of wire back and forth until it broke, the wire felt hot at the break.
9. I'm going to pour diluted acid on rock samples to see which rocks are affected by acid.
10. I think that the steeper a slope is, the faster the soil on it will erode.
11. Since waxing a floor makes it slippery, if I wax the bottom of my toboggan it will slide farther than it did before.
12. The "mystery liquid" turned the litmus paper blue.
13. I put all the liquids in glass containers, and all the solids on aluminum plates.
14. I poured exactly 10 mL into the beaker.
15. The articles inside the locked box seemed to roll around inside. I think these articles are round like marbles.
16. I filled the glass to the very top. I think I can put eight pennies in the glass before the water spills down the side of the glass.
17. I drew a floor plan of my room on graph paper, then added the outlines of my new furniture to see if it would fit into the room.
18. First I divided the animals into those that had hoofs and those that had claws, then I divided each group into those found on the grasslands and those found in the forest.
19. When heat is added to a solid, the heat can cause the solid to become warmer or to melt.
20. If a stack of 10 dimes is about 1 cm high, this eraser is about 4 cm long.

DISCUSSION

1. Share your answers in small groups or with a partner.
2. Were there any skills that you had trouble identifying? If so, go back and review those skills. Make up a statement for each skill you reviewed and share it with your group.
3. Make a list of the subjects besides science that you are studying this year. Beside each subject, list the process skills you would use in the subject and provide an example of how you would use the skill. Below is an example. ❖

Subject	Process skill	Example
Mathematics	Classifying	Dividing numbers into odd or even

REVIEW 1.3

1. Explain the difference between the pairs of skills at the right. An example has been done for you.

Skills	Difference
stating a hypothesis and a theory	A theory is a hypothesis that has been tested many times and never proved to be false.
observing and classifying	
estimating and measuring	
predicting and making inferences	

2. Name two things that predictions, inferences, and hypotheses have in common.
3. Define "data." Describe what you would be doing if you were
   (a) analysing data,
   (b) interpreting data,
   (c) organizing data.
4. Read about how a student conducted an experiment to decide which kind of material would be the most bouncy for a gymnasium floor:

   "The student dropped a basketball and a baseball from different heights. The basketball was dropped on wooden flooring, and the baseball was dropped on rubber flooring."

   Explain whether this was a controlled experiment or not. If you said it was not, how would you make it a controlled experiment?

CHAPTER REVIEW

KEY IDEAS

- Science is a body of knowledge about the world and the universe. Science is also a way of finding out about the world and the universe.
- Technology is the use of scientific knowledge to solve a practical problem.
- The members of society need to know about science and technology in order to make responsible decisions.
- A shared language helps scientists communicate. Many scientific words come from Latin and Greek. If you know what different parts of such words mean, you can tell what the whole words mean.
- Scientists and other investigators use a number of process skills to look for answers to questions. These skills include: observing; classifying; estimating; measuring; predicting; making inferences; stating a hypothesis; experimenting; using models; and recording, analysing, interpreting, and organizing data.
- Scientists develop and use experiments to obtain new knowledge. In a controlled experiment, only one variable is changed at a time. All the other variables remain constant.

VOCABULARY

science
technology
society
process skills
observe
classify
estimate
measure
predict
inference
hypothesis
theory
experiment
controlled experiment
variable
control
model
data
analysing
issues
interpreting
organizing

V1. Use the words from the vocabulary list and any other words you need to make a mind map about science, technology, and society.

V2. Write a short story using 10 of the words in the vocabulary list. Use your imagination!

CONNECTIONS

C1. Design an experiment to find out the answers to these questions:

(a) Does hot tap water make ice cubes faster than cold tap water?

(b) Does one brand of paper towel absorb more water than another brand?

Draw a line down the right-hand side of your page, making a narrow margin. After you have designed your experiment, indicate in the margin which process skills you used. Also indicate which skills you would use in carrying out your experiment.

C2. Review the definitions of "science," "technology," and "society." Write a short explanation about the meaning of the phrase "science, technology, society, and you."

C3. List four different ways that you could record scientific data. Beside each one, give an example of when you might use this method.

C4. Outline the steps you might take to find out more about a scientific issue.

EXPLORATIONS

E1. Divide a sheet of paper into three equal parts. At the top of each part, write one of the three reasons listed below that states why people study science:

(a) Science is a way of knowing more about the world around me.

(b) Science helps me to make decisions about things that are important to me.

(c) Science helps me with career choices I may wish to make.

Under each reason, list several examples of how this use of science is true in your life. When you have finished recording all your examples, exchange your paper with a classmate's and give your opinions on each other's answers. After you have discussed your examples, you may wish to make some changes.

E2. At one time, most people believed that the world was flat. Name another generally held belief that has changed because of changing scientific explanations.

E3. Find out about two Canadian scientists in different branches of science. Prepare a presentation or report describing their contributions.

REFLECTIONS

R1. Go back to Activity 1C. Cover your original responses to "My Personal Environmental Awareness Checklist." Redo the inventory. Have your responses changed? Why do you think that is?

R2. What else would you like to know about science and how it affects your life?

VICTORIAVILLE

UNDERSTANDING YOUR LIVING BODY

Have you ever wondered how your body is able to respond correctly to the world around you? How do you gather information from your environment and make sense of it? How do you make sure that your body's movements are co-ordinated—that is, that your arms, legs, and other body parts work together?

Whether you are actively playing a sport or sitting quietly and reading, your brain is busy. This is because it is your brain that makes sure all parts of your body are working together. Your brain helps you decide what to do next. Your brain is part of one of your most interesting body systems: the nervous system. Your nervous system makes it possible for you to sense and respond to the world around you.

In this unit, you will learn about how your body picks up information from your surroundings by using your senses of sight, hearing, smell, taste, and touch. You may also discover some new senses that you did not know you had. You will then explore what your nervous system does with all this information, and how this system controls your body's actions. Finally, you will look at the ways in which drugs can both help and harm this important body system.

UNIT 1

CHAPTER 2

THE SENSES

Imagine that you are doing your homework and you suddenly notice a burning smell coming from the kitchen. "What's burning?" you shout. Hearing your question, your mother opens the oven door to take a quick peek. She can see that the casserole is bubbling and decides that it is done. Using pot holders to avoid burning her hands, she sets the casserole on the counter. Soon, as the smell of spices and other ingredients reaches you, your mouth begins to water. When you reach the kitchen, you discover that it was only some drippings that caused the burning smell; the dinner itself is perfect, and it looks very tempting. Touching the dish carefully, you discover that it is still hot, so you use pot holders to carry it to the table. "Let's eat — I can taste it already!"

Within this brief period, you would have used many of your body's senses to become aware of sights, sounds, smells, heat, and other features of your surroundings. As the story above shows, your senses are constantly in use, contributing to your health and safety. In this chapter, you will learn more about the human senses: what they are, how they work, and how to protect them.

ACTIVITY 2A / AN ALIEN ADVENTURE

GROUP ACTIVITY CROSS-CURRICULAR

Suppose an alien from outer space has just landed near your school. Its mission is to find out about Earth and report back to others on its own planet. The alien has found this to be a very difficult job. Its own planet is so different from Earth that living things there learn about their surroundings quite differently from the ways humans do. For example, they cannot see or hear. In fact, the alien does not have any of the same senses humans do. This poses a real problem for the alien. How is it going to find out what it needs to know about Earth?

PROCEDURE

1. Work in groups of two or three students. Imagine that each group is part of a scientific team that will help the alien find out about Earth. Give your team a name.
2. In your group, decide which human sense would be the most useful for the alien to have. Your group is able to "lend" the alien a human sense for the time it is on Earth. Imagine that other groups making up the scientific team will lend the alien different senses.
3. On a sheet of paper, describe why the alien needs the sense you have volunteered to lend. Include a description of what the sense does and how it is useful for finding out about the world around you. Your description can include words, diagrams, or whatever you think would be useful.
4. Remember that your job is to assist the alien in exploring Earth. How will the members of your group get along without the sense they have volunteered to lend? In your group, brainstorm ideas about the following questions and record your answers.
   - How could you manage your daily activities — including being part of the scientific team — without the sense you have agreed to lend?
   - How might the other team members help?
   - How might you help team members who are lending a different sense?
5. Make up a team plan. Your plan should show how your scientific team will work together to assist the alien in its explorations. Display your materials for the rest of the class to see.

DISCUSSION

1. (a) List all the human senses you can think of. Beside each sense, record the number of groups that decided to lend the alien that sense.
   (b) Which sense was lent by the largest number of groups? Why do you think this sense was considered to be the most useful sense for the alien to have?
2. Describe what you think the alien might look like. What kind of senses might it have? A picture might help your description.
3. While doing this activity, did you think of any questions about the senses that you would like to have answered? If so, write the questions in your learning journal. ❖

■ 2.1 SENSORY RECEPTORS

Imagine that you are eating the meal described at the beginning of this chapter. Many things are going on inside your body while you are eating. Your lungs are working, allowing you to breathe. Your heart is pumping blood through your whole body. Your stomach and various other body parts are helping digest food. Still other parts of your body

EXTENSION

■ Find out about the life of Helen Keller. How was she able to live without two of her senses?

are also hard at work, gathering information about what is going on inside and outside your body.

This information is gathered by your **sensory receptors**. Sensory receptors are body parts that are specialized to sense or detect (become aware of) changes in your environment. Sensory receptors are located throughout your body. They are especially abundant in your eyes, ears, nose, tongue, and skin. For this reason, these body parts are sometimes called **sensory organs**. An organ is a body part that does a particular job. What job does each of your sensory organs do?

A change in the surroundings that your receptors can detect is called a **stimulus** (plural: stimuli). A stimulus might consist of a single event that occurs quite rapidly, such as the sound made by a door slamming. Other changes, or stimuli, like the smell of dinner cooking or the sight of a mountain, might last for a much longer period of time.

Sensing some stimuli, such as listening to music, simply provides pleasure. Detecting other stimuli is very important to your safety. An ability to sense that something is too hot to touch, for instance, may prevent you from getting badly burned. Being able to see or hear that a car is coming toward you may mean the difference between life and death.

Every day, your sensory organs detect thousands of stimuli. You must be able to interpret, or make sense of, these stimuli as well as detect them. In other words, you need to know what a certain stimulus is and what it means. The process of sensing requires both of these steps: detecting the stimulus (becoming aware of it) and interpreting it (figuring out what it means). In most cases, your brain does the interpreting. For this reason, receptors must be connected to your brain in some way. How are they connected?

Most sensory receptors consist of a single cell. Cells are the tiny subunits that make up all living things. The body of an adult human contains trillions of cells. There are many different kinds of cells in your body. Each type has special features that make it good at performing certain tasks (Figure 2.1). For example, **nerve cells** carry messages from one place to another.

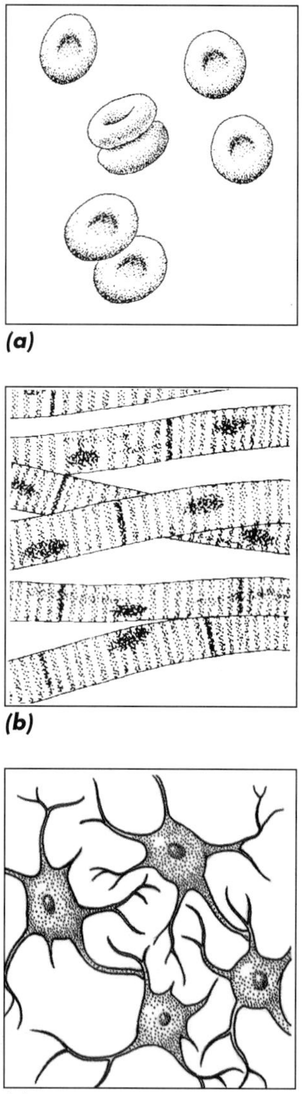

(a) *(b)* *(c)*

FIGURE 2.1
The human body is made up of many different kinds of cells. Shown here are (a) red blood cells, (b) heart muscle cells, and (c) nerve cells.

Most sensory receptors are nerve cells. (You will learn about other kinds of nerve cells in the next chapter.) Often, many nerve cells are joined together into bundles called **nerves** (Figure 2.2). Much like telephone wires, nerves carry messages from one place in your body to another. These messages are called **nerve impulses**, electrical signals that travel along a nerve cell from one end to the other.

What happens in your sensory receptors? Suppose someone suddenly turns on a lamp. Light is a stimulus that would be detected by some of the receptors in your eyes. Nerve impulses would then begin to travel along these cells. When this happens, we say that the sensory receptor has been stimulated.

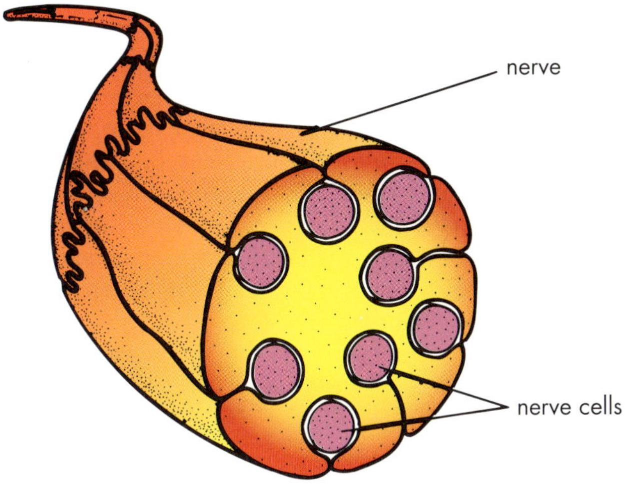

FIGURE 2.2 ◀
Nerves are the cables that connect the brain and the spinal cord with the rest of the body. They consist of nerve cells, tightly packed in bundles, surrounded by connective tissue.

When a nerve impulse reaches the end of a nerve cell, it may then pass on to the next nerve cell. In this way, the message may travel along many nerve cells until it reaches the place where it will be interpreted. Usually this is done in your brain. There, the information in the message is interpreted so that you know what the stimulus is. In the example in the last paragraph, your brain would tell you that the stimulus was light, and that it was coming from a lamp (Figure 2.3).

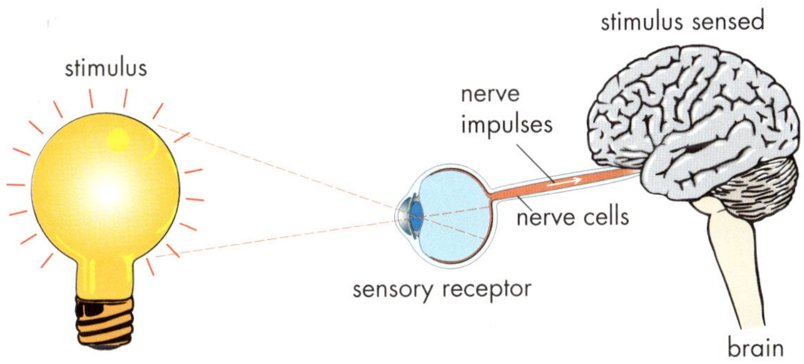

FIGURE 2.3 ◀
In this case the receptor was your eye. If you got closer to the light, what other receptors might start sending signals to your brain?

If incoming stimuli were not interpreted, you might not act properly. For example, the smell of smoke and the smell of a tasty meal are both detected by sensory receptors in your nose. Your actions, however, should be quite different after sensing these two stimuli. Another word for an action is a **response**. You can make the correct response only if your body can both detect and interpret stimuli. And making the correct response may be vitally important to your safety.

Each of your sensory organs contains a different type of sensory receptor. Each type can detect only one kind of stimulus. Receptors in your tongue, for example, can detect chemicals, but they cannot detect sounds. Receptors in your ears are sensitive to sounds, but they cannot taste a thing. In the rest of this chapter, you will look more closely at the different types of receptors.

► REVIEW 2.1

1. What is the difference between a sensory organ and a sensory receptor?
2. (a) Define the term "stimulus."
   (b) Give examples of five stimuli that give us pleasure and five stimuli that are important to our health.
3. Write a paragraph that describes sensory receptors. Include an explanation of what a sensory receptor does, what one is made up of, and where sensory receptors are found.
4. What is a nerve impulse?
5. Why is it that you cannot see with your ears?
6. Write a one-page short story or a poem in which a person responds appropriately to a stimulus. Be sure to use the following words in your story: stimulus, sensory receptor, nerve impulse, nerve cell, and response.

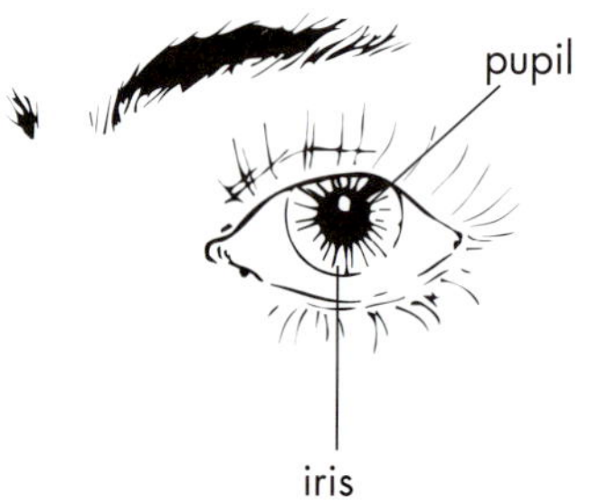

FIGURE 2.4
A human eye. What colour is your iris?

2.2 THE STRUCTURE OF THE EYE

Can you name some parts of your eye? You might want to list these in your learning journal. What job does each part do? As you read this section, you will learn about the structure of your eye (the parts that make it up) and the job, or function, of each part.

The sensory receptors in your eyes detect light energy. They are stimulated by light rays, which enter your eyes after bouncing off objects in the surroundings. (You will learn more about light in Chapter 11.)

Figure 2.4 shows some of the parts of your eye that you can see by looking in a mirror or at your partner's eye. The pupil looks like a black dot in the centre of your eye. The pupil is actually the opening through which light enters your eye. The iris, which is the coloured part of your eye, is a muscle that controls the size of the pupil. Because it can make this opening larger or smaller, your iris controls the amount of light that enters your eye.

Figure 2.5 shows some of the parts of your eye that cannot be seen from outside the body. The muscles attached to your eye allow you to move it up and down and from side to side. A layer of fat surrounds your eye. This helps cushion the eye and protect it from damage. At the back of your eye is the optic nerve. The nerve cells that make up the optic nerve are connected to the sensory receptors located inside your eye. The optic nerve carries impulses from those receptors to your brain.

Inside your eye are more important features, as shown in Figure 2.6. The wall of your eyeball is made up of three layers. The outer layer is called the sclera. It forms a case, which protects the eye and helps it keep its shape. The white part of your eye that you can see in a mirror is part of the sclera. Underneath the sclera is a thin black layer called the choroid, which contains many blood vessels. These vessels bring the nutrients and oxygen needed by the cells that make up the eye.

The vessels also carry wastes away from these cells. The inner layer of the eye's wall is the retina. It contains the sensory receptors (the nerve cells) of the eye.

The centre part of the eye is filled with a jelly-like substance called the vitreous humour. It helps your eyeball keep its round shape and prevents it from collapsing.

The oval-shaped object behind the iris is called the lens. The lens helps to bend the light rays that enter your eye so that you can see objects clearly (Figure 2.7). In other words, the lens helps put whatever you are looking at in focus. (Focusing is discussed further in Chapter 11.)

In front of the lens is a clear covering called the cornea. The cornea helps protect your eye and also helps focus the light rays entering your eye. The space between the lens and the cornea is filled with a watery substance called the aqueous humour. The aqueous humour plays a part in focusing light rays and also helps the front part of your eyeball keep its shape.

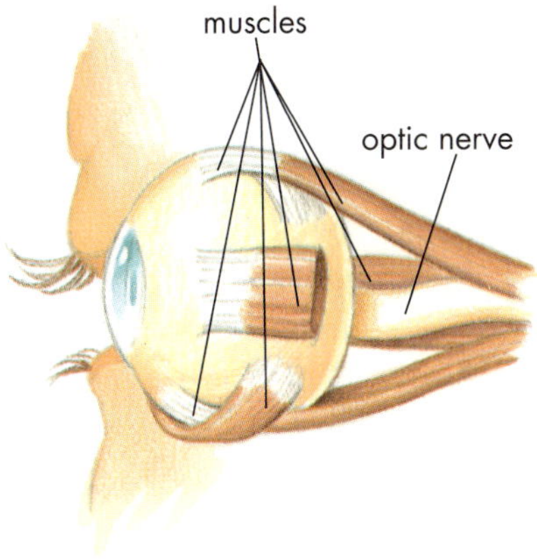

FIGURE 2.5
Six eye muscles control the eyeball, so you can look up, down, right, and left.

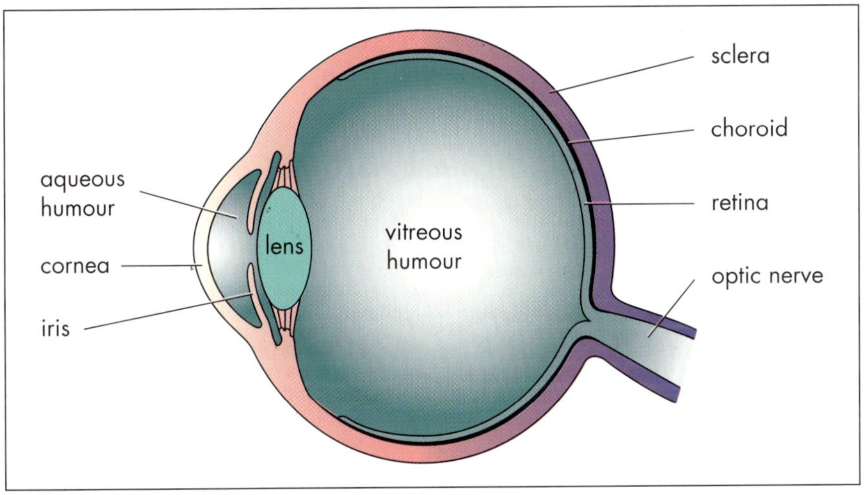

FIGURE 2.6
The inside of the eyeball. A section of the eye from front to back is shown.

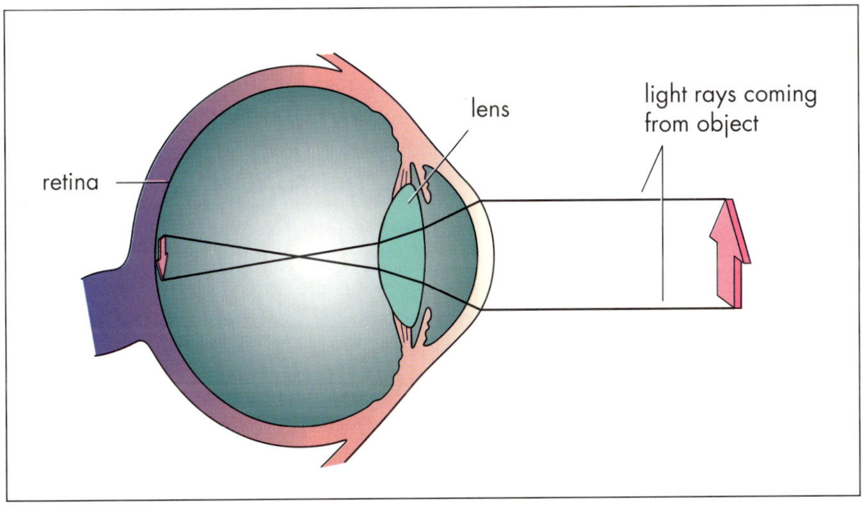

FIGURE 2.7
The lens bends light rays so they all come together in a small image on the retina. Notice that the image is upside-down. Why don't you "see" things as being upside-down?

ACTIVITY 2B / LOOKING AT AN EYE

The eyeball you will dissect has been preserved. This means it has been stored in chemicals. These chemicals help the parts of the eye to stay together for a long period of time. The animal eye you will dissect is very similar to a human eye. It has the same parts and works in the same way. Because the eye came from what was once a living animal, it deserves to be treated with respect. Do not mistreat the eye, and be sure that no parts of the eyeball leave the classroom.

The procedure includes a number of questions. Answer them in your notebook as you do each step.

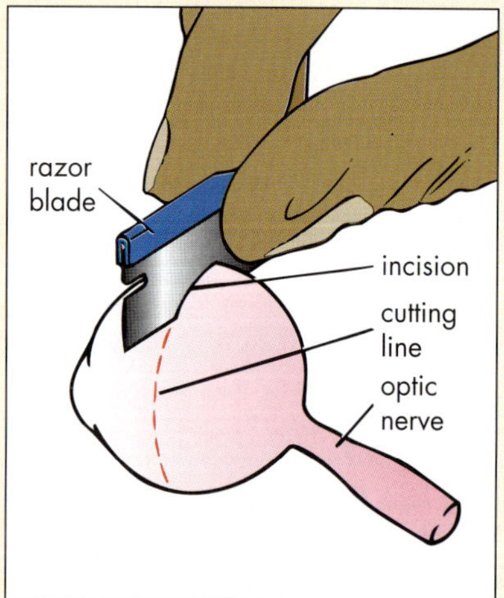

FIGURE 2.8
Making an incision in the eyeball

MATERIALS

Parts I and II
plastic gloves
goggles
apron
preserved cow's or sheep's eye
dissecting tray
single-edged razor blade

PART I Outside the Eye

PROCEDURE

1. Put on the plastic gloves, the goggles, and the apron.
2. Carefully use the razor blade to cut off the muscles and fat that are attached to the outside of the eyeball. The fat is pale yellow or white. Do not confuse it with the muscles that help move the eyeball in its socket. These muscles, which are attached to the sclera, are light brown. In what other way are the muscles different from the fat? Why do you think there are so many muscles attached to the eyeball?
3. Examine the sclera, the outer case of the eye. Around most of the eye, the sclera is white. At the front of the eye, the sclera becomes clear and bulges slightly outward. This bulging part of the sclera is the cornea. In a living animal, the cornea is colourless. In a preserved eye, the cornea is often cloudy.
4. Locate the pupil. Surrounding the pupil is the iris. What colour is the iris in the eye you are dissecting?
5. Find the optic nerve, a smooth, round cord at the back of the eyeball. In a preserved eye, the optic nerve has been cut. In a living animal, where would the optic nerve lead?

PART II Inside the Eye

Dissect the eye carefully. Cut only those structures outlined in the procedure so that the other parts of the eye will not be damaged.

PROCEDURE

1. Place the eye on its side, with the optic nerve to your right. Use the razor blade to cut gently into the eye about 2 cm to the left of the optic nerve (Figure 2.8). Do not squeeze the eye or liquid will squirt out. Cut through the entire eye to separate the eyeball into two parts.
2. Locate and remove the vitreous humour. Place it on the tray. You may notice that the lens is attached to the vitreous humour and has also come out. If not, remove it now. Describe the shape of the lens. In a preserved eye, the lens is usually hard and cloudy. In a living animal (including you), the lens is soft and clear and its shape can be changed by muscles that are attached to it (Figure 2.6).
3. Pick up the front part of the eye — the part that does not have the optic nerve attached to it. Hold it up to a window or light and look through it as the animal might have. Can you see through the pupil?

C A U T I O N !

■ **Handle all sharp or pointed equipment with great care.**
When using a razor blade, cut away from you, not toward you or toward anyone else.
When carrying pointed items, make sure the pointed end is toward the floor.

4. Place the part of the eye that you have been working with in the dissecting tray. Use the other section, which has the optic nerve attached, for the remaining steps.
5. Pick up the back part of the eyeball. Note the thin, skinlike layer stretched over the inside. This layer is the retina. (The retina may be covered with a thin brown layer of blood vessels. If so, this layer can easily be scraped off.) The retina contains the eye's sensory receptors — millions of tiny cells. Describe the retina. Is it coloured?
6. Locate the place at which the optic nerve leaves the inside of the eye. There is a gap in the retina at this point. Therefore, there are no sensory receptor cells here.
7. With the corner of your razor blade, gently lift the retina away from the rest of the eyeball. Notice the black layer underneath the retina. This layer is the choroid. Why do you think this layer is dark-coloured?
8. In your notebook, carefully draw the two parts of the eye that you made with your cut in step 1 of Part II. Label all the parts that you have examined.
9. Wash your hands carefully.

DISCUSSION

1. Why is it important to wear goggles and plastic gloves when dissecting?
2. List the parts of the eye through which light passes as it travels through the eye to the retina. Make up a mnemonic (memory device) to help you remember the order.
3. What does each of these parts do?
4. Write down in your learning journal any questions you have about how the eye works. ❖

EYE PROTECTION

Because your eyes are so important for your survival, they are well protected (Figure 2.9). Lightly run your finger along your eyebrow and then around and under your eye. You can feel the bones that encircle your eye to form the eye socket. These bones help protect your eye from large objects like basketballs.

Your eyelids are very thin layers of skin that are usually folded back when you are awake. When closed, they cover your eyes completely to shut out light and protect your eyes from damage. Your eyelids can close very rapidly — even before you can think about closing them — to shield your eye from approaching objects.

The hair of your eyebrows helps to prevent falling dust and other particles, as well as perspiration, from entering your eye. This is also the job of your eyelashes — the short, strong hairs that are attached to the edges of your eyelids. They form a fine screen to trap particles that might otherwise enter your eye.

If particles do touch the surface of your eyes, they are often washed

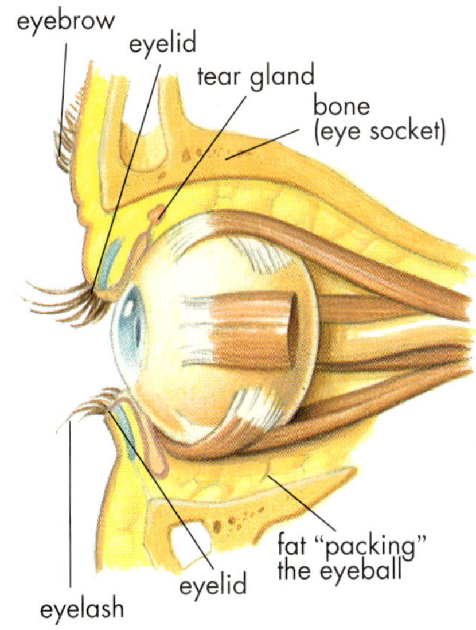

FIGURE 2.9
Body parts that protect the eye

away by tears. Tear glands are located above each of your eye sockets; they produce a watery, salty fluid that flows onto your eyes to keep them moist as well as to wash away particles.

Even with these defences, your eyes are not safe from all harm. It is important to wear proper eye protection when you are working or playing if there is a chance that something could hit your eye or get into it (Figure 2.10). It is also important to wear good-quality sunglasses in sunny weather. Too much sunlight can damage the cornea, lens, and retina. You are usually not aware of this damage when it happens. It occurs slowly and may not cause you problems until you are older.

FIGURE 2.10
What are the eyes being protected from in each photo?

(a) *(b)* *(c)*

► REVIEW 2.2

1. (a) What stimulates the sensory receptors of the eye?
   (b) Where are these receptors found?
2. Construct a table summarizing
   (a) the parts of the body that protect your eyes,
   (b) what each of these parts does.
3. What are some situations in which your eyes might be damaged? What can you do to avoid this damage?

DID YOU KNOW

■ There are about 130 million light-sensitive sensory receptors in each of your retinas. What does this tell you about the size of each of these receptors?

■ 2.3 VISION

Rays of light are continually bouncing off all the objects in your surroundings. When you look at an object or a scene, some of these light rays will enter your eye through your pupil. Inside your eye, the rays hit the retina. Each ray stimulates a different sensory receptor or group of receptors, creating nerve impulses. These impulses are then carried along the optic nerve to the brain where they are interpreted.

Your brain puts together a picture of what you are looking at by interpreting the messages that have come from thousands of stimulated receptors. By itself, your eye cannot "see" anything. Unless your brain interprets what your eye's sensory receptors have detected, sight is not possible.

OPTOMETRIST

Do you wear glasses or contact lenses? If so, you may have had your eyes checked by an optometrist. Here is what Dr. Lindsay Kamachi has to say about his job as an optometrist.

As a student at the University of British Columbia, I was interested in the health sciences. In biology, my studies on vision helped me to decide to be an optometrist. When I first considered this career, I thought I would just examine people's eyes and prescribe glasses and contact lenses. I found out that there is more to being an optometrist than I thought.

After getting my science degree at U.B.C., I studied for four more years at the University of Waterloo to receive my Doctor of Optometry degree. Next I passed provincial exams to work as an optometrist in British Columbia.

An important part of my job is to examine my patients' eyes to see whether they need corrective lenses — eyeglasses or contact lenses — to improve their vision. I also look at how well their eyes move and how well their eyes work as a team. If patients have problems with their eye muscles, I may recommend certain eye exercises or special lenses. An optometrist also examines the patient's eyes to see if they are healthy and may send a patient to a medical doctor for treatment. Sometimes I suggest that patients with poor vision use magnifying devices when regular lenses are not enough. Some of my patients are preschool children, and I check whether their eyes are developing properly.

As an optometrist, I am part of a team that cares for people's eyes. I may send some patients to an ophthalmologist, a medical doctor who specializes in eye diseases and may do surgery. Optometrists and ophthalmologists work closely with family doctors, since many health problems can affect people's eyes.

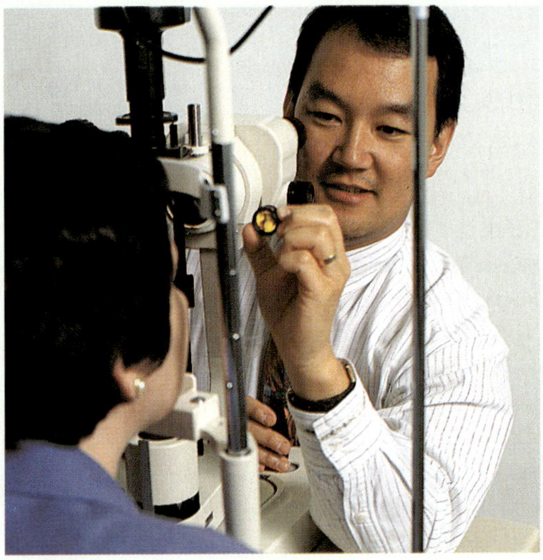

Dr. Kamachi uses a phoropter to help determine whether a patient needs corrective lenses.

If a patient needs corrective lenses, an optometrist or an ophthalmologist will give written instructions (called a prescription) for the lenses. The lenses will be made and fitted by either an optometrist or an optician. Opticians are trained to make and fit lenses but do not examine eyes.

I find being an optometrist a very satisfying career. Optometrists may work on their own, or work in a clinic, or work with a partner. I work in partnership with my wife, Dr. Daphne Wong-Kamachi, who is also an optometrist. We have regular office hours, but with two of us, we can also be flexible. My wife and I find that a career as an optometrist is quite easy to combine with family needs. Although this career requires several years of university training, an optometrist can have a well-paying, interesting job working with people of all ages. I am glad that I decided to become an optometrist and to serve my community as a member of its health team.

TWO TYPES OF RECEPTORS

Your retina contains two types of sensory receptors, named for their shapes. These rod-shaped and cone-shaped receptors are both stimulated by light, but in different situations.

Rods are sensitive to dim light. They allow you to see at night or in places where there is very little light. Rods can only work properly if your body has a good supply of vitamin A. This vitamin can be obtained from various foods, including carrots, milk, and egg yolk. Lack of vitamin A causes a condition called night blindness, in which the eyes adjust to dim light much more slowly than usual (Figure 2.11).

FIGURE 2.11 ▶
Ordinarily, your eyes adjust to being able to see in the dark quite quickly after looking at a light. People with night blindness do not adjust as quickly. They are blinded for several minutes after looking at a light — such as the glare of headlights. How would this affect their ability to drive a car?

DID YOU KNOW

■ Most of the cones in your eye are located near the middle of the retina, whereas rods are found toward the outer edge of the retina. As a result, when you look at an object in dim light, it often helps you to see if you look slightly to one side of the object. This causes a picture of the object to be focused on the sides of the retina, where most of the rods are found. Because rods work better than cones in dim light, focusing on the sides of the retina makes it easier for you to see at night. How could you use this information when looking at the stars in the night sky?

Cones work best in bright light. They allow you to see in colour. There are three types of cones. Some cones are stimulated only by red light, some by green light, and some by blue light. These three types of cones work together to allow you to see a whole range of colours. For example, if both blue and green cones are stimulated at the same time, you can see the colour turquoise.

USING BOTH EYES

When you close one eye, your brain receives only one set of sight messages about the surroundings. When you use both eyes, however, your brain gets two sets of messages. Because your eyes are placed a small distance apart, these messages are slightly different. As a result, when your brain interprets the impulses received from both eyes, it produces two slightly different pictures of what you are looking at. Your brain then blends these two pictures into one, and what you see looks three-dimensional: it has depth as well as length and width. This allows you to see how far apart objects are from one another and how far they are from you.

The ability to judge distances is important in activities such as catching a ball, making a sculpture, and riding a bicycle.

LOSS OF SIGHT

People who have lost their sight (are blind) use various ways to make up for the loss of this sense. Many have friends or volunteers who read books or letters to them — for enjoyment or so they can study. They may borrow recorded versions of books from "talking book" libraries. Some blind people also read using their fingertips. They use a code called Braille, in which combinations of raised dots represent letters, numbers, and punctuation (Figure 2.12). Today, computer programs can translate print into Braille, but many books are still made by volunteers with Braille typewriters or Braille keys on their computers.

Technology assists blind people in other ways too. For example, in some cities in British Columbia, a distinctive noise sounds when traffic lights change from red to green. This sound tells blind people when it is safe to cross the street.

EXTENSION

■ Visit a Motor Vehicles Branch office to find out what visual tests must be passed before you can get a driver's licence. What regulations concerning eyesight are enforced after the driver's licence is issued? Do you think that any of these regulations should be deleted or changed? Should any regulations be added?

FIGURE 2.12
Some blind people learn to rely on their sense of touch to read. With practice, it is possible to read fifty Braille words per minute.

A COMPUTER THAT READS BOOKS

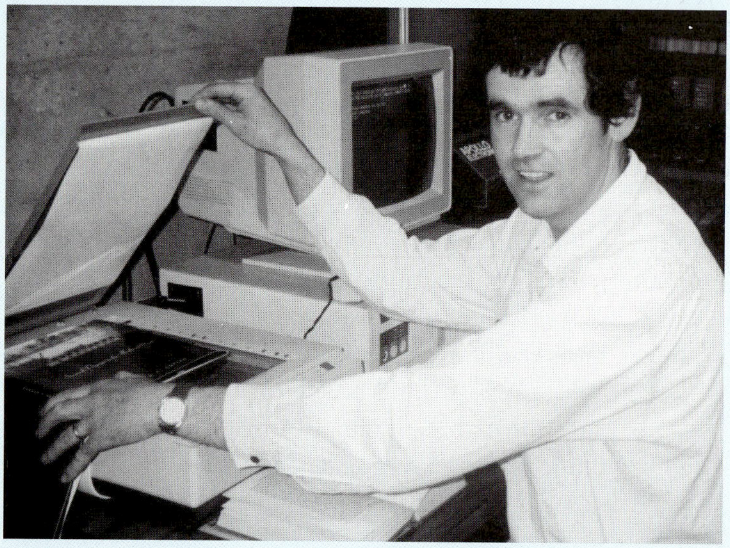

When Peter Booth lost his eyesight in his early twenties, he thought he would never read another book or magazine. Now, thanks to a computer, Booth is able to "read" books. A computer helped him read while he was studying at the University College of the Fraser Valley.

Before computers, people who were blind or had limited vision could only read by listening to taped books, having a person read to them, or using Braille books. Computers have changed all that. Booth used a Kurzweil Personal Reader at the college library to help him read books and other printed materials. Here's how the reader works. When Booth wants to read a book, he places it face down on the scanner, a box that looks like a small photocopier. After he turns on the computer, it tells Booth which keys to press to work the program. The scanner sends an image to the computer, and the page appears on the screen of the monitor. At the same time, the computer reads the page aloud. The computer has a limited vocabulary in its memory, and it does not recognize every word on a page. If the computer does not know a word, it spells it letter by letter.

Although Booth does not have his own scanner to read the printed page, he was able to do some of his reading at home when he was a student. He would copy onto a floppy disk those pages that the computer had read. He would put the disk into his computer at home, which has a speech synthesizer and can read aloud from a disk. Booth often needed to type an essay or report as a student. His home computer is programmed to read aloud each word as he types it.

Some people with limited vision can also use a computer aid called Visualtek. This can enlarge the letters printed on a page. The letters can then be shown on a computer monitor so that they are seen up to 60 times their real size. At this enlargement, only three or four letters of a word appear at a time. Booth, who still has some vision, can use Visualtek, but he says it is as if he is reading a book by looking with one eye through a very long, thin tube.

Although people with vision problems are most likely to use computers that can read, these computers can help others too. People who have difficulty learning to read might use the Kurzweil Personal Reader. It permits them to read the print on the monitor at the same time as they hear it read aloud.

The existence of a computer that reads books has made a tremendous difference to Peter Booth. With its help, he has graduated from college with a social services diploma and is now looking for a job. Can you imagine how such a computer would change your life if you lost your sight?

ACTIVITY 2C / INVESTIGATING VISION

Do these activities with a partner. At each station you can discover something different about how your sense of sight works.

MATERIALS

Station I - Figure 2.13, ruler
Station II - lamp
Station III - sheet of paper, tape
Station IV - Figure 2.17, ruler
Station V - pencil with two-sided picture attached (fish on one side, bowl on the other)

FIGURE 2.13
Figure for Station I

STATION I Blind Spot

PROCEDURE

1. Hold the textbook about 45 cm away from your face so that the X shown in Figure 2.13 is directly in front of your right eye.
2. Close your left eye and then slowly move the book toward you. Keep your right eye on the X. You should be aware that the dot is there, but do not look at it directly. As you move the book toward you, at some point you will notice that the dot entirely disappears from view. Immediately stop moving the book and hold it in place.
3. Have your partner measure and record the distance from your eye to the book.
4. Switch roles with your partner and repeat steps 1 to 3.

DISCUSSION

1. Every person has a "blind spot" in each eye. Think back to your dissection of the eye. Where do you think this blind spot might be?
2. How might this blind spot be related to the disappearance of the dot?
3. Compare the measurement you obtained in step 3 with those of several other members of the class. Did everybody obtain the same measurement? Can you think of a reason why or why not?

STATION II The Size of Your Pupil

PROCEDURE

1. Sit in a brightly lit place in the classroom. Ask your partner to cover his or her right eye with the right hand for 30 seconds. Observe the size of the pupil in your partner's left eye during this time.
2. When your partner quickly removes the hand, stare at his or her right eye. Carefully observe and record any size changes that you notice in the pupil of this eye. If you did not notice any change, ask your partner to repeat steps 1 and 2.
3. Switch roles and repeat steps 1 and 2.

DISCUSSION

1. Describe the change that occurred in your partner's right pupil when it was uncovered.

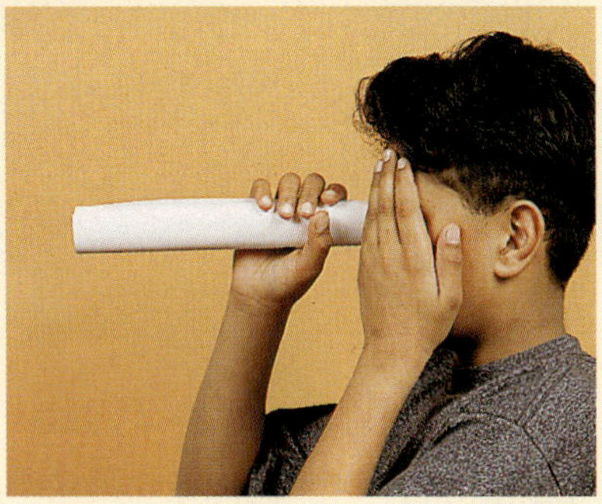

FIGURE 2.14
Position of tube for step 1.

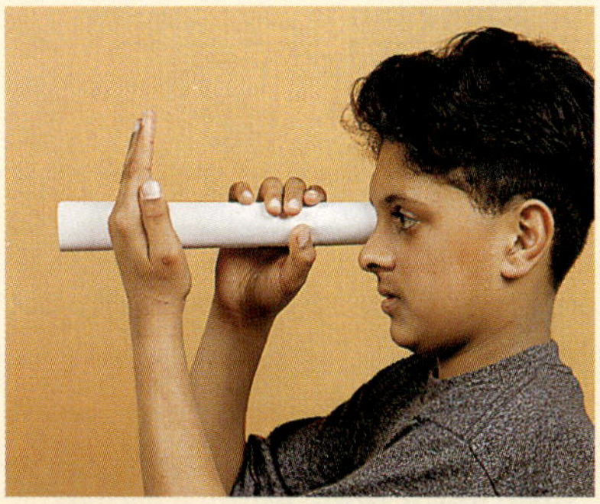

FIGURE 2.15
Slide your left hand away from you in step 2.

FIGURE 2.16
How to hold your fingers in step 4.

2. (a) What do you think is the purpose of this change?
(b) Suggest three situations in which these changes might be helpful to your sense of sight.

STATION III A One-eyed Picture of the World

PROCEDURE

1. Roll a piece of paper lengthwise into a tube about 3 cm in diameter. Tape the loose end in place. Cover your left eye with your left hand while holding the tube with your right hand. With your right eye, look through the tube at an object on the far side of the room (Figure 2.14).

2. Continue to focus on the object on the far side of the room. Open both eyes and slide your left hand (open palm toward you) out along the tube until your hand is near the end (Figure 2.15). Briefly describe your observations to your partner, who will record them.

3. Switch roles with your partner and repeat steps 1 and 2.

4. Hold your index fingers, tips slightly apart, about 12 cm away from your eyes (Figure 2.16). Looking past, or "through," your fingers, focus on an object on the other side of the room. What appears between the tips of your fingers? Draw what you see.

DISCUSSION

1. (a) In steps 1 and 2, your brain received sensory messages about the distant object from only one eye although it was expecting messages from two eyes. How did your brain interpret the stimuli when half of the information was missing?
(b) Why do you think the brain does this? How could this method of interpreting stimuli help you?

2. (a) Does the drawing you made in step 4 show something that was really there?
(b) Do you think both eyes would have to be open to see what you saw? (Try it and see.)
(c) How might you explain your observations in step 4?

STATION IV Optical Illusions

PROCEDURE

1. Look at Figure 2.17a. Predict which of the cylinders in this figure is the largest and which is the smallest. Measure to the nearest millimetre the actual height of each of the three cylinders. Record your measurements in a data table of your own design.

2. Look at Figure 2.17b. Predict which distance is the shortest and which is the longest: a to b, b to c, d to e, or e to f. Measure to the nearest millimetre the lengths of all these distances. Record them in a data table.

3. Predict which of the two diagonal lines (x or y) in Figure 2.17c is longer. Measure the lengths of these diagonal lines to the nearest millimetre. Record your measurements in a data table.

DISCUSSION

1. Were you surprised by any of the measurements you recorded in the steps above? Did your measurements always confirm your predictions? Explain your answer.

2. Why do you think that these pictures might have "tricked" your brain?

STATION V Moving Pictures

PROCEDURE

1. Pick up the pencil with the two-sided picture attached and hold it upright between your palms. Roll the pencil back and forth so that the paper flips from one side to the other (Figure 2.18). Increase the speed of rolling. Describe what seems to happen to the fish and bowl.

DISCUSSION

1. Your eyes hold on to a picture of what you have just seen for a fraction of a second after it has gone out of sight. In other words, they keep seeing an object even after it is no longer there. This feature is called persistence of vision. How does persistence of vision help you explain what you observed with the fish and bowl?

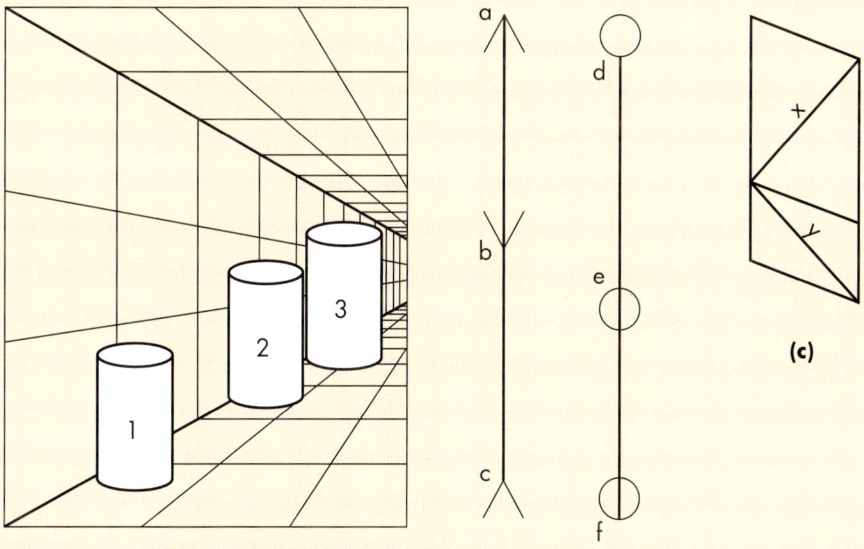

(a) (b) (c)

FIGURE 2.17
Figures for Station IV

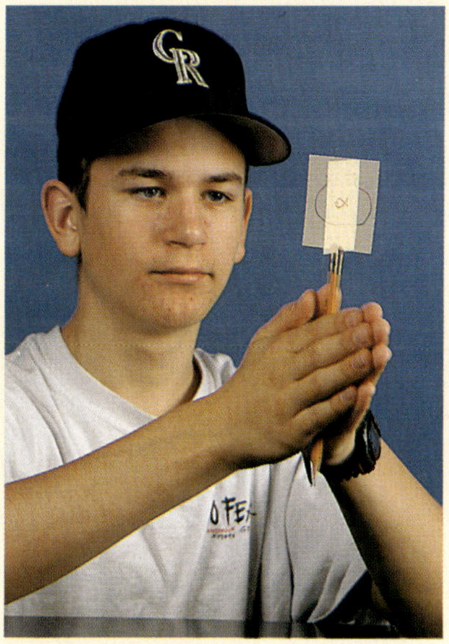

FIGURE 2.18
Twirl the pencil back and forth rapidly so that you see one side of the square, then the other, then the first again, and so on.

FIGURE 2.19
What is the difference between each of the frames in a strip of movie film? If this film were running quickly through a projector, what would the character appear to be doing?

2. Have you ever looked closely at movie film, or watched it roll through a movie projector (Figure 2.19)? Toys that worked like the fish and bowl pictures gave people the idea of how to make movies. How is using this toy similar to using a movie projector? ❖

▶ REVIEW 2.3

1. If your optic nerve was badly injured, how would this affect your sense of sight? Explain your answer.

2. (a) In what ways are rods and cones similar?
(b) In what ways are they different?

3. Why might an activity like driving a car be difficult if one of your eyes was injured?

4. At night, you cannot see colours very well — most of what you see seems to be in black and white. Why do you think this is so?

2.4 THE EAR AND HEARING

Fortunately for us, our sense of hearing never "sleeps." A baby's cry awakens its parent; a pet dog's barking can arouse a household; the buzz of a smoke alarm alerts a sleeping family. Hearing is very important for warning us of possible danger.

Hearing is also important for communicating with others. Babies learn to speak by imitating the words they hear. Imagine how difficult it would be to learn how to speak if you could not hear other people (Figure 2.20). Fortunately, there are other ways to communicate. Many people who are deaf (cannot hear) use sign language to "talk" (Figure 2.21).

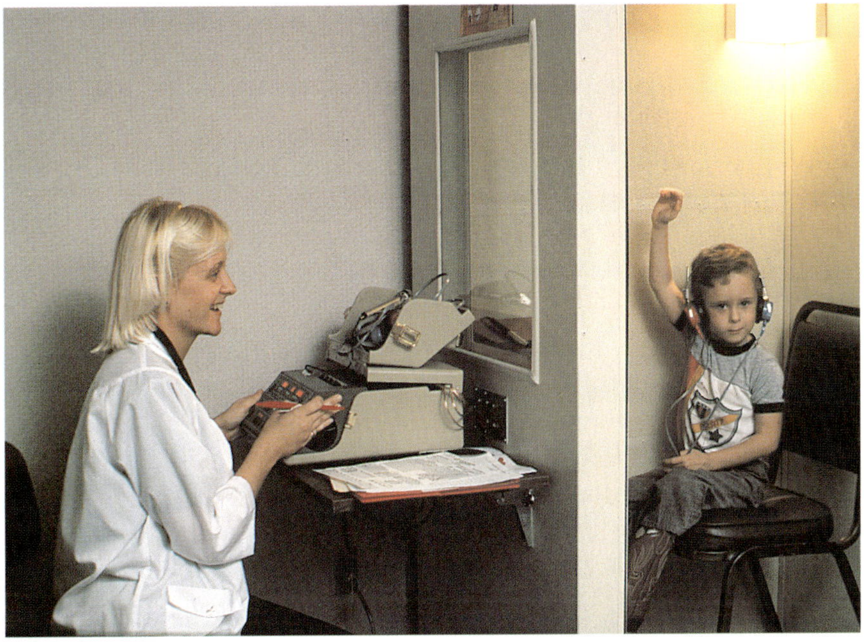

FIGURE 2.20
If your hearing were impaired, how could you tell? With the right equipment, technicians can check your hearing.

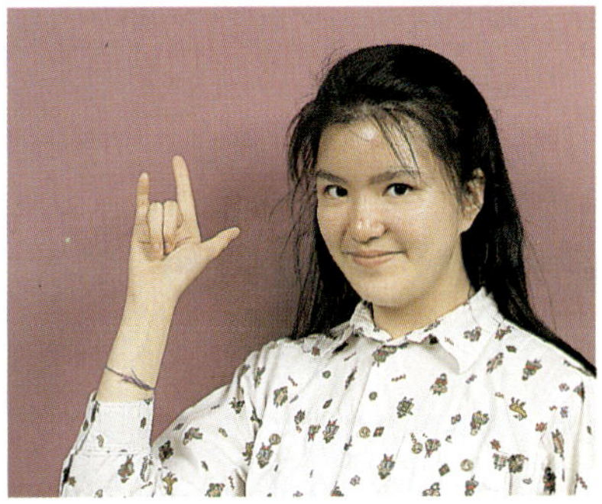

FIGURE 2.21
A type of sign language commonly used in North America is called American Sign Language, or ASL. This person is saying "I love you" in ASL.

ACTIVITY 2D / THE DIRECTION OF SOUND

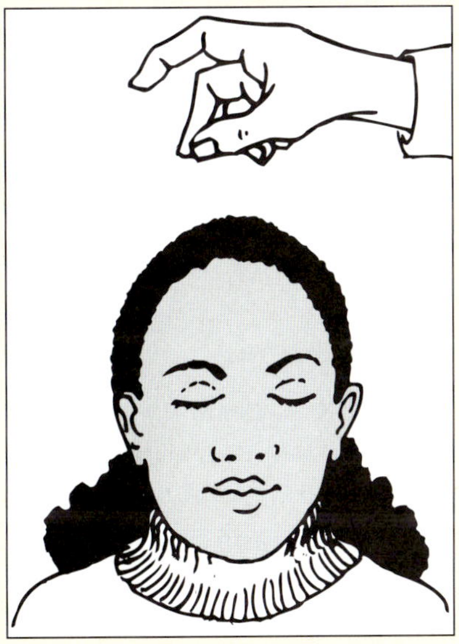

FIGURE 2.22
Have your fingers an equal distance from each of your partner's ears.

Does your ability to hear a sound depend on the direction it comes from?

PROCEDURE

1. Have your partner sit with eyes closed.
2. Snap the fingers of one of your hands above your partner's head. Ask your partner to tell you where you are snapping: near the front, on top, or at the back of his or her head. Try to have your fingers an equal distance from each of your partner's ears each time you snap (Figure 2.22). Design your own data table. Record the location of where you snapped and whether or not your partner guessed this location correctly.
3. Repeat step 2 nine more times, changing the snapping location each time.
4. Switch roles with your partner.

DISCUSSION

1. (a) How many times did you correctly identify the location the snapping sound was coming from?

(b) Were you more successful when the sound came from a particular location or locations?

2. Most people have difficulty determining the location a sound is coming from unless it comes from a place closer to one ear than the other. Why do you think this might be so?

3. Why do you think it is more difficult to hear quiet sounds when they are behind you than when they are in front of you? ❖

THE PARTS OF THE EAR

The sensory receptors that allow you to hear are located in your ears. They gather information about your surroundings by picking up sounds. Your ears have a number of special features that help you detect sound stimuli.

Your ear can be divided into three sections: the outer ear, middle ear, and inner ear (Figure 2.23). You probably think of your ear as the structure on the side of your head. This is part of the **outer ear**. The part of your ear outside your head acts like a funnel, collecting sounds and directing them inside your head.

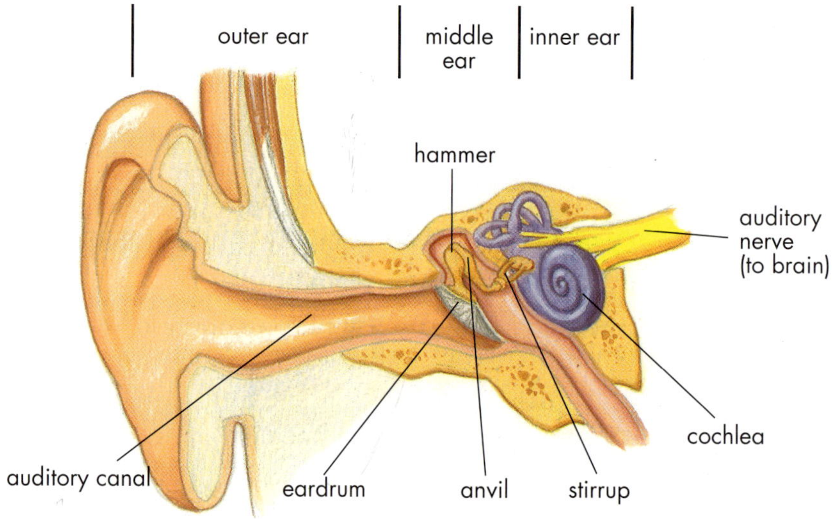

FIGURE 2.23 ▶
The parts of the human ear. The inner ear is deep inside the hard bone of the skull (colour).

After entering your head, the sound travels along the auditory canal to reach the eardrum. The eardrum is a membrane — a thin, flexible layer that is something like skin — that is stretched over the end of the auditory canal. When a sound strikes the eardrum, it starts to vibrate, or move back and forth repeatedly. Your eardrum vibrates the way the top of a drum does when it is hit with a drumstick. The part of the ear outside your head, the auditory canal, and the eardrum make up the outer ear.

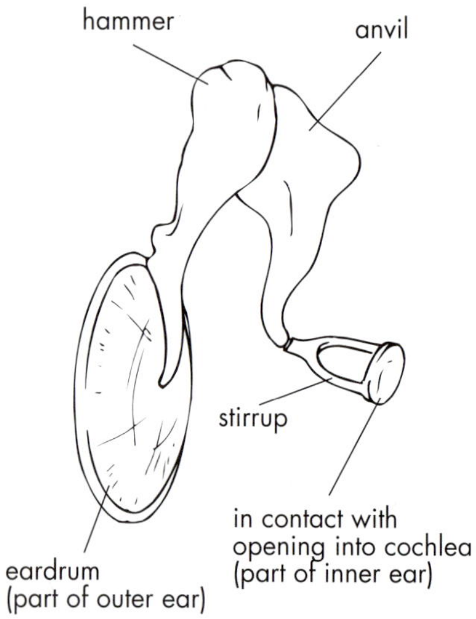

FIGURE 2.24
The bones of the middle ear—the hammer, anvil, and stirrup—are named for their shapes.

On the other side of your eardrum are the three small bones that make up the **middle ear** (Figure 2.24). The eardrum touches the first bone, which is called the hammer. Vibration of the drum, therefore, causes the hammer to vibrate also. The hammer then strikes the second bone, the anvil, causing it to vibrate as well. The anvil pushes against the third bone, the stirrup, so that it vibrates too.

Finally, the vibrations are passed on through a membrane into the **inner ear**. This second membrane covers the opening into the cochlea. The cochlea is a long, funnel-shaped structure that is rolled up so that it resembles a snail-shell (Figure 2.25a.) It is about the size of a pea. The cochlea is filled with fluid and contains many tiny hairs, each of which is connected to a sensory receptor (Figure 2.25b).

When the stirrup vibrates, these vibrations create waves in the fluid inside the cochlea. The movement of the fluid causes the tiny hairs to move. The movement of the hairs stimulates the sensory receptors attached to them. The stimulation creates nerve impulses, which are then sent along the auditory nerve from the cochlea to the brain. Just as you cannot see unless the brain interprets nerve impulses from the eye, you cannot hear unless nerve impulses from the ear reach the brain.

EXTENSION

■ Have your ears ever "popped" while you were riding in an airplane, an elevator, or a car that was driving up and down steep hills? Why does this happen?

PROTECTING YOUR HEARING

Have you ever been told to turn down the volume while you were enjoying some music? You may not have thought the sound was loud at all, especially if you had been listening for a while and had become used to it. Other people near you may have found the volume too high. If you listen to sounds that are too loud, you may damage your ears (Table 2.1).

Loudness (measured in decibels)	Examples
30	Quiet library
40	Leaves rustling
50	Refrigerator
60	Normal conversation
70	City or highway traffic
80	Hair-dryer
90	Food blender, lawnmower
100	Snowmobile, train, video arcade games
110	Racing car, jackhammer, chain-saw
120	Rock concert
130	Jet engine at take-off
140	Firecracker, nearby gunshot blast

TABLE 2.1 ***Loudness of Sounds***

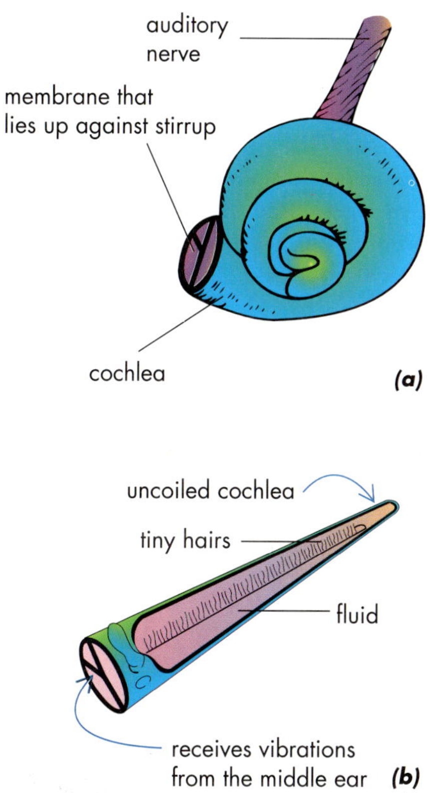

FIGURE 2.25
(a) Inside your ear, the cochlea is coiled. (b) The cochlea is shown as it might look if it were uncoiled.

The sensory receptors or the nerves carrying impulses to the brain can be damaged by sounds that are too loud. Sounds over 120 db can immediately damage your ears. Over time, repeatedly listening to sounds over 85 db can also cause hearing loss. Protecting the ears is a good idea for anyone who is exposed to very loud sounds (Figure 2.26).

FIGURE 2.26
This worker is exposed to noise levels that could damage her hearing if her ears weren't protected. Such damage can be permanent. How would you protect your hearing if you were operating a jackhammer?

And you can always turn down the volume when you listen to music or television.

There are other ways in which your ability to hear may be reduced or destroyed. Some people are born unable to hear or able to hear only a limited range of sounds. Ear infections can cause hearing loss. So can various types of injuries. For example, the eardrum can be damaged by an object stuck into the ear or by very strong vibrations, such as those from a nearby explosion. Damage to the eardrum prevents or reduces the transfer of sound vibrations into the middle ear and inner ear. As a result, the sensory receptors are not stimulated.

Technology can help people with hearing difficulties to hear better or to manage without this sense. Some types of hearing aids carry vibrations into the inner ear if the eardrum or the bones of the middle ear are damaged. Other types of hearing aids are used if the nerves of the ear are damaged. Equipment has been invented that makes it possible for deaf people to use the telephone (Figure 2.27).

FIGURE 2.27
This equipment allows a deaf person to use the telephone. How does this instrument work? What other devices are available for the hearing impaired?

EXTENSION

■ When riding in a boat, car, or airplane, people sometimes feel dizzy. This is called motion sickness. How is motion sickness related to the ear?

► REVIEW 2.4

1. Make up a mnemonic to help you remember the parts of the ear in the order that sound travels through them.
2. Make a table showing (a) the three sections of the ear, (b) the parts in each section, and (c) what each part does.
3. Explain how damage to your eardrum can prevent you from hearing.
4. Many animals, including cats and some types of dogs, can change the position or shape of their ears. How would this ability be useful?
5. Imagine that it is 200 years in the future and it is possible to shrink people down to a height of 1 mm. You are a doctor with a patient who is going deaf for an unknown reason. You shrink down and prepare to travel through your patient's ear to look for the cause of the problem. Describe your voyage through your patient's ear to the brain. Be creative!

2.5 THE CHEMICAL SENSES: TASTE AND SMELL

Humans have two types of sensory receptors for detecting the presence of chemicals in their surroundings — the taste and smell receptors. Although your taste and smell receptors are different in some ways, they also share some similarities.

THE SENSE OF TASTE

When you are at home tonight, look at your tongue in the mirror. Many of the small bumps you will see on your tongue contain **taste buds**. On the top of each taste bud is a tiny opening (Figure 2.28). Chemicals can enter through these openings and stimulate sensory receptors in each taste bud. This stimulation creates nerve impulses. As is true for the other senses, these impulses are then sent to your brain for interpreting.

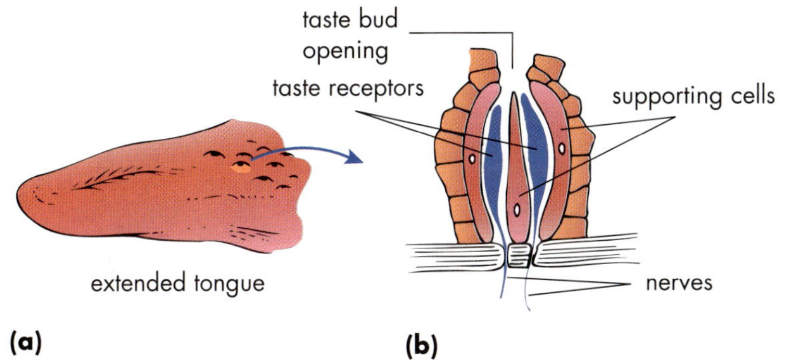

FIGURE 2.28 ◄
(a) Around the tiny bumps on your tongue are many taste buds. (b) A single taste bud enlarged. Supporting cells hold the taste receptors in place and help them do their work.

EXTENSION

■ There are several new terms in this chapter that come from words in other languages. What terms have you seen that use the words in the following list? (The first word is from Greek and the rest are from Latin.)

opti	eye	humor	a fluid
vitri	glassy	cochl	snail
aqua	water	audi	hear

Chemicals from the food you eat cannot enter the taste bud openings in large solid lumps. The chemicals must first be dissolved (broken apart and mixed with water). If you put a lump of sugar on your

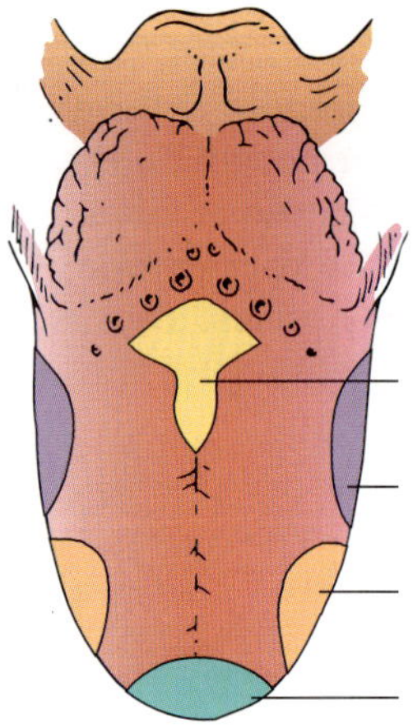

FIGURE 2.29
Map of a human tongue, seen from above. Where on your tongue do you detect the taste of oranges? What about pickles?

tongue, you cannot taste the sweetness right away. At least some of the sugar must first be dissolved. Dissolving solids is one of the jobs of saliva.

There are only four basic tastes: sweet, sour, salty, and bitter. You can probably recognize many different flavours, such as orange, strawberry, and chocolate. These other flavours are made up of combinations of these four basic tastes. Almost all taste receptors are more sensitive to one of the four tastes than to the others. Each of the four basic tastes is detected on a different part of the tongue (Figure 2.29).

The number of taste buds in your tongue will decrease as you get older. This is partly the result of natural wear and tear on the tongue. Certain activities, such as eating very spicy foods, are especially hard on the taste receptors. Smoking also destroys many taste buds.

The sense of taste provides you with information about only a limited part of your surroundings — what you put into your mouth. For many animals, a good sense of taste is very important for survival (Figure 2.30). Humans, however, have other ways to find out about what is safe and healthy to eat, such as reading labels and learning from others. Taste is less important for our safety than sight or hearing.

DID YOU KNOW

■ Human smell receptors become "tired" quickly. When this happens, they stop sending nerve impulses to the brain, even though a particular odour may still be in the air. As a result, we eventually do not notice even very unpleasant odours if they have been all around us for some time.

FIGURE 2.30
In the jungle, if it tastes bad, it's probably a bad idea to eat it. Some animals and plants produce chemicals that are poisonous to others and store them in their bodies. The poisons often taste bad. The bad taste discourages animals from eating them.

THE SENSE OF SMELL

For many animals, the sense of smell is a major source of information about their surroundings. Using smell, they can detect the location of friends, enemies, and food. For example, a dog can find food and learn that visitors have been in the house by using its nose. In general, humans learn more about these things using their eyes and ears. We rarely rely on smell to sense enemies or to find food. Smell can warn us of danger, however, such as when we smell something burning or decide not to eat a bad-smelling substance that might poison us.

Your smell receptors are located inside your nose (Figure 2.31). When these sensory receptors are stimulated by odours, nerve impulses are created. As in the case of the other senses, these impulses are sent to the brain for interpretation.

The two chemical senses — taste and smell — often work together. The brain interprets some flavours, such as chocolate, much better if it receives sensory messages from both taste and smell receptors.

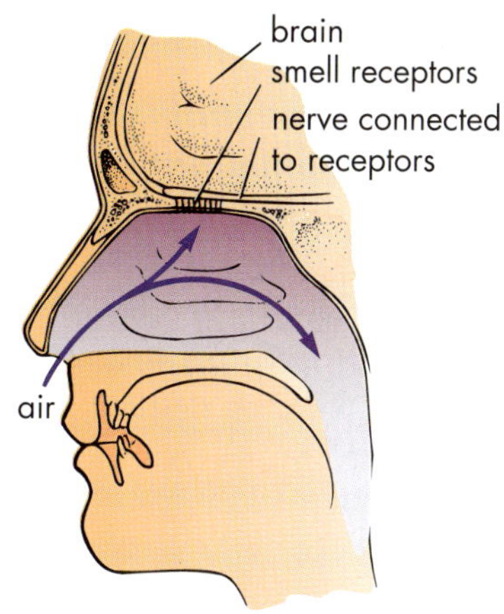

FIGURE 2.31
The smell receptors are located in the nose. When you breathe in, you cause air filled with chemicals (odours) to pass over these nerve cells.

ACTIVITY 2E / HOW DOES SMELL AFFECT TASTE? (TEACHER DEMONSTRATION)

What happens to your sense of taste if your sense of smell is not working?

MATERIALS

five different flavours of soft drinks
five small spoons per taster
glass of water for each taster

PROCEDURE

1. Your teacher will have five different flavours of soft drinks, each in a lettered, unlabelled container. Students will be volunteer tasters.
2. Your teacher or a student should prepare a data table on the board to record observations (Table 2.2).
3. Because the purpose of this test is to investigate the influence of smell (rather than sight) on taste, the taster will be blindfolded.
4. Before tasting each drink, the taster should take a drink of water to rinse off his or her taste buds.
5. The taster will pinch his or her nostrils closed. Using a spoon, your teacher will place a sample of one of the soft drinks on the taster's tongue.
6. The taster will guess the flavour of the drink. Your teacher will record this answer in the table. ➡

Name of taster	Sample A		Sample B		Sample C		Sample D		Sample E	
	Nostrils closed	Nostrils open	Nostrils closed	Nostrils open	Nostrils closed	Nostrils open	Nostrils closed	Nostrils open	Nostrils closed	Nostrils open

TABLE 2.2 ***Sample Data Table for Activity 2E***

DID YOU KNOW

■ Pacific coast salmon hatch from eggs laid in freshwater streams along the coast of British Columbia. The young salmon leave these streams to live in the ocean. When they reach adulthood, they return to breed in the same stream in which they were born. Scientists think the salmon navigate to their home stream by using their sense of smell.

7. Repeat steps 4 to 6 four more times, so that each unknown soft drink is sampled.
8. Repeat steps 4 to 7. This time, the taster should leave his or her nostrils open.
9. Repeat steps 4 to 8 with one or two more volunteer tasters. Samples can be given in a different order for each taster. Use clean spoons and a clean glass of water.
10. Your teacher will add the names of the five soft drinks to the table under the words Sample A, Sample B, etc.

DISCUSSION

1. Why was it important for the tasters to rinse their mouths between tastes?
2. How many drink flavours did the tasters correctly identify
   (a) when their nostrils were pinched shut?
   (b) when their nostrils were open?
3. (a) Did all the tasters guess correctly the same number of times?
   (b) Why do you think people might have different abilities to taste flavours?
4. What effect does the sense of smell have on the sense of taste?
5. What happens to your sense of taste when you have a cold? Explain your answer. ❖

▶ REVIEW 2.5

1. (a) What are the four basic tastes?
   (b) If you can sense only these basic tastes, how can you recognize all the different foods you eat?
2. (a) In what ways are the senses of taste and smell similar?
   (b) In what ways are they different?
3. Do you think that the chemical senses are as important to your health and safety as the senses of hearing and sight? Why or why not?

■ 2.6 THE SKIN: A MULTIPLE RECEPTOR

When you are petting a cat, feeling the warm sun on your face, or holding an ice cube, your skin is acting as a sensory organ. It contains five kinds of sensory receptors. Each type of receptor is sensitive to a different type of stimulus: touch, pressure, pain, heat, and cold (Figure 2.32). These receptors help us avoid injury, find our way around, enjoy our surroundings, and perform a wide variety of tasks, from holding a pencil while doing homework to catching a football. Nerves connect these receptors to the brain.

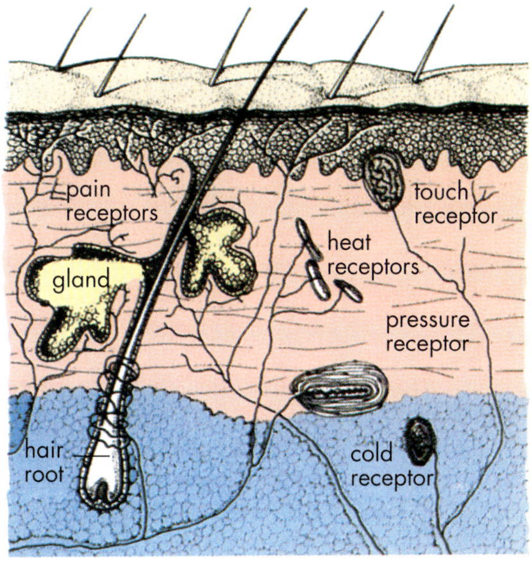

FIGURE 2.32 ▶
A cross-section of human skin, showing the five types of sensory receptors located in this sensory organ.

DID YOU KNOW

■ Your heat and cold receptors only function within a narrow range of temperatures. When you touch something that is too hot or too cold, these receptors do not work. Instead, pain receptors are stimulated. This is why it is sometimes difficult to tell the difference between very hot and very cold objects when they touch your skin.

ACTIVITY 2F / RECEPTORS IN THE SKIN

GROUP ACTIVITY

In this activity, you will locate some of your skin receptors for touch, pain, cold, and heat. Your teacher may ask you to work in a group

MATERIALS

- sheet of paper
- water-soluble felt marker with a fine tip
- pens or pencils in four different colours
- short piece of thread
- straight pin
- metal fork (or paperclip)
- ice cube
- cup of hot water

PROCEDURE

1. Record your predictions for these two questions:
   (a) Which of these four types of sensory receptors (heat, cold, pain, or touch) is most common on the palm of your hand?
   (b) Which of these sensory receptors is most common on the back of your lower arm?
2. In your notebook, trace an outline of your hand (palm up) on a piece of paper. Inside this outline, draw a square about 5 cm on each side. Draw four lines through this square from top to bottom and four lines from side to side to make it into a grid — that is, to divide it into 25 squares of roughly equal size (Figure 2.33).
3. Using the felt marker, draw a grid on the palm of your hand. Make sure it has the same number of small squares inside it as the grid on the hand tracing in your notebook.
4. Dangle the thread over your hand letting it just touch in each of the small squares on your palm. Use one colour of pen or pencil to place a checkmark in squares on the tracing that show where you could feel the touch of the thread. On your tracing, make a key to show which colour indicates touch receptors. ➡

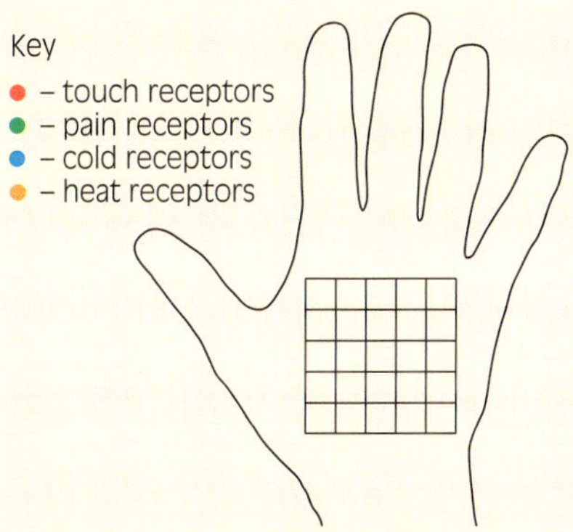

FIGURE 2.33
Trace your hand and draw a grid on it.

CAUTION!

■ **Handle all pointed and hot items with care.**

5. Gently touch the tip of the pin to each square to test for pain receptors. (Do not break the skin.) Using another colour, mark the squares on your hand tracing that show where you felt the pin. Add this colour to the key.
6. Hold a prong of the fork (or the end of a paperclip) against the ice cube until it is very cold. Touch this prong to the squares on your hand, chilling the fork again after every five squares. On the hand tracing, use a third colour to indicate the squares in which you found cold receptors.
7. Put the fork into hot — not boiling — water. Touch a prong to the squares on your skin to locate heat receptors, heating the fork after every five squares. As before, use a different colour to show the location of these on your hand tracing.
8. Repeat steps 2 to 7 with the back of your lower arm.

DISCUSSION

1. (a) List in order (from the most to least common) the types of receptors on
   (i) your palm,
   (ii) the back of your lower arm.
   (b) Do these results confirm your predictions in step 1?
2. (a) Are there more touch receptors on your palm or on the back of your lower arm?
   (b) Why do you think this might be so (that is, how would having more in one place or the other be useful)?
3. (a) Are there more heat or cold receptors on your palm or on the back of your lower arm?
   (b) Why do you think this might be so? ❖

DID YOU KNOW

■ A 1 cm^2 piece of skin on the back of your hand may contain 15 hairs, 150 sweat glands, enough blood vessels to stretch 1 m, 4500 touch receptors, 300 pain receptors, 18 heat receptors, 38 pressure receptors, and enough nerves to stretch 6 m.

THE LOCATION OF SKIN RECEPTORS

You have five different kinds of sensory receptors in your skin. There are different numbers of touch, pressure, pain, heat, and cold receptors in one area of your skin than in another. For example, there are more receptors for touch in the tips of your fingers than in your back. This makes sense because it is easier to obtain information about your surroundings using your fingers than it is using your back. In fact, having so many touch receptors in their fingertips allows blind people to read using Braille.

Touch receptors are found very close to the surface of your skin and around the base of hairs on your skin. These receptors are sensitive to the lightest contact. Pain receptors are also located close to the surface. You need to be able to detect pain quickly if you are to avoid injury. For instance, if you touch a pot that is hot enough to burn you, your pain receptors will send a message along your nerves. When this message is interpreted, you will remove your hand from the pot before it gets badly burnt. Receptors that are sensitive to pressure are usually located deeper in the skin than those for pain.

Receptors that detect heat and cold are also located deeper in the skin. These receptors tell you whether the objects you touch are hot or cold. They also allow you to sense changes in the temperature of your environment. Because you can detect when the temperature outside your body changes, you can behave in ways that help keep the inside of your body at its proper temperature — about 37°C. For example, if it becomes cold, you can put on warm clothes, whereas in hot weather you might look for shade, go swimming, or have a cold drink.

THE BODY'S SENSES: A WINDOW TO THE WORLD

The information gathered by your sensory receptors allows you to know what is going on in the world around you. Your sensory receptors detect a wide range of stimuli in order to give you this information about your surroundings. For example, in the story at the beginning of this chapter, the characters made use of light, sound, chemical, and temperature stimuli to find out about their dinner. In the next chapter, you will learn about how your brain interprets stimuli and co-ordinates your body's responses to them.

DID YOU KNOW

■ Some types of poisonous snakes, including rattlesnakes, have special organs — called pit organs — for detecting heat. These organs help the snakes to locate their food. The snakes feed on animals that have warm bodies and thus give off heat. The pit organs, which are located near the eyes of the snakes, detect the warm bodies of possible prey.

REVIEW 2.6

1. Make up a mnemonic to help you remember the five types of skin receptors.
2. Why is it important to have more skin receptors in some parts of your body than in others?
3. Give an example of how each of the following skin receptors can help you to stay safe or healthy:

   (a) touch
   (b) heat
   (c) cold
   (d) pain
   (e) pressure

CHAPTER REVIEW

KEY IDEAS

■ Sensory receptors provide you with information about your surroundings by allowing you to detect various types of stimuli.

■ When a sensory receptor has been stimulated, a nerve impulse is created and sent to the brain to be interpreted.

■ The eye is a sensory organ that allows you to see by sensing light stimuli.

■ You can hear because of sensory receptors in the ear, which are stimulated by sound.

■ Taste and smell receptors are stimulated by the chemicals in your surroundings.

■ The skin contains five different types of sensory receptors, which are stimulated by touch, pressure, pain, heat, and cold. These receptors have many jobs, including helping you to avoid injury and to control your body temperature.

■ It is important to protect your senses from injury.

■ Technology provides various ways for people to improve their sensory abilities or to manage without certain senses.

VOCABULARY

sensory receptor
sensory organ
stimulus
nerve cell
nerve
nerve impulse
response
rods
cones
outer ear
middle ear
inner ear
taste buds

V1. Create a mind map showing how you think the words in this vocabulary list relate to each other. You can add other words if you wish. Use the words "My senses" as the central theme. Use diagrams to illustrate some of the terms in the list.

V2. Choose one sensory organ. Create a poster to show how this sense works, how you use it, and what you can do to protect it. On your poster, use all the words in the vocabulary list and other words from the chapter that are related to this sense.

CONNECTIONS

C1. (a) List the nine types of sensory receptors covered in this chapter.
(b) What kinds of stimuli does each of these types of receptors detect?

C2. List two ways in which all types of sensory receptors are the same.

C3. Define the following terms: sensory receptor, stimulus, and response. Use an example that will show the role each plays in sensing.

C4. List at least five steps you can take to protect your senses. Beside each step, list the sense that is being protected.

C5. List the senses in what you think is the order of their importance for warning us of danger. Give reasons for your answer.

C6. Complete this sentence: "I think that my sense of ________ is the most important sense because __________."

C7. Describe some of the ways technology is used to help people who have lost or damaged one of their senses.

EXPLORATIONS

E1. Technology has expanded the human senses in many ways. For example, various inventions, such as the microscope, allow us to see more than we could using our eyes alone (Figure 2.34). Technology has also allowed us to detect new types of stimuli — radio waves or infrared light, for example.

Select an invention from the following list. Pretend that you are a newspaper reporter. Write a story about the invention. In your story, explain what type of stimuli the invention can detect and how it is used. Inventions: microscope, telescope, radar, hearing aid, sound parabola, thermometer, seismometer, stethoscope, barometer, fish finder, sonar.

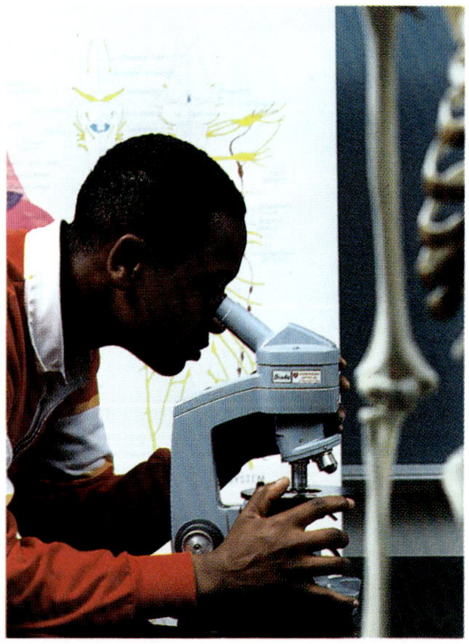

FIGURE 2.34
The microscope improves your vision so you can see small objects.

E2. (a) Think about your school. How could your school be changed to make it easier for a blind student to study there?
(b) How could it be changed for someone who is deaf?

E3. The eye is often compared to a camera. Find out how the following parts of the camera are similar to parts of the eye: lens cap, lens, shutter, film, diaphragm. Present your findings in the form of a poster with labelled diagrams.

E4. Interview someone who is blind or who works at your local Canadian National Institute for the Blind (CNIB) office. Find out more about the types of technology that help people who cannot see. Write up this information in the form of a pamphlet that describes the services available in your area.

E5. With your partner, explore the loss of one of the following senses: sight, hearing, smell, or touch. Do not choose the same sense that your partner chooses. Design a 20 minute exercise that your partner can do to experience life without the use of the sense you have selected. Your exercise must not be dangerous in any way. Check your procedure with your teacher before beginning. Record your partner's actions while he or she is doing the exercise. Then switch roles and do the exercise your partner has designed. Consider the following questions:

- What problems did you have in doing your partner's exercise?
- How did you overcome each problem?
- Which of your other senses was most helpful in overcoming the problems?
- Could this exercise be considered a controlled experiment? Why or why not?

REFLECTIONS

R1. (a) Think back to Activity 2A. Have you discovered any new senses that humans have that you didn't know about at the beginning of this chapter? If so, what are they and what stimuli do they detect?
(b) Have you discovered any other ways you could have helped your fellow team members while they were trying to work "without" one of their senses? If so, describe the methods and which team members they would have helped.

R2. Read over what you have written in your learning journal while working on this chapter. Have any of your questions been answered? If so, write down the answers in your journal. Do you still have questions about how any of your senses work? If so, what are they?

CHAPTER 3

THE NERVOUS SYSTEM

Imagine that you are riding your bicycle, thinking about the snack you will make when you get home. Suddenly a small child chases a ball into the street in front of you — she is heading for the path of a car coming from the opposite direction. You slam on your brakes faster than you thought possible and yell, "Look out!" Hearing this, the driver screeches to a stop just in time: the child makes it to the other side of the street unhurt. Only now do you realize that your stomach is churning, your muscles are tense, and your heart is pounding. Finally, after what seems like forever — but is really only a few moments — your body returns to normal and you continue on your way.

In a very short time, your body has gone through several changes and done many different things. Some of these activities required you to think quickly and make a decision. Others you did automatically, without thinking. Although many parts of your body were involved in these changes and activities, they were all controlled, in one way or another, by your nervous system. How does this important body system work?

GROUP ACTIVITY G CROSS-CURRICULAR C

ACTIVITY 3A / WHAT DO YOU KNOW ABOUT THE NERVOUS SYSTEM?

How much do you already know about your nervous system?

MATERIALS

chart paper
drawing pens
metre stick

PROCEDURE

1. Form a group with two or three other students. Obtain a large piece of chart paper from your teacher. Using a metre stick, divide your paper into six rectangles of equal size. Fill in each of these rectangles by following the instructions in Table 3.1. You might want to use a different coloured pen for each box.
2. Post your chart for other members of the class to see. Read the charts made by other groups.
3. In your learning journal, write a list of things you would like to learn about the nervous system. Also in your learning journal, summarize the entries your group made in boxes A, B, C, and F. ❖

A	B	C
List as many parts of the nervous system as you can. (Use a dictionary if you wish.)	Suggest some reasons why each person needs a nervous system.	Brainstorm as many words as you can that are related to the nervous system.
D	**E**	**F**
Choose an animal. In what ways might the nervous system of this animal be different from yours? How might it be similar?	Write a very short story or draw a picture in which someone makes use of his or her nervous system.	List at least five things about the nervous system that you would like to learn.

TABLE 3.1 ***Instructions for Activity 3A***

■ 3.1 CO-ORDINATION OF THE BODY'S ACTIVITIES

To survive and stay healthy, all living things, including humans, must be able to respond appropriately to changes in their environment. For example, you respond to dust blowing toward your face by blinking or holding your hand in front of your eyes. Many types of birds respond to the coming of winter by flying south to warmer areas. You may recall that these changes in the environment are called stimuli.

In order to respond correctly to stimuli, organisms must have three features. First, they must have a way of detecting the stimuli. This is the job of sensory receptors (you learned about some of these in the last chapter).

Second, organisms must have a way of responding to these stimuli. In humans, responses usually involve two types of body parts: muscles

DID YOU KNOW

■ In some nerve cells, nerve impulses travel at a speed of over 320 km/h.

and glands. Glands are organs that make and release many of the chemicals your body needs in order to work properly. Humans have many types of glands, located throughout their bodies. (In the previous chapter, Figure 2.9 shows a tear gland.)

In the situation described in the opening paragraph of this chapter, both muscles and glands responded. The action of your hand muscles, for example, allowed you to put on your brakes. Some of your glands responded by producing a substance that causes your liver to quickly release large amounts of energy. Your muscles need this sudden burst of energy to perform the many actions that are part of your response to the emergency.

The third feature organisms need in order to respond correctly to stimuli is a co-ordination system. A co-ordination system makes sure that all your body parts work together so that your response is appropriate for the stimulus you have detected. This system needs to be able to interpret the information coming in from sensory receptors and send instructions to the correct body parts about how to respond (Figure 3.1).

(a)

(b)

FIGURE 3.1
Your sense receptors will send out the same kind of information in situations (a) and (b). However, you will react differently. What parts of your body are responsible for deciding what to do in these situations?

Your sensory receptors are constantly receiving many types of stimuli. It is a big job to interpret all this information and co-ordinate many body parts to make a correct response. This job is handled by one of the most important of your body systems, the **nervous system**.

Your nervous system, which runs throughout your body, is made up of billions of cells. These cells are of two major types: nerve cells, and cells that support the nerve cells and help them do their work. Bundles of these cells form the nerves. A very large group of nerve cells and supporting cells makes up your **brain**, one of the most important parts of your nervous system. The sensory receptor cells found in your sense organs — in the retina of your eye, for example — are also nerve cells. They too are part of your nervous system.

The nerves and nerve cells that make up your nervous system carry information — in the form of nerve impulses — from one part of your body to another. Nerve cells are also able to interpret this information. Therefore, your nervous system is perfect for the job of co-ordinating your body's activities. It can receive information from the environment, interpret it, and send out "commands" to the body parts that need to respond.

It is often very important that the information travelling through the nervous system be received, interpreted, and sent out quickly. In some situations, a speedy response could save your life. The length of time it takes you to respond to a specific stimulus is called your **reaction time** for that stimulus. A person's reaction time can vary for many reasons, such as the person's age or health.

ACTIVITY 3B / MEASURING REACTION TIME

How fast can you react to a certain stimulus?

MATERIALS

long strip of paper or cardboard marked in centimetres, with a small weight (such as an eraser) at the bottom

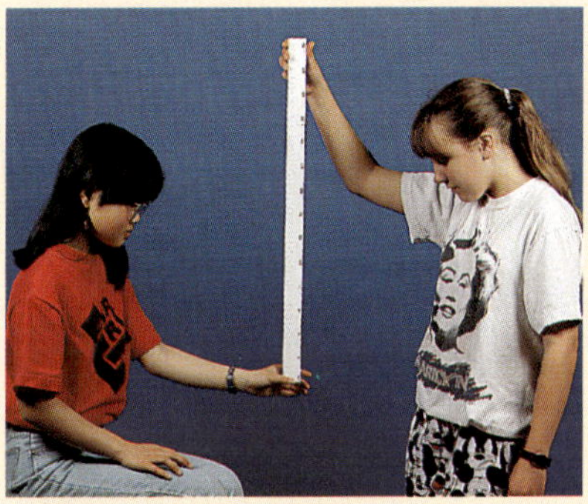

FIGURE 3.2
Be sure that the paper or cardboard strip will fall straight between your thumb and forefinger, without touching them.

PROCEDURE

1. Work with a partner for this activity. First read through steps 3 to 6. Then predict how far the strip will drop before you catch it. Record your prediction in your notebook.
2. Copy Table 3.2 into your notebook.
3. Rest your arm on your desk. Have your partner hold the strip with the 0 cm mark just above your open thumb and forefinger (held 5 cm apart) as shown in Figure 3.2.
4. Keep your eye on the bottom of the strip. Your partner will drop the strip without warning.
5. Catch the strip by closing your thumb and forefinger on it. Keep your arm on the desk as you try to catch it.
6. After you have caught the cardboard strip, read the number (in centimetres) just above your closed fingers. Record the number of centimetres for trial 1 in your table. (The distance the strip fell before you caught it is a way to measure how quickly you responded to the stimulus of the strip falling. The higher the number of centimetres you recorded in Table 3.2, the longer the time between the stimulus and the response.)
7. Before you try steps 3 to 6 again, predict whether or not practice will improve your reaction time.
8. Repeat steps 3 to 6 four more times, recording the distance the strip falls each time.
9. Add the results of your five trials and divide this sum by five to find the average distance the strip dropped before you caught it. Record this in your table.

Trial number	Distance strip fell	Reaction time
1		
2		
3		
4		
5		
Average		

TABLE 3.2 ***Sample Data Table for Activity 3B***

Distance strip fell (in centi-metres)	Reaction time (time required to catch strip) (in seconds)
10	0.14
12	0.16
14	0.17
16	0.18
18	0.19
20	0.20
22	0.21
24	0.22
26	0.23
28	0.24
30	0.25
32	0.26
34	0.27
36	0.28
38	0.29
40	0.30

TABLE 3.3
Reaction Times for Step 9

10. Table 3.3 gives the time required to catch a strip for each of several falling distances. Use this table to determine your reaction time (in seconds) by looking up the distance you allowed the strip to fall on each trial. Then look up the reaction time. Record your reaction times in your data table.

11. Compare your average reaction time with those of other students.

DISCUSSION

1. Compare your prediction of the distance the strip would fall with the results of your first trial. How different were they?

2. What happened to your reaction time with each trial?

3. (a) Does every student in your class have the same average reaction time?
(b) Why might some people have faster reaction times than others?

4. Do you think your own reaction time might be different on a different day? Explain why or why not.

5. (a) Being able to catch a falling strip is not very important for your survival. Think of three situations in which a fast reaction time *would* be important for survival.
(b) Think of three leisure activities for which a fast reaction time is important.

6. What do you think is happening in your body between the time you detect the stimulus (see the strip start to fall) and the time you respond to the stimulus (catch the strip)? ❖

► REVIEW 3.1

1. (a) What three features must organisms have in order to respond appropriately to stimuli?
(b) Describe a situation and identify how these three features allow you to respond to stimuli in this situation.

2. What does your nervous system do?

3. What types of cells make up your nervous system?

4. Define the term "reaction time."

5. (a) Do you think that your body can respond to all the stimuli you detect? Explain your answer.
(b) Which stimuli should your body respond to first?

3.2 REFLEX ACTIONS

Your body responds to some types of stimuli very quickly, without thought. For example, what happens if you step on a tack or touch a hot iron? Stimuli that cause pain usually produce an immediate reaction — people respond rapidly in a way that will cause the pain to stop (Figure 3.3). Other types of stimuli can also produce rapid responses. A sudden, loud noise may cause you to jump or turn your head. A ball approaching your eyes will cause you to quickly shut your eyelids.

A body action that occurs immediately and automatically (without thinking about it) in response to a stimulus is called a **reflex action**. A healthy person always responds with a similar reflex action to a particular stimulus. For example, if you suddenly touch something sharp, your response is always to jerk your hand away. In addition, different people respond with very similar reflex actions to the same stimulus: all people pull their hands away when they suddenly touch something sharp.

Most reflex actions protect your body from harm. They occur quickly so that your body parts are removed from danger as soon as possible. Most reflex actions are very simple responses, involving the action of only one or a few body parts.

FIGURE 3.3
The pan is hot! But when do you know that the pan is hot — before or after you pull your hand away?

ACTIVITY 3C / OBSERVING A REFLEX ACTION

In this activity, you will investigate a reflex action that helps protect certain leg muscles from stretching too much. Doctors make use of this action to test whether parts of your nervous system are working properly.

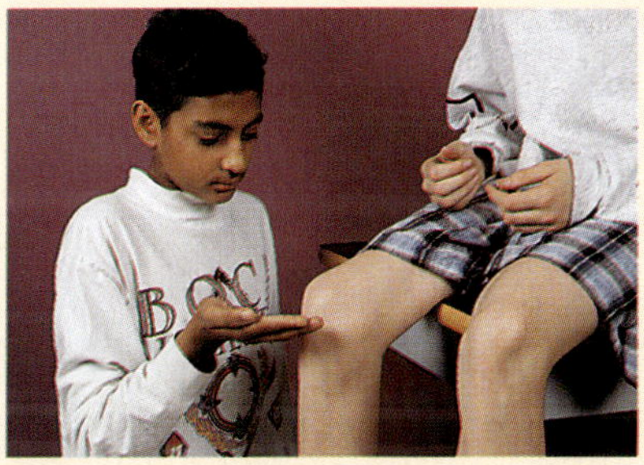

FIGURE 3.4
Testing a reflex action

PROCEDURE

1. Work in pairs for this activity. Have your partner sit on a desk or a stool with his or her legs hanging freely. With the edge of your hand, quickly and lightly tap your partner's leg just below the kneecap (Figure 3.4).
2. Repeat step 1, but this time, have your partner tense his or her leg muscles just before you tap.
3. Ask your partner to count the number of letters on this page. While he or she is involved in this task, tap the area below the kneecap again (without warning your partner).
4. Switch places with your partner and repeat steps 1 to 3.

DISCUSSION

1. (a) What was the stimulus in this activity?
   (b) What was the response?
   (c) Explain why this response is an example of a reflex action.
2. (a) Was the response exactly the same each time you struck your partner's leg? Describe any differences and similarities between the "knee jerk" responses given in steps 1, 2, and 3. ➡

(b) Compare your partner's reflex actions in steps 1, 2, and 3 with yours. Describe any similarities and differences.
(c) Why might there be small differences between people in their responses to this stimulus or even between tests on the same person? ❖

ACTIVITY 3D / WHAT PRODUCES A REFLEX ACTION?

If you accidentally touch a hot element on a stove, you pull your hand away almost immediately in a reflex action. What has happened? Sensory receptors in your finger have sent nerve impulses with the message "I have touched something painfully hot." How does that message reach the arm muscle that you use to pull your arm away? You will find out as you use Figure 3.5 to answer the following questions:

1. What is the stimulus?
2. What part of your body detects the stimulus?
3. What type of nerve cell carries nerve impulses away from the part of the body that detects the stimulus?
4. (a) What type of nerve cell carries impulses to your arm muscle?
   (b) Why do you think this type of nerve cell has this name?
   (c) What is the response of your arm muscle?
5. (a) What is the name of the nerve cell that carries nerve impulses from the sensory nerve cell to the motor nerve cell?
   (b) Why do you think this nerve cell has this name?
6. (a) Notice that the muscle that causes you to move your arm is labelled "effector." Why do you think it is called this?
   (b) What do you think would be the effector or effectors in the reflex action that lifts your foot after you have stepped on a tack?
7. For you to move your hand, nerve impulses did not have to travel to your brain. How, then, do you think you became aware that you touched something hot and moved your arm? ❖

FIGURE 3.5
What are the five parts of a reflex arc? Usually, more than one sensory receptor will be stimulated, so more than one reflex arc will be part of the response.

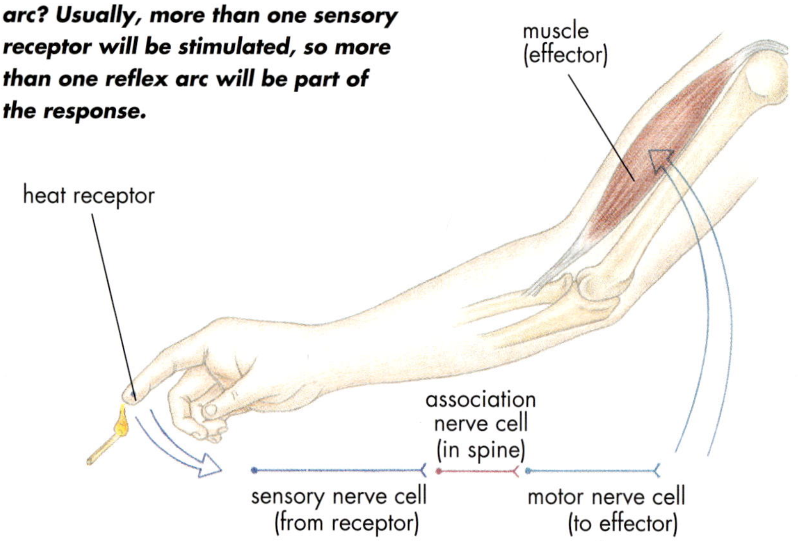

THE REFLEX ARC

The pathway followed by the nerve impulses that produce a reflex action is called a **reflex arc**. As shown in Figure 3.5, a reflex arc consists of five parts.

1. A sensory receptor. Sensory receptors are nerve cells that detect stimuli.
2. A **sensory nerve cell**. Sensory nerve cells carry nerve impulses from sensory receptors to other parts of the nervous system, where these impulses will be interpreted.
3. An **association nerve cell**. In a reflex action, the stimulus is interpreted mostly in association nerve cells. They pass nerve impulses from sensory nerve cells to motor nerve cells.
4. A **motor nerve cell**. Motor nerve cells carry nerve impulses to the parts of the body that will produce the response.
5. An **effector**. Effectors are the body parts — muscles or glands — that respond.

DID YOU KNOW

■ Nerve cells can be very long. For example, a single motor nerve cell may go from the spinal cord down to a muscle in your toe — depending on how tall you are, this cell might be very long! Some of the nerve cells in adult humans can be almost 2 m in length; in a giraffe, they can be close to 5 m long.

REVIEW 3.2

1. (a) What are the five parts of a reflex arc?
   (b) What does each one of these parts do?
2. Make up a mnemonic that will help you remember the five parts of a reflex arc in the correct order.
3. The phone rings. Is your response to this stimulus a reflex action? Why or why not?
4. Why are reflex actions helpful for protecting the body from harm?
5. Give at least one example of a stimulus not mentioned so far in this chapter that causes you to respond with a reflex action.

3.3 THE SPINAL CORD

Reach around and feel the hard bony ridge that runs down the middle of your back. This is your **spine**. The bones that make up your spine protect a very important part of your nervous system: your **spinal cord**. Your spinal cord, which is made up of nerves, runs from the base of your brain down to your lower back (Figure 3.6).

Figure 3.7 shows another reflex action — what happens when you step on a tack. In this diagram, more of the nervous system is shown than in Figure 3.5. Follow the path of a nerve impulse from a sensory receptor to a sensory nerve cell to an association nerve cell.

The association nerve cells that are part of reflex arcs are contained within the spinal cord. In a reflex arc, these cells do most of the interpreting of the information received by your sensory receptors. In most reflex arcs, the association nerve cells have several branches (Figure 3.7). These allow the information coming in from sensory receptors to be sent along several routes — to different parts of your body. As a result, more than one body part can respond at the same time to a particular stimulus. For example, when you step on a tack, muscles in one

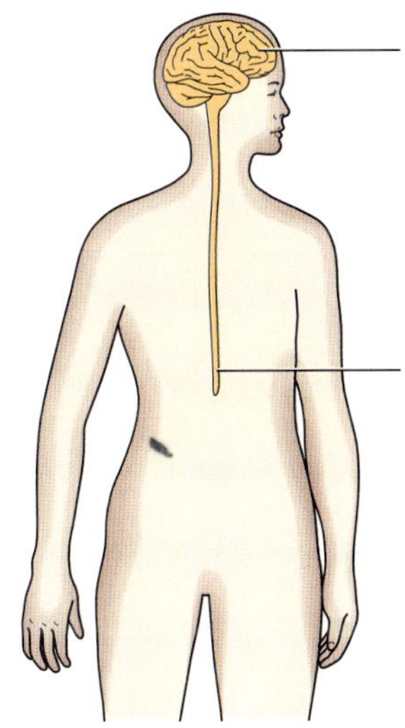

FIGURE 3.6
The spinal cord runs down through your spine from the base of your brain.

leg respond by lifting your foot. The muscles in your other leg also respond at the same time. They tense to allow you to shift your weight and stand on one foot.

Usually one or more association nerve cells connected to a reflex arc send nerve impulses along nerves in your spinal cord up to your brain (Figure 3.8). In your brain, the stimulus is interpreted as pain. Your brain may then send other instructions to your body — to check your injury perhaps.

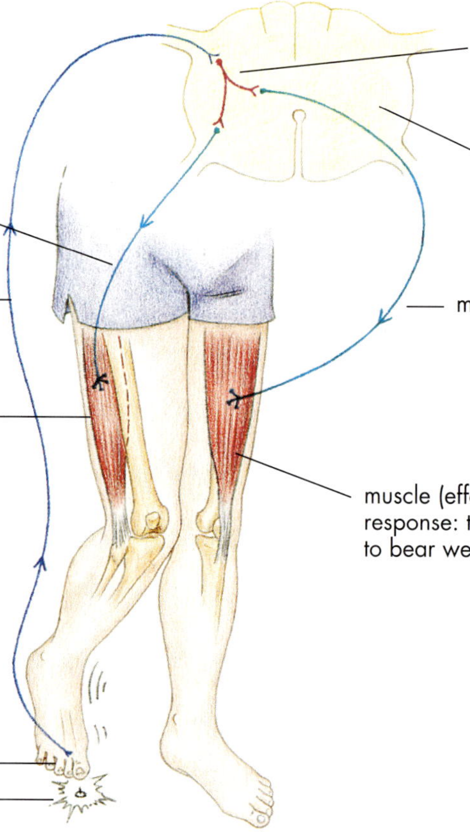

FIGURE 3.7 ▶
In most reflex arcs, the association nerve cells branch to connect with other nerve cells in the spinal cord. As a result, nerve impulses may be sent to more than one effector.

DID YOU KNOW

■ Another name for a nerve cell is a neuron. Sensory nerve cells are sometimes called sensory neurons and motor nerve cells are called motor neurons. Association nerve cells are also known as interneurons. In Latin, the word *inter* means "between." Why is "interneuron" a good name for an association nerve cell?

If you step on a tack, the nerve impulses that reach your brain have to travel farther than those that go along the reflex arc directly to your leg muscles. As a result, you lift your foot even before you actually "feel" pain — and before you have time to think about your response. Because the nerve impulses that produce a reflex action are first interpreted in your spinal cord, your reaction time can be very short. This feature of reflex actions makes them particularly useful for protecting the body from harm.

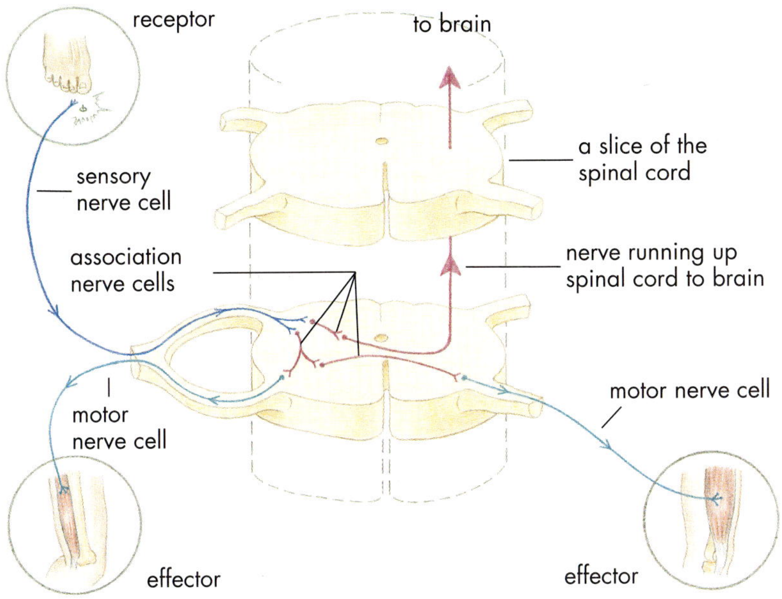

FIGURE 3.8
Some of the association nerve cells in a reflex arc connect with nerves travelling up the spinal cord to the brain. What message do they take to the brain?

PROTECTING YOUR SPINAL CORD

The bones of the spine form a protective case around the spinal cord. Layers of soft **membranes** (thin layers that cover body parts) and a special fluid lie between these hard bones and the fragile nerve cells of the cord (Figure 3.9). These act as a cushion, providing more protection for the spinal cord.

DID YOU KNOW

■ You may one day be at the scene of an accident and suspect that an injured person has a spinal cord injury. Unless there is danger such as fire, it is best not to move the injured person. Some movements can greatly increase any damage to the spinal cord. It is best to wait for people who have been trained in the proper way to handle such injuries.

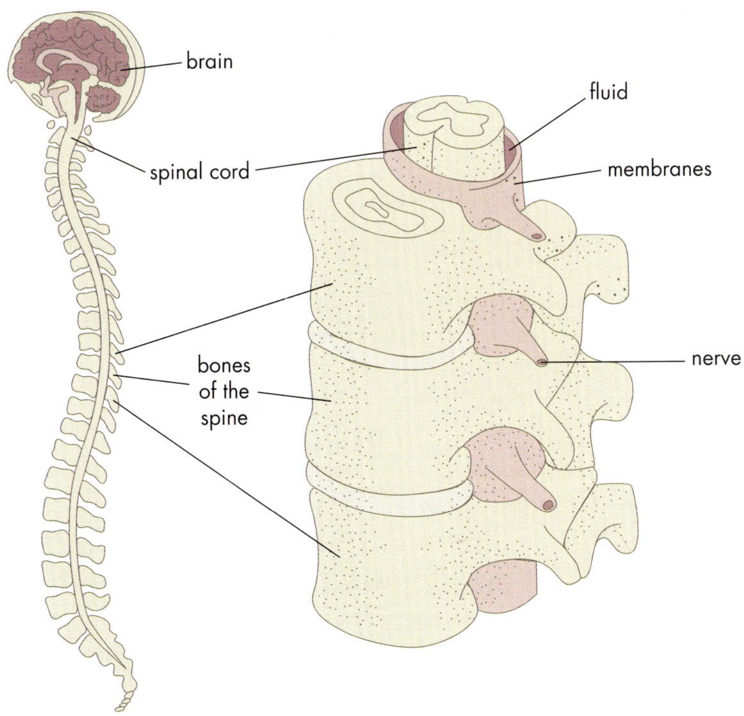

FIGURE 3.9
The spinal cord is protected by bones, membranes, and fluid.

With these body parts to protect it, the spinal cord is safe from many dangers. However, an injury such as a broken neck or back may cut or damage the cord. Many spinal cord injuries are caused by car accidents. Others occur as a result of activities such as diving, skiing, mountain climbing, and motorcycle riding. Being careful and aware of possible dangers when performing such activities will help you avoid spinal cord injuries.

ACTIVITY 3E / TRAVELLING ON WHEELS

CROSS-CURRICULAR

Many people with damaged spinal cords cannot control their leg muscles and must use a wheelchair to move around (Figure 3.10). These people need to get to many of the same places as everyone else. How do they manage? This activity will give you an opportunity to think about how using a wheelchair might affect a person's lifestyle.

PROCEDURE

1. Divide a page or pages of your notebook into three columns. In the first column, make a list of the places you go on a typical day. For buildings, list each of the rooms that you use.
2. In the second column, write a few words to describe why you want or need to visit these rooms or places.
3. In the third column, for each of the places, buildings, and rooms listed, note whether you would be able to get there by yourself if you were travelling in a wheelchair. Which of these locations would be difficult or impossible for you to enter alone?
4. Compare your ideas with those of a partner. Can you add any new ideas to your columns?

FIGURE 3.10 ▶
Rick Hansen, a British Columbian, travelled around the world in his wheelchair.

DISCUSSION

1. Suggest ways that you might change your school building so that people in wheelchairs could use your school more easily.
2. How might you change other buildings or features of your community so that people in wheelchairs can use them more easily? ❖

▶ REVIEW 3.3

1. What is the spinal cord?
2. Why is it helpful for the messages that produce reflex actions to be interpreted in the spinal cord rather than in the brain?
3. If the stimulus that causes a reflex action is interpreted in your spinal cord, how does your brain know that you have detected the stimulus or performed the action?
4. What features of your body protect the spinal cord? What does each of these features do?
5. Think about situations in which your spinal cord could be injured. List three things you could do to help prevent injury in these situations.

3.4 VOLUNTARY ACTIONS

If you hear the phone ringing, you *might* decide to answer it. If you see an interesting book on a table, you *may* decide to pick it up and start reading. These are obviously not reflex actions. In fact, you do not have reflex arcs for these actions. In each case, you have thought about your response — it has not occurred automatically. In a way, you have "volunteered" to make these responses. Responses like these, over which you have control, are called **voluntary actions**.

Voluntary actions are controlled by your brain. In a voluntary action, stimuli are interpreted by some of the nerve cells in your brain, and the instructions for responding are sent out by other brain nerve cells.

Although your spinal cord does not control voluntary actions, it still plays an important role in making sure that they occur. As well as the association nerve cells that are part of reflex arcs, your spinal cord contains many other nerve cells joined together into large nerves. Some of these nerves carry messages from sensory nerve cells in your hands, feet, and other body parts up to your brain for interpreting. Other nerves in your spinal cord carry messages from your brain back to motor nerve cells in all parts of your body. The motor nerve cells pass along the brain's instructions to these body parts so that they can respond appropriately.

In a way, your spinal cord acts like a highway, carrying messages to and from your brain (Figure 3.11). Nerve impulses can travel much faster along this highway than they could along the millions of "back roads" it would take to connect each sensory receptor and effector separately to the brain.

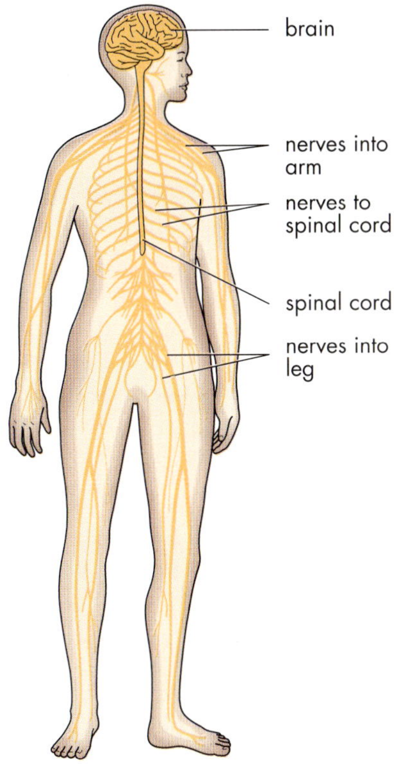

FIGURE 3.11
Your nervous system connects all parts of your body with your brain.

► REVIEW 3.4

1. (a) Define the term "voluntary action."
   (b) Give three examples of voluntary actions.
2. What part of your nervous system controls voluntary actions?
3. What role does the spinal cord play in producing voluntary actions?
4. Imagine that you are travelling on a nerve impulse that has just been created in a sensory receptor. Make up a poem, draw a picture, or write a short story that describes your trip to the brain and back out to an effector. What sensory receptor will you start in? What stimulus makes you start your trip? Where will you end up? Is your response a voluntary or a reflex action? Be inventive! Make your trip into a real adventure.

DID YOU KNOW

■ Your body's cells produce carbon dioxide as a waste product. Your blood picks up the carbon dioxide from your cells and carries it to your lungs. From there, you get rid of it by breathing out. One group of internal sensory receptors detects high amounts of carbon dioxide in your blood. When this happens, your brain sends instructions to your lung muscles that tell you to breathe out.

3.5 INTERNAL STIMULI AND RESPONSES

So far in this chapter, you have learned about how your body detects changes in the environment *outside* your body. For example, pain receptors stimulated by stepping on a tack and sound receptors stimulated by the ringing of a telephone have been mentioned. You also have sensory receptors to detect stimuli *inside* your body. Some of these internal sensory receptors detect the presence of chemicals, such as carbon dioxide, in your body. Others detect how far your muscles have stretched when you use them. Like other sensory receptors, your internal receptors send messages along nerve cells to your brain, where they are interpreted. These internal receptors provide information that helps you keep your balance, control your rate of breathing, avoid muscle injury, and keep the correct amount of various chemicals in your body, among other things (Figure 3.12).

FIGURE 3.12 ▶
Internal sensory receptors constantly let your brain know what the various parts of your body are doing — even in a fast-moving game of soccer.

EXTENSION

■ Use a reference to find out about biofeedback. Compare your findings on biofeedback with what you know about how the nervous system controls the activity of your internal organs.

Most of the motor nerve cells discussed so far in this chapter carry messages to muscles — the muscles that lift your foot or move your arm, for example. These are responses that you can see. There are also many motor nerve cells that carry messages to the muscles and glands that make up your internal body organs, such as your heart, lungs, and stomach. Although these internal organs respond to various stimuli, you cannot usually see their responses. In fact, you are often not even aware of their activity.

The motor nerves that carry messages to the body's organs receive instructions from the brain and do their work automatically. In other words, you usually do not have to think about whether your internal body parts are working properly. When an emergency occurs, such as a child running into the road, motor nerves carry messages that cause your internal organs to respond rapidly. For instance, some motor nerves carry messages to your heart, causing it to speed up. Your heart can then pump more blood throughout your body, allowing your arm and leg muscles to work better.

When the emergency is over, other motor nerves carry instructions from the brain that cause your internal organs to go back to their normal pace of working. For example, some of these messages cause your heart rate to slow down.

REVIEW 3.5

1. (a) List two types of stimuli detected by your body's internal sensory receptors.
   (b) List three things that the information provided by these internal sensory receptors allows you to do.
2. (a) What type of nerve cell carries nerve impulses to your arm muscles?
   (b) What type of nerve cell carries nerve impulses to the muscles and glands that make up your internal organs?
   (c) What do the muscles in your arm and in your body organs have in common?
3. Imagine yourself in an emergency situation. Write a short story that describes the emergency and your feelings during it. Include a description of how your body responds to the situation; what do you think happens to your internal organs? Finish your story with a description of what happens — both inside and outside your body — after the emergency is over.

3.6 THE BRAIN

The human brain is made up of billions of cells. Like the cells in the spinal cord, these cells include both nerve cells and the supporting cells that help the nerve cells do their work. Although scientists have discovered a great deal about the structure of the brain, they have not found out as much about how the brain actually works to allow you to think. Learning about how the brain works is one of the most difficult, but most exciting, subjects of scientific research today.

The mass of a baby's brain is about 350 g. Scientists think that almost all the nerve cells you will ever have in your brain develop before you are born and during your first few months of life. Even after this, however, you get new supporting cells and your brain continues to grow in size. After three years, a child's brain will have a mass of about 1100 g. By about age 20, the brain has reached its maximum mass — about 1700 g. After age 20, the brain starts to decrease slowly in size. Some brain cells — nerve cells as well as supporting cells — die when they get old. Other brain cells are destroyed or damaged. For example, drugs such as alcohol destroy many brain cells. Although some parts of damaged nerve cells can grow back, entire nerve cells usually cannot. Once destroyed, nerve cells in the brain are usually not replaced.

Not everyone has exactly the same size brain. People with larger brains are not necessarily more intelligent. The ability to think depends more on the number of connections, or pathways, among brain cells than on the number of cells. These pathways carry the information that you need to perform all sorts of activities, including thinking. Nerve pathways are developed by actively using your brain, much as a path through a field is created when the same route is used over and over again. Your brain needs to be used to make sure it stays fit and healthy, just as muscles require exercise to keep them in shape (Figure 3.13).

Your brain is made up of many parts. Although each part has its own job, all the parts work together to co-ordinate the activities of your body. In the rest of this section, you will investigate three of the major parts of the brain (Figure 3.14).

FIGURE 3.13
Brain exercise throughout your life can help you avoid a "flabby" brain.

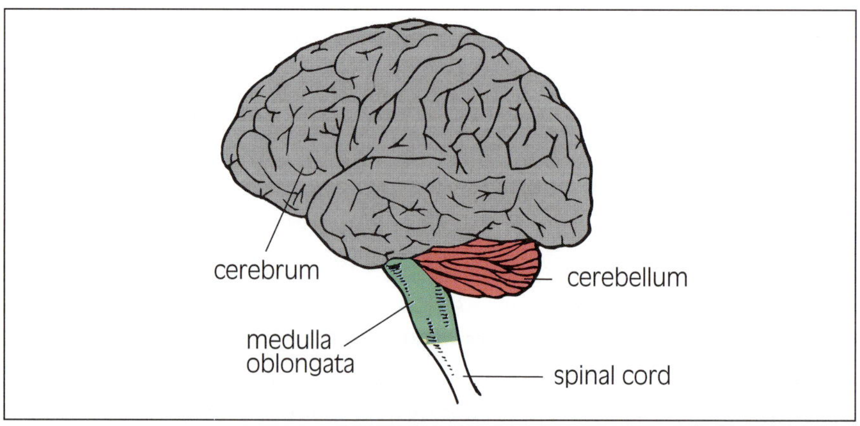

FIGURE 3.14 ▶
The shaded areas show three of the major parts of your brain.

ACTIVITY 3F / THE PARTS OF THE BRAIN

Make a copy of Table 3.4 in your notebook. Fill in the "Brain part" and "Function" columns as you read through pages 69 to 71. (The word "function" means "job.") Use Figure 3.14 to fill in the column labelled "Position." ❖

Brain part	Position	Function

TABLE 3.4 ***Sample Data Table for Activity 3F***

THE MEDULLA OBLONGATA

Imagine what it would be like if you had to think about every breath before taking it or if you had to think about digesting your food. You do not have to do this, because these and other important body functions are controlled by a part of your brain called the **medulla oblongata**. It takes care of these jobs for you automatically. This part of your brain sends out messages that keep your heart beating, your lungs breathing, and other internal body parts working normally.

The medulla oblongata lies at the base of the brain. It looks like a swollen mass at the top of the spinal cord. Although it is quite small, you could not survive without it.

THE CEREBELLUM

One of the most remarkable things you learn in your life is how to stand up and walk. The skills required for standing and walking depend on the action of another part of your brain, the **cerebellum**. The cerebellum helps you keep your balance and perform voluntary actions in a co-ordinated way. How does it do this?

The cerebellum receives messages from your sensory receptors, including those that tell your brain what parts of your body are doing. Your cerebellum also acts as a relay station for outgoing commands. It receives messages or instructions from other parts of your brain and passes them on to nerves that will carry these instructions to your muscles. Before passing them on, however, the cerebellum organizes them: it compares each message with the others and with the information coming in from your sensory receptors. It then passes the messages on in an order that will make sure that your body movements are co-ordinated.

DID YOU KNOW

■ Animals that fly must have a very good sense of balance and must be capable of very rapid, co-ordinated actions. For this reason, birds and bats have cerebellums that are much larger, relative to the size of their entire brains, than the cerebellums of most other animals, including humans.

For example, a while ago you made a decision to pick up this textbook and read. Part of your brain made this decision and sent a command toward your arm muscles. This command had to pass through your cerebellum on its way out to your arm. Your cerebellum compared the command with information about the locations of the book and your arm. Your cerebellum then directed the muscle actions needed to move your hand to the book without missing it or knocking it away, and helped you grasp and lift it. Your cerebellum is now keeping track of changes in your muscles so that you can hold the book steady. At the same time, it is continuing with its other main job of helping you keep your balance. The cerebellum makes it possible for you to perform voluntary actions without thinking about every detailed movement (Figure 3.15).

FIGURE 3.15 ▶
What are the cerebellums of the sky divers doing?

EXTENSION

■ The outer, wrinkled surface of the cerebrum is called the cortex. The many folds and wrinkles in the cortex greatly increase its surface area. Why would this be an advantage? Do you know of any other parts of the human body that have folds in order to increase their surface area? How does a greater surface area help this body part do its job?

THE CEREBRUM

The **cerebrum** is the largest part of your brain. It is responsible for the most complex human activities — voluntary actions and thinking. Although the instructions for voluntary actions are *organized* by your cerebellum, they are *made up* by your cerebrum. The cerebrum allows you to think about the stimuli you have detected and choose which responses to make. For example, you would be using your cerebrum if you decided you were thirsty and needed a glass of juice or milk. Your cerebrum would also send commands toward your muscles to allow you to pour it out and drink it.

Nerve cells in different parts of your cerebrum perform different jobs (Figure 3.16). Large numbers of cells in four different locations are responsible for receiving and interpreting nerve impulses from your eyes, ears, nose, and tongue. Another part of your cerebrum collects the information that comes in from other sensory receptors. Some of the information coming in from your sensory receptors is stored in the cerebrum. This storage is called memory.

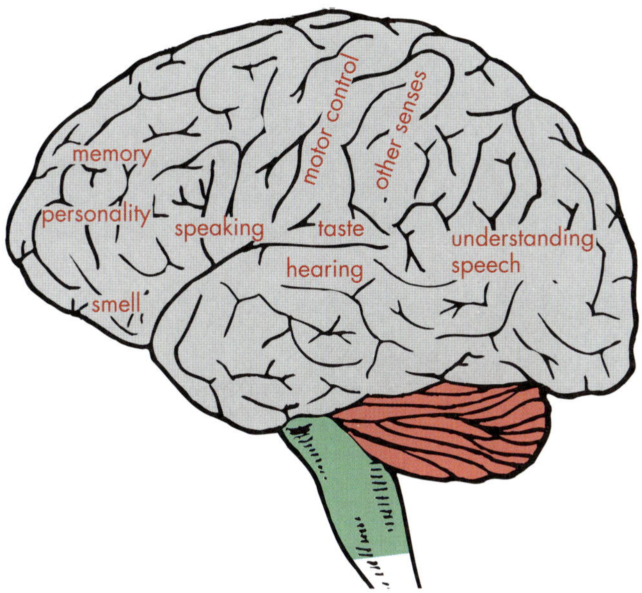

FIGURE 3.16
Different regions of your cerebrum perform different tasks.

Damage to the cerebrum can reduce your ability to sense stimuli. For example, if the part of the cerebrum that interprets sound stimuli is damaged, you may not be able to hear — even if your ears are working properly. Damage to the cerebrum can also cause you to forget some of the information you have stored in your memory.

Other parts of your cerebrum produce outgoing messages — commands to your muscles that control activities such as walking and talking. An area of the cerebrum at the very front of the brain seems to control thinking ability and personality.

For your body to function properly, information must be passed from one area to another within the cerebrum — and also out to the cerebellum and medulla oblongata. Each nerve cell in the brain connects with many others, so information can move rapidly from one area to another.

Your ability to reason — to solve problems based on your experience — is the result of the activity of nerve cells located in the cerebrum. Your ability to memorize is also located there. Scientists are not sure how the cerebrum does these jobs — it is difficult to watch brain cells at work in a living person! However, we can get some clues about the operation of the brain by observing a person doing thinking tasks.

EXTENSION

- Find out how your brain stores all the bits of information that you remember. In what form are they stored? Your research should allow you to explain the difference between short-term and long-term memory and how the two are related.

PROFILE

JULIA BYL

Julia Byl is a student at Trinity Western University in Langley, a small town near Vancouver. She likes studying psychology and sociology; in these courses she learns about individuals and society. After graduating, she plans to work with handicapped people as a counsellor or social worker. When she is not studying, she likes to read books and bake. Although Julia Byl is similar to many other students, in one way she is not a typical university student.

Julia Byl has cerebral palsy. Cerebral palsy is the result of damage to the brain before or during birth. Byl's cerebral palsy was caused by a lack of oxygen to her brain before birth, but cerebral palsy may be caused by other things, such as rubella or the use of certain drugs during pregnancy.

Julia Byl has quadriplegic spastic cerebral palsy. In spastic cerebral palsy, the muscles are tense and contracted, so they do not relax. Walking, talking, and all kinds of movement are difficult. *Quadriplegic* means that all four limbs are affected in this way.

Cerebral palsy cannot be cured, but treatment can help. Byl started treatment at the age of 14 months. Physiotherapy used treatment such as massage, exercise, and heat to help her use her arms and legs better. Speech therapy taught her to speak more clearly. Occupational therapy helped her to learn everyday tasks such as handwriting.

When Julia Byl was in her early teens, she had two operations in the backs of her legs in order to make those muscles less tense. Although the operations did lessen the tension, she says they made her balance worse and she now falls more often.

At university, Byl uses a walker to help her move from one class to another. Although she writes neatly, she is very slow. She uses a portable computer to write essays and class assignments. She writes the same exams as other students, although she needs more time. A two-hour history exam took her six hours to write.

Byl has one piece of advice to students with a classmate or friend who has cerebral palsy or some other physical handicap: "Just because someone is physically handicapped, it does not mean he or she is not mentally capable of doing the same things as you do."

Think about Julia Byl's advice. Make a list of things that a student with cerebral palsy or another physical handicap could do. Then list some ways that you could help that student to do the things that he or she has difficulty doing.

ACTIVITY 3G / EXAMINING MEMORY

This activity will give you an opportunity to learn something about how your memory works.

MATERIALS

Part I
list of 25 common words
clock with second hand

PART I Memory Check-up

PROCEDURE

1. Make a copy of Table 3.5 in your notebook.
2. Get a copy of the list of 25 words. One person in the class — perhaps the teacher — should be appointed timekeeper.
3. Take two minutes to study the list of words, trying to memorize as many as you can. Then turn the list over.
4. Take another two minutes. In the first column ("Trial 1") of your data table, write out as many of the 25 words as you can remember.
5. Compare your list with the original one to see how many words you recalled correctly. Record this number at the bottom of the first column.
6. Repeat steps 3 to 5 twice more, writing down the words in the second and third columns of your data table. Cover the columns you have already used each time you do this. Record the total number of words you recalled correctly at the bottom of the columns.

DISCUSSION

1. Did you find that some words were easier to remember than others? Suggest some reasons for your answer.
2. Did the number of words you could recall increase or decrease from Trial 1 to Trial 3? Explain why you think this result might have occurred.
3. As a class, brainstorm ideas about what factors might affect the number of words a person can remember. List these factors in your notebook. Suggest methods that could be used to help someone memorize a list of words like this one. Write these methods on the board.

PART II Design an Experiment

PROCEDURE

1. Form a group with two to three other students. Imagine that you are a team of research scientists testing ways of improving memory. If possible, each team should choose a different method to help people memorize from those suggested during the class discussion in Part I.
2. Discuss the method with your team. Design an experiment for the whole class that would test whether this method really will help students remember a list of words.
3. Write out the design of your experiment. Be sure to include a description of your hypothesis and methods.
4. With your teacher's permission, try your experiment on the class. Collect the information you need to test the hypothesis and write down your conclusion.

Words Recalled		
Trial 1	**Trial 2**	**Trial 3**

TABLE 3.5 ***Sample Data Table for Activity 3G***

DISCUSSION

1. (a) If you tried your experiment, what problems did you have, if any, in testing your hypothesis?
   (b) How do you think you might have improved your experiment to solve some of these problems?
2. Do you think the method you tested would help you memorize things other than lists of words? Explain your answer.
3. Imagine that your team wanted to publish its results in the *World of Science* magazine. As a team, write a short article that describes your experiment and explains your conclusions. ❖

PROTECTING YOUR BRAIN

Every year, almost 6000 British Columbians suffer serious head injuries. Many of these injuries cause permanent brain damage. Because the brain controls all the body's activities, damage to it can affect all parts of a person's life — as well as the lives of the person's family and friends.

Your brain is protected by the bones of your skull. Like your spinal cord, it is cushioned by membranes and fluid. These lie between the brain and the hard skull bones (Figure 3.17). Despite this protection, the brain can still be injured by a hit on the head — even one that does not appear to be too serious. For this reason, it is very important to wear a helmet when taking part in activities that might cause you to fall, or be hit, on your head (Figure 3.18). Over half of all serious head injuries occur as a result of car accidents. Using your seat-belt, which can keep you from hitting the windshield or being thrown out of the car in an accident, will lower your chance of receiving a head injury in this way.

FIGURE 3.17 ▶
Your brain is protected by membranes and fluid as well as your skull. But if you bang your head, your brain may hit the inside of your skull, causing damage.

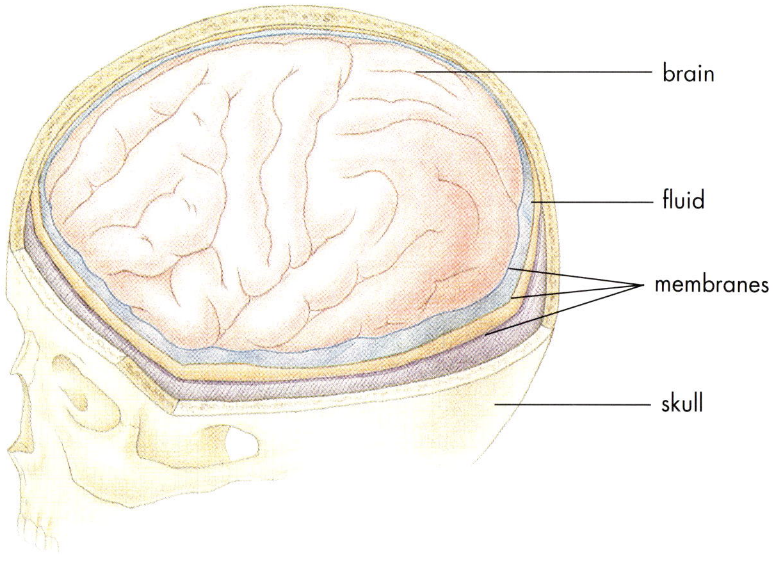

FIGURE 3.18
How are these players protecting their heads? Check out helmets designed for different activities. How are they similar, and how do they differ from each other?

LEARNING

Have you ever found it difficult to understand or remember something that someone else has found quite easy? Situations like this are not unusual, since no two people have brains that are exactly the same. The billions of connections among nerve cells are different in different people. Because of this, some people are good at learning some types of things, but others may find these same things quite difficult. This second group of people may, however, be good at other skills or subjects.

It is a good idea, then, to figure out the method of learning that works best for you. New methods are sometimes difficult the first time you try them. If you practise using the method, you usually become more skilful with it. Sometimes it is easier to learn by using more than one of your senses. For example, some people study by reading aloud whatever they are trying to learn. Their brains are then receiving the same information from two senses (eyes and ears) at the same time. They may thus find it easier to remember what they have been studying. Some people trace the words or diagrams with their fingers as they read for the same reason.

DID YOU KNOW

- Bicycle accidents are a common cause of head injuries in young people. Most of the people who die in bicycle accidents do so because of a head injury. Even when the person survives, a head injury can often lead to permanent brain damage. The Canadian Injury Prevention Program has collected data on thousands of bicycle accidents. These data suggest that wearing a helmet could prevent most serious head injuries. If an accident results in head injuries, cyclists who wear helmets are eight times less likely to have brain damage than those who do not wear one. The helmet needs to meet certain standards to provide protection. What do you think these standards are?

EXTENSION

■ Can you learn things while you are asleep? Use reference books or interview a scientist (perhaps at a university or college) to find out the answer to this question.

You might find that you learn better if you use coloured pens or pencils to underline or circle important words or ideas in your notebook. You may be particularly good at recalling colours or the patterns they form on the page. These can then serve as cues to the ideas you have related to these colours or patterns. Another approach is to draw diagrams, perhaps with circles and connecting lines, that show the relationships between the ideas or facts you are trying to learn. Mind mapping, which you learned about in Chapter 1, is a method of learning that makes use of diagrams like this.

Some people find it easier to learn if they draw or study a picture than if they just read words. For example, you might find it easier to learn about the parts of a reflex arc by drawing and labelling a picture of one than by writing out the names of the parts and their jobs.

Learning is one of the most complicated and interesting things that your brain can do. Many people — scientists and others — spend their time studying how the brain does this job; they are trying to learn how we learn. They have discovered that anything that damages your nervous system (whether the damage is temporary or permanent) can affect how you learn, as well as how you detect and respond to stimuli in your environment.

REVIEW 3.6

1. What types of cells make up the human brain?

2. (a) What does your medulla oblongata do?
(b) Where is this part of the brain located?

3. What might happen if your cerebellum was not working normally?

4. (a) What does your cerebrum do?
(b) Do all parts of your cerebrum do exactly the same thing?

5. What body parts protect your brain?

6. Describe some methods you might use to increase your ability to learn.

7. In some cases, people who have lost certain abilities as a result of damage to some of their brain cells can regain these abilities. How do you think this might be possible?

CHAPTER REVIEW

KEY IDEAS

- Your nervous system interprets information from your sensory receptors and co-ordinates many body parts so that you can respond appropriately to stimuli.
- Your nervous system is made up of billions of cells: nerve cells and supporting cells that help the nerve cells do their work.
- Reflex actions are simple responses that occur quickly and without thought. They usually protect your body from danger. Each reflex action is controlled by a reflex arc, a pathway that includes a sensory receptor, a sensory nerve cell, an association nerve cell, a motor nerve cell, and an effector.
- Responses that you have to think about performing are called voluntary actions. They are controlled by your brain.
- Your body contains sensory receptors that detect stimuli inside your body, and effectors that cause internal responses. You often do not know these internal responses are happening.
- Different parts of your brain, such as the medulla oblongata, cerebellum, and cerebrum, perform different jobs. All these parts must act together to allow you to function properly.
- Your spinal cord and brain are surrounded by protective bones, membranes, and fluid. You still need to give these parts of your nervous system extra protection when taking part in certain activities.
- Learning is a very complicated activity which is not completely understood.

VOCABULARY

nervous system
brain
reaction time
reflex action
reflex arc
sensory nerve cell
association nerve cell
motor nerve cell
effector
spine
spinal cord
membrane
voluntary action
medulla oblongata
cerebellum
cerebrum

V1. Create a mind map using the words in this vocabulary list. Start with the words "nervous system" at the centre of your map.

V2. Imagine that your body is a city and that your nervous system makes up the roads running through the city. Draw a road map that would allow a visitor to travel to important places in the city. Be creative! Study a real road map to see how different types of roads are shown. As on a real map, include a "key" to the different types of roads. What would you include as "points of interest" on your city map? Use as many of the words in the vocabulary list as you can on your key and in your list of points of interest.

CONNECTIONS

C1. (a) Describe two ways in which a reflex action is different from a voluntary action.
(b) Describe two ways in which they are similar.
(c) Give an example of each of these two types of responses.

C2. Describe three ways of reducing your chances of brain or spinal cord injury.

C3. (a) What parts of your nervous system produce and organize the instructions that produce voluntary actions?
(b) What parts of your nervous system produce the instructions for actions that you do not have to think about?

C4. When your finger touches a thorn on a rose bush, your hand jerks away. Using a diagram, trace the path that the impulses will follow in this reflex action. Label the five parts of the reflex arc.

C5. You decide to have a sandwich for lunch and begin to make your favourite kind. What are your cerebrum, cerebellum, and medulla oblongata doing while you do this?

C6. Imagine being awakened from a deep sleep by a loud crash. You jump out of bed. Describe the role of your nervous system in responding to this situation.

EXPLORATIONS

E1. Today we have a variety of methods for studying a person's brain (Figure 3.19). Although these methods cannot show how the brain works, they allow doctors to look at damaged or diseased parts of the brain. Imagine that one of these methods has just been invented. Write a newspaper article that tells people how the method is helpful and why its discovery is exciting. Select one of the following methods to investigate: CAT (**c**omputed **a**xial **t**omography) scanning, PET (**p**ositron **e**mission **t**omography) scanning, EEG (**e**lectro**e**ncephalo**g**raphy), or NMR (**n**uclear **m**agnetic **r**esonance) imaging.

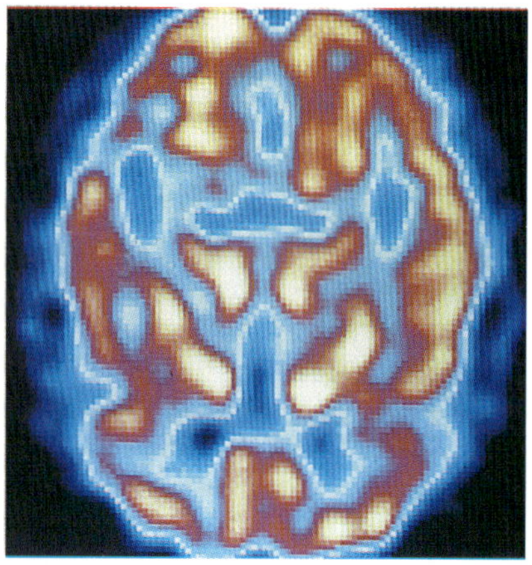

FIGURE 3.19
A picture of the human brain made using PET (positron emission tomography)

E2. Research one of the following illnesses of the nervous system: Alzheimer's disease, amnesia, Parkinson's disease, narcolepsy, migraine headaches, aphasia, tetanus, epilepsy, multiple sclerosis, muscular dystrophy, encephalitis, leprosy, or spinal meningitis. Pretend that you are a doctor who has to explain the symptoms, treatment, and possible effects of the illness to a patient who has it. Share your research with the class in a role play. You should take the part of the doctor, and a classmate can be the patient, who has some questions about his or her illness.

E3. Your cerebrum is divided down the middle into two halves, which are sometimes called the right and left brains. Find out about the two halves of the brain. Choose one of the following topics to investigate: (1) Do the two halves seem to have different roles in thinking activities? (2) Is one half of the brain more in control than the other half in some people? What effect might this have? (3) Are the two halves of the brain ever completely split so that they do not communicate with each other? What problems might people with such "split brains" have?

REFLECTIONS

R1. Look back at the list of things you would like to know about the nervous system that you wrote in your learning journal while doing Activity 3A. Have you learned about some of these things in this chapter? What questions remain? Have you thought of any more questions as a result of reading this chapter? Look at the summaries you made of your group's entries in boxes A, B, and C. Have you changed your ideas on any of these things as a result of reading this chapter? If so, which ideas have changed? What caused you to change your ideas — reading the chapter or doing an activity? Explain your answer in full.

R2. Imagine that you are a scientist studying the nervous system. You have just won an award that gives you a large sum of money for research. You can now investigate any question related to the nervous system (for example, how it works, how to prevent or treat diseases that affect it, or how to repair damage to it). What would you choose to study? Why is your chosen topic important — what will be gained by studying it? Give a brief description of how you will investigate the question.

CHAPTER 4

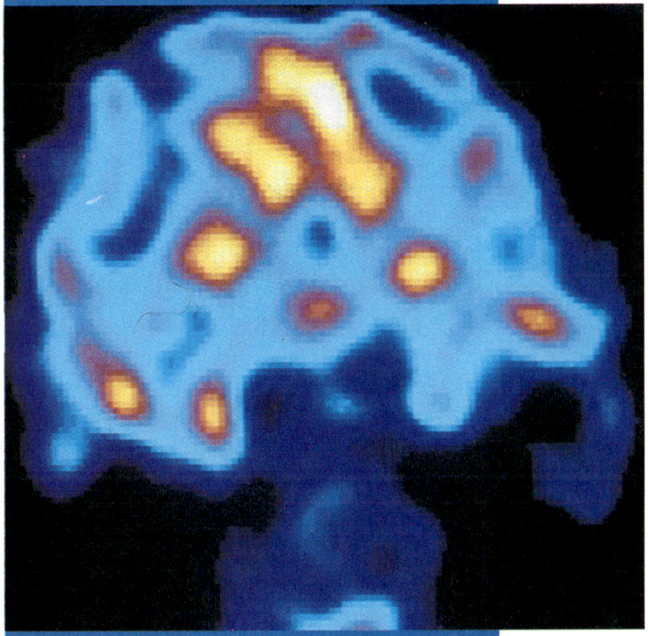

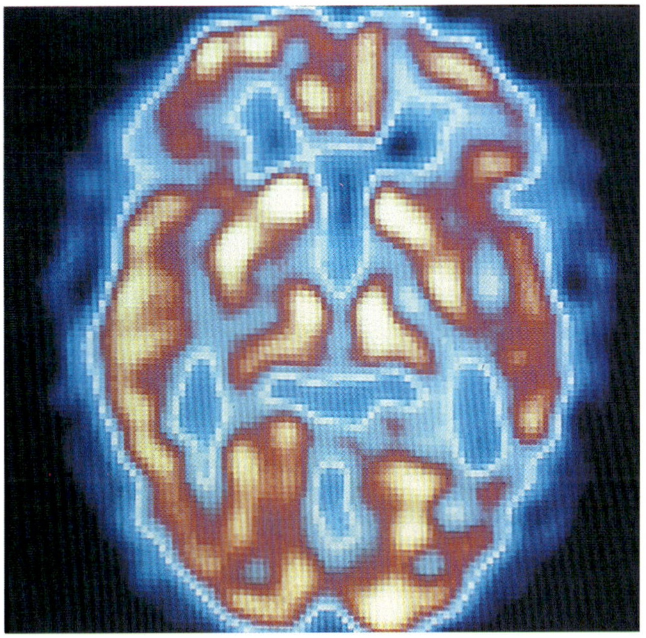

DRUGS AND YOUR NERVOUS SYSTEM

At the beginning of grade 8, Don enjoyed sports and did well in school. During the school year, however, his marks dropped. His teachers and friends noticed that at times he would gaze off into space. One day at school, without warning, he fell to the floor unconscious. Don lay with his arms and legs making rapid, jerking motions. After a few moments, he opened his eyes. Although Don had a headache and was tired, he felt fine after a rest.

The doctor gave Don a complete examination and ran a series of tests. The tests showed that Don had epilepsy. People with epilepsy sometimes have seizures. A seizure occurs when the brain suddenly sends out many nerve impulses all at once. These nerve impulses travel to the person's muscles, sometimes causing them to shake or jerk uncontrollably. The photograph on the left shows a PET scan of a brain during an epileptic seizure. Compare it with the photograph on the right, which shows a brain during normal activity. What differences do you notice?

Although Don started treatment right away, it took several months for his doctor to determine the right combination of drugs to control Don's condition. Now Don once again leads an active life, thanks to the drugs he takes each day.

ACTIVITY 4A / DRUGS IN OUR SOCIETY

What are drugs? Why are they used (Figure 4.1)? This activity may start you thinking about these and other important questions.

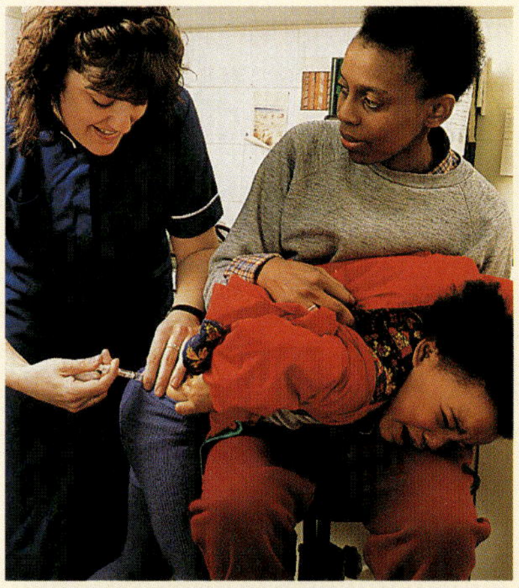

FIGURE 4.1
Drugs can be used for medical and non-medical purposes.

PROCEDURE

1. Form a group with two or three other members of your class. Each group should obtain a large sheet of chart paper.
2. Divide the paper into two columns. Label the left-hand column "Drugs used for medical purposes." Label the right-hand column "Drugs used for non-medical purposes."
3. Discuss these column titles with your group. (You may want to use a dictionary.) Come up with a brief definition (5 to 10 words) for each of the two categories of drugs. Write the definition under the title at the top of the column.
4. List as many drugs as you can in the appropriate column or columns. (Some drugs may have both medical and non-medical uses.)
5. Beside the name of each drug, put a letter "I" if you think the drug is illegal (if it is against the law to buy or use the drug). If you think the drug is legal, put an "L" following the name of the drug. If you know of any laws that limit the use of legal drugs (for example, age restrictions), note these restrictions also.
6. Post your chart. Compare your list of drugs with those prepared by other groups.

DISCUSSION

1. Did your group list any drugs that you thought had both medical and non-medical uses? If so, describe when the drug might be used medically and when it might be used non-medically.
2. (a) Look at the list of drugs used for medical purposes. Are any of these drugs illegal? Or are all or most of them legal? Explain your answer in full.

   (b) Why might some legal drugs be restricted?

   (c) Why do you think that society has decided that some drugs should be illegal to buy or use?
3. Did other groups list any substances that you do not think are drugs? If so, why do you think these substances are not drugs?
4. Think about what you have learned doing this activity. How would you define the term "drug"? ❖

4.1 WHAT ARE DRUGS?

To work properly, your body needs food, water, and oxygen. A **drug** is any other substance which, when taken into your body, can affect how your body works. A drug can also change the way you think, feel, or act. Many different substances fit this definition. As you read the rest of Section 4.1, you might find it helpful to make a chart or web of the key words and ideas.

FIGURE 4.2 ◀
Ben Johnson (left), a Canadian sprinter, took steroids to grow muscles so he would be faster. The gold medal he won in this race was taken from him because he cheated by using steroids.

Many of the chemicals we call drugs are used for medical purposes — to prevent or treat illness or pain. These drugs are often called **medicines**. Other drugs, such as alcohol or nicotine (one of the drugs found in cigarettes), have no medical purpose. Some drugs act directly on your body — they change some part of your body. For example, **steroids** are drugs that affect muscle and bone growth (Figure 4.2). Steroids can increase a person's muscle mass, but can cause a decrease in bone growth. Steroids can also damage the liver and can reduce the ability of some body systems to work properly.

Other drugs affect your body indirectly. They act on organisms that live in or on your body, such as bacteria, some of which can make you ill. **Antibiotics** are drugs that have this kind of indirect effect. Antibiotics kill or slow the growth of some types of bacteria, such as those that give you a sore throat. Penicillin is one type of antibiotic drug.

Did you realize that so many different types of substances are drugs? The substance you might take to relieve a headache is a drug, as are illegal chemicals such as marijuana or cocaine. Alcohol is also a drug,

DID YOU KNOW

- An ancient Egyptian practice was to put mouldy bread on wounds to speed healing. Today we know why this sometimes worked. The antibiotic drug penicillin is made from a type of mould that grows on bread. The mouldy bread used by the Egyptians thus often contained a drug that could kill the bacteria infecting wounds.

EXTENSION

■ Find out more about steroids. Who uses these drugs? Why? What effects do steroids have on the human body? What are the restrictions or laws on steroid use? Your class might want to hold a debate on whether or not people should be allowed to use steroids.

and cigarettes, coffee, and cola drinks contain commonly used drugs. Even the fluoride contained in some toothpastes is a drug: it changes the surfaces of your teeth to protect them against the acids that produce cavities. Many household products can also act as drugs if they are used improperly and taken into the body. For example, if you inhale (breathe in) gasoline or some types of glue, your breathing and heart rates will slow down — perhaps so much that your life may be in danger. If a substance changes the way your body operates, then that substance is a drug.

THE EFFECTS OF DRUGS

The changes in your body caused by drugs are called **drug effects**. Many drugs have helpful or positive effects. Drugs with **positive effects** can help heal injuries, relieve stomach-aches, or ease coughs, among other things. Other drugs have mostly harmful or **negative effects**. For example, glue contains chemicals; when some types of glue are inhaled, these chemicals act as drugs with very negative effects. Once inside the body, these chemicals are carried to organs like the brain and liver. There, they can cause serious, permanent damage, affecting the way these organs work.

How do drugs cause these effects? To do its many jobs, your body uses many different chemicals. Some of these are obtained from the food you eat. However, your body makes most of its own chemicals, using other chemicals (contained in your food) as the raw material. Your body's chemicals control how your bones grow, how your muscles work, and how your nerve impulses travel, and do hundreds of other tasks. For your body to function properly, these chemicals must be present in the proper amounts: too much of one or too little of another may cause you to become ill. In other words, you need the proper chemical balance in your body if you are to be healthy.

Drugs are also chemicals. Taking a drug adds chemicals to the body's own supply. If a drug helps your body perform its usual tasks, then the drug has positive effects. For example, if you are ill and your body is not producing enough of some needed chemical, a drug might help supply the proper amount of this substance. Insulin is a chemical that your body needs in order to work properly. Many people who have a disease called diabetes cannot produce enough insulin in their bodies. People who have diabetes can, however, take insulin as a drug. In this case, the drug replaces a missing chemical and has very positive effects.

If a drug upsets your body's chemical balance, negative effects can occur. This might happen if the drug prevents your body from making a chemical it needs. Or the drug might contain a chemical that your body already has enough of. Adding more of this substance might cause your body to perform some jobs too quickly or too often. Damage to body parts might be the result.

Some drug effects happen very soon after taking the drug and last for only a short time. These are called the **short-term effects** of the drug. Some people drink coffee because they think that it makes them feel more awake. This is because coffee contains a drug called caffeine. One of the short-term effects of caffeine is to speed up the rate at which nerve impulses travel through your body.

Many drugs also have effects that last for a long time — called the **long-term effects** of the drug. In most cases, long-term effects occur only if a person takes too much of a drug, or takes it for a long period of time. The long-term effects of a drug may be different from its short-term effects. People who regularly drink more than eight cups of coffee a day may show some long-term effects of caffeine. These can include depression, an inability to sleep, and an upset stomach. It takes researchers a long time to study long-term effects. As a result, the long-term effects of many drugs are not known.

Because so many different chemicals are needed, your body's chemical balance is very complicated. It is affected by many factors, including your age and weight, as well as whether you are male or female. No two people have exactly the same balance of chemicals in their bodies. As a result, the same drug can sometimes produce different effects in different people. For example, although a certain amount of a drug may have positive effects on an adult, the same amount of this drug could have negative effects on a young child (Figure 4.3).

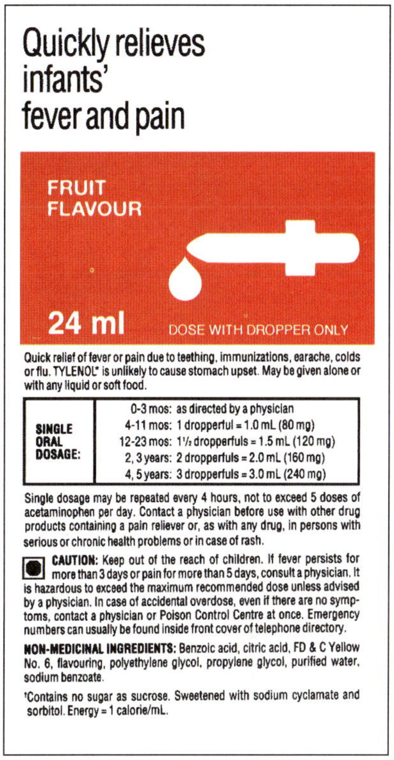

FIGURE 4.3

The amount of this drug that will have positive effects is different for people of different ages. Too much of a drug can have negative effects. Always read the label of a drug you are using.

REVIEW 4.1

1. What is a drug?
2. How do drugs cause their effects on the human body?
3. Does the same drug always affect everyone in exactly the same way? Why or why not?
4. (a) Give three examples of how drugs can help us.
   (b) Can these same drugs also be harmful? If so, explain how.
5. Jatinder's doctor suggested a drug that would help relieve her allergies. Jatinder would need to take the drug for several weeks in spring, when her allergies bothered her. The doctor told her that this drug made some people feel sleepy right after taking it, but that this effect soon wore off. From the following list of terms, choose the ones that apply to this situation and explain why they apply: positive effects, negative effects, medical use, non-medical use, legal drug, illegal drug, short-term effects, long-term effects.

DRUGS FROM PLANTS

What do a flower from Madagascar and a tree from British Columbia have in common? Both these plants provide drugs used to treat cancer.

Madagascar is an island off the coast of Africa. Thousands of the plants there are found nowhere else in the world. The rosy periwinkle from Madagascar is the source of two drugs. Vincristine is used to treat childhood leukemia, and vinblastine to treat Hodgkin's disease. It takes 1000 kg of periwinkle stems and leaves to obtain only 5 g of vincristine. Scientists are researching ways to make the drugs more easily and more cheaply in the laboratory.

The Pacific yew also provides a drug used to treat cancer. The yew is a small, slow-growing coniferous tree found in the forests of the Pacific Northwest, including British Columbia. A drug called taxol can be obtained from the inner bark. Taxol is used to treat cancer of the ovaries and breast, and it may be helpful for other cancers too.

There is a great demand for taxol, but yew trees grow slowly. The bark from three to five 100-year-old trees may be needed to treat one patient. The yew needles also supply some taxol, although much less than the bark does. Needles will grow back, but to get the bark, the trees must be cut down.

The rosy periwinkle and the Pacific yew are just two plants that are sources of drugs. You may have used other medicines that came from plants. About 40 per cent of our modern medicines come from natural sources, mostly plants. The majority of people living in rural areas of the world rely on traditional medicines from plants to treat all sorts of illnesses. Researchers are trying to learn about the plants that traditional healers use. Eventually the drugs may be produced in the laboratory, but first the plants must be studied.

The inner bark of the Pacific yew is a natural source of the drug taxol.

The use of plants for medicines is one good reason to preserve the variety of plants in the world. As forests are cleared, particularly in the tropics, thousands of different kinds of flowering plants may lose their habitat and become extinct. As the plant species are lost forever, so are the possibilities for finding new medicines to treat human disease.

Only a fraction of plant species have been studied for their use as medicines, and new discoveries are made all the time. See if you can find articles in newspapers and magazines on how plants or other organisms may be used as natural sources for new medicines.

4.2 MEDICAL USE OF DRUGS

People have been making and using drugs for thousands of years. Writings left by ancient Egyptians show that more than 4000 years ago, people drank the juices of the poppy plant to relieve pain. Today we know that these juices contain the chemical opium, which slows down the brain's activity and reduces its ability to sense pain.

(a)

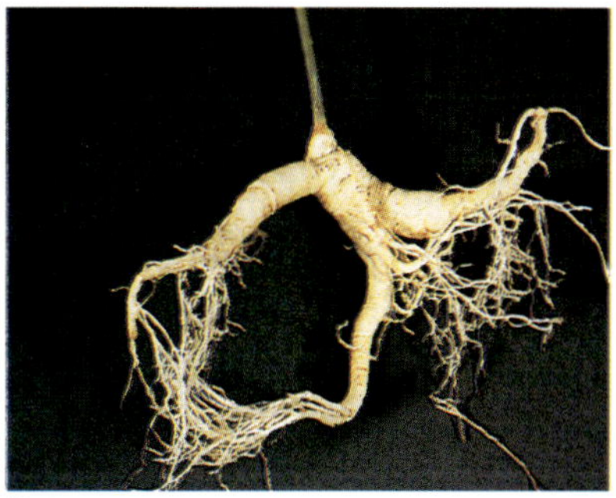

(b)

FIGURE 4.4
(a) Poppies have been the source of the drug opium for thousands of years. Opium, and the drugs that can be made from it, is highly addictive.
(b) Ginseng, an ingredient of many traditional Chinese medicines, is grown in B.C.

Early native people in Canada also used plants to produce medicines. For example, they boiled willow bark to obtain a substance that relieved pain. We now call this substance salicylic acid. You can buy it in products that contain ASA (acetylsalicylic acid). Such products are often taken to relieve headaches and other pains.

Many of the drugs used in the past are still in use today (Figure 4.4). Although some of them are still obtained from plants, many others, like ASA, are now produced in the laboratory. Every year, new medicines are developed from plants.

Drugs can be taken into the body in many ways. Many are swallowed, in the form of pills, capsules, drops, or liquids. Some drugs are applied to the skin as creams, lotions, or drops. You might apply an antibiotic cream to a cut in order to kill bacteria. Other drugs are inhaled, such as nasal (nose) sprays, which are used to clear stuffy noses.

Another common method of getting drugs into the body is by an **injection**. In this method, a syringe — a thin hollow needle attached to a pump — is used to put liquid drugs into the body. At some time in

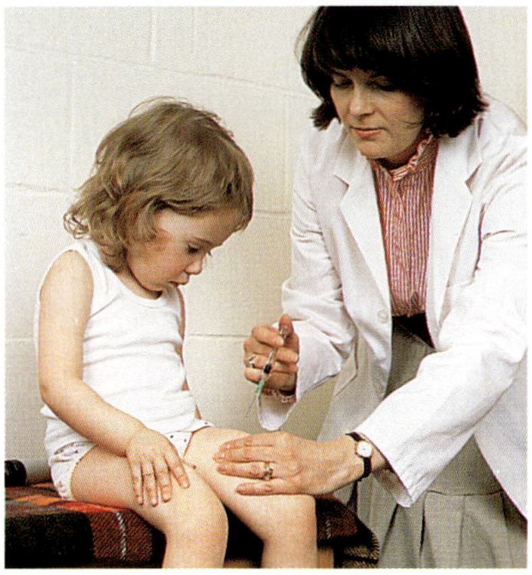

FIGURE 4.5
Many types of vaccines are given by injection. Vaccines have been developed against many diseases, such as diphtheria, tetanus, pertussis, measles, mumps, and rubella. The vaccine against a disease called polio is often given by mouth.

your life, you have probably had injections to protect you against measles, mumps, and other serious diseases. These injections contained **vaccines**. A vaccine is a drug that causes your body to build up its own internal protection against a particular disease. You will not usually catch a disease if you have had a vaccine for it (Figure 4.5).

HOW DRUGS HELP US

Until about 100 years ago, people did not know what caused disease. Some people thought that bad air, or certain types of food, or even witches, were to blame. Then scientists and doctors began working with improved microscopes, which allowed them to see very small living things. Scientists found that some of these tiny organisms caused various types of diseases. Some of these disease-causing organisms are bacteria.

Once scientists had discovered what caused diseases, doctors were able to prevent the diseases and to treat people more successfully (Figure 4.6). In 1900, 190 out of every 100 000 people died from a disease called tuberculosis (TB). Even more people died of pneumonia and influenza. Today few people die of these diseases in North America. Better living conditions, including healthier food and the use of clean water, have helped reduce the number of people dying from these and other diseases.

The development of drugs has also helped to reduce the number of deaths caused by many diseases. Since 1900, many drugs have been developed to treat diseases, including pneumonia and tuberculosis. Some of these drugs kill disease-causing organisms that have entered your body. Others, like vaccines, help your body build up its own defences so that it can kill these organisms. Some drugs help restore your body's balance of chemicals after it has been upset by disease.

FIGURE 4.6 ▶
Influenza, pneumonia, and tuberculosis caused many deaths in North America in the early 1900s. How and why have the data changed?

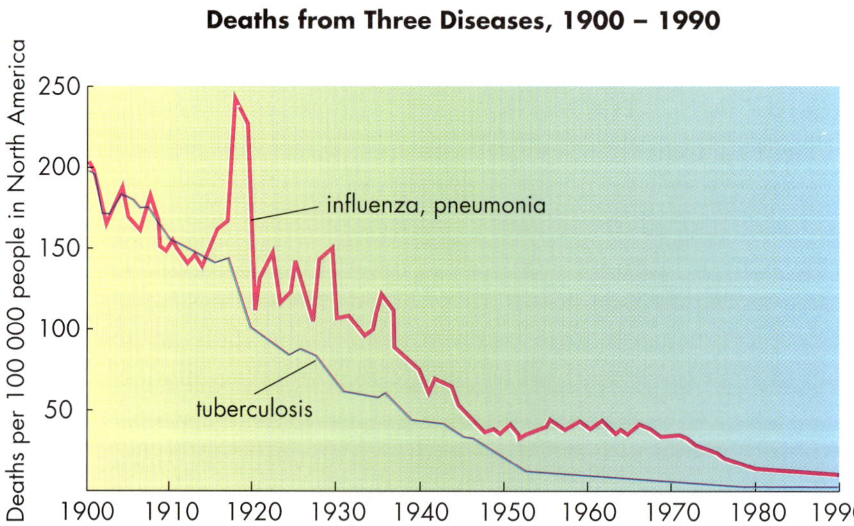

Drugs are also used to treat diseases caused by injuries or by other types of damage to body organs. For example, people with epilepsy and those with diabetes are helped by drugs. (Neither of these diseases is caused by harmful organisms.) At one time, almost everyone with diabetes died. In the early 1920s, John Macleod, Charles Best, and Frederick Banting, working in Canada, discovered how to make insulin in the laboratory. Today many people with diabetes take this drug every day.

Drugs are also taken to reduce or prevent aches and pains. For example, during an operation or when you are having a tooth filled, you may have drugs called **anaesthetics**. These reduce your ability to sense pain. Other drugs have been developed to ease headaches or the pain that results from straining your muscles.

SIDE EFFECTS

People use medicines for the intended, positive effect they will have on the body. Sometimes, however, these same drugs can also cause problems. This is partly because many drugs have side effects. **Side effects** are other body changes a drug causes in addition to its intended effects. Often these side effects are negative. For example, as well as relieving pain (its intended effect), ASA can irritate the lining of your stomach and cause stomach upset.

Some drugs have very serious side effects. For this and other reasons, you need a **prescription** for certain medicines. A prescription is a note, written by a doctor, which allows you to obtain a particular amount of the needed drug at a pharmacy or drugstore. There, prescription drugs (drugs for which you need a prescription) are kept behind the pharmacist's counter (Figure 4.7). The **pharmacist** is the person who reads the prescription and "fills" it by giving you the correct amount of the drug

EXTENSION

- Interview a pharmacist to discover what this job involves. What sort of training does a person need to become a pharmacist? How does a pharmacist learn about all the new drugs that are developed each year?

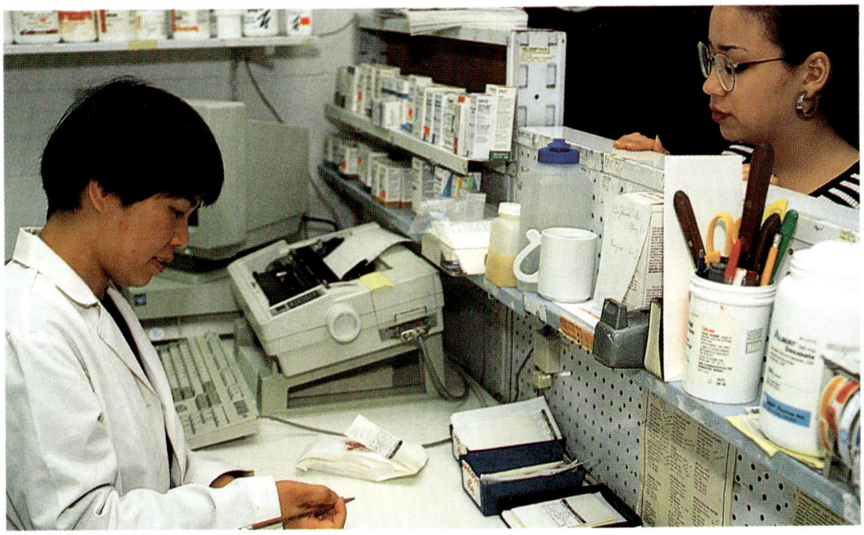

FIGURE 4.7 ◀
This pharmacist is "filling" a prescription. She reads the prescription from the doctor, finds the necessary drugs behind the pharmacy counter, and measures out the correct amount. The doctor's instructions about how much of the drug to take, how often, and for how long will be written on the container she gives the patient.

EXTENSION

■ Some advertisements say that certain over-the-counter drugs relieve headaches, reduce cavities, or ease coughs better than other drugs made for the same purpose. How do the makers of these drugs know that their drugs are better? Design an experiment that would help you to decide which of two drugs does a better job at whatever it is supposed to do. Write out an outline of your proposed experiment. Be sure to describe what experimental controls you will need. Also describe any problems you might run into while doing your experiment. How might these difficulties affect your conclusions? WARNING: It will not be safe for you to carry out this experiment.

you need. Pharmacists are trained to understand drugs and their effects.

Many drugs are not kept behind the pharmacist's counter but are available to anyone without a prescription. These products are often called **over-the-counter drugs**. You may have bought some of these drugs to treat coughs, fevers, headaches, or stomach upset.

Over-the-counter drugs can be very helpful. However, many of these substances also have side effects, especially if they are used improperly. Taking too much of a drug at one time, or taking it repeatedly over a long period of time, can cause problems. Too much ASA, for example, can cause bleeding inside your body. Continued use of ASA can damage organs such as your kidneys.

In addition, some over-the-counter drugs can be dangerous if used in combination with other drugs. Mixing two drugs can produce effects greater than, or different from, the same amount of one of the drugs used alone (Figure 4.8).

To avoid problems with over-the-counter or prescription drugs, you must be an informed consumer. Informed consumers know how and when drugs should be used and what their effects are.

CAUTION: For occasional use in adults only. Do not take within 1½ hours of time you plan to sleep. Do not take with caffeine-containing beverages. Consult your physician before using this product if you are taking other medication or under doctor's care.

DIRECTION: 1 or 2 tablets every 4 hours as required. Do not exceed recommended dose or more than 8 tablets in any 24-hour period.

NOT TO BE GIVEN TO CHILDREN.

INGREDIENTS: CAFFEINE ALKALOID 100 mg PLUS INERT FILLERS

FIGURE 4.8 ▶
It is sometimes dangerous to take two different drugs at the same time. If you are taking a prescription drug, ask your doctor or pharmacist what over-the-counter drugs you should avoid.

ACTIVITY 4B / INVESTIGATING OVER-THE-COUNTER DRUGS

This activity will give you an opportunity to become an informed consumer.

Select an over-the-counter drug to investigate. Read the instructions that come with the product. Get more information from reference books or interview a pharmacist or a doctor to help you answer the following questions about this drug:

1. What disease or condition is this drug used to treat?
2. What is the intended effect of this drug?
3. What is the recommended dose of this drug? That is, how much of the drug does the package recommend that you should take and how often can you take it?
4. What are the possible side effects of using this drug? Are these side effects listed on the label or container?
5. Do you think that the intended effects and side effects of this drug have been explained well enough on the label or container? Why or why not?
6. Are there any methods other than using a drug or drugs that you could use to treat the condition referred to in question 1? ❖

PREMARKET TESTING

Imagine that you have developed a new drug to treat a disease like leukemia or a condition like a headache. You would want to be sure that the drug was safe for people to use. What do you think you would have to do before the drug could be sold in Canada? How much of the drug should people take and how often? Does the drug have any side effects? Are there people who should not take any of the drug, perhaps because of their age, or because they have another condition that would make the drug dangerous to them (Figure 4.9)?

New drugs are being developed all the time. Before these drugs can be sold (before they can "go on the market"), they must be carefully tested to make sure the chemicals they contain are not harmful. This testing is called **premarket testing**.

In the past, some drugs were not carefully tested. When people began using them, these substances were discovered to have harmful side effects. Today, Canada has stricter laws to control premarket testing.

DIRECTIONS FOR USE — ADULTS: Dissolve the contents of one pouch in a 225 mL (8 oz.) glass of hot water. May be repeated in 3 to 4 hours. Do not exceed 3 doses in 24 hours.

CAUTION: ALTHOUGH THIS PRODUCT HAS A LOW SUGAR CONTENT, IT MAY NOT BE APPROPRIATE FOR DIABETICS. Individuals with high blood pressure, diabetes, heart, thyroid or lung diseases, prostate diseases, glaucoma, the elderly or children under 15 years of age, pregnant women or nursing mothers should use only as directed by a physician. May cause drowsiness. Do not drive or operate machinery and avoid alcoholic beverages as well as other depressants while taking this medicine. If symptoms persist, consult your physician. Keep safely out of reach of children.

CONTENTS: Each pouch contains: Active ingredients: Acetaminophen 325 mg. Phenylephrine Hydrochloride 10 mg, Pheniramine Maleate 20 mg. Non-medicinal ingredients: Corn syrup solids Aspartame (contains phenylalanine). Sodium 31 cal.pouch. Also contains: Vitamin C, 50 mg.

FIGURE 4.9
Pregnant women should avoid using drugs, including over-the-counter products, unless they have been advised to do so by their doctor. This is because the drugs they take may also affect the developing baby.

ACTIVITY 4C / DRUG TESTING

CROSS · CURRICULAR

Watch the newspapers and magazines for articles that mention the discovery or development of new drugs. Post these articles on a class bulletin board. Use this information, and any other information you can find, to hold a class discussion on one of the two questions on the right.

1. Do you think that drugs are tested for a long enough period of time? Why or why not?
2. What are the advantages and disadvantages of having laws that require companies to test drugs before selling them? ❖

► REVIEW 4.2

1. (a) Describe some ways in which drugs are helpful. Include some examples of helpful drugs.
   (b) When might helpful drugs become harmful?
2. Imagine that a new antibiotic lotion has been developed to kill bacteria that get into cuts and other skin injuries. Some people who use the lotion find that although their cuts heal, an itchy rash appears wherever the lotion has touched their skin.
   (a) What is the intended effect of this drug?
   (b) Does this drug have any side effects? If so, describe the side effect or effects.
3. (a) What is the difference between prescription drugs and over-the-counter drugs?
   (b) Why is the sale of some drugs restricted by requiring a prescription?
4. (a) What is premarket testing?
   (b) Why is it necessary?

PROFILE

DR. FRANCES OLDHAM KELSEY

Have you ever thought about how much difference one person can make? Thousands of children may have been born healthy because of a key decision made by Dr. Frances Kelsey.

Born in Canada, Kelsey moved to the United States to study drugs and medicine. Just after she began to work for the Food and Drug Administration (FDA), she received an application to approve a new drug. The year was 1960 and the drug was thalidomide. Kelsey's job was to make sure that thalidomide had been properly tested and that it produced no serious side effects.

Dr. Frances Kelsey with President John F. Kennedy

Thalidomide had been used in Europe since 1956. Anyone who wanted a drug for a good, sound sleep relied on thalidomide. Pregnant women were among those who used this drug. Thalidomide was very popular and could be bought without a prescription. It had a reputation as a safe drug and seemed to have no side effects. The American manufacturer of the drug wanted to begin selling thalidomide to the public and counted on speedy approval by the FDA.

Kelsey noted, however, that certain basic tests had not been done. She questioned the claim that thalidomide was completely safe. At the time, there did not seem to be a good reason to delay approval, except for a few missing test results. The drug had sold widely in other countries, and there was no public evidence of damage to humans. Kelsey's growing awareness of the effects of drugs on unborn babies made her cautious. She would not yet approve the drug for use in the United States.

By the early 1960s, unfavourable news about thalidomide surfaced. Researchers in Great Britain and Germany found that the drug caused numbness and tingling in the fingers and toes of some users. Soon nerve damage was directly linked to the drug. Women who had taken thalidomide during early pregnancy were giving birth to babies whose arms or legs did not develop properly. With this evidence of serious side effects, the American manufacturer withdrew its application to the FDA.

Since thalidomide had to be tested before the FDA could give approval, there had been some premarket testing in the United States. From these tests, there were some "thalidomide babies," but the number was much lower in the United States than in countries where thalidomide had been widely sold.

Kelsey had delayed approval of thalidomide because she had asked exactly the right question: Is the drug safe for pregnant women? For her insight and efforts, Kelsey received a medal from President John F. Kennedy.

Do you know of other drugs that can harm unborn babies? How do you think women should be warned about the possible side effects of drugs?

4.3 DRUG ABUSE

Since drugs change the way your body works, they must be used with care. Sometimes the use of drugs causes problems. **Drug abuse** is any use of a drug that causes a problem other than the side effects of medicine. Drug abuse can cause problems at school, at home, and with the law, and can cause physical harm to the body. Sometimes it is illegal drugs, such as heroin, marijuana, or cocaine that are abused. More commonly, however, it is alcohol, which is legal for adults, that is abused. Any drug can be abused if it is not used carefully.

A drug abuser may use too much of a drug or may use it for too long a period of time. (Some people must take drugs all their lives for diseases such as epilepsy or diabetes, but this is not drug abuse.) Drinking too much alcohol, or drinking it too often, can cause serious problems. Even a small amount of alcohol can be deadly if a person drives a car after drinking. Not following your doctor's directions for the use of prescription drugs, or taking drugs prescribed for someone else, can also have dangerous effects.

A drug can also be abused if it is taken for the wrong reasons. A liquid drug used to ease a stomach ache is a medicine. If a person drinks this liquid in order to feel "relaxed" or because the person's friends are doing it, then the drug is not a medicine. In other words, whether or not a drug is a medicine depends on how the drug is used, as well as on what its effects are. Using drugs that are usually medicines for non-medical purposes is a type of drug abuse.

Another type of drug abuse is taking illegal drugs that have no medical use at all, such as LSD (**lys**ergic acid **d**iethylamide) or PCP (phencyclidine or **p**henyl**c**yclohexl**p**iperidine). These drugs change the way a person perceives the world. Although these drugs can temporarily make a person feel "good," they can also cause people to feel confused, depressed, or terrified. These drugs sometimes cause serious physical or mental damage and even death. LSD, PCP, and other illegal drugs like them can cause problems no matter how and when they are taken. In these cases, there is no difference between "use" and "abuse." If you use them, you are abusing them.

DID YOU KNOW

The most commonly abused drug in Canada is alcohol. In B.C. hospitals, 50 per cent of all emergency cases and 20 to 40 per cent of all admissions to hospitals are linked to alcohol.

EXTENSION

What is meant by the term "drug trafficking"? Who are drug traffickers? What are the penalties for drug trafficking in Canada? Do research to answer these questions, perhaps by interviewing a police officer. Write a brief report about your findings.

DRUG ADDICTION

Using a drug for a long period of time may lead to drug **addiction**. Drug addiction is the repeated use of a drug, which the user finds difficult to stop. Another term for addiction is **drug dependence**. A person who is addicted has become dependent on the drug: he or she cannot carry out daily activities without using it.

There are two kinds of drug dependence. **Physical dependence** occurs when a person's body has become so used to the drug that the body needs the drug in order to work properly. Drugs that can cause physical dependence include alcohol, nicotine, morphine, heroin, and opium. The second type of drug dependence is **psychological dependence**. It occurs when a person has a strong emotional need for a drug, feeling lost or desperate without it. People can become psychologically dependent on caffeine, sleeping pills, marijuana, and cocaine, among other drugs (Figure 4.10). Many of the drugs that can cause physical dependence also cause psychological dependence.

FIGURE 4.10 ▶
The leaves this worker is picking will be dried and made into tea. Tea contains caffeine, a drug that can be harmful if a person consumes too much of it. What other foods and drinks contain caffeine?

If an addict (a person who is addicted to a drug) stops using the drug, he or she suffers a **withdrawal reaction**. The type of withdrawal reaction depends on which drug has been abused, and for how long. A withdrawal reaction may be simply physical discomfort, such as diarrhea or headache. In some cases, however, a withdrawal reaction may cause severe illness and even death. Some withdrawal reactions are more psychological, such as sleeplessness or unhappiness.

BECOMING ADDICTED

How does a person become addicted to a particular drug? In some ways, the process of becoming addicted depends on the drug being taken and on the person taking it. However, it usually follows the same basic steps. The process may begin the first time a person uses a drug. A person might use a drug because of feeling worried or depressed or because of wanting to do what it seems "everyone else" is doing. After using the drug, the person might feel more relaxed or happier. Even if the experience was not really enjoyable, the person may have felt like "one of the crowd."

Eventually, the effects of the drug wear off. The person may then feel upset or left out again. In order to feel "better," the person takes the drug again. Using a drug repeatedly like this causes a person to develop **tolerance** to the drug. This means that the person feels the effects of the drug less and less each time he or she uses it. As the user builds up tolerance to a drug, more of the drug is needed to create the desired feelings (Figure 4.11).

As always, the effect of the drug eventually wears off. At some point, the person will have become so used to taking the drug that he or she needs it just to feel "normal." The person must now take more of the drug and must take it more often. Soon, the drug user may spend much of his or her time thinking about using or obtaining the drug. This person has become addicted. Without help from a doctor or other trained person, it is very difficult to recover from addiction to some drugs.

EXTENSION

■ Find out what people, organizations, or agencies there are in your community to help people who have a drug dependence. Make a pamphlet that describes these services and how to reach them.

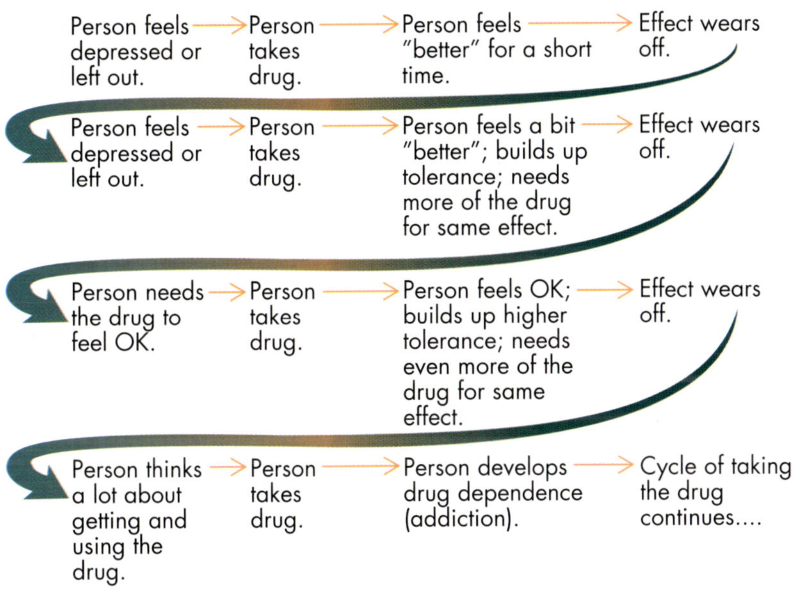

FIGURE 4.11 ◀ ***This flow chart shows how a person can become addicted to a drug. How can you break the cycle?***

▶ REVIEW 4.3

1. (a) Define the term "drug abuse."
   (b) What are some ways in which drugs can be abused?
2. What is the difference between physical and psychological drug dependence?
3. (a) Think about addiction to a drug such as alcohol, heroin, or the nicotine in tobacco. How might becoming addicted to that drug affect a person's life?
   (b) How might the drug addiction affect the lives of the person's family and friends?
4. Describe how a person becomes addicted to a drug. You might choose to do this in the form of a short story or a poem about a particular person and a particular drug. Or you might choose to draw a picture or a flow chart that illustrates this story.

4.4 ALCOHOL — A LIQUID DRUG

Many people do not think of alcohol as a drug. Did you include it on your chart in Activity 4A? Think about the definition of a drug given earlier in this chapter — alcohol certainly fits this description.

ACTIVITY 4D / WHAT DO YOU KNOW ABOUT ALCOHOL?

In your learning journal, write "True" or "False" beside the number that represents each of the following statements. This is not a graded quiz, so just write down what you think. Once you have completed the activity, there will be a class discussion on each statement.

1. Alcohol makes you more alert.
2. Alcohol affects everybody the same way.
3. A person who is upset can be calmed down by a drink of alcohol.
4. A person who has had too much alcohol can "sober up" by drinking a cup of coffee or taking a cold shower.
5. The rate at which alcohol is removed from the body depends on a person's weight.
6. Alcohol can be removed from your body faster if you walk or run than if you just sit.
7. The legal age for purchasing or drinking alcohol in British Columbia is 19.
8. Drinking alcohol is not as hazardous to a person's health as smoking cigarettes.
9. Drinking too much alcohol can lead to brain and liver damage and can even cause death.
10. A person who has just had three drinks containing alcohol can drive just as well as he or she would after three glasses of juice. ❖

THE EFFECTS OF ALCOHOL

Alcohol is a chemical substance contained in beer, wine, and other types of liquor, such as rum, gin, vodka, and whisky. Alcohol is also a drug. When a person drinks alcohol, the first part of the body to be affected is the nervous system, particularly the brain. Alcohol slows down the nerve impulses that travel through the brain and around the body. As a result, all the body's activities are affected when a person drinks. It takes the person longer to respond to the stimuli his or her senses pick up, and the responses are less co-ordinated.

Since alcohol affects the brain, a person's ability to think clearly and to control body movements decreases after drinking alcohol. Because no two people have brains that are exactly the same, the effect of a certain amount of alcohol on one person may be different from its effect on another person. Even the same individual may experience different effects each time he or she drinks alcohol, depending on the person's general health and tiredness.

People who have been drinking may appear to be acting normally and may think that they are all right. However, the alcohol has actually had negative effects on many of their brain functions. For example, their ability to judge distances decreases. Their eyes become less able to adjust to seeing in the dark after looking at a bright light. These difficulties reduce a person's ability to perform tasks such as driving a vehicle (Figure 4.12). Drinking alcohol greatly increases a driver's chances of being involved in an accident in which someone is killed. This is particularly true for drivers 16 to 19 years of age.

Alcohol also has harmful effects on other parts of your body. Long-term use or heavy drinking can damage internal organs such as the liver and heart. Some research suggests that alcohol may cause certain types of cancer. Alcohol can also injure the lining of the stomach, leading to ulcers (sores in the stomach's lining) and other problems.

FIGURE 4.12
This crash claimed a life. The driver had been drinking alcohol. How does alcohol impair driving ability?

RIDDING THE BODY OF ALCOHOL

When a person drinks, alcohol is absorbed into the bloodstream and carried to all parts of the body. Like other types of food and drink, most of the alcohol a person drinks must be broken down into very small particles before it can be removed from the body. This is done mostly in the liver. After alcohol has been broken down, it is removed from the body in the urine. It takes much longer for the body to get rid of this drug than it does to drink it.

Alcohol is broken down and removed from the body at a constant rate, regardless of a person's size, weight, or experience with the drug.

There is nothing anyone can do to speed up this rate. Taking a cold shower or drinking coffee may make a person feel more in control. In fact, the alcohol is still present, and is still slowing down the nervous system. Only a very small amount of alcohol leaves the body with perspiration, so exercise does not help. Neither does going to the bathroom frequently. Only time will do the job. It takes about an hour for the body to rid itself of the amount of alcohol contained in one 340 mL bottle of beer.

DID YOU KNOW

- In Canada, it is illegal to drive with a blood alcohol content higher than 0.08 per cent. Blood alcohol content is a measurement of the amount of alcohol in a person's bloodstream. Someone with a blood alcohol content of 0.08 per cent has 80 mg of alcohol in each 100 mL of his or her blood. Depending on a person's height, weight, and other factors, a blood alcohol level this high could be reached after having only a single drink. A driver with a blood alcohol content of more than 0.08 per cent has a much higher chance of being in a serious car accident than a driver who has not had any alcohol.

ALCOHOL ABUSE

Alcohol is the most commonly abused drug. Long-term use can cause dependence on alcohol. This addiction is called alcoholism. People find it very difficult to recover from alcoholism. It poses major problems for individuals who are alcoholic as well as for their families and friends. Heavy drinking over a long period of time can cause enough damage to body organs to result in death. Thousands of Canadians die each year of diseases related to abusing alcohol.

Even short-term abuse — drinking too much alcohol at dinner or at a party, for example — can have very serious results. Drinking a large amount of alcohol over a short period of time can result in death. Drinking alcohol is particularly dangerous if the drinker then drives (Figure 4.13). Each year in British Columbia, approximately 200 people die and 7000 people are injured in accidents caused by drivers who have been drinking. In fact, drunk driving is the leading cause of accidents that result in death.

Why is alcohol abuse so common? Alcohol is fairly easy to obtain, even though it is illegal in British Columbia for people under 19 years of age. Sometimes people drink to fit in with their friends and be part of the group. Advertising may also contribute to the problem. To convince you to buy a product, advertisers often use hidden persuaders — things that stretch the truth or that make you feel that using the product will lead to success, happiness, or popularity (Figure 4.14).

FIGURE 4.13 ▶
Using a small instrument called a breathalyser, a police officer can determine how much alcohol is in a driver's blood.

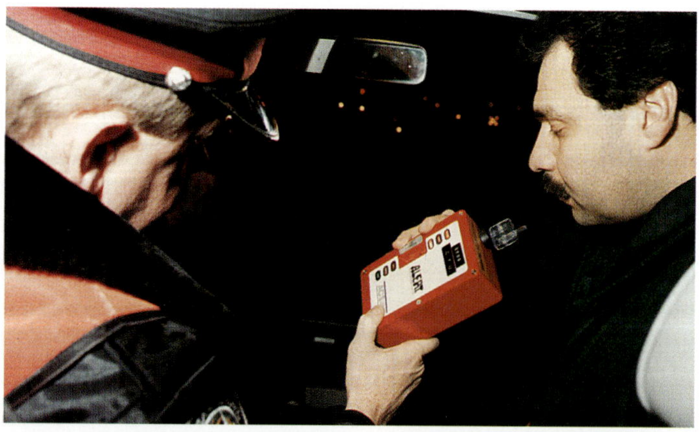

FIGURE 4.14
What hidden persuaders are used in this advertisement?

ACTIVITY 4E / ALCOHOL ADVERTISING

CROSS • CURRICULAR

This activity will give you an opportunity to look for hidden persuaders in alcohol advertising. You might work individually or with a partner.

PROCEDURE

1. Study three advertisements for beer, wine, or liquor from magazines, newspapers, or television.
2. Identify any hidden persuaders in your three advertisements. Explain how you think the hidden persuaders stretch the truth or link alcohol with a desirable lifestyle.
3. Design an advertisement for a drug-free product, event, or activity using one of the same hidden persuaders.
4. Select one of the advertised products from step 1. Make a poster that shows what you think might really happen if people use this product.

DISCUSSION

1. Why do you think hidden persuaders are used in advertising?
2. What are some of the facts that are left out of these alcohol advertisements?
3. Do you think that the advertisements used in step 1 are made for a particular audience? Explain your answer in full. ❖

REVIEW 4.4

1. Why is alcohol considered to be a drug?
2. (a) How does alcohol affect the nervous system?
   (b) In what ways can alcohol affect other parts of the body?
3. How is alcohol removed from the body?
4. Why is it dangerous to drink and drive?
5. Why do you think alcohol is so commonly abused?
6. What do you think are some of the costs to society of alcohol abuse?

DID YOU KNOW

Smoking and drinking alcohol are particularly dangerous during pregnancy, since the drugs a pregnant woman takes can also reach her developing baby. Babies born to women who smoke while pregnant have a higher chance of being born too early and with nervous system damage than those born to non-smokers. Drinking during pregnancy can cause a number of birth defects, including mental retardation and heart problems. Because no one knows just how much alcohol is harmful to the developing baby, pregnant women are advised not to drink at all.

4.5 WHAT DOES TOBACCO CONTAIN?

Tobacco smoke contains many chemicals. One of these chemicals is a drug called nicotine. Nicotine affects the nervous system, increasing the rate at which nerve impulses travel through the body. Some smokers say that nicotine helps them "get going." This is because they have become dependent on the drug and need to smoke to get this feeling.

Smokers usually begin by having a cigarette on a few occasions. Gradually they start to smoke more cigarettes and inhale more tobacco smoke into their lungs. If they continue, they can become addicted to the nicotine in the smoke. Many smokers have 10 to 20 cigarettes every day. People who regularly smoke this much would suffer a withdrawal reaction if they quit. You might be able to see this yourself if a relative or family friend quits smoking. He or she may be nervous and easily upset, and want very much to smoke a cigarette.

Nicotine is the chemical in smoke that people become addicted to; it is what keeps them smoking. However, tobacco smoke also contains other chemicals that are harmful to your health, including substances called tars. Tars have been shown to cause lung cancer. Although much of the tar that enters a smoker's lungs is coughed up, the average cigarette smoker deposits about 124 g of tar in his or her lungs every year (Figure 4.16).

Tobacco smoke also contains gases such as carbon monoxide. This potentially deadly gas is also found in automobile exhaust fumes. Although you cannot see, smell, or taste carbon monoxide, it is present whenever tobacco burns. Carbon monoxide prevents your body's cells from getting the oxygen they need to perform their usual jobs. The lack of oxygen can make you feel weak.

Tobacco smoke contains other harmful substances as well. Scientific studies have shown that these chemicals may cause heart disease, liver disease, various types of cancer, and several different lung diseases. Health and Welfare Canada has estimated that over 38 000 Canadians die each year from tobacco-related diseases.

Statistics from Health and Welfare Canada show that in recent years, British Columbia has had the lowest percentage (26.3 per cent) of smokers of any province in Canada. This survey includes people of all ages. When male and female smokers were counted separately, it was found that fewer females (23.6 per cent) than males (29.0 per cent) smoke.

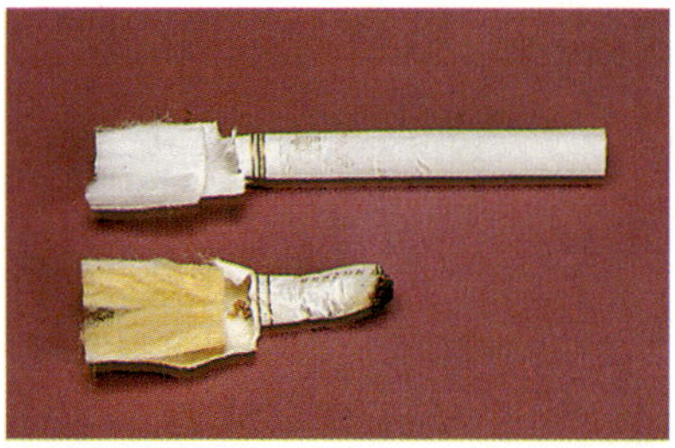

FIGURE 4.15
What evidence can you see in this picture that cigarette filters remove only some of the tar from cigarette smoke? Other harmful substances, such as carbon monoxide, pass right through the filter.

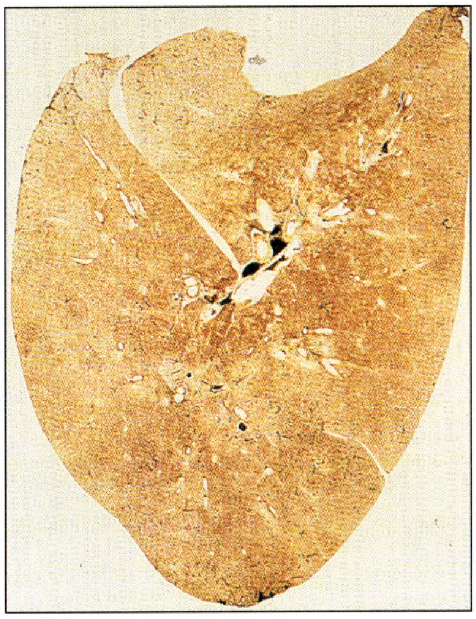

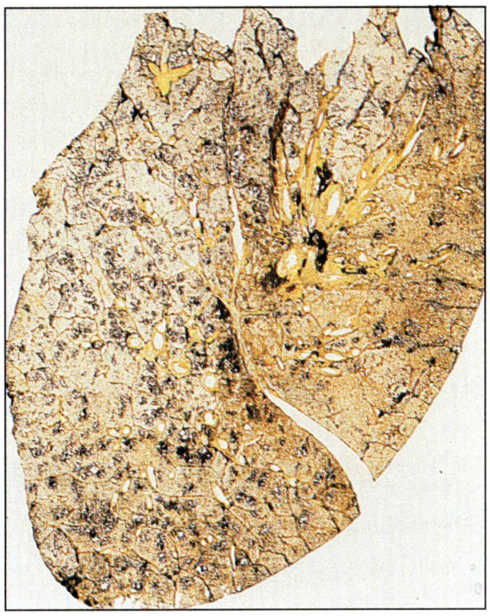

FIGURE 4.16
The lung of a non-smoker is shown on the left. The lung of a smoker is on the right. What differences do you notice?

ACTIVITY 4F / ANALYSING CHANGES IN SMOKING HABITS

Table 4.1 shows the percentage of current cigarette smokers (male and female) in Canada aged 15 to 19 for several years between 1965 and 1989. Current smokers are those who had had one or more cigarettes in the past day when this survey was done. Study the table and answer the following questions:

1. Graph the percentage of male and female smokers on the same graph. Put years on the x-axis and the percentage of smokers on the y-axis.

2. Compare the changes in the percentages of male and female smokers from 1965 to 1989.
(a) Why do you think these changes occurred?
(b) In which group, male or female, did the percentage change the most? Why do you think this happened?

3. Predict what effect, if any, you think the changes you have observed will have on the number of people who will get lung cancer in Canada. ❖

Percentage of smokers aged 15–19					
Year	**Males**	**Females**	**Year**	**Males**	**Females**
1965	55	37	1981	45	42
1970	56	43	1983	38	39
1974	54	48	1986	24	28
1977	49	47	1989	22	24
1979	47	46			

TABLE 4.1 ***Current Cigarette Smokers, Aged 15–19, in Canada***

EXTENSION

■ Do a survey in your school to find out the percentage of smokers in a certain group (for example, those 16 years and older). Compare your results with the data in Table 4.1. Are there any differences? If so, explain why you think these might exist.

THE NON-SMOKER

Between puffs, a smoker usually holds a cigarette in his or her hand or leaves it in an ashtray. As a result, cigarette smoke goes directly into the environment. This unfiltered smoke is called **second-hand smoke**, or sidestream smoke. This smoke may contain twice as much tar and nicotine, and five times as much carbon monoxide, as smoke that has passed through the filter of a cigarette. Think of what this might mean for a non-smoker in the same room as the smoker! Research has suggested that several breathing diseases, as well as roughly 300 lung cancer deaths each year in Canada, are due to second-hand smoke.

Today, non-smokers are speaking up about their desire to breathe smoke-free air. Many Canadian cities have passed by-laws restricting smoking in public places. In some buildings, smoking is allowed only in specific places. Other buildings are now completely smoke-free (Figure 4.17).

FIGURE 4.17 ▶
Do you think it's fair for smokers to smoke near non-smokers?

▶ REVIEW 4.5

1. (a) What is the drug in tobacco that causes addiction?
   (b) Why does it cause addiction?
2. (a) What are some of the other substances that a smoker inhales?
   (b) Are these substances considered drugs? Why or why not?
3. (a) How does smoking act on the nervous system?
   (b) What are some effects smoking has on other parts of the body?
4. (a) What is second-hand smoke?
   (b) Why is it dangerous?
5. What can be done about limiting or eliminating the amount of second-hand smoke in the environment?
6. What do you think are some of the costs to society of smoking?

4.6 DRUGS AND THE NERVOUS SYSTEM

There are drugs that act on almost all parts of the human body. The two most commonly abused drugs, alcohol and nicotine, affect the nervous system. This section is about some other drugs that affect the nervous system.

As shown in Appendix B (Table B.1), most of the drugs that affect the nervous system fall into three major groups: stimulants, depressants, and hallucinogens. **Stimulants** speed up the activity of the nervous system. Some increase the rate at which nerve impulses travel. Others act in different ways. Stimulants can make you feel alert and keep you awake. Caffeine, a drug found in coffee, tea, cola drinks, and chocolate, is a stimulant. The nicotine in tobacco is also a stimulant. The illegal drug cocaine is a very dangerous stimulant. People who take cocaine can easily become dependent on it.

Depressants slow down, or depress, the nervous system. Although they do it in different ways, both depressants and stimulants make users feel "good" for a short time.

There are many different kinds of depressants. Some are medicines that can be obtained only with a prescription. Others, including codeine, are contained in many over-the-counter products, such as cough syrups. Still other depressants, such as heroin, are not used medically in Canada and are illegal to have. Alcohol is the most commonly abused depressant drug.

A third group of drugs that affect the nervous system is made up of substances called **hallucinogens**. Hallucinogens cause people to see or hear things that do not exist. When a person has taken a hallucinogen, his or her brain sometimes acts as if it is receiving nerve impulses from various sensory receptors even though no impulses are being sent. In other words, these drugs cause hallucinations. Hallucinogens include drugs such as LSD and PCP, as well as the chemicals found in certain types of mushrooms.

DID YOU KNOW

■ Combining alcohol with other drugs — particularly other depressants — can be very dangerous. Combining two depressants can slow nerve impulses down so much that a person may stop breathing. Death may result. Alcohol combined with stimulants may lead to a false sense of security. The person may feel sober and may therefore go ahead and do something dangerous — like driving a car. What is one stimulant drug that people often use after drinking alcohol?

CANNABIS

You may have heard of cannabis in one of its three forms: marijuana, hashish, and hash oil. All three come from a plant known as *Cannabis sativa*. Cannabis is another drug that affects the nervous system. It is often described as a hallucinogen because users seem to detect things that are not really there. As well, their sense of time and space is distorted. However, in some ways, cannabis acts like a depressant. It slows down parts of the nervous system. It usually makes people who use it feel relaxed. In other ways, cannabis is a stimulant. For example, using it increases the heart rate.

All three forms of cannabis have similar effects on the nervous system. The drug interferes with the user's memory, as well as with his or her ability to learn and think logically. Although cannabis makes most users feel "good" for a short time, it causes other users to feel panicky, depressed, and confused. Some users become dependent on the drug.

Cannabis also has negative long-term effects. Smoking it can cause more lung damage than smoking ordinary cigarettes. In addition, the amount of one cancer-causing substance is much higher in cannabis smoke than it is in the smoke from tobacco. Some scientists have suggested that cannabis may also interfere with the chemicals in your body that control reproduction, growth, and development. Cannabis may have particularly serious effects, therefore, for people 11 to 16 years of age, who are undergoing rapid growth and sexual development. It may also be dangerous for pregnant women to use cannabis, since it may affect their developing babies.

FIGURE 4.18
People with the disease called asthma have difficulty breathing. Often, they must inhale drugs to clear their breathing passages.

INHALANTS

As you have learned, drugs can be taken in different ways. Some drugs are taken by being inhaled, or "sniffed." These drugs are called **inhalants**. Although some inhalant drugs have medical uses (Figure 4.18), many do not. Inhalants used for non-medical purposes include such things as glue, gasoline, nail polish remover, paint thinner, correction fluid, and products that come in spray cans, such as cooking oil and hair spray.

Some of the chemicals present in these products are depressants. Others act like hallucinogens. Most inhalants are very dangerous (see Appendix B, Table B.2). Long-term use leads to forgetfulness and an inability to think clearly, among other nervous system problems. Internal organs, such as the liver and kidneys, may also be damaged by using inhalants. Regular sniffing of these drugs can lead to dependence.

REVIEW 4.6

1. (a) What is the difference between stimulants and depressants?
(b) In what ways are these two types of drugs similar?

2. (a) What are some medical uses for depressant drugs?
(b) Give three examples of depressant drugs that are used for non-medical purposes.

3. (a) What do hallucinogenic drugs do?
(b) How might this be dangerous?

4. Why does cannabis not fit well into one of the three major groups of drugs?

5. What are some of the negative effects of cannabis on the human body?

6. (a) Define the term "inhalants" and give three examples of non-medical inhalant drugs.
(b) Why are inhalant drugs dangerous?

4.7 MAKING CHOICES

Using drugs for non-medical purposes affects more than the user. The person who sells illegal drugs in order to have enough money to buy drugs for his or her own use, the person who insists on drinking and driving, the smoker whose second-hand smoke bothers non-smokers, even the person who misuses over-the-counter drugs — all these people endanger both themselves and others.

If using drugs for non-medical purposes can have so many negative results, why do people do it? Some say that they try drugs just to see what these substances are like. Other people take drugs because they feel worried, unhappy, or under stress. They think that using drugs will make them feel better. Still others say that they see, or read about, or hear about people all around them using drugs. Therefore, they think it must be "normal" to use drugs. Many people give "peer pressure" as their reason for using alcohol, tobacco, or other drugs. In other words, they feel pressured by their peers (people their own age) to act in a particular way so that they will become part of the group (Figure 4.19).

DID YOU KNOW

- Drugs bought on the street are often impure. Buyers can never be sure what they are getting, so they cannot predict exactly what effect the drug will have on them. This is particularly true for cannabis. It is often mixed with harmful chemicals (pesticides or fertilizers) that were used on the plants while they were growing. In addition, cannabis sometimes has very dangerous drugs such as PCP mixed with it. What effect might this have?

FIGURE 4.19 ◀
How might peer pressure be at work in this situation?

One way to resist this type of pressure is to realize that in fact, many people do not use drugs for non-medical purposes. In 1990, the British Columbia Ministry of Health conducted a survey in which they asked more than 14 000 students in grades 8 to 12 whether they had used drugs in the previous year. (The students did not have to give their names when answering.) Here are some of the results:

- 73 per cent had not smoked tobacco
- 77 per cent had not used cannabis
- 91 per cent had not used LSD
- 90 per cent had not used other hallucinogenic drugs
- 97 per cent had not inhaled solvents
- 98 per cent had not inhaled glue

Alcohol is different. In this survey, only 28 per cent of students had not used alcohol in the previous 12 months. It is the most commonly abused drug. People need a different response to the peer pressure that urges them to try alcohol.

ACTIVITY 4G / DEALING WITH PEER PRESSURE

GROUP ACTIVITY G

CROSS-CURRICULAR C

How does peer pressure work? How can you deal with it? The next activity will give you an opportunity to investigate these questions.

Situation #1
After school, Richard, David, and Parminder are walking to the mall. Richard takes out a package of cigarettes and lights one. After giving a cigarette to Parminder, Richard offers one to David, who refuses it. David's friends accuse him of being chicken. After all, they say, "One smoke isn't going to hurt." What should David do?

Situation #2
Nava, Elissa, Indira, and Rachel are spending the night at Giselle's house. Giselle's older sister Marie is upstairs doing homework, but their parents are out for the evening. Elissa suggests that the girls sample some of the alcohol belonging to Giselle's parents. The other three girls go along with Elissa, saying, "It's OK. We'll only have a little." Giselle does not like the idea at all. Her parents have trusted her to have her friends over without causing any trouble, and she has never let them down. What should Giselle do?

PROCEDURE

1. Have small groups of students role-play the situations described at left. Each group might want to rehearse briefly before presenting the situation to the class, but the lines should not be written out — let the story develop as it goes along. Because different people might deal with these situations in different ways, more than one group could role-play each of the situations.

2. While these role plays are being carried out, watch for ways in which peer pressure is applied. Try to identify the methods used to apply the pressure.

3. During the role play, also look for how people respond to the peer pressure. One choice is to give in and go along with the group. There are, however, ways to resist peer pressure. Here are some of the methods you might use:
   (a) Turn the tables — say that you would not want the others to do something harmful because you are their friend. Similarly, you hope they would not want you to do something harmful.
   (b) Recognize false arguments — point out that someone's idea that a certain drug is not harmful may be false.
   (c) Recognize consequences — point out what might happen if you take the drug.
   (d) Leave the group.
   (e) Suggest an alternative activity.
   (f) Change the subject — talk about something else.
   (g) Take a stand — state your position and your right to say no.

DISCUSSION

1. What pressure tactics were used in the role plays?

2. (a) Did the role players use any of the methods described in step 3 to resist peer pressure?
   (b) Did the method or methods they used work? Why or why not?
   (c) What other methods might you have used?

3. What do you think might have happened if the role players did not resist the peer pressure?

4. Do you think you would lose friends if you do not go along with the activities of a group? Why or why not?
5. (a) Do your peers affect your behaviour? Why or why not?
   (b) Do you think that what your peers do should affect your behaviour? Why or why not?
6. How can role plays such as these help you resist peer pressure? ❖

A HEALTHY LIFESTYLE

In this chapter, you have learned that various types of drugs can be valuable for treating disease and easing pain. In some situations, it is necessary to take drugs for medical purposes.

Unfortunately, many drugs also have negative side effects, so a lifestyle that keeps your need for drugs as low as possible would be best. Factors such as a healthy diet, exercise, and enough sleep can reduce your chance of becoming ill. You will then be less likely to need medical drugs.

Activities that increase your self-confidence and reduce worry, fear, or tension are also important. Many people find playing or watching sports relaxing (Figure 4.20). Others enjoy activities like reading, woodworking, hiking, or just talking with friends. People who have a positive outlook on life are less likely to feel that they need to take drugs to make them "happy" or "relaxed."

Although many drugs can be helpful, many are dangerous. All drugs must be used with care. Only if our nervous systems are functioning normally can we respond to the demands and pleasures of everyday life — the stimuli in our environments.

FIGURE 4.20
What activities do you think are part of a healthy lifestyle?

REVIEW 4.7

1. (a) What are some of the reasons people give for taking drugs for non-medical purposes?
   (b) Do you think that these are good reasons? Why or why not?
   (c) What do you think are some other things people could do, other than taking drugs, to satisfy the needs or solve the problems mentioned in (a)?
2. (a) What is peer pressure?
   (b) How can you resist peer pressure?
3. (a) Do you think that well-known people, such as musicians or athletes, who take drugs for non-medical purposes have an effect on others? If so, describe this effect.
   (b) How might well-known people help reduce drug abuse in society?
4. (a) How do you think that your behaviour affects people younger than yourself — younger brothers or sisters, for example?
   (b) What could you do to encourage younger people not to abuse drugs?
5. In what ways can you get the same effects produced by some drugs without taking drugs?

CHAPTER REVIEW

KEY IDEAS

- Drugs are substances (other than food, water, and oxygen) which, when they are taken into your body, change the way your body works.
- Many drugs are helpful to the body. Some drugs have no medical use and are harmful. Even medicines can have negative effects, so all drugs should be used with care.
- Drugs may have both short-term effects and long-term effects.
- Every drug used for medical purposes has one or more intended effects — to treat or prevent a specific disease or condition. Many of these drugs also have side effects.
- Before they can be sold, new drugs must undergo premarket testing to be sure they are safe for use.
- The long-term use or abuse of drugs can lead to physical and/or psychological dependence on these substances. Repeated use causes the drug user to develop tolerance and can lead to addiction.
- Alcohol and nicotine are the two most commonly abused drugs.
- Most drugs that affect the nervous system fall into three major groups: stimulants (like nicotine, cocaine, and caffeine), depressants (such as alcohol, heroin, and codeine) and hallucinogens (for example, LSD and PCP). Each of these types of drugs has a different effect on the nervous system.
- People use drugs for many reasons, including peer pressure, curiosity, and a desire to feel "better." A healthy lifestyle can reduce the need for medical drugs and make other drug use unnecessary.

VOCABULARY

drug
medicine
steroid
antibiotic
drug effect
positive effect
negative effect
short-term effect
long-term effect
injection
vaccine
anaesthetic
side effect
prescription
pharmacist
over-the-counter drug
premarket testing
drug abuse
addiction
drug dependence
physical dependence
psychological dependence
withdrawal reaction
tolerance
second-hand smoke
stimulant
depressant
hallucinogen
inhalant

V1. Create a mind map using the word "drugs" as the central theme. Show how you think the terms in the vocabulary list relate to each other. Also include on your map some of the names of specific drugs mentioned in this chapter. If you feel it would be helpful, use diagrams to illustrate some or all of the terms.

V2. Make a poster expressing some of the ideas you have about drugs that you would like other people to consider. Use as many of the words from the vocabulary list as you need to. You might choose to "use" the words by illustrating them with pictures, rather than writing them out.

CONNECTIONS

C1. What types of drugs match the following descriptions:
(a) drugs that cause people to "see" things that are not really there
(b) drugs that slow down the nervous system
(c) drugs that are sniffed
(d) drugs that speed up the rate at which nerve impulses travel

C2. What type of drugs do you think are more commonly abused — illegal or legal drugs? Explain your answer.

C3. Why do you think people become psychologically dependent on drugs that affect the nervous system?

C4. Why do you think people drink alcohol? Give several reasons.

C5. (a) Why do you think people start smoking?
(b) Why do you think people continue to smoke even when studies have shown that it is hazardous to their health?

C6. Write a one-page essay, write a poem, or design a poster describing your views on smoking. You might consider some of the following ideas in your essay, poem, or poster: Do you think it is a good or bad habit? What do you enjoy or dislike about smoking? How do you feel about second-hand smoke? You might direct your essay or poster to people who are considering taking up smoking. What might you say to them?

C7. What are the short-term and long-term effects on your body of
(a) drinking alcohol?
(b) smoking cigarettes?
(c) using cannabis?

C8. A survey of Canadians showed that individuals who drink a lot of alcohol are more likely to smoke than those who drink only moderately or not at all. Why do you think drinking might be connected with smoking?

EXPLORATIONS

E1. Discuss the following in class:
(a) What role do you think the law can have in reducing alcohol and tobacco use?
(b) What other means do you think can be used to reduce use of these drugs?

E2. Choose one of the following topics. Use books, magazines, and pamphlets, or interview appropriate people, to get the most current information. Then have a debate on the issue.
(a) Non-smokers have rights.
(b) No drug should be sold without a prescription.
(c) Marijuana use should be legal.
(d) All alcohol and tobacco advertisements should be banned.

E3. Organize a panel discussion on drinking and driving. You might invite speakers from the police department, an insurance company, and an organization that works to prevent drinking and driving (such as CounterAttack or MADD — Mothers Against Drinking Drivers). List the main points made by each panel member. What do you think are the best reasons for not drinking and driving? Write a short paragraph to explain your answer.

E4. Read reference books or interview people from appropriate agencies to find out how people overcome physical or psychological dependence on drugs such as alcohol, tobacco, cocaine, or heroin.

E5. Before they begin a study, scientists often write out a research proposal that explains what it is they are trying to do. Pretend that you are a scientist who is planning to investigate the effects of caffeine on the human body. Design an experiment to look at this. What predictions will you make and what hypothesis will you test? What controls will you need to use? Write out a research proposal, and include the answers to these questions in your proposal.

WARNING: Do not carry out this experiment without your teacher's permission.

REFLECTIONS

R1. Alcohol, nicotine, and caffeine are sometimes called "invisible" drugs. Why do you think this might be a good name for them? How might their "invisibility" contribute to their abuse?

R2. (a) Look back at the chart your group made in Activity 4A. What substances have you learned about in this chapter that you might now add to the chart as drugs? Would you remove any of the substances that you listed from your chart?
(b) How have your ideas about "what is a drug" changed after reading this chapter? What have you read or talked about while studying this chapter that caused you to change your ideas? Write an entry in your learning journal that describes your feelings about drugs.

INVESTIGATING MATTER

Gold: Why do people go to such trouble to search for tiny gold nuggets in a stream or to mine gold deep in the Earth? Gold is just one kind of matter among millions of others. What makes it so special? What could you do to tell real gold from "fool's gold," which looks similar but is almost worthless? Look at the nuggets carefully? Bite them or hit them with a hammer to test the hardness? Weigh them? Try to dissolve them? Before you did any of these things, it would help you to know about the many kinds of matter.

Some kinds of matter, such as air and water, are much more common than gold. Air and water are worth less money than gold, but they are considerably more important to your daily life. What other types of matter are important to you? Clothes? Food? Soft drinks?

In this unit, you will investigate some of the many types of matter. You will find out how all types of matter can be classified. You will also learn how to make mixtures, how to separate them, and how they are used in your daily life. Finally, you will explore how matter is used in personal care products, such as soap, shampoo, and cosmetics, and how these products affect the environment.

UNIT 2

CHAPTER 5

WHAT IS MATTER?

Matter is all around you. You eat it, breathe it, wear it, and sit on it. Everything is made of matter, including your own body, as well as all the other things that you see on Earth. In fact, the kinds of matter seem to be almost endless. What do bowls, air, fingers, and sauce have in common? They are forms of matter.

In this chapter, you will observe, measure, and compare many different kinds of matter. As you do this, you will notice how these kinds of matter are the same and how they are different. You will also learn how scientists classify all matter.

ACTIVITY 5A / MATTER IN YOUR WORLD

GROUP ACTIVITY

MATERIALS

safety goggles
apron
a collection of different kinds of matter that are commonly found at school, at home, and in the workplace

CAUTION!

If these samples are in closed containers, do not open them and do not taste them, since they might be toxic. If you wish to smell any of these items, be sure to use the correct technique.

PROCEDURE

1. Put on your safety goggles and apron.
2. With three or four other students, examine the samples of matter your teacher has prepared.
3. Identify the samples of matter.
4. Work together to classify the samples into groups. Each sample in one group should have something in common with the other samples in that group. Agree on a name for each of the groups.
5. After you have finished examining and classifying the samples, wash your hands.
6. Prepare a chart in your learning journal so that you will have a record of your classification system. For example, you might list the groups in one column. In the second column, you might describe what the items in each group have in common.
7. Share your classification system with other groups of students in your class. Be prepared to describe the reasons behind your classification system.

DISCUSSION

1. Why was it necessary to wear safety goggles and an apron for this activity?
2. How was your group's classification system similar to those of the other groups in your class? How was it different?
3. Would your classification system work for all samples of matter? Why or why not? ❖

5.1 MEASURING

In Activity 5A, you examined many kinds of **matter**. They are just a small sample of all the matter in the world. Wherever you look, whether in a science classroom, your home, or outside, there are millions of different kinds of matter. Different as they are, all kinds of matter have two things in common: they all have mass, and they all have volume.

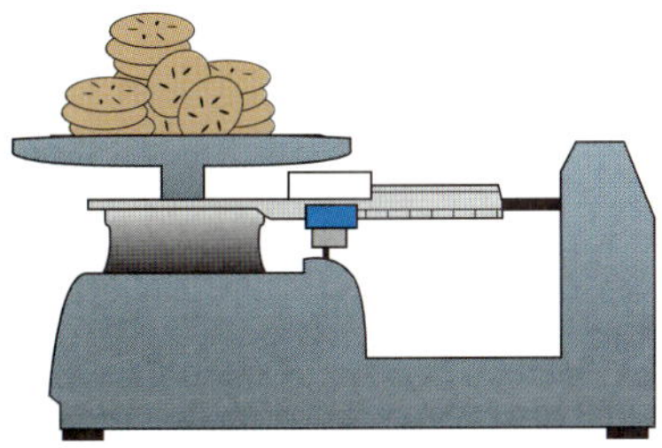

FIGURE 5.1
You can measure mass in grams by using a centigram balance.

MASS

The amount of matter in an object is called its **mass**. When you buy a package of crackers or a bag of raisins, you are buying a certain mass of the product (Figure 5.1). Small masses, such as the mass of a package of crackers, are often measured in grams. Larger masses, such as the

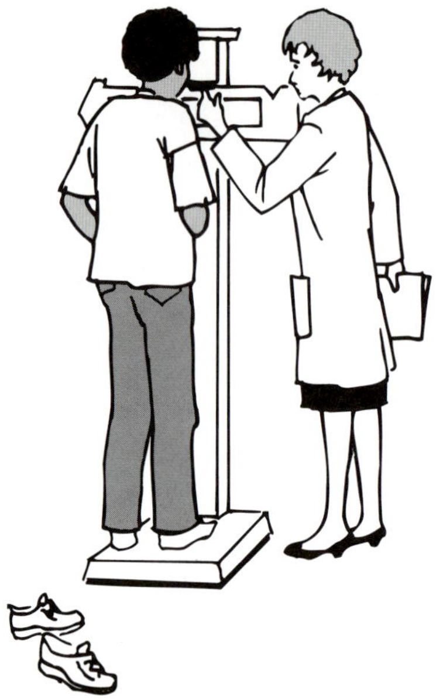

FIGURE 5.2
Balances like this one give masses in kilograms.

mass of a person, are often measured in kilograms ("kilo" means 1000) (Figure 5.2). Very small masses, such as amounts of certain medicines, are measured in milligrams ("milli" means one-thousandth, or 1/1000).

1000 mg = 1 g
1000 g = 1 kg

When you measure the mass of an object on a balance or a scale, you are measuring it directly. This is an example of **direct measurement**. When you use direct measurement, you need to have only the measuring device and the object you are measuring.

Sometimes you need more than one step to measure matter. For example, to find the mass of a sample of a liquid, you would first need to find the mass of a dry, empty container. Then you would pour the liquid into the container and find the mass of the container with the liquid in it. Finally, you would subtract the mass of the empty container from the mass of the container with the liquid in it. This is an example of **indirect measurement**.

ACTIVITY 5B / ESTIMATING AND MEASURING MASS

In this activity, you will estimate the mass of several samples of matter and then measure their mass, using direct measurement.

MATERIALS

Parts I and II
safety goggles
apron
centigram balance

Part I
several solid objects

Part II
dry beaker
liquid sample A

PART I Mass of Solids

PROCEDURE

1. In your notebook, prepare a data table similar to Table 5.1. List the objects in the first column of your table.
2. Put on your safety goggles and apron.
3. Estimate the mass of the first object and record your estimate in your table.
4. Use the centigram balance to measure the mass of the object. Record the measured value in your table.
5. Repeat steps 3 and 4 for the other objects.

DISCUSSION

1. (a) Which of your estimates were most accurate?
   (b) Explain how your results in steps 3 and 4 could help you make more accurate estimates in step 5.
2. In your notebook, list several items at the grocery store that are purchased by mass.
3. Estimate the mass of
   (a) an apple,
   (b) your science textbook,
   (c) a penny,
   (d) any other small object (choose your own).

Object	Estimated mass (in grams)	Measured mass (to the nearest 0.01 gram)
1.		
2.		
3.		
4.		

TABLE 5.1
Sample Data Table for Activity 5B

4. What is your mass in kilograms?
5. Estimate approximately how many kilograms of food you eat in one week. In your notebook, show how you calculated this amount.
6. Cindy has a jar full of quarters. Suggest a method that she could use to estimate the number of quarters in the jar.

PART II Mass of a Liquid

PROCEDURE

1. Estimate the mass of liquid sample A and record your estimate in your notebook.
2. Plan how you could measure the mass of the sample. In your notebook, write the steps of the procedure. (Hint: You will need four steps.)
3. Carry out your procedure to determine the mass of the sample.

DISCUSSION

1. How close was your estimate to your measured value?
2. Estimate the mass of
   (a) a glass of water,
   (b) 1 L of milk,
   (c) a bathtub full of water.
3. Why is it important to be able to measure mass accurately?
4. Explain why accurate measurement of mass is important to
   (a) a shopper buying apples in the supermarket,
   (b) a pharmacist filling prescriptions in a drugstore,
   (c) a scientist working in a laboratory. ❖

VOLUME OF LIQUIDS

When you want to measure the space that an object occupies, you measure its volume. You also measure volume when you measure the space inside a container, such as a spoon, a glass, a room, or a swimming pool. **Volume** is the amount of space that a sample of matter occupies.

The basic unit for measuring the volume of liquids is the litre. Products such as those shown in Figure 5.3 are measured in litres and millilitres.

1000 mL = 1 L

You can measure small volumes of a liquid directly in a graduated cylinder. A graduated cylinder is a tall, narrow container with a scale of numbers on the side (Figure 5.4). To measure the volume of a liquid in a graduated cylinder, you read the scale of numbers. You must be sure to read from the bottom of the curved surface of the liquid, called the **meniscus**. For an accurate measurement, you should have your eye at this level, as shown in Figure 5.5.

FIGURE 5.3
A liquid product is measured by its volume, which is shown on the label. Check out some household products. Which are measured by mass? Which are measured by volume?

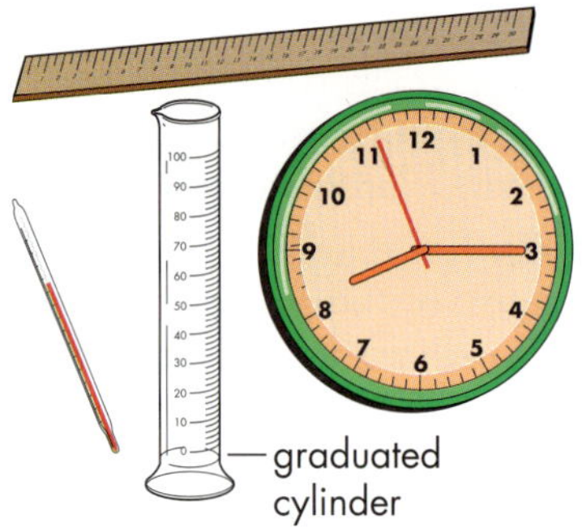

FIGURE 5.4
A graduated cylinder, like other measuring devices, has a scale of numbers printed on it. Not every number in the scale is written on the cylinder. How do you determine the values between the marks?

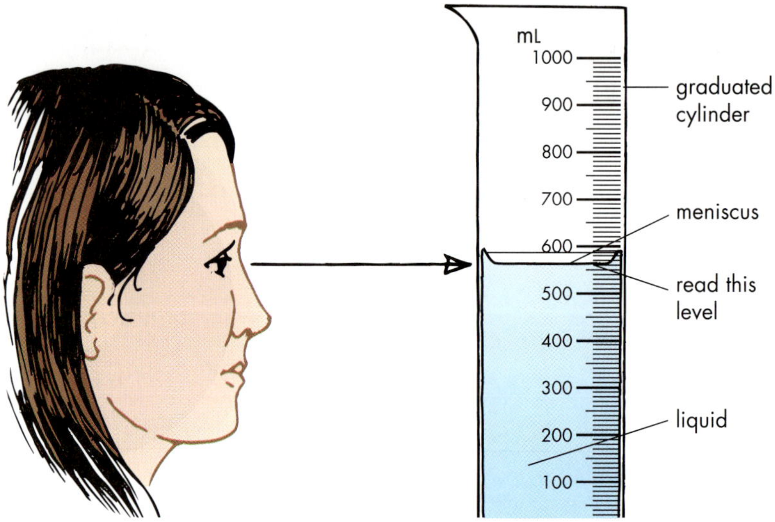

FIGURE 5.5
Reading the volume of a liquid accurately

ACTIVITY 5C / MEASURING THE VOLUME OF LIQUIDS

In this activity, you will use a graduated cylinder to directly measure the volume of several liquid samples.

MATERIALS

safety goggles
apron
several samples of coloured liquids, labelled A, B, C, and so on.
graduated cylinders of various sizes

PROCEDURE

1. Prepare a table in your notebook to record the estimated and measured volumes of the liquid samples. List the samples in the first column of your table. Record your estimated volumes in the second column and the measured volumes in the third column.
2. Put on your safety goggles and apron.
3. Estimate the volume of each sample and record your estimate in your table.
4. Use a graduated cylinder to measure the volumes. Remember to read at the bottom of the meniscus. Record the volumes in your table.

DISCUSSION

1. (a) How close were your estimates to the actual volumes of the liquids?
   (b) For each of the various samples, state which size of graduated cylinder gives a more accurate measurement of volume. Explain your answer.
2. State the unit of measurement (mL, L) you would use to measure the volume of each of the following examples:
   (a) the air in your lungs
   (b) a soft drink in a bottle
   (c) shampoo in a squeezable tube
   (d) the gasoline in a car
3. Is measuring the volume of a liquid using a graduated cylinder an example of direct or indirect measurement? Explain your answer.
4. (a) Estimate the volume of water you use for all purposes (drinking, washing, and so on) in one day.
   (b) Using your estimate in (a), estimate how much water is used in one day by all the people in your home, in your school, in your town or city, and in all of Canada.
   (c) Suggest ways in which people could conserve water. ❖

FIGURE 5.6
What shapes make it difficult to estimate volume?

EXTENSION

■ Your teacher will provide a variety of drinking glasses like the ones in Figure 5.6. Estimate the volume of liquid that each could hold. Then use a graduated cylinder to check your estimates.

VOLUME OF SOLIDS

To calculate the volume of a solid object such as a box, multiply the length by the width by the height of the box:

volume = length × width × height

If all the sides are measured in centimetres, the volume will be in cubic centimetres (cm^3). If all the sides are measured in metres, the volume will be in cubic metres (m^3). For the small cubes shown in Figure 5.7, it is most convenient to measure the sides in centimetres. Here is how to calculate the volume in cubic centimetres:

volume = 1 cm × 1 cm × 1 cm = 1 cm^3

You cannot measure the length, width, and height of an irregularly shaped object such as a spoon or a piece of rock. You cannot directly measure its volume in a graduated cylinder either. For an object such as this, you must use indirect measurement.

One type of indirect measurement you could use is called **displacement of water**. With displacement of water, you measure a volume of water and then place the object to be measured in the water (Figure 5.8). You measure the volume of liquid again and subtract the original volume of the water. This difference is equal to the volume of the object.

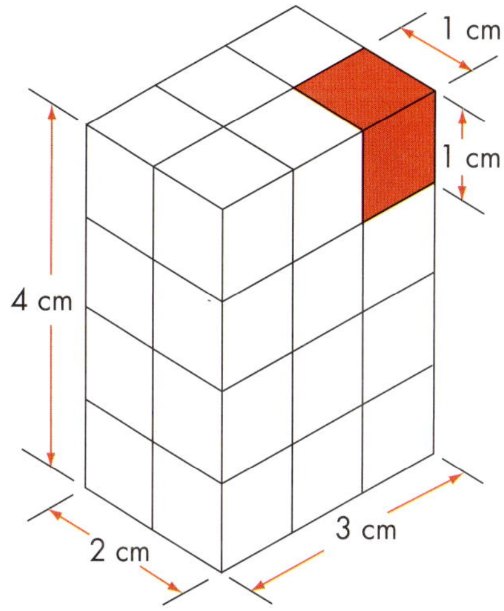

FIGURE 5.7
Count the number of 1 cm^3 blocks in the larger block. Then calculate the volume of the large block in cubic centimetres. Are the two numbers the same?

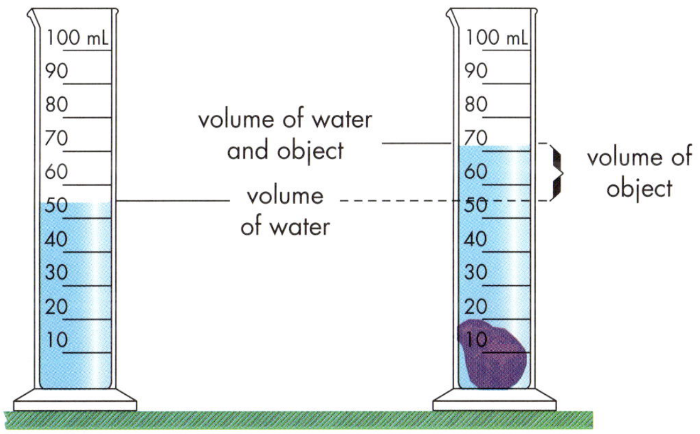

FIGURE 5.8 ◄
Measuring volume by displacement of water

ACTIVITY 5D / MEASURING THE VOLUME OF SOLID OBJECTS

In this activity, you will use displacement of water to find the volume of irregularly shaped objects.

MATERIALS

safety goggles
apron
water
graduated cylinder
small objects such as erasers, spoons, stones

PROCEDURE

1. Put on your safety goggles and apron.
2. Pour some water into a graduated cylinder and measure its volume. Record the volume in your notebook.
3. Tilt the graduated cylinder a little, and gently slide a small object into it (Figure 5.9). Do not allow any water to splash out. Any loss of water will cause an error in your results.
4. In your notebook, record the total volume of the object and the water in the cylinder. Calculate the volume of the solid object as shown in Figure 5.9.
5. Repeat steps 2 to 4 for the other objects.

DISCUSSION

1. (a) Suppose you are asked to compare the volume of an eraser and the volume of a pencil that is the same length as the eraser. Which do you predict has the larger volume?
   (b) Describe how you could test your prediction.
2. Estimate the volume of
   (a) an orange,
   (b) a grape,
   (c) a cup of tea,
   (d) yourself.
3. Think of different everyday situations in which measurement of volume is important. In your notebook, describe two or more of these situations. ❖

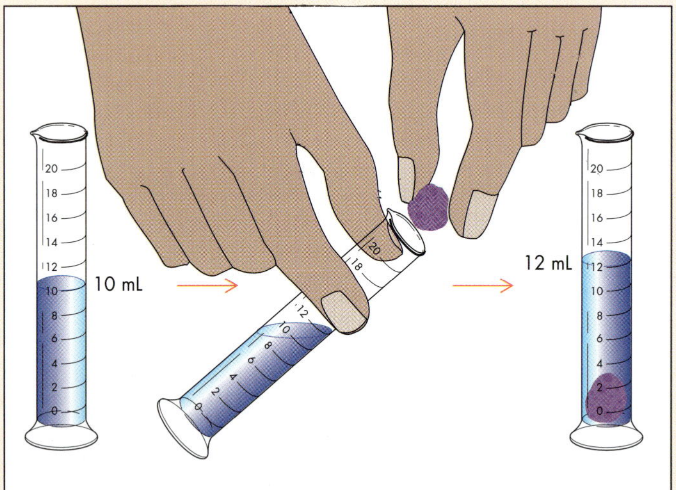

Volume of object = volume of water + solid object – original volume of water
= 12 mL – 10 mL
= 2 mL

FIGURE 5.9 ◀
Why should you slide the object gently into the graduated cylinder?

EXTENSION

■ For a regularly shaped object such as a block of butter, determine the volume in two ways — by reading the volume marks on the package, and by displacement of water. Which method was more accurate?

TEMPERATURE

Temperature is a way of measuring how hot or how cold something is and of communicating that information. A "hot" cup of coffee is quite a different temperature from a "hot" bath, and both of those are hotter than the air on a "hot" day. A number scale makes it possible to give an accurate description.

A thermometer measures temperature. In a thermometer, the level of a small amount of liquid, usually mercury or alcohol, rises or falls in a narrow tube, depending on how hot or cold the liquid is. A scale of numbers is marked on the tube so that the position of the liquid can be described. One temperature scale was invented by Anders Celsius (1701–1744), a Swedish scientist. In this scale, 0°C (read as "zero degrees Celsius") is the temperature at which pure water freezes, and 100°C ("one hundred degrees Celsius") is the temperature at which pure water boils. Between these two temperatures, the scale is divided into 100 parts. The scale also extends above 100°C and below 0°C. Ordinary room temperature is usually around 20°C. A common type of laboratory thermometer is shown in Figure 5.10.

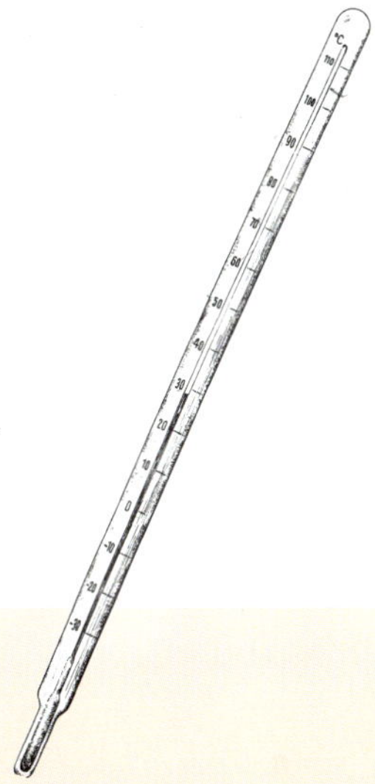

FIGURE 5.10
This thermometer is made of glass. Why should you handle it carefully?

ACTIVITY 5E / THE LABORATORY THERMOMETER

In this activity, you will observe and use a laboratory thermometer.

MATERIALS

laboratory thermometer
cold tap water

PROCEDURE

1. Examine the thermometer carefully. Draw a full-size diagram of the thermometer in the centre of a page of your notebook.
2. On your diagram, label:
   the liquid
   the bore (the narrow tube through which the liquid moves)
   the bulb (storage space for the liquid)
   the number scale
   0°C (freezing point of pure water at sea level)
   100°C (boiling point of pure water at sea level)
3. Look at the thermometer and record the temperature in your classroom in your notebook. Then put your thermometer into cold water from the tap. Record the temperature in your notebook.
4. (a) Wrap your hand gently around the middle of the thermometer and record what happens to the level of the liquid.
   (b) Wrap your hand gently around the bulb and describe what happens to the level of the liquid.
5. Label the temperature of the classroom and the temperature of the water on your drawing.

DISCUSSION

1. What do you think would happen if you put this thermometer into an oven at 300°C?
2. What do you think would happen if you placed the thermometer outside when the temperature is –70°C? ❖

KALIYA YOUNG

Have you ever wondered how the temperature of the water affects your family's wash? Grade 9 student Kaliya Young tried to answer this question as part of her award-winning science project.

Young entered her first science fair in grade 7. For that fair, she compared the effects of water, bleach, and vinegar on a piece of cotton thread. "How to Weaken Your Wash" was the catchy slogan for her project, which went to the Canada Science Fair for the best entries from regional fairs across the country.

Two years later, Young decided to compare the effects of regular bleach, bleach for coloured fabrics, vinegar, lye, and water on various types of thread at four different temperatures. The types of thread included silk, wool, rayon, nylon, cotton, polyester, and a cotton-polyester blend. To obtain accurate results, she built her own apparatus, which included a special testing device that she borrowed from the University of British Columbia. She ran three tests for each kind of thread, using each cleaner at each temperature. Altogether, she conducted 320 tests, which took about 35 hours to complete.

For Young, the hardest parts of the project were preparing her proposal before she started and writing her report after she had finished the experiment. Young has a learning disability that makes writing difficult for her. She found that using a computer helped her.

For the second time, Young reached the Canadian finals. Although she did not win a medal, she won the Ingenuity Award given by the Canadian Society for Women in Science and Technology. She also won a cash prize from the B.C. chapter of the Physics Teachers of America.

For her next science project, Young plans to test the hydrodynamics of swim caps and goggles. She hopes to make science her career, specializing in chemistry or physics. In the meantime, she is helping to organize a group called Young Scientists of Canada. She also plays trombone, sings in a choir, throws the discus, swims competitively, and plays water polo so well that she hopes to make the national team. She also finds time to help with the family wash!

If your school doesn't have a science fair, maybe you could enter the science fair in your region. A useful book is *Science Fare: A Practical Guide for Parents and Students*, by Wayne T. Connors. It can be purchased from:

Science World British Columbia
1455 Quebec Street
Vancouver, B.C. V6A 3Z7

▶ REVIEW 5.1

1. (a) Define mass.
   (b) State the units used to measure mass.
   (c) Define volume.
   (d) State the units used to measure the volume of liquids.
   (e) State the units used to measure the volume of solids.
2. (a) Name two pieces of apparatus used for measuring mass and volume.
   (b) Explain how these pieces of apparatus improve the accuracy of measurements.
   (c) How do these types of apparatus improve people's ability to communicate with each other?
3. For each of the following, state which is the larger value.
   (a) 340 mL or 1 L of apple juice
   (b) 100 g or 0.5 kg of laundry soap
   (c) 50 L or 500 mL of water in a bathtub
   (d) 2 kg or 500 g of potatoes
4. What is the difference between direct measurement and indirect measurement?
5. (a) What problem could you have if you tried to use displacement of water to find the volume of a sugar cube? What could you do to solve the problem?
   (b) List two other objects for which the displacement of water would not work well to measure the volume of the object. Explain why not.

■ 5.2 MATTER

Matter is anything that has mass and volume. Bricks, feathers, notebooks, clothes, cosmetics, snow, rain, lakes, trees, the Earth, the air, and you yourself are all examples of matter. All these things, even a tiny feather or the air you breathe, have mass. In addition, they all occupy space, so they all have volume (Figure 5.11). Not everything, however, is matter. Forms of energy, such as light or sound, have no mass. Neither do feelings such as happiness or anger, or ideas such as justice, truth, knowledge, or honesty. None of these things are matter.

FIGURE 5.11
Air is matter. You can show that by holding an "empty" bottle under water with the opening pointing down. Why doesn't the water enter the bottle? What happens when you tilt the bottle?

THE STATES OF MATTER

Look around you, and you will see many different kinds of matter. But any kind of matter can be described as a solid, a liquid, or a gas. These are known as the three **states of matter**. Both a brick and a feather are examples of solid matter. A brick has a relatively large amount of mass and a simple shape. A feather has much less mass, and its shape is quite complicated. But both bricks and feathers have mass and have a shape that does not change, and both take up a certain amount of space. These are the characteristics of solids. A **solid** has a fixed (unchanging) mass, a fixed volume, and a fixed shape.

What about liquids, such as water, gasoline, vegetable oil, and soft drinks? They have a fixed mass and a fixed volume. When you fill the tank of your car, for example, you buy a certain volume of gasoline. When you follow a recipe, you use a certain volume of vegetable oil. Both the gasoline and the vegetable oil also have a fixed mass. Liquids do not have a fixed shape, however. They take the shape of the container that is holding them (Figure 5.12). Thus, a **liquid** has a fixed mass and a fixed volume, but its shape depends on the shape of the container it is in.

FIGURE 5.12 ▶
All of these containers hold the same volume of the liquid. How could you show this?

FIGURE 5.13
The air being pumped here will fill this tire. The same amount of air would fill many balloons.

Oxygen, helium, and carbon dioxide are examples of gases. Gases have a fixed mass, although the mass of a sample of gas may be so small that you could not measure it on a centigram balance in your classroom. Gases do not have a fixed volume, however (Figure 5.13). A gas always fills its container completely. Nor do gases have a fixed shape (Figure 5.14). A gas always takes the shape of the container it is in. Thus, a **gas** has a fixed mass, but its volume and shape depend on the container it is in.

Table 5.2 summarizes the characteristics of solids, liquids, and gases.

State	Mass	Volume	Shape
Solid	Fixed	Fixed	Fixed
Liquid	Fixed	Fixed	Takes shape of its container
Gas	Fixed	Fills its container	Takes shape of its container

TABLE 5.2 ***The Three States of Matter***

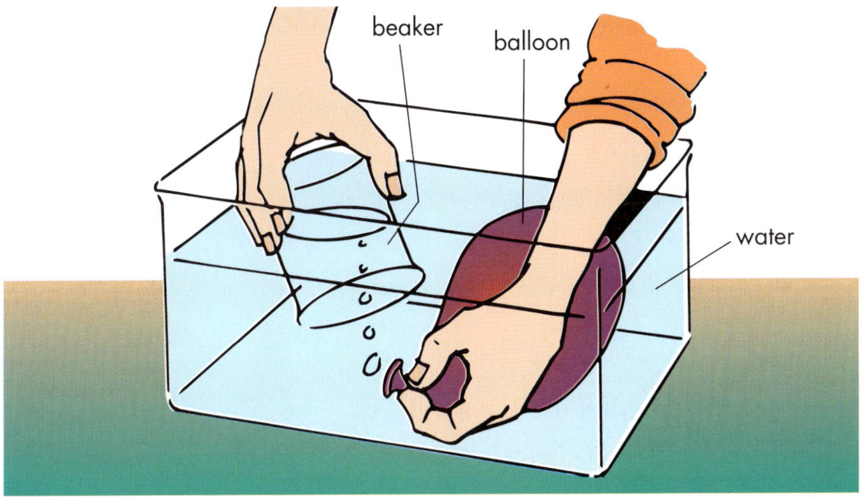

FIGURE 5.14
Inside the balloon, the air is balloon-shaped. In the beaker, it is beaker-shaped.

FIGURE 5.15
A chain of paperclips can be used to illustrate the hypothesis of Democritus. The chain represents matter, and each paperclip represents one particle. You can divide a long chain of particles into two chains, which can be divided into smaller and smaller chains. Eventually, each chain will have only one paperclip. If you break one of these into smaller pieces, it will no longer have the characteristics of a paperclip. Similarly, there is a limit to how far matter can be subdivided and still retain the characteristics of that type of matter.

THINKING ABOUT MATTER

More than 2000 years ago in ancient Greece, a philosopher named Democritus suggested that all matter is made up of tiny particles too small to be seen. He thought that if you kept cutting a piece of matter into smaller and smaller pieces, you would eventually come to the smallest possible particle (Figure 5.15). He called such particles *atomos* (meaning "cannot be divided"), from which we get our English word "atom."

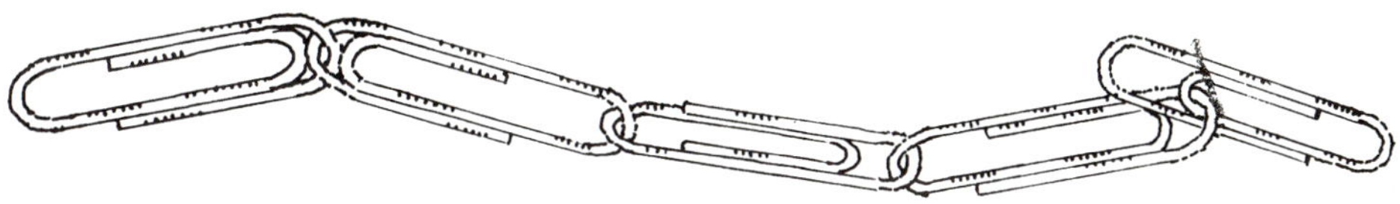

ACTIVITY 5F / INVESTIGATING CHANGES IN MATTER

In this activity, you will observe what happens when two liquids mix together.

MATERIALS

safety goggles
apron
250 mL beaker
water
piece of notepaper
ink in dropper bottle

PROCEDURE

1. Put on your safety goggles and apron.
2. Half-fill the beaker with water. Place a piece of notepaper under the beaker and let it sit for about 1 min to let the water become perfectly still.
3. Hold the dropper of ink just above the water and place a single drop in the centre of the beaker (Figure 5.16).
4. Sketch the contents of the beaker as it appears immediately after the ink has been added.

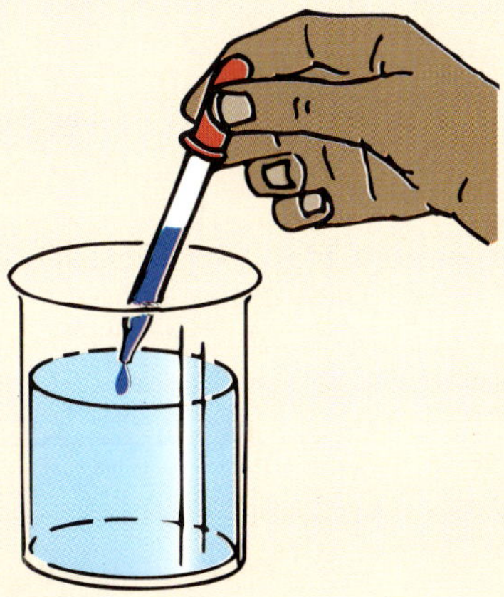

FIGURE 5.16
Why should you add the ink with as little disturbance as possible?

5. Leave the beaker undisturbed for 5 min.
6. Sketch the contents of the beaker as it appeared after 5 min.

DISCUSSION

1. Describe how the colour spread in the beaker.
2. Sketch the water in the beaker as you predict it would look in (a) 30 min and (b) 24 h.
3. What could have caused the ink and the water to behave in this manner? ❖

THE PARTICLE MODEL OF MATTER

Over many centuries, scientists have carried out many investigations of matter. The hypothesis that matter is made up of tiny particles has been further developed and today is called the **particle model** of matter (Figure 5.17). This model has been useful in explaining some observations about matter.

FIGURE 5.17 ▶
The particle model of matter

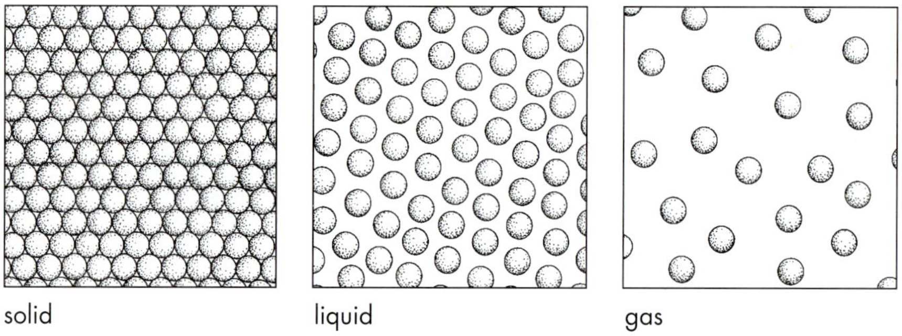

The particle model states the following:

1. Solids, liquids, and gases are made up of particles that are too small to be seen.
2. The particles in solids are held tightly together, and the spaces between the particles are very small.
3. The particles in liquids are separated by spaces that are large enough to allow the particles to slide past each other.
4. The particles in gases are separated by much larger spaces. Gases are mostly empty space.

THE KINETIC MOLECULAR THEORY

The particle model of matter has been useful in explaining some, but not all, observations that can be made about matter. For example, the model does not explain why gases occupy much more space than liquids. To explain observations such as this one, scientists revised the particle model. The result is called the **kinetic molecular theory**. According to this theory:

1. All matter is made up of very small particles.
2. These particles are in constant motion.
3. There are empty spaces between the particles.
4. The particles and spaces are so small that they cannot be seen.
5. In a solid, the particles are so close together and move so slowly that they can only vibrate (move back and forth).
6. In a liquid, the particles are slightly farther apart and move slightly faster than those in a solid.
7. In a gas, the particles are far apart and move very quickly.
8. Heat and other forms of energy make particles move faster.

The kinetic molecular theory is nearly 200 years old. Scientists find it useful for two reasons. First, it provides a reasonable explanation for the behaviour of matter. Second, it presents a very important idea. Matter that seems perfectly motionless is not that way at all. Your books, your desk, the air you breathe — all consist of matter in constant motion.

DIFFUSION: EVIDENCE FOR THE KINETIC MOLECULAR THEORY

When a drop of ink is put into water, the colour gradually spreads throughout the container, even if the liquid is not stirred. This gradual movement is called **diffusion**. How do scientists explain diffusion? According to the kinetic molecular theory, tiny particles of ink are continually moving about and bumping into each other. Similarly, the tiny particles of water also move about and bump into each other. When a drop of ink is put into the water, the particles of ink slowly spread out. After some time, the particles of ink and water are equally mixed throughout the container.

Have you ever wondered how you can detect the presence of perfume from across a room? If someone opens a bottle of perfume in a far corner of your classroom, you are soon aware of it. The particles of perfume bump into each other and gradually move away from the crowded bottle. Because of diffusion, the fragrance spreads (Figure 5.18).

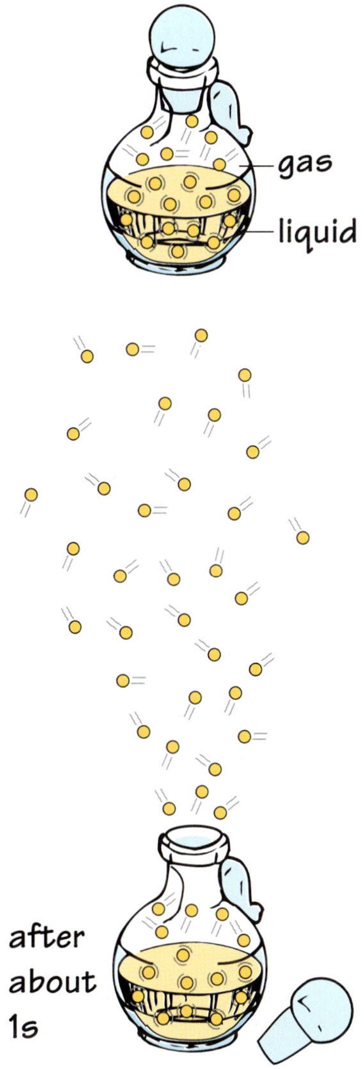

FIGURE 5.18
Diffusion. Particles of perfume spread throughout the room, mixing with the other gases in the air.

SOLIDS, LIQUIDS, AND GASES

The kinetic molecular theory is useful in explaining the differences between solids, liquids, and gases (Figure 5.19). Solids have an unchanging shape because the particles can move only a little — they vibrate back and forth but remain in a fixed position.

A liquid takes the shape of its container because the particles can move around more freely than they can in solids. The particles in a liquid can slide past one another. They are held close together, however, so a liquid, like a solid, has a fixed volume.

A gas always fills whatever container it is in. The individual particles of a gas are quite far apart, with large spaces between them. Since gas particles are moving constantly in all directions, they spread throughout their container, whatever its volume or shape.

FIGURE 5.19 ▶
What does this illustration tell you about the kinetic molecular theory? Which substance(s) would escape if you took the stoppers out of the flasks?

CHANGES OF STATE AND THE KINETIC MOLECULAR THEORY

According to the kinetic molecular theory, particles with more energy move faster than particles with less energy. One way of adding energy to a material is to heat it. As a solid is heated, the particles vibrate faster and faster until they have enough energy to break away from their fixed positions. If this happens, the particles can move about more freely; we say the material has melted. **Melting** is the change of state from a solid to a liquid. The reverse of melting is called **freezing** (or solidification), which is the change from a liquid to a solid. As a liquid cools, the particles in the liquid lose energy and thus move more and more slowly. When they settle into fixed positions, the liquid has frozen or solidified (Figure 5.20).

FIGURE 5.20
Steel melts when it is heated to a very high temperature. The liquid steel solidifies (changes from a liquid to a solid) when it cools below the same temperature.

Some solids can change directly to a gas without first becoming a liquid. This change of state is called sublimation. In **sublimation**, individual particles of a solid gain enough energy to break completely away from the other particles, forming a gas.

Sublimation occurs, for example, as the material in a room deodorizer gradually "disappears" into the air. You can also see sublimation by observing the "disappearance" of blocks of dry ice used in ice cream carts (Figure 5.21). The reverse process — a direct change of state from a gas to a solid — is also called sublimation (Figure 5.22).

When a liquid absorbs heat energy, the particles move about more and more quickly. Some of the particles gain enough energy to break free of the other particles. When this happens, the liquid changes to a gas. The change from a liquid to a gas is called **evaporation**. The reverse process — the change from a gas to a liquid — is called **condensation** (Figure 5.23).

FIGURE 5.21
Ice cream carts like this one use blocks of dry ice to keep the ice cream frozen. Dry ice seems to disappear as it changes directly from a solid to a gas.

FIGURE 5.22
This pattern is a result of sublimation. Water particles from the air formed solid ice on the window, without becoming a liquid first.

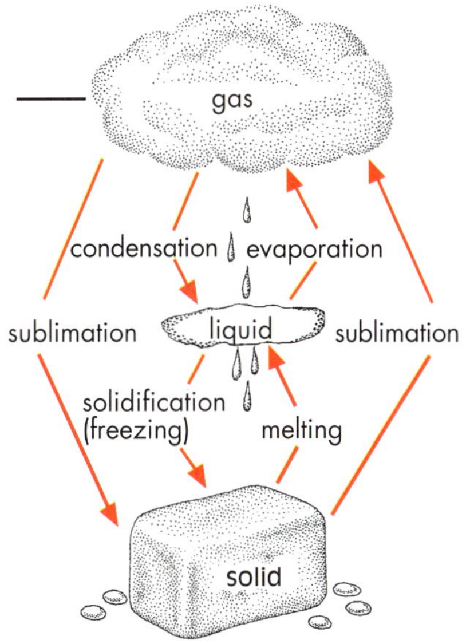

FIGURE 5.23
Changes of state

► REVIEW 5.2

1. How are all types of matter similar?
2. Which of the following are examples of matter? Explain your answers.
   (a) candle wax
   (b) milk
   (c) heat energy
   (d) colours
   (e) clouds
3. In your notebook, draw a table like Table 5.3. Complete the table by writing "yes" or "no" in each column.
4. What evidence do you have from your everyday life that
   (a) matter is made of particles?
   (b) the particles are in motion?
5. Use the kinetic molecular theory to explain the differences between
   (a) solids and liquids,
   (b) liquids and gases,
   (c) solids and gases.
6. Name the change of state that occurs when
   (a) butter is warmed on the stove,
   (b) water vapour cools and forms raindrops,
   (c) liquid wax hardens,
   (d) water boils,
   (e) frost forms on the window of your family car.
7. Give one example from your everyday life of each of the following changes of state (use examples that are not listed in question 6): evaporation, condensation, and sublimation.

	Fixed mass?	Fixed volume?	Fixed shape?
Solid			
Liquid			
Gas			

TABLE 5.3
Characteristics of Solids, Liquids, and Gases for Review Question 3

FIGURE 5.24
Concrete has useful properties. When first mixed, it can be poured. After it has been left standing for a while, it becomes a hard solid. If a smooth surface is desired, it must be smoothed at the right time — too late and the concrete will be too hard.

5.3 PROPERTIES OF MATTER

Have you ever tried to describe some new clothes to a friend over the phone? Perhaps you described characteristics such as the colour, shape, and cost of the clothes. Characteristics are also called **properties**. The properties of a sample of matter include what it looks like, how it feels, how it acts when it is heated or cooled, and what happens when it is mixed with other types of matter (Figure 5.24). For example, think of some of the properties of pure water. (You can buy pure water in grocery stores — it is often labelled "distilled water.") Pure water is a clear, colourless liquid with no taste and no odour. Below a certain temperature, it freezes, and above a certain temperature, it boils. It mixes easily with some solids and liquids, such as sugar, salt, vinegar, and milk, but does not mix well with others, such as pepper, stones, salad oil, and gasoline. Pure water does not burn or explode. Table 5.4 lists the properties of several other familiar materials.

Types of matter	State	Colour	Other properties
Concrete	Solid	Grey	Hard, may contain small pebbles
Salad dressing	Liquid	Yellow-brown	Separates into layers when left standing
Copper	Solid	Reddish-brown	Hard, shiny, bendable
Salt	Solid	White	Crystals dissolve in water
Gasoline	Liquid	Clear	Has a strong odour, flammable

TABLE 5.4 ***Properties of Some Common Kinds of Materials***

PURE SUBSTANCES

Properties can help you sort out all the thousands of different types of matter that you see every day. For some types of matter, called **pure substances**, the properties are always the same. All samples of a pure substance have the same properties, whether the sample is large or small, wherever the sample is found in the world. In Table 5.4, salt and copper are examples of pure substances. There are many thousands of other pure substances. Examples are aluminum, baking soda, carbon dioxide, hydrogen peroxide, mercury, sulphur, and silver. Scientists have studied the properties of many pure substances and have listed them in reference books. Because all samples of a pure substance have the same properties, these reference lists can help you to identify unknown substances. A short reference list, called the Table of Properties, is included in Appendix C.

For matter that is not a pure substance, the properties may be different in different samples. Look again at the list in Table 5.4. Three of the materials listed there are not pure substances. There can be different kinds of concrete, for example, used for different purposes in construction. There are also various kinds of salad dressings — they may contain different proportions of oil and vinegar, as well as various herbs and spices. And different kinds of gasoline are sold as "regular unleaded" or "super unleaded."

DID YOU KNOW

■ Truly "pure" pure substances are not easy to find. For example, most city water contains chemicals added to kill bacteria, most well water contains dissolved solids, and all tap water contains dissolved air.

ACTIVITY 5G / IDENTIFYING PURE SUBSTANCES

In this activity, you will use a list of properties to identify some unknown pure substances.

MATERIALS

safety goggles
apron
samples of four unknown pure substances in small bottles
information in Table 5.5
hand lens

CAUTION!

■ **If you spill any of the solids, notify your teacher, who will tell you how to clean the spill. Copper sulphate is poisonous. If any chemical comes in contact with your skin, wash it off thoroughly with a large amount of cold water.**

PROCEDURE

1. Put on your safety goggles and apron.
2. Briefly examine the pure substances in the bottles. Match each sample with one of the descriptions in Table 5.5.
3. Using a hand lens, examine the pure substances more carefully.
4. Sketch what you see. Can you identify any more of the substances? Explain.
5. After you have completed the activity, wash your hands.

DISCUSSION

1. (a) Which substances could you identify?
   (b) List the substances about which you were uncertain.
2. (a) Were there any substances you could not identify by appearance alone?
   (b) What further tests could you do? (Hint: Think about other properties of these materials. Check the Table of Properties in Appendix C.) ❖

Name of pure substance	Appearance
(a) Sucrose (icing sugar)	Powdered white solid
(b) Sodium chloride (table salt)	Small white solid crystals
(c) Calcium carbonate (chalk)	Powdered white solid
(d) Sulphur	Powdered yellow solid
(e) Calcium hydroxide (slaked lime)	Powdered white solid
(f) Copper sulphate (bluestone)	Blue solid crystals
(g) Aluminum potassium sulphate (alum)	Small white solid crystals

TABLE 5.5 ***The Appearance of Selected Pure Substances***

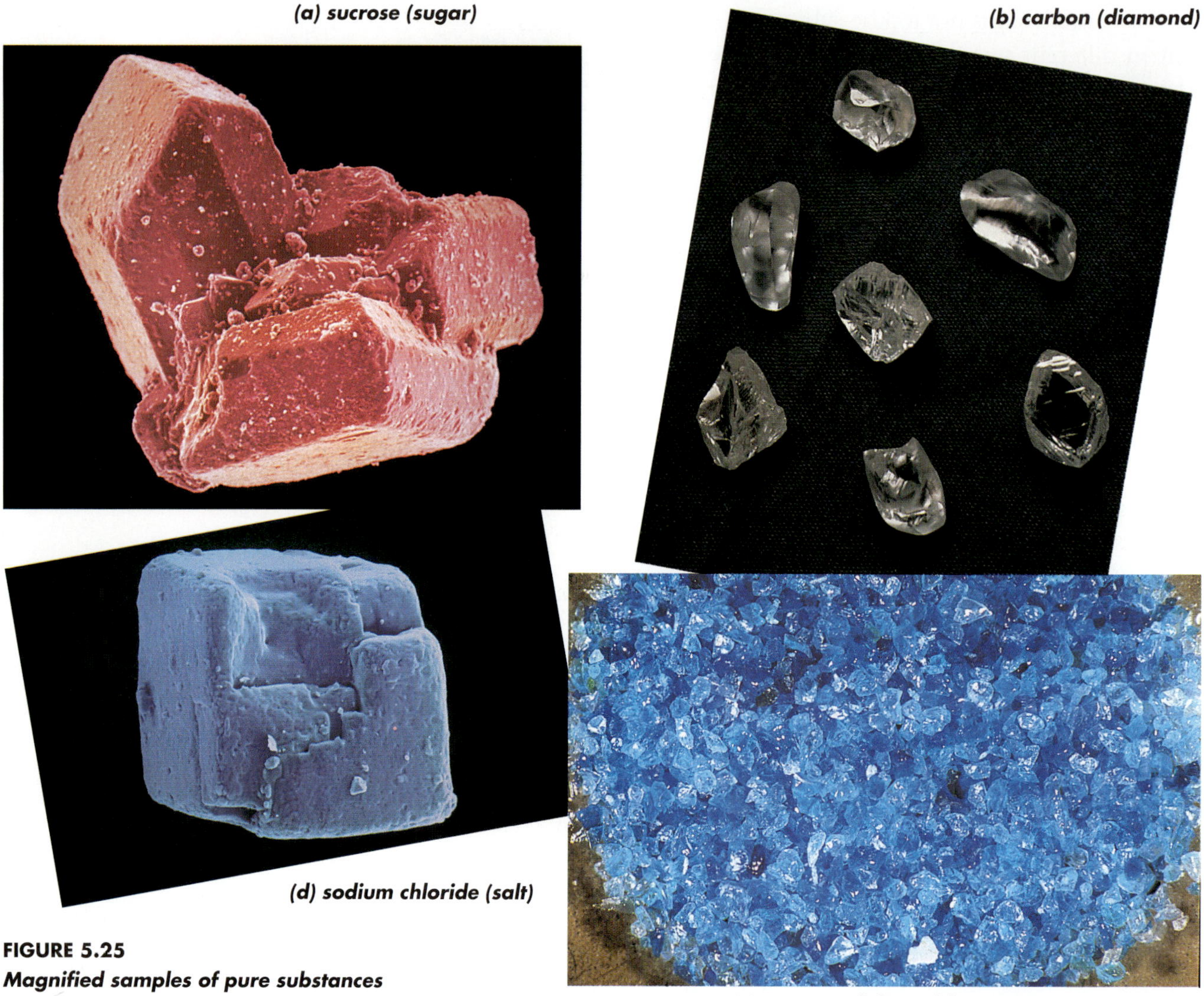

(a) sucrose (sugar)

(b) carbon (diamond)

(d) sodium chloride (salt)

(c) copper sulphate (bluestone)

FIGURE 5.25
Magnified samples of pure substances

FIGURE 5.26
This drink is a mixture. What pure substances have been mixed together?

THE NATURE OF PURE SUBSTANCES

Why do pure substances have fixed properties? Scientists believe that all the particles in a pure substance are the same. One particle of pure water is like any other particle of pure water; one particle of sugar is like any other particle of sugar (Figure 5.25).

In other types of matter, there are two or more kinds of particles. Concrete, for example, may have different types of stones in it. Gasoline is a blend of several different liquids. Air contains not only oxygen particles but also particles of other gases. In these types of matter, the properties change in different samples because there may be more or less of the different types of particles (Figure 5.26). All these types of matter are called **mixtures**. A mixture is made up of two or more pure substances.

REVIEW 5.3

1. (a) Define properties of matter.
   (b) List three examples of properties that you can describe just by looking at a sample of matter.
2. In your notebook, make a table with headings like those in Table 5.4 on page 126. In the first column, list 10 common materials that are not mentioned in this chapter. Describe several properties of each in the other columns.
3. In your notebook, set up a table with two columns, labeled "Matter" and "Pure Substance?" In the first column, list the five examples from Table 5.4 on page 126 and fill in the second column with "yes" and "no." Add to your table the 10 materials you described in question 2. Be prepared to defend your classification.
4. Look at the Table of Properties in Appendix C.
   (a) List the names of at least three substances in the table that are gases at room temperature.
   (b) How many of the substances in the Table of Properties are described as a "colourless liquid"?
   (c) From the table, find the names of two colourless liquids that are poisonous or corrosive.
   (d) Of the white solids that are listed, name two that are edible, two that are not edible but are not dangerous to eat, and two that are hazardous to people in some way.
5. Examine the photograph in Figure 5.27. If the three glasses were mixed up, what properties could you use to identify the three liquids?

FIGURE 5.27
These liquids look similar. What properties do they have that make them different?

CHAPTER REVIEW

KEY IDEAS

- Knowing how to measure mass, volume, and temperature is an important skill for investigating matter.
- Both direct measurement and indirect measurement are needed to measure and compare different states of matter.
- There are three states of matter: solid, liquid, and gas.
- According to the particle model, all matter is made up of tiny particles.
- According to the kinetic molecular theory, particles are in a constant state of motion. The particles of solids, liquids, and gases move at different rates.
- Solids, liquids, and gases can change to other states. These changes are called changes of state and include melting, freezing, sublimation, evaporation, and condensation.
- The kinetic molecular theory can be used to explain diffusion and changes of state.
- Properties can be used to tell different types of matter apart.
- Pure substances have properties that are always the same, since all the particles in a pure substance are identical.
- Mixtures have properties that may be different, depending on the sample of the mixture that you choose.

VOCABULARY

matter
mass
direct measurement
indirect measurement
volume
meniscus
displacement of water
temperature
states of matter
solid
liquid
gas
particle model
kinetic molecular theory
diffusion
melting
freezing
sublimation
evaporation
condensation
properties
pure substance
mixture

V1. Use all the words from the vocabulary list, and any other words or ideas you need, to make a mind map about matter. You may connect any two parts of your map with lines and words describing how they are linked.

V2. Using the vocabulary list, write in your notebook six examples of things that have mass and volume, four words that are ideas or concepts, and five words that describe changes in matter.

CONNECTIONS

C1. The volume of a sample of water can be measured more easily than the volume of a chunk of rock. Why?

C2. Milk will mix in tea even if the liquid is not stirred. Explain this according to the kinetic molecular theory.

C3. Refer to the Table of Properties in Appendix C and describe how you could tell the difference between samples of (a) iron and tin, (b) ethanol (a type of alcohol) and water, (c) nitrogen gas and oxygen gas.

C4. Examine the graduated cylinder in Figure 5.28 and read the explanation below it. Use the kinetic molecular theory to explain the appearance of the liquid when the photograph was taken.

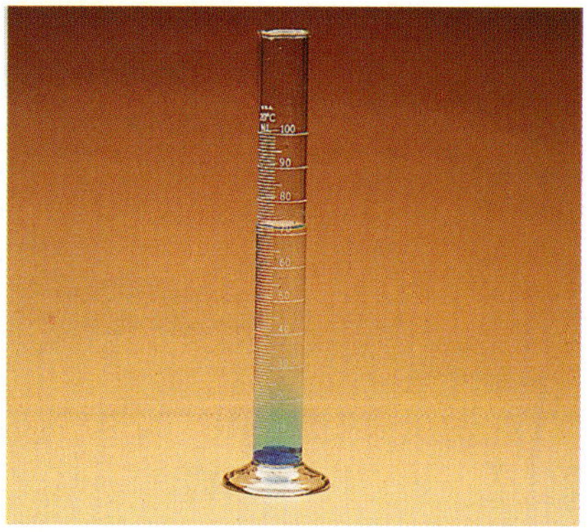

FIGURE 5.28
Twenty minutes before this photo was taken, a small piece of a solid was dropped into the water in this cylinder. Since then, the cylinder has remained undisturbed.

EXPLORATIONS

E1. Use a reference to prepare a report on two of the pure substances listed in Table 5.5 on page 127. Include a description of where the substances are found in nature, how they are produced, and how they are used by humans.

E2. In a reference book, find out what "fool's gold" is and what properties you would use to distinguish it from gold.

E3. The human body is approximately 70 per cent water. However, people do not appear to be made of liquid. Find out where all this liquid water is and why we appear to be mostly solid.

REFLECTIONS

R1. (a) In this chapter, you have learned about two ways that scientists classify matter. In your notebook, list the categories in each of these ways.
(b) In Activity 5A, your class classified materials into groups. Refer to the chart from Activity 5A in your learning journal. How many classification systems did you think of?
(c) Are there any advantages to your systems of classification over the two that scientists use? Explain.
(d) Are there any advantages to the scientists' classification systems? Explain.

R2. Suppose that all kinds of particles of matter were held together more strongly than they are now. How would the properties of substances be changed? Imagine how that would change your life. Write an imaginative paragraph or a story describing some way in which you would personally be affected by this change. (As an alternative, suppose the particles of matter were held together less strongly.)

R3. Philosophers say, "You can't buy happiness." Explain why you can't.

CHAPTER 6

CLASSIFICATION OF MATTER

What bursts from a pop bottle when it is opened? What causes the bubbles to come out of the drink? A "flat" soft drink is certainly different from a fizzy one, but what causes this difference? You may have questions about other ordinary kinds of matter. What happens to wood when it burns? Why can't you see sugar when it is dissolved in water? What happens to an egg when it cooks? Learning about matter and its properties can help you understand everyday events and how things change.

You learned in Chapter 5 that you can classify all the millions of kinds of matter into just two categories — pure substances and mixtures. But the classification of matter does not stop there. There are also classifications of pure substances and of mixtures. These other classifications can help you understand the properties of matter.

The classification of matter can also help you understand how matter changes. You have already observed some changes — melting and diffusion, for example. In this chapter, you will try changing matter in other ways. In your investigations, you will learn more about both pure substances and mixtures.

ACTIVITY 6A / CLASSIFYING MATTER

GROUP ACTIVITY

How many ways can you think of in which you could classify matter? Discuss this question with your group. List your answers in your learning journal.

Have each student in your group choose one of the ways of classifying matter and draw an illustration to explain it. ❖

EXTENSION

■ Your teacher may have labelled samples of elements available for you to look at. Examine the samples and describe each of the elements in your notebook.

CAUTION!

■ **If any of the samples are in sealed containers, do not open the containers.**

■ 6.1 ELEMENTS AND COMPOUNDS

There are millions of kinds of pure substances. How can anyone expect to learn about all of them? Which ones would you start with? How would you find out which ones are useful to humans?

About 200 years ago, scientists asked these same questions. They began to investigate pure substances in many ways. For example, they heated pure substances and mixed them together in various ways. They found that some pure substances could be broken down into other pure substances, but some could not. For this reason, pure substances are classified into two types.

ELEMENTS

Elements are pure substances that cannot be broken down into any other pure substances. By the early 1900s, after many more investigations, scientists found that there are only about 100 substances that are elements (Figure 6.1).

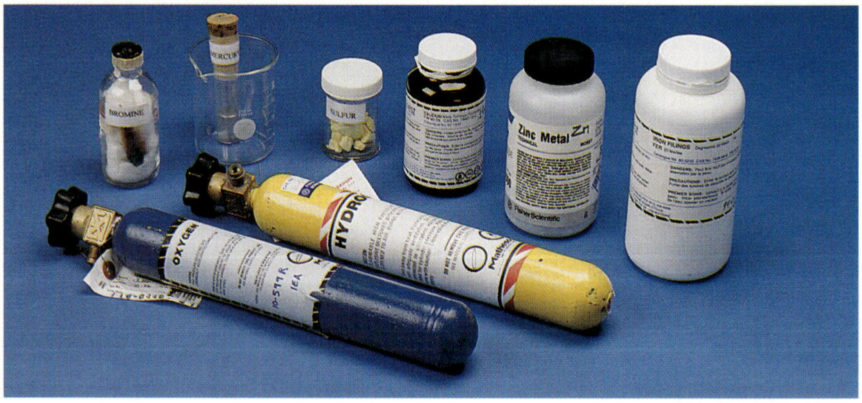

FIGURE 6.1 ▶
Some elements. Most elements are solids at ordinary temperatures. Only two elements (mercury and bromine) are liquids. Several elements are gases.

The smallest particles of an element are called atoms. Each element has its own kind of **atom**. Since there are about 100 elements, there are about 100 kinds of atoms. The properties of the different elements are different because their atoms are different. Figure 6.2 gives the names of the elements. Some elements, such as iron, copper, and oxygen, are common in nature. Other elements, such as krypton, are extremely rare. Some elements are considered safe to humans, whereas others, such as sodium and chlorine, are explosive or poisonous.

actinium, aluminum, antimony, argon, arsenic, astatine, barium, beryllium, bismuth, boron, bromine, calcium, cadmium, carbon, cesium, chlorine, chromium, cobalt, copper, curium, dysprosium, erbium, europium, fluorine, francium, gadolinium, gallium, germanium, gold, hafnium, helium, holmium, hydrogen, indium, iodine, iridium, iron, krypton, lanthanum, lead, lithium, lutetium, magnesium, manganese, manganese, mercury, molybdenum, neodymium, neon, nickel, niobium, nitrogen, osmium, oxygen, palladium, phosphorus, platinum, polonium, potassium, praseodymium, protactinium, radium, radon, rhenium, rhodium, rubidium, ruthenium, samarium, scandium, selenium, silicon, silver, sodium, strontium, sulphur, tantalum, tellurium, terbium, thallium, thorium, thulium, tin, titanium, tungsten, thulium, tin, titanium, tungsten, uranium, vanadium, xenon, ytterbium, yttrium, zinc, zirconium

FIGURE 6.2
These are the names of all the elements that are found in nature. There are other elements that have been created by scientists.

DID YOU KNOW

The element carbon forms many different compounds. These are so important that an entire field of chemistry — organic chemistry — studies compounds of carbon. New carbon compounds are still being discovered.

COMPOUNDS

Elements can combine with other elements to form new pure substances that are called **compounds**. Compounds are pure substances that are made up of two or more elements combined. Compounds are related to elements in the same way that words are related to letters of the alphabet. Compounds are made by combining elements, just as words are made by combining letters. Many thousands of words can be made from the 26 letters of the English alphabet. Similarly, although there are only about 100 elements, millions of compounds can be made by combining elements. A very few examples are shown in Table 6.1.

TABLE 6.1
Elements in Some Common Compounds

Compound	Elements combined in compound
Water	Hydrogen, oxygen
Table salt (sodium chloride)	Sodium, chlorine
Carbon dioxide	Carbon, oxygen
Sugar (any type)	Carbon, hydrogen, oxygen
Alcohol (any type)	Carbon, hydrogen, oxygen
Copper sulphate	Copper, sulphur, oxygen
Chalk (calcium carbonate)	Calcium, carbon, oxygen
Baking soda	Sodium, hydrogen, carbon, oxygen

A compound always contains two or more different kinds of atoms. The atoms of the elements in a compound are joined together to form larger particles called **molecules**. Each molecule of a compound contains at least two atoms.

All the molecules in a compound are identical. For example, look at the molecule illustrated in Figure 6.3. This is a molecule of methane, the main component of natural gas, which is used in home heating and the Bunsen burners in your classroom. All methane molecules are exactly like this one, containing one carbon atom joined to four hydrogen atoms. Figure 6.4 shows models of some other molecules. These are all fairly small molecules, with two to eight atoms each. Many compounds, however, contain large molecules that have many thousands of atoms (Figure 6.5).

FIGURE 6.3
A model of a molecule of natural gas (methane)

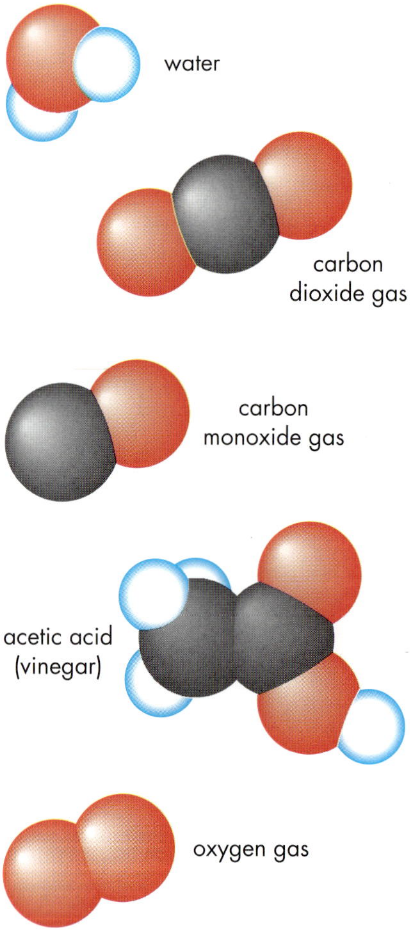

FIGURE 6.4
Models of molecules. Water, carbon dioxide gas, carbon monoxide gas, and acetic acid are compounds — they contain more than one kind of atom. Some molecules contain only one kind of atom, like the oxygen gas molecule shown here.

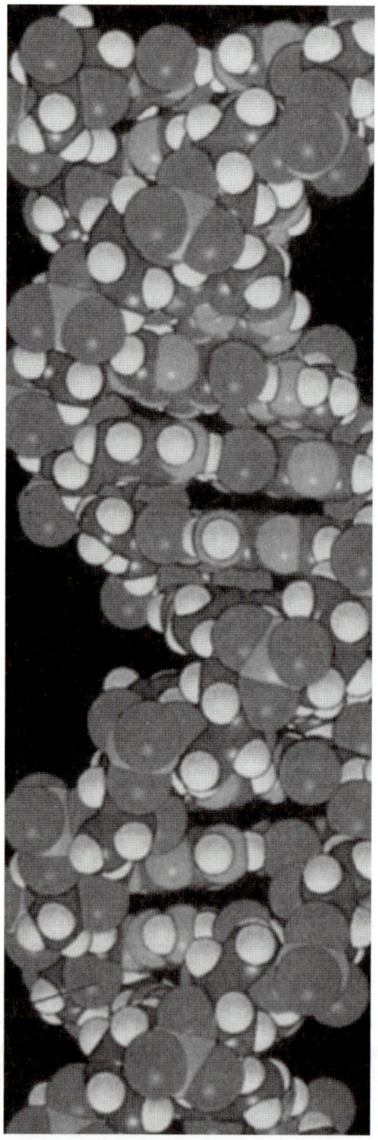

FIGURE 6.5 ◀
This is a model of DNA, an extremely large molecule found in cells of living things. It is made up of thousands of atoms, but only five elements — carbon, hydrogen, oxygen, nitrogen, and phosphorus.

Different elements have different properties because their atoms are different. In the same way, different compounds have different properties because their molecules are different. Some compounds, such as baking soda and salt, are solids at room temperature. Some compounds, such as water and acetic acid, are liquids at room temperature. Other compounds, such as carbon dioxide and methane, are gases at room temperature.

REVIEW 6.1

1. Explain the relationship between the following pairs of words:
   (a) atom and element
   (b) atom and molecule
   (c) element and compound
2. Use examples to explain the differences between an element and a compound.
3. Use the particle model to explain the differences between an element and a compound.
4. Approximately how many kinds of atoms are there?
5. In your notebook, sketch a molecule of a compound that contains
   (a) two atoms,
   (b) five atoms,
   (c) eight atoms.

DID YOU KNOW

Experiments have shown that the water in one ordinary drinking glass has about 10 000 000 000 000 000 000 000 000 molecules (that's 10 million million million million). Could you count that high? Suppose you start counting when you are born, counting one every second. In one year you would count to 31 557 600. If you lived to be 317 years old, you would reach 10 thousand million (10 billion). By the time you finished counting, you would be 317 000 000 000 000 000 years old.

6.2 CHANGES IN MATTER

Matter — whether it is water, concrete, steel, natural gas, butter, or fresh milk — does not stay the same forever. The world around us is continually changing. Water evaporates, concrete cracks, steel rusts, natural gas burns, butter melts, and milk goes sour.

ACTIVITY 6B / WHAT IS CHANGING? (TEACHER DEMONSTRATION)

GROUP ACTIVITY

Watch carefully as your teacher carries out the investigations shown in Figure 6.6. What happens to the sugar cube in each of the investigations? Where does it go? If you tasted any of the materials remaining, would they taste sweet? Do you think that you could get any of the sugar cubes back somehow? In your group, discuss these questions and try to explain what happened in each investigation. Write your group's explanations in your learning journal. Share your explanations with other groups.

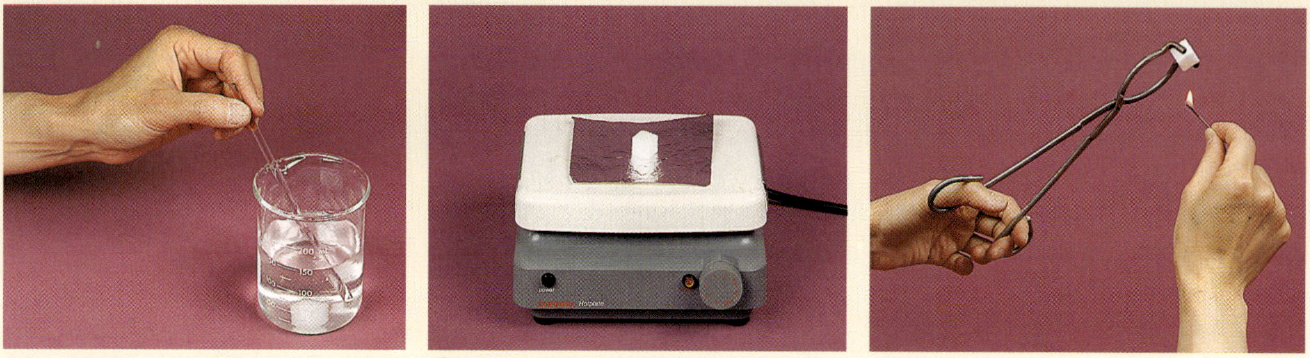

(a) (b) (c)

FIGURE 6.6
(a) A sugar cube is put into a beaker of water. The water is stirred until a change is observed. (b) A sugar cube is placed on a piece of aluminum foil on a hotplate. It is heated until changes occur. (c) A sugar cube is held with tongs over a lighted match. ❖

FIGURE 6.7
When food is cooked, chemical changes occur. What changes do you notice here?

CHEMICAL CHANGES

Changes in which new substances are produced — substances with properties that are different from those of the starting material(s) — are called **chemical changes**. Think of the changes that occur when food is cooked. When an egg is heated, for example, the liquid changes colour and becomes solid. The cooked egg has properties that are quite different from the properties of the uncooked egg (Figure 6.7). As another example, think of the changes that can happen to the body of a car when it is exposed to wet weather over several years. Where the steel was once hard and shiny, a crumbly reddish-brown substance forms; the steel has changed into rust (Figure 6.8). You can wipe away the soft rust and polish the steel again, but eventually holes will appear. Both cooking and rusting are examples of chemical changes.

In a chemical change, molecules are rearranged into different kinds

FIGURE 6.8 ◀
The rusting of steel is an example of a chemical change.

of molecules. Another example of a chemical change, the burning of charcoal, is illustrated in Figure 6.9. Charcoal, a black solid, consists of the element carbon. When charcoal burns, atoms of carbon combine with oxygen from the air. The new substance produced in this chemical change is carbon dioxide gas.

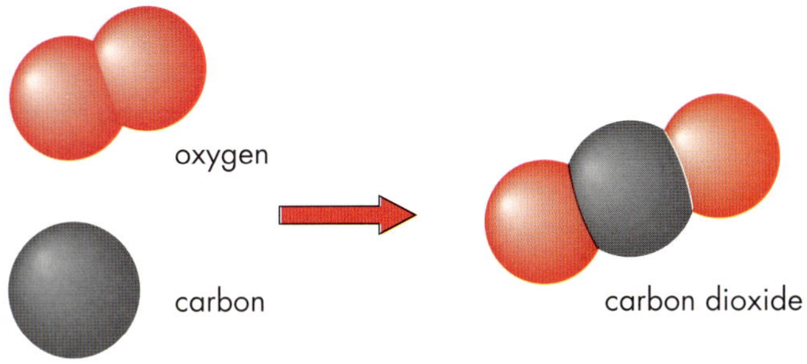

FIGURE 6.9
The burning of charcoal is another example of a chemical change.

PHYSICAL CHANGES

When water changes to ice, is a new substance produced? When ice melts, is a new substance produced? The answer to both questions is no. When a liquid freezes or when a solid melts, it is still the same material. Melting and freezing are examples of **physical changes** in matter — changes in which no new substance is produced. When ice melts, the molecules do not break apart — they just become more free to move around. In other changes of state, too, such as boiling and condensing, no new substances are produced. Changes of state are examples of physical changes.

Dissolving is another example of a physical change (Figure 6.10). When you dissolve a drink mix in water, the flavour is still there. You may not be able to see the flavour crystals, but you can taste the flavour. If you let the water evaporate, you would find the crystals left in the container. Other examples of physical changes are mixing substances together, cutting objects into pieces, and moulding a sculpture. In physical changes, the particles of substances may move closer together or farther apart, or they may mix with particles of other substances, but no new kinds of particles are produced.

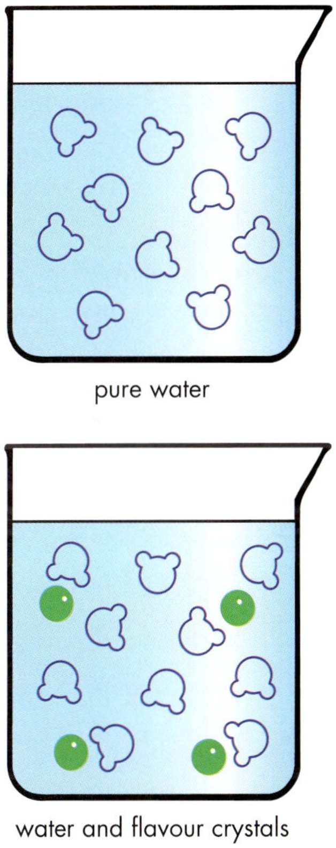

FIGURE 6.10
When flavour crystals are mixed with water, no new molecules are produced.

Certain clues may help you tell the difference between a chemical change and a physical change. There may have been a chemical change if:

- a new colour appears
- heat energy or light energy is given off
- the change is difficult to reverse
- bubbles of gas are produced

When considering changes, don't jump to conclusions too quickly. Any of these clues could also occur with a physical change. You need to consider several clues in order to determine what type of change has taken place.

ACTIVITY 6C / PHYSICAL AND CHEMICAL CHANGES

In this activity, you will observe physical and chemical changes.

MATERIALS

Parts I and II
safety goggles
apron

Part I
rubber gloves
lump of modelling clay
small candle
glass plate
water
scoopula (or 2 mL measuring spoon)
copper sulphate crystals
two test tubes
stopper for test tube
watch glass or shallow dish
small piece of steel wool

Part II
electrolysis apparatus
power supply
electrical wires and clips
water containing some dissolved sodium sulphate
wooden splints

FIGURE 6.11
What changes do you think will occur in the liquid over time?

PART I Student Experiments

PROCEDURE

1. Put on your safety goggles and apron.
2. Using the lump of modelling clay, make a secure stand for the candle. Light your candle. Hold a glass plate under it, and tip the candle slightly until some wax drops onto the glass plate. Blow out the candle after it has melted down a bit. In your notebook, record your observations in a table like Table 6.2.

Procedure step	Description of starting materials	Changes observed
2.		
3.		
4.		
5.		

TABLE 6.2 ***Sample Data Table for Activity 6C***

3. Put water into a test tube to a depth of about 4 cm. Add one scoop of copper sulphate crystals, put the stopper into the tube, and mix the water and copper sulphate by turning the tube upside down several times. Pour several drops of the liquid onto a watch glass (Figure 6.11) and record your observations. Set the watch glass aside until the next class.
4. Put on rubber gloves and gently push the piece of steel wool to the bottom of a test tube. Add a few drops of water, and stopper the tube. Record your observations, then set the test tube aside until the next class or for a few days.
5. In the next class, examine the materials from steps 3 and 4. Record any changes.

DISCUSSION

1. For each type of change that you have observed, decide whether it is a physical change or a chemical change and give reasons for your answer. (Hint: You observed four changes in steps 2–4.)

PART II (Teacher Demonstration) Electrolysis

PROCEDURE

1. Put on your safety goggles and apron.
2. Your teacher will assemble the apparatus shown in Figure 6.12 and turn on the electricity. (Note: the sodium sulphate in the water is there simply to allow the electric current to pass through the water.)

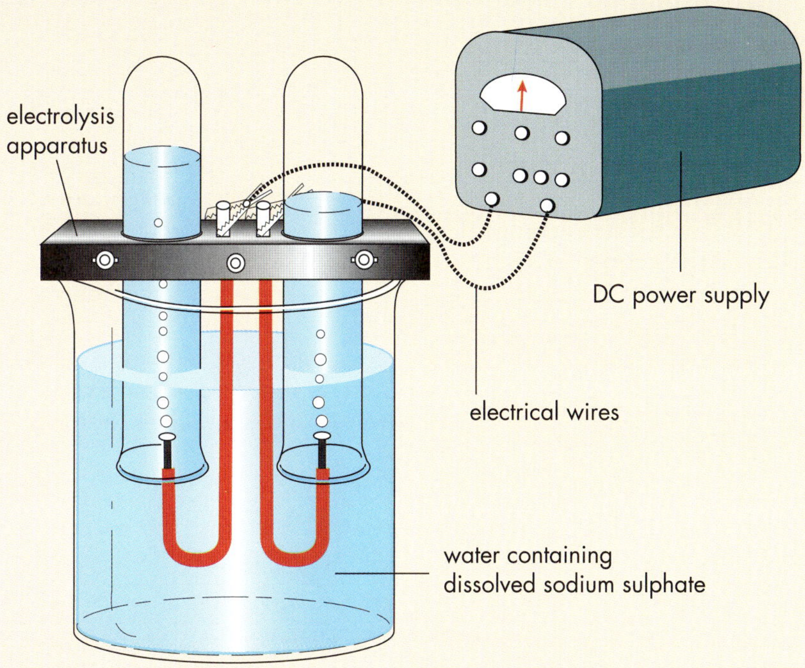

FIGURE 6.12
Electrolysis apparatus

3. Observe the apparatus and record in your notebook what happens when the electricity is turned on.
4. When one of the test tubes is almost full of gas, your teacher will turn off the power.
5. Your teacher will stopper the test tubes containing gas, lift them out, and test them by putting a flaming or glowing wooden splint into the test tubes.
6. In your notebook, record the results of each test.

DISCUSSION

1. When did bubbles of gas form and when did bubbles stop forming?
2. Describe what the two gases looked like.
3. How much of each gas was collected?
4. What evidence do you have that a chemical change occurred in the apparatus?
5. Describe what happened when the splint was held to each gas in the test tubes.
6. Examine Figure 6.13. Identify the molecules and explain what the drawing represents. ❖

CAUTION!

■ **Do not try to do this experiment at home. It is dangerous and can result in a strong electrical shock.**

EXTENSION

■ Collect some or all of the following: vinegar, sugar, lemon juice, baking soda, steel wool. Carefully mix small amounts of these materials in pairs and watch for evidence of a chemical change. Describe the chemical changes that you observed. Make sure that you wear your safety goggles and apron when you mix these materials, and wear rubber gloves when you handle steel wool.

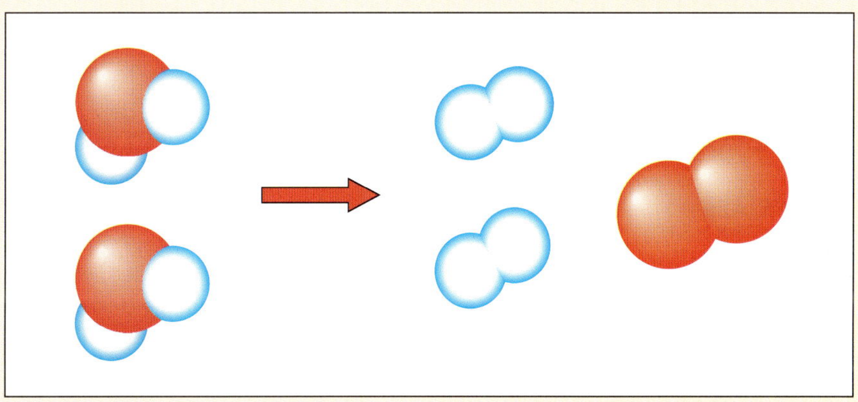

FIGURE 6.13
What does this drawing represent?

▶ REVIEW 6.2

1. For each of the following changes, state whether it is a physical change or a chemical change. Give at least one reason for your answer in each case.
   (a) Frost forms on windows.
   (b) Tea is made using hot water and a tea bag.
   (c) A firecracker explodes.
   (d) Concrete becomes hard after it is poured.
   (e) The burner on an electric stove glows red.
   (f) Coffee changes colour when cream is added.
   (g) Liquid nitrogen boils at −196°C.
   (h) In a frying pan, butter is heated until it turns brown.
   (i) When a flame is brought near hydrogen gas in a test tube, there is a loud pop.
2. Use the kinetic molecular theory to explain the difference between a chemical change and a physical change.
3. (a) In Activity 6B, you observed a sugar cube being mixed with water, being heated, and then being burned. Examine your written explanations of those changes. How have your ideas changed?
   (b) In your learning journal, write your own explanation of those three changes.

■ 6.3 QUANTITATIVE PROPERTIES

It is possible to describe the properties of any material, whether it is a mixture or a pure substance. Those properties that describe materials without using numbers are called **qualitative properties**. For example, when you describe the colour of a material, its state, what it feels like, or how it burns, you are describing qualitative properties. Properties you can measure or calculate are called **quantitative properties**. Quantitative properties always include numbers.

ACTIVITY 6D / MELTING POINT

In this activity, you will use a thermometer to determine a quantitative property of ice.

MATERIALS

safety goggles
apron
crushed ice in beaker
stirring rod
thermometer
watch or timer

PROCEDURE

1. In your notebook, draw a table similar to Table 6.3, leaving space to include minutes to 12 min.
2. Put on your safety goggles and apron.
3. Carefully stir the crushed ice with a stirring rod (Figure 6.14). Place the thermometer in the beaker and record the temperature at 0 min. Take out the thermometer and stir the ice again. After 1 min, replace the thermometer and record the temperature. Remove the thermometer while you stir the ice again.
4. Repeat step 3 several times, recording the temperature every minute. In the right-hand column of your data table, describe any changes you observe.
5. Continue to repeat step 3 until 3 or 4 min after all the ice has melted.

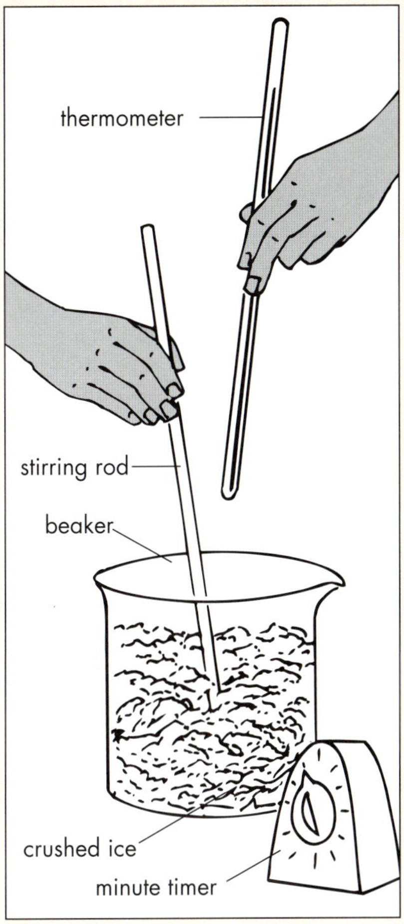

FIGURE 6.14
Remove the thermometer from the beaker before you stir the ice. Thermometers are easily broken.

FIGURE 6.15 ▶
Graph the temperature of the ice/water mixture against the time of each observation. Show the time when all the ice has melted.

DISCUSSION

1. Describe how the temperature changes during this change of state.
2. Prepare a line graph like the one in Figure 6.15. Plot your data on the graph. Describe the shape of the line during the time the ice is melting.
3. What is the melting temperature of ice?
4. Predict what would happen to the line on your graph if you had started with more ice.
5. Predict what would happen to the line on the graph if you heated the water after all the ice had melted. ❖

Time (min)	Temperature (°C)	Observations
0		
1		
2		
etc.		

TABLE 6.3
Sample Data Table for Activity 6D

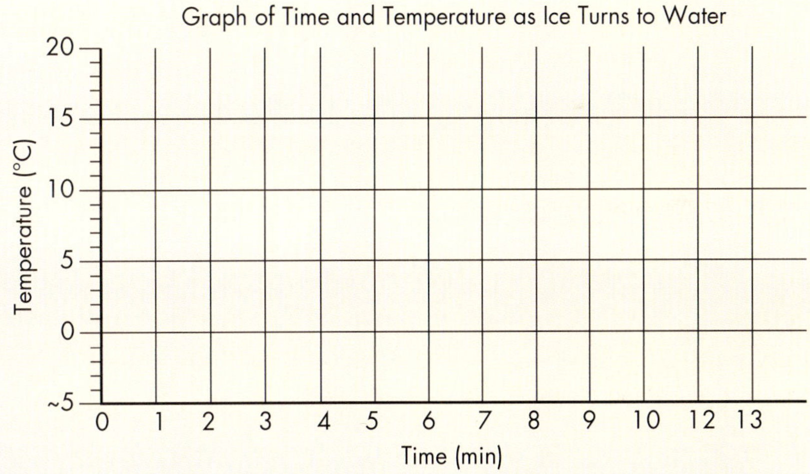

MELTING, FREEZING, AND BOILING

Scientists have observed again and again that each pure substance changes from one state to another at a certain temperature (Figure 6.16). The **melting point** of a pure substance is the temperature at which it changes from the solid state to the liquid state. For example, pure ice always melts at 0°C. The **freezing point** of a pure substance is the temperature at which it changes from the liquid state to the solid

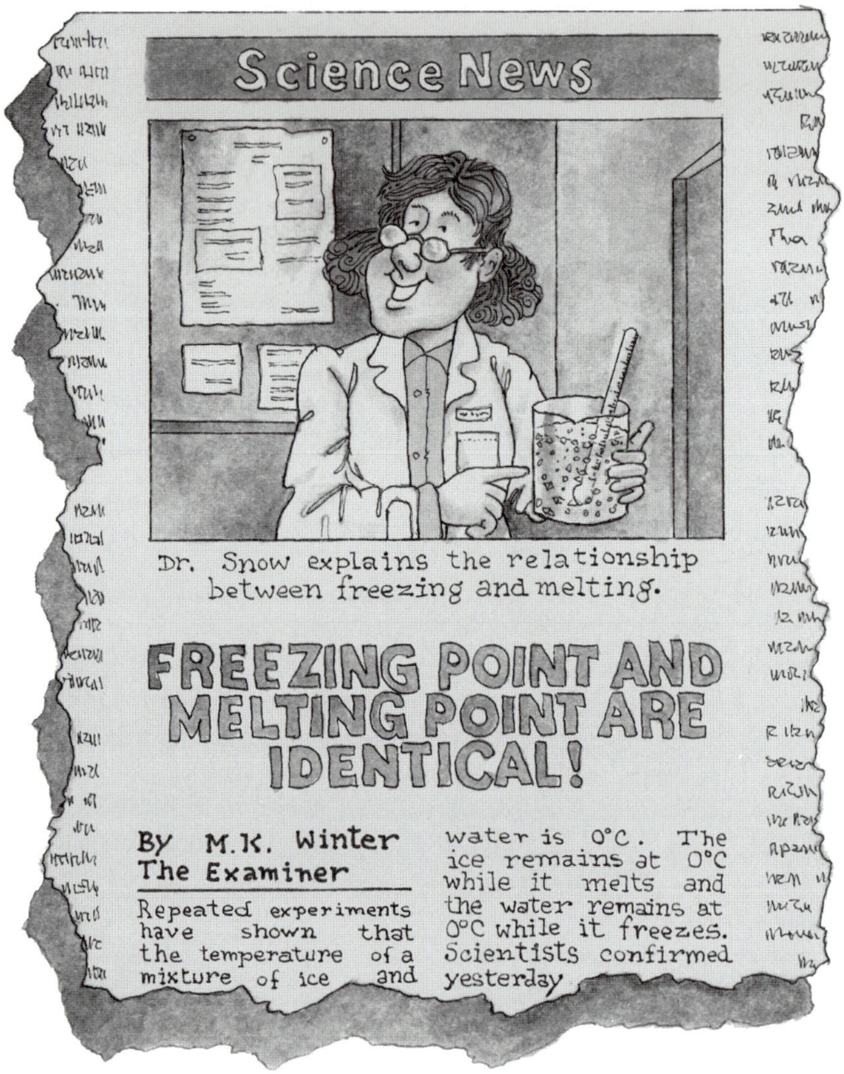

FIGURE 6.16 ▶
How could you verify this scientist's results?

state. The freezing point of water is 0°C. Every pure substance has its own freezing point, which is the same temperature as its melting point (Table 6.4).

TABLE 6.4 ▶
Melting Points and Boiling Points of Some Pure Substances.

Substance	Melting point (°C)	Boiling point (°C)
Alcohol (ethanol)	−115	78
Copper	1084	2336
Oxygen	−218	−183
Sodium chloride (table salt)	801	1465
Sulphur	113	445
Water	0	100

Another change of state, evaporation, can occur slowly at almost any temperature. But if enough heat is added to a liquid, it will begin to bubble rapidly, or boil. The temperature at which this rapid change of state occurs is the **boiling point** of the liquid. Boiling point is another quantitative property of matter.

Table 6.4 lists the melting points and boiling points of several pure substances. Three of these substances melt at temperatures higher than the melting point of ice. These three — copper, sodium chloride, and sulphur — are solids at ordinary temperatures. What does it mean to say that "ethanol melts at −115°C?" If ethanol melts at such a low temperature, it must be a liquid at ordinary temperatures. It is a liquid, and it boils when it is heated to only 78°C. You can see in the table that solid oxygen also has a very low melting point. In addition, liquid oxygen has a very low boiling point. Oxygen melts and boils at extremely low temperatures — meaning that at ordinary temperatures it is a gas.

ACTIVITY 6E / WATER TO STEAM (TEACHER DEMONSTRATION)

For the boiling point of water, find out how close your experimental result is to the value given in the Table of Properties in Appendix C.

MATERIALS

thermometer (accurate at temperatures above 90°C)
stand
ring clamp
clamp
beaker
water
source of heat (Bunsen burner or hotplate)
watch or timer

PROCEDURE

1. In your notebook, draw a table similar to Table 6.3 on page 141. The time column should continue to 15 min.
2. Predict how the temperature of water will change as it is heated to boiling. Predict as well how the temperature will change as the water continues to boil.

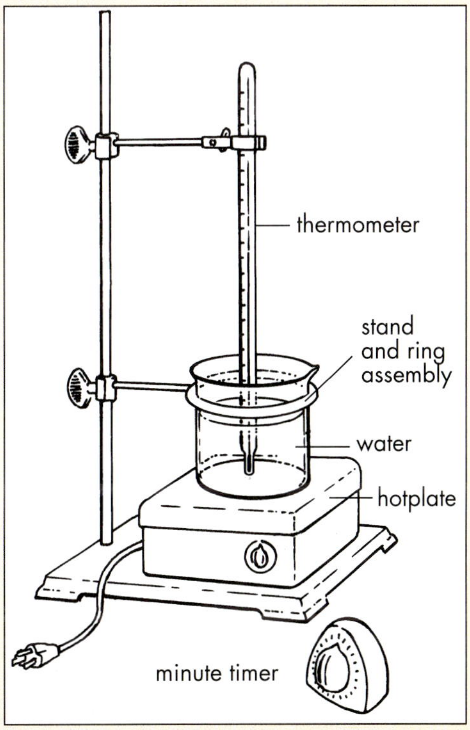

FIGURE 6.17 ▶
Apparatus for Activity 6E

3. When the apparatus is set up as shown in Figure 6.17, with about 100 mL of water in the beaker, the water will be heated.
4. Record the temperature when you start (0 min).
5. Record the temperature every minute as the water is heated.
6. In the right-hand column of your table, describe any changes you observe.
7. Continue recording the temperature for at least 5 min after the water has been boiling rapidly. ➡

EXTENSION

■ How do you think your results would have been different if you had used 250 mL of water instead of 100 mL? Make a prediction, then design an experiment to check your prediction. Check your design with your teacher before conducting your experiment.

DISCUSSION

1. Describe how the temperature changes as the water comes to a boil.
2. Was your prediction correct? Explain why or why not.
3. Prepare a graph for your data similar to the graph in Figure 6.15 on page 141. The range of temperatures shown should be from 60°C to about 110°C. Plot your data on the graph.
4. Describe the shape of the line as the heating continued.
5. What was the boiling point of your sample of tap water? ❖

DENSITY: ANOTHER QUANTITATIVE PROPERTY

Why does a block of wood float on water, whereas a piece of copper sinks? You might say that the copper is "heavier" than the water, but that is not necessarily true. The water that fills a 1 L beaker has a mass of 1000 g, but a copper earring with a mass of 1 g will sink to the bottom of the beaker. To compare the "heaviness," you need to compare the mass of equal volumes of different materials. Table 6.5 shows the mass of 1 cm^3 of wood, water, and copper.

TABLE 6.5 ▶
Mass of Equal Volumes of Three Substances

Substance	Mass of 1 cm^3 (g)
Wood (western red cedar)	0.37 (approximate)
Pure water	1.00
Copper	8.92

When you compare the masses of equal volumes of different kinds of matter, you are comparing their **densities**. Density is the mass (in grams) of each cubic centimetre (or millilitre) of a material. Density is a quantitative property of substances — a number that helps in identifying and comparing materials. You cannot measure density directly; you must calculate it after you know the mass and the volume of a sample of the substance.

$$\text{density} = \frac{\text{mass}}{\text{volume}}$$

If you have measured the mass in grams (g) and the volume in millilitres (mL), the units of density will be grams per millilitre (g/mL). The density of a liquid is usually written in this way. You can also measure the volume in cubic centimetres (cm^3) and calculate the density in grams per cubic centimetre (g/cm^3). The density of solids is usually written in this way.

The information in Table 6.5 tells you that the density of one kind of wood is 0.37 g/cm^3, the density of pure water is 1 g/mL, and the density of copper is 8.92 g/cm^3. Now you can see why copper does not float on water. Copper sinks in water because it is more dense than water. The wood is less dense than water, so it floats (Figure 6.18).

Scientists have calculated the densities of many types of matter (see the Table of Properties in Appendix C). Density can help you to identify pure substances. It can also be used to predict whether a substance will float or sink in a liquid.

FIGURE 6.18
These logs have a very large mass. Using the property of density, can you explain why they float in water?

ACTIVITY 6F / FLOATING AND SINKING

In this activity, you will find out whether various solids will float or sink in three liquids.

MATERIALS

safety goggles
apron
three 250 mL beakers
rubbing alcohol (isopropanol; density 0.8 g/cm^3)
water (density 1.0 g/cm^3)
glycerol (glycerine; density 1.3 g/cm^3)
small pieces of various solids, such as ice, wax, linoleum, asphalt
reference data: densities of the solids to be tested

PROCEDURE

1. In your notebook, draw a table like Table 6.6. In the first column, list the solid materials you will test. Obtain the data about their densities from your teacher and fill in the second column.
2. Use the information about densities to predict which solids will float in which liquids. Write your predictions in your table.
3. Put on your safety goggles and apron.

Solid	Density (g/cm^3)	Will solid float or sink?		
		In rubbing alcohol	In water	In glycerol
Ice				
Wax				
etc.				

TABLE 6.6 ***Sample Data Table for Activity 6F***

EXTENSION

■ Determine for yourself the densities of some common materials. All you need to do is measure the mass and the volume, then calculate the density.

$$\text{density} = \frac{\text{mass}}{\text{volume}}$$

If you use a pure substance listed in the Table of Properties in Appendix C, you can then compare your result with the value given there.

4. Test your predictions for the solids by placing them one by one in the three liquids. Indicate in your data table which of your predictions were correct.

DISCUSSION

1. Summarize your results in a few sentences.
2. Explain how you can use density to predict whether or not a solid will float in a liquid.
3. All metals are solids at room temperature except one — mercury, which is a liquid (Figure 6.19). Find the density of mercury in the Table of Properties in Appendix C. Then find the density of at least three solid metals, such as aluminum, gold, and lead. Write the densities in your notebook (remembering to include units). Predict whether or not each of the solid metals will float in liquid mercury. Give reasons for your predictions. ❖

FIGURE 6.19 ▶
Mercury has many properties common to all metals, but it has one that is unique — it is a liquid at ordinary temperatures. Note: Mercury is very toxic. Do not touch it and do not breathe its vapours.

FIGURE 6.20
Density can be used to identify an unknown substance.

CALCULATING DENSITY

Density is a characteristic property of pure substances. This means that you can use density to identify a pure substance. Suppose you find a large, clear, colourless crystal and you want to determine whether it is a diamond or a piece of quartz. It is beautiful, so you don't want to do anything to damage it. In a reference book, you find out that the density of diamond is 3.51 g/cm^3 and the density of quartz is 2.65 g/cm^3 (Figure 6.20). To determine the density of your crystal, all you need to do is

- measure its mass
- measure its volume
- calculate the density by dividing the mass by the volume

Using a balance, you find that the mass of the crystal is 21.6 g. You decide to determine the volume of the crystal by displacement of water. You gently lower the crystal into a graduated cylinder containing exactly 50 mL of water. The new volume reading is 58 mL (Figure 6.21).

$$\begin{aligned} \text{volume of water and crystal} &= 58\text{ mL} \\ \text{volume of water} &= \underline{50\text{ mL}} \\ \text{volume of crystal} &= 8\text{ mL} \end{aligned}$$

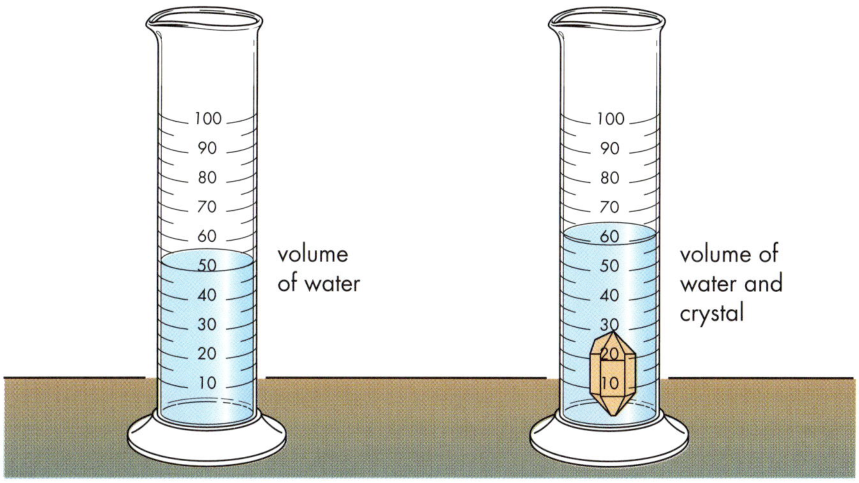

FIGURE 6.21
Determining volume by displacement of water

The volume of the crystal in millilitres is the same as its volume in cubic centimetres (1 mL = 1 cm^3). The density of the crystal is

$$\frac{21.6\ \text{g}}{8\ \text{cm}^3} = 2.7\ \text{g/cm}^3$$

You compare your result with the reference values and sadly conclude that what you have found must be quartz. (Your result is not exactly the same as the reference value for quartz, but small errors are always possible when you are using standard laboratory equipment. Your result is close enough.)

REVIEW 6.3

1. (a) In what ways are boiling and evaporation similar?
(b) Explain the differences between boiling and evaporation.

2. In the Table of Properties in Appendix C, find
(a) three colourless liquids that boil at temperatures lower than 100°C,
(b) the substances in the table with the highest and lowest melting points,
(c) the substance in the table with the highest density.

3. Calculate the density of the following kinds of wood:
(a) a child's block made of birch wood with a volume of 510 cm^3 and a mass of 306 g
(b) a log of pine with a volume of 240 000 cm^3 and a mass of 96 000 g
(c) a sculpture made of ebony, whose volume is 81 cm^3 and whose mass is 96 g

4. (a) Calculate the density in grams per millilitre of a liquid, if 8.0 mL of the liquid has a mass of 108.8 g.
(b) Refer to the Table of Properties in Appendix C and indicate what liquid this might be.

5. A graduated cylinder containing 40 mL of water has a mass of 60 g. As you carefully place an object into the graduated cylinder, the total volume increases to 70 mL and the total mass becomes 95 g. Determine the object's
(a) mass,
(b) volume,
(c) density.

6. A block of grey metal has the dimensions 10 cm x 5 cm x 3 cm. Its mass is 1700 g.
(a) Calculate its density in grams per cubic centimetre.
(b) Refer to the Table of Properties in Appendix C and indicate what metal this might be.

COMPUTERIZED CONTROL IN THE DAIRY INDUSTRY

Doug Karlson is in charge of the laboratory of a large dairy company that produces a wide variety of milk products as well as fruit juices. These products are tested throughout the production process to make sure that they are safe to use. In the past, the results of these many tests were handwritten in notebooks. Today Karlson and his technicians use a computer to record the results. Not only is using a computer faster, but Karlson can find the results of a particular test by pressing a few keys on the computer instead of hunting through pages of data in notebooks.

Dave Hsin uses a Bactometer to test milk and fruit juice for bacteria.

Karlson also uses automatic temperature devices. It is important that dairy products be stored at the correct temperature. An increase of even 2°C can cause products to spoil. A small device can be attached magnetically to a storage tank, delivery truck, or refrigerated display case to record the temperature over a two-week period. The device is then returned to the laboratory, where Karlson reads the results on a computer. If there is a problem, it can be corrected right away.

In another plant of the company, Dave Hsin uses a computerized testing machine called a Bactometer to test for bacteria in cartons of UHT (ultra-high temperature)-treated milk and fruit juices. The milk or juice is poured into small cups in a tray. Each cup has electrical contacts on opposite sides. The tray is then placed in the incubator of the Bactometer, where it is kept at a constant temperature. The contacts in the cups are connected to an electrical current and to a computer. The amount of current passing through each cup remains the same unless bacteria start to grow. If that happens, the current increases. At any point during the 24 hours of incubation, Hsin can turn on the computer and see how much current is flowing in each cup.

Computers have made a big difference in ensuring that dairy products are safe to eat or drink. Can you think of other situations in which a Bactometer or a computerized temperature recorder might be useful?

6.4 MIXTURES

Very few things in our environment are completely pure. For example, products such as hand lotion and soap are made of many substances mixed together, including colouring materials and perfumes. You see other common mixtures every day. Foods, for instance, contain preservatives and other additives. Even fruit juice labelled "100% pure" is actually a mixture of water, citric acid, and other substances.

ACTIVITY 6G / MAKING MIXTURES

In this activity, you will make some mixtures and discuss several ways of classifying them.

MATERIALS

safety goggles
apron
six (or more) test tubes
test tube rack
rubber stoppers for test tubes
tape for labels (or wax pencil)
scoopula
graduated cylinder (10 mL)
a variety of solids and liquids, such as salt, sand, pepper, salad oil, vinegar, copper sulphate, sugar, ethanol, water

CAUTION!

Copper sulphate and ethanol are poisonous. Do not touch them. Ethanol is flammable. Do not use it near an open flame.

PROCEDURE

1. Put on your safety goggles and apron.
2. Set up the test tubes in your test tube rack and label them.
3. Copy Table 6.7 into your notebook, listing all the materials you will use in the left-hand column.

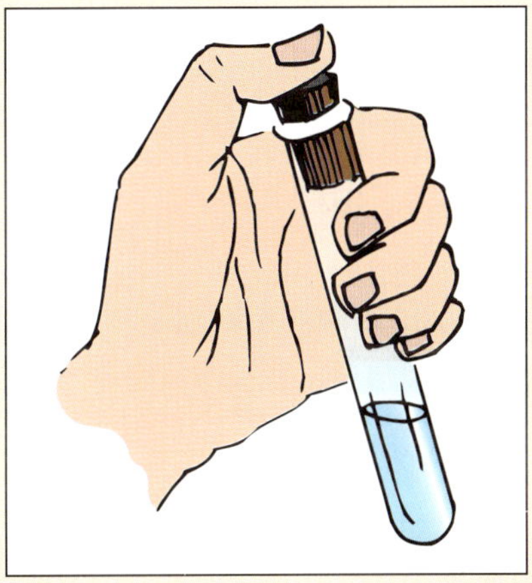

FIGURE 6.22
Hold the test tube like this when you turn it upside down.

4. Make each mixture by combining the two substances in the appropriate test tube. Use 10 mL of the substances that are liquids and one small scoop of the substances that are solids.
5. To mix the two substances in each test tube, put the stopper in the test tube, hold it with your thumb, and turn the tube upside down several times (Figure 6.22). Then remove the stopper.
6. Record your observations in your table. (See the sample entry in Table 6.7 for mixture 1.)
7. After you have completed the activity, wash your hands thoroughly.

TABLE 6.7
Sample Data Table for Activity 6G

Substances mixed	How many parts are visible?	Does the mixture contain solids, liquids, or both?	What changes, if any, occurred during mixing?
Salt and sand	2	2 solids	No change
Copper sulphate and water			

DISCUSSION

1. Classify the mixtures that you made. List the mixtures
   (a) that were made from two solids
   (b) that were made from two liquids
   (c) that were made from a solid and a liquid
   (d) in which one of the substances could no longer be seen
   (e) in which one of the substances appeared to change colour
2. Think of at least one other way of classifying the mixtures, besides those in question 1. Record your method in your notebook. Compare your idea with those of your classmates. In your notebook, describe some of your classmates' suggestions. ❖

FIGURE 6.23
Granola cereal is a mechanical mixture. What other foods can you classify as mechanical mixtures? As solutions? As suspensions?

CLASSIFYING MIXTURES

One way that scientists classify mixtures is to group them according to their appearance. A **mechanical mixture** is a mixture in which two or more parts can be seen with the unaided eye. Granola cereal is an example of a mechanical mixture (Figure 6.23). A **solution** is a mixture that appears to be only one substance. The parts of a solution are so completely mixed that they cannot be seen even under a microscope. Apple juice (a liquid), clean air (a mixture of gases), and stainless steel (a solid mixture of metals) are all solutions. More examples are listed in Table 6.8. Can you explain the classification of each of the substances listed?

Mechanical mixtures	Solutions
Dirty, sooty air	Clear air
Salad	Vinegar (a solution of water and acetic acid)
Cornflakes and milk	Tea
A fizzy soft drink	A "flat" soft drink
Concrete (cement, sand, and gravel)	Clear shampoo
Sand and pebbles	Bronze (a solid solution of tin and copper)

TABLE 6.8 ***Examples of Mechanical Mixtures and Solutions***

If you did Activity 6G, reread the observations you recorded. Which of the mixtures could you classify as solutions? Which could you classify as mechanical mixtures? (Liquid solutions are often the most difficult to identify. It may help to remember that water solutions are always clear — that is, you can see through them. They may be coloured, like one of the solutions in Activity 6G, but they are never cloudy.)

There is a third type of mixture, called a **suspension**. A suspension is a cloudy mixture in which clumps of a solid or liquid droplets are scattered throughout a substance (Figure 6.24). Muddy water is one example of a suspension. Tomato juice is another example. The parts of a suspension are easier to separate than those of a solution. Without constant stirring, the parts of a suspension may not stay mixed.

Farm-fresh milk is a typical suspension. As with all suspensions, its components eventually separate. If the milk is left to stand, the fatty part floats to the top, while the watery part sinks to the bottom. Shaking breaks up the fat into small globules, which stay suspended for a while. Eventually, however, the fat floats to the top again.

Commercially available milk, however, does not separate in this way. It is a special kind of suspension called an emulsion. An **emulsion** is a suspension that has been treated to keep it from separating. Equipment at the dairy sprays the milk through very small openings. This process, called homogenization, breaks the fat into droplets so tiny that they stay suspended.

DID YOU KNOW

■ Your body contains many solutions. You have probably noticed the taste of tears, which is caused by dissolved salt. Saliva, sweat, and urine are also solutions. Blood is more complicated. It consists of many kinds of cells — including the red cells that give the blood its colour — suspended in a clear yellow solution that contains many substances.

FIGURE 6.24 ◀
Which of these beakers do you think contain suspensions? Which beakers contain solutions?

CLASSIFYING MATTER

You can classify all mixtures as mechanical mixtures, suspensions, or solutions, depending on what they look like. But how can you tell whether a liquid is a solution or a pure substance? A pure substance has fixed properties that are always the same. For example, the properties of any sample of pure water are always exactly the same as those of any other sample of pure water. In contrast, the properties of a solution depend on the amount of each substance in the solution. For example, clear tea may be strong or weak depending on how long the tea bag has been left in the pot. You may add sugar to it — a little sugar will make it slightly sweet, and a lot makes it much sweeter.

Solutions look like pure substances. To tell the difference between a solution and a pure substance, you might need to carry out some investigations. The classification of matter into mechanical mixtures, suspensions, solutions, compounds, and elements is based on the observations and experiments of many scientists over hundreds of years. Figure 6.25 summarizes the classification.

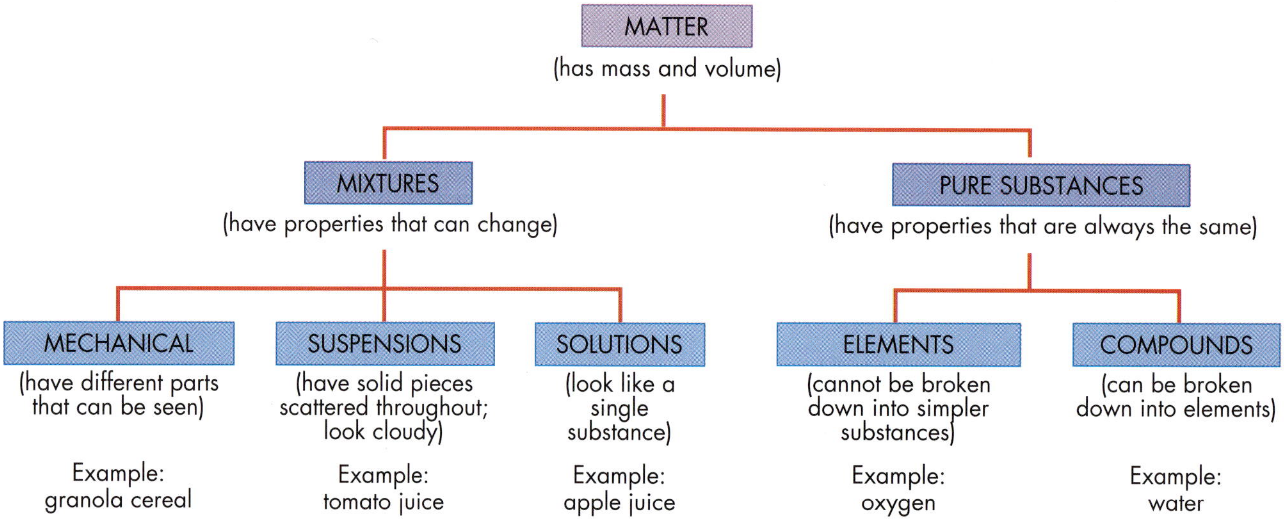

FIGURE 6.25
Classification of matter

SOLUTIONS

Why does a sugar cube seem to disappear in water? Where does it go? Think back to the kinetic molecular theory (page 122). Solid sugar crystals consist of very tiny particles packed tightly together. Although the particles vibrate, they stay locked in place. Water is made up of tiny particles that are able to move around. When water particles collide with solid sugar, individual sugar particles are broken off and carried away. These individual sugar molecules are much too small to be seen, so the sugar seems to disappear. In this way, sugar **dissolves** in water. When one substance dissolves in another substance, the tiny particles of the substances mix so completely that you cannot tell the substances apart (Figure 6.26).

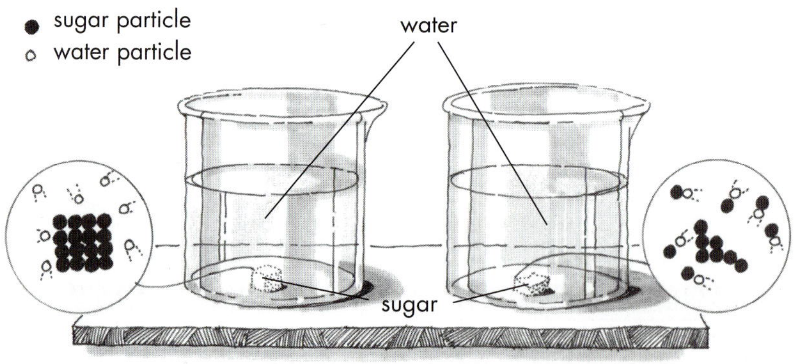

FIGURE 6.26 ▶
Sugar dissolving in water. Why can't you see the sugar after it has dissolved?

Another way of saying that a substance dissolves in water is to say that it is **soluble** in water. For example, salt, sugar, copper sulphate, ethanol, and carbon dioxide are soluble in water. An **insoluble** substance is one that does not dissolve. Pepper, sand, and oil are insoluble in water.

When a solid dissolves in a liquid, the liquid that does the dissolving is called the **solvent**, and the solid that dissolves is called the **solute**. For example, in a solution of orange-drink crystals and water, water is the solvent and the orange crystals are the solute. Water is the solvent in juices, soups, and milk. Other substances can act as solvents too.

ACTIVITY 6H / USING DIFFERENT SOLVENTS

In this activity, you will compare two different solvents.

MATERIALS

safety goggles
apron
four small cups
tape for labels
salad oil
water
four popsicle sticks
salt
petroleum jelly

PROCEDURE

1. Copy Table 6.9 into your notebook.
2. Put on your safety goggles and apron.
3. Label the four cups 1, 2, 3, and 4 (Figure 6.27). Pour salad oil into cups 1 and 2 to a depth of about 2 cm. Pour the same amount of water into cups 3 and 4.
4. Using the popsicle sticks, add a little salt to cups 1 and 3 and a little petroleum jelly to cups 2 and 4, as shown. Stir each mixture thoroughly.
5. Examine the contents of each cup and record whether the solute has been dissolved completely, partially, or not at all. Under "Observations," describe each mixture.

Cup	Solute	Solvent	Observations
1			
2			
3			
4			

TABLE 6.9
Sample Data Table for Activity 6H

DISCUSSION

1. In which liquid was the petroleum jelly more soluble? What observation suggests this?
2. Which solvent dissolved more salt? What observation suggests this? ➡

FIGURE 6.27 ▶
Testing two solutes and two solvents

3. All three cloths shown in Figure 6.28 had identical tar stains, which were then treated in different ways. Compare the effect of washing the cloth in Varsol with the effect of washing it in water. Use the words "solvent" and "dissolve" in your answer. ❖

FIGURE 6.28 ▶
The cloth on the left is unwashed. The cloth in the middle was washed in Varsol, and the cloth on the right was washed in water.

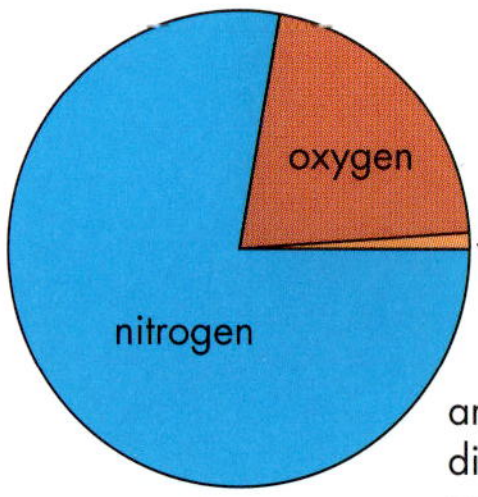

FIGURE 6.29
The proportions of gases in air. Why is nitrogen considered the solvent? What are oxygen and the other gases?

ALL KINDS OF SOLUTIONS

Solids, liquids, and gases can all form solutions. You know that soft drinks are solutions. The solvent is water. Besides the various flavourings, colourings, and sugars, a gas — carbon dioxide — is also dissolved in the water. When you open a soft-drink bottle or can, you can see bubbles of carbon dioxide separating from the solution. This gives the soft drink its "fizz."

In any solution, there is always more of the substance that does the dissolving (the solvent.) There is always a smaller amount of the solute. Clean air is a solution of about 80 per cent nitrogen and 19 per cent oxygen. About 1 per cent is a mixture of argon gas, carbon dioxide gas, water vapour, and other gases (Figure 6.29). In this example, nitrogen is the solvent, and oxygen and the other gases are solutes.

Some of the metals we use are really solid solutions of metals called **alloys**. To produce an alloy, different metals are heated together until they melt and form a liquid solution. When the solution is cooled, it changes to a solid. For example, to make brass (Figure 6.30b), copper and zinc are heated together and then cooled.

ACTIVITY 6I / SOLUTE AND SOLVENT

Copy Table 6.10 into your notebook. Using the information on these pages and in Figure 6.30, as well as your general knowledge, complete the table by naming the solvent and the solute for each solution.

TABLE 6.10 ▶
Sample Data Table for Activity 6I

Solution	Solvent	Solute(s)
Tea		
Air		
Ocean water		
Soft drink		
"Gold" jewellery		
Brass		

FIGURE 6.30

(a) Soft drinks are solutions of solids (such as sugar), liquids (such as flavourings), and a gas (carbon dioxide) in water. When the drink is poured, the carbon dioxide gradually comes out of solution, appearing as little bubbles rising through the liquid and clinging to the glass.

(b) Brass is an alloy made of copper and zinc. The alloy is stronger than copper alone. Brass is used to make household articles like these ornamental pots, as well as bathroom taps and inexpensive gold-coloured jewellery.

(c) Steel is an alloy made of iron with a small amount of carbon in it. The added carbon makes the steel harder. Many steels also contain other metals, such as nickel, chromium, and tungsten.

(d) This "gold" jewellery is made of an alloy of copper and gold. The copper makes the jewellery less expensive and much stronger than gold alone. Gold is too soft to use by itself in jewellery.

SOLUTIONS AND THE KINETIC MOLECULAR THEORY

In solutions, the tiny particles of both the solvent and the solute are completely mixed. Because the individual particles of the solute are small and far apart, you cannot see them. However, you can make some observations that indicate that the solute is present. Sometimes you can taste the solute; for example, you can taste sugar dissolved in your tea, or salt dissolved in your soup. (Remember that taste is not a property that should be tested in your science classroom.) Sometimes the particles of a solute, such as those of copper sulphate, colour the solution.

The explanation for the classification of matter into mechanical mixtures, solutions, compounds, and elements is summarized in Figure 6.31. Compare this chart, which is based on the kinetic molecular theory, with the chart in Figure 6.25 on page 152.

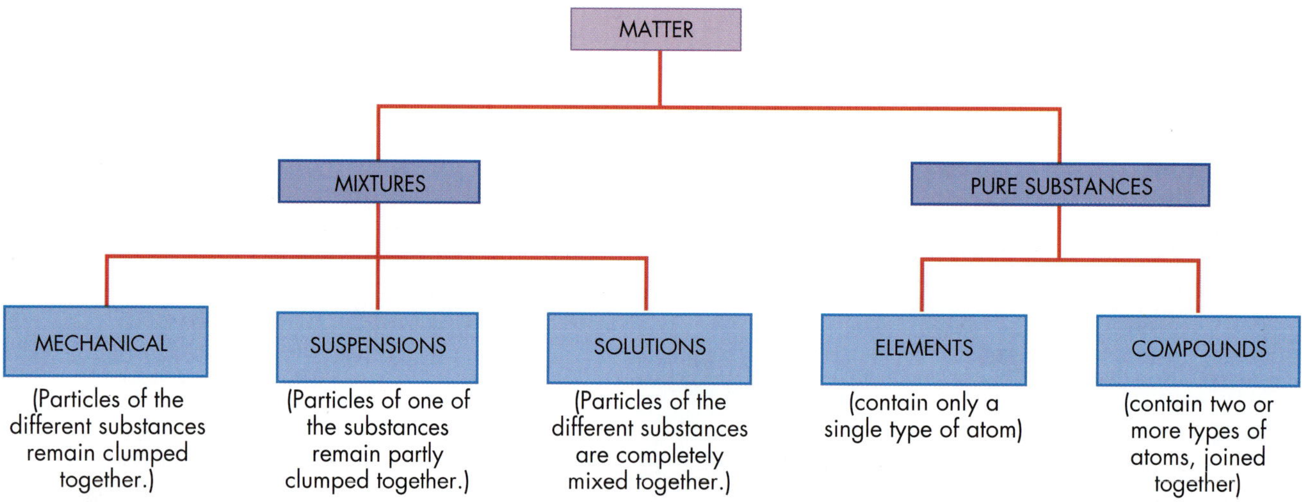

FIGURE 6.31
The classification of matter according to the kinetic molecular theory

▶ REVIEW 6.4

1. List at least three mechanical mixtures and three solutions from your everyday life that have not been mentioned in this chapter.
2. (a) How are suspensions and solutions similar?
   (b) How are they different?
3. The following sentences about solutions are either incomplete or incorrect. In your notebook, write the complete, correct version of each sentence.
   (a) A solvent is a liquid that dissolves salt.
   (b) A solute is part of a liquid.
   (c) Oil is insoluble.
   (d) A solution can always be distinguished from a pure substance by how it looks.
4. Give at least one example from everyday life of each of the following:
   (a) a solid solution
   (b) a liquid solution that does not contain water
   (c) a solution of gases

5. For each of the following statements, identify the solute and the solvent.
(a) Varsol dissolves the grease from a mechanic's clothes.
(b) Ocean water tastes salty.
(c) Bubbles of gas are produced when a soft-drink bottle is opened.
(d) Some jewellery is made of copper and gold.
(e) Tea is a clear, brownish liquid.

6. (a) Describe how a solution differs from a mechanical mixture.
(b) Explain this difference using the kinetic molecular theory.

CHAPTER REVIEW

KEY IDEAS

- There are two kinds of pure substances — elements and compounds.
- An atom is the smallest possible particle of an element.
- A molecule is a particle consisting of two or more atoms joined together.
- In a chemical change, a new substance is formed; in a physical change, no new substance is formed.
- Qualitative properties describe the colour of a material, its state, what it feels like, and so on.
- Quantitative properties are properties you can measure or calculate, such as melting point, freezing point, and density.
- Mixtures can be classified as mechanical mixtures, suspensions, or solutions.
- All matter can be classified into mechanical mixtures, suspensions, solutions, elements, and compounds.
- The classification of matter can be explained by the kinetic molecular theory.

VOCABULARY

element
atom
compound
molecule
chemical change
physical change
qualitative properties
quantitative properties
melting point
freezing point
boiling point
density
mechanical mixture
solution
suspension
emulsion
dissolve
soluble
insoluble
solvent
solute
alloy

V1. Use all the words from the vocabulary list and any other words you need to make a mind map about classifying matter.

V2. (a) You have been learning about mixtures whose parts cannot be seen. Three words (all are nouns) related to such mixtures begin with s-o-l. Find these three words in the vocabulary list. Using your own words, write a definition for each one in your notebook.
(b) You have learned three other words (one is a verb and two are adjectives) that also contain the letters s-o-l. Find these three words in the vocabulary list. Using your own words, write a definition for each one in your notebook.

CONNECTIONS

C1. What three clues can you use to determine whether a change is physical or chemical?

C2. Which of the following changes are physical changes? Which are chemical changes? Give reasons for your answers.
(a) an apple core rotting by the side of the highway
(b) covering garbage with soil in a compost box
(c) cutting up carrots with a knife
(d) burning wood in a fireplace

C3. All types of matter can be classified into one of five categories, as shown on page 156. In each of the following lists, three of the materials are classified in the same way, and one does not belong. For each list, indicate how the materials are classified and explain why one is different.

(a) salt water, concrete, chocolate-chip cookie batter, granola cereal
(b) water, baking soda, chalk, salt water
(c) orange juice, clear tea, chicken soup, muddy water
(d) carbon dioxide, oxygen, water, copper sulphate
(e) carbon, hydrogen, oxygen, water

C4. Refer to the kinetic molecular theory in Chapter 5 (page 122).

(a) Which part(s) of the theory explain what happens when liquid candle wax solidifies?
(b) Use the theory to explain what happens when salt is dissolved in water.

C5. Different samples of a compound always have the same properties, but different samples of a mixture may have different properties. Explain this statement, using the kinetic molecular theory in your explanation.

C6. Flour is stirred into water. Will this mixture be a suspension or a solution? Explain.

C7. The pie graph in Figure 6.32 shows the elements that are present in the crust of the Earth. Compare this pie graph with the illustration of the elements present in the human body (Figure 6.33).

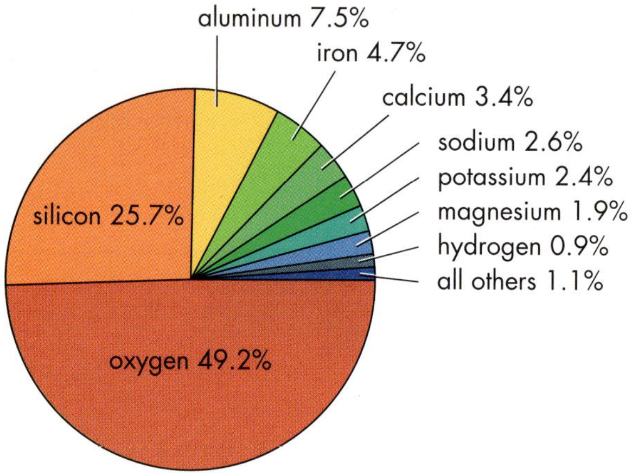

FIGURE 6.32
The proportions of elements in the Earth's crust

(a) What similarities can you see?
(b) What element makes up a large part of the crust of the Earth but very little of the human body?
(c) What element makes up a large part of the human body but less than 1 per cent of the crust of the Earth?

C8. In a supermarket, items for sale are arranged on the shelves according to several systems of classification.

(a) How are the items classified?
(b) How do these systems of classification help you?
(c) Describe at least three other ways in which supermarket items could be classified.
(d) Would any of these classification systems make it easier to find what you want in the store? Explain.

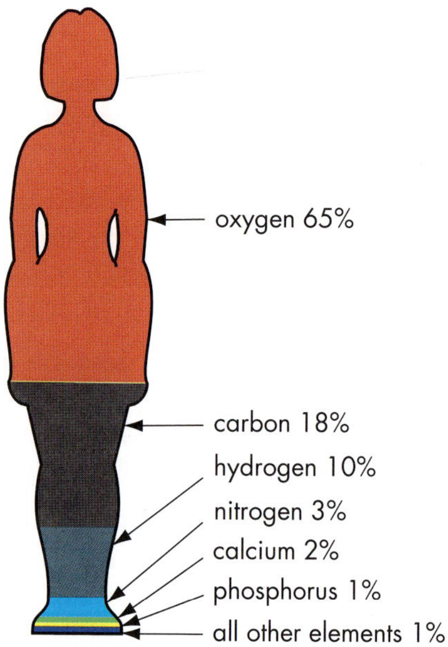

FIGURE 6.33
The proportions of elements in the human body

C9. Create your own original version of Figure 6.25; instead of boxes, use your own creative set of shapes. You could use a theme for your picture. For example, you could use a tree to represent matter and parts of the tree to represent the types of matter.

EXPLORATIONS

E1. With the permission of your parent or guardian, try eating a soft-boiled egg with a silver teaspoon. Afterward, observe how the spoon has changed. Find out how you can restore its original appearance and then do so. Using a reference book, identify any physical or chemical changes.

E2. At home, investigate the densities of some common fruits and vegetables such as apples, grapes, carrots, or lettuce. List the names in two lists, entitled "Density less than 1.0 g/cm^3" and "Density more than 1.0 g/cm^3."

E3. (a) Solder, an alloy of lead and tin, has a low melting point. Solder is used to join metals together. You may see solder in electrical wiring in your house or in some tins of canned food. Find out why lead solder is used in some tins but is not allowed in others. Examine some empty tins and bring examples of different types to show to the class.

(b) In the past, lead has been used in the glaze on dishes, in cooking pots, and in household water pipes. Lead is no longer used for these purposes. If people take lead into their bodies with their food or water, the nervous system can be damaged. Using sources in the library, find out the maximum recommended lead levels in blood, and how high lead levels affect the nervous system. Report to your class about an incident in which someone suffered from lead poisoning.

E4. There are many kinds of steel with many different properties. These different properties are the result of different materials added to iron to make the steel. In a reference book, find out how steel is made. Choose one kind of steel and create a poster illustrating how it is made, what it is made of, and how it is used.

E5. Suppose you accidentally invented a solvent in the laboratory. When this substance is in the liquid state, between –5°C and 25°C, it dissolves everything. Draw a cartoon strip or write an illustrated story describing the problems this new solvent might cause.

E6. Examine the list of elements in Figure 6.2 on page 133.

(a) Name at least five elements that appear to have been named after countries or other land areas.

(b) Name at least three elements that appear to have been named after people.

(c) Find out who these people were and why they were important.

REFLECTIONS

Think back over what you have learned in this chapter. How have your ideas about classification of matter changed? How have they remained the same? In what ways is the classification of matter related to your daily life? Write your ideas in your learning journal.

CHAPTER 7

WORKING WITH MIXTURES

Does your family have a "junk drawer" somewhere, maybe in the kitchen or near the door? Have you ever tried to sort all the pieces of junk that have collected? You might pick out old toys, broken gadgets, pieces of wire and string, or maybe an old shopping list. If you're lucky, you might find a few coins.

In everyday life, there are many situations when people want to separate the parts of mixtures. You don't want to find mud or algae or fish from the river in your drinking water — you prefer to have these removed from the water before it is pumped to your house. In factories, harmful or toxic substances must be removed from any waste products before they can be released into the environment. Depending on the mixture involved, separating the parts can be easy or difficult.

In this chapter, you will learn some skills that are useful in working with mixtures. You will find out how to separate different types of mixtures, how to make solutions, and how some simple mixtures are used.

ACTIVITY 7A / BRAINSTORMING SEPARATION METHODS

How can you separate the parts of mixtures?

MATERIALS

safety goggles
apron
mixtures prepared by your teacher

PROCEDURE

1. Put on your safety goggles and apron.
2. In a small group, examine the mixtures that your teacher has prepared and the ones shown in Figure 7.1. Brainstorm ways in which the parts of each mixture could be separated. (Hint: Think of the properties of each part. Does one part float or sink in water? Does one of the parts dissolve in water? Could you separate the parts with tweezers?)
3. Discuss the methods the students in your group have suggested. Predict whether or not these methods of separating mixtures would work well.

DISCUSSION

1. Make a list of the methods suggested by the students in your class.
2. For each method, try to explain why you think it would or would not work. ❖

FIGURE 7.1
Mixtures

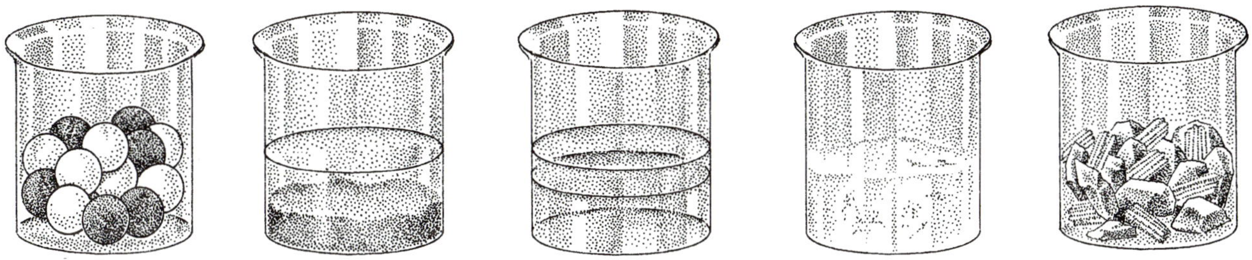

(a) marbles and Styrofoam balls **(b)** soil and water **(c)** oil and water **(d)** salt and pepper **(e)** wood chips and pieces of brick

7.1 SEPARATING MECHANICAL MIXTURES AND SUSPENSIONS

Would you drink the water from the river shown in Figure 7.2 on page 162? This water probably contains a mixture of soil, tiny plants and animals, and dissolved chemicals. Many cities obtain their water supply from a source such as this. The water is first treated at a water treatment plant to make it safe. One of the techniques used to make the water safe to drink is **filtration**. The water is passed through a **filter**, which allows the liquid to go through but holds back larger objects. The liquid that passes through the filter is called the **filtrate**. The solid material that does not pass through the filter is called the **residue**. A filter can be made from a wire screen or mesh with holes, but it can also consist of a material such as sand or charcoal.

FIGURE 7.2
The Fraser River

ACTIVITY 7B / MAKING A FILTER

In some water treatment plants, water is filtered through sand filters. In this activity, you will make a sand filter.

MATERIALS

safety goggles
apron
plastic bottle with bottom cut off (transparent if possible)
support stand
ring clamp
250 mL beaker
chunks of clay
fine sand
coarse sand
small stones
large stones
muddy water (or water and sawdust)
timer or watch

FIGURE 7.3
Once you have set up the equipment, you still have a few practical details to work out. Write them in your notebook.

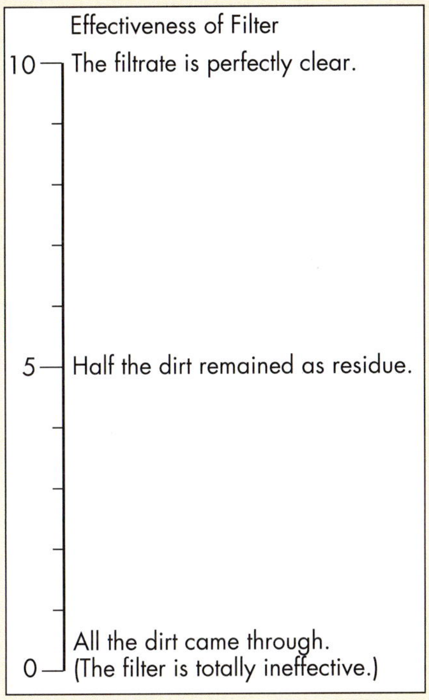

FIGURE 7.4

On your scale, add more labels to show your meaning for each number.

PROCEDURE

1. Put on your safety goggles and apron.
2. Plan how you could use the set-up shown in Figure 7.3 to make a filter to separate the "dirty" matter from the water.
3. In a group design your own filter. Inform your teacher of your plans. Try out your filter and make any changes that you think will make it work better.
4. Pour 250 mL of the dirty water through your filter. In your notebook, record the number of seconds it takes for all the water to pass through.

DISCUSSION

1. Examine your filtrate. Compare it with the original mixture. How effective was your filter in separating solid material from the water? Use a scale from 0 to 10, similar to the one in Figure 7.4. Give your filtrate a rating and record it in your notebook.
2. One student will record the data from the class, including filtering time and the effectiveness rating for each of the filters made by the groups of students in the class. What observations can be made about the data presented?
3. What materials or combinations of materials made the filters that worked best? Explain why you think these worked best.
4. (a) What was the fastest filtering time in your class?
   (b) What was the slowest filtering time?
   (c) More effective filters are often slower than less effective ones. Was this true in your class? If so, explain why.
5. In your notebook, draw a diagram of the best filtration apparatus you can design. Use features from any of the filters made by the students in your class, and any other features you can think of.
6. Would you be prepared to drink the clear filtrate from the best filter in your class? Explain why or why not. ❖

FILTERS

Filters are commonly used whenever solid pieces of matter must be removed from other solids, liquids, or gases (Figure 7.5). For example, air is filtered in car engines, factory smokestacks, and hospital operating rooms. Window screens act as filters, keeping annoying insects out of houses. Workers who use spray paint wear face masks so that they don't breathe in droplets of paint. Tea bags keep tea leaves out of tea, and coffee filters keep coffee grounds out of coffee. Can you think of other examples of filters?

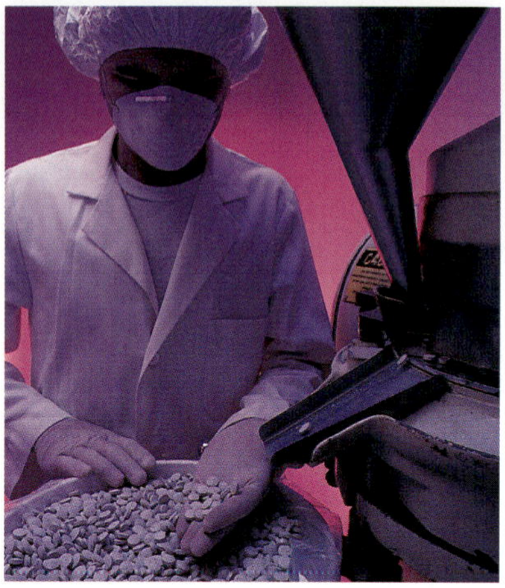

(a)

(b)

FIGURE 7.5
(a) Some industrial workers use face filters to keep particles in their breath from reaching the product. (b) Smokestacks have filters to remove some of the solid particles from the gases that are released.

ACTIVITY 7C / USING FILTER PAPER

Even very fine sand cannot remove the smallest bits of solids from water. To do this, a filter with much smaller holes is needed. In this activity, you will use filter paper to separate mixtures.

MATERIALS

safety goggles
apron
funnel
support stand
ring clamp
250 mL beaker
filter paper
stirring rod
liquid mixtures, such as tomato juice, soil and water, flour and water, charcoal powder and water, or a cloudy filtrate from Activity 7B

PROCEDURE

1. Put on your safety goggles and apron.
2. Set up a support stand, ring clamp, and funnel. Place an empty beaker under the funnel.
3. Prepare the filter paper as shown in Figure 7.6.

(a)

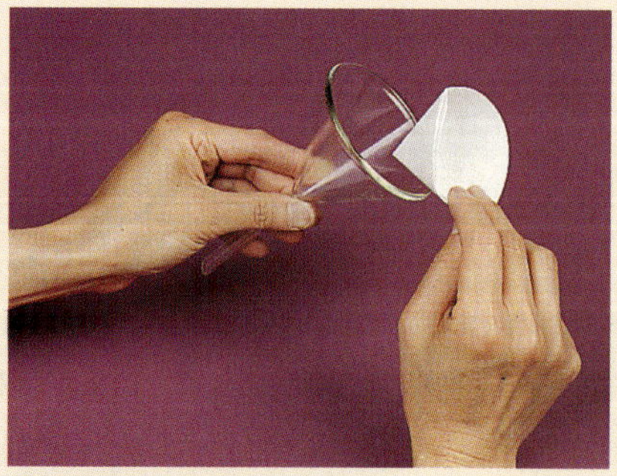

(b)

FIGURE 7.6
(a) Fold the filter paper twice, then shape it into a cone.
(b) Wet the funnel and fit the cone of filter paper into it.

FIGURE 7.7
Pour slowly so that the level of liquid in the funnel stays below the edge of the filter paper.

4. After you have put the cone of filter paper into the funnel, gently place the funnel into the ring clamp (Figure 7.7).
5. Pour the mixture assigned to your group into the filter paper and collect the filtrate in the beaker.
6. While your mixture is being filtered, prepare a table in your notebook with these headings: "Description of Mixture," "Description of Filtrate," and "Description of Residue."
7. In your table, list all the mixtures that were filtered by the class. Describe the appearance of each filtrate and each residue.

DISCUSSION

1. Compare the appearance of the filtrates for the groups in your class. How are they the same?
2. For any filtrate that looked cloudy, suggest what caused its cloudiness.
3. Draw a labelled diagram of the equipment you used in this activity.
4. (a) Suggest at least one advantage of using filter paper over using a sand filter like the one used in Activity 7B.
   (b) Suggest at least one advantage of using a sand filter over using filter paper.
5. List as many kinds of filters as you can. Ask your family and friends for suggestions. Ask office workers, mechanics, restaurant employees, factory workers, engineers, and people in other occupations to suggest examples of filters. Make a sketch of one or more of these filters and explain how it works. ❖

WHEN DOES FILTRATION WORK BEST?

Even very small bits and pieces of substances can be removed from mixtures by filtration if the holes in the filtering material are small enough. Liquids and gases have no bits and pieces that can be held back by a filter. Thus, filters can be used to separate solids from mechanical mixtures or suspensions, but can not be used to separate the parts of solutions.

WATER TREATMENT PLANTS

Water treatment plants use separation methods to produce clean, drinkable water from a lake or a river. The diagram in Figure 7.8 shows you the inside of a water treatment plant. Intake pipes covered with screens filter out larger material such as plants, fish, or pieces of debris. In a process called sedimentation, a chemical is added to the water to make small pieces of mud stick together in clumps; after several hours, these heavier clumps settle to the bottom of the sedimentation tanks and are removed. The water then passes through sand filters that

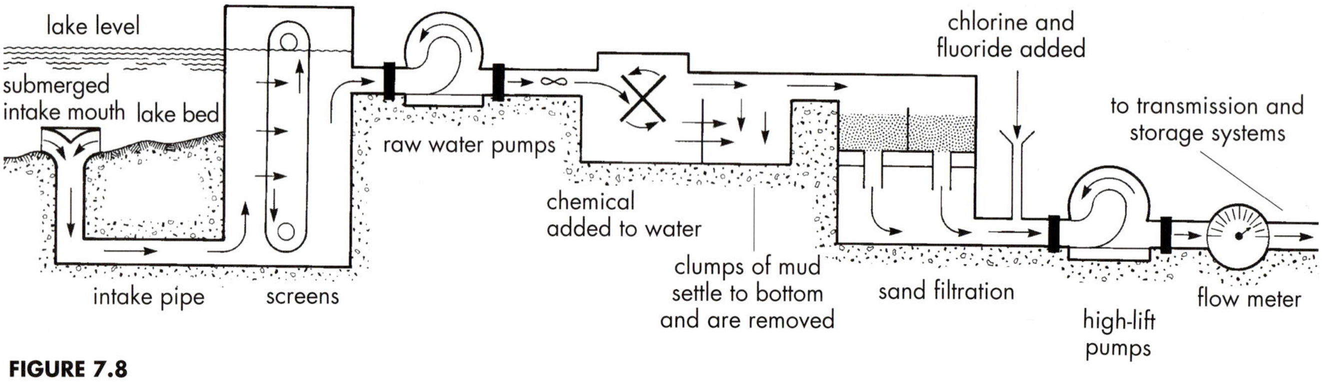

FIGURE 7.8
How a water treatment plant works

remove smaller bits of dirt from the water. Finally, small amounts of chlorine are added to kill tiny plants and animals, and a chemical called fluoride may be added to the water to help prevent tooth decay.

PREVENTING SEPARATION

Sometimes it is necessary to prevent mixtures from separating. In the food industry, several substances may be used to do this. In salad dressings, for example, oil and vinegar separate into layers unless another substance, called an **emulsifier**, is added to the mixture (Figure 7.9). The emulsifier in a salad dressing helps the oil and vinegar stay mixed as the liquid is being poured. Egg is often used as an emulsifier in foods.

FIGURE 7.9 ▶
Egg yolks can be used as emulsifiers in salad dressings.

ACTIVITY 7D / USING AN EMULSIFIER

In this activity, you will see how an emulsifier works.

MATERIALS

safety goggles
apron
salad oil
vinegar
egg yolk
two test tubes
rubber stoppers for test tubes

PROCEDURE

1. Put on your safety goggles and apron.

2. In each test tube, pour oil to a depth of about 1 cm, and add an equal volume of vinegar. To the first test tube, add two drops of egg yolk.

3. Put the stoppers into the tubes and turn them upside down several times to mix the contents thoroughly.

DISCUSSION

1. What happened when you mixed the contents in each test tube? Use a sketch of the test tubes in your description. Colour and label your sketch to show any differences in the test tubes.

2. Egg yolk, gelatin, corn syrup, and cornstarch are all common emulsifiers. In your kitchen at home, find five products that contain one or more of these emulsifiers. List these products in your notebook. ❖

► REVIEW 7.1

1. List five uses for filters. You may include examples from home, leisure activities, and the workplace.

2. Describe how you would separate the parts of the following mixtures. For each mixture, explain what makes the separation method work.
(a) sand and salt
(b) dust in a fluffy blanket
(c) sawdust and sand
(d) pebbles and sand
(e) flour and water

3. Describe two examples of mixtures that you think could not be separated by filtration. Explain in each case why this method would not work.

4. (a) Where is the filter located in a vacuum cleaner?
(b) Describe the residue and the filtrate.
(c) What problems do you think would occur if the holes in the filter in a vacuum cleaner were too small or too large?

7.2 SEPARATING SOLUTIONS

It is not always easy to tell whether you are looking at a solution or a pure substance. For example, most water, even rainwater, contains dissolved substances. As rain or snow falls through the air, it dissolves some carbon dioxide gas from the air. On reaching the ground, the rainwater trickles over soil and rocks, dissolving chemicals as it goes. The familiar taste of your drinking water is caused by all these solutes (Figure 7.10).

DID YOU KNOW

■ Have you ever visited another town or city and thought that the tap water tasted strange? In a different area, with different rocks and soils, the water contains a different combination of dissolved chemicals. It may taste strange to you but quite normal to someone who lives there. How do you think pure water, with no solute dissolved in it, would taste?

There are many ways to separate the parts of solutions. Many of these methods involve changes of state such as boiling, condensing, solidifying, or evaporating. In this section, you will investigate several of these methods.

FIGURE 7.10
Trace the path of the water. What kinds of substances will it pick up in its journey from clouds to the sea?

CHEW A PETROPRODUCT

Did you chew some gum today? Or listen to music on a tape player? If so, you used some "petroproducts." In fact, you use hundreds of products made from petroleum every single day.

The products of petroleum (crude oil) range from fuels for cars, planes, and other vehicles to plastics and synthetic fibres such as nylon, to sunscreen lotions, paints, cosmetics, dental floss, plastic pens and tapes, medicines, glues, mattresses, food preservatives, and even one of the ingredients in chewing gum. These diverse products have one thing in common: they all start out deep underground as crude oil.

Changing a blob of crude oil into useful products doesn't require any magic. All it takes is some science and technology.

Crude oil is first separated into its liquid parts, or fractions. To do this, the crude oil is heated to about 370°C so that most of the liquids turn into gases, or vapours. These vapours are channelled into the bottom of a tall tower called a fractionating column. As the vapours rise in the column, they cool and condense back into liquids. Since each substance in the crude oil condenses at a different temperature, each one also condenses at a different level in the fractionating column. Trays located at various heights in the column collect the different liquids. Then pipes transport the liquids away for further processing.

Some of the liquids are blended and purified to make fuels such as gasoline, kerosene, propane, motor oil, and home heating oil. Others are used as petrochemicals, the building blocks of plastics, vinyls, synthetic fibres, and many other petroproducts.

Check out the petroleum in your wardrobe. Which clothes are made of synthetic fibres? List the names of the synthetic materials that are printed on the labels.

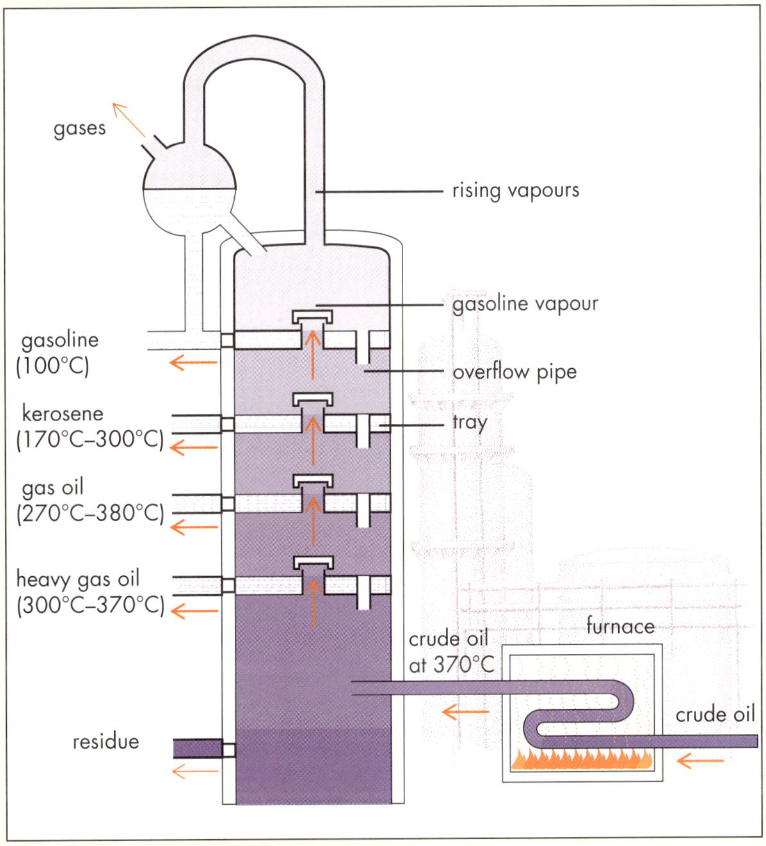

ACTIVITY 7E / EVAPORATION

In this activity, you will use evaporation to compare solutions and to find out whether an unknown liquid is a solution or a pure substance.

MATERIALS

Parts I and II
safety goggles
apron

Part I
three watch glasses
three samples of water, such as ocean water, city tap water, and distilled water

Part II
watch glasses
samples of unknown liquids

EXTENSION

■ Water is described as being "hard" or "soft" depending on what chemicals are dissolved in it. Rainwater is "soft" because it does not contain chemicals that prevent soap from foaming. Water in the ground, especially in areas where there are limestone rocks, may be "hard." In a reference book, read about "hard" and "soft" water.

PART I Comparing Samples of Water

PROCEDURE

1. Put on your safety goggles and apron.
2. Half-fill a watch glass with each of the samples of water.
3. Set the watch glasses aside for a few days or until all of each liquid evaporates.

DISCUSSION

1. Use the kinetic molecular theory to explain what has happened to the water in each watch glass.
2. After the water evaporated, were any of the watch glasses perfectly empty? Explain why or why not.
3. (a) Describe the three watch glasses after the water evaporated and sketch the appearance of each.
   (b) Explain how the three samples of water were different from each other.

PART II Pure Substance or Solution?

PROCEDURE

1. Put on your safety goggles and apron.
2. Half-fill the watch glasses with the unknown liquids supplied by your teacher.
3. Set the watch glasses aside for a few days or until all the liquids evaporate.

DISCUSSION

1. Identify which materials were mechanical mixtures, which were solutions, and which were pure substances. Give reasons for your answers.
2. What happened to the liquids? (Explain according to the kinetic molecular theory.)
3. What differences between the particles of solute and particles of solvent cause them to separate by evaporation? ❖

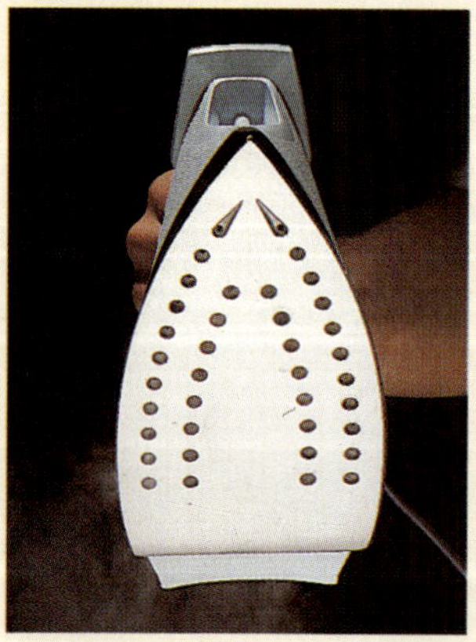

FIGURE 7.11 ◀
Why do you think that distilled water, rather than tap water, is recommended for use in steam irons?

CRYSTALLIZATION

When part of a solution evaporates, the solute may begin to **crystallize**, or form crystals. **Crystals** are solids that occur in nature. They have straight edges, flat sides, and regular angles. Not all pure substances can form crystals. But each substance that forms crystals has its own special crystal shape. Some crystals are soluble in water, but others are not. Figure 7.12 shows several types of crystals.

EXTENSION

■ Use a hand lens to examine a variety of crystals, such as the ones in Figure 7.12. Sketch one crystal of each substance and describe its shape.

(a)

(b)

(c)

(d)

FIGURE 7.12
Crystals of common substances: (a) tungsten, (b) cane sugar (sucrose), (c) calcite, and (d) sea salt

DISTILLATION

You have seen how the solute can be recovered from a solution by evaporation. Using the process of **distillation**, you can separate the parts of a solution and recover both the solute and the solvent. The liquid solvent that is collected during distillation is called the **distillate**. The mixture of substances that remains in the original container is called the residue. To distill a solution quickly, you need to add a lot of heat.

DID YOU KNOW

■ Your body produces a solution, called urine, to get rid of wastes. Usually the waste solids remain dissolved in the liquid. Sometimes, however, substances that were once dissolved in urine may solidify and form a lump, called a kidney stone, within the kidney. If this lump blocks the flow of urine, intense pain can result. Occasionally a small stone may pass out of the body along with the urine. Usually, however, the stone must be broken up or removed.

ACTIVITY 7F / DISTILLATION (*TEACHER DEMONSTRATION*)

In this activity, you will observe how both solvent and solute can be separated and recovered from a solution.

MATERIALS

safety goggles
apron
250 mL flask
hotplate
clamp
test tube
support stand
beaker
rubber stopper
boiling chips
solution, such as copper sulphate solution
glass and rubber tubing apparatus

PROCEDURE

1. Put on your safety goggles and apron.
2. Your teacher will set up the apparatus as shown in Figure 7.13, heat the solution until it boils, then turn down the heat and allow the solution to boil gently.
3. The heat will be turned off while there is still about 1 cm of solution in the flask.

DISCUSSION

1. In your notebook, describe the solution in the flask at the beginning of the demonstration.
2. Describe the residue at the end of the demonstration. Does the residue look different from the original solution?
3. Describe the distillate at the end of the demonstration. How is it different from the solution in the flask?
4. What observation indicates that the solute and solvent have separated?
5. (a) Identify the changes of state in this distillation.
   (b) Where did each change of state occur?
6. Why do you think that the heat must be turned off while there is still solution in the flask?
7. Two safety precautions are included in Figure 7.13. For each one, suggest what danger or problem is prevented.
8. Use the kinetic molecular theory to explain the changes of state that you observed during distillation. ❖

CAUTION!

■ The glass tube must be removed from the test tube and left out in the air before the heat is turned off. The heat must be turned off while there is still liquid in the flask. The flask must not be allowed to boil dry.

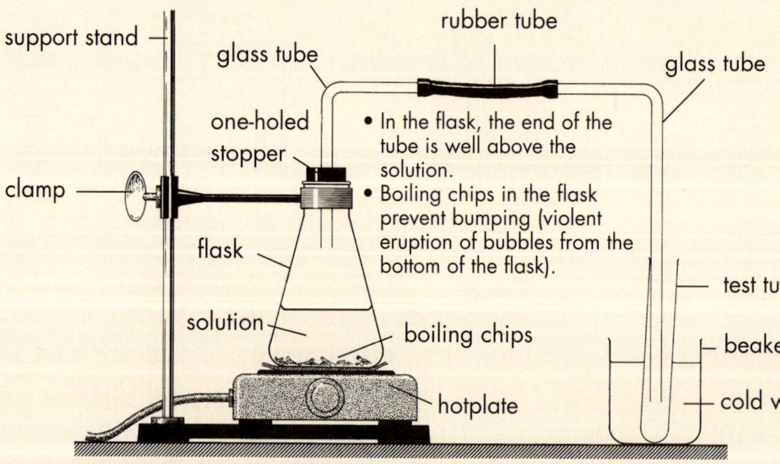

FIGURE 7.13 ▶
Apparatus for distillation

SEPARATION METHODS

You have learned several ways to separate the parts of mixtures, and you have tried several techniques yourself. You should be familiar with:

- dissolving one part but not the other
- filtering (using a variety of filters)
- picking apart the bits (with or without a hand lens)
- floating and/or sinking the parts in water
- evaporating part of a solution
- crystallizing part of a solution
- distilling a solution

ACTIVITY 7G / USING SEPARATION METHODS

GROUP ACTIVITY

In this activity, you will design an efficient and practical way to solve a separation problem.

MATERIALS

safety goggles
apron
mixture of three or more substances
your choice of the equipment available

CAUTION!

- **Check with your teacher about safety precautions.**

PROCEDURE

1. Put on your safety goggles and apron.
2. Examine your mixture carefully. In your group, discuss the properties of the various substances in it. Then brainstorm how your mixture could be separated (Figure 7.14).
3. List the steps in the separation procedure you have devised. Beside each step, predict what will happen.
4. Obtain your teacher's permission, then carry out your procedure.
5. (a) Several groups should list their separation procedures on posters or on the board.
   (b) Discuss each procedure. What problems occurred? Were any steps left out?
   (c) Would it help to change the equipment or procedure? How?
6. In your notebook, write a summary of your group's work.
7. Wash your hands thoroughly after you have completed the activity. ❖

FIGURE 7.14 ▶
Consider a variety of separation procedures.

▶ REVIEW 7.2

1. In your notebook, write the descriptions of separation methods in list A and match each description with the separation technique in list B.

LIST A

(a) One substance changes to a gas and then changes back to a liquid.

(b) The solute separates from the solvent, forming a solid.

(c) One substance changes to a gas more readily than the other.

(d) One of the substances has pieces of a different size than those of the other substance.

LIST B

1. crystallization
2. filtration
3. evaporation
4. distillation

2. Explain the meaning of: filtrate, distillate, crystal. If you like, use diagrams in your explanations.

3. Use the kinetic molecular theory to describe what occurs in one of the separation methods listed in question 1.

4. Examine the diagram of a solar still in Figure 7.15. This is a device used to produce pure water from sea water.

(a) What mixture is being separated?

(b) What is the effect of the heat from the sun?

(c) What separation process does the solar still use?

(d) Identify the distillate in this separation.

(e) How do you think the residue in the dishpan is different from the original mixture?

(f) Why do you think this device is called a solar still?

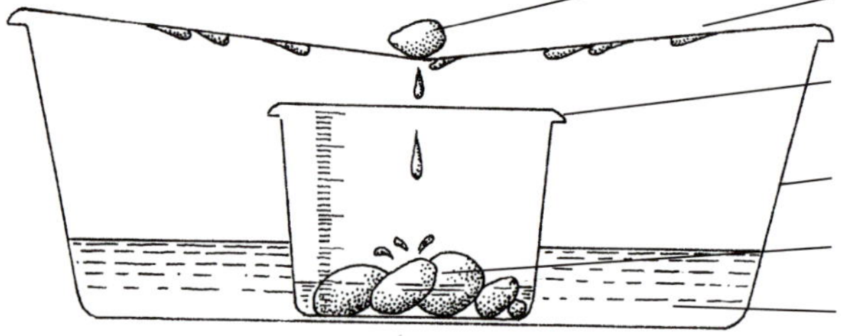

FIGURE 7.15
A solar still (solar distillation apparatus)

■ 7.3 DISSOLVING

Have you ever tried to mix an ice-cold drink, such as lemonade, in a hurry and found that the sugar seemed to take forever to dissolve? What could you do to speed up the dissolving process? Would you heat the solution? Cool it? Stir it or shake it? Put it in the dark or in the light? Transfer it to a larger or a smaller container? Grind up the solute or leave it in large pieces? In this section, you will investigate these questions and other questions and see how the kinetic molecular theory can be used to explain your results.

ACTIVITY 7H / TESTING PREDICTIONS

In this activity, you will work with a group of students to investigate how quickly solids dissolve.

MATERIALS

safety goggles
apron
solid solute, such as sugar, table salt, potassium chloride, aluminum sulphate
beakers, test tubes, stirrers, etc., as needed
timer or watch

PROCEDURE

1. With your group, brainstorm all the factors that could possibly affect how quickly a solute dissolves. List these factors in your notebook.
2. Use the key points of the kinetic molecular theory on page 122 to make a hypothesis about at least two methods you could use that might make a solid dissolve faster in water.
3. Choose *one* of the methods and design a controlled experiment that will allow you to test your hypothesis. List the factors that will be controlled in your experiment.
4. Check your procedure with your teacher.
5. Put on your safety goggles and apron, and try out your procedure. Use a watch or clock to measure from the time the solute is added to the water until it has completely dissolved.
6. Wash your hands thoroughly after you have completed the activity.

DISCUSSION

1. List all the procedures tested by the groups in your class. Beside each procedure, indicate whether it speeded up the dissolving process, slowed it down, or did not affect the speed at all.
2. For each procedure that speeded up the dissolving process, use the kinetic molecular theory to explain what happened.
3. Suggest at least two procedures that you predict would have no effect on the speed of dissolving. ❖

CONCENTRATION OF SOLUTIONS

Solutions made up of the same substances may contain different amounts of each substance. The solution with less solute is said to be more **dilute**. The solution with more solute is said to be more **concentrated**. For example, lemonade with a small amount of dissolved sugar in it is a more dilute solution of sugar than lemonade with a lot of sugar dissolved in it. The lemonade with more sugar is more concentrated and tastes sweeter than the more dilute solution does (Figure 7.16).

FIGURE 7.16
When you add sugar to your lemonade, do you prefer a more dilute or a more concentrated solution?

There is a limit to how concentrated a solution can become. When a solution contains as much solute as it can possibly hold at that temperature, it is said to be **saturated**. If more solute is added to the solution, the solute will not dissolve. A solution of one substance in water may be saturated when only a little solute has dissolved. A saturated solution of another substance may contain a lot of solute.

ACTIVITY 7I / COMPARING SOLUTES

GROUP ACTIVITY G

In this activity, you will compare saturated solutions of various solutes.

MATERIALS

safety goggles
apron
test tube
rubber stopper for test tube
graduated cylinder
solid solute, such as table salt, sugar, potassium chloride, aluminum sulphate, or other substance
scoopula (or 2 mL measuring spoon)

PROCEDURE

1. Each group of students will use a different solute. To compare the results of different groups, all groups must use identical methods of mixing. Decide exactly how to mix the solution and how much time to allow for the last bits of solute to dissolve.
2. Put on your safety goggles and apron.
3. Pour 10 mL of water into the test tube. Add 1 scoop of the solute assigned to your group, insert the stopper, mix the contents, and then remove the stopper.
4. If all the solute dissolves, add another scoop, insert the stopper, and mix. Keep track of how many scoops you have added.
5. Repeat step 4 until some undissolved solute remains at the bottom of the test tube. The solution is now saturated.
6. Record the total number of scoops of solute that dissolved. Save or dispose of your solution as your teacher directs.
7. Summarize the class results in a table.
8. Wash your hands thoroughly after you have completed the activity.

DISCUSSION

1. Record the number of scoops of the various solutes that were needed to make a saturated solution in 10 mL of water. List the solutes used by your class in order, from the most soluble to the least soluble.
2. Draw a bar graph like the one in Figure 7.17 to illustrate how many scoops of the various solutes were required to make a saturated solution in 10 mL of water. ❖

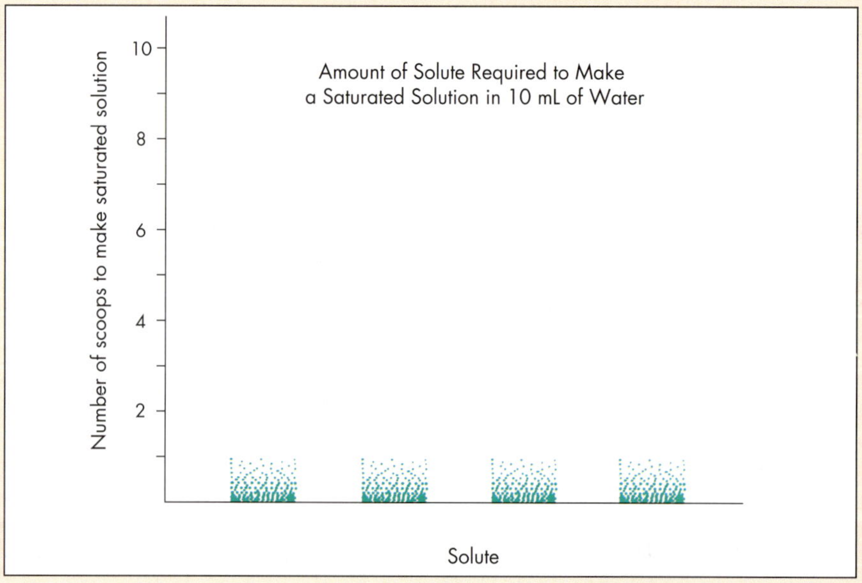

FIGURE 7.17 ▶ ***Include a bar of appropriate height for each solute used in your class. Label the bars.***

DISSOLVING AND THE KINETIC MOLECULAR THEORY

To speed the dissolving process, you can stir or shake the mixture of solute and solvent to increase the mixing of the two kinds of particles. Heating the mixture also speeds dissolving. As you have learned, increasing the temperature makes the particles of the mixture move about more than they do at lower temperatures (Figure 7.18). This explains why raising the temperature speeds dissolving — the particles of both the solute and the solvent are moving about more quickly, so they mix more quickly.

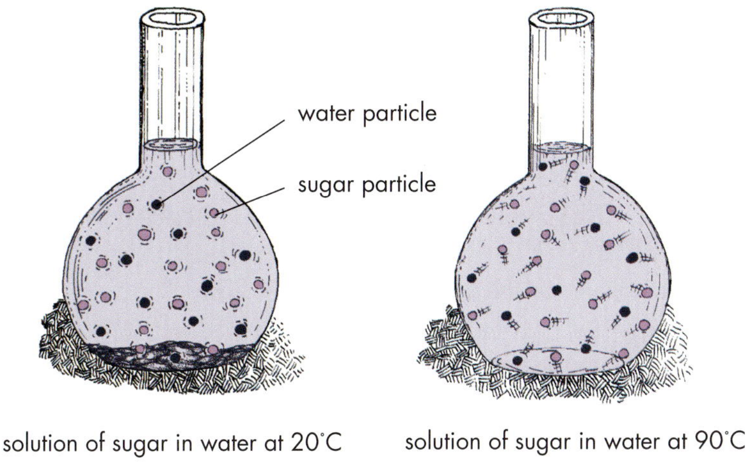

FIGURE 7.18
At a higher temperature, the particles of both the solid and the liquid are moving more quickly, so they mix together more quickly.

REVIEW 7.3

1. Read the following statements. Indicate which solution in each statement is more dilute and which is more concentrated.
   (a) Rainwater contains a small amount of dissolved carbon dioxide gas, but a soft drink contains much more of this gas.
   (b) Amin mixed so much sugar in his tea that he did not want to drink it, but Rachel added only one lump of sugar to hers.
   (c) Angela thought the fruit punch was much too sweet; the apple juice was more to her liking.

2. Which of the solutions mentioned in question 1 might be saturated? Give a reason for your answer.

3. Describe two situations in everyday life in which it is important to know how much solute is being added to a solvent. Do not use examples described in this chapter.

4. "Dilute" and "concentrated" are words that are used to describe solutions *qualitatively*. A *quantitative* description involves measurement or counting. Think of three ways in which you could describe the concentration of a solution in a quantitative way. Include information about both the amount of solute and the amount of solvent or solution. (Hint: The descriptions could involve measurements of mass and/or volume.)

7.4 USING SOLUTIONS IN A COLD CLIMATE

As you have learned, different substances have different properties because every pure substance is made up of different kinds of atoms. Thus, each pure substance has its own melting point, freezing point, and boiling point. Adding a solute to a substance changes the melting point, freezing point, or boiling point of the solution.

ACTIVITY 7J / CHANGING THE FREEZING POINT OF A SOLUTION

GROUP ACTIVITY

In this activity, you will investigate the effect of solutes on the freezing point of water.

MATERIALS

Parts I and II
safety goggles
apron
mixture of crushed ice and water (or snow and water)
250 mL beaker
large demonstration thermometer (optional)
thermometer
centigram balance
stirring rod

Part I
table salt (sodium chloride)

Part II
various solutes, such as sugar, antifreeze, calcium chloride, propanol, aluminum sulphate

CAUTION!

Some solutes may be poisonous or flammable. Follow your teacher's instructions for using them and disposing of them.

PART I (Teacher Demonstration) Salt

PROCEDURE

1. Put on your safety goggles and apron.
2. Your teacher will half-fill a beaker with a mixture of ice or snow and a little water. Let it sit for 5 min. Occasionally observe the temperature during this time.
3. Your teacher will use the balance to measure 20 g of salt.
4. Your teacher will add 20 g of salt to the beaker and gently stir the mixture with the stirring rod. Observe the temperature again.

DISCUSSION

1. Describe the effect of the salt on the temperature in the beaker.
2. What do you think would have happened if 40 g of salt had been added instead of 20 g?

PART II How Cold Will It Get?

PROCEDURE

1. With your group, decide which solute to investigate.
2. Design an experiment to test the effect of the solute on the temperature of a mixture of ice or snow and water. Questions that you might investigate include:
   (a) How does this solute change the temperature of the mixture?
   (b) How do different amounts of solute change the temperature of the mixture?
   (c) What is the lowest temperature that can be reached using this method?
3. Write a step-by-step procedure and get the approval of your teacher to carry it out.
4. Put on your safety goggles and apron.
5. Carry out your experiment.
6. Wash your hands thoroughly after you have completed the activity.

CAUTION!

■ Use a stirring rod to stir the mixtures. Do not use the thermometer for stirring.

DISCUSSION

1. Summarize your class results in a table.

FIGURE 7.19 ▶
An old-fashioned ice-cream maker

2. (a) Homemade ice cream (Figure 7.19) requires a mixture of ingredients, an ice-cream maker, and lots of salt. The salt is not added to the ice cream. Why do you think salt is needed?
   (b) Design an apparatus that you could use to freeze the ice cream as you continue to stir the ingredients. Draw a diagram of the apparatus in your notebook. ❖

SALTING ROADS

In winter, snow and ice can make driving dangerous. To melt the ice and reduce the danger, salt (sodium chloride) is often spread on roads. As the salt comes in contact with the snow, it dissolves. The dissolved salt lowers the freezing point of the liquid, causing some of the snow to melt. The resulting salt solution spreads out and prevents falling snow from sticking to the surface of the road. Snowploughs can then remove the mixture of unmelted snow and salt-water solution.

Salting roads makes driving safer, but it also causes some serious problems. In cities where salt is used, cars rust much more quickly. Salt also damages metal bridges, concrete parking garages, and the pavement itself (Figure 7.20). Spray from passing cars damages plant life up to 500 m from the road. If the concentration of salt in soil and streams increases, it may make the water in springs and wells unfit to drink.

DID YOU KNOW

■ In Canada's prairie provinces where temperatures often fall below −15°C, calcium chloride is sometimes spread on roads. Although calcium chloride works better than sodium chloride at lower temperatures, it costs more and causes similar environmental damage. Research is under way to find another solute that will work as well as sodium chloride and calcium chloride, that is cheaper, and that causes less damage to cars, bridges, pavement, and living organisms.

FIGURE 7.20 ◀
In the winter, salty water can trickle into cracks in a concrete road and cause the reinforcing steel to rust. The rust takes up more space than the steel, so the cracks get wider. Eventually, the road must be repaired and the rusty steel replaced.

ANTIFREEZE

The cooling system of a car contains liquid that circulates through the engine. The moving liquid, which is called a coolant, removes heat from the engine and transfers it to air passing through the radiator. If pure water were used as the coolant, the water would freeze when the engine was shut off in the winter. The engine might crack from the pressure of the ice forming inside. To prevent the liquid in the engine from freezing, antifreeze is added to the cooling system (Figure 7.21). Antifreeze (usually a mixture of water and ethylene glycol) has an extremely low freezing point. Depending on the lowest temperature expected, different concentrations of antifreeze are used.

FIGURE 7.21
Antifreeze can keep a car engine from freezing up in winter. This is because the freezing point of antifreeze is lower than the freezing point of water.

FIGURE 7.22
Antifreeze in the cooling system can keep a car engine from overheating. The boiling point of antifreeze is higher than the boiling point of water.

There is another reason to use antifreeze in a car engine. On a hot summer day, especially in slow-moving traffic, the engine temperature of a car can rise above 100°C, the boiling point of water (Figure 7.22). If the water in your car's cooling system were to boil, it would soon evaporate, causing the engine to overheat and be damaged. Antifreeze is used in the engine's cooling system in the summer as well as in the winter, because the antifreeze in the solution raises the boiling point above 100°C.

FIGURE 7.23
Snow-making equipment at Whistler Mountain

DID YOU KNOW

At ski resorts, artificial snow is made by spraying water into the air from high-pressure equipment (Figure 7.23). The water freezes in the cold air, forming crystals that fall as snow. Ski-resort operators want ice to form as quickly as possible, even when the temperature is fairly high. Researchers have developed a product that helps ice crystals form. When this product, which is made from a type of dead bacteria, is mixed with the spray, snow-making becomes easier.

REVIEW 7.4

1. For each group of words below, write an accurate statement containing all the words.
   (a) dilute, solvent, solute
   (b) concentrated, dilute, solution
   (c) saturated, solvent
   (d) solvent, solute, temperature
   (e) diffusion, soluble

2. (a) How is the freezing point of water affected by dissolved solutes?
   (b) Describe two ways in which this effect of solutes on freezing point is useful.

3. Cooks who make homemade candy from sugar and water usually use a specially made candy thermometer with temperature markings up to about 175°C. Explain why the sugar-water solution can be heated to such a high temperature.

4. In some Canadian cities, salt is used regularly on streets in the winter. But where there is too much snow or when the temperature is lower than –15°C, salt is no longer useful. In which of the cities listed in Table 7.1 do you think salt would be effective in melting the snow on roads? Explain your answer.

City	Average January temperature (°C)	Average January snowfall (cm)
Vancouver, British Columbia	3	26
Prince George, British Columbia	–12	61
Kamloops, British Columbia	–6	32
Calgary, Alberta	–12	19
Edmonton, Alberta	–17	29
Toronto, Ontario	–5	36
Montreal, Quebec	–10	53
Halifax, Nova Scotia	–6	63

TABLE 7.1 ***Temperature and Snowfall in Eight Canadian Cities***

CHAPTER REVIEW

KEY IDEAS

- Filtration can be used to separate the parts of mechanical mixtures and the parts of suspensions.
- Methods for separating the parts of solutions include evaporation, crystallization, and distillation.
- Dissolving can be speeded up by using a higher temperature, by stirring, or by using more solvent.
- If two solutions are compared, the solution with less solute is said to be more dilute and the one with more solute is said to be more concentrated.
- A solution that contains as much dissolved solute as possible at that temperature is said to be saturated.
- Dissolved solutes affect the freezing point and boiling point of liquids.
- Knowing about solutes and solvents can help you understand many everyday situations in which dissolving is important.

VOCABULARY

filtration
filter
filtrate
residue
emulsifier
crystallize
crystal
distillation
distillate
dilute
concentrated
saturated

V1. Use all the words from the vocabulary list and any other words you need to make a mind map about mixtures.

V2. Explain how the following pairs of words are related.
(a) filtrate, residue
(b) distillation, residue
(c) dilute, concentrated

CONNECTIONS

C1. Describe
(a) two mixtures that can be separated by filtration
(b) two mixtures that cannot be separated by filtration

C2. Write the letters (a) to (e) in your notebook. Then read the following statements. Beside each letter, write T if the statement is true and F if the statement is false. Rewrite each false statement, changing it to make it true.
(a) "Mixing" and "dissolving" have the same meaning.
(b) "Melting" and "dissolving" have the same meaning.
(c) In both filtration and distillation, there is a residue.
(d Water dissolves most solids.
(e) Antifreeze changes the freezing point of water.

C3. What separation methods could you use most easily to separate the parts of the following mixtures?
(a) copper sulphate and water
(b) oil and water
(c) feathers and sand
(d) wood chips and marbles

C4. Figure 7.24 shows identical uncooked eggs, one in a beaker of pure water and one in a beaker of salt water. Which beaker do you think contains pure water? Explain your answer.

C5. Use the kinetic molecular theory to explain what happens when sugar dissolves in water. Include a sketch in your answer.

C6. Think of a mixture that would be useful to separate. Describe the mixture and how you would separate the parts.

EXPLORATIONS

E1. Using only a cardboard box, cardboard, scissors, and tape, construct a mechanical sorter for pennies, nickels, dimes, quarters, and loonies. Compare your construction with a coin sorter used in your school office or cafeteria.

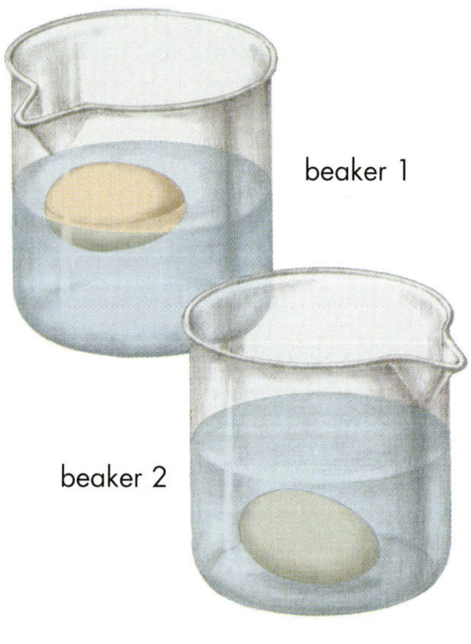

FIGURE 7.24
Why does one of the eggs float?

E2. (a) Sewage is an interesting mixture of substances! Besides food scraps, human waste, and chemicals, it also contains things that are dropped into street sewers — for example, wallets, coins, and watches. Design a method of separating and treating sewage so that it can be returned to the river as clean water. Your method may be similar, but not identical to, the treatment of drinking water described on pages 165–166.

(b) Arrange to tour a sewage treatment plant in your community. Find out when it first began operating and how it has been improved since that time.

E3. Soft drinks contain a lot of dissolved carbon dioxide gas. What keeps this gas dissolved in the liquid? Examine some pop bottles and cans and discuss the following questions with your class.

(a) Why do bottled soft drinks go "flat" if the top is not replaced tightly?

(b) Why do you think soft drinks are not sold in cardboard containers like milk cartons?

(c) Which remain fizzy for a longer time after they are opened, cold soft drinks or soft drinks that are left at room temperature? Explain your answer.

(d) Sketch and describe your own design for a new soft drink container. It should be

- reusable (so that the materials are not wasted)
- cheap (so that you will make a profit on sales)
- in one piece (so that discarded lids will not litter the landscape)
- convenient to store in your refrigerator

Evaluate the designs suggested by your classmates. Think of other features besides those mentioned here that you want to include in your own design.

E4. (a) How much carbon dioxide do you think there is in a typical soft drink? Ask your teacher to help you design an experiment to find out.

(b) Repeat your investigation, comparing the volumes of carbon dioxide in different kinds of soft drinks.

E5. Have you ever noticed that honey, once it starts to crystallize, rapidly becomes solid? It may remain liquid for months, then solidify in a week. Why does this happen so quickly (Figure 7.25)? Try putting two samples of liquid honey in clean jars. To one jar, add a spoonful of solid honey. Store both jars in the same place. After you have completed your observations, develop a hypothesis to explain what happened.

FIGURE 7.25
How does the addition of solid honey affect the crystallization of liquid honey?

REFLECTIONS

R1. How have your ideas about mixtures changed as you have worked through this chapter? In your learning journal, write a list of new things you have learned and how these are different from what you used to think.

R2. Many cities and towns use a river as their source of water. Their sewage treatment plant may empty into the same river, as shown in Figure 7.26. Some people say that towns should be required by law to have their intake pipe downstream from their sewage discharge pipe (that is, the reverse of the arrangement shown in Figure 7.26). Discuss with your class the advantages and disadvantages of this arrangement.

R3. Some factories that produce necessary and valuable products also contribute to air pollution because of the substances that are released into the air through their smokestacks. Removing these pollutants may be difficult, but it is not impossible. What do you think could be done to encourage industries to develop new ways of separating harmful substances so that they are not released into the environment?

FIGURE 7.26

Why might you want your town to have its water intake pipe upriver from its sewage treatment plant discharge pipe? What are the advantages to other river users if the intake pipe is downriver?

CHAPTER 8

MATTER FOR PERSONAL USE

Since the beginning of history, people have been painting their faces and bodies. In ancient Egypt, women used a black substance called kohl to line the edges of their eyelids. The Haida people painted their faces with charcoal, blue-green clay, and ochre, or iron ore, before attending a potlatch. Today many women in Canada and other countries use cosmetics such as lipstick and eyeshadow.

Cosmetics are one type of personal care product. Every day, you are bombarded with information and advertising about hundreds of personal care products. You are told to use Brand X toothpaste, wash your hair with Brand Y shampoo, use hand lotions, soaps, antiperspirants, foot powders, deodorants, hair gels, tissues, make-up, after-shave lotions, perfumes, hair conditioners, and dozens of other products. How do you decide what to buy? Are all these products really essential? What should you know about the products that you buy? For example, you might want to know what a product is made of and whether it contains any substance that might be harmful to the environment.

In advertisements, manufacturers make certain claims for their products. You can evaluate the claims by comparing one product with another or by testing how well an individual product works. You can also tell whether claims are based on scientific evidence or simply on personal opinion.

Science can help in your evaluation, but it cannot tell you everything. You must make the final decisions about personal care products, based on what you value most.

ACTIVITY 8A / PERSONAL CHOICES

CROSS · CURRICULAR

What do you want to know about the personal care products that you buy? What properties do you look for in personal care products? Do you care how the environment is affected by the products? To clarify these questions in your own mind, construct a mind map centred on the phrase "Personal Care Products." Write the names of some products that are familiar to you around this phrase. Then write down your ideas about how necessary these products are, how they affect the environment, and so on. Use lines and phrases to connect your ideas to each other, to the personal care products, and to the centre. ❖

8.1 PERSONAL CARE PRODUCTS

Personal care products are products you use to clean your body or to make yourself look or smell good. Think about the personal care products you use every day (Figure 8.1). For example, you probably use soap and toothpaste every day. Perhaps you also use lipstick, cologne, or hair gel. Most likely you buy all these products at a store.

FIGURE 8.1 ▶
Some personal products, like toothpaste, are good for your health. Name some products that are not necessary for your health, but help you feel good about yourself.

The personal care products you buy at a store are made by chemists, using scientific principles. Most of these products contain very simple ingredients, and anyone can use the same scientific principles that chemists use to make these products at home or in the laboratory.

EXTENSION

■ Make a list of all the brands of toothpaste available in a drugstore, indicating which brands contain fluoride. In a reference book, read about the effect of fluoride on teeth and report to your class.

TOOTHPASTE

Unpleasant odours in the mouth are caused by bacteria acting on leftover food particles. These bacteria also cause a more serious problem: tooth decay. The best way to avoid these problems is to floss your teeth and brush them with toothpaste every day.

ACTIVITY 8B / MAKING AND TESTING TOOTHPASTE

CROSS • CURRICULAR

In this activity, you will make homemade toothpaste and compare its cleaning ability with that of a commercially made toothpaste.

CAUTION!

- **Do not taste the homemade toothpastes.**

MATERIALS

Parts I and II
safety goggles
apron

Part I
centigram balance
beaker (100 mL)
5 mL measuring spoon
stirring rod
glycerine (glycerol)
distilled water
paper square (5 cm x 5 cm)
powdered castile soap
baking soda
mortar and pestle
blackboard chalk (about 2 cm long)
commercial toothpaste

Part II
three glass slides
aluminum foil
marking pen
hand lens

PART I Making Toothpaste

PROCEDURE

1. Put on your safety goggles and apron.
2. Mix 5 mL of glycerine and 5 mL of distilled water in a small beaker. Measure 0.5 g of Castile soap on a balance. Put the 0.5 g of soap on the paper square. Add the soap to the beaker and stir thoroughly.
3. Add baking soda a little at a time and mix until the consistency is similar to that of commercial toothpaste.
4. Divide your homemade toothpaste into two samples. Set one aside, labelled as sample A.
5. Use a mortar and pestle to grind the blackboard chalk to a fine powder. Add the chalk to the second sample of homemade toothpaste and stir thoroughly. Label this as sample B.
6. Label the commercial toothpaste as sample C.

DISCUSSION

1. Which of the functions listed here do you think your homemade toothpastes can perform?
   (a) act as an abrasive, polishing the teeth
   (b) whiten the teeth
   (c) taste good
2. Years ago, many toothpastes contained sugar. What problems might have resulted from the addition of sugar?

PART II Testing Cleaning Ability

PROCEDURE

1. Cover each of the three slides with aluminum foil, shiny side up. Label the slides A, B, and C. Make sure that the slides are on a flat surface so that they do not break.
2. Place a dab of sample A, sample B, and sample C on its proper slide. With your finger, rub the samples repeatedly on the same spot for about 1 min each.
3. Rinse the slides and examine them with a hand lens.

DISCUSSION

1. (a) Compare the effect of each test paste on the aluminum foil.
   (b) What effect do you think each paste would have on tooth enamel?
2. Many toothpastes contain an ingredient called precipitated chalk. This is similar to ground-up blackboard chalk.
   (a) What do you think the purpose of this ingredient is?
   (b) What might be the result of its continued use?
3. (a) Does this experiment actually test a toothpaste's cleaning ability?
   (b) Is this an example of a controlled experiment? Explain your answer.
4. Would you be willing to use homemade toothpaste regularly? Why? ❖

SOAP

Soap is the most widely used of all personal care products. Today many brands are available, but this has not always been so. In early pioneer times, families made soap from fats and the ashes of plants (Figure 8.2). Mixed with water and boiled in a kettle over an open fire, these simple ingredients were all that the soap-makers required.

Later, pioneer women were able to buy lye, which they used instead of ashes. Lye is a powerful chemical that is used in oven cleaners today but is considered much too strong for the skin. If too much lye was used in making the soap, it was very hard on the skin of people who used it.

FIGURE 8.2
Early Canadian pioneers making soap

All soaps contain the same type of cleaning agent, called a **surfactant**. The molecules of surfactants attach themselves to dirt, pull the dirt out into the water, and hold it there until it can be washed away (Figure 8.3). Modern soaps, made with scientifically produced ingredients and accurate measurement, are not generally harmful to your skin. People who have allergies, though, must be careful about what kind of soap they use, since other ingredients may be added. Soap may contain additional cleaning agents as well as perfumes, cold cream, colouring, and substances that discourage the growth of bacteria.

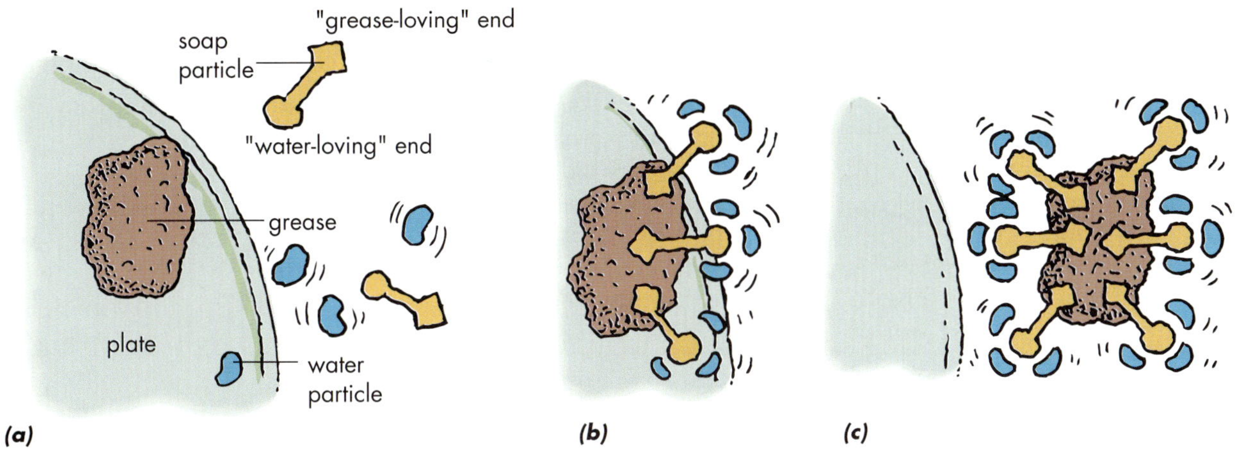

FIGURE 8.3
How soap cleans — a close-up view of surfactant molecules.
(a) Each soap molecule has one end that is attracted to grease and one end that is attracted to water.
(b) The grease-loving ends attach themselves to bits of dirt.
(c) Soap molecules pull the dirt away. The bits of dirt stay suspended in the water so they can be easily washed away.

DEODORANT

Body odour is produced by bacteria that live on the skin, especially in areas where there is perspiration. Perspiration, or sweat, normally evaporates quickly. Under the arms, however, perspiration cannot easily evaporate. As a result, bacteria thrive there and may produce odour.

Body odour can be controlled by frequent washing to remove perspiration. In addition, some personal care products control body odour for longer periods of time. Deodorants are products that contain perfume to mask the body's odour. They may also contain chemicals to halt the growth of bacteria. Antiperspirants are products that contain a chemical to halt the production of perspiration by the sweat glands in the skin.

REVIEW 8.1

1. (a) Describe how soap removes dirt.
(b) Many commercially prepared soaps contain perfume, cold cream, or deodorant. Why do you think these ingredients are added?

2. How is the cleaning action of soap different from the cleaning action of toothpaste?

3. Which of the following statements about a personal care product could be tested scientifically? Explain your answer.
(a) Now 10 per cent more for your money!
(b) Tastier!
(c) Longer-lasting than ever before!
(d) Maximum shrinkage 5 per cent (for a pair of jeans).
(e) Wetness protection for 24 hours (for a deodorant).
(f) Keeps your teeth whiter than white!

4. You have been asked to test two brands of white shoe polish to determine which one is more waterproof. ➡

(a) Describe briefly how you would set up a controlled experiment.
(b) What factors would you think about before carrying out your investigation?

5. A researcher is planning to compare two brands of deodorant.
(a) What are the properties of a good deodorant?
(b) What variables should be controlled in a fair test of the two deodorants?
(c) Describe in detail how you would set up the controlled experiment and how you would assess the results.

6. (a) Suppose your local store sells two brands of perfume in bottles of equal size. Brand X, described as being "super long-lasting," costs 10 dollars. Brand Y costs 7 dollars. Assuming that "long-lasting" is the most important property of perfume, how could you test the two brands to determine which supplies greater value for your money?
(b) What other factors, besides how much it costs and how long it lasts, might affect your choice of brands?

7. (a) What are the advantages of making your own personal care products instead of buying them?
(b) What are the disadvantages?

FIGURE 8.4
Fifteenth-century spinners and weavers of wool

8.2 TESTING AND THE FABRIC INDUSTRY

Many of the materials in the clothes you wear were unknown to your ancestors. Until the middle of the twentieth century, clothes were made only from natural materials such as cotton, wool, leather, and fur (Figure 8.4). Although these materials are still used, many clothes now include some synthetic materials. Rayon, nylon, and polyester, for example, are made from chemicals that come from wood, petroleum, and coal.

NATURAL FIBRES

Most clothes are made by weaving or knitting to produce cloth. If you pull a piece of cloth apart, you will find that it separates into thin, hair-like strands. These strands are the **fibres**. For centuries, only **natural fibres**, which come from animals or plants, were used for weaving into fabrics. On the coast of British Columbia, the Haida people used fibres from the bark of cedar trees. Europeans prepared long strands made from cotton and wool in a slow and laborious process (Figure 8.5). First the individual fibres were separated and made to lie parallel by a process called carding. Then the fibres were spun into thread or yarn. The thread or yarn was then woven into cotton or wool.

Now there are modern, automated methods for producing cotton and wool, but these natural fibres are still widely used. The four most common natural fibres in use today are cotton, linen, wool, and silk (Figure 8.6).

FIGURE 8.5
Carding wool. If you go to a museum displaying tools used by pioneers, you may see how wool was carded and spun.

(a)

(b)

(c)

(d)

FIGURE 8.6
Many fabrics are prepared from natural sources. (a) Wool is made from the hair of animals such as sheep or goats. (b) Linen is produced from soaked stems of the flax plant. (c) Cotton comes from the seed pod of the cotton plant. (d) Silk comes from the cocoon of the silkworm moth. This larva will spin its cocoon and become a pupa inside the cocoon. A silk harvester will unwind the silk from the cocoon in one long strand (up to 3 km long).

ACTIVITY 8C / FABRICS FROM NATURAL FIBRES

CROSS-CURRICULAR

In this activity, you will examine four fabrics made from natural fibres: cotton, linen, wool, and silk.

MATERIALS

Parts I and II
safety goggles
apron
samples of cotton, linen, wool, and silk (10 cm x 10 cm)

Part I
hand lens
tweezers
ruler

Part II
pie plate
support stand and ring
wire gauze
Bunsen burner
tongs
fireproof mat ➡

CAUTION!

■ **This activity requires adequate ventilation.**

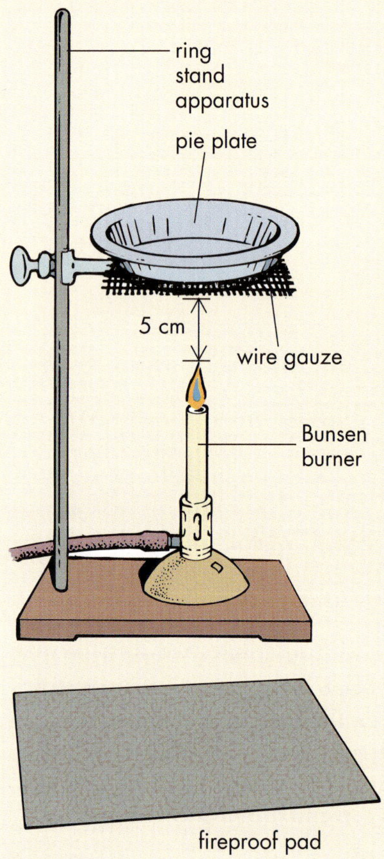

FIGURE 8.7
Apparatus for testing the effect of heat on fabric samples

PART I Fibres

PROCEDURE

1. Use a hand lens to examine the cotton sample. Draw a sketch showing how the threads of cotton are woven together.
2. Use the tweezers to pull out a single cotton thread. Try to separate the thread into individual fibres.
3. Repeat steps 2 and 3 for each of the other fabrics.

DISCUSSION

1. (a) How long is an average cotton fibre from your sample?
   (b) How do you think these fibres are made into longer lengths of thread?
2. Repeat question 1 for linen, wool, and silk.

PART II Effect of Heating

PROCEDURE

1. In your notebook, make a table like Table 8.1.
2. Put on your safety goggles and apron and ensure that loose clothing is restrained and hair is tied back. Have a beaker of water handy to put out flames if necessary.
3. Set a pie plate on a support stand as shown in Figure 8.7. Place your cotton sample on the pie plate and heat with a burner. Does the fabric melt? Does it burn? Record your observations in your table.
4. With tongs, hold the cotton fabric near the flame for 1 s. Hold it in the flame for 1 s and then remove it. Hold the fabric over the fireproof pad. How quickly does the fabric burn? Does it continue to burn when it is removed from the flame? Record your observations.
5. Carefully note the odour of the fabric after it has been in the flame. (Use the wafting technique for smelling. Do not place the fabric near your nose.) Describe any ash. Record your observations.

DISCUSSION

1. How could a police investigator use your table to identify fibres in a scrap of fabric found at the scene of a crime?
2. Suppose you are given a fabric sample. When held in a flame, the sample burns quickly and sputters, with a smell like burning meat. When removed from the flame, the sample continues to burn. Is this information enough to let you identify the sample as cotton, linen, wool, or silk? Explain your answer. ❖

Fibre type	Heated indirectly (on pie plate)	Heated directly (near flame)	Heated directly (in flame)	Odour	Ash
Cotton					
etc.					

TABLE 8.1 ***Sample Data Table for Activity 8C***

PROPERTIES OF NATURAL FIBRES

Cotton and linen fibres come from plants. Cotton fibres are flat and twisted, whereas linen fibres look like sets of joined tubes (Figure 8.8). Linen produces a stronger material that lasts longer than cotton. Since linen is more expensive to produce, however, it is not used as much as cotton.

Silk and wool fibres come from animals. Silk fibres are like long tubes, so smooth on the outside that they give silk fabric a beautiful sheen. Wool fibres have scales on the outside (Figure 8.9). When wool fibres are spun into yarn, the scales trap air. When the yarn is knitted or woven, it forms a fabric that traps even more air. As a result of these air pockets, wool keeps you warm in cold weather.

All these natural fibres have some undesirable properties. For example, wool may shrink when washed, and it is a favourite food of some moths. Linen and silk wrinkle easily. Cotton, like wool, may shrink when it is washed.

Early in this century, chemists began to look for ways to produce new fibres in the laboratory. They hoped to create fibres that did not have the undesirable properties of natural fibres. In addition, some natural fibres had become scarce and expensive.

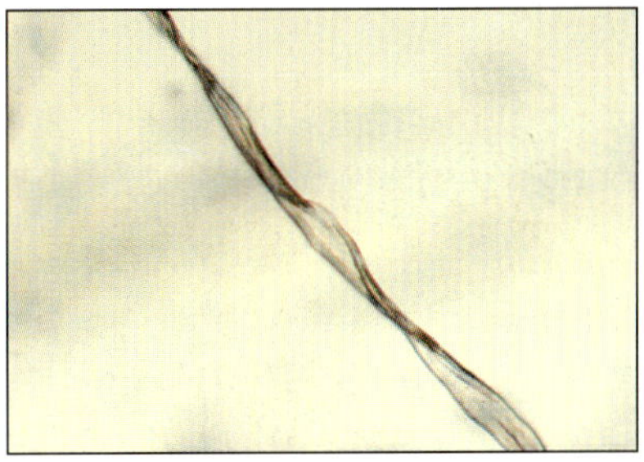

(a)

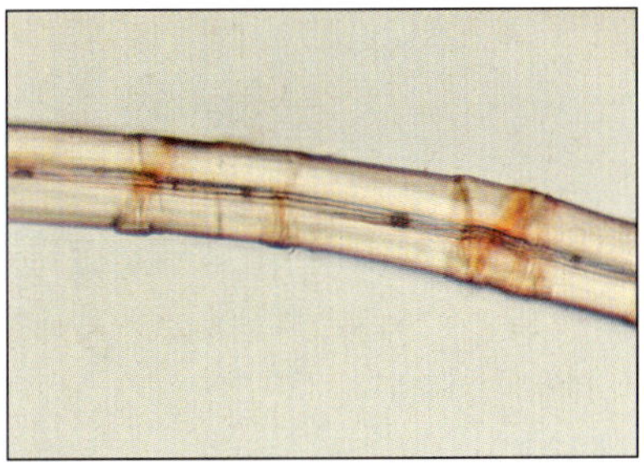

(b)

FIGURE 8.8
Microscopic view of two plant fibres: (a) cotton and (b) linen

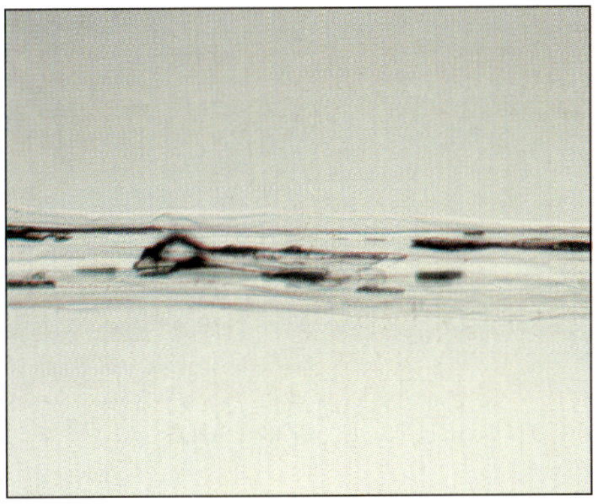

(a)

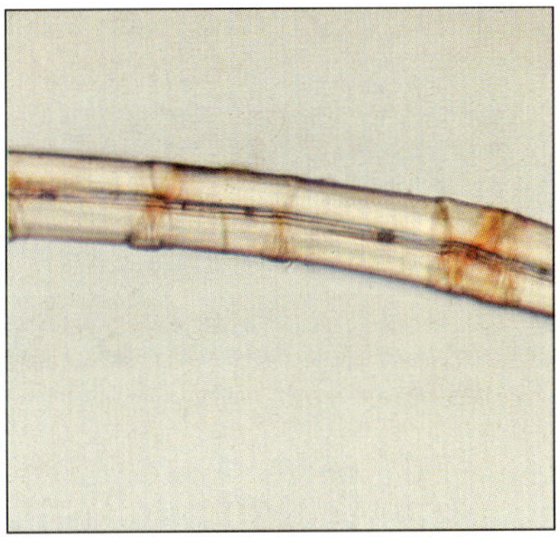

(b)

FIGURE 8.9
Microscopic view of two animal fibres: (a) silk and (b) wool

EXTENSION

■ In your classroom, set up a laboratory bench for a police investigation, including a microscope and the materials used in Activity 8C. Add a mystery fibre found at the scene of a crime and samples of the clothing of the suspects. Ask other students in your class to identify the criminal. For the court case, write a complete description of the tests done and the process that led to the identification of the criminal.

SYNTHETIC FIBRES

The new fibres developed by chemists are known as **synthetic fibres**, or fibres made by humans. They are not found in nature but are produced in laboratories and factories by a series of chemical changes. The world's first synthetic fibre — rayon — was made from wood toward the end of the nineteenth century. It looked like silk but was very flammable. In the 1930s, chemists found a way to rearrange the molecules of coal, oil, and natural gas into long chains. These chains could be combined to form long fibres of nylon, which were less expensive to produce than silk.

EXTENSION

■ Write an advertising brochure for an imaginary new synthetic fabric, describing all of its advantages over present-day materials.

People soon realized that synthetic fibres were not just substitutes for natural ones but were stronger and could last longer. Alone, or combined with natural fibres, synthetic fibres could be used to produce fabrics with a wide range of desirable properties. You can now choose clothes that are:

- water-resistant
- wrinkle-resistant
- insulating
- stretchable
- windproof
- crease-retaining
- colourfast
- drip-dry
- dirt-resistant
- flame-resistant
- rot-resistant
- pre-shrunk
- tough and durable
- absorbent

Some properties of fabrics can be produced as the cloth is being made. For example, coloured fibres that do not fade are produced by melting coloured pigments and glue-like substances with the fibres. Wrinkle-resistant fabrics are soaked in a resin and dried before being made into a garment. The garment is then pressed and baked at a high temperature (Figure 8.10). Other properties, such as stretchiness, are a result of the way the fibres are woven, knitted, or "double knitted" into the material.

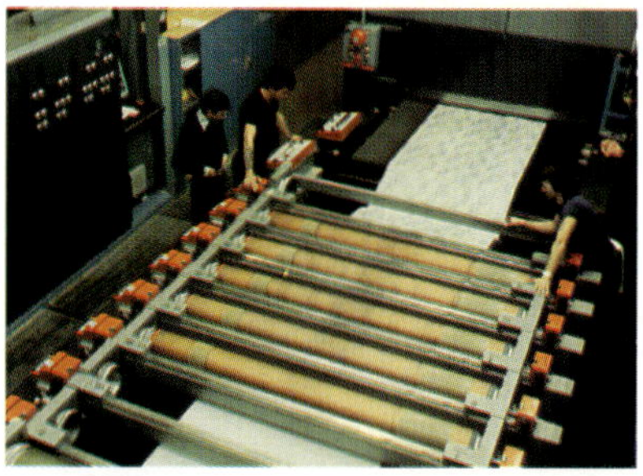

FIGURE 8.10
Special processing of permanent-press fabrics causes them to hold their creases even after washing.

ACTIVITY 8D / FASHION OR FUNCTION?

CROSS • CURRICULAR

In this activity, you will test and compare some properties of fabrics.

MATERIALS

safety goggles
apron
waterproof marker
masking tape
two samples each of three different fabrics, that have never been washed
three 250 mL beakers
small pieces of paper
laundry detergent
bowl or large beaker
stirring rod
tweezers
ruler
hair dryer
white paper or cardboard
drawing paper

PROCEDURE

1. In your notebook, make a table like Table 8.2. Use it to record the results of your tests.
2. Using a waterproof marker to write on a strip of masking tape, label your fabric samples A, B, and C. For each sample of material, carry out the four tests described.
3. Put on your safety goggles and apron before carrying out each test.

Property	Sample A	Sample B	Sample C
Crease resistance			
Wind resistance			
Colourfastness			
Shrinkage			

TABLE 8.2
Sample Data Table for Activity 8D

FIGURE 8.11
Test 1

FIGURE 8.12
Test 2

Test 1 *Crease Resistance*

1. Tie a knot in each sample of material and leave it for 5 min (Figure 8.11).
2. Untie the knot, smooth out the material, and note its appearance. Are many creases visible?
3. In your table, describe each sample as good, moderate, or poor for this property.

Test 2 *Wind Resistance*

1. Hold a sample of fabric taut. With your lips almost touching the fabric, try to blow through it (Figure 8.12). Does the material allow air to pass through it?
2. See if you can blow enough air through the fabric to move some small pieces of paper on the other side of the fabric. In your table, describe each sample as having good, moderate, or poor wind resistance.

Test 3 *Colourfastness*

1. Place a sample of each fabric in a separate beaker of hot water that contains 1 mL of laundry detergent. (You may need to remove the tape from the fabric and stick it on the beaker instead during this test.) Let the samples soak for 5 min, stirring occasionally.
2. Observe whether any of the colour has been transferred to the water. Hold a white sheet of paper or cardboard behind the beaker to see the water colour more clearly (Figure 8.13). In your table, record whether the colour bleeds or does not bleed. ➡

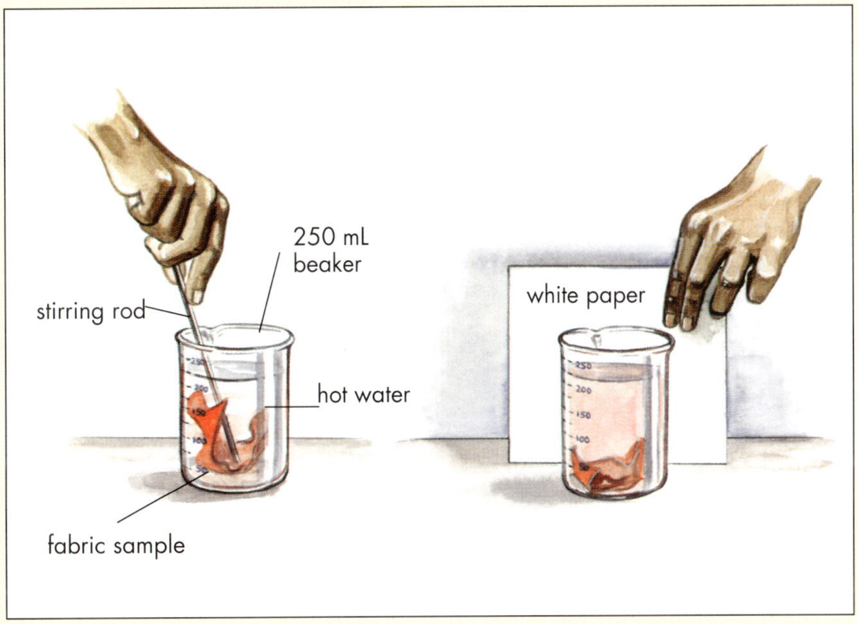

FIGURE 8.13
Test 3

FIGURE 8.14
Test 4

Test 4 *Shrinkage*

1. Lay a flat, dry sample of each fabric on a separate sheet of paper and carefully trace around the edges of the samples (Figure 8.14). Do not include the frayed ends in your outline.
2. Soak one fabric sample in hot water for 5 min.
3. Use tweezers to remove the fabric. Let it cool enough to touch safely and squeeze out the water. Dry the sample with hot air from a hair dryer.
4. Smooth out the dry fabric sample and place it back on the paper tracing. Describe any change in the size of the sample; record the result.
5. Repeat the procedure for the other samples.

DISCUSSION

1. In your notebook, write a summary of the data you have recorded in your table. Your summary should describe the properties of samples A, B, and C.
2. (a) Which one of the fabric samples would you recommend using in a spring or fall jacket? Why?
   (b) Why are the other two fabrics less suitable for this use?
   (c) How could you use the materials that are less suitable for a jacket?
   (d) What other factors, not tested in this activity, might be important in the choice of fabric for a spring or fall jacket?
3. What other tests could you conduct to determine whether the fabrics are suitable for a spring or fall jacket?
4. Examine each type of material through a magnifying lens. From your observations, compare the properties that you tested and
   (a) the length and thickness of the fibres,
   (b) the way the fibres are woven or pressed together.
5. For 4(a) and (b), explain the relationship, if one exists, between the properties and your observations. ❖

REVIEW 8.2

1. Explain the difference between fibre and fabric. Give an example of each.
2. Name two fibres that come from plants and two fibres that come from animals that are used to make fabric for clothing.
3. Explain the difference between natural fibre and synthetic fibre. Give examples of each.
4. (a) Name two important properties you would want in a shirt or a blouse to wear at a dance.
   (b) What properties would you want in a shirt to wear on a camping trip in the mountains?
   (c) Which of the properties you listed in (a) and (b) can be tested in a controlled experiment?
5. Rajid and Jill each got a new backpack. Both packs were of the same design and made of the same material. After six months, Jill's backpack had a ripped seam and a broken zipper, whereas Rajid's looked as good as new.
   (a) Suggest two reasons for these differences.
   (b) Describe an experiment that you could use to test one of your reasons.

8.3 PRODUCT TESTING

It is easier to compare the properties of similar products than to test how good a single product is. If you wanted to test fabrics used in ski pants, for example, you would need some quantitative measure of how much wind resistance is enough, or how much snow and ice the fabric can slide over before it is damaged.

If a product has several parts, each part must be tested. For example, even a simple hair dryer like the one in Figure 8.15 has several parts. If you were testing a hair dryer like this one, you would need to check that the heater can produce three different levels of heat, that the fan works, that the switches are properly connected, and that the casing meets whatever standards are set for strength.

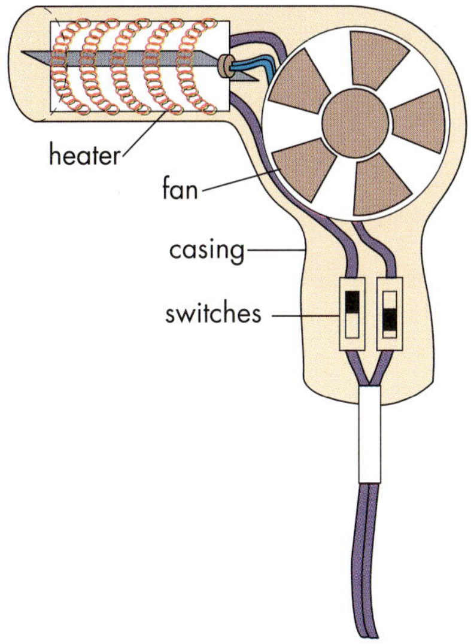

FIGURE 8.15
The parts of a hair dryer

Manufacturers may test every part of every product several times. A scientific test must be repeatable — that is, the same result should be obtained each time the test is carried out. Tests may require elaborate laboratory equipment or almost no equipment at all. Testing must be carried out in a controlled manner.

Tests on different parts of a product can be carried out at different stages of production, both while a product is being made and after it has been completed. For example, a fan may be tested before it is installed in a hair dryer to make sure that it works. The fan may then be tested again after the hair dryer has been assembled to ensure the fan has been installed correctly.

SPOT TESTING OR RANDOM SAMPLING

For mass-produced and inexpensive products, it may not be practical or necessary to test every item. Instead, individual items may be selected at random — or every so often — and tested. This technique is known as **spot testing**, or **random sampling**. Researchers assume that the randomly chosen products are like the other items that are produced in the same way. Thus, the untested items should have the same properties as the tested items.

DID YOU KNOW

- Some products are tested by human senses. For example, certain people are employed as professional tasters or sniffers to evaluate the quality of products such as tea, wines, perfumes, deodorants, and water.

ACCELERATED AGING

One type of testing carried out on samples may actually damage the product. This technique, called **accelerated aging**, is used to determine how long a product will last. For example, a hair dryer might be turned on continuously for several hours, or it might be turned on and off every 30 seconds until the switch wears out.

Samples of some products are tested until they break to determine how strong they are. One well-known furniture manufacturer tests how strong chairs are by pummelling them up to 60 000 times with a 70 kg mass (Figure 8.16). This company also tests desk drawers by filling them with objects of a certain mass and sliding them in and out over and over again. The Canadian Standards Association (CSA) tests some consumer products in this way. For example, a 133 kg mass is placed inside a bathtub to determine if the tub cracks or bends too much under this load (Figure 8.17).

FIGURE 8.16
This chair is being pummelled to test its strength. Can you think of other ways that a manufacturer could test a chair?

FIGURE 8.17
Bathtubs, bathroom fixtures, and other products are tested by the Canadian Standards Association. How would you test a faucet?

FIELD TESTING

In a **field test**, a product is actually used, rather than tested in a laboratory. People simply use the product and then tell researchers whether they liked it. Field tests may reveal problems that were not found in the lab tests. For example, a hair dryer may be well made and may work properly, but it may be too heavy. A hand lotion may smooth skin but have a fragrance that some people find irritating.

CONSUMER SURVEYS

People who buy products or services are called consumers. In a **consumer survey**, people who have used a product answer a questionnaire. Such a survey is more accurate if many people answer the questions. The questionnaire results are analysed to find out if a product has any recurring problems.

ACTIVITY 8E / SOFT BUT STRONG

CROSS-CURRICULAR

In this activity, you will test the strength of facial tissues when they are dry and when they are wet.

MATERIALS

safety goggles
apron
samples of two different brands of facial tissue, A and B
500 mL beaker
masking tape
coarse, dry sand or other mass
metric measuring spoon
centigram balance
water
dropper

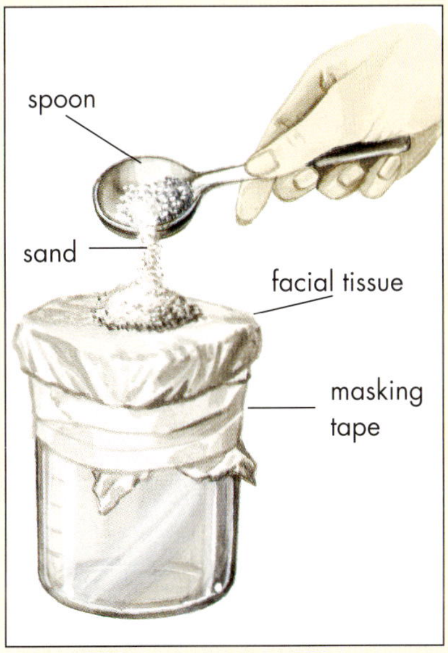

FIGURE 8.18
How could you test the tissue's strength if sand isn't heavy enough to tear it?

PROCEDURE

1. Put on your safety goggles and apron.
2. Based on the appearance and feel of the tissues, predict which of the two brands will be the stronger. Record your prediction in your notebook.
3. Stretch a sheet of facial tissue A across the top of a clean dry beaker and tape it firmly in place.
4. Measure and record the mass of the beaker, tissue, and masking tape.
5. Carefully place a spoonful of sand in the centre of the tissue, as shown in Figure 8.18. Continue adding sand, a little at a time, until the tissue tears.
6. Use the balance to measure the mass of the beaker and the sand used. Calculate the mass of the sand and record it in your notebook.
7. Repeat steps 3 to 6 with tissue B.
8. Stretch a new sheet of tissue A across the top of the beaker and tape it firmly in place. Use the dropper to add 10 drops of water to the tissue, wetting it evenly.
9. Repeat steps 4, 5, and 6.
10. Stretch a new sheet of tissue B across the top of the beaker and tape it firmly in place. Use the dropper to add 10 drops of water to the tissue, wetting it evenly.
11. Repeat steps 4, 5, and 6.

DISCUSSION

1. (a) Which brand of facial tissue was stronger when dry?
   (b) Which brand was stronger when wet?
2. Was the stronger dry tissue also stronger when wet?
3. Was there any other property that you might have used to predict strength?
4. (a) From the cost of each box of tissues and the number of tissues in the box, calculate the cost of the two types of tissues.
   (b) If strength and cost are the only considerations, which brand is the better buy?
5. (a) Name a property other than strength that might be important to consider when buying facial tissue. Explain.
   (b) How could you test for this property?
6. Suggest other products that could be tested for strength. Could your products be tested using the method in this activity? If not, suggest a method that could be used. ❖

FIGURE 8.19
Consumer magazines publish the results of tests that consumer groups and other organizations conduct. These results can help consumers decide which products are best. You can find consumer magazines in your library.

CONSUMER GROUPS

You might think that testing has been completed once a product is ready to be shipped to the stores. But at this stage, products may still be tested. Government agencies may test a product to make sure that it is safe or of good quality. Such agencies may also check that the information on the label and in advertisements is accurate. Besides government agencies, various consumer groups also test products to discover which ones work best. The results of their tests are published in various magazines (Figure 8.19). If a consumer group finds that a manufacturer is making false claims for a product, the group may inform the public or take the manufacturer to court.

Other groups may be formed when people have a particular concern about a product. One group may be concerned about an ingredient that is used in an anti-ageing skin cream. Another group may work to prevent the testing of cosmetics on animals. Other groups may organize recycling programs for glass or plastic so that materials are conserved and the amount of garbage is reduced. Non-smokers may demand a smoke-free environment in their workplace. By working together, consumers can affect governments, large companies, and the public.

ACTIVITY 8F / YOU BE THE INVESTIGATOR

Imagine that you are in a team of reporters for a consumer magazine. Your job is to choose a product, test it, and report your findings for a special article in the next issue of the magazine. Choose a product that interests you, and keep your questions simple. Remember that to produce a recommendation that the readers of your magazine can rely on, you need to repeat your tests a few times to confirm your results.

- Which of the product's properties will you test?
- What are the variables in your test?
- How will you control the variables?

PROCEDURE

1. Design a procedure for testing your product. Be sure to define what you mean by "best," "least," "most," and so on.
2. Write a list of the materials you will need to carry out your test.
3. Make a table for recording your results.
4. Discuss your plans with your teacher.
5. After you have your teacher's approval, carry out your tests, being sure to follow all proper safety procedures.

DISCUSSION

Present your findings in the form of a magazine article. Give your article an interesting title and draw one or two illustrations. Include recommendations based on your findings. ❖

REVIEW 8.3

1. Describe how you could test how well a hair conditioner works.
2. For a sample of perfume, suggest at least two properties that you could test and describe how you would carry out the tests.
3. (a) Does it matter to you what kind of container a personal care product has? For example, would you want to buy a certain type of container to use in your bathroom at home?
   (b) What other factors would you take into account when choosing one type of container over another?
4. Give two examples of products (not mentioned in this chapter) that are suitable for testing in each of the following ways. Explain your answer in each case.
   (a) product testing
   (b) random sampling
   (c) field testing
   (d) accelerated ageing

8.4 ADVERTISEMENTS AND LABELS

Think about something you bought recently. Why did you buy that product? Did advertising affect your choice? Are advertisements an accurate source of information about that product or any others?

ADVERTISING CLAIMS

Consider the two advertising claims in Figure 8.20. Could you test these claims? The claim for product A — "Has more vitamins than product B!" — can be tested. Scientists could analyse the products to find out exactly how much of the vitamins are present. If this information is printed on the boxes, you could read the lists of ingredients and compare the two.

What about the claim for product B? It claims to be "good for you." This claim might be true, but how could you test it? You may eat product B and feel good. But how do you know that feeling good was a result of consuming product B? You could also have had the same feeling after eating something else — or even after eating nothing at all! This claim would be hard to test.

Some television advertisements claim to show products being tested. A car is dropped from a helicopter; a wristwatch is strapped to a deep-sea diver's wrist; a spot of glue is used to suspend a construction worker from a girder. Many TV commercials show "tests" in which one product is compared with another: one laundry detergent makes clothes whiter than another; one type of soft drink tastes better than its competitors; one brand of battery lasts longer than others. In another advertisement, a battery manufacturer claims that its brand of battery was not included in the famous comparison test shown in the advertisements of its competitor.

FIGURE 8.20
Labels and advertisements affect the way consumers think of products, even if they don't supply any real information.

Are these tests fair? Do you have enough information to evaluate such tests? Knowing how scientific tests are designed will help you to assess the advertisements.

ACTIVITY 8G / ANALYSING ADVERTISEMENTS

GROUP ACTIVITY

CROSS-CURRICULAR

In this activity, you will watch TV (or listen to the radio or read newspapers or magazines) to determine whether advertisements are an accurate source of information about products.

PROCEDURE

1. Select three or four advertisements from television, radio, newspapers, or magazines to analyse.
2. For each advertisement, record the following.
   (a) Describe where the advertisement appeared. If it was on TV or radio, at what time of day was it aired and how long did the advertisement last? If it was in a newspaper or magazine, how much space did it take up?
   (b) Describe in detail the people, activities, and background in each advertisement. (For example, a young woman with a baby is shown using the product in a kitchen; three young women and three young men are shown splashing in the sea or playing a game on a beach while the product is shown in a separate scene; a famous sports figure is shown in a locker room, talking about the product he is holding up.)
   (c) Record what facts, if any, each advertisement told you about the product.
   (d) Record whether any scientific terms or claims were featured in the advertisements.

DISCUSSION

1. (a) Do the advertisements show or tell you how the product is used?
   (b) If not, how would you obtain this information?
2. (a) Is the product compared with other, similar products?
   (b) If so, how is this done?
   (c) Do you think that the comparison is fair?
3. (a) What sort of people (old or young people, men or women, people with special interests) would you expect to buy and use the product?
   (b) Are these the same sort of people as the ones shown in the ad?
4. Is the background or setting of the advertisement related to the way the product is actually used? Explain your answer.
5. (a) Does the advertisement make any claims about how well the product works?
   (b) Do you think that these claims can be scientifically tested?
   (c) Design an experiment for testing one claim used in an advertisement.
6. Form small groups in class. Using your analysis of the advertisements, debate the following statement: "Only factual statements should be allowed in advertisements." Some students in your group should argue in favour of the proposal, and some should argue against it. ❖

EXTENSION

■ Advertisements for a brand of shampoo may claim that that brand makes hair "softer" or "more manageable." In a group, discuss how you could test the truth of an advertisement such as this. Devise a testing procedure, writing down all the steps.

MAKER OF PERSONAL CARE PRODUCTS

Ron Reynolds has a small company that manufactures personal care products, detergents, and fabric softeners. Here is his story.

I never dreamed that my career would be such fun when I took a two-year chemical technology course at the Southern Alberta Institute of Technology in Calgary. I followed this with a degree in business and computers at the University of Alberta. It was while I was managing a chain of gas stations in the Okanagan Valley that I met a herbalist. He knew about herbs and I knew about chemistry and business, so we became partners.

Now I have my own business, which makes personal care products such as shampoos, hair conditioners, skin lotions, and deodorants. We also make detergents, cleaners, and fabric softeners. Some of our products are "no-name" brands for large grocery stores or drugstores, and some are for companies that want their own line of products. We also make our own brands, which we sell to stores, beauty salons, and so on.

How do I make a new product? After many years, I have a good idea of the materials that are required to produce a particular product. As I work, I keep very careful records of what I do. It is no use making a fabulous new product if you cannot repeat what you have done.

All the substances that we use have already been tested for purity and safety and are certified as safe by government testers. Since many people are allergic to the perfumes in personal care products, I use natural scents from herbs and fruits.

My work requires that I keep up with the latest trends in personal products. This means attending trade shows and reading chemical journals.

If a young person wants to go into a career like mine, I suggest taking a two-year chemical technician's course to learn the basics of chemistry, laboratory techniques, report-writing, and record-keeping. A knowledge of computers will help you to computerize your records. Training or experience in the cosmetic business would also be helpful. Above all, be prepared to never stop learning in the most enjoyable job you may ever have.

LOOKING AT LABELS

What do labels and packaging tell you about a product? Can you use this information to help you to decide which products to buy? For example, Canadian law requires that the list of ingredients on any food product tell you if the food contains artificial flavouring or colouring. Labels on specific products may give further information for people who have allergies or who want to reduce the sugar or salt in their diet. The law also requires that all ingredients be listed in order of decreasing quantities.

Non-food products must also be labelled. For example, the labels inside clothing tell you the size of the clothes, what materials they are made from, and how to clean and care for them (Figure 8.21). Hazardous products have warning labels, such as the WHMIS (Workplace Hazardous Materials Information System) labels shown on page xi. Labels on electronic equipment tell you how to use the product, what kind of batteries it requires, and so on.

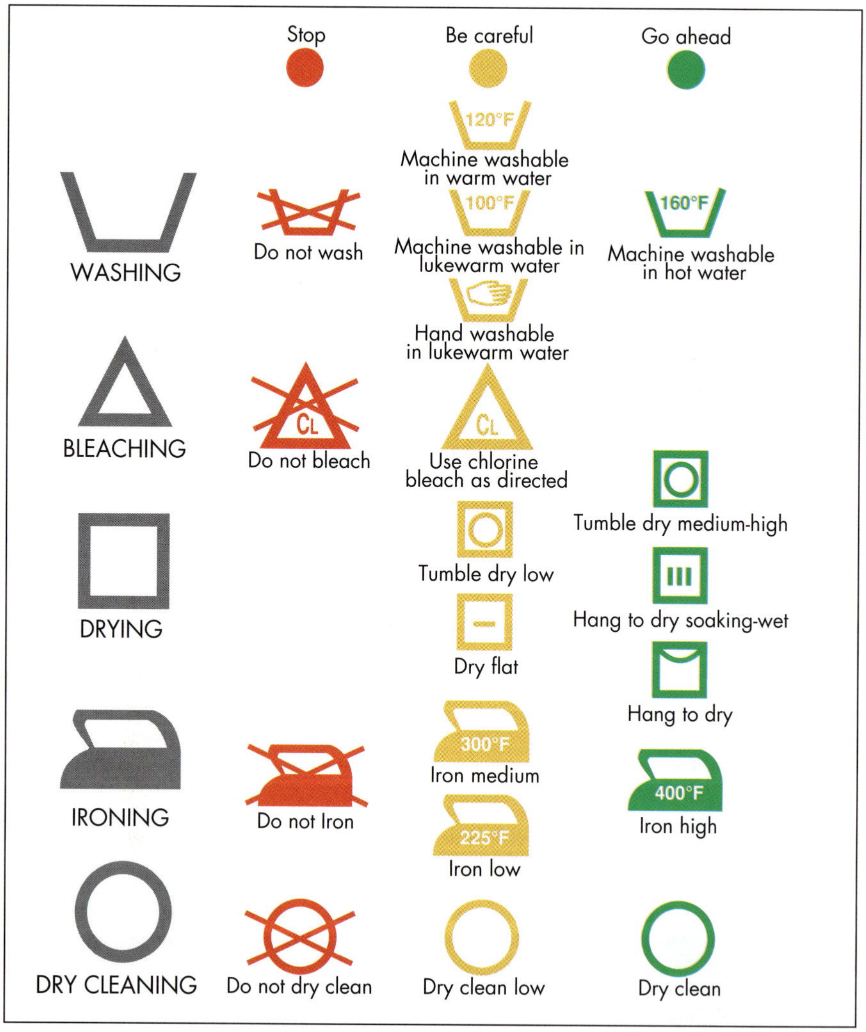

FIGURE 8.21 ▶ ***Washing instructions are found on clothing labels. Compare the label on a winter coat with the label on a summer shirt. How should each be cleaned?***

Have you seen products with labels that say "vitamin enriched" and "pH balanced"? These terms sound scientific, but what do they mean? Do they tell you what you want to know about the product? If a product has "with vitamin C" on its label, does that mean that similar products without this claim do not have vitamin C? Interpreting the meaning of labels is not always easy.

REVIEW 8.4

1. Which of the following advertising claims can be tested and which cannot? Explain your answer.
   (a) "More people choose brand X than any other leading brand."
   (b) "Brand Y gets your bathroom cleaner, faster."
   (c) "Dogs live longer if they eat brand A dog food."
2. (a) List, in order of their importance to you, three things that you would like to see printed on a bottle of shampoo.
   (b) Explain why each of these things is important to you.
   (c) What information is printed on a shampoo container that is not important to you? Explain your answer.
3. (a) A brand of sunscreen advertises that its chemical ingredient provides more protection from sunburn than any other brand. How could you test this claim?
   (b) Suggest an experiment that you could use to carry out this test. (Remember that your experiment must be absolutely safe.)
4. (a) Which of the three tubes of toothpaste in Figure 8.22 seems to be the best value for the money? Explain how you arrived at your answer.
   (b) What other factors do you think are important in deciding which product gives you the best value for money?
5. Write a set of instructions for consumers telling them how to use a hair dryer safely.

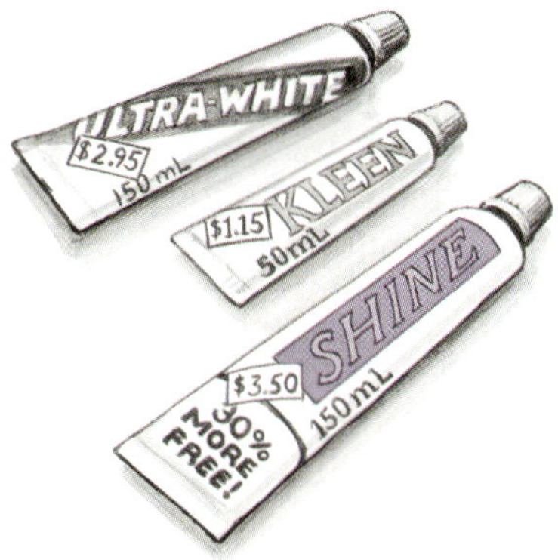

FIGURE 8.22
What is the difference between "the most for your money" and "the best value for your money"?

CHAPTER REVIEW

KEY IDEAS

- Some personal care products, such as lipstick and hair gel, help you look good. Others, such as soap and toothpaste, help to keep you clean and healthy.
- There are alternatives to commercial personal care products; these can have advantages over the store-bought ones.
- Personal care products are developed and made by scientists using scientific principles.
- Natural fibres such as cotton, linen, wool, and silk have many useful properties and are widely used in clothing.
- Chemists have developed synthetic fibres with new and useful properties.
- Consumer products are tested in many different ways, both while they are being produced and after they are already on the market.
- Consumers, in choosing what products to buy, have a responsibility to consider how these products affect other people and how they affect the environment.
- Some information in advertisements and labels may be verified by scientific tests, but other information is simply not testable.

VOCABULARY

personal care product
surfactant
fibre
natural fibre
synthetic fibre
spot testing
random sampling
accelerated ageing
field test
consumer survey

V1. Create a mind map using the terms in the vocabulary list. Use the title of the chapter or any other key word or phrase for the centre of your map.

V2. "If you are a rock climber, dangling from a cliff, you need a rope that is [_ _ _ _ _ _ _ _]!" To find the missing word in the sentence, first identify the words described in clues (a) to (h) below. The highlighted letters in the clues will spell the mystery word.

(a) _ _ _ _ _ _ _ ▮ _ _ _ _ _ _
(to test a product, people who have used the product answer a questionnaire)

(b) _ _ _ _ _ ▮ _ _ _ _ _
(another term for random sampling)

(c) _ _ _ _ _ _ _ _ _ _ ▮ _ _ _
(a single product is picked from many and is tested)

(d) _ ▮ _ _ _
(a natural fibre)

(e) _ _ _ _ _ _ _ ▮ _ _ _
(speeded up)

(f) _ _ _ _ _ _ _ ▮ _ _
(a test that has the same results again and again)

(g) _ _ _ ▮ _ _ _ _ _
(a test on a product carried out under actual conditions of use)

(h) _ _ _ _ ▮ _ _ _ _ _ _ _ _ _
(made using chemical changes)

CONNECTIONS

C1. "Modern products have better designs and are made of better materials than products in the past. Modern products also have fewer problems than products in the past." Do you agree or disagree with this statement? Give examples, along with the reasons for your answer.

C2. Analyse the manufacturers' claims below. Explain why the claim would or would not convince you that the testing was adequate.

(a) "We know that our product is reliable. We have said that it is fireproof, and we know that it is because we have tested it repeatedly. We have done over 100 tests, and the material has never caught fire."

(b) "Our calculators can be depended upon. We tested the first 100 that came off the assembly line, and each of them worked perfectly for the period of time that we guarantee."

(c) "Our consumer survey of high school students throughout Canada showed that our brand of soft drink is their favourite — we are pleased to state that Canadians prefer our brand."

C3. What is essential in a fair test for any product?

C4. List properties of a hand lotion

(a) that can be scientifically tested,
(b) that are a matter of opinion.

C5. Explain why you agree or disagree with each of the following statements:
(a) Products need to be tested only once before they are ready to be sold.
(b) If spot testing is used, many individual samples do not need to be tested.
(c) Field tests of personal care products are unnecessary.

C6. Describe two ways in which a consumer can obtain reliable information about the quality and safety of a product.

C7. (a) Write an advertising claim that can be scientifically tested.
(b) Describe how you would test the claim.

C8. Create an advertisement for a pair of running shoes. Include a drawing that makes the shoe look attractive and use statements that
(a) will make the product sound good to consumers,
(b) can be scientifically tested.

EXPLORATIONS

E1. In a reference, find out what the safety symbols shown in Figure 8.23 indicate about a product.

E2. (a) Find out, from a clerk in a bicycle store, a consumer group, or a government regulatory agency, the safety specifications for bicycle safety helmets.
(b) Design a fair test that will allow you to compare at least two factors that affect the quality of different brands of helmets.

E3. Design your own symbol to communicate to consumers that a product has been specially designed to have a minimum effect on the environment.

E4. There are many kinds of shampoos, made for a variety of types of hair. Examine the following types of shampoo in a drugstore and find out the purpose of each: plain shampoo, cream shampoo, egg shampoo, non-stripping shampoo, dry shampoo, soapless oil shampoo, and dandruff shampoo. Put the information on a poster and display it in your classroom.

REFLECTIONS

R1. (a) Think of ways in which the production, use, or disposal of personal care products can affect the environment.
(b) Suggest ways in which ordinary people could help to reduce or eliminate these effects.

R2. (a) To ensure that products are safe for humans to use, they must be carefully tested. For personal care products such as lotions or make-up, the tests may involve trying out the product on an animal such as a rabbit or a guinea pig. Do you think such tests are justified? Why or why not?
(b) Drugs are also often tested on animals. Is your opinion about testing drugs the same as your opinion about testing cosmetics? Explain your answer.

R3. How has this chapter changed the way you think about advertisements on television?

R4. Are all the personal care products you use necessary? Could you do without any of them? Explain.

FIGURE 8.23
What does each of these safety symbols mean?

DISCOVERING ENERGY AROUND YOU

The sights and sounds of a busy city are evidence for many different forms of energy in the world around you. You can hear the noises of sirens, buses, trucks, and cars because of sound energy. Your family can drive through the city because of the energy in the gasoline in your car. As you drive through the city, you stop and go at traffic lights that use electrical energy to create light energy that keeps traffic moving safely. How many other different forms of energy do you think are used in the city in the photograph?

You may have already learned about matter and energy in Unit II (Chemistry). In this unit, you will explore the importance of energy and how energy changes from one form to another. You will learn about the forms of energy produced by the sun, and how both humans and plants use them. You will also learn about thermal energy, heat, and temperature, how thermometers work, and how you can keep warm.

In addition to thermal energy, you will explore light energy and some of the ways in which you use light energy every day. Finally, you will investigate sound energy, how it travels, and how it is used.

UNIT 3

CHAPTER 9

FORMS OF ENERGY

How did you travel to school today? Whether you walked, rode your bicycle, or took the school bus, like the students in the photograph, you used energy. When you arrived at school, your classroom was warm and bright. Energy heats and lights our schools, homes, and other buildings. At home, when you are making toast or watching television, you are using energy. You use energy for everything you do, every day. Your life depends on energy. In this chapter, you will explore the different kinds or forms of energy, and how energy changes from one form to another. You will also learn how important the sun is in providing energy.

ACTIVITY 9A / HOW DO YOU USE ENERGY?

GROUP ACTIVITY · CROSS-CURRICULAR

Think about all the different ways in which you use energy. Get together with three other students. Use a metre stick to divide a large sheet of poster paper into six boxes. Use the instructions below to fill in the boxes.

With your group, present your poster to the rest of the class.

Later in this chapter you will compare your idea of energy with a scientific description of energy. ❖

Print the names of at least 10 devices that use energy.	Draw a large picture of at least 3 of these devices.	Draw a mind map of how you use energy every day.
Write a short story about how life on Earth would be different without energy.	List the names of as many different kinds of energy as you can think of.	Print at least five questions about energy you would like to know the answers to.

9.1 WHAT IS ENERGY?

Every day we hear the word "energy" used in expressions such as "energy crisis," "energy food," and "energy saver." But these expressions do not tell us what energy is. **Energy** is the ability to make things move. Without energy, you would not be able to walk, planes could not fly, and television sets would not work.

ENERGY'S MANY FORMS

When you wash your clothes, toast marshmallows over a campfire, or wind a watch, you are using different forms of energy. Energy has many different forms that allow us to use it in many different ways. How many forms of energy do you think Masako and Juan are using in Figure 9.1? You will learn more about the forms of energy in this section.

EXTENSION

■ Try to list all the different ways that you use energy indirectly. For example, think about the energy used to make your clothing, bicycle, or sports equipment. Also think about the energy used to build houses, your school, and the roads you use. Is energy needed to make other products that you use each day? List some of these products.

FIGURE 9.1
How many forms of energy can you see?

ACTIVITY 9B / INVESTIGATING ENERGY

In this activity, you will look for evidence of different forms of energy. Equipment will be set up at stations around the room. Move with your group from station to station, following your teacher's instructions.

At each station, follow the procedures given on the facing page, and observe what happens.

MATERIALS

Station I
bar magnets
paperclips, thumb tacks, nails, rubber stoppers, pennies

Station II
tuning fork
rubber mallet
beaker of water

Station III
hand drill or egg-beater or bicycle

Station IV
water wheel

Station V
cart and ramp

Station VI
springs
rubber bands
rubber ball

Station VII
light meter
light source

PROCEDURE

STATION I

1. Slowly lower the bar magnet over the objects (paperclips, thumb tacks, nails, rubber stoppers, pennies). In your notebook, describe what happens to the objects.

CAUTION!

■ Do not touch the sides of the glass beaker with the tuning fork. The beaker may break.

STATION II

1. Gently strike the tuning fork with the rubber mallet. Record what happens.
2. Strike the tuning fork again, and slowly lower it into the beaker of water. In your notebook, describe what happens.

STATION III

1. Turn the crank of the hand drill or the egg-beater. What do you see?
2. If you are using a bicycle, make sure that it is well supported, so that the rear wheel is off the ground and free to turn. Turn the pedal. Record your observations.

STATION IV

1. Observe the flow of the water from the faucet onto the water wheel. Increase the flow of water slightly. In your notebook, describe what happens.

STATION V

1. Bring the cart to the top of the ramp and allow it to roll down. Why do you think this happens? Write your explanation in your notebook.

CAUTION!

■ Do not stretch the rubber bands or springs too far. They can cause injury when released.

STATION VI

1. Stretch the rubber bands or springs slightly. Release one end. Describe what happens in your notebook.
2. Drop the ball to the floor from shoulder height. What happens to the ball? Record your observations.

STATION VII

1. Hold the light meter so that it faces the light source. Cover the front of the light meter with your hand. In your notebook, describe what happens to the needle on the light meter.
2. Remove your hand from the front of the light meter. What happens to the needle? Record your observations.

DISCUSSION

1. Using your own words, make a list of the forms of energy that you observed at each station.
2. Think about the definition of energy given earlier in this chapter. How do you know that energy was involved with the equipment at each station?
3. In Activity 9A, you listed some of the different ways that you use energy. Compare these uses with the forms of energy from this activity. How are they similar? How are they different?
4. Think about the motion you observed at each station. Was the motion you observed at each station caused by the form of energy or was the energy caused by the motion? For example, when the rubber ball was dropped, did a form of energy cause the motion or did the motion cause a form of energy to be produced? Explain your answer. ❖

THE FORMS OF ENERGY

Are you using energy right now? Even if you are sitting perfectly still, your heart and other organs are working. They use the energy from the food you have eaten today to keep going. You can see these words because of light energy. Sound energy lets you hear cars driving by on the street. These are some of the forms of energy that are around you. The 10 common forms of energy are shown on these two pages. Can you think of other examples of each one, besides those shown here?

Light energy *is the form of energy that you can see. You will learn more about light energy in Chapter 11.*

Gravitational energy *is the energy that an object has when it is above the surface of the Earth. Any object that can drop, roll, or slide down has gravitational energy. You have gravitational energy if you are sitting up in a tree.*

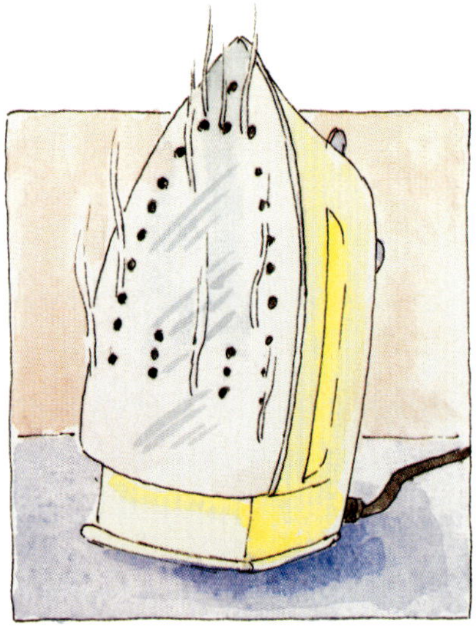

Thermal energy *is the energy of the particles in an object. The greater the movement of particles, the more thermal energy the object has. "Thermal" is from the Greek word* therme, *meaning heat. You will learn more about thermal energy in Chapter 10.*

Magnetic energy *(magnetism) is the form of energy that causes some kinds of metal to attract (pull together) or repel (push apart) some metal objects.*

Nuclear energy *is the energy stored in the central part of an atom, called the nucleus. This energy is used for producing electricity.*

Electrical energy *is the energy of moving electrical particles. Electrical energy runs your stereo, your toaster, and the light bulbs in your lamps.*

Elastic energy ***is the energy stored in an object when its shape is changed by stretching (pulling apart) or compressing (pushing together). A stretched rubber band has elastic energy.***

Sound energy ***is the form of energy that you can hear. It travels as vibrations through materials and through air. You will learn more about sound energy in Chapter 12.***

Chemical energy ***is the form of energy stored in matter, such as the fuel for your family's car and the food that you eat.***

Mechanical energy ***is the energy in any set of moving parts. Your bicycle has mechanical energy.***

You cannot see most of these forms of energy because only the particles in the substance are moving. These are the particles you learned about in Unit II when you studied the kinetic molecular theory.

Many forms of energy occur with other forms; for example, chemical energy and thermal energy often occur together. When the furnace in a house burns fuel, the chemical energy in the fuel becomes the thermal energy that keeps you warm. You will learn more about these relationships in the rest of the chapter.

▶ REVIEW 9.1

1. What is energy?
2. Which forms of energy are being used when you
   (a) prepare a meal in the kitchen?
   (b) watch television?
   (c) ride a bicycle?
3. Sometimes, when there is a long list of unfamiliar terms to remember, people use a mnemonic sentence, which is an aid to memory. The first letters of the words in a mnemonic sentence represent the words to be remembered. Examine the first letters of the words of the following sentence. "*M*onkeys *e*at *s*paghetti, *g*orillas *e*at *l*asagna, *t*urtles *m*unch *c*anned *n*oodles." List the forms of energy represented by these first letters.
4. Make your own mnemonic sentence to help you remember the 10 forms of energy. The forms of energy may be in any order you choose.
5. Using the list you made in question 3, give examples of each form of energy. Use different examples from those given in the text.
6. Identify the form(s) of energy involved in each of the following examples. You may need to give more than one form of energy for some examples. ➡

(a) a sling shot
(b) firewood
(c) bungee jumping
(d) downhill skiing
(e) a compass
(f) a nuclear reactor
(g) drums
(h) an electric fan
(i) a star
(j) a motorcycle

7. How would your life change if each of the following forms of energy did not exist?
(a) elastic
(b) chemical
(c) thermal
(d) gravitational
(e) nuclear

8. How would life on Earth change if each of the forms of energy listed in question 7 did not exist?

EXTENSION

■ Go through today's newspaper and find every story that talks about energy. In a group, discuss the importance in your lives of the energy in these stories. Think about all the costs of this energy. What are the problems with the energy in the newspaper stories? Can you think of any other problems with energy?

■ 9.2 ENERGY TRANSFORMATIONS

You have learned that there are many different forms of energy. You often find these forms together. For example, when you turn on a light, the source of energy for the light bulb is electrical energy. The light bulb produces both thermal energy and light energy. If you attract a nickel with a magnet, the nickel obtains mechanical energy as it moves toward the source of the magnetic energy. If you drop a tennis ball, it will fall to the floor because of gravitational energy. It will produce some sound energy, and it will bounce back because of elastic energy.

What is happening to the energy in these examples? When you turn on a lamp, for example, the electrical energy changes into thermal energy and light energy. When energy changes from one form to another, we say that it is being transformed. These changes are called **energy transformations**. Energy cannot be used without these energy transformations.

FROM ONE FORM TO ANOTHER

Every time you use energy, it changes from one form to another. For example, when you ride a bicycle, your body's chemical energy is being transformed into the mechanical energy of the bicycle.

Sometimes when energy is used, several energy transformations take place. Think about the headlights in a car. The chemical energy of the fuel is first transformed to thermal energy by burning. Then the thermal energy is transformed to mechanical energy by the engine. The mechanical energy is then transformed to electrical energy, which is transformed to light energy and thermal energy by the headlight.

In any energy transformation, the starting energy is called the **input energy**. A form of energy that results from the transformation is called an **output energy**. In the example of the car headlight, the input energy is the chemical energy in the fuel, and the output energies are light energy and thermal energy.

All energy transformations start with an energy source. The **energy source** is the substance or object that provides the input energy. The fuel in the car example is an energy source because it provides the chemical energy as the input energy.

ACTIVITY 9C / ENERGY TRANSFORMATIONS

To be useful, energy must be transformed from one form to another. In this activity, you will examine a number of devices that transform energy.

MATERIALS

devices supplied by your teacher

PROCEDURE

1. Copy Table 9.1 into your notebook.
2. A number of energy-transforming devices will be placed at stations around the room. Following your teacher's instructions, you will move with your group from station to station.
3. At each station, write the name of the device in the first column of your data table. Observe the device in action. In the table in your notebook, record the form of energy the device uses and the form(s) of energy it produces.

DISCUSSION

1. Although many devices are designed to produce one main form of energy, they also produce other forms. For example, a candle is used to produce mainly light energy, but it also produces thermal energy. In your table, underline the main output energy for those devices that produce more than one form of energy at the same time.
2. Did any of the devices you examined perform two or more energy transformations in a row? If so, identify the device and list all the energy forms produced in order. For example, with a flashlight, the battery's chemical energy produces electrical energy, which produces thermal energy and light energy.
3. Name devices you use often that transform energy in each of these ways:
(a) electrical energy into thermal energy
(b) elastic energy into mechanical energy
(c) electrical energy into light energy
(d) electrical energy into sound energy
(e) chemical energy into thermal energy
(f) elastic energy into gravitational energy ❖

TABLE 9.1 ▶
Sample Data Table for Activity 9C

Device	Energy form used (input energy)	Energy form(s) produced (output energy)
Candle	Chemical	Thermal, light

POTENTIAL AND KINETIC ENERGY

The energy forms that you have studied in this chapter can also be classified as either potential energy or kinetic energy. **Potential energy** is stored energy. The spring in a wind-up toy stores elastic energy that is transformed into mechanical energy when the spring is released. The elastic energy is potential energy. Any object that has stored energy has potential energy, which can be released to move things.

Kinetic energy is the energy of anything in motion. "Kinetic" comes from the Greek word *kinein*, to move. Look at the skiers in Figure 9.2. Can you see where the skiers have potential energy and where they have kinetic energy? The skier standing at the top of the ski hill has gravitational potential energy because she is high above the surface of the earth. This gravitational energy is stored in the skier's body, so it is called gravitational potential energy. It is transformed to kinetic energy when the skier starts down the slope. The skier also has kinetic energy as she moves back up the hill on the chair lift. This kinetic energy is transformed into potential energy when the skier stops at the top of the hill, waiting to ski down again.

FIGURE 9.2 ▶
Which skiers have more potential energy and which have more kinetic energy?

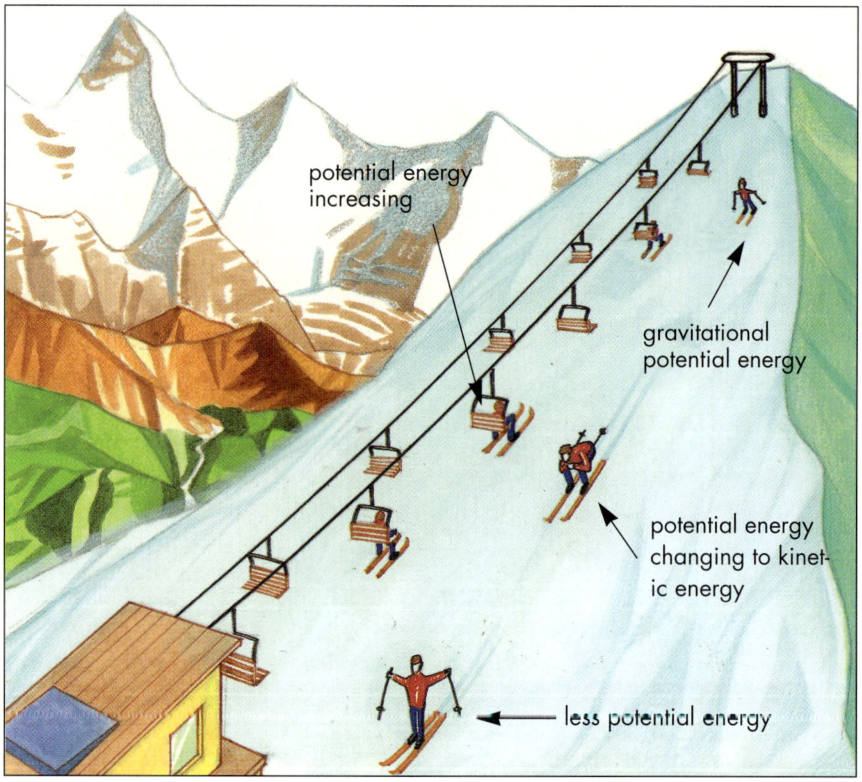

▶ REVIEW 9.2

1. Explain what "energy transformation" means.
2. Copy the headings for columns A and B from Table 9.2 into your notebook. Under column A, copy the list of devices, (a) through (f). Now match the correct energy transformation in column B with each device.
3. (a) Use a series of diagrams to show the energy transformations in a car run by a gasoline engine. Show each of the transformations in order.

(b) Does all the energy go to moving the car? Explain your answer.

4. List all the energy transformations that occur with each of the devices listed below (Figure 9.3). Include any transformations to unwanted energy forms.
   (a) curling brush
   (b) hydroelectric dam
   (c) electric blender
   (d) child on a swing set

5. What is the energy source in each of the devices listed in question 4?

6. Explain the terms "input energy" and "output energy."

7. How would your life be different if energy could not be transformed?

8. Choose one common energy transformation and describe how life on Earth would be affected if this transformation did not occur.

(a)

A Devices	B Energy transformations
(a) whistle	1. Chemical energy is transformed into mechanical energy.
(b) fan	2. Mechanical energy is transformed into sound energy.
(c) tape recorder	3. Chemical energy is transformed into gravitational energy.
(d) rocket	4. Electrical energy is transformed into mechanical energy.
(e) motorcycle	5. Electrical energy is transformed into sound energy
(f) flashlight	6. Electrical energy is transformed into light energy.

TABLE 9.2
Energy Transformations

(b)

FIGURE 9.3
What energy transformations occur with each device?

(c)

(d)

9.3 ENERGY FROM THE SUN

Most of us, like the people in Figure 9.4, enjoy a sunny day at the beach. There we can feel the sun's light energy and thermal energy. Think about all the ways the sun is important to us throughout the year. The sun is responsible for the air we breathe, the food we eat, the clothes we wear, the fuels we burn, and our weather. The sun is the source of almost all the world's energy. **Solar energy** is the general term for the forms of energy we receive from the sun. In this section, you will learn how important the sun is to your life.

FIGURE 9.4 ▶
On the beach, you can feel the energy of the sun. It is important to protect yourself from the sun whenever you are outside.

GREEN LEAVES: NATURE'S ENERGY TRANSFORMER

Have you ever thought about what the Earth would be like if there were no plants? Plants are important to life on Earth because they provide shelter, fuel, food, and even the oxygen we breathe. However, plants, like those in Figure 9.5, cannot do this without a source of energy. That source is the light energy from the sun.

Plants are able to transform light energy into chemical energy using a process called **photosynthesis**. The word "photosynthesis" comes from the Greek terms *photo*, meaning light, *syn*, meaning together, and *thesis*, meaning putting. Green plants are able to capture the sun's energy because they have a green chemical called **chlorophyll** (from the Greek words *chloro*, meaning green, and *phyll*, meaning leaf).

Using water from the ground and carbon dioxide gas from the air, plants transform light energy into chemical energy. The first food produced by the plant is sugar. The plant then changes the sugar into starch. Some of the starch is used as the plant grows. The plant also stores some of the starch, which it uses for food when there is not enough light for photosynthesis. The whole process of photosynthesis can be written in a short form this way:

FIGURE 9.5
Green plants are natural energy transformers. Why can't you perform the same energy transformation that plants can?

$$\text{water} + \text{carbon dioxide} \xrightarrow[\text{chlorophyll}]{\text{light energy}} \text{sugar} + \text{oxygen}$$

As shown in Figure 9.6, the plant takes water from the ground and carbon dioxide from the air. Using light energy and the chlorophyll in its leaves, the plant produces sugar and oxygen.

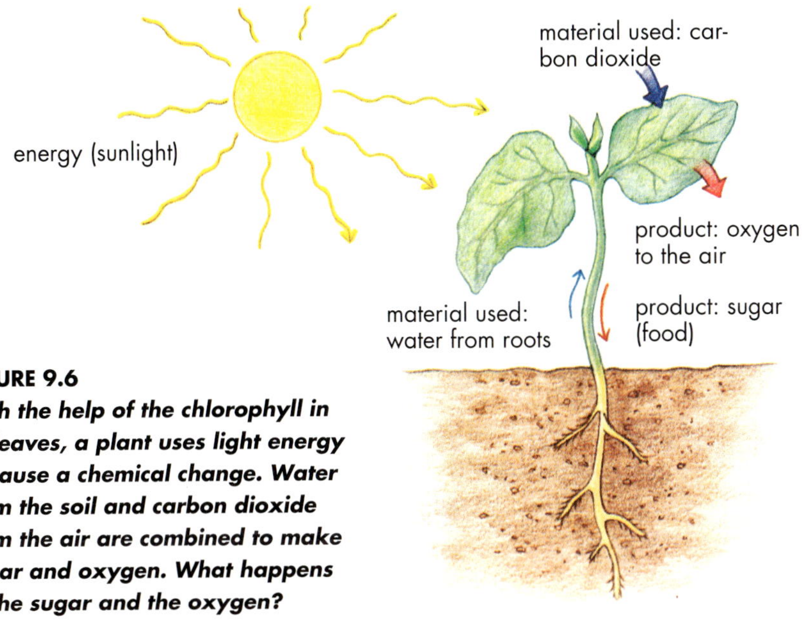

FIGURE 9.6
With the help of the chlorophyll in its leaves, a plant uses light energy to cause a chemical change. Water from the soil and carbon dioxide from the air are combined to make sugar and oxygen. What happens to the sugar and the oxygen?

DID YOU KNOW

You know that plants need the sun, but did you know that animals need it, too? Photosynthesis in plants produces food for animals as well as for the plants. The oxygen in the air you breathe is a product of photosynthesis, too. Humans and many other animals also need the sun so that a chemical called vitamin D can be produced in the skin. Vitamin D is sometimes referred to as the "sunshine vitamin." The production of vitamin D is necessary for the growth of strong, straight bones and healthy teeth. Lack of vitamin D can lead to poor teeth and a condition called rickets, in which the legs can become bowed.

ACTIVITY 9D / LIGHT AND PHOTOSYNTHESIS

In this activity, you will use a green plant to find out if light is needed for photosynthesis to occur.

MATERIALS

Part I
safety goggles
apron
starch
watch glass
IKI solution or Lugol's iodine
dropper

PART I A Test for Starch

PROCEDURE

1. Put on your safety goggles and apron.
2. Place a small amount of starch on a watch glass.
3. Place a few drops of IKI solution or Lugol's iodine on the starch. Observe what happens when the iodine solution is added to the starch. Record your observations in your notebook.

PART II Photosynthesis and Starch Production

PROCEDURE

1. Place the geranium plant in a warm, dark place for at least 48 h. During this period in the darkness, the starch stored in the leaves moves to other parts of the plant, such as the roots. ➡

MATERIALS

Part II
safety goggles
apron
geranium plant, or other green plant
aluminum foil or stiff black paper
paperclips
masking tape
grow light
scissors
600 mL beaker
hotplate
large test tube
test tube clamp
methanol (or denatured ethanol)
long forceps
three Petri dishes
IKI solution or Lugol's iodine

CAUTION!

■ Methanol is a poisonous, flammable liquid. Before proceeding, make sure that there are no open flames in the classroom. Always wear safety goggles when handling hazardous materials.

FIGURE 9.7
Geranium plant prepared for Activity 9D

2. After 48 h, remove the plant from the dark. Choose three leaves on the plant. Cover one leaf completely with a folded piece of aluminum foil or stiff black paper a little larger than the leaf, as shown in Figure 9.7. Make a mask from a second piece of foil or paper large enough to cover about one-third of a leaf. Attach the mask to the second leaf with masking tape or paperclips, as shown in Figure 9.7. Take care not to damage the leaves or the plant in any way. Do not cover the third leaf at all, but identify it with a piece of tape wrapped around the base of the leaf stem. This leaf will act as a control (Chapter 1 explains what a control in an experiment is).
3. In your notebook, draw and label the plant and the three leaves, showing which parts were covered and which were not.
4. Place the plant in a bright, sunny spot for 2 d. If grow lights are used, make sure that the leaves do not become too hot from the lights.
5. After 2 d, remove the three leaves chosen in step 2. Cut the leaf stems to different lengths so you will be able to tell the leaves apart. Remove the coverings from the leaves.
6. Put on your safety goggles and apron.
7. Half-fill the 600 mL beaker. Place the beaker on the hotplate, and heat the water to boiling (Figure 9.8). Place the leaves in the boiling water for 5 min to soften them. This will allow the iodine to mix more easily with the starch inside the cells of the leaves.
8. Half-fill the large test tube with methanol (or denatured ethanol). Using long forceps to handle the leaves, place them in the test tube. Using the test tube clamp, place the test tube in the hot water bath (the same 600 mL beaker as in step 7).
9. Boil the leaves in the methanol (or ethanol) for 8 min or until the leaves are colourless. This boiling dissolves the chlorophyll from the leaf. If the leaves are still green, repeat this step using fresh methanol (or ethanol).

FIGURE 9.8
Always be careful when working with hot liquids.

10. The leaves will be quite brittle now. Rinse them in the hot water bath to soften them.

11. Lay each of the three leaves flat in separate Petri dishes. Cover each of the leaves with IKI solution or Lugol's iodine. Let the leaves sit for 15 min.

12. Holding the leaves with forceps, rinse them thoroughly in warm water.

13. Using your observations from Part I of this activity, draw each leaf in your notebook showing where the starch is.

14. Clean your hands, work surfaces, and all the equipment that you used.

DISCUSSION

1. Why do you think iodine is used to test for the presence of starch in the leaves?
2. What were the variables in this activity? (See Chapter 1 for information on designing experiments.)
3. What were the controlled factors in this activity?
4. Why do you think the starch had to be moved out of the plant's leaves before you could start?
5. Why was one leaf covered completely, one partially covered, and one left uncovered?
6. Why were the leaves boiled in water?
7. List all the safety measures taken during this activity. Explain why each one was necessary.
8. Is light needed for photosynthesis to occur in the leaves of the plants you used? Explain your answer, using your observations from Part II of the activity. ❖

EXTENSION

■ Design a controlled experiment to see how the colour of the light that shines on a plant affects photosynthesis and the production of starch. You can use coloured cellophane placed in front of grow lights. If the plants are grown in natural light, you can wrap them loosely in the coloured cellophane.

STORED ENERGY FROM THE SUN

The sun provides us with energy both directly and indirectly. When there are no energy transformations between the sun and us, we are receiving the energy directly. For example, when we are outside, we can feel the sun's energy. In Canada, unfortunately, the sun's energy is not always available to us directly.

One way that we can stay warm is by using the sun's energy that has been stored in the form of chemical energy in wood. Many people throughout Canada still use wood to heat their homes (Figure 9.9). The sun provides trees with light energy, which they transform through photosynthesis and store as chemical energy. When you burn the wood, you are transforming the energy that originally came from the sun. When energy transformations allow us to use stored energy from the sun, we say that we are receiving the sun's energy indirectly.

FIGURE 9.9
Trees store energy from the sun. The energy is released when you burn firewood.

CAREER

SCIENCE TEACHER

Do you like teaching other people new things? If so you'll be interested in what Pavola Marra, a science teacher at Vanier Secondary School in Courtenay, British Columbia, has to say about her career in education.

When I was in secondary school, I already knew that I wanted to be a teacher. Now, after five years at the University of British Columbia, I am teaching chemistry, earth science, and junior high science.

Science is a great area to be involved in. It's always changing, with new discoveries being made every day that increase our understanding of the world. It's an exciting field.

Science is an area that many people used to think was mainly for boys, and I'm concerned that some people may still think that way. If they looked at my chemistry classes, they'd see that boys and girls who take the subject do equally well. If you enjoy a subject you should feel confident to take it and do well in it.

What I like best about teaching is getting to know students. Seeing students get excited about something I have just taught them is really rewarding for me. My students particularly enjoy investigating the natural world. Students are often amazed when they learn about the various applications of science in the real world.

Investigating and understanding nature is fun for me as well. I've always been fascinated by how things operate. In the summertime, and when I was going to university, I had several jobs including heavy-duty mechanic's apprentice. I really enjoyed the work, and it was a great experience.

We live in a society based on science and technology. Applications of science touch our lives constantly, at home, at work, shopping for groceries, and in our recreational activities. This is why it is important that students become interested in and involved with science. If you keep an open mind about science, you will learn many things that you can use throughout your life. Perhaps you will be able to make a great discovery or become a teacher and help others learn about science and technology.

Do you enjoy helping others learn? Interview your teachers and ask them what they like best about teaching. Find out what qualifications you would need to become a science teacher.

ACTIVITY 9E / HOW YOU USE ENERGY TRANSFORMED FROM THE SUN

The following section describes some of the ways that the sun's energy can be used directly and indirectly. In your notebook, make a list of all the forms of energy that you use or see being used all day today. Remember to include forms of energy like the chemical energy in the fuel of the bus you rode to school. Put a check mark next to the forms that you think come from the sun directly or indirectly. Beside each form that has a check mark, write a short explanation of how this form of energy was transformed from the sun's energy. As you read this section, add or subtract information, if necessary, to make your explanations complete. Add to your list any forms of energy that you did not have on your list before reading the following section. ❖

OTHER TRANSFORMERS OF SOLAR ENERGY

Figure 9.10 shows some of the forms of energy that are supplied to us indirectly by the sun.

FIGURE 9.10
Each of these energy sources transforms, or has transformed, the energy of the sun. How has the energy been stored?

EXTENSION

■ Hydroelectric dams are huge projects, often built in wilderness areas. Do research at the library to find out how hydroelectric dams can affect the environment. Make a poster showing these possible effects.

The chemical energy stored in fossil fuels is one way that we use the sun's energy indirectly. Coal, oil, and natural gas are called fossil fuels because they were made from the remains of ancient plants and animals. When the plants and animals died, they were slowly buried under layers formed by other plants and animals, soil, and rocks. As they were buried deeper and deeper, pressure and heat in the Earth slowly changed their remains over millions of years into fossil fuels. We use fossil fuels to heat buildings, to operate vehicles, and to produce electricity.

Electricity produced by hydroelectric dams, like the one in Figure 9.11, also comes indirectly from the sun. The sun provides the heat that evaporates the water from oceans and lakes. The water then falls as rain and snow. Rain and melt water from the snow run off the land into rivers, lakes, and oceans. Dams for electricity are built across rivers. When a dam blocks a river, a large lake called a reservoir forms behind the dam. Figure 9.11 shows how water moves through a dam.

Water in a reservoir has gravitational potential energy. This energy is transformed to mechanical energy as the water turns the large water wheels, called turbines. The turbines use this mechanical energy to turn the shafts of the generators that produce electricity. Most of British Columbia's electrical energy comes from hydroelectric dams and so, indirectly, from the sun.

Whereas fossil fuels and hydroelectricity are energy sources that we use daily, the wind is a less common energy source. Winds are caused by the sun heating the Earth's surface, which creates movements in the air.

FIGURE 9.12
This vertical-axis windmill can rotate no matter which way the wind is blowing. How does a windmill transform the energy in the wind into electrical energy?

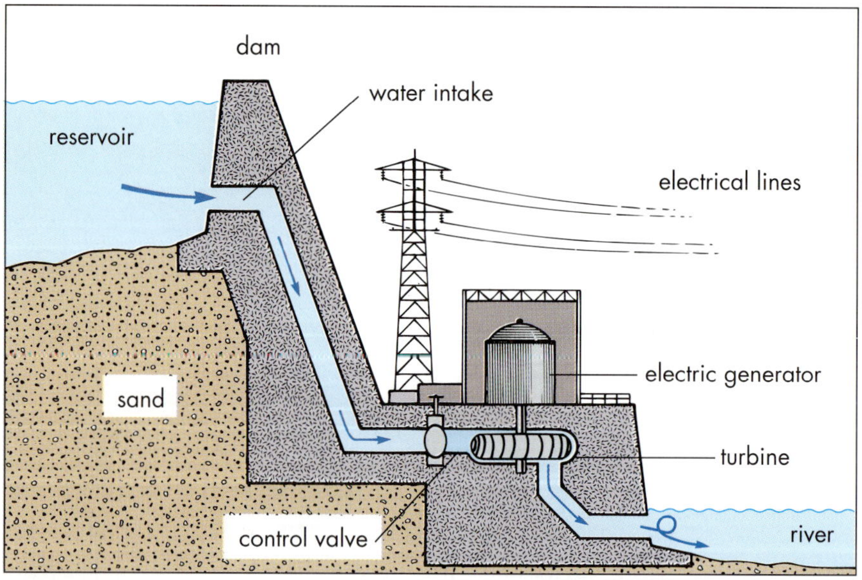

FIGURE 9.11
The potential energy stored in the water behind this dam originally came from the sun. The hydroelectric power plant transforms the gravitational energy of the water in the reservoir into electrical energy.

In Chapter 17, you will learn how the sun's energy affects winds. In the past, the mechanical energy of windmills was used to grind grains, pump water, and cut wood. Modern windmills are used to produce electricity. Figure 9.12 shows a windmill designed to produce electricity.

FIGURE 9.13
Active solar collectors have been built into the roof of this house. What might the home-owner do with the heat energy they provide in the summer?

CAPTURING THE SUN'S ENERGY

Earlier in this section, you learned that solar energy is the energy that comes from the sun. Solar energy can be collected, stored, or transformed to other forms of energy.

There are two types of collectors of solar energy, passive and active. A passive solar heating system lets solar energy in and prevents heat from getting out. In Canada, this can be as simple as building a house with most of the windows on the south side. Active solar heating systems are designed so that as much heat from the sun as possible is absorbed by a substance, usually a liquid. This liquid is then carried through pipes throughout the building. Figure 9.13 shows an active solar collector on the roof of a house.

FIGURE 9.14
The photoelectric cell in this calculator transforms the sun's light energy into electrical energy. Does this mean you could plug your radio into your calculator?

Other active solar systems can transform energy from the sun to produce another form of energy. Solar-powered calculators transform light energy into electrical energy using small panels called photoelectric cells (Figure 9.14). Electricity can also be produced by using solar energy to heat water and create steam. The steam runs a turbine, which is connected to a generator for producing electricity.

REVIEW 9.3

1. (a) What is photosynthesis?
(b) What chemical in plants is necessary for photosynthesis?

2. (a) What substances are used by green leaves when they make food by photosynthesis?
(b) What do plants make through photosynthesis?

3. (a) What is the original source of the energy that is stored in green plants?
(b) What energy transformation takes place in photosynthesis?

4. Criticize or defend the following statement: The sun is the major energy source for Earth.

5. Imagine that you have developed a cheap energy source that gives the world a nearly unlimited supply of electricity. It produces no air pollution or waste material. Give your new energy source a name.
(a) How would your energy source be distributed?
(b) What benefits would your energy source create for people and the environment?
(c) What problems might your energy source create for the environment, even though it does not produce air pollution or waste material?
(d) What fuels that we use now could we stop using because of your energy source?
(e) Draw a poster advertising your new energy source.

CHAPTER REVIEW

KEY IDEAS

- Energy is the ability to make things move.
- Energy affects our lives in many ways.
- Energy has many different forms.
- An energy transformation occurs when one form of energy changes into another form.
- The sun is the main source of the Earth's energy.
- The sun provides us with energy both directly and indirectly.
- Plants use the sun's light energy to manufacture food through the process called photosynthesis.
- Fuels contain stored chemical energy that was transformed from the sun's light energy.
- Many of the sources of energy that you use every day come directly or indirectly from transformations of the sun's energy.

VOCABULARY

energy
electrical energy
magnetic energy
thermal energy
sound energy
light energy
mechanical energy
gravitational energy
elastic energy
chemical energy
nuclear energy
energy transformation
input energy
output energy
energy source
potential energy
kinetic energy
solar energy
photosynthesis
chlorophyll

V1. Create a mind map showing how each of the 10 forms of energy, which you learned about in this chapter, can be transformed from one form to another form. Show the connections between the forms of energy by drawing lines from one to another. On these lines, print an example of a device that could make the transformations. (Show transformations going both ways. For example, a turbine transforms mechanical energy to electrical energy, and an electric fan transforms electrical energy to mechanical energy.) Do this for all the forms of energy, showing the connections between them. Remember to include the sun as the major source of energy for the Earth. Also include the forms of energy that the sun produces.

V2. Create a poster that shows examples of all the 10 forms of energy in the vocabulary list.

CONNECTIONS

C1. What form or forms of energy are produced by each of the following:
(a) a lightning bolt?
(b) a lawnmower?
(c) a personal computer?

C2. What devices could you use to make the following energy transformations:
(a) electrical energy to sound energy?
(b) chemical energy to thermal energy and light energy?
(c) gravitational energy to mechanical energy?
(d) mechanical energy to sound energy?
(e) thermal energy to mechanical energy?
(f) chemical energy to mechanical energy?

C3. Explain the difference between kinetic energy and potential energy.

C4. Explain the short-form equation for photosynthesis given in Section 9.3, on page 221.

C5. Trace the energy from the sun through its transformation(s) to its form in each of the following energy sources:
(a) wood
(b) wind
(c) coal
(d) hydroelectricity
(e) solar energy

EXPLORATIONS

E1. Make a poster showing a labelled plan of a farm or a town where all your energy needs would be provided by the sun, and no fossil fuels would be used. Make sure to include all the energy sources used and show how the energy is carried to the places where it is used.

E2. Investigate and write a report on the advantages and disadvantages of operating vehicles using any of these sources of energy: (a) hydrogen gas, (b) alcohol, (c) solar energy, or (d) rechargeable batteries. Prepare a presentation of your findings for the class.

E3. Think of one of your favourite activities, such as bicycling or skiing. Now trace back to its source all the energy that is required for you to be able to enjoy this activity. Think of all the equipment or materials required for the activity. What forms of energy are required to manufacture the equipment or materials? Include all the energy transformations required for this activity. Design a poster that follows your activity back to its energy beginnings. Show all the equipment, forms of energy, and energy transformations involved.

E4. Design a "whatzit machine" like the one in Figure 9.15. This is an impractical device that uses several forms of energy to perform a simple chore. As a class project, you may want to build a "whatzit machine" that works.

FIGURE 9.15
A "whatzit machine"

REFLECTIONS

R1. After completing this chapter, you have a better understanding of energy. Look again at the poster that you completed in Activity 9A. In a paragraph, compare your new ideas about energy with those on the poster. How have your ideas about energy changed from the beginning of the chapter? Why did your ideas change? What else do you want to know about energy?

R2. Did you know that the sun provides us with the materials for the clothes we wear? Fossil fuels are used to make synthetic materials (materials made by humans) such as nylon, Spandex, acrylic, and polyester. Natural materials also come indirectly from the sun: cotton comes from plants, wool from sheep, silk from silkworms, and leather from animal hides. At the library, find out how both synthetic and natural fibres are made.

(a) For polyester, list all the energy transformations that occur from the original source of energy (the sun) to the finished product.

(b) For each of the natural materials given above, list the energy transformations that occur from the original source of energy (the sun) to the finished product.

(c) In a group, discuss which type of clothing material, synthetic or natural, affects the environment more.

CHAPTER 10

THERMAL ENERGY AND HEAT

When the temperature drops outside, you put on your winter clothes. By wearing heavier, thicker clothing, you are preventing your body from losing too much heat. Keeping heat in is important in your life in other ways too. Your home stays warm in winter because it was built to prevent heat transfer. A heavy mug keeps your hot drink warm longer than a thin-walled china cup does.

Keeping things cool by keeping heat out is often just as important as keeping heat in. For example, at the beach you may use a cooler to keep your drinks and food cold. When you are out in the sun, you may wear a hat to keep your head cool.

People have developed many ways of living more comfortably by preventing heat transfer. In this chapter, you will learn how you can control heat transfer. You will also learn about the differences between thermal energy, temperature, and heat.

ACTIVITY 10A / THINKING ABOUT THERMAL ENERGY

GROUP ACTIVITY

In this chapter, you will learn a great deal about thermal energy. What do you already know about thermal energy? One way to find out is to create a mind map. In your learning journal, use a phrase such as "Thermal Energy in My World" for the centre of your mind map. For your ideas on thermal energy, think about the activities you do every day, about your house and your school, and about events that occur in the world around you. On the connecting lines, write a word or phrase to describe how the ideas are connected.

Your teacher may ask you to work together with two other students. Create a group mind map by selecting, in order, one idea from each student's learning journal. Go around the group as often as time allows. ❖

10.1 THERMAL ENERGY AND TEMPERATURE

In Chapter 9, you learned that thermal energy is one of many forms of energy. Understanding thermal energy is important because other forms of energy can be changed into thermal energy. For example, the thermal energy that keeps you warm at home in the winter may be transformed from the chemical energy in the gas or oil used in the furnace. If your home is heated by electricity, the thermal energy is transformed from electrical energy. What other examples can you think of where a form of energy is transformed into thermal energy?

ACTIVITY 10B / MAKING THERMAL ENERGY

In this activity, you will explore two ways in which thermal energy can be transformed from another form of energy.

MATERIALS

Part II
two plastic foam cups
sand
thermometer
masking tape
timer
pencil

PART I Handiwork

PROCEDURE

1. Rub your hands together rapidly for 10 seconds. What do you feel? Record your observations.

DISCUSSION

1. What form of energy was produced when you rubbed your hands together?
2. Was this energy transformed from another form of energy? If so, what was the original form of this energy?

PART II Shake, Shake, Shake. . .

PROCEDURE

1. Half-fill a foam cup with sand. Using a thermometer, measure and record the temperature of the sand.
2. Securely tape a second foam cup to the first, as shown in Figure 10.1. Shake the taped cups vigorously for 5 min. You may take turns with your partner, but make sure you keep the cups moving for the full 5 min. ➥

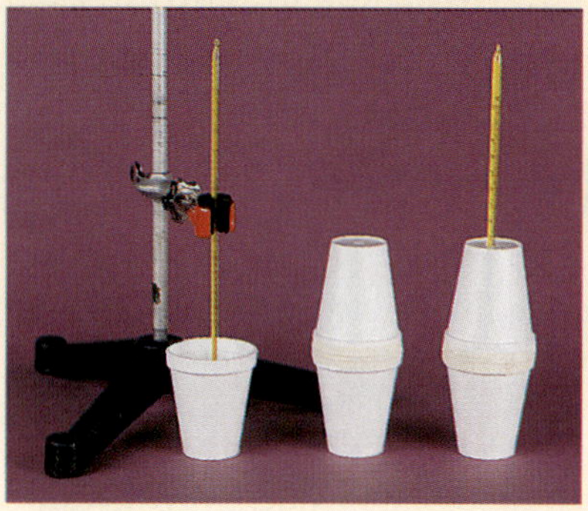

FIGURE 10.1
Apparatus for Activity 10B, Part II

CAUTION!

■ **Always be very careful when handling thermometers. The glass is easily broken.**

3. In your notebook, predict what you will find when you measure the temperature of the sand.
4. At the end of 5 min, make a small hole in the end of the top cup with a pencil. Carefully insert a thermometer into the sand (Figure 10.1). Do not damage the cups; they can be used again. Measure and record the temperature of the sand.

DISCUSSION

1. What form of energy was produced when you shook the sand in the cups?
2. (a) What was the temperature of the sand before it was shaken?
   (b) What was the temperature of the sand after it was shaken?
   (c) How does this compare with your prediction?
3. Was the thermal energy of the sand transformed from another form of energy? If so, what was the original form of the energy?
4. Why do you think that you used plastic foam cups instead of another kind of container such as a glass bottle or a tin can? ❖

THERMAL ENERGY, TEMPERATURE, AND THE KINETIC MOLECULAR THEORY

Thermal energy and temperature are closely related, but they are not the same. To understand the difference between thermal energy and temperature, think about the kinetic molecular theory. In Unit II, you learned that the particles in a solid, liquid, or gas move more quickly when they have more energy. When they have less energy, they move more slowly. Moving particles are the reason that objects are hot or cold. When an object is hot, the particles in it are moving more quickly. When the object is cold, the particles in it are moving more slowly.

Thermal energy is the total energy of all the particles in an object. The amount of thermal energy depends on the size of the object, because the larger the object, the more moving particles it contains. For example, a pot of tea has more thermal energy than a cup of tea.

Not all the particles in an object move at the same speed. Some particles move more quickly than others because they have more energy. **Temperature** is a way of measuring the average energy of all of the particles in an object. If most of the particles in an object are moving very quickly, the average energy of the particles is high. So, the object would have a high temperature. If most of the particles of an object are moving very slowly, the average energy of the particles is low. The object would then have a low temperature.

Suppose that you have a pie in the freezer. The pie is cold because the particles in the pie are moving slowly. Some of the particles are moving more slowly than others, but none of them are moving very fast. The average energy of the particles is low, so the pie's temperature is low.

If you take your pie out of the freezer and put it into a hot oven, the pie eventually becomes hot. The pie is hot because the particles in it are now moving much more quickly than they did when the pie was frozen. The temperature of your pie is now much higher because the average energy of the particles is greater.

Temperature is a way of measuring the average energy of the particles in an object, so it does not change when the size of the object changes. If you take a piece out of your pie, it will be the same temperature as the whole pie.

Imagine that you are sitting down to lunch with a bowl of soup in front of you. You take your first spoonful of hot soup. If you measure the temperature of the spoonful of soup before it cools off, would it be different from the temperature of the soup in the bowl? The soup in the bowl has much more thermal energy than the soup in the spoon, because the total amount of soup in the bowl is greater than in the spoon. The temperature, however, would be the same, because the average energy of all the particles would be the same in the spoon and in the bowl (Figure 10.2).

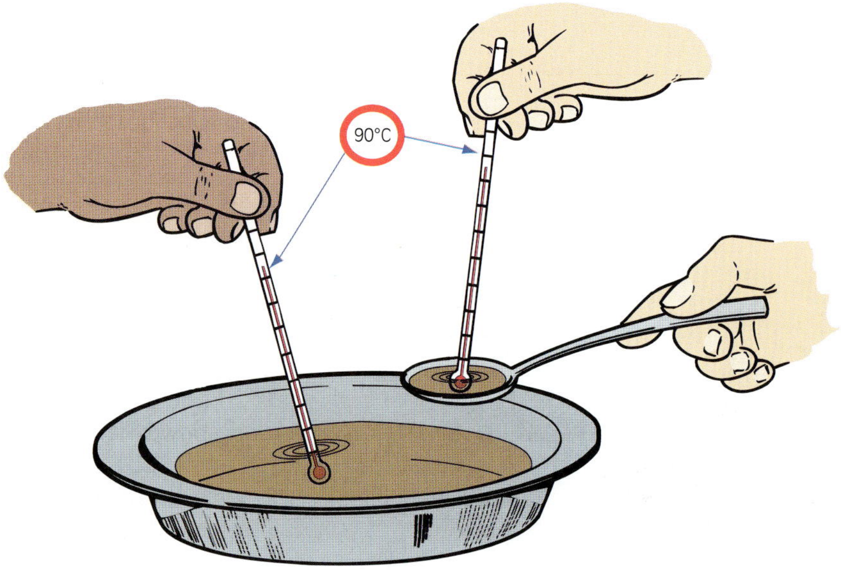

FIGURE 10.2
The temperature of the soup is the same in the bowl and the spoon.

Why does a spoonful of soup cool off much more quickly than a bowl of soup, if the starting temperatures are the same? Where would you expect to take the "coolest" spoonful of soup? Why does blowing on your soup cool it down? You will learn the answer to these and other questions later in the chapter.

REVIEW 10.1

1. Think about the three situations shown in Figure 10.3. In each situation, which of the containers has more thermal energy? Which has the higher temperature? Give reasons for your answers.
2. Describe two ways that mechanical energy can be changed into thermal energy.
3. Use the kinetic molecular theory to explain the difference between thermal energy and temperature.

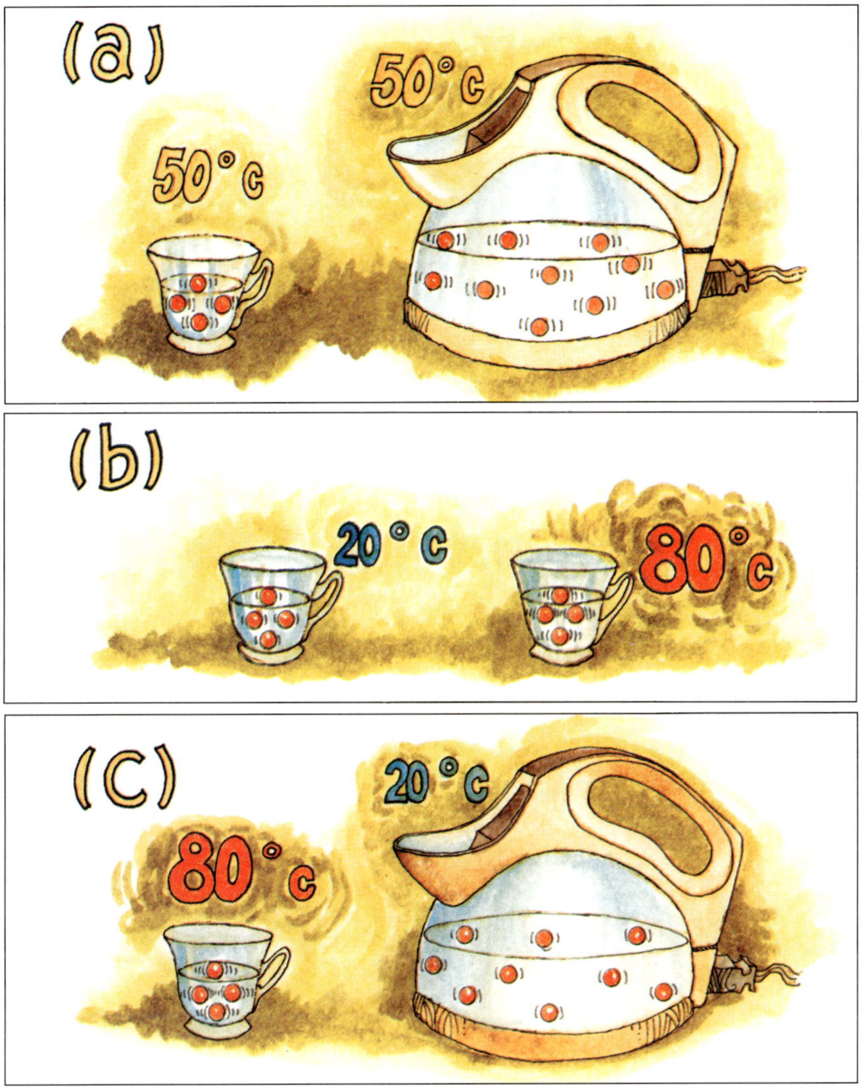

FIGURE 10.3 ◀
Which container in each pair has more thermal energy? See Review Question 1.

■ 10.2 HOW A THERMOMETER MEASURES TEMPERATURE

You can usually tell if an object is hot or cold by how it feels or by its appearance. When you take a can of pop out of the refrigerator, it feels cold. You know that water is hot when you see that it is boiling. But how can you tell how hot or cold something is?

You learned in Section 10.1 that temperature is a way of measuring the average energy of the particles in an object. The temperature indicates how hot an object is. How can you determine the temperature of something?

A **thermometer** is an instrument that is used to measure temperature ("thermo-" means heat; "-meter" means measure). To under-

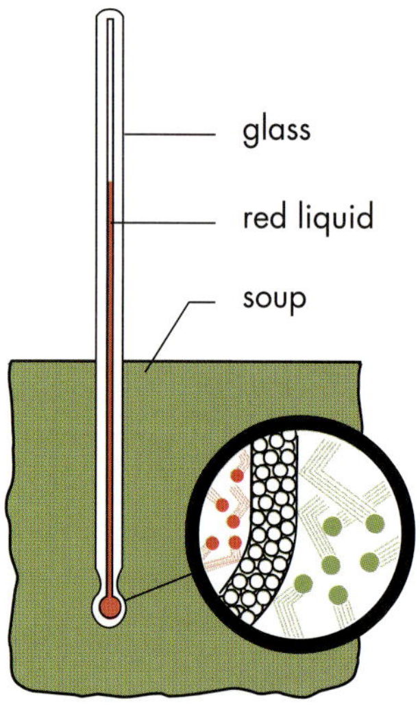

FIGURE 10.4
Soup particles hitting a thermometer. What happens to the particles of the red liquid?

stand how a thermometer works, think about the kinetic molecular theory.

Figure 10.4 shows a thermometer that has been placed in a bowl of hot soup. The particles in the soup are moving quickly because they have a great deal of energy. As they bump into the glass of the thermometer, some of their energy is transferred to the particles of the glass. As the particles in the glass begin to move faster, some of their energy is transferred to the red liquid inside the thermometer.

This extra energy causes the particles of the red liquid to move faster and to push each other farther apart. The only place for the particles of the red liquid to go is up the narrow hole inside the glass tube of the thermometer. How high the red liquid rises depends on the average energy of the particles in the red liquid. The energy of these particles increases because of the greater energy of the particles in the soup. So, the reading on the thermometer is a measurement of the average energy of the particles in the soup. This measurement is the temperature of the soup.

HOW HOT? HOW COLD?

FIGURE 10.5
Galileo Galilei

Advances in science have always depended on good measuring techniques. The invention and improvement of the thermometer was one of the most important developments in measuring techniques. As often happens in science, this development was the work of many different people.

Near the end of the 1500s, the Italian scientist Galileo, shown in Figure 10.5, experimented with measuring temperature. He took a glass bulb with a long tube attached and turned it upside down into a container of water. He would heat the air in the bulb with his hands or another heat source. As the temperature rose, the particles in the air moved faster and pushed each other farther apart. This forced bubbles out of the bottom of the tube. When the air cooled, the particles moved closer together and the water level rose in the tube. Changes in air temperature caused the water level in the tube to rise or fall. As the air temperature dropped, the level of the water in the tube rose. The level of the water gave the temperature reading. This device was not very accurate because it was not sealed. Also, Galileo used different number scales whenever he designed a new thermometer. Figure 10.6 shows one of Galileo's thermometers.

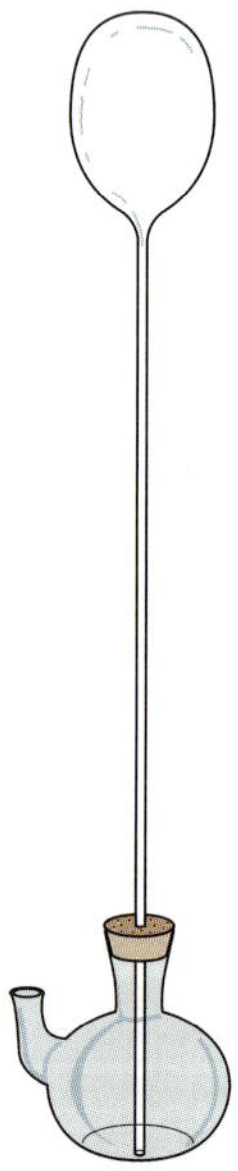

FIGURE 10.6
Galileo's thermometer

By the year 1700, many people were making thermometers. The problem was that each thermometer maker used a different number scale, and even two thermometers by the same maker could show different readings. In 1717, Gabriel Fahrenheit, a Dutch maker of scientific instruments, developed the first truly accurate thermometers. These thermometers used mercury.

In 1742, Anders Celsius, a Danish astronomer, devised the centigrade scale ("centi-" means 100; "-grade" means gradations or steps). On this scale, water freezes at 0° and boils at 100°. Now called the **Celsius scale**, it is used in most countries of the world.

ACTIVITY 10C / MAKING A THERMOMETER

In this activity, you will make a thermometer and compare its accuracy with that of a laboratory thermometer.

MATERIALS

Part I
safety goggles
apron
glass tubing (30 cm)
one-holed rubber stopper
500 mL Florence flask
test tube clamp
clamp stand
250 mL beaker
water
candle
wet cloth

CAUTION!

- **Always be very careful when handling the glass tubing. Do not try to remove the tubing from the stopper.**

PART I Making an Air Thermometer

PROCEDURE

1. Put on your safety goggles and apron.
2. Your teacher already has the rubber stopper and tubing assembly prepared. Insert the rubber stopper into the Florence flask. Half-fill the beaker with water. Support the Florence flask upside down with the clamp stand, so that the end of the glass tubing is in the 250 mL beaker (Figure 10.7).
3. In your notebook, predict what will happen when the Florence flask is heated. Then warm the flask with your hands. What happens? Record your observations.
4. Lightly heat the flask with the flame of a candle. Record your observations.
5. In your notebook, predict what will happen to the level of the water in the tube when the flask is cooled. After heating the flask with the candle flame, cool the flask with a wet cloth. Observe what happens. Record your observations.

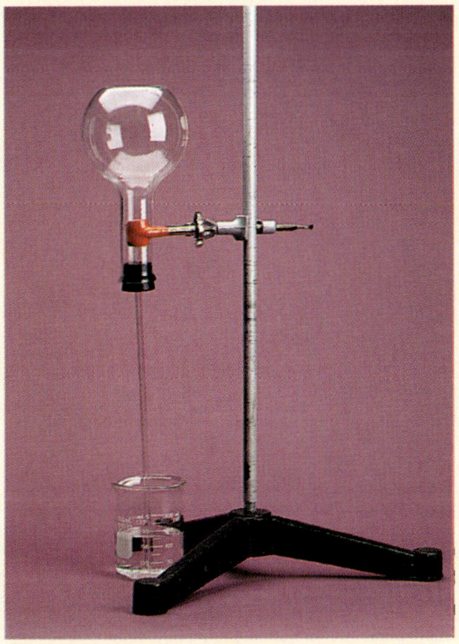

FIGURE 10.7
How to set up the apparatus for Activity 10C, Part I

DISCUSSION

1. Do you think that this type of thermometer is convenient to use to measure body temperature or the temperature of a bowl of soup? Explain your answer.
2. Why was the large container (the Florence flask) used instead of a smaller container?
3. Why do you think that the bubbles appeared at the bottom of the glass tubing? Use the kinetic molecular theory to explain your answer.
4. The beaker containing the water was open to the air. How do you think this affects the level of the liquid in the glass tubing?

MATERIALS

Part II
safety goggles
apron
glass tubing (50 cm)
one-holed rubber stopper
ethylene glycol
food colouring
test tube (125 mm x 15 mm)
tape
strip of paper
test tube clamp
clamp stand
two 400 mL beakers
water
hotplate
ice

CAUTION!

- **Ethylene glycol is poisonous. Be careful in handling it. Wash your hands thoroughly at the end of this activity.**
- **Be very careful when using a hot water bath. The hot liquid can cause severe burns.**

EXTENSION

- Make a thermometer from a water-filled Florence flask. Have the flask sit upright, with a piece of glass tubing inserted in a rubber stopper at the top. Use coloured water so that you can see the level easily. What happens when you cup your hands around the flask?

PART II Making a Liquid Thermometer

PROCEDURE

1. Put on your safety goggles and apron.
2. Fill the test tube with ethylene glycol that has been coloured with food colouring.
3. Your teacher already has the rubber stopper and tubing assembly prepared. Insert the rubber stopper and glass tubing into the test tube. Tape a strip of paper onto the glass tubing, as shown in Figure 10.8. You will use this paper to record your readings.
4. Half-fill one of the beakers with water. Heat it on the hotplate until the water boils.
5. While you are waiting for the first beaker to heat up, half-fill the second beaker with crushed ice.
6. Using a test tube clamp and clamp stand, carefully place the test tube and glass tubing assembly into the boiling water in the beaker. When the level of the ethylene glycol stops changing, mark the final position on your paper strip as 100°.
7. Remove the test tube from the hot water bath. (If the level of the ethylene glycol goes over the top of the tubing, wait until it stops flowing and mark the top of the tubing as 100°.)
8. Place the test tube and glass tubing assembly in the ice. Support it with the test tube clamp and the clamp stand. When the level stops changing, mark the final position of the ethylene glycol on the paper strip. This time, mark it as 0°.
9. Divide the space between the two marks on your paper strip into 10 equal sections. Label the divisions from 10° up to 90°. Divide every 10° section in half with another mark.

DISCUSSION

1. Make a list of all the safety precautions you took while doing Part II. Explain why each one was necessary.
2. (a) What happened to the level of the ethylene glycol in the glass tubing when the test tube was placed in the water bath?
   (b) What happened to the level of the ethylene glycol in the glass tubing when the test tube was placed in the crushed ice?
3. The end of the glass tubing was open to the air. How do you think this could affect the level of ethylene glycol in the glass tubing?
4. Why was a large container (the test tube) needed on the end of the glass tubing?
5. How could the size of the container

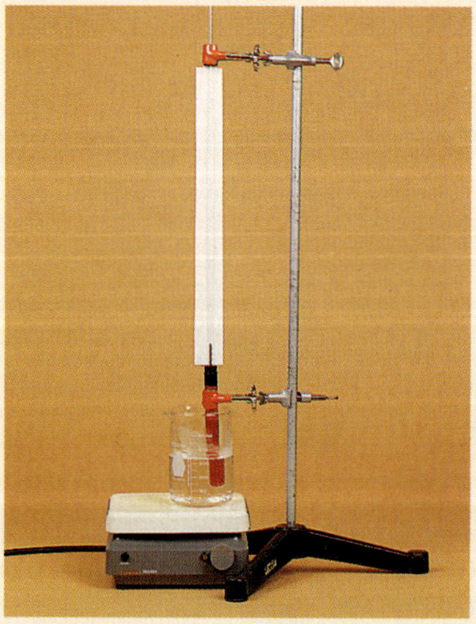

FIGURE 10.8 ▶
Apparatus for Activity 10C, Part II

affect the temperature of the liquid being measured? Explain your answer.

6. Why did you wait for the level of the ethylene glycol to stop changing before you marked the scale?
7. Ethylene glycol is used in car engine radiators as an antifreeze and to keep the radiator from boiling over. Why do you think that ethylene glycol was used in your thermometer?

MATERIALS

Part III
your thermometer from Part II
laboratory thermometers
beakers of water at different temperatures

PART III Testing Your Thermometer

PROCEDURE

1. Your teacher has placed a number of beakers containing water at different temperatures around the room. At each station, there is a laboratory thermometer. Move from station to station and measure the temperature of the water in each beaker using your thermometer. Make sure that you allow your thermometer to remain in the sample long enough for the level of the ethylene glycol to stop changing. Record your reading.
2. Measure the temperature of the water in the beaker using the laboratory thermometer. Record the reading.

DISCUSSION

1. Compare the temperatures you obtained using your thermometer with those of the laboratory thermometers. Suggest some reasons why the readings from your thermometer might be different from those on the laboratory thermometer.
2. How could you improve the design of your thermometer so that the temperature readings would be closer to those of the laboratory thermometers?
3. Using the kinetic molecular theory, explain how your thermometer works. ❖

HOW LOW CAN YOU GO?

Think about the thermometer in the soup that you read about earlier in this section. In the example, the energy of the particles in the soup are transferred to the particles in the glass of the thermometer and then to the particles in the liquid of the thermometer. The extra energy causes the particles in the thermometer's liquid to move faster and farther apart. This movement of the particles causes the volume of the liquid to increase. (Volume is the amount of space something occupies.) This increase in volume is called **expansion**.

What would happen if you took the thermometer out of the soup and put it into a dish of ice cream? From the kinetic molecular theory, you know that particles in a warm substance move more quickly than those in a cold substance. The particles in the thermometer move more quickly than those in the ice cream. They have more energy than those in the ice cream. The quickly moving particles start transferring energy to the slower-moving ones as soon as the thermometer is placed in the ice cream.

EXTENSION

■ The fluid-filled glass thermometers used to take your body's temperature are called clinical thermometers. When the thermometer is heated, the fluid can squeeze by the narrow place at the bottom of the tube, but it cannot return into the bulb when it has cooled. The column of fluid remains at the highest temperature measured. Why is this type of thermometer used for taking body temperature? How is the fluid in the thermometer returned to the bulb?

DID YOU KNOW

In 1848, William Thompson (Lord Kelvin), a Scottish mathematician and physicist, suggested a new temperature scale. This scale has its zero mark at absolute zero and the degrees are the same as those on the Celsius scale. The scale is called the Kelvin scale and temperatures are written as K (without the ° symbol). Because nothing is colder than absolute zero, Kelvin temperatures are always positive. This makes the Kelvin scale easier to use than the Celsius scale.

As the faster-moving particles in the liquid of the thermometer transfer their energy, they begin to move more slowly. They also move closer together because they no longer have enough energy to move apart. The movement of the particles closer together causes the volume of the liquid in the thermometer to decrease. This decrease in volume is called **contraction**.

The particles in gases move even more freely than those in liquids, so gases expand and contract in a similar way to liquids. Thermometers that contain air or gases also use contraction and expansion to determine temperature readings. Particles in all substances reach their lowest level of energy at **absolute zero**, the lowest temperature possible. Using the Celsius scale, absolute zero is –273°C.

REVIEW 10.2

1. Use the kinetic molecular theory to explain how a thermometer measures temperature.
2. Why is coloured water not commonly used as the fluid in thermometers? (Hint: Think about the boiling point and the freezing point of water.)
3. Why are thermometers sealed?
4. Explain expansion and contraction using the kinetic molecular theory.

10.3 TRANSFERRING HEAT

Earlier in this chapter, you learned the difference between thermal energy and temperature. Another important term used in studying thermal energy is "heat." **Heat** is the energy transferred from an object at a higher temperature to one at a lower temperature. If you have ever cupped your hands around a mug of hot chocolate or touched a car on a hot day, you have felt heat.

Energy always transfers from matter with a higher temperature to matter with a lower temperature. That is, energy transfers from particles of greater average energy to particles of lower average energy. This process is called heat transfer. **Heat transfer** from one object to another only takes place as long as the temperatures of the objects are different. There are three methods of heat transfer: conduction, convection, and radiation.

Today, you can explain heat transfer using the kinetic molecular theory, but 18th century scientists used another theory. The **caloric theory** suggested that heat was a fluid called "caloric," and every object contained caloric. Caloric flowed from hot objects into cold ones. By 1800, however, the caloric theory was proven wrong by Benjamin Thompson, also known as Count Rumford. Rumford believed that, if caloric existed, any object being heated or cooled should change mass as the caloric flowed into it or out of it. Rumford designed experiments to test this idea. His findings showed that the mass of an object did not change in any way when it was heated. Rumford concluded that caloric did not exist, and heat was not a fluid. Rumford was an inventor, as well as a scientist. He invented the double boiler for cooking, the kitchen range, and the drip coffee pot.

CONDUCTION

Imagine grabbing the steel handlebars of your bicycle after it has been sitting out in the sun on a hot summer day. Now imagine picking up a piece of wood that is about the same size as the handlebars and that has also been sitting out in the sun. Which do you think would feel hotter? Can you suggest a reason?

The handlebars are hot because of the metal's ability to transfer the heat to all parts of it. The transfer of heat by the collision of particles in a solid is called **conduction**. A substance that conducts heat well, like steel, is called a **conductor**. Wood is not a good conductor.

ACTIVITY 10D / HEAT TRANSFER IN SOLIDS

In this activity, you will investigate heat transfer in solids and the ability of different materials to transfer heat.

MATERIALS

Part I

- safety goggles
- apron
- gloves
- copper pipe or steel rod (12 mm diameter)
- wooden dowel (12 mm diameter)
- paper
- tape
- candle
- beaker
- water
- stopwatch ➡

CAUTION!

- **Be prepared to extinguish any flame that cannot be blown out by drowning it in a beaker of water.**

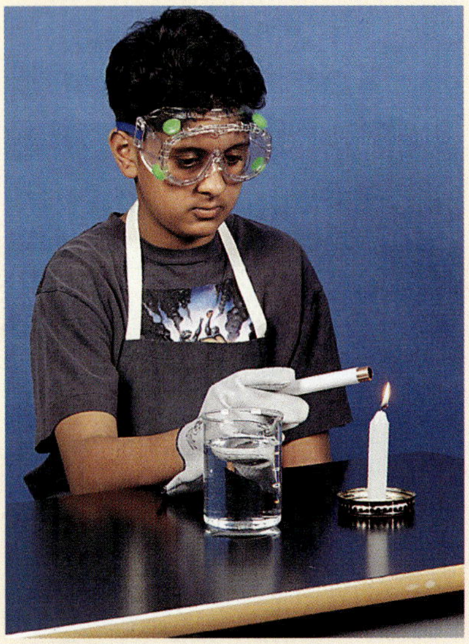

FIGURE 10.9
Hold the paper-wrapped copper pipe in the candle flame.

MATERIALS

Part II
copper wire
pencil
beaker
water
candle

PART I Conduction in Two Solids

PROCEDURE

1. Put on your safety goggles, apron and gloves. Ensure loose clothing is secured and long hair is tied back.
2. Wrap three-quarters of the sections of copper pipe and wooden dowel tightly with paper one layer thick. Fasten the paper with tape.
3. Predict what will happen to the paper as the copper pipe and the wooden dowel are held in a candle flame. Write your prediction in your notebook.
4. Fill the beaker with water and place it close to where you are working.
5. Hold the paper on the pipe in a candle flame as shown in Figure 10.9. Carefully observe what happens. Using a stopwatch, measure the time it takes for the paper to begin burning. Record your observations.
6. Repeat step 5 above using the wooden dowel.

DISCUSSION

1. How did your predictions from step 3 compare with your observations in step 5?
2. Using the kinetic molecular theory, explain
   (a) what happened to the paper on the copper pipe,
   (b) what happened to the paper on the wooden dowel.
3. From your observations, why do you think a wooden pot would not be a good container to use in cooking even if it could not burn?

PART II Caging the Flame

PROCEDURE

1. Construct a copper coil by wrapping the copper wire loosely around a pencil about 15 times. Predict what will happen when the copper coil is lowered over the candle flame, as shown in Figure 10.10. Do you think the flame will increase in size, decrease in size, or stay the same? Write your prediction in your notebook.
2. Fill the beaker with cold water. Cool the copper coil in the water. Shake the coil to remove as much water as possible.
3. Lower the copper coil over the candle flame. Make sure that you surround the flame and that you do not press the wick into the melted wax. Quickly record your observations.
4. Repeat step 3 using the heated copper coil. Record your observations in your notebook.

DISCUSSION

1. How did your prediction in step 1 compare with your observations from step 3?
2. Using the kinetic molecular theory, explain your observations from steps 3 and 4.

FIGURE 10.10
Caging the flame

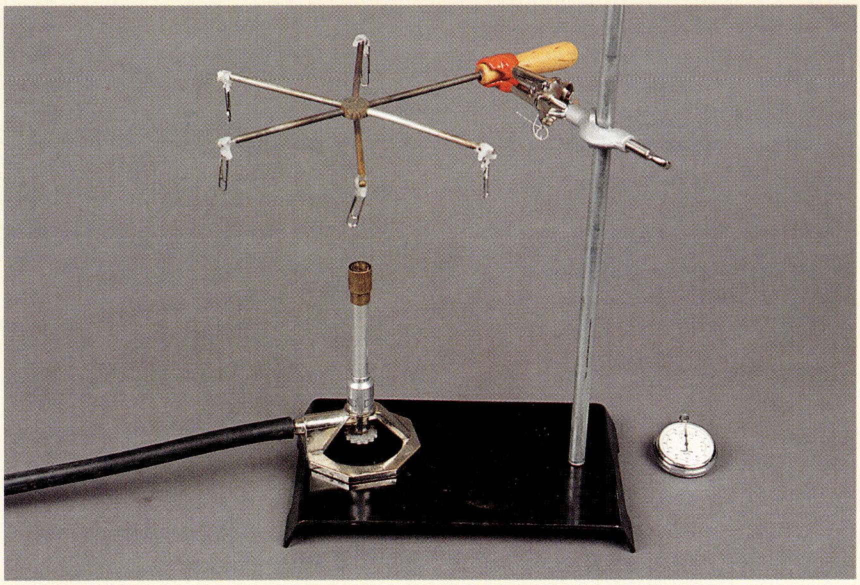

FIGURE 10.11
A conductometer

3. Why did the cool coil have a different effect on the candle flame than the heated coil did?

MATERIALS

Part III
six-rod conductometer
paper clips or finishing nails (2.5 cm)
wax
Bunsen burner

PART III Using a Conductometer (Teacher Demonstration)

PROCEDURE

1. Your teacher will prepare the apparatus shown in Figure 10.11. Each rod on the conductometer is made of a different metal. When the temperature at the end of each rod is high enough to melt the wax, the paperclip or nail will drop. Predict the order in which the paper clips or nails will drop. (Hint: Think of the different uses of each metal on the conductometer.) Write your prediction in your notebook.

2. Carefully observe as your teacher places the hub of the conductometer in the flame. Record your observations.

DISCUSSION

1. List the metals in the order (from fastest to slowest) that energy travelled through them. Were your predictions correct?

2. The ability of materials to allow the transfer of heat is important in many things you use at home. Choose three of the metals tested, and write down some of the uses for each one where the ability to conduct heat is important. For example, copper is used on the bottom of some cooking pots.

Part IV
right-angle clamp holder
support stand
four rods (60 cm long and 6.3 mm diameter), one each of aluminum, brass, copper, and steel
finishing nails (2.5 cm) or paperclips
wax
Meker-type burner
stopwatch
graph paper

PART IV Graphing Conduction Rates (Teacher Demonstration)

PROCEDURE

1. Copy Table 10.1 in your notebook to record your data. ➥

CAUTION!

■ **Do not touch the hot metal. Cool and hot metal rods look the same.**

EXTENSION

■ Your graph will level off if, after a long time, no more nails fall. This occurs when the heat transfer from the rod to the surrounding air is taking place faster than the heat transfer from the flame to the rod. Draw a diagram of this idea showing particles of matter.

2. Using the support stand and clamp holder, your teacher will set up the four 60 cm metal rods, as shown in Figure 10.12. Mount the nails on the rods every 5 cm using the wax.
3. Your teacher will take each rod, one at a time, and place the free end in the hottest part of the flame of a Meker-type burner. Using a stopwatch, start timing from when the rod is placed in the flame. Record the time it takes for each nail to drop. Continue until all the nails have dropped or to a maximum of 10 minutes for the rod.
4. Your teacher will repeat steps 2 and 3 for each of the other rods. Each time, the end of the rod will be at the same height in the burner flame. Also, the burner flame will stay constant.
5. Prepare a sheet of graph paper as shown in Figure 10.13.
6. Make a graph using the data collected in steps 3 and 4. Graph the results from all four rods on the same piece of paper. Use a different symbol or colour for plotting the points for each.

FIGURE 10.12
How to set up apparatus for Activity 10D, Part IV

DISCUSSION

1. (a) Why was it important to have the rods set at the same position above the burner?
   (b) Why was it important to keep the burner flame constant?
   (c) What other factors must be kept the same for all the rods? ❖

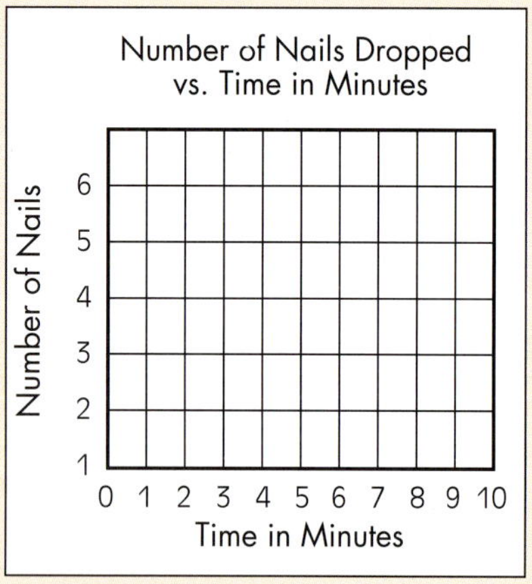

FIGURE 10.13
Sample graph for Activity 10D, Part IV

Number of nails	Aluminum	Brass	Copper	Steel
1				
2				
3				
4				
5				
6				
7				

TABLE 10.1 ***Sample Data Table for Activity 10D, Part IV***

CONDUCTION AND THE KINETIC MOLECULAR THEORY

As you stir a pot of soup on the stove with a metal spoon, you can feel the spoon become hot. Heat is being transferred by conduction along the spoon. The ability of a material to transfer heat through conduction is called its conductivity.

The kinetic molecular theory explains how conductivity works. The fast-moving particles in the hot soup transfer energy to the spoon by colliding with the particles in the metal of the spoon. The particles in the spoon begin to move faster. But the entire handle of the spoon is not in the soup. Why does it become hot? As the particles in the spoon move faster, they collide with their neighbours more often. Energy is gradually transferred to particles all through the spoon, so the cool handle of the spoon becomes hot.

Table 10.2 lists the conductivity of a number of different substances. Good conductors, such as many metals, have high conductivities. Air and human skin have low conductivities. Figure 10.14 shows how the transfer of energy occurs when a metal rod is held in a flame.

Material	Conductivity
Air	1.0
Down from birds	1.1
Cork	1.8
Human skin	8.7
Glass	25
Water	26
Brick	30
Concrete	73
Ice	94
Iron and steel	2 000
Brass	4 600
Aluminum	8 600
Copper	16 000
Silver	18 000

TABLE 10.2
Conductivity of Materials Compared with Air (at about 20°C)

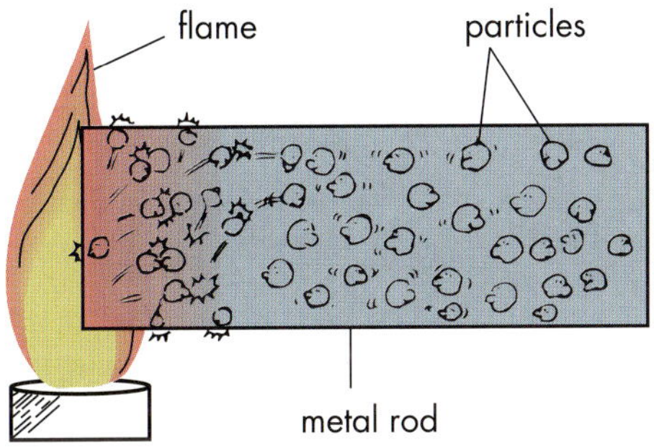

FIGURE 10.14
Heat transfer by conduction in a metal rod. The particles near the source of heat begin to vibrate quickly. As they collide with other particles, they transfer energy to them. This way, the energy spreads along the rod. If you were holding the end of the rod farthest from the heat, what would you feel?

CONVECTION

You have learned how heat transfer takes place in solids by conduction. But not all matter is solid. Liquids and gases are states of matter in which the particles flow from place to place. They are called **fluids**, and they are poor heat conductors. If liquids and gases do not conduct heat as well as solids do, how does heat transfer take place in fluids?

Think about soup again. How does the soup in a pot on the stove become hot enough to boil? To help heat the soup more quickly, you can stir it with a spoon. This hints at another method of transferring heat. As soup is heating, some parts of it, near the heat source, will be hotter than other parts. By stirring, you are mixing higher-temperature soup with lower-temperature soup. This also occurs naturally, because particles in liquids and gases can flow and move past each other. This movement is called convection. **Convection** is the transfer of heat in fluids by the movement of particles from one part of the fluid to another.

ACTIVITY 10E / HEAT TRANSFER IN FLUIDS

In this activity, you will investigate how heat transfer by convection occurs in liquids and gases.

MATERIALS

Part I
safety goggles
apron
convection ring apparatus
(glass tubing ring)
cold water
test tube clamp
support stand
Bunsen burner (or candle)
food colouring (with dropper)

Part II
safety goggles
chimney box apparatus
candle
smoke paper

CAUTION!

- **Be careful with open flames. Discard smouldering paper in water.**

PART I Observing a Convection Ring

PROCEDURE

1. Put on your safety goggles and apron.

2. Fill a convection ring apparatus with cold water and support it with a test tube clamp and support stand as shown in Figure 10.15. Predict what will happen when the glass test tube is heated at the position indicated in Figure 10.15. Write your prediction in your notebook. Give reasons for your prediction.

3. Test your prediction. Heat one corner of the convection ring apparatus with a Bunsen burner or a candle. Just as heating begins, place a drop of food colouring in the open tube at the top of the ring. Record your observations.

DISCUSSION

1. (a) From your observations, describe any evidence that convection is taking place in the water.
(b) What is the source of the heat?
(c) Where does the heated water go?
(d) If you did not have food colouring, what data could you collect to show that heat is being transferred by convection in the water?

2. Use the kinetic molecular theory to explain why the water moves around in the convection ring apparatus.

PART II Observing a Chimney Box

PROCEDURE

1. Put on your safety goggles.

2. Using a chimney box similar to the one shown in Figure 10.16, place a candle in the holder under one of the chimneys. Predict what will happen when smoke paper is held above the chimney over the candle. Also predict what will happen when smoke paper is held above the other chimney.

3. Use the apparatus to test your prediction. Hold a piece of smoke paper above the chimney over the candle, then above the other chimney. Record your observations.

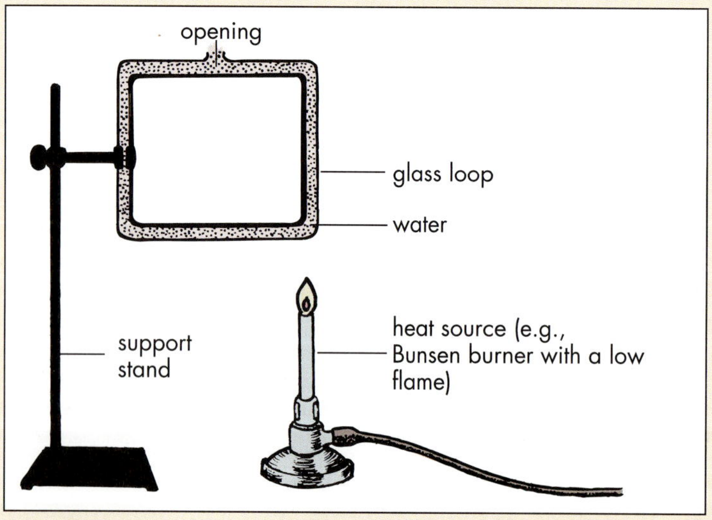

FIGURE 10.15 ◀
Convection ring apparatus for Activity 10E, Part I

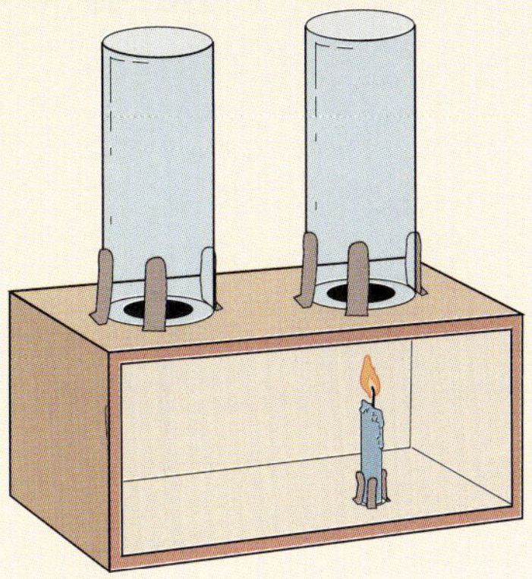

FIGURE 10.16
Chimney box apparatus for Activity 10E, Part II

DISCUSSION

1. (a) What evidence do you have that heat transfer was taking place in the chimney box apparatus?
   (b) What is the heat source?
   (c) Where does the heated air go?
   (d) If you could not see the movement of the smoke, what data could you collect to show that heat transfer is taking place in the chimney box apparatus?
2. (a) Describe the similarities in the way the water moved in the convection ring apparatus in Part I of this activity and the way the air moved in the chimney box apparatus in Part II.
   (b) Describe the differences in the way the water moved in the convection ring apparatus in Part I of this activity and the way the air moved in the chimney box apparatus in Part II.
3. From your observations and your knowledge of the kinetic molecular theory, draw a diagram to explain why the air in the chimney box moves as it does. ❖

CONVECTION AND THE KINETIC MOLECULAR THEORY

The kinetic molecular theory explains convection in fluids such as air and water. When soup particles on the bottom of a pot are heated, they gain speed and move farther apart. This part of the soup is less dense than the cooler parts of the soup. This less dense soup then rises to the top of the pot, and the denser soup sinks.

While the pot is heating on the stove, it contains a rising stream of warmer soup and a sinking stream of cooler soup. These streams are called **convection currents**. Heat transfer in fluids takes place because of convection currents.

Convection in liquids and in gases is very similar. You read about convection currents moving in a liquid like soup. How do they move in a gas? Imagine that you have an electric heater along the floor on one side of a room, as shown in Figure 10.17. As the particles of air collide with the particles of the heater, they gain heat. The particles of air begin to move faster and farther apart. As the particles move apart, the heated air becomes less dense than the cooler surrounding air. This heated air rises and is replaced by cooler, denser air. As this pattern continues, a convection current develops in the room.

RADIATION

You have learned that heat transfer by conduction and convection depends on the motion of particles. In conduction, the particles move

FIGURE 10.17
A convection current in a room with a heater along one wall. What would happen to the current if you opened the door?

FIGURE 10.18
Radiant energy from the sun reaches the Earth through 149 million kilometres of space, where there are almost no particles.

back and forth, colliding with each other. These collisions transfer the energy from one particle to the next, but the particles themselves do not move very far. In convection, the particles move through a fluid, transferring energy as they collide with other particles.

In Chapter 9, you learned that the sun is the main source of Earth's energy. The space between the Earth and the sun contains almost no particles, so heat transfer by either of these two methods, conduction or convection, is impossible. How is the sun's energy transferred to the Earth?

A third method of transferring heat is called **radiation**. Radiation does not require particles to transfer energy. Energy transferred by radiation is called **radiant energy**. Both light and heat come to us from the sun as radiant energy (Figure 10.18).

ACTIVITY 10F / HEAT TRANSFER BY RADIATION

In this activity, you will discover some of the properties of radiant heat.

CAUTION!

- **Be careful with the hotplate as it will remain hot long after it has been turned off.**

MATERIALS

Part I
radiometer
incandescent light source
fluorescent light source
hotplate
brick

Part II
two-container radiation apparatus
graduated cylinder
water
two thermometer clamps (or burette clamp)
two thermometers
incandescent light source (200W lamp or floodlight)
stopwatch
graph paper

FIGURE 10.19
Place a radiometer near an incandescent light bulb in Activity 10F, Part I.

PART I The Radiometer

PROCEDURE

1. Hold your hand briefly near the incandescent light source. Record what you feel.
2. Examine a radiometer like the one shown in Figure 10.19. Bring the bright incandescent light source near the radiometer. Record your observations.
3. Hold your hand near the fluorescent light source. Record what you feel.
4. Bring a fluorescent light source near the radiometer. Record your observations.
5. Set a hotplate on its side so that it is stable and resting on a non-flammable surface such as a brick. After the hotplate has been turned on, bring the radiometer toward the face of the hotplate. Record your observations.
6. Turn off the hot plate.

DISCUSSION

1. (a) Does the incandescent light source produce radiant heat? How do you know?
   (b) Does the fluorescent light source produce radiant heat? How do you know?
2. (a) How are the hotplate and the incandescent light similar?
   (b) How are they different?
3. The vanes of the radiometer are in a partial vacuum. This means that there are few air particles within the radiometer bulb. What method of energy transfer caused the movement you observed?

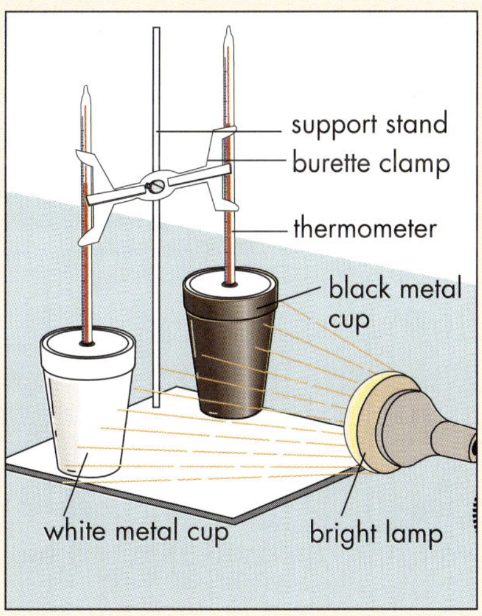

FIGURE 10.20
Apparatus for Activity 10F, Part II

PART II Making Use of Radiant Heat

PROCEDURE

1. Copy Table 10.3 in your notebook to record your data.
2. Set up the two-container radiation apparatus as shown in Figure 10.20. Use a graduated cylinder to accurately measure an equal amount of water into both containers so that they are about half full. Using the thermometer clamps, support the thermometers so that they are held away from the insides of the containers. Be sure that the light source is the same distance from both containers (Figure 10.20).

Time	Temperature (°C)	
	White container	**Black container**
0		
1		
2		
3		
4		

Table 10.3 Sample Data Table for Activity 10F, Part II

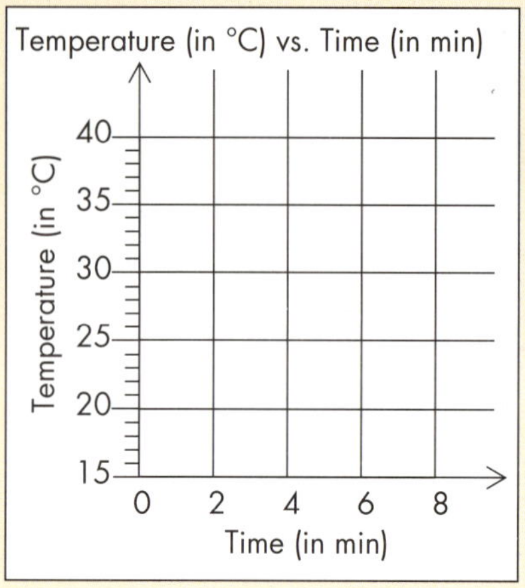

FIGURE 10.21
Sample graph for Activity 10F, Part II

EXTENSION

■ Using the same containers as in Activity 10F, predict which one would cool off more slowly, if they were both filled with the same quantity of hot water. Give reasons for your prediction. Test your prediction.

3. In your data table, record the starting temperature of the water in each of the containers.
4. Turn on the lamp and start the stopwatch. After 1 min, measure the temperature in each container and record the value in the data table.
5. Continue to measure the temperature every minute up to a total of 10 min.
6. Prepare a sheet of graph paper as shown in Figure 10.21. Make a graph using the data collected in steps 3, 4, and 5. Put the data from both containers on the same graph. Use a different symbol or colour for plotting the points for each container.

DISCUSSION

1. (a) Which container showed the greatest increase in temperature?
   (b) Which container absorbed the most energy?
2. (a) What was the source of heat?
   (b) How did the energy from the light bulb reach the water in the containers?
3. (a) What were the controlled factors in this experiment?
   (b) Why was it important to keep these factors the same for both containers?
4. What do you think happened to the energy when it reached
   (a) the dark container?
   (b) the bright, shiny container? ❖

THE PROPERTIES OF RADIANT ENERGY

Light energy and radiant heat have some common properties. Both can travel where there are few particles of matter; for example, in space. Both travel at the speed of light: about 300 000 km/s. This means that they could travel across Canada about 60 times in one second! Both forms of radiant energy travel only in straight lines and therefore cannot travel around corners.

On a hot sunny day, if you stand in the shade of a building, the light is much less bright and you feel cooler. The building is blocking the sun's radiant energy from reaching you. Would there be any shade if the energy radiating from the sun could travel around corners?

Radiant energy can be either reflected or absorbed by objects. It can also be transmitted; that is, radiant energy can pass through materials such as glass. Uses of radiant heat are all around us. Figure 10.22 shows some devices that use heat transfer by radiation. What do you think happens in each case?

(a) Car radiator

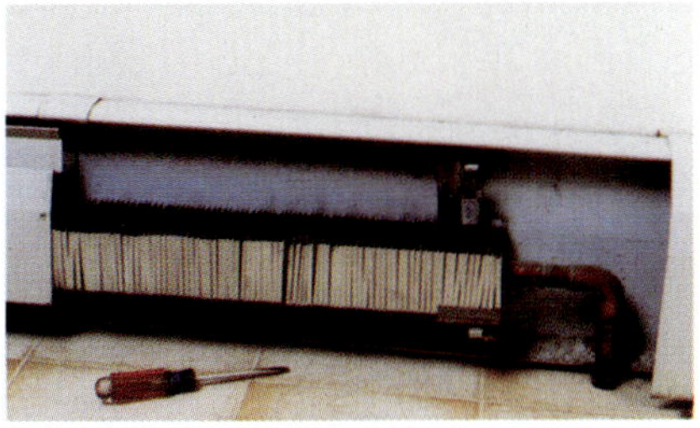

(b) Baseboard radiator

(c) Fins on a motorcycle engine

FIGURE 10.22
Devices that transfer heat by radiation

REVIEW 10.3

1. Which of the three methods of heat transfer occur in the following situations?
   (a) Ice forms on the inside of a window.
   (b) A cat stays warm by sitting on the hood of a recently parked car.
   (c) A glider soars upward as it hits some air currents.
   (d) Black pipes are used for a solar energy collector.
   (e) Curtains gently sway above an electric radiator.
   (f) You hold a cup of hot cocoa tightly to warm your hands.
2. Use the kinetic molecular theory to explain how heat is transferred in each of the following ways:
   (a) conduction
   (b) convection
3. (a) Name the theory used by early scientists to explain heat transfer before the kinetic molecular theory was accepted.
   (b) How did this theory explain heat transfer?
   (c) How did the scientists learn that this theory did not describe heat transfer accurately?
4. Examine the list of conductivities of various substances given in Table 10.2 on page 245.
   (a) What do the five substances with the highest conductivity have in common?
   (b) What would be the problems of living in a house entirely made of copper or silver? Explain your answer.
   (c) A baker can choose between using a glass pan or a metal pan. In which pan would the bread develop a firm brown crust on the bottom and the sides? Explain.
5. (a) In which of the three states of matter does convection occur?
   (b) Why can convection not occur in the other state(s) of matter?
6. Name three things that may happen to radiant heat when it strikes a surface.
7. What colour clothing would be worn to keep cool on a hot sunny day in summer? Explain your answer.

10.4 PREVENTING HEAT TRANSFER

In this chapter, you have examined three ways that heat can be transferred: conduction, convection, and radiation. In what you have learned so far, can you find clues to ways that you could prevent or slow down heat transfer? By controlling heat transfer, we can conserve (save) fuel and money, and reduce pollution. This is important in business, at home, at school, and in your leisure activities. In this section, you will learn more about ways to slow heat transfer and how they are applied in everyday life.

INSULATION

Substances that prevent or slow down the transfer of heat are called **insulators**. Insulators are used anywhere that it is important to reduce heat transfer by conduction, convection, and radiation. The use of insulators is called **insulation**. The heavy coat that you wear during the winter is insulation for your body. The insulator used in your coat may be down feathers from birds or an artificial fibre. You may think that insulation is only a way of preventing heat loss. There are many situations, however, where insulation is used to prevent heat gain as well.

ACTIVITY 10G / DISCOVERING INSULATION

CROSS-CURRICULAR

Think of as many different uses of insulation as you can. At the top of a page in your notebook, write the title "Insulation to Keep Heat In." Halfway down the page, write the title "Insulation to Keep Heat Out." Below each title, make a three-column table like Table 10.4. You will have two tables on your page.

Use Figure 10.23 to help you start thinking about insulation. After you have completed your tables, your teacher may ask you to combine your ideas with those of other students. From these tables, you can determine what some of the most common insulation materials are.

Insulation use	Type of insulation material	Method of heat transfer prevented
Hot drink mug	Plastic	Conduction

TABLE 10.4 ***Sample Data Table for Activity 10G***

(a) (b) (c) (d)

FIGURE 10.23
How is heat transfer reduced in each of these situations? ❖

INSULATION AND THE KINETIC MOLECULAR THEORY

What does the word "insulation" make you think of? You may think of the pink or yellow fibreglass batts used in house construction. If you have ever felt this material, you know that it is very light. The reason for this lightness is the air trapped between the fibres of the fibreglass.

Air is not a good conductor of heat. The particles in a gas are spread out, so that heat transfer by conduction is very slow. In Section 10.3, you learned how heat could be transferred in gases by convection. But the air spaces in insulation like fibreglass batts are too small for convection to take place. Air spaces also provide insulation in clothing, such as lined gloves, thermal underwear, and ski jackets.

A different method is used to prevent the transfer of radiant heat. Radiant heat can be reflected, and it cannot be transferred to any material that reflects it. Builders can use reflecting materials on windows to prevent the loss of heat from a building. A reflective coating on the inside of windows reflects radiant heat back into a house. This helps to keep the house warm in winter. Similarly, windows with a reflective coating on the outside reflect radiant heat from the sun and stop much of it from entering the house. This helps to keep the house cool in the summer. These windows still allow visible light to enter.

INSULATING YOUR HOME

A house can lose heat in many ways, and there are just as many ways to insulate against this loss of heat. Figure 10.24 shows where heat is lost through single-glazed windows. Insulating your house can also help to keep the inside of your house cooler on hot days in summer.

(a)

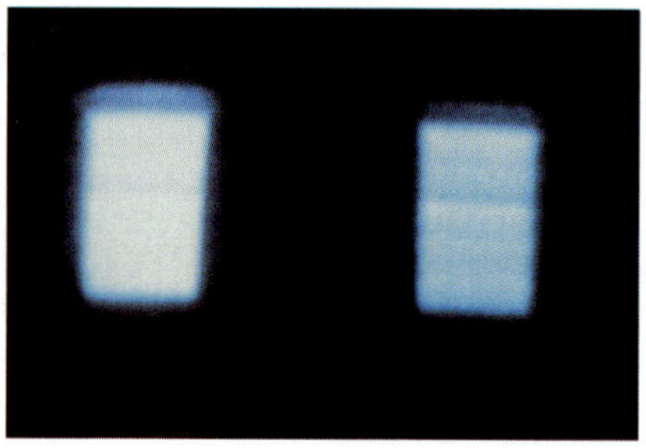

(b)

FIGURE 10.24 ▶

(a) Photograph of a single-glazed window (on the left) and a double-glazed window (on the right). (b) Thermograph of the same windows. Light blue shows the most heat loss, dark blue shows less, and black shows the least heat loss. Thermographs are similar to photographs, but are sensitive to radiant heat instead of light (thermo- is Greek for "heat" and photo- is Greek for "light").

Insulation between the outside and inside surfaces of a house prevents heat transfer by conduction, convection, and radiation. The inside walls of the house stay warm, and the outside walls stay cool and do not conduct or radiate heat in the winter. Insulating the roof is especially important, because this is where a house loses most of its heat.

Windows need special treatment because glass both conducts heat and transmits radiant heat. The reflective coatings described earlier in this section can help, but two other methods of preventing heat transfer through windows are used more commonly. One is adding extra panes of glass. Trapping air between two panes of glass (double glazing) greatly reduces the loss of heat by conduction. However, the air space must be small enough that convection currents cannot develop (Figure 10.25). A double-glazed window insulates 30 times better than a single-glazed window.

Curtains are another way to make windows better insulators. Cloth is a poor conductor of heat, and lined or padded curtains can prevent heat transfer by trapping air. Light-coloured curtains can reflect

EXTENSION

■ Some homes in Canada are being built as part of a government program to make energy conservation in new houses as good as possible. This is called the R2000 Program. Research the benefits of R2000 homes and some of the differences between R2000 construction methods and those of regular homes.

radiant heat. But even well-insulated windows lose more heat than the walls or roof of a house.

Heat can also be lost by air leaking around windows and doors. Weather stripping is material used around windows and doors to reduce heat loss by convection through cracks. Figure 10.26 shows some examples of building insulation.

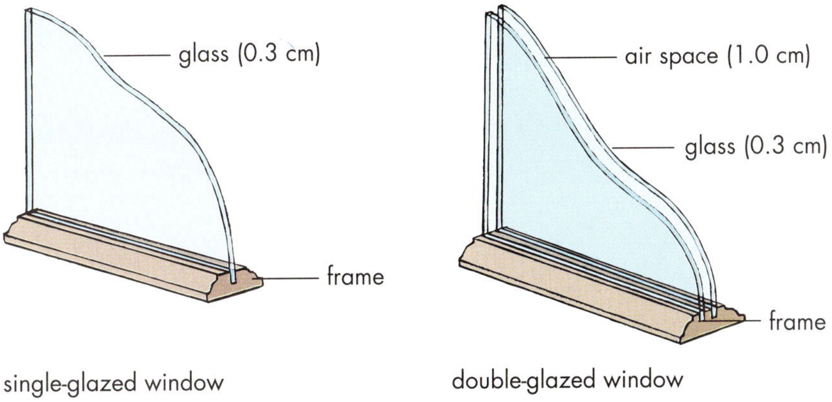

FIGURE 10.25 ◀
Double-glazed windows help to conserve energy by trapping a layer of air, which is a poor conductor of heat.

(a)

(b)

(c)

(d)

FIGURE 10.26 ◀
There are many different ways to insulate a building to reduce heat loss:
(a) weatherstripping around a door,
(b) insulation in the attic and walls,
(c) double sets of doors, and
(d) rigid roof insulation.
How does (c) differ from the other photographs? How does it compare with the double-glazed window shown in Figure 10.25?

ACTIVITY 10H / KEEPING THE HEAT IN

In this activity, you will design the best insulating container you can. You will use your knowledge of heat transfer, a set of guidelines for the container, and the materials available. Your challenge is to design an insulating container that will keep water as hot as possible.

MATERIALS

Part I

insulation materials (for example, fibreglass, Styrofoam, excelsior, vermiculite, fabric, paper, large cans, beakers, aluminum foil)
metal can (250 mL or other standard)
thermometer
support stand and clamp to hold the thermometer (if necessary)

Part II

boiling water
your container from Part I
timer
uninsulated metal can
graph paper

CAUTION!

■ Be careful when handling insulation materials. Fibreglass can cause skin irritation. Wear rubber gloves if they are available.

PART I Making Your Container

PROCEDURE

1. Using the insulation materials available, insulate the 250 mL metal can to a maximum size of 30 cm in any dimension. You want your insulated can to be able to keep 150 mL of water hot as long as possible.
2. Your design must allow some way of easily and frequently measuring the temperature in the centre of the water, using the thermometer. Use the support stand and clamp to hold the thermometer, if necessary. You may use any materials available. Do not do anything to the inside of the metal can.
3. In your notebook, draw a labelled, cross-sectional diagram of your container, identifying the material(s) you used.

DISCUSSION

1. Explain which features of your container are designed to prevent
   (a) conduction,
   (b) convection,
   (c) radiation.

PART II Testing Your Container

PROCEDURE

1. In your notebook, make a data table like Table 10.5.
2. When you are ready, your teacher will pour 150 mL of boiling water into your container. Use a thermometer to measure the temperature immediately after the water has been poured into your container. Measure the temperature every minute after that. Use a timer to time your readings. Continue taking readings for 20 min. Record your readings in the data table.
3. As a control, your teacher will conduct the same test on an uninsulated can. This will allow you to determine if the insulation on your can was effective.
4. Prepare a sheet of graph paper as shown in Figure 10.27. Draw a graph using the data collected in steps 2 and 3. Graph the results for your container and for your teacher's control on the same piece of paper. Use a different symbol or colour for plotting the points for each container.

DISCUSSION

1. By how many degrees did the temperature drop after 20 minutes
   (a) in the uninsulated container?
   (b) in the insulated container?
2. Did the insulation slow down the heat transfer from the hot water? How do you know?
3. Explain how you could improve your container's design.

Time in minutes	Temperature of water in °C
0	
1	
2	
3	

TABLE 10.5 ***Sample Data Table for Activity 10H, Part II***

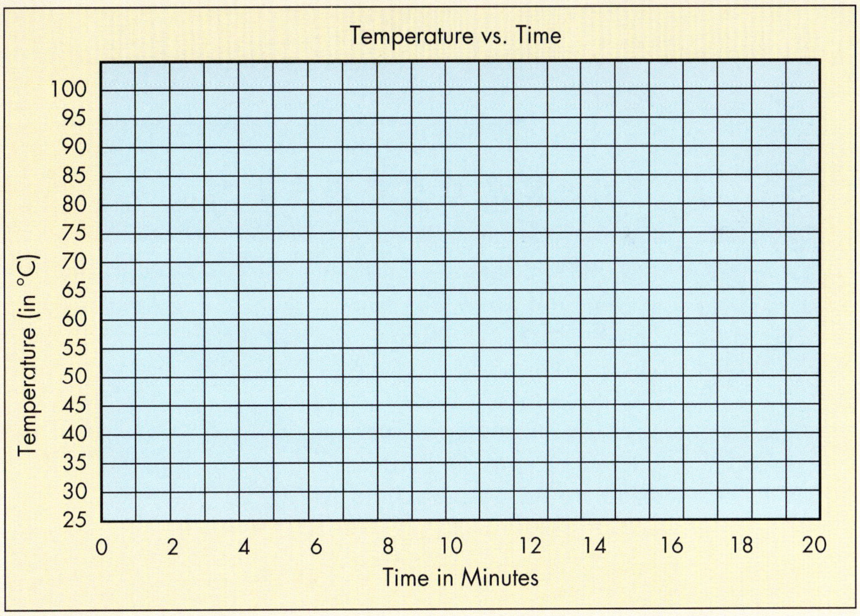

FIGURE 10.27
Sample graph for Activity 10H, Part II

4. The temperature of the hot water usually drops noticeably when the water is first poured into the container. Suggest a reason for this drop in temperature.

5. Choose one of the following appliances and describe how it is designed to reduce the loss or gain of heat: hot water tank, refrigerator, oven. ❖

EXTENSION

■ Conduct the same experiment to prevent heat gain. See how long you can keep an ice cube from melting completely. Use the same size ice cube for each group.

▶ REVIEW 10.4

1. Give some examples of heat insulators.

2. Use the kinetic molecular theory to explain how insulators prevent heat transfer by
(a) conduction,
(b) convection.

3. How do insulators prevent heat transfer by radiation?

4. (a) Why is down from birds an excellent insulator?
(b) Why is down not a good insulator when it gets wet?

5. (a) Why is home insulation so important in countries like Canada?
(b) Why is home insulation also important in warmer climates?

6. If you use aluminum foil to keep a baked potato hot, should you have the dull side or the shiny side facing inward, next to the potato? Why?

7. Temperatures in space are extremely low. Describe how an astronaut could be protected from the cold.

8. Without insulation, our lives would be very different.
(a) How would life on Earth be different?
(b) How would your everyday life be different?

THERMOGRAPHY

Your family's heating bills are too high!

Is warm air leaking out from the roof? Is cold air coming in around the windows or doors? If only you could see what is happening.

Actually, you can. You need help from an instrument called a thermal scanner. It measures invisible radiant heat. Then, with the help of a computer, the scanner changes the measurements into a "picture of heat" that you can see on a video screen. This process is called thermography.

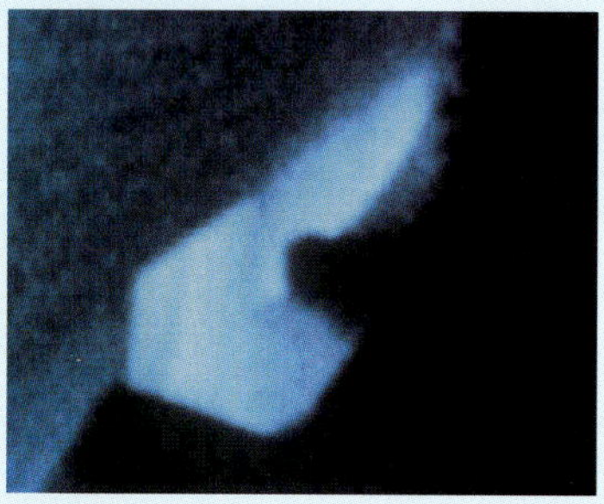

The thermograph on the left and the photograph on the right were taken at the same time and place. The blue colour in the thermograph shows the areas of greatest heat loss. Can you see why heat is being lost by looking at the photograph?

Here's how it could happen at your house. Your parents call a professional thermographer, who brings a scanner, which looks somewhat like a videocamera. The thermographer walks around the outside and inside of the house, aiming the scanner at the walls. As the walls are scanned, images appear on a small screen. You would recognize the images as "pictures" of parts of your house, but the colours would be different.

When the entire house has been scanned, the thermographer sits down with your parents. They review the videotape. "See this bright patch on the outside of your basement wall?" the thermographer says. "Remember—on this thermogram, dark means cold and bright means warm. You're losing heat from your basement, especially from around that basement window."

"I'll show you the difference in temperature," the thermographer continues. He or she presses some buttons, and numbers appear on the screen. "This section is several degrees warmer than the rest of the outside wall."

"However, your biggest problem is here." The thermographer shows them a picture taken from the inside where the roof and wall meet. "See the dark patches? It looks like the roof is not properly sealed. That is something you need to fix now, before the moisture damages the wood in your roof."

The thermographer takes the videotape away to examine it more carefully. A computer is used to blow up the dark patch and add colours so that the temperature differences show up better. The computer also helps to pinpoint the exact place on the roof where cold air is coming in.

The thermographer offers to come back and do another thermogram when the repairs are finished. The scanner's computer will then be able to compare the "before" and "after" images to ensure that the problem has been fixed.

Thermography can also be used in other situations where it is important to "see" heat. In electrical inspections, thermography can detect hot spots that indicate faulty equipment. In fire-fighting, it can detect hot spots where a fire might break out. It can be used in search-and-rescue work to find plane-crash victims. Can you think of other ways thermography might be useful?

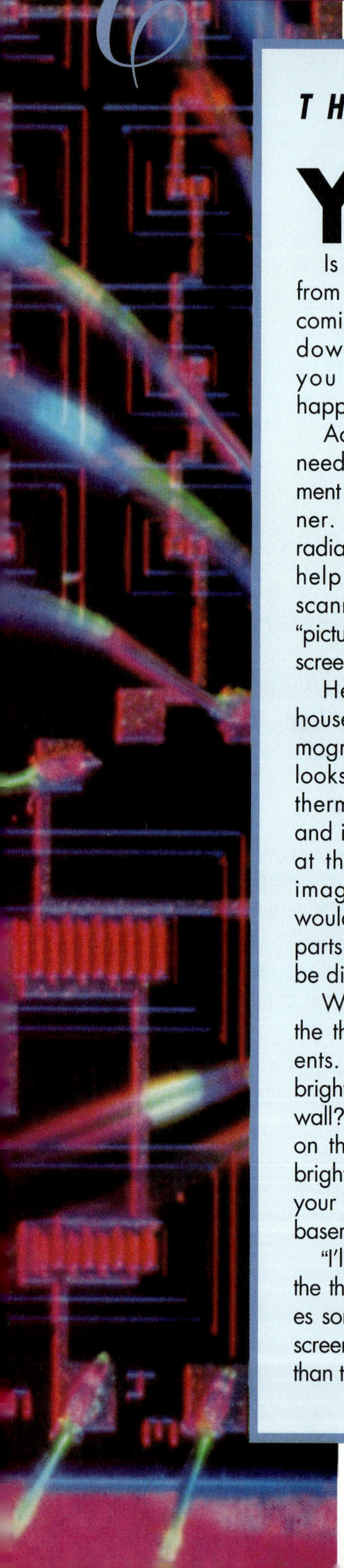

10.5 TEMPERATURE AND THE HUMAN BODY

When you feel sick, have you ever been told "you have a temperature"? What does this mean? Your body's normal temperature is 37°C. But when your temperature is higher than normal, you say you "have a temperature."

When your body temperature is higher than normal, you have a **fever**. A fever can be caused by illness, but it can also be caused by too much exercise or by over-exposure to the sun.

Normally your body keeps its temperature down by sweating. The sweat evaporates from your skin and keeps you cool. If you are suffering from **heat stroke**, your ability to sweat is affected. Heat stroke causes high fever, and can cause convulsions, fainting, and even death.

When your body temperature drops below normal, **hypothermia** results (*hypo-* is Greek for below or less than normal; and *thermia* is Greek for heat). Hypothermia is the loss of too much heat from your body. Because sweating helps to cool your body, sweating in a cold environment can lead to hypothermia if you are not dressed warmly. This sometimes happens to people hiking in the mountains. They become so warm that they take off their warm outer clothes. The low temperature of the mountain air cools their bodies down, and sweating cools their bodies even more. Soon they are suffering from hypothermia.

Hypothermia can occur in other situations. For example, if you were caught in a cold rain or wet snow, and your clothes were soaked through, you would lose body heat. The water in your clothes would conduct heat away from your body.

Anyone who stays in cold water too long also risks hypothermia, even a swimmer (Figure 10.28). In very cold water, like the ocean, you can lose body heat very quickly. So if someone, even a good swimmer, falls overboard, he or she must be rescued quickly.

When it is cold, the body uses shivering to try to keep its temperature up. Shivering is a form of exercise, which generates heat, so it uses up the body's energy stores. However, hypothermia prevents the body from shivering. When shivering stops, the person may become confused and start losing muscle control. Without immediate help, breathing and heart rate slow down, the person becomes unconscious, and death follows.

Sweating and shivering are two ways your body controls its temperature. Another way is to reduce the amount of skin surface exposed to the cold. You can curl up into a ball to prevent heat loss. Swimmers do this when they are cold in the water. It is like making a fist with your hand; your open hand has much more skin surface exposed. But your body does not have to rely only on itself to stay warm or keep cool. You can do many things to prevent your body from becoming too hot or too cold.

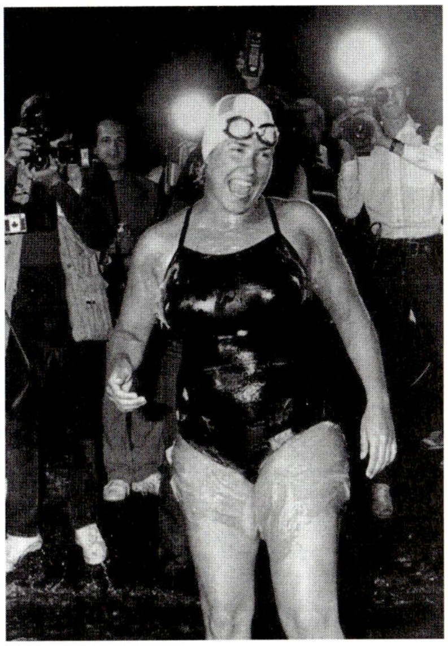

FIGURE 10.28
Long-distance swimmers can lose heat rapidly in cold water. Often, they cover their bodies with grease (animal fat) before they start their swim. The grease helps to hold in body heat.

EXTENSION

- Find out how you can prevent hypothermia. Do research in the library to find out how you can safely enjoy the outdoors all year long. You can also contact local medical offices, fire departments, or rescue and ski patrols to find out more about this condition.

ACTIVITY 10I / WHAT SHOULD I WEAR TODAY?

CROSS-CURRICULAR

In this activity, you will consider the right clothing to wear in a specific situation. Imagine that you will be making a day hike on a mountain in the fall. When the sun is out on the slopes and there is no wind, the radiant heat reflecting off the snow can make you feel quite warm. At other times, however, the weather can become severe, with strong winds and below-zero temperatures. There is no shelter on the trail you are taking.

PROCEDURE

1. In your notebook, make a table like Table 10.6.
2. In column 1, list all the clothing you would wear or take with you on the hike. In column 2, describe the purpose of each item. In column 3, identify the method of heat transfer it prevents (conduction, convection, or radiation). The weather can change suddenly, so you should be able to easily change the amount of clothing you have on. Remember that you have to carry everything that you decide to take.
3. Make a labelled diagram of the outfit you have chosen.
4. Draw a series of pictures to show the different weather conditions you might face on your mountain hike. Show the clothing you would wear in each of the weather conditions. ❖

TABLE 10.6 ▶
Sample Data Table for Activity 10I

What Should I Wear Today?		
Item of clothing	**Purpose**	**Method of heat transfer prevented**

EXTENSION

■ Wool is an excellent natural insulator. It insulates by trapping air between the wool fibres. These air spaces are so small that convection currents cannot develop. Conduction of heat is also reduced because few of the fibres are actually in contact with the skin. Wool absorbs water and yet still feels dry. Water causes the wool fibres to swell. This makes it harder for the wind to pass through the material, so you do not feel cold.

WHAT TO WEAR

How do you decide what to wear each day? One thing you probably consider is the weather. Another is what you will be doing during the day. If you will be sitting all day in school, you dress differently than if you will be outside riding your bike. How comfortable do you think the girl and boy in Figure 10.29 will be during the day?

In Figure 10.24, in the section on home insulation, you saw how a thermograph is used to show heat loss. In the thermograph in Figure 10.30, you can see the heat loss from a person's head. Windproof clothing and head coverings are very important in preventing heat loss from your body by convection. Heat loss from your head can lower your body temperature quickly.

FIGURE 10.29
Why think about the weather?

FIGURE 10.30
A thermograph of someone drinking something hot

You can prevent heat loss from your body by conduction in two ways. You can wear a bulky covering that traps the air, such as a fur coat or a down-filled parka. Or you can use several layers of clothing, which trap air between each layer. The inner layer of your clothing absorbs the radiant heat lost by your body. In gloves, the use of good insulating materials can prevent heat transfer from your hands to cold objects you may touch.

It is important to remember that you must keep your clothes dry. Clothes lose their insulating qualities when wet because the material mats together, and the small insulating air spaces disappear. The water in the clothing then acts as a heat conductor.

▶ REVIEW 10.5

1. What is your normal body temperature?

2. Use each of the following terms in a sentence that clearly shows their meaning:
(a) fever
(b) hypothermia

3. Explain how proper insulation can prevent hypothermia.

4. Why should residents of British Columbia understand the dangers of hypothermia and how to prevent it?

5. Figure 10.31 shows a person in a cold-weather survival suit. The suit has a shiny lining, and its only opening is a small breathing hole. How do you think this suit prevents the loss of body heat by
(a) conduction?
(b) convection?
(c) radiation?

6. What are some ways that your body controls its temperature?

FIGURE 10.31 ▶
A cold-weather survival suit

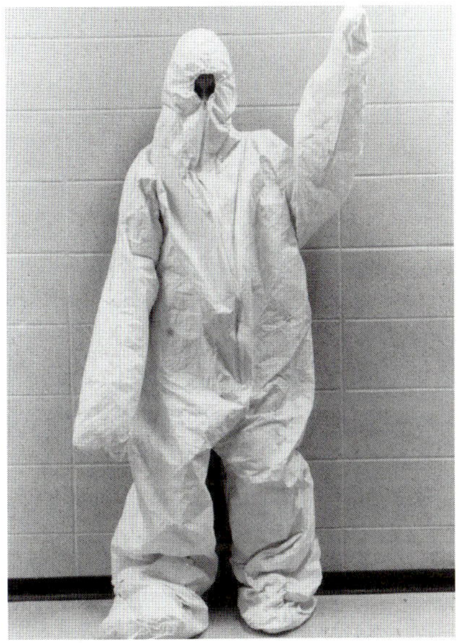

PROFILE

JOHN HAYWARD

Are you a practical person? Can you fix a flat tire on your bike, or repair the toaster when it will not pop up?

John Hayward was practical when he was a teenager. He had no idea then that he would become a scientist and inventor. Later, when he was given an award for his work, he thanked his father. "He made his workbench available to me when I was a boy and taught me how to use tools and fix things."

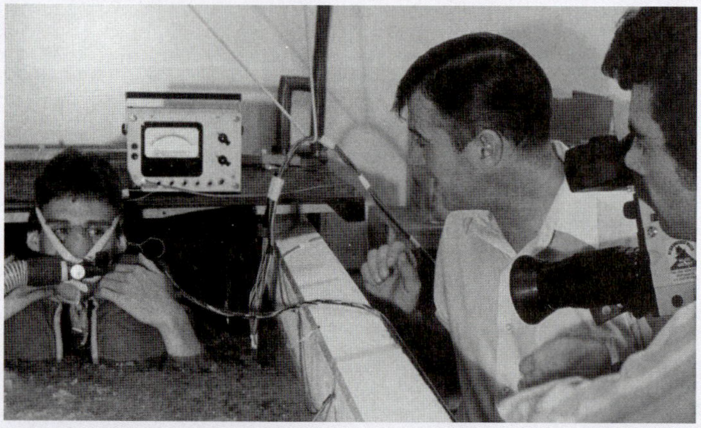

Dr. John Hayward (centre) researching hypothermia with a volunteer (left) and a technician.

Hayward is one of the inventors of the Thermofloat jacket—a jacket that can keep you afloat and help keep you warm in cold water.

As a zoologist, Hayward studied animal hibernation (zoology is the study of animals and animal life). He wondered how animals like squirrels kept warm through the cold winter. Later, when he decided to study humans, he asked similar questions, such as "How does the human body respond to cold?"

This information cannot be found in a warm laboratory. Instead Hayward and others had to spend a lot of time in the ocean. They would stay for about an hour in very cold water (10°C) until their inner body temperature dropped from 37°C to 35°C. At this stage, they had mild hypothermia. This provided Hayward with information such as how much heat is produced by shivering, and what parts of the human body lose heat fastest.

Hayward's studies showed that by curling up, you expose less body surface to the water and you stay warmer. Huddling with other people in the water also helps slow down how quickly your body cools.

At first, Hayward's research was purely scientific. But it led to a practical application—the Thermofloat jacket.

There are better survival suits than the Thermofloat available, but they are expensive and bulky. Hayward designed the Thermofloat jacket to be both inexpensive and comfortable so that people would wear it. "If it's stowed in the front of the boat, it's not a life jacket," he explains.

Today, Thermofloat jackets are sold worldwide, and Hayward has gone on to other inventions. "Once you sample being an inventor, your whole thinking pattern changes around and you're very likely to be an inventor again."

His advice to today's practical students? "Don't be afraid to be a novel [original] thinker," he says. "Have a passion for solving problems, and don't always leave it up to somebody else."

Hayward used student volunteers for his research. They had to stay in cold water until they were shivering and uncomfortable. Why do you think people were willing to volunteer? Would you?

CHAPTER REVIEW

KEY IDEAS

- Thermal energy and temperature are closely related, but they are not the same. Thermal energy is the total energy of all the particles in an object. Temperature is a way of measuring the average energy of all the particles in an object.
- Heat is the energy transferred because of a temperature difference between objects. There are three methods of heat transfer: conduction, convection, and radiation.
- Conduction is the transfer of heat through a solid by the collision of particles.
- Convection is the transfer of heat in fluids by the movement of particles from one location to another.
- Radiation is a method of heat transfer that does not depend on particles. Heat transferred by radiation is called radiant heat. It can be reflected, absorbed, or transmitted.
- Insulation reduces heat transfer by conduction, convection, and radiation. It is used to control heat transfer in many applications.
- You can save money and make your house more comfortable by making sure it is well insulated. Insulation in the roof and the walls is important. Double-glazed windows and weather stripping also reduce heat loss.
- Your body uses a number of ways, including sweating and shivering, to help control its temperature. When your body is unable to control its temperature, fever or hypothermia can result.

VOCABULARY

thermal energy
temperature
thermometer
Celsius scale
expansion
contraction
absolute zero
heat
heat transfer
caloric theory
conduction
conductor
fluids
convection
convection current
radiation
radiant energy
insulator
insulation
fever
heat stroke
hypothermia

V1. Create a mind map of what you have learned about thermal energy and heat, using as many of the vocabulary words as possible.

V2. Create a poster showing everyday uses of thermal energy and heat. Include ways in which you can improve or prevent heat transfer.

CONNECTIONS

C1. Explain the difference between thermal energy and temperature.

C2. (a) What device is commonly used to measure temperature?
(b) What temperature scale is commonly used?
(c) What is the lowest possible temperature on this scale? What is it called?
(d) What other scale do scientists use to measure temperature?
(e) What is the lowest possible temperature on this scale? What is it called?

C3. You are using a long metal fork to hold a hot dog over a campfire. The end you are holding heats up very quickly.
(a) Which method of heat transfer is involved here?
(b) Use the kinetic molecular theory to explain what happens to the particles of the metal fork as heat is transferred along it.
(c) Explain why a wooden handle on the fork would help to keep it cool.

C4. How is a conductor different from an insulator?

C5. (a) Air is a poor conductor. However, heat can be transferred through air. Name the method of heat transfer involved.
(b) Under what conditions can air act as a good insulator?

C6. Can convection occur in solids? Explain your answer.

C7. Can conduction occur in gases and liquids? Explain your answer.

C8. Explain why each of the following people would be concerned about heat transfer:
(a) an architect
(b) a hot air balloonist
(c) a chef in a restaurant
(d) a manufacturer of winter boots
(e) a runner on a cold day

C9. (a) How does blowing on soup or other hot foods help to cool them?
(b) In which container would the same amount of soup cool more quickly: a wide, shallow bowl or a deep bowl?

EXPLORATIONS

E1. Snow and low temperatures go together, but did you know that snow can be an excellent insulator? Explain how snow could be used as an insulator. Describe how the insulating properties of snow are useful for
(a) plants,
(b) animals,
(c) the people living in Canada's north.

E2. What do you think would happen to a fluid being heated in space, where there is no up or down, and there is no gravity? Would convection occur or would another form of heat transfer take place? (Hint: Think about the kinetic molecular theory.)

E3. Design your own home so that it would be as energy-efficient as possible; that is, it would use little energy in winter and stay cool in summer. Draw a diagram of your energy-saving house. Show and label some of the features that you would include in it. Explain how you would control the three methods of heat transfer.

REFLECTIONS

R1. After completing this chapter, you have a better understanding of thermal energy and heat. Find Activity 10A in your learning journal. Compare the ideas about thermal energy that you have now with those that you wrote down at the beginning of this chapter. How have your ideas changed? What else do you want to know about thermal energy?

R2. In this chapter, you have learned about thermal energy and how heat is transferred. Think about why our society should be concerned about conserving energy.

CHAPTER 11

LIGHT ENERGY

Fireworks lighting up the night sky show us light energy in a spectacular way. Light energy can be fun in fireworks and laser shows, but it is also important to life on Earth. Without light energy, plants could not make their food through photosynthesis. Everything you eat comes in some way from plants.

Light energy is important to your life in other ways too. When you wake up on a dark winter morning, one of the first things you do is switch on a light. This light allows you to see yourself in the mirror as you get ready for school. At school, the lights in your classroom help you to see your work. At night, you need light to do your homework. You use light energy all day, from the time you wake up until you go to sleep at night.

Light energy has properties that are similar to the properties of other forms of energy. For example, light energy can be transformed into other forms of energy, and light energy can cause motion. In this chapter, you will learn about the properties of light.

ACTIVITY 11A / LIGHT ENERGY IS...

GROUP ACTIVITY

You may already know some of the ways you use light energy every day. In this activity, you and a partner will think about the many different sources and uses of light energy in the world.

Working with your partner, brainstorm all the different sources of light energy that you can. List them in your learning journal.

Now list all the important uses of light energy that you can think of. (Hint: Think about the different types of equipment that produce or use light energy in science, medicine, recreation, and industry.)

Your teacher may ask you to compare your lists with those of other students. Add to your lists any new ideas that are different from the ones you wrote down. At the end of the chapter, you can compare what you know now about sources and uses of light energy with what you learn in this chapter. ❖

11.1 HOW LIGHT ENERGY TRAVELS

You can see the world around you because of light energy. Light energy travelling from its source to your eyes allows you to see other students, your teacher, desks, and everything else in the room.

You learned in Chapter 9 that light is radiant energy. It radiates from a source in lines called **rays**. Do light rays travel in straight lines from a source or do they curve and bend?

ACTIVITY 11B / OBSERVING LIGHT AND SHADOWS

In this activity, you will investigate what happens to light rays as they travel from a source.

MATERIALS

Part I

film-strip projector (or laser light source)
projector screen
chalk brushes
chalk dust
ray box
incandescent light bulb
rubber stopper

PART I Light Beams and Shadows (Teacher Demonstration)

PROCEDURE

1. Your teacher will shine a light beam from a film-strip projector (or a laser) at a screen and then use chalk brushes to tap chalk dust into the beam. Describe the beam of light.
2. Your teacher will make shadows on a screen using a point source of light, such as a ray-box lamp. A point source of light is a tiny source of light that seems as big as this dot (.). Then your teacher will make shadows with a broader source such as an incandescent light bulb. In your notebook, describe the path of the light for each light source. How are the shadows from the point source different from those of the broad source of light?
3. A student will move the stopper closer to, and farther from, the screen. How does the size of the shadow change when the stopper's position changes? Record your observations.

DISCUSSION

1. Why was the chalk dust tapped into the beam of light? Explain.

MATERIALS

Part II
point light source
rubber hose
ray box with five-slit baffle
ruler

PART II The Path of Light

PROCEDURE

1. Look at a point light source through a piece of rubber hose. Can you see the light when the hose is curved? Can you see the light when the hose is straight? Record your observations.
2. Darken the room. Observe the paths of the light rays produced by the ray box. In your notebook, record what happens to the light rays as the two halves of the ray box are slid together and apart. What happens when the baffle is moved back and forth in front of the ray box? Use a ruler to draw the ray box and the path of each of the five light rays.

DISCUSSION

1. Using your observations from the rubber hose, describe the path of light rays from a source. Do the light rays travel in straight lines or curved lines?

Part III
rubber stopper
screen (sheet of white paper)
ray box with single-slit baffle

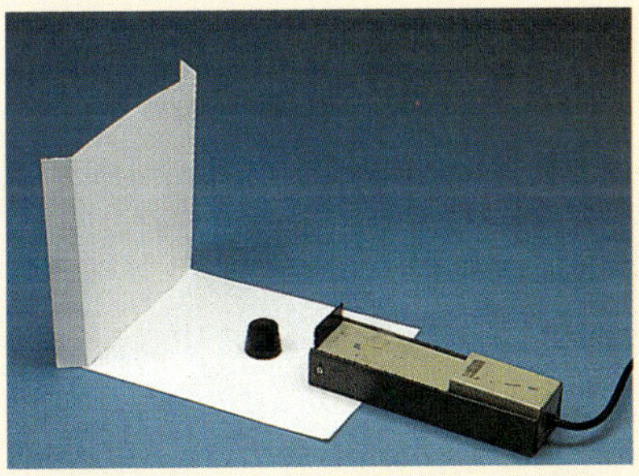

FIGURE 11.1
How to set up the apparatus for Activity 11B, Part III

PART III Predicting Shadows

PROCEDURE

1. In your notebook, sketch what you think the shadow will look like when a rubber stopper is placed halfway between a screen and a light source (Figure 11.1). Will the shadow be the same size as the stopper? Will it be the same shape as the stopper?
2. With the room darkened, test your prediction. If your observations are different from your predictions, draw a new sketch to show what you observed.
3. Draw the two sketches of what you think the shadow will look like
   (a) when the stopper is brought closer to the screen,
   (b) when the stopper is brought closer to the light source.
4. Test your predictions. If your observations are different from your predictions, draw new sketches to show what you observed.

DISCUSSION

1. Describe what happened to the size of the shadow as the rubber stopper was
   (a) moved closer to the screen,
   (b) moved closer to the light source.
2. Describe what happened to the sharpness of the edge of the shadows as the rubber stopper was
   (a) moved closer to the screen,
   (b) moved closer to the light source.
3. From your observations of shadows, what general statement can you make about the path of light? (Hint: Why do light rays not reach the area behind the object?) ❖

USING LIGHT'S PATH

Shadows show us that light rays travel in straight lines. A **shadow** is the dark area behind an object, created when the object blocks the light rays from a source that is in front of the object. When you stand outside on a sunny day, you can see your shadow clearly. Your body blocks the path of the sun's light rays. Because light rays travel in straight lines, they cannot bend around you to light you or the ground on all sides.

The sharpness of the edges of a shadow depends on the size of light source and the positions of the object and the light source. The smaller the source of light, the sharper the edges of the shadow. A shadow becomes larger as the object moves closer to the light source. These observations are all evidence that light travels in a straight line.

The fact that light rays travel in straight lines explains why images form. **Images** are formed whenever you see an object that looks like an object but is not the object itself. A photograph is an example of an image, and so is your reflection in a mirror. You will learn more about images later in this chapter.

ACTIVITY 11C / MAKING IMAGES WITH A PINHOLE

You have learned that light rays travel in straight lines. In this activity, you will use what you know about light rays and shadows to produce images of objects on a screen.

MATERIALS

construction paper
(21.6 cm x 27.9 cm)
scissors
tape
aluminum foil
pin
white loose-leaf paper
(21.6 cm x 27.9 cm)
metre stick
candle and holder (Petri dish)
pencil crayons
centimetre ruler

PROCEDURE

1. Cut a hole 3 to 5 cm in diameter in a piece of construction paper so that the centre of the hole is about level with the top of the candle you are using. Tape a piece of aluminum foil over the opening. Use the pin to make one small hole in the aluminum foil.
2. Fold the edges of the construction paper so that it will stand by itself. Fold the edges of the white paper so that it will also stand by itself. Set up the candle and the white-paper screen so that they are 40 cm apart, as measured with the metre stick. Place the construction paper with the pinhole halfway between the candle and the screen as shown in Figure 11.2. Adjust the height of the candle or the pinhole with supports if necessary.
3. In your notebook, sketch the arrangement of the candle flame, construction paper with pinhole, and screen. What do you think will happen when you light the candle? In your sketch, use a pencil crayon to show what you think the path of a light ray will be from the top of the flame. Use a different-coloured pencil crayon to show what you think the path of a light ray will be from the middle of the flame. Use a third pencil crayon to show what you think the path of a light ray will be from the bottom of the flame.
4. Light the candle and turn off the room lights to test your prediction. Use the centimetre ruler to measure the size of the image on the screen. Record it in your notebook.

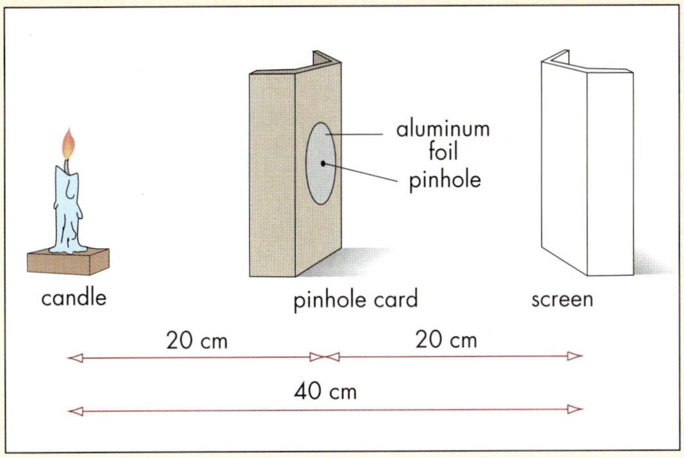

FIGURE 11.2
How to set up the apparatus for Activity 11C

5. Predict what will happen to the position of the candle's image on the screen when the candle is (a) moved to the right, and (b) moved to the left. Write both your predictions in your notebook. Test your predictions. Record your observations.
6. Predict what will happen to the size of the image on the screen when you move the candle (a) twice as far from the pinhole (40 cm), and (b) half as far from the pinhole (10 cm). Write both your predictions in your notebook. Test your predictions.
7. Measure the sizes of the images on the screen and record them. What do you notice about the brightness of the image on the screen in each situation? Record your observations.

DISCUSSION

1. Describe the image of the candle produced by the pinhole. Use a diagram to explain why it appeared as it did.
2. What happened to the position of the candle flame's image when you moved the candle to the right and to the left? Use a diagram to explain why this happened.
3. Describe two ways in which you can make the image of the candle flame larger.
4. In what two ways can you make the image of the candle brighter?
5. How can you make the candle flame's image both larger and brighter at the same time?
6. Construction paper and aluminum foil do not permit light to pass through them; white loose-leaf paper does. Why were these materials used where they were? ❖

REVIEW 11.1

1. Why can you not see an object that is behind another object?
2. List some uses of light energy that depend on the property that light rays travel in straight lines.
3. Think about walking down a street lit by street lamps at night.
   (a) What happens to your shadow as you walk farther away from a street lamp?
   (b) Suggest reasons for this. Use a diagram to help you explain your answer.
4. Suppose you are standing at the side of the road. You know that there are several telephone poles along the road, but you can only see the one closest to you. How do you know that the telephone poles are in a straight line? How could this knowledge be used by surveyors?
5. On a sunny day, when do you think your shadow would be shortest?
6. How would life on Earth be different if light rays did not travel in straight lines?

11.2 THE COLOUR OF LIGHT

What colour is light from the sun? What colour is the light from the lamp in your living room at home? A rainbow, like the one in Figure 11.3, is made up of many colours. Where do these colours come from? You will find the answers to these questions in this section.

FIGURE 11.3
Rainbows are beautiful, but why do we see these colours?

ACTIVITY 11D / THE COLOUR OF LIGHT

In this activity, you will use two devices, a prism and a spectroscope, to investigate light. A prism and a spectroscope are devices used to observe the colour of light.

MATERIALS

Part I
ray box
single-slit baffle
two equilateral prisms
white loose-leaf paper
pencil crayons
coloured cellophane

PART I Using a Prism

PROCEDURE

1. With the room darkened, adjust a ray box so that the edges of the beam of light are parallel. Insert a single-slit baffle. Aim the ray box at the prism (Figure 11.4). Slowly turn the prism. What do you observe? Place the sheet of white loose-leaf paper in the path of the light leaving the prism so that you can see this light more easily. In your notebook, use pencil crayons to draw what you have observed.
2. Place the other prism in the path of the light leaving the first prism. Can you recombine the bands of light to produce white light? Can you use the second prism to separate the bands of light even more?
3. In your notebook, predict what will happen when a piece of coloured cellophane is placed between the prism and the white screen. Test your prediction. What part of the white light was able to pass through to the screen? Does placing the cellophane between the ray box and the prism make any difference? Record your observations.

MATERIALS

Part II
hand-held spectroscope
pencil crayons
candle
incandescent light bulb

CAUTION!

■ **Never look directly at the sun because it can cause permanent damage to your eyes.**

DISCUSSION

1. How does the light leaving the prism compare with the colours of the rainbow in Figure 11.3?
2. (a) What colour of light can pass through red cellophane?
   (b) Why is coloured cellophane sometimes called a "light filter"?

PART II Using a Spectroscope

PROCEDURE

1. Using a hand-held spectroscope, examine the light from a candle. Record your observations by making a drawing with pencil crayons.
2. Use the spectroscope to examine the light produced by an incandescent light bulb. Record your observations using pencil crayons.
3. If possible, examine natural sunlight by aiming a spectroscope at the sky or at a window. Record your observations using pencil crayons.
4. Use the spectroscope to examine the light produced by the fluorescent lights in your classroom. Record your observations using pencil crayons.

DISCUSSION

1. (a) Compare the colours you saw when you used the spectroscope to observe the different light sources in steps 1, 2, 3, and 4 of the Procedure.
   (b) How do these colours compare with the colours of the rainbow in Figure 11.3?
2. Explain why the position of the sun is important to the formation of a rainbow. ❖

FIGURE 11.4
How to set up the apparatus for Activity 11D, Part I

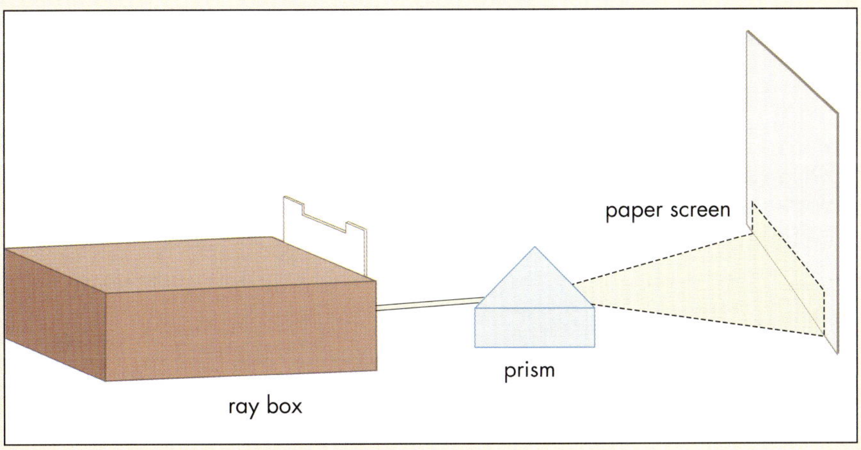

A RAINBOW OF COLOURS

The light you see from the sun or from a lamp may seem to be all one colour, but it is made up of light of many colours. You can see these colours in a rainbow. You can also separate the light from the sun or from other sources into its many colours by using a prism. A **prism** is a clear object that can separate light into its colours. A rainbow is created when light passes through raindrops, which act as prisms.

EXTENSION

■ You can create your own mnemonic sentence to help you remember the colours of the spectrum in order. Using seven words that have ROYGBIV as their first letters, make up a sentence that you find easy to remember.

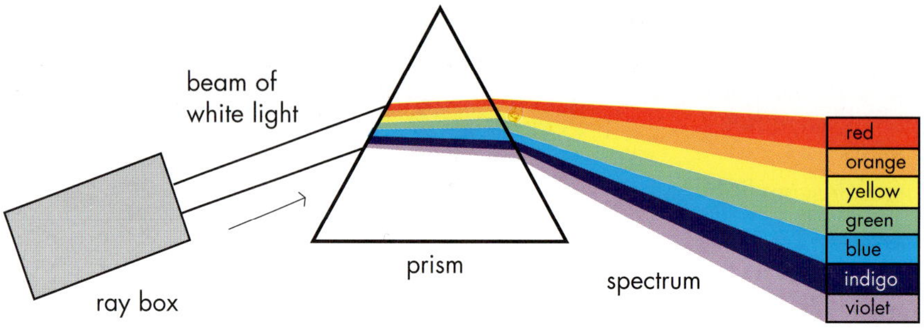

FIGURE 11.5
A prism can separate white light into its component colours.

FIGURE 11.6
A boy with a colourful name

The colours you see in a rainbow are the same as those produced by a prism like the one in Figure 11.5. This set of colours is called the **spectrum**. The spectrum is always made up of the same colours in the same order: red, orange, yellow, green, blue, indigo, and violet. Together these colours make up white light. Any light that does not appear to be coloured is called white light. For example, the sun, the headlights of a car, and the lights in your classroom all produce white light.

There is an easy way to remember the colours of the spectrum in order. If you take the first letter of each colour and put them together, they make the "name" ROY G. BIV. Think of ROY G. BIV in Figure 11.6 when you want to remember the colours of the spectrum.

A COLOURFUL WORLD

In Chapter 10, you learned that radiant energy can be transmitted, absorbed, or reflected. Light energy is a form of radiant energy. You can see colours because light energy can be reflected. You see green grass, red stop signs, and blue jeans because they contain substances that reflect those colours of light. A yellow pencil reflects yellow light. All the other colours of the spectrum are absorbed by the pencil.

REVIEW 11.2

1. Define the terms:
   (a) spectrum
   (b) prism
2. What does ROY G. BIV stand for?
3. What colours of light are reflected by a piece of white paper?
4. How would life on Earth be different if the light produced by the sun suddenly turned
   (a) red?
   (b) green?
   (Hint: Think about why plants appear green.)
5. Many cities use sodium vapour street lamps because they conserve energy. However, these lamps produce a yellowish light. Why might this be a problem?

11.3 REFLECTION

Have you ever seen yourself in mirrors like the ones in Figure 11.7? How often do you look in a mirror—several times a day? What do you know about the image a mirror produces? For example, why does a mirror flip right for left and not top for bottom? In this section, you will find out how an image is produced in a mirror.

FIGURE 11.7
We can have fun with mirrors, but how do they produce the images that we see?

WHAT IS A MIRROR?

If you look into a polished tabletop, a storefront window, or the back of a soup spoon, you can see your image. These surfaces all act as mirrors, but some surfaces give clearer images than others do (Figure 11.8). A **mirror** is anything that reflects light so that it produces a visible image. A visible image in a mirror is called a **reflection**. All objects that we can see reflect light, but they do not all produce images on their surfaces.

FIGURE 11.8
What are the properties of this lake that allow it to reflect light so clearly? What part might the wind play in this picture of beauty?

Figure 11.9 shows what happens to a light ray when it strikes the surface of a mirror. An **incident ray** is the ray of light travelling from a light source to a mirror's surface. A **reflected ray** is the ray of light that leaves the mirror's surface. The reflected light rays travel to your eyes and allow you to see the image in the mirror.

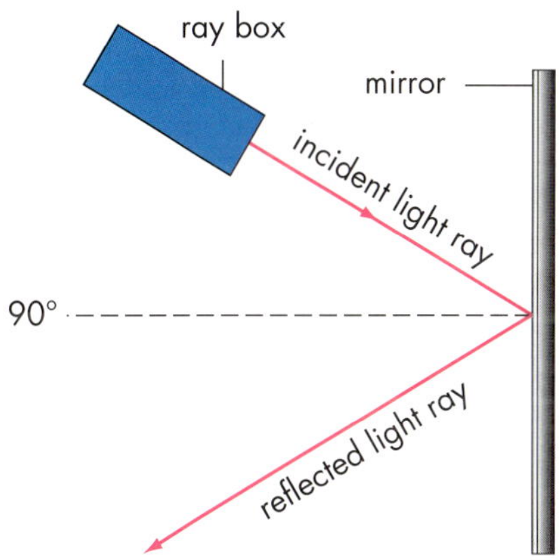

FIGURE 11.9
A light ray reflecting off a mirror. What do you notice about the angles the incident ray and the reflected ray make with the mirror?

ACTIVITY 11E / REFLECTED LIGHT

In this activity, you will see how images in mirrors are different from the objects reflected. You will learn what type of surface makes a good mirror.

MATERIALS

Part I
mirror
15 cm ruler
shoe box
scissors
paper

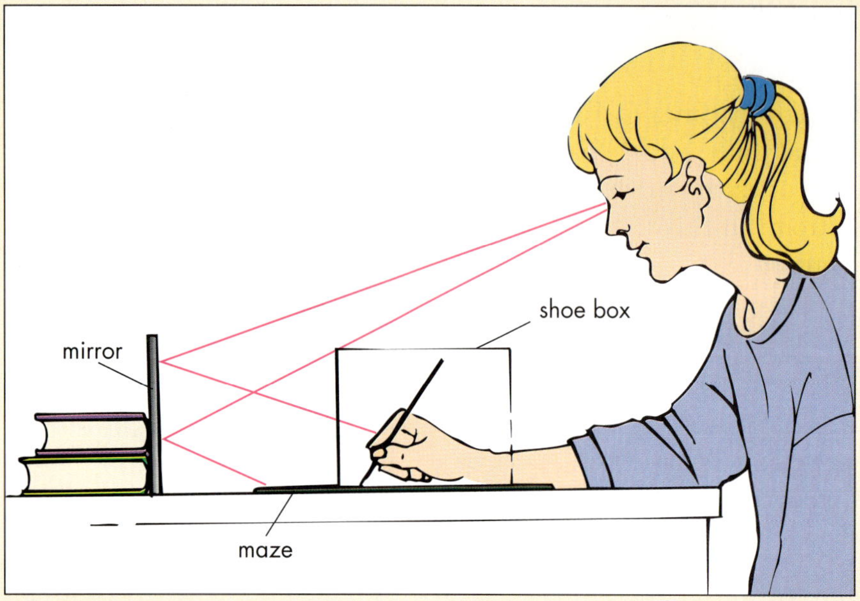

FIGURE 11.10
Apparatus for Activity 11E, Part I

PART I Amazing Mirror

PROCEDURE

1. Look at your image in the mirror. Predict which eye your image would appear to wink if you winked your right eye. Write your prediction in your notebook. Test your prediction. Record your observation.
2. Place the 15 cm ruler so that one end touches your nose and the other end touches the mirror. Record your distance from the mirror's surface. Using the image of the ruler in the mirror, measure how far your image appears to be from the mirror's surface. Record your measurements.
3. Print several letters on a piece of paper (e.g., R, S, b, e). Predict how the letters will appear in the mirror when you hold the paper in front of it. Write down your predictions. Test your predictions. Record the appearance of the mirrored letters.
4. Write your name on a piece of paper. How do you think your name will appear when you hold it up to the mirror? Write down the way you think it will look. Test your prediction. Describe the image. Try to write your name on the paper so that it appears normal when you hold it up to the mirror.
5. Cut the long sides out of a shoebox so that the ends and the bottom remain. Turn it upside down and place it in front of a mirror on your lab bench as shown in Figure 11.10. Place the maze design in Figure 11.11 (or your own pattern) under the shoebox. Sit in front of the shoebox and position the mirror so that you can see the image of the maze in the mirror but not the maze itself. You may need to place the mirror on a book or at an angle.
6. Have your partner sit in front of the mirror. Make sure that your partner can see only the reflection of the design in the mirror and that the direct view of the design is blocked. Have your partner draw a line along the path in the maze design only by looking at it in the mirror.

FIGURE 11.11
Draw this design onto a piece of paper for the mirror maze, or make your own design.

DISCUSSION

1. Describe the reflections produced by a mirror.
   (a) Are they upside down?
   (b) Are they backwards?
   (c) Does the distance between the reflection and the surface of the mirror seem to be the same as the distance between the object and the mirror?
2. How is your mirror image different from you?
3. Explain why following the maze design by looking at its mirror image was difficult.

MATERIALS

Part II
ray box
five-slit baffle
mirror
aluminum foil
paper
ruler
single-slit baffle

PART II Mirrors and Reflection

PROCEDURE

1. With the room lights off, adjust the ray box so that the edges of the light beam are parallel. Insert a five-slit baffle. Shine the light rays at the mirror at about a 45° angle. Describe the pattern of the light rays reflected from the mirror.

2. Repeat step 1 using a crumpled piece of aluminum foil instead of the mirror, and then using a vertical piece of white paper. Record your observations each time.

3. Place the mirror upright on a piece of white paper. Draw a line on the paper along the face of the mirror. Label this line "mirror." Without moving the mirror, use a ruler to draw a line on the paper at a 90° angle to the face of the mirror.

4. Replace the five-slit baffle in the ray box with a single-slit baffle. Shine a light ray along the line that you drew at a 90° angle to the mirror's surface (Figure 11.12). What happens to the reflected ray of light?

5. Move the ray box into different positions so that the incident light ray strikes the mirror at a different angle each time. Make sure that it strikes the mirror at the point where the 90° angle line meets the face of the mirror. On the paper, use a pencil and a ruler to trace the incident ray and the reflected ray of light produced in each position. Label each pair of light rays with a number. Use arrows to indicate the direction of the light rays.

DISCUSSION

1. How does the reflection of light rays from rough surfaces, like the white paper, differ from their reflection from polished flat surfaces, like the mirror? Which type of surface reflects light rays the best?

2. Movie screens must be good reflectors. Why do you think polished glass mirrors are not used as screens?

3. Describe what happens to the angle of the reflected light ray as the angle of the incident light ray becomes steeper?

4. If you wanted to take a photograph of yourself in a mirror 2 m away, what distance setting should you use to make sure that the camera is properly focused? ❖

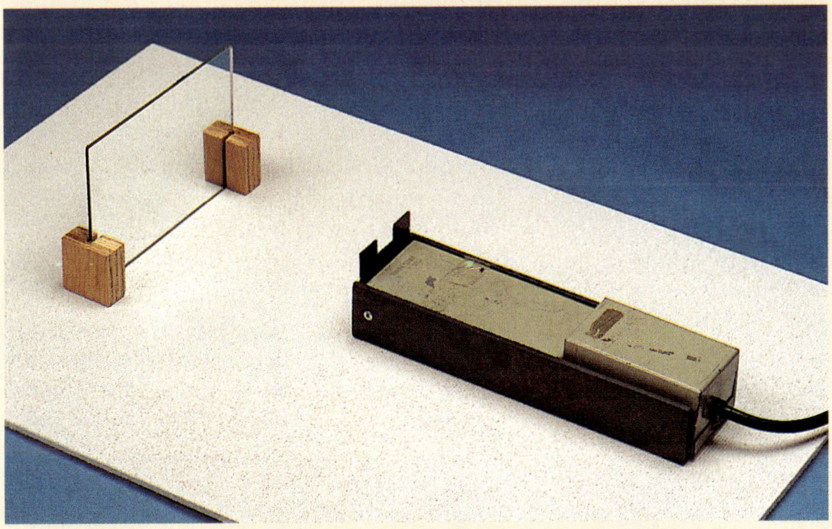

FIGURE 11.12
In Part II, Step 4, shine a light ray along the line at 90° to the mirror's surface.

CAREER

LIGHTING TECHNICIAN

Colleen Warnock is a lighting technician. She works in theatres and at rock concerts. Here she talks about her work.

If you can wire a lamp at home, you know more or less what I do at work. For my job, you need to understand electricity and not be afraid of it.

We hang lights in theatres. A show could use as many as 140 lights. Then we connect all of them with cables, and hook them up to dimmers. These are switches that we use to change the brightness of the lights. You have to know where to use the different sizes of cables so that you don't start a fire. Then we focus each light, and put a filter over it to make it the right colour for the scene.

In a theatre, the set doesn't look very good close-up. The lighting improves everything. It also sets the time and location of the scene—daytime or night-time, inside or outside. The mood, the emotions—all that is done with lighting.

Sometimes I run the console, which is the board that holds the controls for all the lights. These boards are computerized.

Trouble can happen on opening night. The computer may crash, or there may be a break in a cable, but you don't know where.

What makes my work interesting is that every show is different, with different people, in a different place. It is almost like a different job every time. Once in a while I see a really good show.

It is hard work, but I enjoy that. You have to lift heavy cables, and you can't be scared of heights.

I don't know why there aren't more women working as lighting technicians and stagehands. Other theatre jobs are cleaner, but they don't pay as well. Most of what I know I learned just by doing it. I started out by working for a country rock band. I drove a truck, loaded the truck, and worked with the person who looked after the sound. I also volunteered at a local radio station. That helped me to learn about sound, and I went from sound into lighting. I didn't know that it would turn into a trade, but I'm glad that it did.

Volunteering is a good way to get started. You meet people, you learn, and it doesn't cost very much. Then you have a better idea of whether you want to do the job.

Where could you volunteer? You could help at your local theatre, building sets or doing other things. Or you could work with the band or drama club at your school. That's how I started.

CURVED MIRRORS

While they may look very different, curved mirrors have the same rules for reflecting light rays as flat mirrors. There are two types of curved mirrors: convex and concave. Convex mirrors are curved mirrors that have their reflective surface bulging outward (Figure 11.13). **Convex** means "curved outward." This type of mirror is used in many ways, such as in stores to guard against shoplifters, and in hospital hallways to prevent people from crashing into each other where hallways cross.

Concave mirrors have a curved reflective surface that curves inward, like a cave. **Concave** means "curved inward." This type of mirror is also used in many different ways, such as in the headlights of cars, in camera flashes, and in some telescopes (Figure 11.14).

Both convex and concave mirrors can be either spherical or cylindrical. Spherical mirrors are shaped like a bowl. Cylindrical mirrors are shaped like a cylinder.

DID YOU KNOW

Most mirrors have their reflective surfaces on the back of a clear piece of glass. The glass at the front acts as a flat support. Polished metal mirrors and some expensive mirrors for precision optics have the reflective surface on the front of the mirror. How do you think the location of the reflective surface affects the reflected light rays?

FIGURE 11.13
The balloon in this picture is acting like a convex mirror. What can you see that you probably wouldn't see if the shiny surface were flat? Can you think of places where convex mirrors would increase safety?

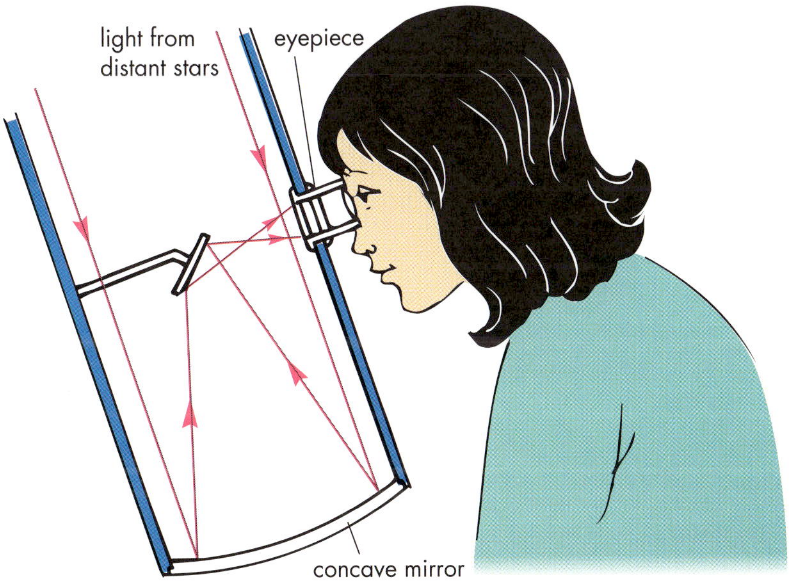

FIGURE 11.14
The concave mirror in this telescope concentrates the light so that the distant stars appear brighter.

ACTIVITY 11F / CURVED MIRRORS

In this activity, you will learn how light rays are affected by curved mirrors.

MATERIALS

Part I
large spherical concave mirror
candle

Part II
ruler
ray box
five-slit baffle
cylindrical concave mirror
paper

Part III
ruler
ray box
five-slit baffle
cylindrical convex mirror
paper

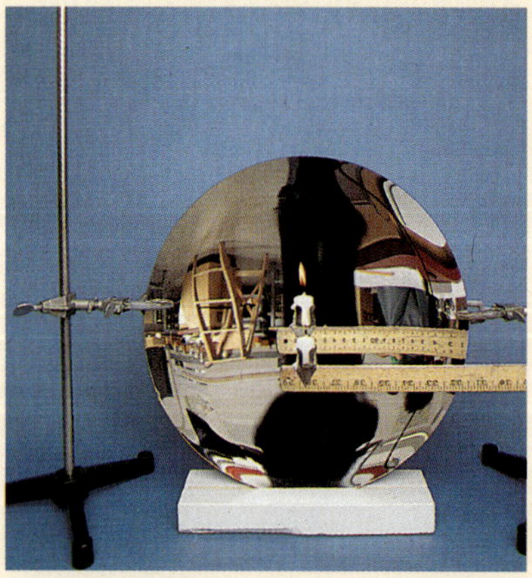

FIGURE 11.15
A large spherical concave mirror for Activity 11F, Part I

PART I A Spherical Concave Mirror (Teacher Demonstration)

PROCEDURE

1. In a darkened room, your teacher will demonstrate a large spherical concave mirror as shown in Figure 11.15. A candle will be placed in front of the mirror.
2. In your notebook, draw a labelled diagram to show the paths of the light rays from the candle to the mirror. Then draw the paths of the light rays that are reflected from the mirror.
3. Predict what will happen when the candle is moved
   (a) closer to the mirror,
   (b) farther from the mirror.
4. Test your predictions. Record your observations.

DISCUSSION

1. What happened to the image as the candle was moved closer to the mirror and farther from the mirror? Explain your observations.
2. Suggest some uses for a concave mirror like the one you have just seen.

PART II Using a Concave Mirror

PROCEDURE

1. Trace Figure 11.16. Predict the paths of the reflected rays from the light rays aimed at the concave mirror by drawing them on the diagram, using a ruler. Label this drawing "My Prediction."
2. Test your prediction. With the room lights off, adjust the ray box so that the edges of the light beam are parallel. Insert the five-slit baffle. Place the concave mirror on a piece of paper, and draw a line on the paper along the face of the mirror.
3. Shine the light rays from the ray box at the concave mirror so that the middle incident ray hits the centre of the mirror straight on, as shown in Figure 11.16. On the paper, trace the paths of the reflected rays. Label the incident and reflected rays. Use arrows to indicate the direction of the rays. Label this drawing "My Observations."

DISCUSSION

1. Compare your observations of the paths of the reflected light rays with your prediction.
2. Suggest a reason to explain why a concave mirror reflects light rays in this way.

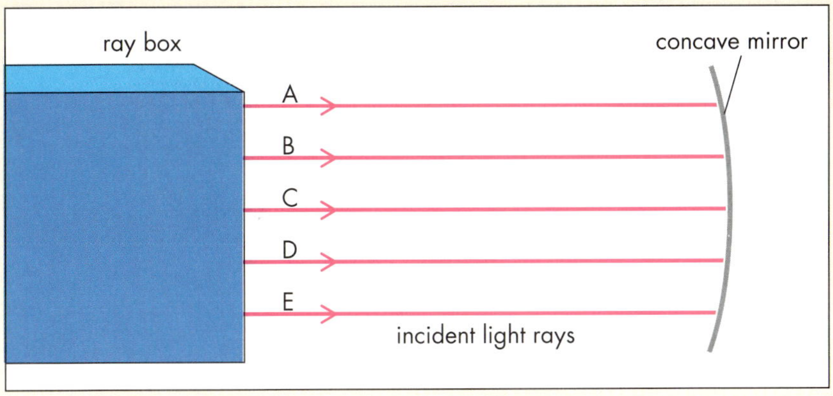

FIGURE 11.16
Trace this diagram and predict the paths of the reflected light rays. Use an arrow to show the direction of each ray and label the reflected rays.

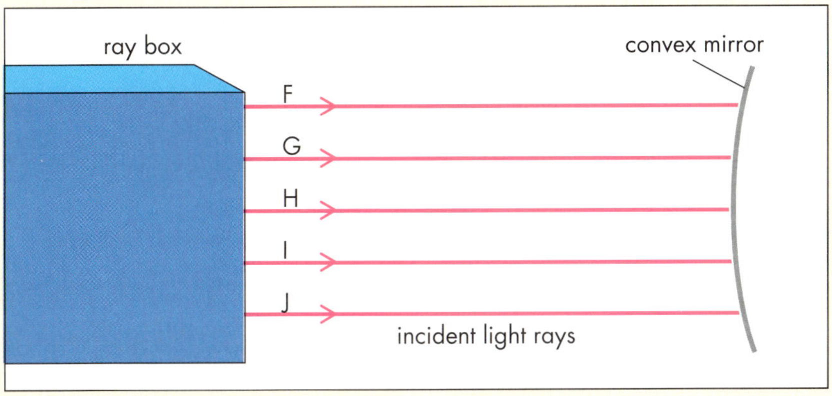

FIGURE 11.17
Trace this diagram and predict the paths of the reflected light rays. Use an arrow to show the direction of each ray and label the reflected rays.

PART III Using a Convex Mirror

PROCEDURE

1. In your notebook, trace Figure 11.17. Predict the path of the reflected rays from the light rays aimed at the convex mirror by drawing them on the diagram, using a ruler. Label this drawing "My Prediction."
2. Test your prediction. Use the same set-up of the ray box as in Part II. Place the convex mirror on a piece of paper and draw a line on the paper along the face of the mirror.
3. Shine the light rays from the ray box at the convex mirror so that the middle incident ray hits the centre of the mirror straight on, as shown in Figure 11.17. On the paper, trace the paths of the reflected rays. Label the incident and reflected rays, and draw arrows to indicate the direction of the rays. Label this drawing "My Observations."

DISCUSSION

1. Compare your observations of the paths of the reflected light rays with your prediction.
2. Suggest a reason to explain why a convex mirror reflects light in this way. ❖

BRINGING IT TOGETHER

The two types of curved mirrors cause parallel incident rays to behave in two different ways. Concave mirrors cause the reflected light rays to converge; this means that they come together at a single point. This point is called the **focus**. However, when a source of light is placed at the focus of a concave mirror, a parallel beam of reflected light is formed. This is how a car headlight works (Figure 11.18).

Convex mirrors cause the reflected light rays to diverge; this means that they spread the rays apart. The incident rays coming from a wide angle are reflected for the viewer, as shown in Figure 11.19.

EXTENSION

■ Solar furnaces are concave mirrors that focus solar radiation onto a small area. Fluid in a pipe located in that area is heated to very high temperatures. This hot fluid can be used to produce steam, which can then be used to generate electricity. Solar furnaces can be very large, with hundreds of mirrors. Find out how concave mirrors are used in solar furnaces.

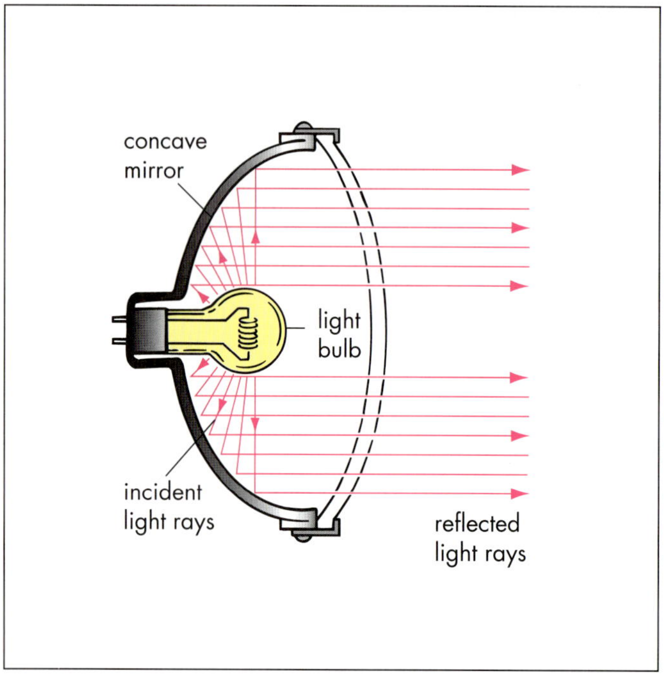

FIGURE 11.18
The light bulb in a car headlight is placed in the focus of the concave mirror so a beam of light is formed.

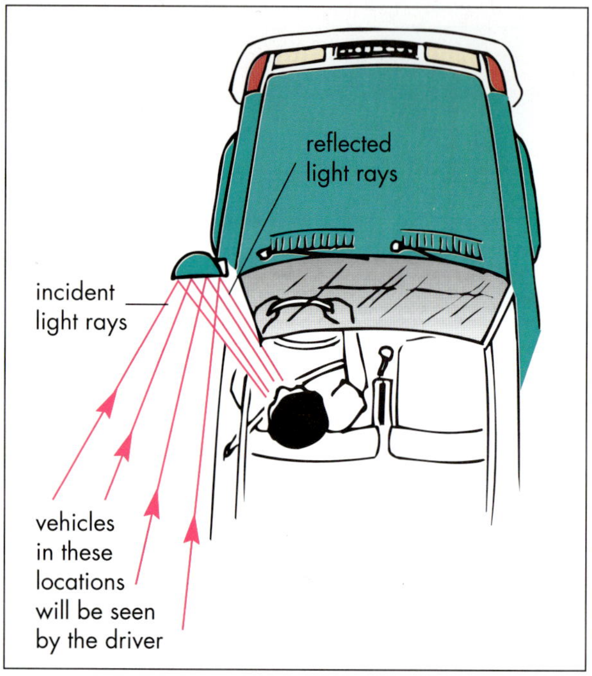

FIGURE 11.19
Convex mirrors allow drivers a wide field of view.

► REVIEW 11.3

1. Define the terms "mirror" and "reflection."
2. If the only light source in a room is a single light bulb, why are you able to see everything in the room?
3. Explain the difference between diverging and converging rays.
4. Astronomers are scientists who study the universe. Why do you think astronomers use very large concave mirrors in some telescopes?
5. What everyday uses of mirrors have not been mentioned in this section?
6. Explain how a concave mirror could be used to start a fire. Use a diagram to explain your answer.
7. Use a diagram to show how a flashlight bulb and a reflector produce a beam of light. Label the incident and reflected light rays. Use arrows to show the direction of the light rays.
8. Using a diagram, show how a convex mirror is used to help with security in a store. Label the incident and reflected light rays. Use arrows to indicate the direction of the rays.

■ 11.4 REFRACTION

Figure 11.20 shows two cups; one is filled with water. You can see a coin in the bottom of the cup filled with water, but the empty cup also has a coin in it. Why are you not able to see the coin in the bottom of the empty cup? The coin in the cup full of water is visible because of the property of light called "refraction."

FIGURE 11.20
There is a coin at the same place in each cup. Why can you see much more of the one in the water-filled cup?

Light rays travel in a straight lines, but when they hit a reflective surface, they change directions. The direction of a light ray can also change when it passes from one substance to another. This change in direction is called **refraction**. The light ray that passes through one substance and hits the surface of a different substance is the **incident ray**. The light ray that bends at this surface and passes through the different substance is called a **refracted ray**.

In Figure 11.20, the light rays bend at the water's surface, where the air and water meet. This change in direction allows you to see the coin in the cup containing water. You cannot see the coin in the empty cup because the light rays reflected from the coin travel straight out of the cup. Figure 11.21 shows the paths of the light rays that can reach the eye from both cups.

Substances that allow light rays to pass through them are said to be **transparent**. Light rays are refracted as they pass from one transparent substance to another. Substances that do not allow any light to pass through are **opaque**. Substances that allow some light to pass through but do not allow you to see clearly through them are said to be **translucent** (Figure 11.22).

FIGURE 11.21
Refraction allows you to see the coin in the water-filled cup.

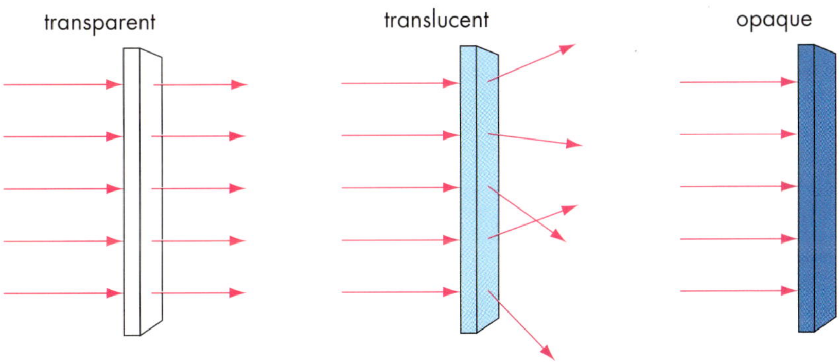

FIGURE 11.22
Objects can affect transmitted light in three ways. Look for examples of transparent, translucent, and opaque objects in your classroom. Which are hardest to find?

ACTIVITY 11G / REFRACTED LIGHT

In this activity, you will see what happens to light rays when they pass from air into plastic or glass.

MATERIALS

plastic or glass block with polished sides
paper
ruler
ray box
single-slit baffle

PROCEDURE

1. Place the plastic or glass block on a piece of paper. Trace the outline of the block on the paper. From the middle of the front of the block, use a ruler to draw a line on the paper at a 90° angle to the block. Figure 11.23 shows the set-up for this activity.
2. With the room lights off, adjust the ray box so that the edges of the light beam are parallel. Insert the single-slit baffle.
3. Shine a light ray from the ray box along the line at 90° to the block. What happens to the ray of light as it enters the block? Record your observations in your notebook.
4. Move the ray box to a different position so that the light ray strikes the front of the block at a different angle. Make sure that it strikes the block at the point where the 90° line meets the face of the block.
5. With a pencil and a ruler, trace the incident ray on the paper. Mark the point where the refracted ray meets the back of the block. Trace the line of the light ray leaving the block. Label this pair of incident and refracted light rays "A." Use arrows to indicate the direction of the light rays.
6. Remove the block and draw in the refracted ray by connecting the point where the incident ray enters the block and the light ray leaves the block. Draw the 90° angle line across the area where the block sat.
7. Repeat steps 4, 5, and 6, changing the position of the ray box so that the incident ray enters the block at a different angle each time. Label each new pair of incident and refracted light rays with a different letter.

FIGURE 11.23
How to set up the apparatus for Activity 11G

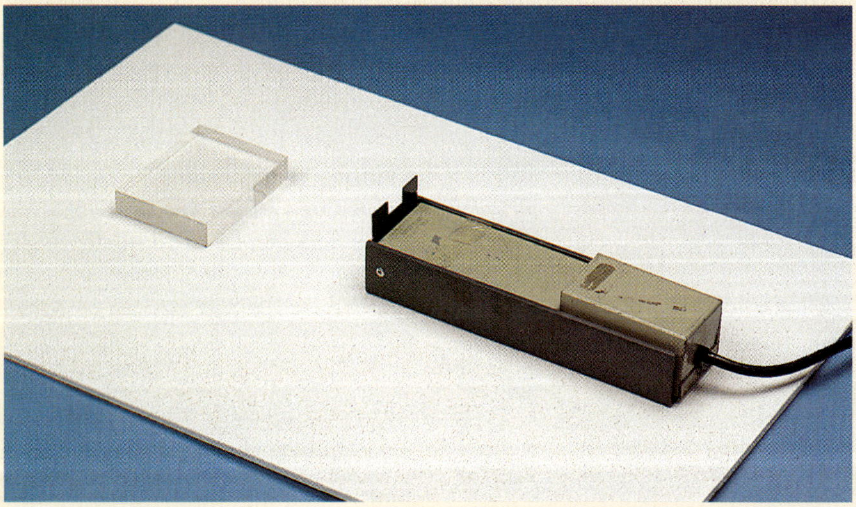

DISCUSSION

1. (a) Describe what happens to the light ray when it enters the block along the 90° line.
   (b) What happens to the light ray when it enters the block at other angles?
   (c) What happens to the refracted ray when the angle at which the incident ray hits the block is increased?
2. Compare the light ray's entry into the block with its exit. How is it similar? How is it different?
3. What happens to light as it passes from one substance to another? ❖

PUTTING REFRACTION TO WORK

Every time light rays pass from one substance into and through another, they are refracted. A lens is a good example of how refracted light can be used. A **lens** is a transparent device, with at least one curved surface, that can refract light rays. If you wear glasses, your lenses are refracting light into your eyes so you can see better.

There are two types of lenses: convex and concave. Convex lenses have surfaces bulging outward; this means that they are thicker in the centre than at the edges. Convex lenses are used by people who are far-sighted and need glasses to read. They are also used in optical equipment such as microscopes and telescopes. Concave lenses have a surface that is curved inward, like a cave. A concave lens is thinner at the centre than at the edges. These lenses are used by people who are near-sighted and need glasses to see objects in the distance. You can learn more about eye problems and how they can be corrected with lenses in Chapter 2.

EXTENSION

■ Some people who need corrective lenses wear contact lenses instead of glasses. Find out how contact lenses correct eye problems. Why do some people prefer to wear them? Are there any problems with contact lenses? Visit an optometrist or ophthalmologist to learn about the different kinds of contact lenses and how they are fitted.

ACTIVITY 11H / LENSES

In this activity, you will observe what happens to light rays when they pass through concave and convex lenses.

MATERIALS

Part I
ruler
ray box
five-slit baffle
convex lens
paper

PART I A Convex Lens

PROCEDURE

1. In your notebook, trace Figure 11.24. Using a ruler, predict the paths of the refracted rays as they leave the right side of the convex lens.
2. Test your prediction. With the room lights off, adjust the ray box so that the edges of the light beam are parallel. Insert a five-slit baffle. Place the convex lens on the paper, and trace around the outside of the lens.
3. Shine the light rays at the convex lens so that the middle refracted ray makes a straight line through the middle of the lens.
4. On the paper, trace the refracted rays as they leave the other side of the lens. Label the incident rays and refracted rays, using the letters A, B, C, D, and E. Use arrows to indicate the direction of the light rays.

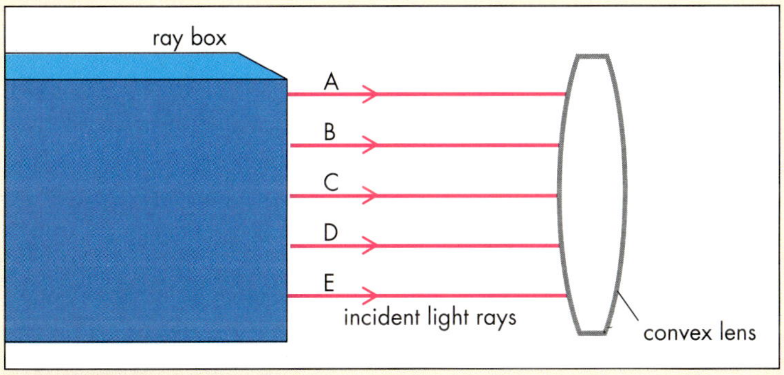

FIGURE 11.24
Trace this diagram and predict the paths of the refracted light rays. Use an arrow to show the direction of each ray and label the refracted rays.

DISCUSSION

1. Compare your prediction with your observations.
2. Examine the lens at the front of your ray box. What kind of lens is it? Why do you think this kind of lens is used for the ray box?

MATERIALS

Part II
ruler
ray box
five-slit baffle
concave lens
paper

PART II A Concave Lens

PROCEDURE

1. Trace Figure 11.25 in your notebook. Using a ruler, predict the paths of the refracted rays as they leave the right side of the concave lens.
2. Test your prediction. Use the ray box with the five-slit baffle as in step 2 of the Procedure in Part I. Place the concave lens on the paper, and trace around the outside of the lens.
3. With the room lights off, shine the light rays at the concave lens so that the middle refracted ray makes a straight line through the middle of the lens.
4. On the paper, trace the refracted rays as they leave the lens. Label the incident rays and refracted rays, using the letters F, G, H, I, and J. Use arrows to indicate the direction of the light rays.

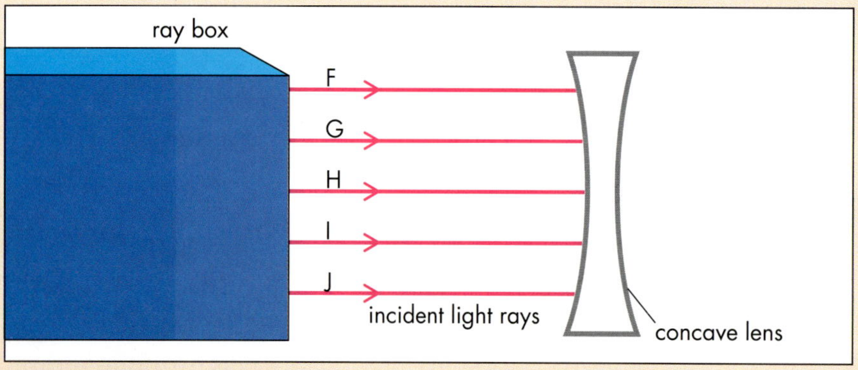

FIGURE 11.25
Trace this diagram and predict the paths of the refracted light rays. Use an arrow to show the direction of each ray and label the refracted rays.

DISCUSSION

Compare your prediction with your observations. ❖

USING LENSES AND MIRRORS

In Section 11.3, you learned that concave mirrors cause reflected light rays to converge at a focal point. Convex mirrors cause reflected light rays to diverge.

Lenses also cause light rays to converge and diverge. However, it is convex lenses that cause refracted light rays to converge to a focus. Figure 11.26 shows how a convex lens can converge light rays from the sun to a focus. Concave lenses cause light rays to diverge.

Mirrors and lenses are all around you. You may use a mirror in the morning to get ready for school, but you can also see yourself in the shiny surface of a toaster. A shiny spoon is a concave mirror on one side and a convex mirror on the other. Glassware, water, and windows all refract light rays. Without the lenses in their eye glasses, many people would not be able to see clearly. Figure 11.27 shows some of the ways that mirrors and lenses are used every day.

Through lenses and mirrors in instruments like microscopes and telescopes, the reflection and refraction of light shows us a world we would not otherwise be able to see. Understanding light and its properties helps us to understand the universe.

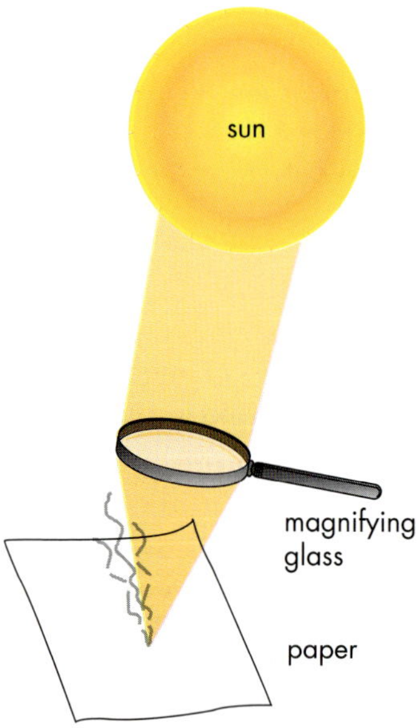

FIGURE 11.26
A magnifying glass is a convex lens, which makes light rays converge. Why is the paper burning?

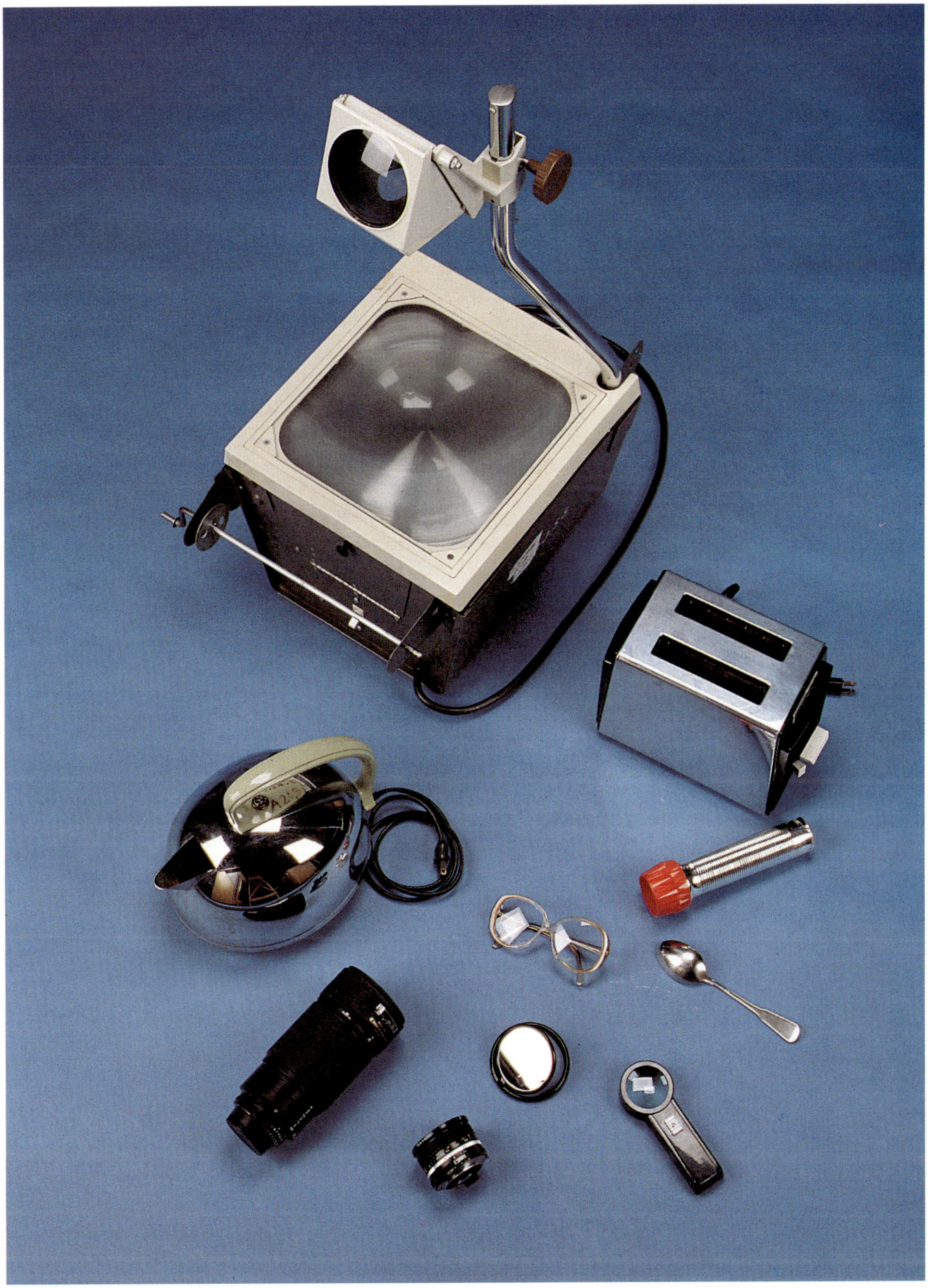

FIGURE 11.27
Mirrors and lenses are all around you. Look for other examples in your home and school.

► REVIEW 11.4

1. Define the following terms:
   (a) incident ray
   (b) refracted ray
2. Name five devices that use refraction.
3. Make a drawing to show how a convex lens refracts light rays.
4. Use a diagram to show how a drop of water sitting on a piece of paper can act as a convex lens.
5. Explain how a convex lens could be used to start a fire.
6. (a) Why are convex lenses sometimes called "converging lenses"?
   (b) Why are concave lenses sometimes called "diverging lenses"?

CHAPTER REVIEW

KEY IDEAS

■ Light is a form of energy. Like other forms of energy, light energy can cause motion, and light energy can be transformed into other forms of energy.

■ Light rays travel in straight lines, but they can change direction by being reflected or refracted.

■ White light can be separated into bands of coloured light, which form a spectrum. These colours can be seen when white light passes through a prism or a spectroscope.

■ Reflection occurs when light rays are bent by hitting a shiny surface.

■ Refraction is the change of direction of light rays when they pass from one medium to another.

■ Mirrors are any objects that reflect light so that a visible image is produced. A visible image in a mirror is called a reflection.

■ Lenses are transparent devices with at least one curved surface that can refract light rays. Lenses have many uses in science, medicine, and everyday life.

■ Substances can be transparent, translucent, or opaque. A transparent substance allows light to pass through it. An opaque substance allows no light to pass through it. A translucent substance allows some light to pass through it.

VOCABULARY

rays
shadow
image
prism
spectrum
mirror
reflection
incident ray
reflected ray
convex
concave
focus
refraction
refracted ray
transparent
opaque
translucent
lens

V1. Make a mind map of what you have learned about light energy, using as many of the words in the vocabulary list as possible.

V2. Make a poster showing everyday uses of mirrors and lenses. Write the words in the vocabulary list on the poster and connect them as they relate to the pictures.

CONNECTIONS

C1. Use two labelled drawings to explain the differences between reflection and refraction.

C2. Name three devices that use both lenses and mirrors together.

C3. If you wear glasses, you may know that glasses will not help your vision when you are swimming. Corrective lenses must be mounted in goggles or a mask in order to help you see clearly under water. Explain why this is so.

C4. Draw a top-view diagram to show how you would place a mirror that would allow you to see around a corner.

EXPLORATIONS

E1. The lens of a camera is similar in shape to the lens in your eye. Consult a reference book to find out how the lens in your eye is able to focus on objects that are different distances from you.

E2. Prepare a report on how fibre optics and lasers are used for sending voices and computer data.

E3. Examine a fish tank (or another large, clear container of water). Explain, using diagrams, how refraction appears to change the position of the fish or other objects in the tank when you look at the fish tank at different angles.

E4. Good-quality concave mirrors are usually parabolic in shape. Find out what a parabolic shape is. Use a diagram to help you explain why mirrors of this shape are used for the reflectors in flashlights, headlights, and solar furnaces.

REFLECTIONS

R1. Find Activity 11A in your learning journal. How has your knowledge of the sources and uses of light energy changed after studying this chapter?

R2. Every day, your life is affected directly and indirectly by mirrors and lenses. List at least five ways that you see lenses or mirrors used. Think about how your life, and life on Earth in general, would be different without mirrors or lenses.

CHAPTER 12

SOUND ENERGY

Think of a world with no sound. Without sound, you would not be able to enjoy music or the singing of birds, or be aware of a fire alarm. You would also not be aware of noise — the crash of thunder, the roar of jets, the hammering of construction tools, the dripping of a tap. In this chapter, you will learn how sounds are made, and how they travel.

ACTIVITY 12A / THE SOUND OF SILENCE

Think about the importance of sound energy in the world. In your learning journal, make a list of all the ways in which sound affects your life. Your teacher may ask you to work together with other students. In your group, make a list of all the ways that sound energy affects daily life. Add any new ideas to your own list.

In your group, discuss all the ways you think that the world would be different without sound energy. Divide a page in your learning journal into two columns. Title the first column "Problems," and the second column "Solutions." In the first column, make a list of the possible problems of living in a world without sounds. In the second column, list the possible solutions to these problems.

Later in this chapter, you will have an opportunity to think about these questions again. ❖

■ 12.1 WHAT IS SOUND?

Sound is a form of energy. It can be transformed into other forms of energy, and other forms of energy can be transformed into sound energy. Because it is a form of energy, sound energy can cause motion. This motion is not always easy to see, but we can sense it using our ears and sensitive electronic equipment.

EXTENSION

■ You may know people who cannot hear very well. How are they able to understand you when you talk to them? Find out about the variety of devices that people who cannot hear well can use to help them communicate.

ACTIVITY 12B / SOMETHING IN COMMON

Imagine the sound of a pin dropping. Then imagine the blast of an exploding firecracker. These sounds are very different, but they do have something in common. In this activity, you will discover a property shared by all sources of sound energy.

CAUTION!

■ **Never strike a tuning fork against a desk or any other hard surface.**

MATERIALS

Part I
safety goggles
tuning fork
rubber mallet
pith ball
thread
water
beaker

PART I A Moving Experience

PROCEDURE

1. Put on your safety goggles.
2. Strike a tuning fork with the rubber mallet or against your hand. Touch the tuning fork to the pith ball, which is hanging on a thread. In your notebook, describe what happens when the tuning fork touches the pith ball. ➡

C A U T I O N !

- Be careful not to touch the sides of the beaker with the tuning fork.

3. Predict what will happen when you strike the tuning fork and touch it to the surface of the water in the beaker. Record and test your prediction. Strike the tuning fork and allow the prongs to touch the surface of the water in the beaker as shown in Figure 12.1. Record your observations.

DISCUSSION

1. Why did you protect your eyes in this activity?
2. Compare your observations from step 2 and step 3. How are they similar?
3. You learned in Chapter 9 that energy is the ability to make things move. What evidence do you have from your observations that sound is a form of energy?
4. (a) Can a tuning fork make a sound if it has not been struck?
   (b) From your observations, what is necessary for sound to be produced?

MATERIALS

Part II
tuning forks
resonating boxes
rubber mallet

FIGURE 12.1
What happens when the tuning fork touches the surface of the water?

PART II Resonating Boxes

PROCEDURE

1. Mount a pair of tuning forks on resonating boxes as shown in Figure 12.2. Strike one of the tuning forks with a rubber mallet. Allow it to sound for a few seconds and then stop it with your hand. Listen for a sound at the other resonating box. Record your observations.

DISCUSSION

1. In Unit II, Investigating Matter, you learned about the kinetic molecular theory. All matter is made up of moving particles. Particles that move quickly have more energy than particles that move more slowly. Use the kinetic molecular theory to explain your observations in step 1 of Part II.
2. A tuning fork receives energy when it is struck. What happens to this energy when the tuning fork prongs stop moving? ❖

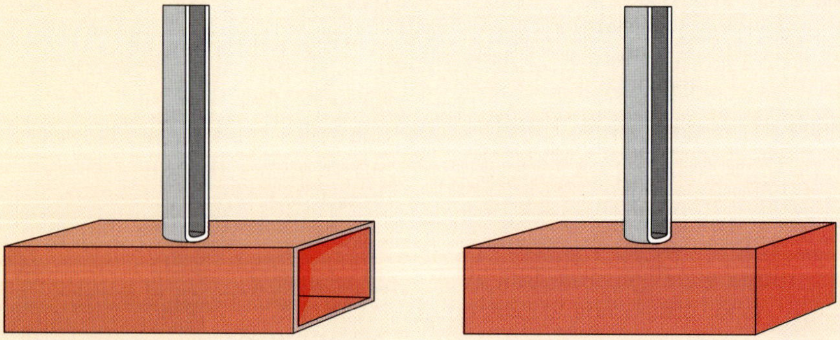

FIGURE 12.2
A pair of tuning forks mounted on resonating boxes

SOUND AND MOVEMENT

When an object moves back and forth, we say that it vibrates. These back-and-forth movements are called **vibrations**. All sounds are caused by vibrations. For example, when you strike a tuning fork or pluck the string of a guitar, it vibrates.

Every musical instrument has a part that vibrates to produce the sounds that we hear. Figure 12.3 shows a number of these instruments. Stringed instruments have strings that are plucked (guitar), struck (piano), or stroked with a bow (violin) to produce the sound. Reed instruments such as clarinets, saxophones, and accordions have thin pieces of wood, bamboo, or plastic that vibrate.

Drums, cymbals, xylophones, and other percussion instruments are all struck, like a tuning fork, to produce vibrations. Wind instruments, including pipe organs, have vibrating columns of air.

Trumpets and other brass instruments rely on the vibration of the player's lips and a vibrating column of air to produce the sound. Electric instruments, such as organs and guitars, use electrical energy to move the membranes in speakers to produce the sound.

EXTENSION

- Find out about your vocal cords. Where are they? How do they work? Why is everyone's voice different?

FIGURE 12.3
All musical instruments have a part that vibrates to produce the sound you hear. What is the vibrating part on each of these instruments?

THE SPEED OF VIBRATIONS

At the end of a concert, you clap your hands to show that you enjoyed the performance. If you enjoyed it very much, you might clap your hands as fast as 20 claps in five seconds.

Frequency is the number of times an event, such as clapping or vibrations, occurs in a given length of time. Usually the length of time is one second. In the example above, you are clapping at a frequency of four claps in one second. We could write this as: frequency = 4 claps per second (per means "for each") or $f = 4$ claps/s.

When you strike a tuning fork, its prongs move back and forth just as your hands do when you clap. The prongs move much more quickly and many more times per second than your hands do. We say that the prongs are moving at a higher frequency than your hands are.

The unit for measuring frequency is the **hertz**. One vibration in one second is called one hertz (Hz). This unit was named after the German physicist Heinrich Rudolf Hertz (1857–1894). The tuning forks in your school probably have frequencies between 128 and 1024 Hz. The frequency is usually stamped on the side of the fork.

ACTIVITY 12C / FREQUENCY

In this activity, you will investigate frequency and see how it can be changed.

MATERIALS

Part I
safety goggles
two clamps
assorted elastic bands
support stand

CAUTION!

- **Elastic bands can cause serious injuries if misused. Do not release elastic bands toward other people.**

PART I Rubber Bands and Frequency

PROCEDURE

1. Put on your safety goggles.

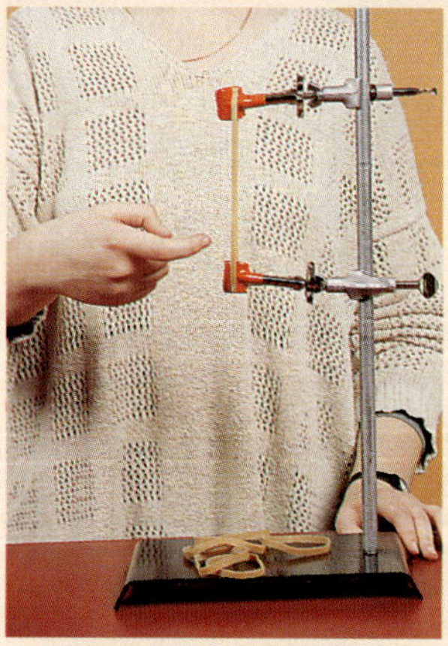

FIGURE 12.4
What happens to the sound when you stretch the elastic band or use a thicker one?

2. Mount an elastic band around two test tube clamps on a support stand so that the elastic band just becomes tight, as shown in Figure 12.4. Pluck the elastic. Look and listen. Record your observations.
3. Predict what will happen to the frequency of the vibrations and the sound produced when you stretch the elastic to (a) two and (b) three times its original length. Record your predictions in your notebook.
4. Test your predictions. Look and listen. Record your results.
5. Replace the elastic band with a thicker elastic band of the same length. Repeat steps 2 to 4 above.
6. Experiment with other elastics of different

MATERIALS

Part II
two C-clamps
metre stick
clock or stopwatch
100 g masses
masking tape
clock or stopwatch

FIGURE 12.5
What happens to the sound and to the frequency when the length of the metre stick and the mass on the end are changed?

thickness and lengths if available. Change the tightness of the elastic bands. Record your observations.

DISCUSSION

1. (a) How did the frequency of the vibrations change as the elastic band was stretched?
   (b) How did the sound change as the elastic band was stretched?
   (c) How are the changes in the sound produced related to the frequency?
2. Make a general statement about the differences in the sound and the frequency produced by thin and thick elastic bands.

PART II Metre Sticks and Frequency

PROCEDURE

1. Using the C-clamps, clamp a metre stick to the edge of a table so that a 50 cm section extends beyond the edge of the table, as shown in Figure 12.5. Pull down and release the free end of the metre stick. Be careful not to bend the metre stick too far. Record your observations in your notebook.
2. Predict what will happen to the sound and to the frequency when the length of the metre stick hanging over the table edge is
   (a) reduced to 25 cm,
   (b) increased to 75 cm.
   Record your predictions in your notebook.
3. Test your predictions. Record your observations in your notebook.
4. Copy Table 12.1 in your notebook.
5. Predict what will happen to the frequency if a 100 g mass is taped to the end of the metre stick that extends over the table edge by 75 cm. Write your prediction in the table in your notebook.
6. Test your prediction by pulling down and releasing the free end of the metre stick as before. Be careful not to bend the metre stick too far. If possible, count the frequency of the vibrations over a 10s period using a clock or stopwatch. Record the count in the table.
7. Tape an additional 100 g mass to the end of the metre stick. Repeat steps 5 and 6.

Mass added to metre stick	Predicted frequency	Observed frequency
100 g		
200 g		

TABLE 12.1
Sample Data Table for Activity 12C, Part II

MATERIALS

Part III
sonometer or guitar

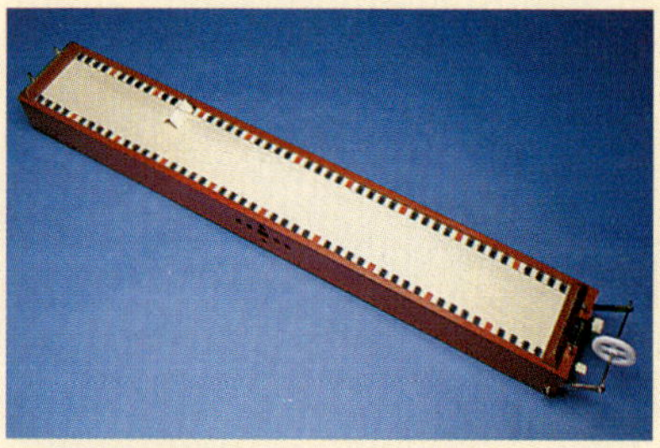

FIGURE 12.6
A sonometer

DISCUSSION

1. What happens to the frequency of the metre stick as the section extending past the edge of the table is
   (a) decreased?
   (b) increased?
2. What happens to the frequency of the metre stick as the mass taped to the end of the stick is increased?
3. Why was 10 s used as the time period for measuring the frequency in step 6?
4. (a) Which would have a higher frequency, a short tuning fork or a long tuning fork? Explain your answer.
   (b) Which would have a higher frequency: a short piano wire or a long piano wire?

PART III A Sonometer (Teacher Demonstration)

PROCEDURE

1. Your teacher will demonstrate a sonometer (Figure 12.6) or a guitar. Observe what happens to the sound produced when
   (a) a string is shortened,
   (b) a string is tightened,
   (c) a thinner string is plucked.
   Record your observations.

DISCUSSION

1. Describe three ways in which the frequency of sound produced by a sonometer or a guitar can be increased.
2. Think of all of the musical instruments you can and the sounds they produce. In general, what can you say about the size of an instrument and the sound that it produces? Give two examples that explain your answer. ❖

DID YOU KNOW

■ Pitch increases as frequency increases. Although pitch and frequency are closely related, there is more to pitch than the frequency of the vibration. The pitch you hear depends on other factors, such as the loudness of the sound. Can you think of other factors that might affect pitch?

THE QUALITY OF SOUND

The frequency of an object can be changed. For example, you can change the frequency of a guitar string by making the string shorter or by making it tighter. The shorter the string, the higher the frequency. The tighter the string, the higher the frequency.

Other methods are used to change frequencies in other kinds of instruments. The length of a vibrating air column in a brass instrument, such as a trumpet, is changed by opening and closing valves. How can you tell which sounds have higher frequencies?

Sometimes you may describe sounds as being "higher" or "lower" than other sounds. For example, a truck's horn has a much deeper (lower) sound than a car's horn. **Pitch** is used to describe the highness and lowness of sounds. A scream has a high pitch. A person with a deep voice talks in a low pitch. Pitch is determined by frequency. A sound with a high pitch has a high frequency (for example, over 440 vibrations per second). A sound with a low pitch has a lower frequency (for example, below 440 vibrations per second).

FREQUENCY RANGES

A sound that you can hear is called an **audible** sound. Those sounds that are too low or too high for you to hear are called **inaudible**. The range of frequencies from the lowest to the highest that you can hear is called your audible frequency range. For humans, the range of normal hearing is from a low of about 20 Hz to a high of about 20 000 Hz.

Many animals have an audible frequency range different from that of humans. The upper end of the audible range of dogs is much higher than that of humans, while the lower end of an elephant's range is much lower than a human's range (Figure 12.7).

Age, injury, or disease can cause hearing to become less sensitive, so that a person may only be able to hear part of the normal range.

Hearing specialists can check you for hearing loss by testing your audible frequency range. In the last section of this chapter, and in Chapter 2 on the senses, you can learn about your hearing and how to protect it.

FIGURE 12.7
Many animals can hear higher or lower frequencies than humans can. How does a dog whistle differ from the whistle used by your physical education teacher?

ACTIVITY 12D / YOUR FREQUENCY RANGE

GROUP ACTIVITY

In this activity, your teacher will set up a frequency generator and speaker so that you can find out the range of frequencies you can hear.

MATERIALS

frequency generator with speaker

PROCEDURE

1. The generator will be started at a high frequency (100 000 Hz or higher), which will gradually be lowered. As this is happening, listen for a high-pitched whistle. Your teacher will call out the frequency settings. In your notebook, record the first frequency that you are able to hear. Record the frequencies that are uncomfortable to listen to. Continue listening until you can no longer hear the sound. Record this frequency.
2. Repeat step 1 in reverse, so that the generator is started at a low frequency and gradually raised. Record your range of frequencies again.
3. Record the range of frequencies of everyone in the class in a data table on the chalkboard.

DISCUSSION

1. What range of frequencies can you hear?
2. What was the common frequency range for the class?
3. What frequency range did you find uncomfortable to listen to?
4. You may have found that high-frequency sounds are similar to those produced by sirens, alarms, and smoke detectors. Why do you think high-frequency sounds are used for these devices?
5. How is it helpful to hear a wide range of frequencies? ❖

▶ REVIEW 12.1

1. What is sound?
2. What is meant by the frequency of a vibration?
3. What is the difference between frequency and pitch?
4. Which would have a higher pitch: a string vibrating at 500 Hz or one vibrating at 1000 Hz? Explain your answer.
5. (a) Suggest three ways in which a violinist can make a note higher in pitch.

   (b) What happens to the frequency of the sound produced when any of these changes are made?

■ 12.2 THE TRANSMISSION OF SOUND ENERGY

In the first section of this chapter, you learned that all sounds come from vibrating sources. The transmission of sound energy also has two other parts: a medium and a receiver. The **medium** is the material that carries or transmits the sound energy. The **receiver** receives the sound energy that came from the source and travelled through the medium. Your ear is an example of a receiver.

ACTIVITY 12E / LOST IN SPACE (TEACHER DEMONSTRATION)

In this activity, you will discover how important a medium is for transmitting sound energy.

MATERIALS

electric bell
bell jar
vacuum pump, plate, and hose
power supply or batteries

PROCEDURE

1. Your teacher will suspend an electric bell inside a bell jar, and place the jar on a vacuum pump, as shown in Figure 12.8. The bell will then be connected to a power source. Is the striker hitting the bell? Can you hear the bell ringing inside the bell jar? Record your observations.

FIGURE 12.8 ▶ ***What happens to the sound from the bell when the air is removed from the bell jar?***

2. The vacuum pump will be turned on for several minutes, until the air inside the bell jar has been removed. Predict what will happen to the sound of the bell when the air is removed. Write your prediction in your notebook.
3. The valve to the bell jar will be closed, and the pump turned off. The jar now contains a vacuum, which is a space from which all the air has been removed. Is the striker hitting the bell? Can you hear the bell ringing inside the bell jar? Record your observations.
4. The valve to the bell jar will be opened slowly. What do you notice as the air flows back into the bell jar? Record your observations.

DISCUSSION

1. How did your prediction in step 2 compare with your observations in step 3?
2. What is needed in order for sound energy to be transmitted?
3. Why do you think that the bell was suspended from the top of the bell jar, rather than sitting on the bottom or leaning against the side of the bell jar?
4. Can sound energy travel through a vacuum? Explain your answer. ❖

SOUND MEDIUMS

Most sounds that you hear come to you through the air, which is a gas, but sound energy can also travel through liquids and solids. For example, if someone taps on the railing of a metal fence, you can hear the tapping by placing your ear to the railing, even if you are far enough from the source that you cannot hear the tapping through the air. The metal is the medium that carries the sound in this case. A medium that allows sound energy to travel through it is called a **conductor**.

ACTIVITY 12F / FINDING A GOOD MEDIUM

In this activity, you and your partner will experiment with different materials to see whether they are good mediums for sound transmission.

MATERIALS

Part I
tuning fork
rubber mallet
various materials (rubber eraser, steel rod, book, glass square, sponge, copper rod, Styrofoam, and anything else that might be available)

PART I Sound Transmission in Solids

PROCEDURE

1. Place your finger in your ear so that your hand and arm are in a line, as shown in Figure 12.9. Tap your elbow with a finger from your other hand lightly. What do you hear? Now, move your finger out of your ear (a few centimetres) and repeat the tapping. In your notebook, describe any differences in the sounds that you hear.
2. You and your partner will stand some distance apart beside a lab counter or at opposite ends of a lab counter. Put your ear to the surface of the counter, as shown in Figure 12.10. Your partner will strike the tuning fork with the rubber mallet, and then press the handle of the tuning

➥

FIGURE 12.9
What do you hear when you tap your elbow?

MATERIALS

Part II
hammer
nail
tin cans
string
copper wire
nylon wire

fork against the counter. How does the sound that you hear through the table compare with the sound that you hear through the air? Record your observations. Switch positions with your partner and repeat.

3. Predict how each of the materials supplied by your teacher will affect the sound when it is placed between the tuning fork and the counter. Write your predictions in your notebook. Test your predictions by repeating step 2 using each material. Record your observations.

DISCUSSION

1. Through which materials that you tested did sounds
   (a) travel well?
   (b) not travel well?
2. Suggest a test to measure accurately how well sounds can travel through different materials.

PART II Making Tin-can Telephones

PROCEDURE

1. Using a hammer and a nail, punch a small hole in the centre of the bottom of two tin cans. Thread 2 to 10 m of string through the holes. Tie a knot in each end of the string so that it will not slip through the holes.
2. You and your partner each hold one can. Stand far enough away from your partner so that the string is tight. Have your partner talk into one can while you listen at the other one. What do you hear? Try plucking the string lightly. What do you hear? Record your observations.
3. Predict what you will hear if you take a step toward your partner so that the string hangs loosely. Write down your prediction. Test your prediction by talking into the cans. What do you hear? Record your observations.
4. Make a set of tin-can telephones using copper wire or nylon wire (a set may already be prepared). Repeat step 2. In your notebook, describe how the tin-can telephones made using this material compare with those made using the string.

DISCUSSION

Use your observations to explain the differences in the sounds that you heard in steps 2 and 3. ❖

FIGURE 12.10
Can you hear the tuning fork through the counter?

WAVES OF SOUND

It is Saturday morning and you are going to visit a friend. When you arrive at the front door of your friend's house, you remember that the doorbell is broken, so you knock hard to make sure that someone hears you.

You have learned in this chapter that all sounds are caused by vibrations. Your knock caused the door to vibrate, which produced the sound energy. You have also learned that sound energy needs a medium in order to be transmitted. The air on both sides of the door is a medium. The air carries the sound of the knock to your ears and to your friend inside the house. But how does sound energy travel through the air to your ears?

The way that sound energy travels can be compared to the way that waves spread out when a stone is dropped into a pond of water, as shown in Figure 12.11. If you watch the waves carefully, you may notice that only the wave travels outward from the source—the water itself does not move outward from the source, only up and down. To prove this, you could drop a leaf on the water. You would see that the leaf bobs up and down as the wave passes. But the leaf stays the same distance from the point where the stone was dropped. The type of wave produced in water is called a transverse wave.

Another model of wave motion is the "wave" created by spectators in a stadium or arena. The groups of fans jump up in their seats and then sit down quickly so that you see what looks like a wave passing through the crowd. The fans do not move away from their seats; they only move up and down to create the "wave" like the one shown in Figure 12.12.

Sound waves are different from water or spectator waves, but these examples are useful models of how a wave passes through a medium.

FIGURE 12.11
The ripples created by a falling drop of water are a model of sound waves.

FIGURE 12.12
A spectator "wave" is another model of sound waves.

HOW ARE ELECTRIC GUITARS MADE?

The next time you listen to your favourite electric guitar music, you might think about what you learned in science class. The sound of an electric guitar depends on the properties of the materials used to make the guitar.

Maple is often used for the neck of the guitar because it is a strong wood (a). The neck must be strong enough to withstand the pull of the strings without bending. The best necks use one piece of wood that runs the length of the guitar. A metal rod inside the neck helps to keep it from bending.

(a) An outline of the neck is traced on to a maple board.

Ebony, a very hard wood, is a good choice for the finger board of a guitar (b).

The body is made of wood. The wood must be of good quality and prepared properly. The type of wood affects the quality of sound. A guitar made of dense maple will have a harsh, metallic sound. Red alder and butternut, which are less dense woods, produce a more mellow sound. The amount of moisture in the air (humidity) must be controlled while the guitar is being made.

(b) Ebony, a hard dark wood, is used to hold the frets.

Even the finish applied to the guitar affects the sound. Some finishes deaden the sound. Other finishes change colour or crack with time. The last finish sprayed on the guitar must be long-lasting and attractive. The best choice is acrylic lacquer (c).

The pick-ups on the guitar detect the vibrations of the strings (d). The pick-up closest to the neck detects sounds of low pitch (bass response). The pick-up near the bridge detects higher-pitched sounds (treble response). Controls allow the player to modify the sound.

The strings contain the metals iron, chromium, and nickel. This combination has two properties that are needed: it is magnetic, so it can affect the pick-ups; and it does not readily rust.

The final product is unique. It produces a sound affected by the properties of all its parts: wood, metal, acrylic—and, of course, the talent and skill of the player!

Choose any other musical instrument and find out what materials it is made of. List as many of the materials as you can, and describe what properties affect the quality of the sound.

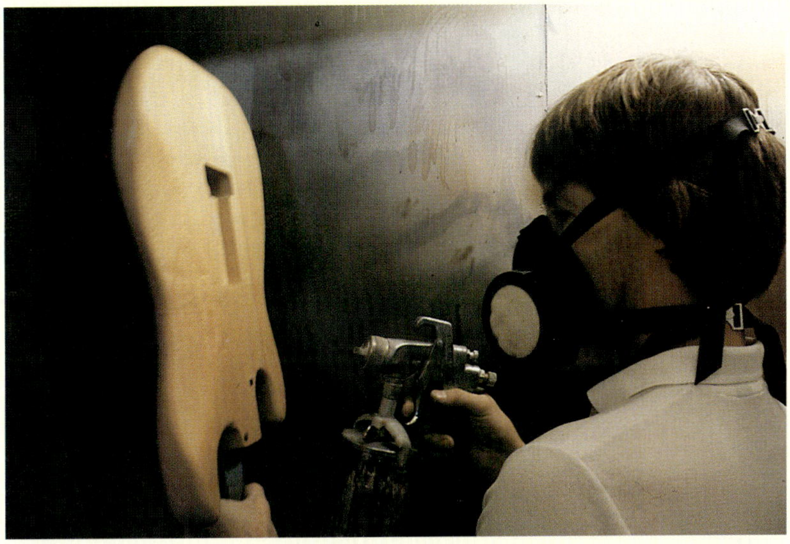

(c) The body of the guitar is coated in acrylic lacquer.

(d) The electronic pick-ups are hooked up.

ACTIVITY 12G / WHAT I KNOW ABOUT SOUND WAVES

Copy Table 12.2 in your learning journal. In the first column, write what you already know about sound waves. In the second column, write questions you have about sound waves.

As you read the following section, write down new ideas, details, or examples that you learn about sound waves. When you have finished reading, put a check mark beside the ideas that your reading has confirmed, and a question mark beside the ideas that you are still not sure about. ❖

TABLE 12.2 ▶
Sample Data Table for Activity 12G

What I already know about sound waves	Questions I have about sound waves	What I have learned about sound waves

FIGURE 12.13
Vibrations of a tuning fork cause compressions and rarefactions.

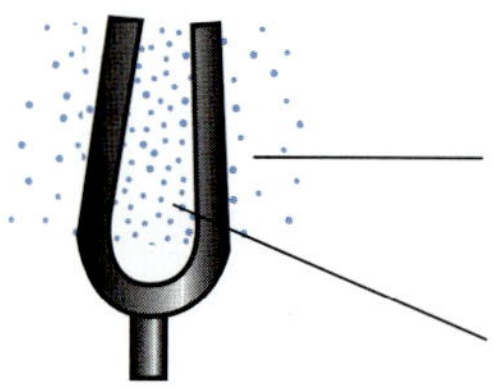

(a) Prongs coming together

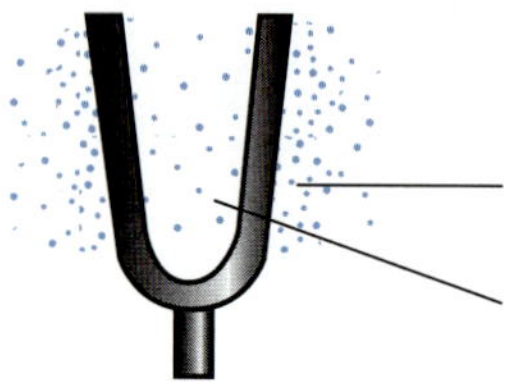

(b) Prongs spreading apart

HOW SOUND WAVES TRAVEL THROUGH AIR

When you knock on your friend's door, the sound energy travels outward in all directions from the door. Sound energy is like light energy in the way it radiates (moves outward) from a source. But sound energy needs a medium, like air or water, in order to travel.

The kinetic molecular theory tells us that all substances are made up of particles. Sound energy is transmitted by the particles of the medium moving back and forth and bumping into other particles. This movement is caused by the vibrations of the object producing the sound energy.

As the prongs of the tuning fork vibrate, they move outward, forcing the particles of the air next to the prongs closer together. This is called a **compression** (from the Latin *com-*, meaning "together," and *pressere* meaning "press"). When the prongs move inward, the particles beside the prongs move apart again. This is called **rarefaction** (from the Latin *rare*, meaning "less dense," and *facere*, meaning "make"). The movement of the prongs causes the particles in the air all around the tuning fork to move, forming compressions and rarefactions.

A sound wave is called a **compressional wave** because it is made up of compressions and rarefactions. The particles of the medium do not

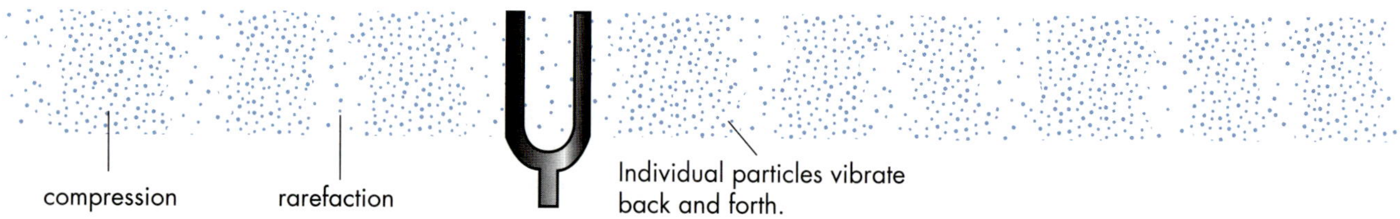

(c) Compressional waves coming from a tuning fork

move very far. Compressions and rarefactions move out in all directions from a sound source, like the tuning fork. This is similar to the waves in a pond moving away from the spot where a stone has been dropped.

Figure 12.14 compares transverse and compressional waves. Transverse waves are often used in diagrams to represent sound waves because they are easier to draw than compressional waves.

The length of compressional waves can be measured from the middle of one compression to the middle of the next one. This is called one **wavelength**. In a transverse wave, the wavelength can be measured from the highest point of one wave to the highest point of the next wave.

The **amplitude** of a transverse wave is the distance from the highest point of the wave to the rest line, as shown in Figure 12.14. In a compressional wave, the amplitude is measured as the farthest distance a particle moves from the rest position. For example, with the tuning fork, the bigger the back-and-forth movement of the prongs, the farther the particles are pushed from their starting or rest position. This means that the larger the vibration, the larger the amplitude of a compressional wave.

DID YOU KNOW

■ When an airplane is flying, it produces sound waves, which move out in all directions. As the airplane approaches the speed of sound, the sound wave compressions in front of the plane become closer together. When the speed of sound is reached, the sound wave compressions build up to produce a powerful wave in the air called a shock wave. When this shock wave reaches you on the ground, you hear a sonic boom. As the plane travels faster than the speed of sound (also called the sound barrier), it is said to be supersonic. What kind of airplanes do you think are most likely to produce sonic booms? Why?

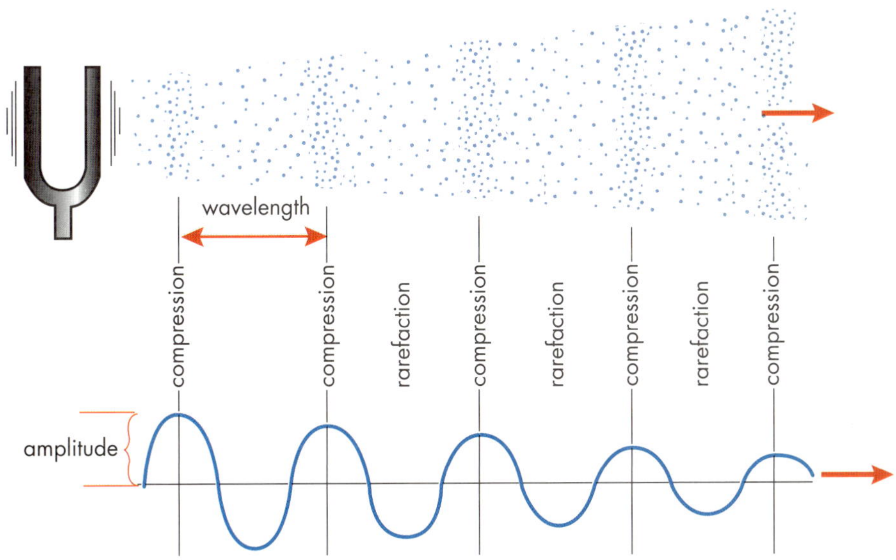

FIGURE 12.14 ◀
How do compressional and transverse waves compare?

AMPLITUDE AND VOLUME

In the first section of this chapter, you learned that pitch describes the highness or lowness of a sound. A sound with a high frequency has a high pitch, while a sound with a low frequency has a low pitch. Another way of describing sounds is by loudness. **Volume** describes the loudness of a sound. A loud sound has a high volume, and a quiet sound has a low volume. Volume is determined by the amplitude of the sound wave. The greater the amplitude of the wave, the louder the sound.

ACTIVITY 12H / A SOUND MODEL

In this activity, you will use springs as models of sound waves.

MATERIALS

Part I
Slinky
ribbon

Part II
Slinky
2.5 cm diameter tightly coiled spring

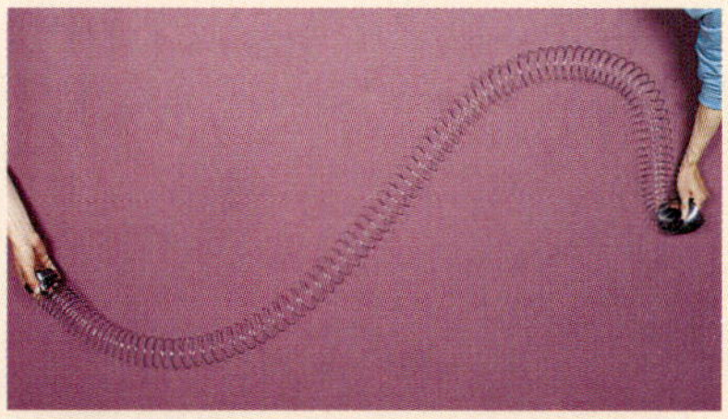

FIGURE 12.15
A Slinky can be used to model transverse waves.

PART I Making Waves (Teacher Demonstration)

PROCEDURE

1. Use a Slinky on the floor, as shown in Figure 12.15, to show compressional waves and transverse waves. Observe compression, rarefaction, amplitude, wavelength, and frequency.
2. Tie a small piece of ribbon to the middle of the Slinky. Predict what will happen to the ribbon when the Slinky forms (a) a compressional wave and (b) a transverse wave. Will the ribbon move along the Slinky? Write your predictions in your notebook. Test your predictions. Record your observations.

DISCUSSION

1. Make a drawing of a Slinky producing a transverse wave. Label the amplitude and wavelength of the wave.
2. A wave appears to travel down the length of the Slinky, but the individual coils of the Slinky move very little. Explain how this happens.

PART II Comparing Mediums

PROCEDURE

1. Use the 2.5 cm diameter spring as a model of another wave medium. Lay the Slinky and the tightly coiled spring together, as shown in Figure 12.16. Hold them tightly.
2. Create a compressional wave in both springs. Which spring produces a faster wave?
3. Create a transverse wave by either plucking the spring or shaking the end of the spring with your hand. Which spring produces the faster wave?
4. Using the Slinky, first create a small transverse wave, then create a large one. Does the amplitude affect the speed of the wave produced?

FIGURE 12.16
Which spring represents the denser medium?

CAUTION!

■ **The release of a stretched spring can injure your partner and damage the spring. Do not over-stretch the springs.**

5. Stretch the Slinky more and create a transverse wave. What happens to the frequency of the waves as the Slinky is stretched?
6. Repeat steps 4 and 5 with the 2.5 cm diameter spring.

DISCUSSION

1. What happens to a wave when it hits the end of the spring?
2. What happens to the amplitude of the wave as it moves away from the source?
3. What were the differences in the waves produced in the Slinky and the 2.5 cm diameter spring? Which represents the denser medium: the Slinky or the other spring?
4. How does the tightness of the spring affect the frequency of its vibrations? ❖

REVIEW 12.2

1. What are the three parts of sound transmission?
2. Explain how sound energy is transmitted using compression and rarefaction.
3. What is the difference between volume and amplitude?
4. In some science fiction movies, you see spaceships being blown apart and then you hear the sound of the explosion. What is wrong with these scenes?
5. Explain why sound energy cannot travel in a vacuum.
6. Use the kinetic molecular theory to explain why sound energy can travel faster through rock than through air.

■ 12.3 SOUND ENERGY AND TECHNOLOGY

Technology allows us to put sound energy to work in many ways. The study of sound energy is called **acoustics**. Acoustical engineers are people who design anything related to sound energy, including hearing aids, car horns, concert halls, and stereo speakers. In this section, we will look at some of the ways that sound energy is controlled and used.

ECHOES

Have you ever shouted in a large, empty room? It may have sounded as if two people had shouted almost at the same time, one a little less loudly than the other. This double sound is caused by the sound waves you created reflecting back from the walls, the ceiling, and the floor of the room. These reflected sound waves are called an **echo**.

We can use a model to help us understand how an echo forms. Figure 12.17 shows what happens when you drop a beachball into a

EXTENSION

■ Blind people can use echo location to help them "see" where they are going. Hand-held units send out sound waves that bounce off objects. Earphones carry a tapping noise that speeds up as the wearer approaches an object. Find out how these systems work. How many blind people use them? If possible, talk to blind people who use an echo location system. Have they found the system easy to use? What difference has the system made to their lives?

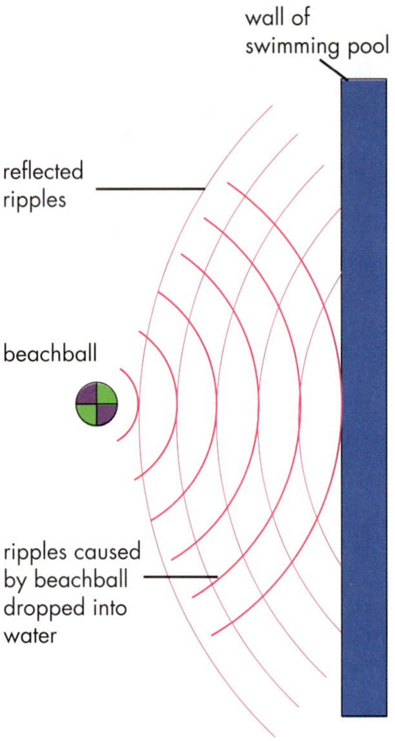

FIGURE 12.17
Reflected ripples are a model of an echo. Will the amplitude of the reflected ripples be greater or smaller than that of the original ripples?

swimming pool. Ripples move out in all directions until they hit the sides of the pool. The ripples then bounce off the sides and are reflected back across the water. They form an echo.

Sound waves form an echo in the same way. The sound waves travel from their source until they hit a hard surface and are reflected. You can hear echoes outdoors, as well as indoors; for example, anywhere there are high brick or stone walls.

USING ECHOES

Animals such as whales and dolphins use echoes to keep track of their surroundings. As the animal swims, it makes high-frequency sounds that go out in all directions. When these sounds meet an object, such as a rock, a boat, or a fish, they are reflected and travel back as echoes. The longer the echo takes to come back, the farther away the object is.

The animal's brain sorts out all these echoes and forms a "sound picture" of its surroundings. This sound picture helps the animal to decide which way to go to find food and to avoid obstacles. Using echoes to find the positions of objects is called echo location.

Humans have learned to use echo location by developing special technology, such as sonar. (The word "sonar" is formed from the phrase "*so*und *n*avigation *a*nd *r*anging.") Sonar systems are made up of a high-frequency transmitter, a high-frequency sound receiver, and a clock. By measuring the time it takes for echoes to return, the sonar system can compute the distance from, for example, a boat to the ocean floor as shown in Figure 12.18. Sonar is also used to find schools of fish.

DID YOU KNOW

■ Bats use ultrasonic sounds at about 50 000 Hz for echo location. They can locate their insect prey in flight and find their way easily in the dark by listening for the echoes of these sounds.

FIGURE 12.18 ▶
A ship's sonar uses echoes of sound waves to detect objects below the water's surface. How could you tell if there was a submarine beneath your ship?

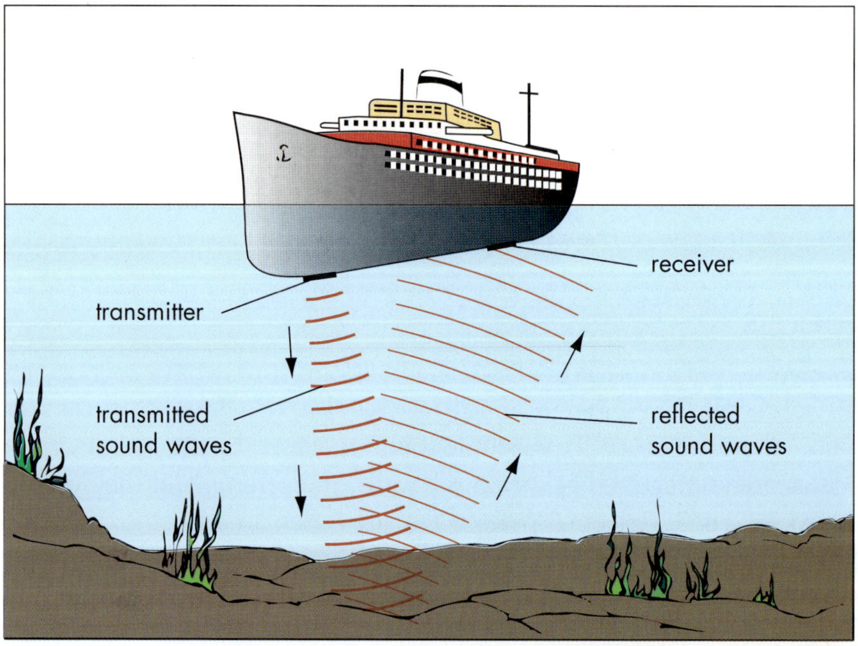

BEYOND OUR HEARING

The very high frequencies used in sonar are also used on land. **Ultrasonic** describes those frequencies above 20 000 Hz (*ultra-* is the Latin word meaning "beyond"). Humans cannot hear sounds much above 20 000 Hz. Engineers use ultrasonic frequencies to inspect pipes and airplane parts for faults in the metal. Manufacturers cut and drill metal by using ultrasonic frequencies.

Ultrasonic drilling is also used by some dentists. They can drill and clean teeth using ultrasonic frequencies.

One of the most important uses of ultrasonic frequencies is in ultrasound. Ultrasound is a procedure that uses sound waves to "see" inside a patient (Figure 12.19). It is often used to examine unborn babies (Figure 12.20), but it can also be used to look at organs inside our bodies. The benefits of ultrasound are that the body does not need to be cut, it is quick, and it does not harm the unborn baby as X rays might.

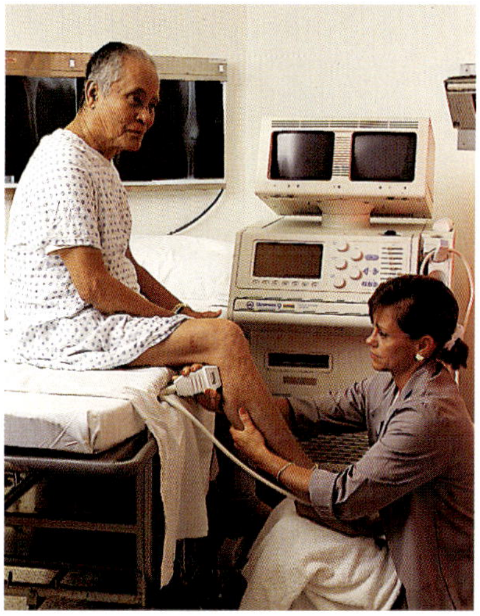

FIGURE 12.19
Ultrasound being used to measure blood flow in a vein. If ultrasound were not available, how would this be done?

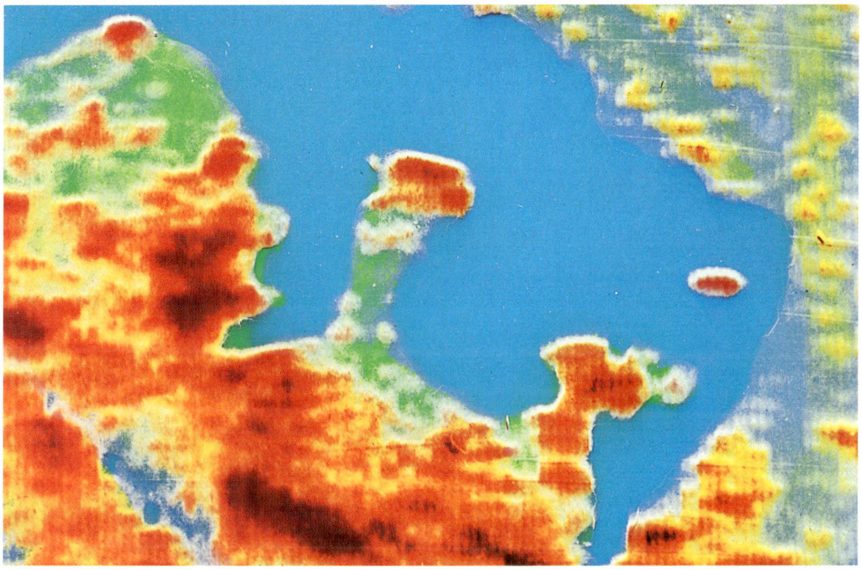

FIGURE 12.20 ◀
The size, position, and health of a fetus can be seen using ultrasound. The results of the examination can be seen on a display screen as the ultrasound is being taken.

WHEN SOUND IS NOISE

Any unwanted sound is called **noise**. It may be loud, like the engine of an airplane taking off, or it may be quiet, like the sound of another student tapping a pencil constantly. Noise is all around us. We cannot always eliminate the source, but there are ways of reducing the transmission of noise. Figure 12.21 shows some examples of noise sources.

Noise can be harmful to you. Noise can lead to a lack of concentration, fatigue, irritability, tension, backache, and headache. Continued exposure to loud noises can also lead to dizziness and nausea. Continuous or repeated exposure to loud noises can permanently damage the nerve endings in your ears. If a noise is extremely loud, it may even split your eardrum.

FIGURE 12.21
Music to one person's ears can be noise to another's!

ACTIVITY 12I / REDUCING NOISE

GROUP ACTIVITY

In this activity, you will experiment with various methods of reducing the noise produced from a sound source.

MATERIALS

alarm clock, speaker, or some other device that makes a loud noise
materials for building a container

PROCEDURE

1. You will work with other students in teams to design and construct the container that best reduces the level of noise. Your teacher will give you directions about your sound source and the materials available.
2. Make a labelled diagram of your team's container, giving reasons for each feature used.
3. Your whole class will judge the containers. Listen to the sound coming from each container when the noise source has been placed inside. Vote on which containers are quietest. List the containers on the blackboard, with the quietest at the top of the list and the loudest at the end.

DISCUSSION

1. What features of your container helped reduce the noise level?
2. What changes would improve the ability of your container to reduce the noise level?
3. What features did the better containers have in common?
4. What other method could be used to determine which one is the quietest container?

5. Imagine that the noise source was placed outside your container and a microphone was placed inside to measure the noise level. Would your container be as successful at keeping the noise out as it was at keeping the noise in? Explain your answer. ❖

NOISE INSULATION

Noise insulation works the way heat insulation does, by preventing the transfer of energy. Noise insulation either absorbs or reflects sound energy. Hearing protection, such as that pictured in Figure 12.22, is usually made of foamy material. This type of material is comfortable to wear and it absorbs sound waves. It is important to wear hearing protection whenever you are near loud noises. Regular exposure to loud noises will damage your hearing.

In hotels, apartments, offices, and schools, fibreglass insulation is often used in the walls to reduce the transmission of noise from room to room. Simply having carpeting in a car or truck, instead of rubber mats, can reduce the noise in the vehicle.

EXTENSION

■ If a sound meter is available, use it to measure as many different noise-making devices in your school as possible. Make a list of the devices, with the quietest at the top of the list and the loudest at the end of the list.

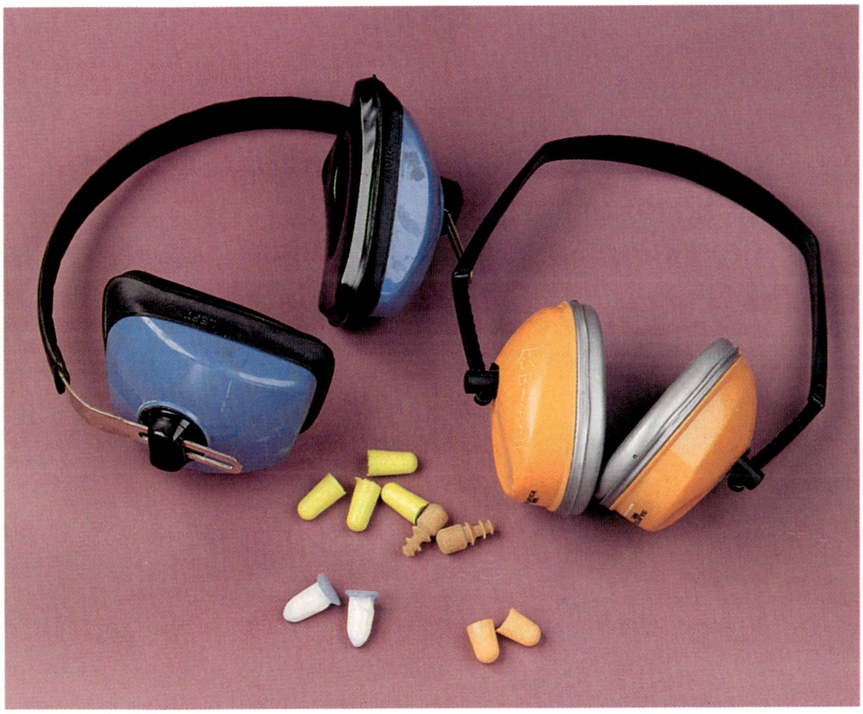

FIGURE 12.22 ◀
Hearing protection comes in many shapes and sizes. Some devices are so small that they can't be seen when they're being worn.

When houses or hospitals are built next to busy roadways, walls, trees, or berms of earth may be used to either reflect or absorb the noise. Figure 12.23 shows some examples of these structures.

Noise is a form of pollution. The reduction of noise, like other pollution, is everyone's business. It depends on acoustical engineers, city planners, lawmakers, and you.

FIGURE 12.23 ▶
Walls, trees, and berms of earth all reduce noise from traffic and industry. How does this barrier compare with the heat energy barriers in Figure 10.26?

▶ REVIEW 12.3

1. (a) What is noise?
   (b) How is it measured?
2. List five effects that noise can have on human health.
3. "One person's sound is another person's noise." Explain this statement. Give an example.
4. List ways in which ultrasonic sound can be used.
5. In what two main ways can materials and structures reduce noise?
6. What are some ways used to improve sound transmission or reception?
7. (a) How do echoes occur?
   (b) How are echoes used by animals?
   (c) How are they used by humans?

CHAPTER REVIEW

KEY IDEAS

- All sounds are caused by vibrations.
- The transmission of sound energy has three parts: a source, a medium, and a receiver.
- Sound energy is transmitted in waves by the particles of a medium moving closer together and farther apart. These movements form compressions and rarefactions.
- Pitch describes the highness or lowness of a sound. It is determined by the frequency of the sound. A high frequency causes a high-pitched sound.
- Volume describes the loudness of a sound. It is determined by the amplitude of a sound wave. The greater the amplitude of the wave, the greater the volume of the sound.
- Various materials can be used to insulate against noise. These materials either absorb or reflect sound energy.
- Science and technology allow us to use sounds that we cannot hear. Ultrasound and sonar are just two examples of how we can "see" with sound.

VOCABULARY

vibrations
frequency
hertz (Hz)
pitch
audible
inaudible
medium
receiver
conductor
compression
rarefaction
compressional wave
wavelength
amplitude
volume
acoustics
echo
ultrasonic
noise

V1. Create a mind map using a sound wave as the central theme. Show how the terms in the vocabulary list are related to each other. Use diagrams to illustrate each term.

V2. Make a poster with drawings of some of the ways that sound energy is used as mentioned in this chapter. Add those terms from the vocabulary list that are related to your drawings.

CONNECTIONS

C1. What range of frequencies is audible to a person with normal hearing?

C2. How are the following terms related: audible, inaudible, ultrasonic, frequency range?

C3. Suppose you are watching a large tree being cut down 500 m away. When it strikes the ground, do you see it first, hear it first, or see it and hear it at the same time? Explain your answer.

C4. If you were on the moon and you hit a golf ball, would you expect to hear the sound of hitting it? Explain your answer.

C5. Suppose that you are standing 170 m away from a tall, rocky cliff. You shout at the cliff and hear an echo one second later. Use this information to calculate the speed of sound in kilometres per second.

C6. How do you know that sound is a form of energy?

EXPLORATIONS

E1. Research one of the following topics in the library. Prepare a report that explains the science involved and the technology used. Use illustrations to help with your explanation.
(a) sonic boom
(b) Mach number
(c) supersonic transport
(e) tinnitus

E2. Scientists have determined that sound is transmitted better nearer the ground than it is higher up, for example, on top of a mountain. Find out why this is.

E3. Examine a compact disc with a magnifying glass. Find out how a CD is made, and how it is used to reproduce sound.

E4. Your science classroom may have "acoustic" tiles on the ceiling. These tiles are designed to reduce echoes in the room. Prepare a report describing how these tiles and other techniques are used to reduce noise in classrooms and other public buildings. Find out how these tiles are able to reduce noise in the room. Examine one of these tiles if possible.

REFLECTIONS

R1. Sound energy is very important in our world. Make a list of all the ways your life is affected by sound. How does this list compare with the one you prepared in Activity 12A?

R2. Look at the table you made for step 2 of Activity 12A. You listed the ways that the world would be different without sound, and solutions to problems of such a world. Can you add anything else to the list of problems? What are their possible solutions?

R3. In the review of Section 12.3, you read that "One person's sound is another person's noise." Think about the noise that other people make that really bothers you. Also think about noise that you make that may be too loud or irritating to someone else. Why do people complain about noise? What can each person do to reduce noise pollution?

EXPLORING SPACE

From far away, the Earth appears to be round, as you can see in the photograph. This photograph was taken from a space vehicle sent up from the Earth. Only in the past 35 to 40 years have such photographs been possible. Before that, people used other ways to find out that the Earth was shaped like a ball.

Hundreds of years ago, many people believed that the Earth was flat. If you could go back hundreds of years, how would you convince people that the Earth was not flat? What other ideas about the Earth in space could you tell them? What could you tell them about the moon and the sun that they did not know?

As you study this unit, you will learn how our ideas about the Earth, moon, and sun have changed over the past hundreds of years. Some of these ideas are still changing. New ideas come from astronomers and other space scientists who use telescopes and computers that are more powerful now than ever before. New ideas also come from people who look at the night sky through telescopes and binoculars as a hobby. Many of these amateur astronomers started their hobby when they were about your age. Some of them have made important discoveries about objects in space.

The topic of space is connected to other topics found in this book. Much of what we know about space comes from observing the light energy that comes from our sun or other stars. The study of space also teaches us about heat and climate. Knowing about space helps us understand our environment and appreciate our place in the universe.

As you study this unit, try to remember to look at the sky on clear nights. Observe the moon, the stars, and the planets as they seem to move in the night sky. You will discover that, as you learn more about astronomy and space science, you will be able to understand more about the world in which you live.

UNIT 4

CHAPTER 13
The Earth and Moon in Space

CHAPTER 13

THE EARTH AND MOON IN SPACE

Many songs have been written and stories told about the moon that travels around the Earth. How much do you know about the moon? For example, why can you see half the moon so clearly in the photograph on the left, yet the other half is in darkness? What method was used to take this photograph? Would such a method have been possible thousands of years ago?

This chapter is about the Earth and its moon in space. You will learn about the causes of day and night, and the causes of the changing seasons on the Earth. You will study the moon's motion around the Earth. And you will discover how the sun's light is sometimes blocked, causing eclipses. The chapter ends with a brief look at the Earth's location among the planets that travel around the sun.

The most important part of this chapter is a paper model of the Earth/moon/sun system that you will build. This model has movable parts, which you will use in four different activities. The model is fun to assemble and use, and it helps to make the ideas in this chapter easier to understand. You can be creative with your model by adding drawings and colour. (It is a good idea to keep this model to study other science topics and space science in future grades.)

ACTIVITY 13A / THINKING ABOUT THE SUN, PLANETS, AND MOON

CROSS • CURRICULAR

PROCEDURE

In your learning journal, write as many words, phrases, sentences, or paragraphs as you can that describe your ideas about the sun, planets, and moon. Include diagrams to illustrate your descriptions. Your teacher may ask you to share your ideas with other students. ❖

13.1 A DAY ON THE EARTH

Tony asks his older sister, Maria, who is in grade 8, where the sun rises and sets. Maria replies, "It rises in the east and sets in the west." Why does the sun appear to travel across the sky from east to west?

People have always wondered about the motion of the sun in the sky. Throughout history, different groups of people have had different explanations for the sun's movement. More than 4000 years ago, the Egyptians thought that the sun was a god named Ra (rah). Each morning, Ra sailed in a golden boat across the sky (Figure 13.1). After sunset, Ra traded the golden boat for a different boat so that he could ride through the dangerous underworld of the night.

FIGURE 13.1 ◀
Ra, the Egyptian sun god, sails in his boat across the sky.

Natives in North America have legends about the sun and other objects in nature. A legend of the Nuxalk of British Columbia tells of their most important god, Alkuntam. He could enter the sun and use it as his canoe. When Alkuntam entered the sun, he wore a cloak with salmon in its lining. Whenever he turned his cloak inside out, the rivers on the Earth became filled with salmon.

Many things about the sun have been discovered since the times of these explanations. The sun does not travel across the sky. It only appears to travel because the Earth is spinning, like a huge merry-go-round. The spinning of an object is called **rotation**. A spinning object rotates around an imaginary line called an **axis**. For the Earth, the axis is an imaginary line passing through the North and South Poles, as shown by the globe in Figure 13.2.

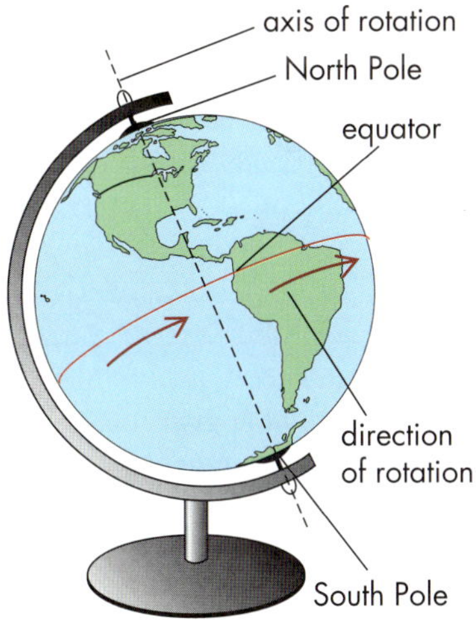

FIGURE 13.2
A globe shows that the Earth rotates on its axis, which is an imaginary line passing through the North and South Poles. If you have a globe in your classroom, use it to discover why the sun rises in the east and sets in the west.

ACTIVITY 13B / A MODEL OF THE EARTH/MOON/SUN SYSTEM

In this activity, you will construct your own model of the Earth/moon/sun system. This model is important because you will use it throughout this chapter. Build your model carefully, and find a place to store it neatly when you are not using it.

There are several parts to this model. You will use only a few of the parts for Part II of this activity. The remaining parts will be used later in other activities.

MATERIALS

diagrams of the Earth, moon, and sun
scissors
masking tape
thick thread (or thin string)
a pin or needle to make holes in the paper Earth, moon, and sun

CAUTION!

- **Handle pins and needles carefully; they are very sharp.**

PART I Constructing the Model

PROCEDURE

1. Cut out all the diagrams provided for this activity. Place a small piece of masking tape under each of the eight solid dots on the diagrams. Carefully make a small hole through each dot and the tape beneath it. The holes should be large enough for the thread to pass through.
2. Figure 13.3 shows how to assemble your model. Attach the circular moon to the moon with the handle by passing the thread through the hole in each one. Tie knots in the thread, and wrap small pieces of masking tape around the knots so the thread cannot go back out through the holes.
3. Place the end of the handle of the moon in the centre of the Earth with the handle, as shown in Figure 13.3. Attach Earth X, the moon's handle, and Earth Y by using a thread and masking tape. Make sure the side of Earth Y with the drawing is facing downward, away from the Earth with the handle.
4. Face sun X the same way as Earth X. Then attach the Earth's handle to the middle of the sun using thread and masking tape (Figure 13.3). Label the reverse side of the sun "sun Y."
5. Print your name on the Earth's handle.

PART II Day and Night

PROCEDURE

1. Face sun X toward you with Earth X to the right of it. Label the curved arrow on Earth X "direction of rotation." This is the way you will rotate the Earth in the steps that follow.
2. Notice that there are two open circles on Earth X, one in Newfoundland (Nfld.) and one in British Columbia (B.C.). You may want to colour them

FIGURE 13.3
How to assemble your Earth/moon/sun model

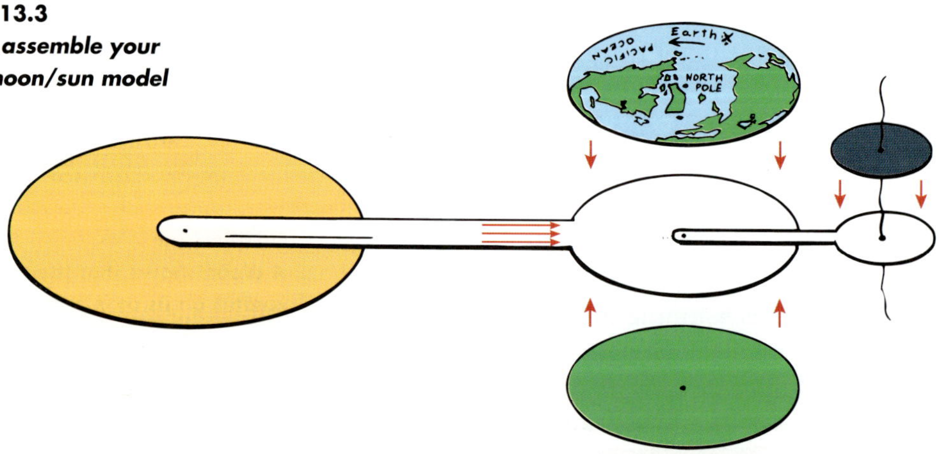

in, using a different colour for each one. These circles represent two observers on opposite sides of Canada.

3. Assume you are looking at the Earth/sun system from far above the North Pole of the Earth. The half of the Earth farthest from the sun is in darkness, while the other half is in daylight. Rotate Earth X so that the Nfld. observer just sees the sunrise. In other words, the Nfld. observer is just coming out of the darkness and into daylight. Check with other students and your teacher to be sure that the Earth is in the correct position.
4. Now rotate the Earth farther until the B.C. observer just sees the sunrise. Does the B.C. observer see the sunrise at the same time as the Nfld. observer?
5. Learn how to position the Earth so that the B.C. observer sees the following four events in order: sunrise, noon, sunset, and midnight. Discuss the four positions with other students and your teacher to be sure you have the right idea.

DISCUSSION

1. Around what point does your model of the Earth rotate?
2. When viewed from far above the North Pole of the Earth, does the Earth rotate clockwise or counterclockwise? Use your model to explain how you know. (Clockwise is the direction in which the hands of a clock rotate. Counterclockwise is the direction opposite to clockwise.)
3. Does the Earth rotate eastward or westward? Explain your answer. (Hint: Is the Nfld. observer east or west of the B.C. observer?)
4. Use your answer in Discussion question 3 above to explain why the sun appears to travel westward across the sky. (It may help to look at your model.)
5. In your notebook, draw a diagram of the sun and the Earth. Label the North Pole, the direction of the Earth's rotation, and the equator. Because your model has the North Pole in the centre, the equator is the outside edge of the Earth in your model. On your drawing of the Earth, show where an observer near the equator must be in order to observe sunrise, noon, sunset, and midnight. ❖

OUR DAY AND NIGHT CYCLE

Every day, the sun appears to rise in the east, travel westward across the sky, and set in the west. Then darkness follows to complete the **day and night cycle**. (A cycle is a series of actions repeated in the same order every time.) The day and night cycle is caused by the Earth's rotation on its axis in the eastward direction. If you were far above the Earth's North Pole, you would see the Earth rotating counterclockwise. This rotation causes the sun to appear to rise in the east and travel westward across the sky (Figure 13.4).

The amount of time that the Earth takes to complete one rotation is called a **day**. As you know, we split one day into 24 equal periods

FIGURE 13.4
The rotation of the Earth on its axis as viewed from above the North Pole. An observer at point A is about to see the sunrise.

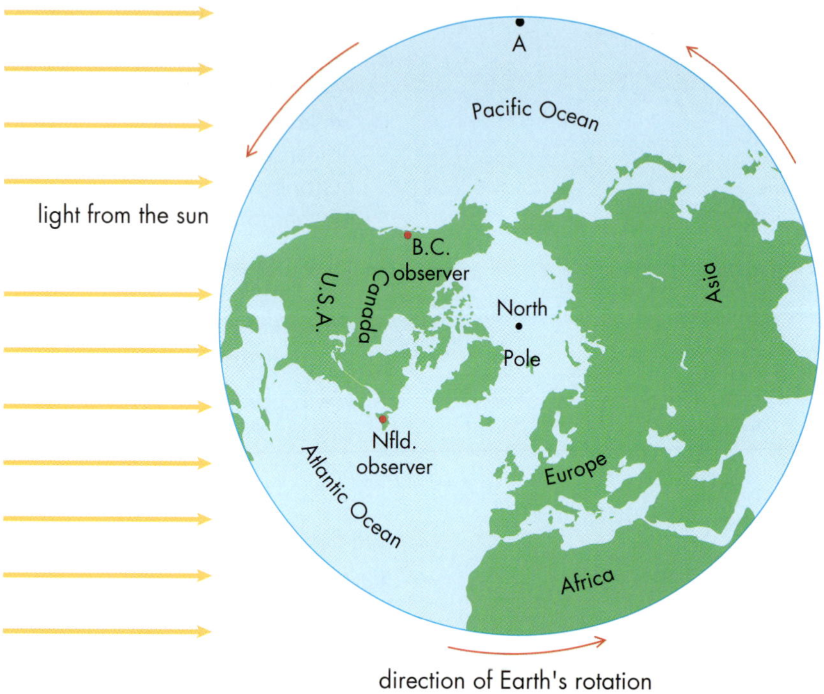

EXTENSION

- By using a camera with a shutter that can be kept open, you could take a photograph similar to the one in Figure 13.5. On a clear night, set up the camera on a tripod in a dark location. Aim the camera toward the North Star, then keep the shutter open for an hour or more. The North Star is the bright star at the end of the handle of the group of stars called the Little Dipper.

called hours, and we split the hours into minutes and seconds. A person living at or near the Earth's equator has about 12 hours of daylight and 12 hours of darkness each day.

Now imagine that you are standing at the North Pole. It is night and you are looking straight up into the sky, where you can see thousands of stars. If you were to watch for a long time, what do you think you would observe? Remember that the Earth is rotating on its axis. Because the axis passes through you at the North Pole, all the stars would appear to be moving in circles around a point above you in the sky. Figure 13.5 shows a photograph of this motion. The photograph was taken using an exposure time of more than one hour. This is more evidence that the Earth rotates in space.

FIGURE 13.5
This time-exposure photograph of the night sky directly above the North Pole shows that the stars appear to travel in circles around a single point. What causes this effect?

▶ REVIEW 13.1

1. What does the expression "day and night cycle" mean?
2. (a) What are two possible ways of explaining why the day and night cycle occurs?
   (b) What explanation do we use today?
3. Jason lives in Corner Brook, Newfoundland, and Anitra lives in Cranbrook, British Columbia. When Jason has lunch at 12:00 noon, is it morning or afternoon for Anitra? Explain why this is so.
4. The circle in Figure 13.6 represents the Earth as viewed from above the North Pole. The numbers shown are eight locations near the Earth's equator. Which location represents each of the following situations:
   (a) sunrise?
   (b) noon?
   (c) sunset?
   (d) midnight?
   (e) bright morning sunlight?
   (f) bright afternoon sunlight?

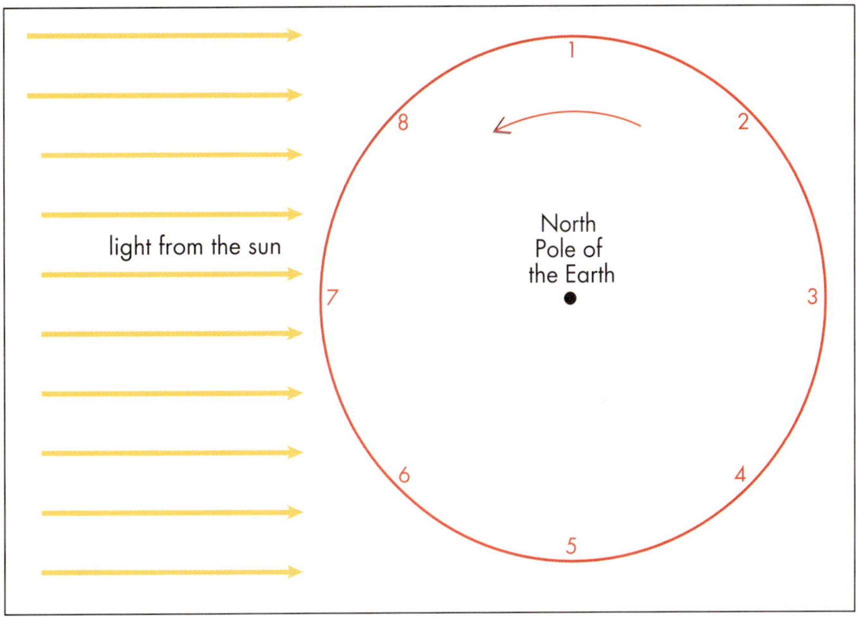

FIGURE 13.6
Match the numbers on the Earth with the six situations in Review question 4.

5. The model you assembled in Activity 13B is two-dimensional; in other words, it is flat. Describe how you could demonstrate the day and night cycle of the Earth using one student to act as the Earth and another student to act as the sun.

13.2 A YEAR ON THE EARTH

In Section 13.1, you learned that the rotation of the Earth on its axis causes the day and night cycle. Another cycle that is important to life on the Earth is the **summer and winter cycle**. As you will see, this cycle is caused by another type of motion of the Earth.

What evidence can you see of the summer and winter cycle? Probably the most obvious evidence is that our summers are warm and our winters are cold. Can you think of other differences between summer and winter? Is sunlight different in summer and winter?

One result of our summer and winter cycle occurs each spring. As the weather becomes warmer, snow in the mountains begins to melt. The water runs into the rivers, so they flow more rapidly.

For the native peoples of North America, the warmer weather meant that a new season of hunting and trapping could begin. The Ojibway tribe of Northern Ontario considered the beaver to be sacred.

Every spring, they had a special ceremony when the first beaver of the season was caught. They believed that this ceremony would help to bring good luck in catching beaver for the rest of the season.

The type of motion that causes the summer and winter cycle is called revolution. **Revolution** is the movement of an object in a path around another object. It comes from the verb "revolve." The Earth revolves around the sun. The time it takes the Earth to revolve once around the sun is called one **year**.

Revolving is different from rotating (Figure 13.7). One way to remember the difference is to think of a spinning top. The many t's in "tops rotate" should help you remember rotating. Revolving has no t's.

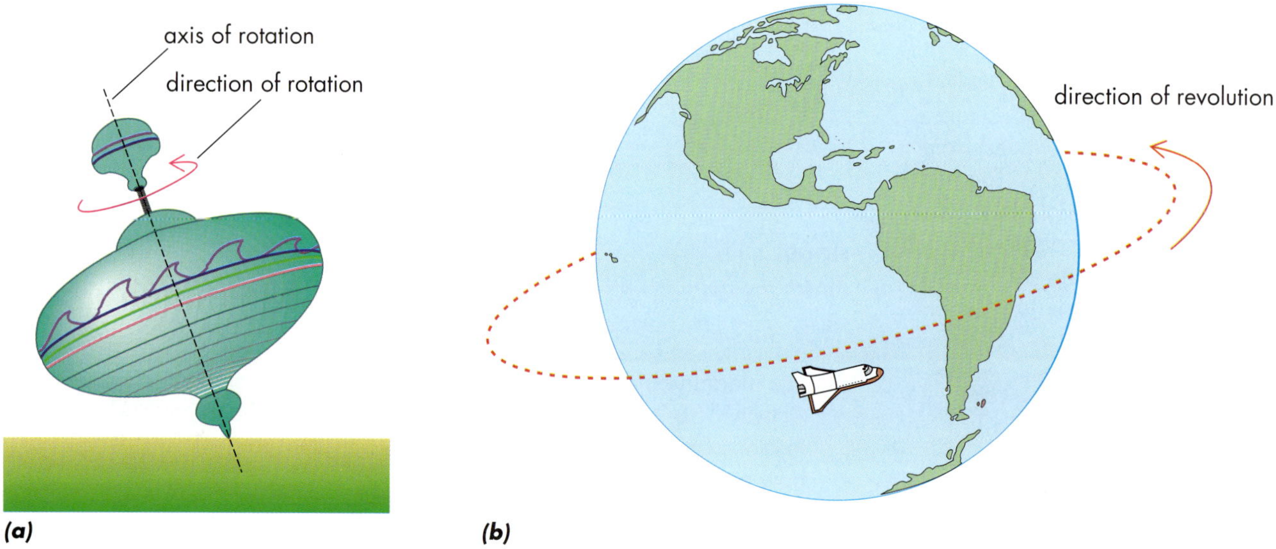

FIGURE 13.7
Comparing rotation and revolution: (a) a top rotates, and (b) a space shuttle revolves around the Earth.

ACTIVITY 13C / THE EARTH'S MOTION AROUND THE SUN

In this activity, you will use your Earth/moon/sun model to learn more about the summer and winter cycle.

MATERIALS

the Earth/moon/sun model assembled in Activity 13B

PROCEDURE

1. Place the model so sun Y and Earth Y are facing toward you, with Earth Y to the right of the sun. Draw a dashed line along the middle of the strip of paper joining the Earth and the sun. Continue this dashed line through the middle of sun Y across to the opposite edge of sun Y (Figure 13.8).
2. Learn about the features of Earth Y. This view of the Earth is from the side. (Remember that Earth X was the view from above the Earth, looking down at the North Pole.) Label the equator, which is the solid line through the middle of Earth Y. Label the northern hemisphere (the half of the Earth above the equator) and the southern hemisphere. Label the North Pole and the South Pole. Then draw a solid line joining the North and South Poles, and label it "axis of rotation."

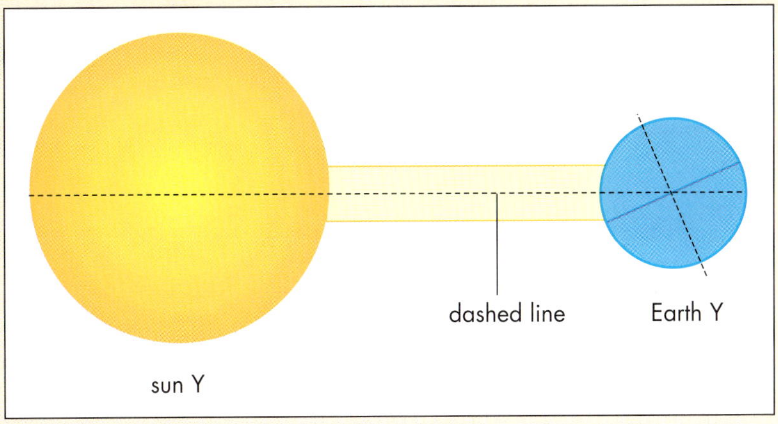

FIGURE 13.8
Draw a dashed line on your model as described in step 1. (The moon is not shown in this diagram.)

3. Place Earth Y so that the dashed line on it is lined up with the other dashed lines that you drew in step 1. These dashed lines are a way of showing the Earth's position as it travels around the sun. Notice that the Earth's equator is tilted at an angle to the dashed lines. This occurs because the Earth's axis of rotation is tilted at an angle to the path of the Earth's revolution. Discuss with other students and your teacher whether this position of the Earth represents summer or winter in the northern hemisphere, where British Columbia is. (Hint: Look at the way the light from the sun hits the Earth.) Be sure you understand this before going on.
4. With Earth Y still to the right of sun Y, draw an arrow facing upwards on the arm joining the Earth to the sun. Label the arrow "direction of revolution." This is the way you will move the Earth in the next step.
5. To keep the tilt of the Earth at the same angle, hold onto the North Pole of Earth Y, and move Earth Y around the sun until it reaches the left side of sun Y. Line up all the dashed lines. This shows that the Earth's axis of rotation faces the same way it did in step 3. Discuss with other students and your teacher whether this position represents summer or winter for the northern hemisphere. Be sure you understand why.
6. Use your model to discover other aspects of summer and winter. For example, can you see why parts of the Earth receive 24 hours of daylight in the summer and 24 hours of darkness in the winter?

DISCUSSION

1. Refer to Figure 13.9, in which the dashed line represents the Earth's path around the sun (as seen from the side). What position is the Earth in, A or B, during summer in the northern hemisphere? Explain why summer occurs in this situation.
2. In Figure 13.9, what position is the Earth in, A or B, during winter in the northern hemisphere? Why?

FIGURE 13.9
For Discussion questions 1, 2, and 3

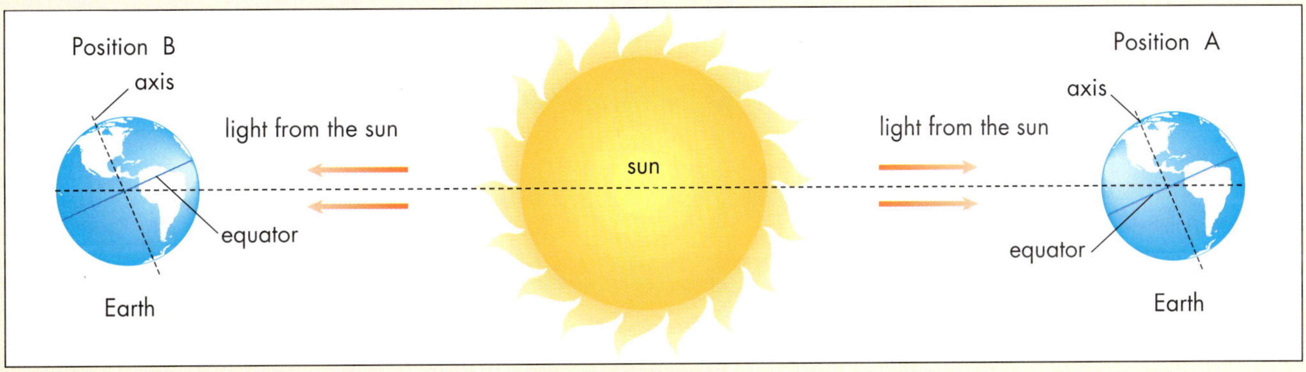

3. How long does it take the Earth in Figure 13.9 to travel from position A to position B on the opposite side of the sun?

4. When it is summer in Canada and other countries in the northern hemisphere, what season is it in countries in the southern hemisphere, such as Australia? Why? ❖

THE EARTH'S CHANGING SEASONS

The **summer and winter cycle** is split into four seasons: winter, spring, summer, and fall. In the northern hemisphere, the first official day of winter is December 21. That day has the least amount of daylight and the greatest amount of darkness of any day of the year. In far northern regions of the Arctic, the sun does not appear above the horizon.

After December 21, the number of hours of daylight increases as winter passes and spring arrives. The number of hours of daylight in one day is greatest on June 21. This is the longest day (and shortest night) of the year. It is called the first day of summer. In the far north, such as in Canada's Arctic region, the sun does not set on this date (Figure 13.10).

FIGURE 13.10
This artistic representation shows the sun staying above the horizon all day on June 21 in northern Canada. Do you think the artist has drawn the true path of the sun on that day?

DID YOU KNOW

■ In Norway, which is a far northern country in Europe, the sunless winter months are called *morketiden*, which means the murky times. Can you suggest a reason for this name?

After June 21, the number of hours of daylight gradually decreases as summer passes and fall arrives. Finally December arrives, and the cycle of the seasons begins again.

One reason our summers are warmer than our winters is that we receive more hours of sunlight each day in the summer. But there is a second very important reason. In our summer, the light rays from the sun hit the northern hemisphere more directly than they do in winter. Figure 13.11 shows that when light rays from a source strike an object directly, they reach a small area. Then they provide a lot of light and heat to each

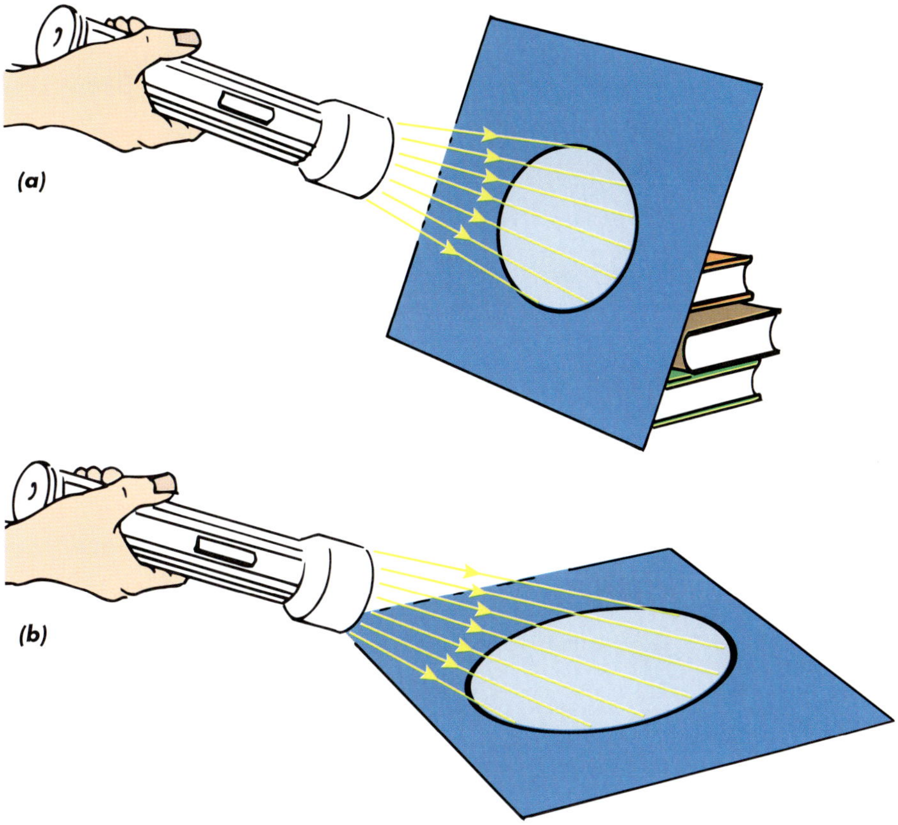

FIGURE 13.11
Light hitting an object directly and at an angle.
(a) Light rays from this flashlight hit the screen directly, giving all their light to a small area. (b) Light rays from the same flashlight hit the screen at an angle. The light is spread out over a much larger area, so each spot on the screen that receives light has less light than in (a).

spot in that area. However, when light rays from the same source strike an object at an angle, they spread out more. Thus, they reach a larger area and provide less light and heat to each spot in the larger area.

As you learned in Activity 13C, it is the tilt of the Earth's axis that causes the sun's rays to strike the surface of the Earth at different angles as the Earth revolves around the sun. In our summer, the sun's rays hit the northern hemisphere more directly, as shown in Figure 13.12a. This helps to cause the countries in the northern hemisphere, such as Canada, to become warmer.

During our winter, the northern hemisphere is tilted away from the sun. Canada and other northern countries become colder. At the same time, the sun's rays hit the southern hemisphere more directly because of the tilt of the Earth. This helps to cause the countries south of the equator, such as Australia, to become warmer. Thus, they have summer while we have winter, as seen in Figure 13.12b. The positions of the Earth for all four seasons are shown in Figure 13.12c.

DID YOU KNOW

■ Some people think that the distance between the Earth and the sun is less in summer, because we have higher temperatures in summer. This is not true. The Earth is actually about 3 per cent closer to the sun during northern winter than it is during northern summer.

EXTENSION

■ The development of the calendar we now use went through many stages. Research that development, and write a report or make a poster presenting what you discover. Be sure to include the meaning of leap years. How do we determine which years are leap years?

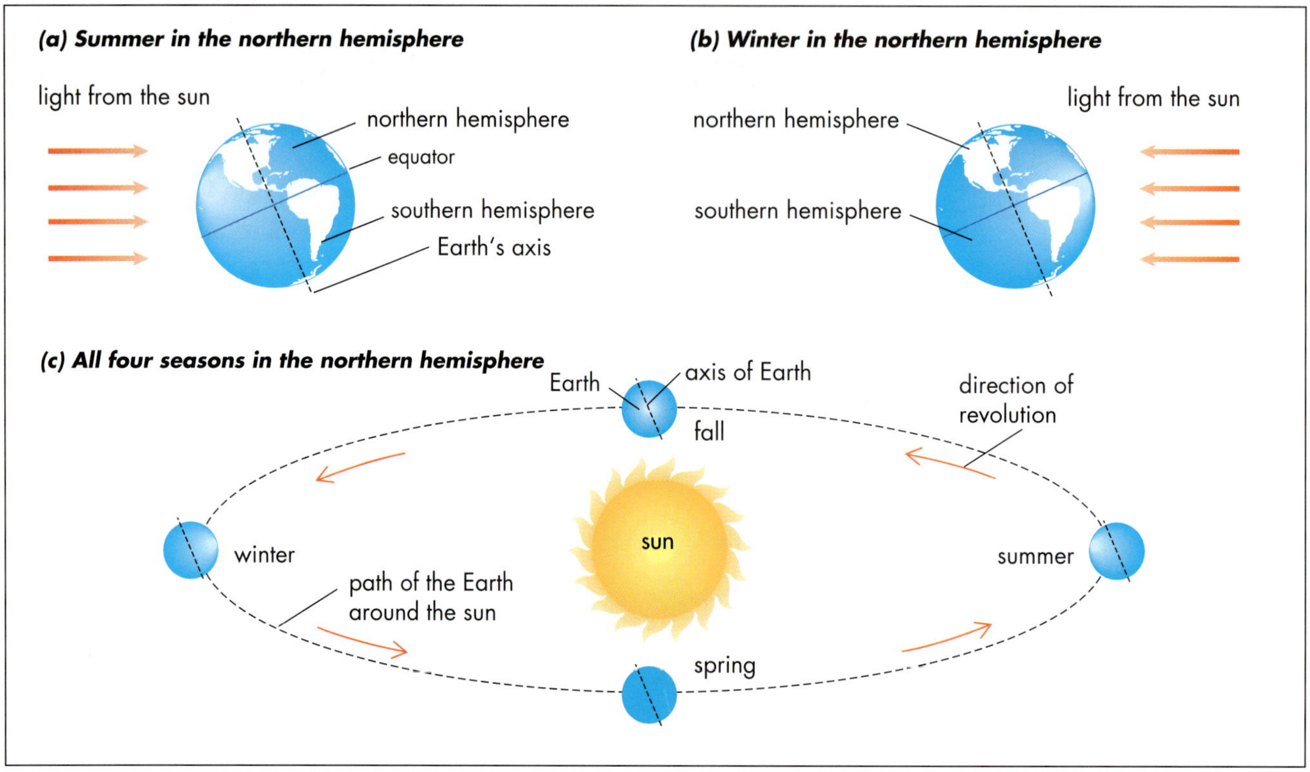

FIGURE 13.12
The seasons are caused by the tilt of the Earth's axis combined with the Earth's motion around the sun. Notice that the axis always points in the same direction.

▶ REVIEW 13.2

1. Explain the difference between rotation and revolution. Use the Earth as an example.
2. How long does the Earth take to complete one revolution around the sun? Give the length of time in:
   (a) years
   (b) months
   (c) weeks
   (d) days
3. Why do you think Canada's far north is sometimes called the land of the midnight sun?
4. The model you used to learn about the summer and winter cycle is two-dimensional; in other words, it is flat. Describe how you could demonstrate the summer and winter cycle using one student to represent the Earth and another to represent the sun.
5. Imagine that somehow the Earth's axis was not tilted. In this situation, the equator would line up exactly with the Earth's path around the sun. Would there be any changing seasons? Explain your answer. (You may want to use your model to help you understand this.)

13.3 THE EARTH-MOON SYSTEM

The moon is the Earth's nearest neighbour in the sky. It travels with the Earth as the Earth revolves around the sun. That is why you attached the moon to the Earth and not to the sun on your Earth/moon/sun model.

The moon is the second brightest object we can see in the sky. (The sun is the brightest.) The moon is bright enough to be seen during the day. You may have noticed a crescent-shaped moon early in the morning before sunrise, or late in the day before or after sunset (Figure 13.13). However, the moon cannot be seen during the day if its path causes it to be almost in line with the sun.

The moon does not give off its own light, the way the sun does. So why can you see the moon? The reason is that the moon reflects the light that comes from the sun.

FIGURE 13.13
A crescent-shaped moon. The dark part of the moon can be seen because of "earthshine," sunlight reflected off the Earth, and then back to us from the moon.

ACTIVITY 13D / THE MOON'S MOTION AROUND THE EARTH

In this activity, you will use your Earth/moon/sun model to help you understand the revolution and rotation of the moon.

MATERIALS

the Earth/moon/sun model assembled in Activity 13B
pencil

PROCEDURE

1. Set up your model so that you can view sun X, Earth X, and the moon all at once. This is the view from above the North Pole of the Earth. Arrange your model so that the sun, Earth, and moon are in a straight line, with the moon farthest from the sun (Figure 13.14). Rotate the moon so the open circle near its edge is closest to the Earth. In pencil, label this point "A."
2. Label the direction shown by the arrow on the arm joining the moon to the Earth "direction of revolution of the moon." Keeping point A closest to the Earth, move the moon through one complete revolution around the Earth in the direction shown by the arrow. In reality, this motion takes one month to complete. Does the same side of the moon always face the Earth? ➡

FIGURE 13.14 ◀
How to arrange your model for Activity 13D

3. Have the moon revolve around the Earth again, as you did in step 2. This time observe how the moon rotates slowly about its centre. Does the moon rotate in a clockwise or counterclockwise direction?

DISCUSSION

1. Does the moon revolve around the Earth in a clockwise or counterclockwise direction when viewed from above the Earth's North Pole? How does this direction compare with the direction of the Earth's revolution around the sun?
2. What do you think the expression "the far side of the moon" means?
3. For your Earth/moon model, is the moon's rotation around its centre clockwise or counterclockwise? ❖

DID YOU KNOW

■ Many of the ancient people who thought that the sun was a god who ruled the day also thought that the moon ruled the night. The Romans, for example, called the goddess of the moon Luna, which is the Latin word for moon. The word "lunatic" comes from Luna. People used to call an insane person a lunatic because they thought that the moon caused insanity.

A MONTH ON THE EARTH

So far in this chapter, you have learned that there are different types of motion in space. Every object in space is rotating or revolving or moving in some way when compared to all other objects. The moon, for example, revolves around the Earth.

As the moon revolves around the Earth, the Earth revolves around the sun. Figure 13.15 shows both of these motions. The time for the moon to revolve once around the Earth and line up again with the sun is called one **month**. Although one month on our calendars is usually 30 or 31 days, this motion actually takes about 29.5 days.

As the moon revolves around the Earth, the same side of the moon always faces toward the Earth. To some people, this surface of the

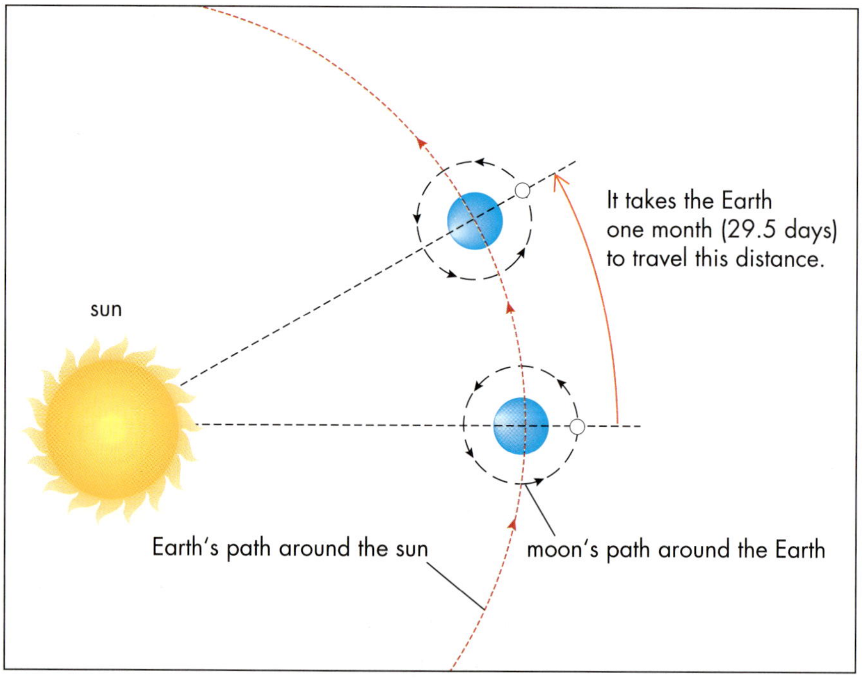

FIGURE 13.15 ▶ ***Just as the Earth revolves around the sun, the moon revolves around the Earth. It takes one month for the moon to make a complete revolution around the Earth, and line up again with the sun on the far side of the Earth.***

moon has features that look a little like a human face. Can you see the "man in the moon" in Figure 13.16?

Not everyone thinks that the surface of the moon resembles a human face. To the Loucheux, who are natives of northern Canada, the features of the moon look like a boy with one of his legs bare. The Loucheux have a legend about a hunter's son who warned his father that he was going to visit the moon. One day the boy was missing, and when the hunter searched for him, all he found was one leg of his son's trousers hanging from the top of a pole. That night when the moon rose, the hunter looked up and saw the boy standing in it with one leg of his trousers torn off.

While the moon revolves around the Earth, it is rotating around its centre, or axis. Figure 13.17 shows the moon's rotation as it revolves around the Earth. In (a), the same side of the moon always faces toward the Earth. This means that the moon must be rotating as it is revolving. In (b), the moon is shown by itself, to illustrate its rotation. Notice that both the revolution and rotation are counterclockwise, looking down from above the North Pole.

FIGURE 13.16
The full moon. The next time your calendar tells you the moon will be full, look for the "man in the moon." Maybe you will see the hunter's son instead.

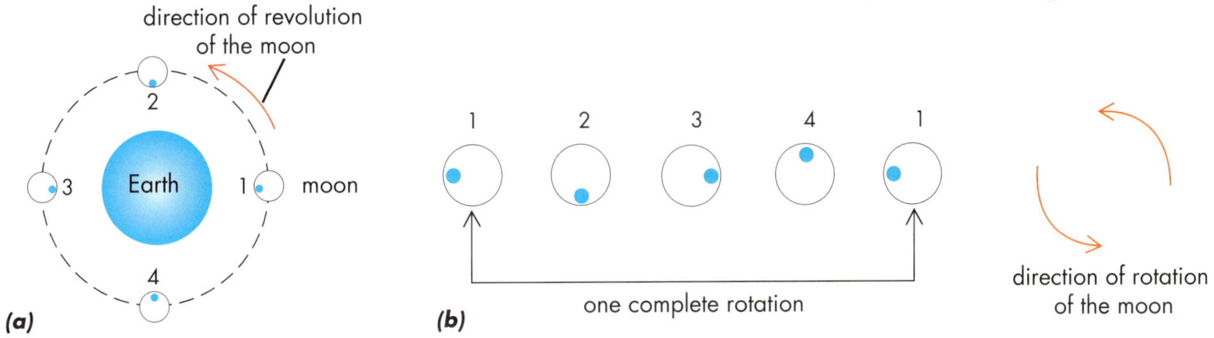

FIGURE 13.17
The revolution and rotation of the moon. (a) As the moon revolves around the Earth, the same side always faces the Earth. (b) Looking at the moon alone, you can see its rotation. The numbers match the positions shown in (a).

TIDES

Anyone who lives near or has visited the ocean is familiar with tides. **Tides** are the regular rise and fall of the water level in bodies of water on the Earth. Figure 13.18 shows the effects of high and low tides in one fishing village.

Tides are caused by gravity, which is the force that also holds you on the Earth. Gravity is the attraction between any two objects in the universe. When objects are large and close together, the pull of this attraction is strong. The pull of gravity between the Earth and the moon is very strong. The pull of the moon on the Earth does not affect the solid part of the Earth very much. However, the oceans and other bodies of water are more easily pulled, resulting in tides. The sun's pull on the Earth also adds to the tide (Figure 13.19).

DID YOU KNOW

■ Some human activities depend on a knowledge of tides. For example, tides are important in fishing. Certain types of fish are easier to catch at high tide, but shellfish, such as clams, mussels, and oysters, are easier to gather at low tide.

FIGURE 13.18
These photographs show high and low tides at Grand Manan Island, New Brunswick. This island is in the Bay of Fundy, which has one of the highest tides in the world.

EXTENSION

■ If you watched the moon every night for a month, you would see that the moon *appears* to change its shape during that time. Sometimes it seems to be a crescent shape. Sometimes it looks like a perfect circle. These different shapes are called the phases of the moon. Research the phases of the moon, including their names, appearances, and causes. Draw a poster showing all the phases and their names. Learn how to set up your Earth/sun/moon model to observe each of the phases and to see what each phase would look like from the Earth.

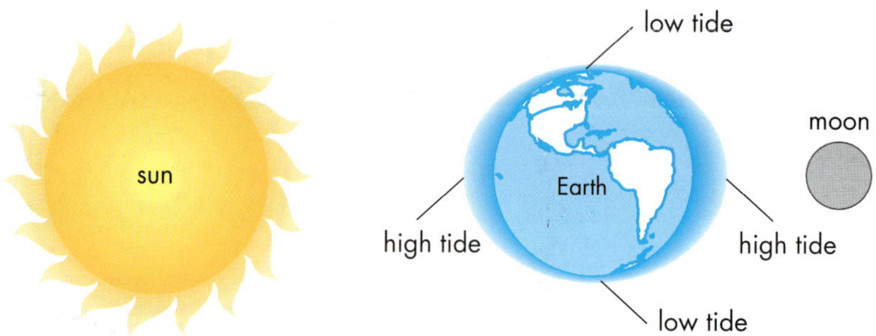

(a) When the moon is directly in line with the sun and the Earth, there is a big difference between the high and low tides.

(b) When the moon and sun are not lined up, their forces on Earth work against each other. Then there is little difference between high and low tides.

FIGURE 13.19
Tides

ACTIVITY 13E / A DISPLAY CALENDAR

GROUP ACTIVITY G — CROSS-CURRICULAR C

In this activity, you will design a one-month calendar that can be displayed in the classroom.

MATERIALS

Bristol board or poster paper

PROCEDURE

1. Form the same number of groups as the number of months of the calendar that your class will make. For example, to make a 12-month calendar you will need 12 groups.
2. In your group, choose one month different from all the other groups. Draw a display calendar for your chosen month. Put the days and dates in the appropriate places, but leave a lot of space to add more information in words and drawings.
3. Add as much information as possible about space and astronomy to your group's calendar. Try to make your calendar interesting and appealing. Some references to help you are newspapers that state times of sunrise and sunset or high and low tides, and a Canadian almanac. (An almanac is a book containing a calendar and information about the weather, sun, moon, stars, and tides.) ❖

▶ REVIEW 13.3

1. How many days does the moon take to revolve once around the Earth? What do we call this period of time?
2. What does the expression "the man in the moon" mean?
3. Figure 13.17a shows the rotation of the moon as it revolves around the Earth. Draw your own diagram to show what would happen if the moon did not rotate as it revolves around the Earth.
4. Assume that three students are acting as the sun, moon, and Earth in a play titled "A Month on Earth." Describe what the students should do to act out the title of the play.
5. What are tides? What causes them?

■ 13.4 ECLIPSES OF THE SUN AND THE MOON

Imagine that a bright projector light is aimed toward a screen in your classroom. You place your hand about 10 cm in front of the screen in the light beam. You notice the shadow of your hand on the screen. A **shadow** is the dark area behind an object, created when the object blocks the light rays from a source that is in front of the object. You have seen your own shadow many times, especially outdoors on sunny days.

Shadows form because of an important property of light: light rays travel in straight lines. (If you have studied Chapter 11, you observed this property.)

A shadow can have more than one part. The **umbra** is the part of a shadow where all the light rays have been blocked. It is the darkest part of the shadow. The **penumbra** is the part of a shadow where only some of the light rays have been blocked. Such shadows can be demonstrated in the classroom using devices called ray boxes, as seen in Figure 13.20.

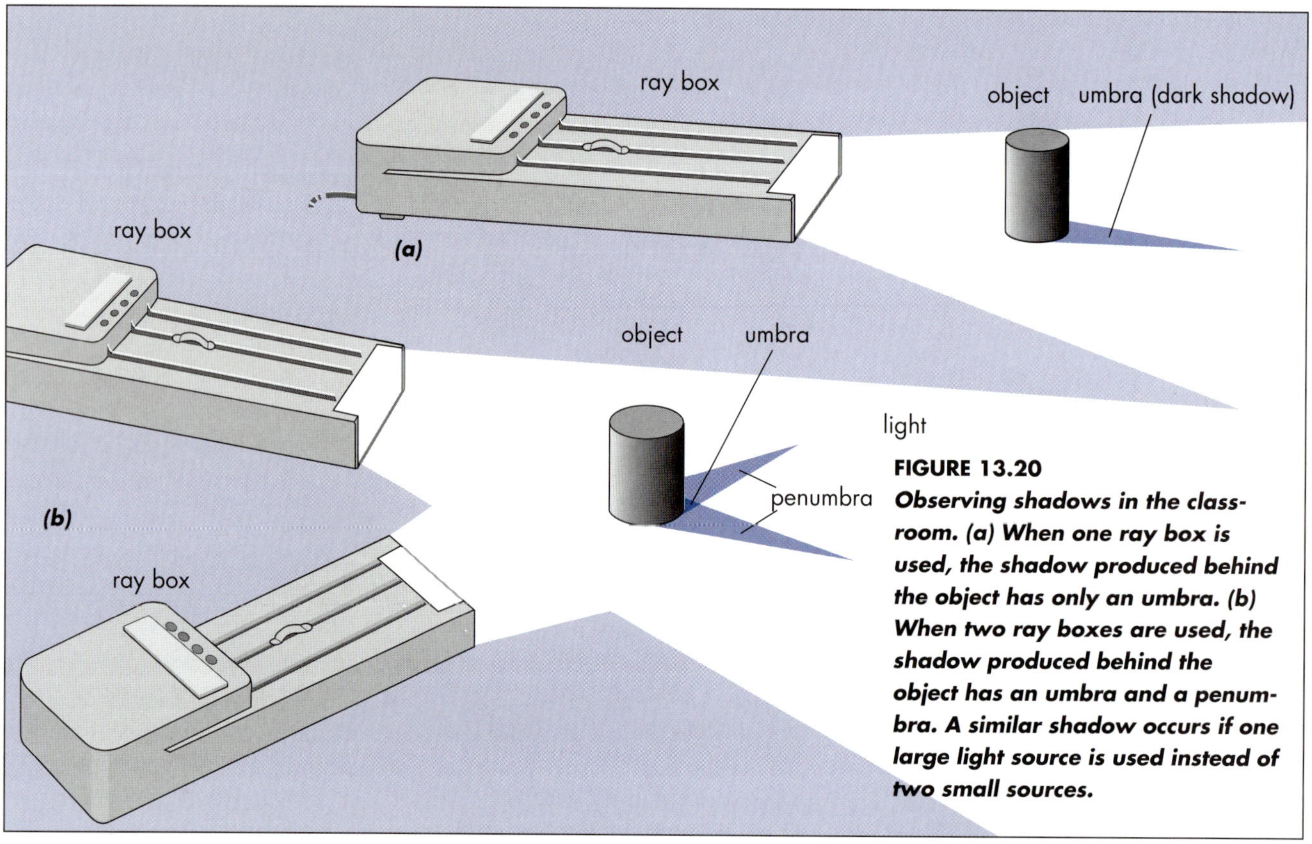

FIGURE 13.20
Observing shadows in the classroom. (a) When one ray box is used, the shadow produced behind the object has only an umbra. (b) When two ray boxes are used, the shadow produced behind the object has an umbra and a penumbra. A similar shadow occurs if one large light source is used instead of two small sources.

In nature, a shadow forms when light from the sun is blocked. This is shown in Figure 13.21. The four straight lines in the diagram are the fewest number of lines needed to find the edges of the umbra and penumbra.

When one object in space blocks the light rays from the sun to another object, we say an **eclipse** occurs. In the Earth/moon/sun system, two important types of eclipses occur.

FIGURE 13.21 ▶
A shadow forms when light from the sun is blocked. This shadow has both an umbra and a penumbra. In this drawing, only light rays from the edge of the sun are shown. If you added more light rays to the diagram, would they change the size or location of the umbra and penumbra?

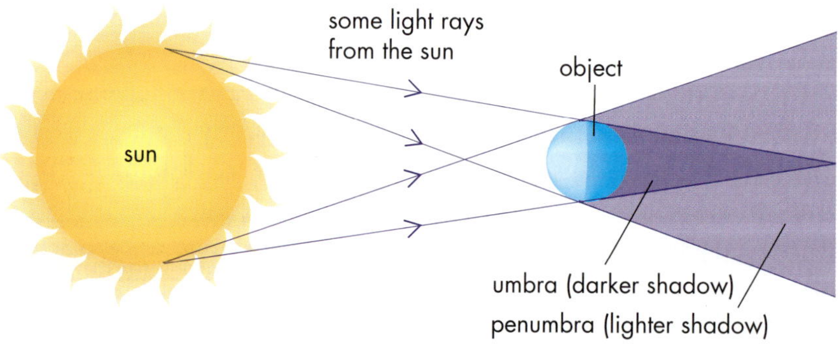

ACTIVITY 13F / ECLIPSES

In this activity, you will learn how eclipses of the sun and moon happen.

MATERIALS

the Earth/moon/sun model you assembled in Activity 13B
two rulers

PROCEDURE

1. Set up side X of your model so the moon is located directly between the sun and the Earth. This set-up illustrates an eclipse of the sun. Can you see why?
2. Place a ruler so that it just touches the bottom outer edges of the sun and the moon. Place a second ruler touching the top edges of the sun and the moon. As shown in Figure 13.22, this arrangement allows you to observe the umbra produced by the moon. Does the umbra touch the Earth?
3. Set up your model to illustrate an eclipse of the moon. (You should be able to do this without detailed instructions.) Again use the rulers to locate the umbra of the Earth. Notice the size of the Earth's umbra compared with the moon's umbra.

FIGURE 13.22
Apparatus for Activity 13F, Step 2

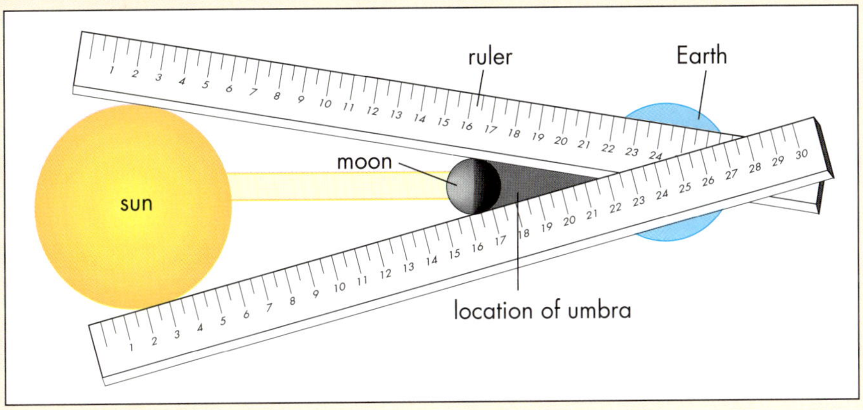

DISCUSSION

1. For a person on the Earth, would an eclipse of the sun be visible during the day or at night? (You may want to refer to your model to help you understand this question and the next one.)
2. For a person on the Earth, would an eclipse of the moon be visible during the day or at night?
3. How does the size of the Earth's umbra compare with the size of the moon's umbra? Suggest a reason why this is so. ❖

SOLAR ECLIPSES

Probably nothing in the sky was more frightening to ancient peoples than a total eclipse of the sun. In bright daylight, the sun would become completely blocked. The sky would grow dark when it should have been light. No one knew how long this darkness would last. Some people in ancient China thought that evil dragons were blocking out the life-giving light of the sun. People screamed and yelled, and threw spears at the dragons to scare them away. Of course, their methods worked; the sun returned to its usual appearance and life soon returned to normal.

An eclipse of the sun is called a **solar eclipse**. (The word "solar" comes from the Latin word *sol*, meaning sun.) A solar eclipse occurs when the moon is between the sun and the Earth, and directly in line with them. Although the moon almost comes between the sun and the

Earth once a month, its path is not often directly in line with the sun and the Earth. For this reason, a solar eclipse does not occur very often. You can demonstrate the situation by pretending that your head is the Earth, your hand is the moon, and a distant object is the sun. If you move your hand across your face in front of your eyes, the distant object can be blocked out. But if your hand is too low or too high, it will not block out the distant object.

When a solar eclipse occurs, only a small part of the moon's umbra reaches the Earth. The only people on the Earth who see a total eclipse of the sun are those in the moon's umbra. The time of complete darkness during a solar eclipse lasts from about two to seven minutes. At other locations, people are in the penumbra of the moon's shadow. They see a partial solar eclipse, which means that they can still see part of the sun. Figure 13.23 shows the position of the sun, moon, and Earth during a solar eclipse.

DID YOU KNOW

■ The last total solar eclipse that could be seen in Canada was in 1979. The next total solar eclipse that can be seen in Canada will occur in the year 2024. It will be visible in parts of Ontario and Quebec. People on the West Coast can see a total solar eclipse on August 21, 2017, in the state of Oregon.

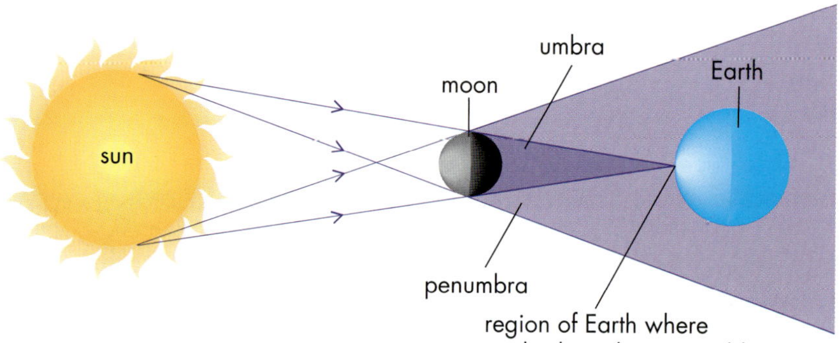

FIGURE 13.23 ▶
During a solar eclipse, the umbra of the moon's shadow covers a very small area of the Earth. In this drawing, only light rays from the edge of the sun are shown.

When a total solar eclipse is about to happen, professional and amateur astronomers travel to the best location to see it. The experience of total darkness in the middle of a bright day is unforgettable. Scientists have learned much about the sun during total eclipses (Figure 13.24).

DID YOU KNOW

■ The total solar eclipse on June 30, 1973, lasted for seven minutes for observers on the ground. For some observers, however, the eclipse lasted 72 minutes. They were in a Concorde jet following the moon's shadow as it moved across northern Africa.

FIGURE 13.24 ◀
One of nature's most exciting sights occurs when the moon passes directly in front of the sun during a total solar eclipse. This is the only time that the sun's outer gas layer, the corona, can be seen without special instruments.

LUNAR ECLIPSES

An eclipse of the moon is called a **lunar eclipse**. This type of eclipse can be observed at night when the moon is full (Figure 13.25). A full moon occurs once every 29.5 days, so you may expect that a lunar eclipse would occur just as often. However, it does not happen that often because the sun, Earth, and moon must line up exactly to produce a lunar eclipse.

Just as they did for solar eclipses, many groups had legends to explain lunar eclipses. For example, the Kwakiutl people of the West Coast believed that a lunar eclipse was caused by a sky monster who tried to swallow the moon. By dancing around a smoky fire of clothing and hair, they hoped to force the monster to sneeze and let the moon go free.

Figure 13.26 shows a diagram of a lunar eclipse. Notice that the umbra of the Earth is much longer than the umbra of the moon in Figure 13.23. The Earth is much larger than the moon. Its diameter is about four times bigger than the moon's diameter. This causes a larger shadow.

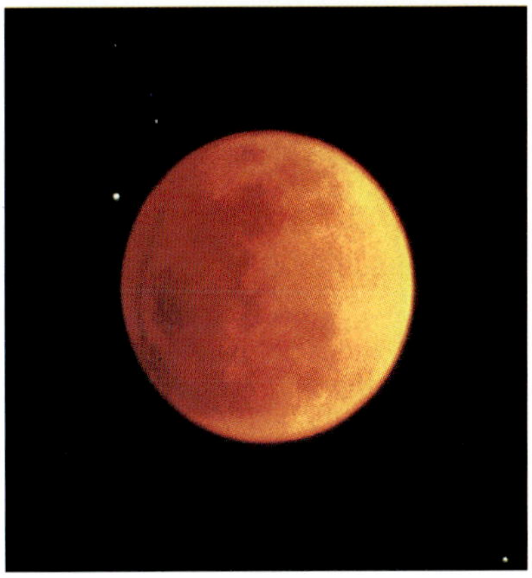

FIGURE 13.25
A lunar eclipse. Often the moon looks red during a lunar eclipse. This is because of the Earth's atmosphere, which acts like a prism for sunlight (see Figure 11.5). Can you draw a model showing how this works?

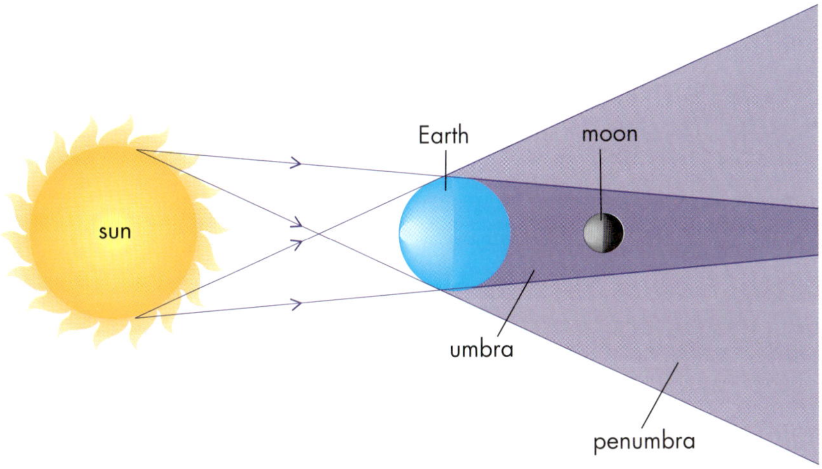

FIGURE 13.26 ◀
Diagram of a lunar eclipse. Compare the umbra of the Earth shown here with the umbra of the moon shown in Figure 13.23.

▶ REVIEW 13.4

1. What arrangement of the Earth, moon, and sun causes
   (a) a solar eclipse?
   (b) a lunar eclipse?
2. Why does a solar eclipse not occur every month?
3. When a solar eclipse occurs, would you expect more people to see a total eclipse or a partial eclipse? Why?
4. Create a one-page travel poster advertising a trip to a location on the Earth to view a total solar eclipse. Choose one location from the following list of the dates and locations for viewing total solar eclipses:
   October 24, 1995: India, Thailand, Viet Nam
   March 9, 1997: Siberia
   February 26, 1998: Galapagos Islands, Venezuela, Guadaloupe
   August 11, 1999: England, France, Germany, Austria, Hungary, Romania, Turkey, Pakistan, India

➡

5. Describe how you would demonstrate solar and lunar eclipses using yourself as the sun and two friends as the Earth and the moon.

6. If the moon were the same size as it is now but were located closer to the Earth than it is, would the number of people on the Earth who could see a total solar eclipse be greater, smaller, or the same? Explain your answer.

13.5 OUR NEIGHBOURS IN SPACE

To complete this chapter on space, we will look briefly at where the Earth and moon fit into the solar system. As you have learned, solar refers to the sun. Our **solar system** consists of the sun and all the objects that travel around it. These objects include planets, such as the Earth, and moons that travel around some of the planets. Other smaller objects you may have heard of are comets, meteors, and asteroids. In this section, you will read about only the sun and planets.

The sun is a huge ball of hot materials that gives off light, heat, and other forms of energy. It is the biggest body in the solar system. More than one million Earths could fit into a space the size of the sun.

The sun may seem big compared with the Earth, but it is only an average-sized star. There are billions and billions of stars in the universe. All stars are extremely hot and give off their own light and other forms of energy. Every year more stars are discovered. Even with binoculars or a telescope, you can see only a small number of all the stars in the universe. The reason the other stars appear so small compared with our sun is that they are very, very far away.

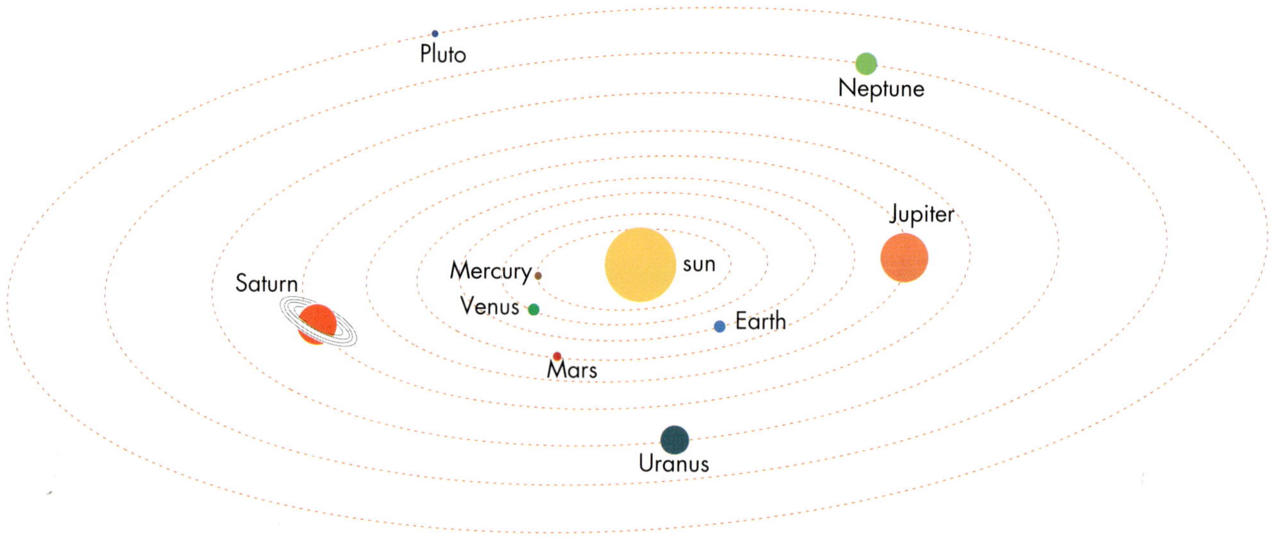

FIGURE 13.27
The planets of the solar system. (The sizes of the sun and the planets, and their distances from each other, are not drawn to scale.)

The Earth is one of nine known planets that travel around the sun. It is the third planet from the sun, as shown in Figure 13.27. In the sky at night, you can sometimes see the other planets that are closest to the sun. These planets are Mercury, Venus, Mars, Saturn, and Jupiter. We can see them because they reflect light from the sun. Often these planets are brighter than stars, and they do not appear to twinkle the way the stars do. If you observe the sky for several nights, you will notice that the stars always appear in the same pattern as they move across the sky. The planets, however, appear to move slowly within the star patterns. For this reason, the early astronomers called the planets the wandering stars.

Astronomy is probably the oldest of all the sciences. But in many ways it seems new because so many new things are discovered each year (Figure 13.28). Astronomy can be enjoyed by everyone, from the scientist who is trying to learn more about life and the universe, to young students who are just finding out how small the Earth is in the huge universe.

EXTENSION

- Share ideas about amateur astronomy with another student. If you know a lot about this hobby, show other students how to pick out star patterns (constellations) and how to identify planets. If you have never observed the night sky, find somebody who can help you use a telescope or a pair of binoculars to view stars, constellations, the planets, and their moons.

FIGURE 13.28
In recent years, spacecraft travelling to planets in the solar system have sent back photographs that help us learn much about the universe. This image, from photographs taken by a Voyager spacecraft, shows the planet Saturn with its rings and some of its many moons.

ASTRONOMY AS A HOBBY

The Milky Way is a cluster of billions of stars.

Have you ever looked — really looked — at the sky on a clear, dark night? Maybe you've noticed the dazzling cloud of light that is the Milky Way with its billions of stars. Or you've found the Big Dipper, and followed its pointer stars to the North Star. Perhaps you've seen shooting stars streaking across the sky.

Away from the lights of the city, you can see so many stars that it may seem overwhelming at first.

"It's something that people know so little about," says 15-year-old stargazer Brandy Maisine. "It's like a mystery, and I like mysteries."

"I know it sounds sort of corny to say it's a spiritual experience," says 17-year-old Christie Cunningham, "but it is, in a sense. It fills you with wonder — you wonder what's out there."

Many people enjoy astronomy as a hobby. Maisine started when she was about five. "I'd look at the sky and ask questions," she says, "and then my family started buying books for me." Since grade 4, she has been doing science fair projects on astronomy, and last year, she won a national award for her project on the planet Mars.

Cunningham's interest in astronomy was sparked by her father. "He'd be out there at night and I'd wonder what he was doing, so I'd go out and look through the telescope. I was really amazed at some of the things I could see."

Astronomy is a hobby that anyone can do. Amateur astronomers have made many important discoveries in star science. While a good telescope is useful, you can see a great deal with the naked eye or a pair of binoculars. You can learn to locate constellations (star patterns). You can find the more visible planets such as Venus, Mars, and Jupiter. Looking at the moon, you can learn to identify the large dark "seas" (they don't really contain water) and mountain ranges.

Both Maisine and Cunningham suggest starting at the library. "Books can give you a lot of information and a lot of hints," says Maisine.

Occasionally stargazers get together for a "star party." They meet on a mountain on a night with no moon. On Mount Kobau, near Osoyoos, B.C., astronomers from around the world gather in August to watch the sky.

Cunningham joined other astronomers in Baja, Mexico, last year to watch an eclipse of the sun. "When the shadow comes rushing over you and you're enveloped by darkness at 12 o'clock in the middle of the day, it's just amazing!" she says. "That was one great experience — I'll be at the next one!"

Why do you think so many people are fascinated when they look up at the sky at night? Is astronomy a hobby that might interest you?

▶ REVIEW 13.5

1. (a) What object is the centre of the solar system?
(b) Describe this object.

2. Each statement listed below applies either to a planet or to a star. For each one, state whether it is about a planet or a star, and explain your answer.
(a) They appear in constant patterns.
(b) They are visible because of reflected light.
(c) They are extremely hot.
(d) They are fairly near to us.
(e) They appear to twinkle.
(f) They revolve around the sun.

3. Suppose the Earth was in Mercury's position in the solar system. Describe the changes this would cause in the surface conditions of the Earth.

4. Suppose the Earth was in Pluto's position. Describe the changes this would cause on the Earth.

5. Prepare an advertisement for a school newsletter to attract students (and teachers) to attend a meeting of an amateur astronomy club.

CHAPTER REVIEW

KEY IDEAS

■ Rotation and revolution are two important types of motion of objects in space. To rotate means to spin, and to revolve means to travel around another object.

■ The Earth rotates once a day on its axis. This causes the day and night cycle. Because the rotation is from west to east, objects in the sky appear to rise in the east and set in the west.

■ The Earth revolves around the sun once a year, and the Earth's axis is tilted at an angle to its path. These situations combine to cause our changing seasons.

■ As the Earth revolves around the sun, the moon revolves around the Earth. It takes 29.5 days for the moon to complete one revolution around the Earth.

■ Tides on the Earth are caused by the pull of gravity from the moon and the sun on the Earth.

■ A solar eclipse occurs when the moon blocks the light rays travelling from the sun to the Earth. A lunar eclipse occurs when the Earth blocks the light rays travelling from the sun to the moon.

■ The sun is only one of billions of stars in the universe. Our solar system includes the sun, nine known planets, the moons that travel around some of the planets, and other moving bodies.

VOCABULARY

rotation
axis
day and night cycle
day
summer and winter cycle
revolution
year
month
tide
shadow
umbra
penumbra
eclipse
solar eclipse
lunar eclipse
solar system

V1. Create a mind map using the vocabulary list and other words in this chapter. Begin with the sun, and focus on the Earth and moon. Wherever possible, show how ideas link to each other, and include ideas from other topics you have studied, such as energy and light.

V2. Use as many words from the vocabulary list as you can to create a crossword puzzle about the Earth/moon/sun system in space.

CONNECTIONS

C1. Describe how you would set up a demonstration in your classroom to show the difference between rotation and revolution. Use your own body as the "object" in motion.

C2. Suppose you were looking down on the Earth from a position far above the Earth's North Pole. State whether each motion listed below would appear to be clockwise or counterclockwise:
(a) the Earth's rotation
(b) the Earth's revolution around the sun

(c) the moon's revolution around the Earth
(d) the moon's rotation

C3. What causes
(a) a day?
(b) a year?
(c) a month?

C4. Arrange your Earth/moon/sun model to demonstrate each of the situations listed below. In some cases, you may need to move the Earth or the moon. Draw each situation in your notebook, using a ruler.
(a) A student in British Columbia has just observed sunset.
(b) It is December 21 in the southern hemisphere.
(c) The moon rotates as it revolves around the Earth.
(d) The moon is located in the Earth's umbra. Name the type of eclipse that is occurring.
(e) A very high tide is occurring on the east coast of Canada.

C5. "If one side of the moon always faces the Earth, the other side must always be in darkness." Is this statement true or false? State reasons to support your answer. (You may need to use your model to help you understand this question.)

C6. In Figure 13.29, the dot represents an observer who lives on the coast, by an ocean. Compare the size of the tide when the moon is at position A with the size of the tide when the moon is at position B. Explain your answer.

C7. Although the moon revolves around the Earth once a month, a solar eclipse does not occur that often. Explain why.

C8. Draw a neat labelled diagram to show a solar eclipse. Use a straight edge to draw the four light rays needed to locate all parts of the shadow. Place the Earth at the tip of the moon's umbra. Label locations on the Earth where a person would see a total solar eclipse and a partial solar eclipse.

C9. Consider the reasons that we are able to see stars, planets, and the Earth's moon. Is the moon more like a planet or more like a star? Explain your answer. (Hint: Which objects give off their own light, and which ones reflect light?)

C10. Describe the sun's importance in our solar system.

C11. Some stars are much bigger and hotter than our sun. Why do we not feel warmth from such stars?

EXPLORATIONS

E1. In this chapter, you have read about legends or myths that were used to explain events such as the day and night cycle. Create your own legend or myth to explain something you have read about in this chapter. For example, you might write a story about why the moon always faces the Earth, or why solar eclipses occur.

E2. Many songs, poems, and stories have been written that mention the sun, moon, or stars. Make a list of titles of, or phrases from, songs, poems, and stories that have something to do with these bodies. You may want to write your own song, poem, or story.

E3. You are a reporter for a local newspaper, and you have just returned from a visit to Canada's Arctic. There you interviewed students to find out what it is like to live in a place where the sun never sets in June and never rises in

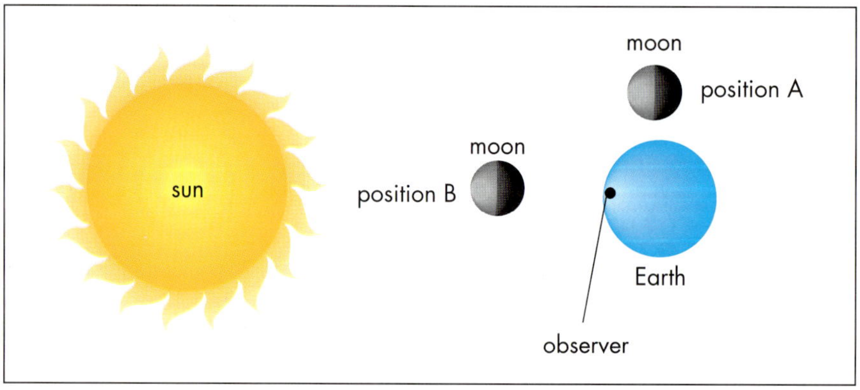

FIGURE 13.29
For question C6

December. Write a summary of your interview.

E4. You are the director of a movie about the great King Xerxes (pronounced zerk´-seez) of Persia. In your movie, he is preparing his army to battle the Greeks in the year 478 B.C. Suddenly the sun begins to disappear from the sky. As the movie director, you must decide if this is a good or bad sign for Xerxes. Describe how you would make this part of the movie exciting.

E5. Choose one room in your school or home. Describe how you would change that room so it could be used as a planetarium. (A planetarium is a room that is set up to show the sun, moon, planets, and stars.) The design should be attractive enough that anyone entering the room immediately wants to learn about the solar system.

REFLECTIONS

R1. Look back in your learning journal to what you wrote in Activity 13A. Have any of your ideas changed? If so, in what way? What questions would you now like answered about the Earth/moon system or the solar system?

R2. In ancient times, many people had different ideas about the Earth, moon, sun, stars, and planets. For example, one idea was that the Earth was the centre of the universe.

(a) Describe the reasons that ideas about space and astronomy have changed over the past several hundred years.

(b) What changes in ideas do you think may occur in the next 50 years?

(c) Suggest reasons why you think our ideas about the sun and the planets may change.

EXAMINING THE EARTH

The Earth has not always looked as it does today in this photograph. The beach, point, and rocks that you see have changed during our planet's long history. Even the plants that you see in the photograph are different from those that lived on Earth in the past. In this unit, you will explore some of the facts that allow us to understand these changes.

You will discover that different rocks were formed in different ways, and at different times. From the clues in the rocks, you may find that the very ground that you are standing on may have been a river bed, or part of the ocean floor, or may even have flowed out of a volcano. In some rocks, you can find fossils — the remains of organisms that no longer live on the Earth. Other rocks show how the Earth's climate was very different in the past from the way it is in this photograph.

All the many processes that have changed the rocks of the Earth, the land surface of the Earth, and the living things on the Earth are still going on in the world today. One of the most important things that affects the land and us is the weather. In the last chapter of this unit, you will investigate how changes in the weather occur.

UNIT 5

CHAPTER 14

ROCKS AND MINERALS

Have you ever eaten bits of rock? Almost certainly, you have — in the form of salt. Those tiny white grains in the salt shaker may be ground-up particles of rock salt, mined from the earth. Do you wear bits of rock? There may be metals in your wristwatch or buttons or zippers that come from rocks, and the gems or precious stones in jewellery may come from rocks. Rocks also contain the materials we use to make many other everyday products, from glassware, toothpaste, baby powder, and pencils to buildings, automobiles, and computers.

In this chapter, you will investigate what rocks are made of and learn how to classify different types of rocks. You will also look for clues in rocks that tell you how they were formed. You will look at evidence that shows how rocks have changed in the past, and may still be changing today. If you think of rock as something solid and unchanging, you may be in for a surprise.

ACTIVITY 14A / WHAT I KNOW ABOUT ROCKS

In this activity, you will record some of the things that you already know about rocks, and list some questions that you would like to answer as you study this unit.

With three other students, obtain a large piece of chart paper and drawing pens from your science teacher. Divide the chart into six rectangles (you may use a metre stick to do this). Follow the instructions in the chart. ❖

Print the names of at least five different types of rocks or minerals in this box.	Draw a large picture that has something to do with rocks.	Print at least five things that you already know about rocks.
Print your names in this box.	List several types of rocks that you have used and tell why they are important.	Print at least five questions that you would like to find the answers to in this chapter.

14.1 IDENTIFYING EARTH MATERIALS

If you look carefully at rocks, you will soon see that they are not all the same (Figure 14.1). Some may be white, some black, and others may be brightly coloured. Some rocks have several different colours. One rock may be soft and dull, whereas another may be hard and shiny. An important step in learning to understand rocks is to find ways of classifying them into groups, based on their properties. Properties are observable facts about materials, such as colour. You can find out more about properties in Chapter 5. Scientists who identify, classify, and study rocks are called **geologists**.

FIGURE 14.1
Rocks contain clues about the Earth's past — and its future.

ACTIVITY 14B / CLASSIFYING ROCKS

In this activity, you will classify rocks based on their properties.

MATERIALS

collection of rock samples

PROCEDURE

1. Either collect your own rock samples or examine samples provided by your teacher.
2. List as many different properties of each rock as you can observe.
3. Using your list of properties, how would you organize the collection into different groups? All the rocks in each of your groups must have a property that the rocks in the other groups do not have. Give each group a name to identify it. ➡

DISCUSSION

1. Suppose that a geologist visits your classroom. Write down several questions you would ask about the rocks in your collection.
2. Think of another way to classify your rock samples.
3. Suppose you wanted to select a kind of rock to make a fireplace. List the properties that you would look for. Classify your rocks in order of usefulness for making the fireplace. ❖

ROCKS AND MINERALS

The appearance and properties of each rock depend on the materials it contains. All rocks are made of solid materials that occur in nature. These materials are called **minerals**. A **rock** is usually a combination of two or more minerals. Although more than 3000 different minerals have been identified, most of them are quite rare. Only a few minerals, such as quartz and mica, are common all over the Earth's surface (Figure 14.2).

You have probably seen a type of rock called granite (Figure 14.2). It is commonly found in the Coast Mountains in British Columbia. Polished granite is often used in shopping malls and as facing on large buildings. If you look at granite closely, you may see tiny sparkling white or pink mineral grains, mixed with glass-like white or colourless crystals, and some silvery-white or black flakes. The sparkling white and pink grains are a mineral called feldspar. The glassy crystals are the mineral quartz, and the flakes are usually pieces of mica (Figure 14.2). Each of these minerals may also be found in other kinds of rocks.

Most minerals are chemical compounds. (You can look back to Chapter 6 to review the meaning of compounds, elements, and chemical formulas.) Quartz, for example, is a form of the compound silicon dioxide. Other minerals are made up of a single chemical element,

FIGURE 14.2 ▶ ***There are many kinds of granite. The piece of granite in this picture contains the minerals mica, quartz, and feldspar.***

such as sulphur or copper. Properties of minerals are related to their chemical formulas.

To identify minerals, it is usually necessary to examine several properties. Before you begin your study, you need to know the meaning of the terms used to describe some of these mineral properties:

- **Colour** is useful to identify some minerals. However, many minerals occur in many different colours, and different minerals may be the same colour. You can see through some minerals, just as you can see through glass. They are transparent. Some samples of quartz and calcite are like this. A transparent mineral that has no colour is described as colourless.
- The **hardness** of a mineral can be found by scratching one mineral against another. The harder mineral leaves a scratch on the softer one. The hardness of a mineral is measured with a number scale developed by a German scientist named Friedrich Mohs (1773–1839). The **Mohs hardness scale** is a list of 10 minerals ranked in order of hardness. These 10 are used to compare the hardness of all other minerals found on Earth. However, if you cannot obtain a set of Mohs hardness scale minerals, you can make a similar scale using everyday materials (Table 14.1).

Mohs hardness scale		Hardness scale of materials you can easily find
1. Talc	SOFTEST	1 soft pencil point
2. Gypsum	↓	
3. Calcite		2–3 fingernail
4. Fluorite		3–4 copper penny
5. Apatite		
6. Feldspar		5–6 nail, glass bottle
7. Quartz		6–7 steel file
8. Topaz		7–8 sandpaper
9. Corundum		9 emery paper
10. Diamond	HARDEST	

TABLE 14.1 ***Scale for Comparing the Hardness of Minerals***

- **Lustre** is a word used to describe how the surface of a mineral reflects light rays to your eye. Some minerals have a metallic lustre like polished gold, or steel. Others are called non-metallic. They may have lustre like glass, plastic, or oil.

EXTENSION

■ To help you remember the correct order of the minerals in the Mohs hardness scale, write down the first letter of each of the 10 minerals (t, g, c, f, a, f, q, t, c, d). Now make up a sentence or phrase that contains 10 words beginning with these same 10 letters in the same order.

- **Streak** describes the colour of the powdery mark that some minerals make when they are scratched against a hard surface. To see the streak clearly, scratch a mineral on a streak plate. A streak plate is an unpolished piece of porcelain tile. The colour of the streak may be the same as the colour of the mineral, or it may be different. Streak is more constant than colour and is very useful for identifying some minerals.
- **Magnetism** is the ability of the mineral to attract a magnet or compass needle. (A compass is an instrument with a magnetized needle that always points in the same direction.) Magnetism is found only in certain minerals that contain iron. Magnetism is not found in most minerals, but it is easy to demonstrate.

ACTIVITY 14C / MINERAL MYSTERY

In this activity, you will be able to identify several different minerals by examining the properties you have just read about. Geologists use the same properties, as well as others, to identify unknown minerals.

MATERIALS

safety goggles
apron
set of numbered mineral samples
Mohs hardness scale set of minerals (or substitutes)
nail
penny
hand lens
streak plate (unglazed tile)
magnet

PROCEDURE

1. Copy Table 14.2 into your notebook.
2. Put on your apron and safety goggles.
3. Take a mineral sample and record its number in the first column.
4. *Colour.* In the next column, record the mineral's colour.

FIGURE 14.3 ◀ ***You can identify many different minerals using simple equipment and your senses.***

Mineral no.	Colour	Hardness	Lustre	Streak	Magnetism	Other	Name

TABLE 14.2 ***Sample Data Table for Activity 14C***

EXTENSION

■ Re-examine the minerals in Activity 14C that have non-metallic lustre. Describe the lustre of each mineral in more detail using the following terms or terms that you invent yourself.

- glassy (like the broken edge of a piece of thick glass)
- waxy (like polished wax)
- pearly (like mother-of-pearl)
- silky (like the shine on a piece of silk fabric or fibreglass cloth)
- greasy or oily (like a piece of fat or soap)
- dull (with no shine at all, like a piece of chalk)
- brilliant (sparkly like a diamond)

5. *Hardness.* Scratch your sample with Mohs mineral #5 (or the nail). If that does not leave a scratch or groove on your sample, continue along the scale toward #10. If mineral #5 does leave a scratch on your sample, move along the scale toward #1. Rank the hardness of your sample. (It will be between two numbers unless your sample is identical to one of the samples in the Mohs hardness scale).

6. *Lustre.* Describe the lustre of the sample as either metallic (like polished metal) or non-metallic.

7. *Streak.* Rub the mineral across the streak plate and brush off the extra powder with your fingers. Record the colour of its streak, if any.

8. *Magnetism.* Record whether or not a magnet attracts the sample.

9. *Other.* What else is special about this mineral? Record your observations under "Other."

10. Repeat steps 2 to 8 for the remaining mineral samples in your set.

11. Try to identify your samples by comparing their characteristics with the minerals listed in Table 14.3. Write the mineral's name in the last column of Table 14.2. If there are any minerals in your set that you could not name, print "Do not know." ➡

Mineral	Colour	Hardness	Lustre	Streak	Other
Graphite	Black	1–2	Metallic	Black	Slippery feel
Galena	Grey	2–3	Metallic	Grey	Square corners
Halite	White	2–3	Glassy	Colourless	Square corners
Biotite	Black	2–3	Glassy/brilliant	White/pale grey	
Calcite	White	3	Glassy	Colourless	
Pyrrhotite	Yellow-brown	4	Metallic	Black	Magnetic
Serpentine	Shades of green	2–5	Silky/waxy	Colourless	
Magnetite	Black	6	Metallic	Black	Strongly magnetic
Hematite	Red/ black	5–7	Metallic/dull	Red	
Feldspar	White/ pink/greenish	6	Pearly	Colourless	
Pyrite	Yellow	6–7	Metallic	Brown/black	
Quartz	Colourless/ white/rose	7	Glassy	Colourless	

TABLE 14.3 ***Characteristics of Some Common Minerals***

DISCUSSION

1. Why is it important to wear safety goggles when examining rock samples?
2. Suggest one advantage of using colour to identify a mineral.
3. Suggest one disadvantage of using colour to identify a mineral.
4. Did lustre help you identify any of the minerals in your set? If so, which one(s)?
5. Do you think that streak is more useful for identifying minerals than colour or lustre? Explain your answer, using an example.
6. Do you think magnetism is a useful property for identifying minerals? Suggest a reason for your answer.
7. Suggest other characteristics of minerals that you think might be useful for identifying them. ❖

FLUORESCENCE

A few minerals have a property called **fluorescence** (Figure 14.4). These minerals change colour when you look at them using ultraviolet light. (See Chapter 11 to read about how light from the sun can be broken into a spectrum. Beyond the violet end of the visible spectrum is a form of light called ultraviolet. We can't see ultraviolet light, which carries more energy than visible light.) Fluorescence is named after the mineral fluorite, because this was the mineral in which scientists first observed fluorescence. In daylight, fluorite is a glassy mineral that occurs in several colours. In ultraviolet light, fluorite is deep blue or purple. Calcite, another mineral, may fluoresce red, pink, or yellow. Fluorescence is not always present, however. Some specimens of a mineral show it, and some do not.

(a) *(b)*

FIGURE 14.4

A specimen containing willemite appears red under natural light (a) but fluoresces green under ultraviolet light (b).

JESSICA MARTIN, ROCKHOUND

It is the crystals that Jessica loves best: sparkling, beautifully formed clear or coloured chunks of rock that look like cut-glass treasures. "I like collecting fluorite — it has such beautiful colours in it," she says, "and quartz crystals." She has made jewellery out of some of her favourites.

Jessica Martin lives in the town of Fruitvale, in southern British Columbia. For years, prospectors and miners have travelled to this area in search of gold, silver, copper, lead, and zinc. The mountains are dotted with abandoned diggings and old mine sites. It is a good place to be a rockhound.

Rockhounding, as rock collecting is sometimes known, is a fascinating hobby. Jessica and her family belong to a rock club in their area. The club organizes expeditions. The Martins pack their lunch and rock-collecting tools into a bag, and take along the dog. It's a pleasant way to spend a day outdoors.

They may hike up to an old mine site where rock has been left lying around the hillside. There may even be good rock collecting right beside a highway, where road construction has exposed the underlying minerals.

Jessica pokes around the area, picking up whatever catches her eye. She puts on her goggles and uses a pick and chisel to break open rocks and chip out the crystals that are hidden inside. After they have had time to explore, club members get together to show each other what they have found. There are usually a few experts with the group who can suggest what to look for and help identify rocks.

Jessica first became interested in rocks in grade 2 when her teacher gave the students egg cartons filled with little rocks to look at. Her mother, also a keen rock collector, encouraged Jessica to continue her interest. The family now has boxes full of neatly arranged and numbered rock samples that they've found on their trips. They enjoy finding out about the rocks they have collected. Sometimes they find fossils, too.

Some good rock-collecting sites have become very popular and well known. Can you imagine what a site might look like after dozens or even hundreds of rockhounds explore it with picks and chisels? "There used to be lots of minerals in some places, but when you go there now, there are hardly any," says Jessica. Responsible rock collectors are aware of the problem. "You take as little as possible," explains Jessica. "Just take the best ones that you find."

Jessica isn't planning a career as a geologist, although her uncle is one and they occasionally go on trips together. "I just do it for fun," she says. Although none of her friends are rockhounds, "I find it interesting — I like being outside, and looking around in the dirt. . . . you never know what you'll find."

Is rockhounding something you might enjoy? Where could you go in your area to look for interesting rocks?

CRYSTALS

Minerals found in nature are often in the form of crystals (Figure 14.5). **Crystals** are solids with straight edges, flat sides, and regular angles. However, the large and beautiful crystals seen in photographs and museums are quite rare. Most crystals are too small to be seen without magnification. Each mineral has its own special crystal shape. The crystal shape may help to identify the mineral. You can find out more about crystals in Chapter 7.

(a) *(b)* *(c)* *(d)*

FIGURE 14.5
You can identify minerals by the shape of their crystals. These photographs show crystals of (a) wulfenite, (b) fluorite, (c) pyrite, and (d) calcite. How are crystals formed?

CLEAVAGE AND FRACTURE

Have you ever dropped a rock on the ground and had it break apart? A mineral may also break when dropped or hit sharply. The way a mineral breaks may be used to help identify it. Minerals break in two ways. Those that split apart along smooth, flat surfaces are said to show **cleavage**. Some examples are mica, galena, and feldspar. Minerals that break into rough fragments are said to **fracture**. An example is quartz. Even though a quartz crystal shows smooth surfaces, the crystal will break into irregular fragments like a piece of glass when dropped.

Apart from helping to identify the minerals in a rock, crystals also provide clues to the way some rocks were formed. You will discover more evidence about rock formation in the next section.

REVIEW 14.1

1. What does a geologist do?
2. Explain the statement: "You can have minerals without having a rock, but you cannot have a rock without having minerals."
3. List five properties that can be used to identify minerals.
4. What is meant by the terms:
   (a) fluorescence?
   (b) crystals?
   (c) cleavage?
   (d) fracture?
5. List some of the uses of minerals, and say what properties make the minerals most suitable for each use.
6. Can streak be used to help separate minerals with metallic lustre from those with non-metallic lustre? Give reasons for your answer.
7. What property do you think is most useful as a first step in identifying a mineral?

14.2 CLASSIFYING ROCKS

Can you imagine finding rocks in British Columbia made of substances that were blown out of a volcano? In the mountains of British Columbia, you may also find rocks that were once deep on the ocean floor or many kilometres below the Earth's surface. How do scientists know where these rocks came from? The evidence is in the rocks themselves. Although there are many different kinds of rock, all rocks can be grouped into three major families or types, depending on the way the rocks were formed. The three families of rock are named igneous, sedimentary, and metamorphic.

IGNEOUS ROCK — "BORN OF FIRE"

The "shell" of rock that forms the hard surface of our planet is called the **crust**. The crust is about 5 km thick under the ocean floor and may be as much as 50 km thick under the continents. Over four-fifths of the Earth's crust is made up of **igneous** rock. The word "igneous" comes from the Latin word *ignis*, meaning "fire." Igneous rocks are formed by the cooling of hot, liquid rock, or **magma** (Figure 14.6).

Magma is formed many kilometres below the Earth's surface. At these great depths, temperature and pressure are extremely high. (Pressure is the force exerted on an area, like the force that pushes water through a fire hose.) Occasionally, magma is forced into cracks in the solid crust around it. There, it slowly cools and hardens to form **intrusive rock** (Figure 14.7). This type of igneous rock may be seen on the Earth's surface only after years of erosion have worn away the rock that once lay above it. The granite in Figure 14.2 is an example of an intrusive rock.

DID YOU KNOW

Diamonds are formed in intrusive rocks. In South Africa, diamonds are mined in the intrusive rocks over a kilometre below the Earth's surface. Diamonds are the hardest natural substance known and are made of the element carbon. Only the finest crystals are cut and used in jewellery. However, many diamonds are flawed. What do you think the flawed diamonds could be used for?

FIGURE 14.6 ▶
When this hot lava from a Hawaiian volcano cools and hardens on the Earth's surface, it will form igneous rock. How hot must lava be to flow out of a volcano?

FIGURE 14.7 ▶
Two types of igneous rock

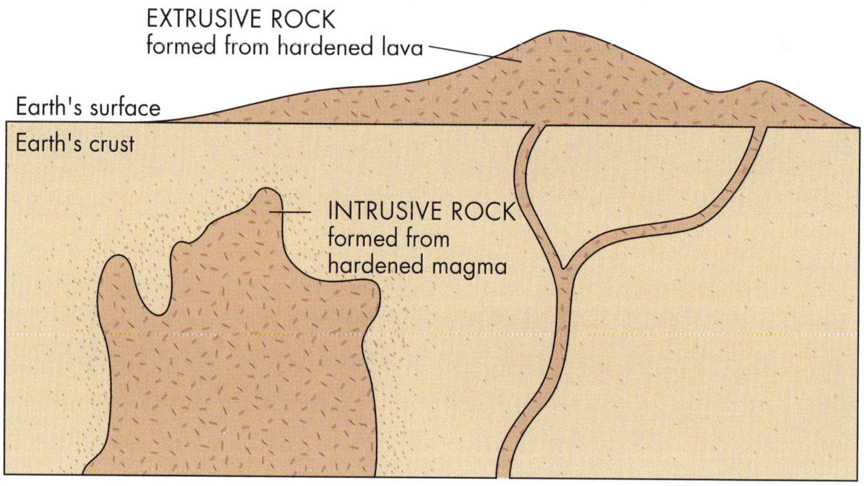

EXTENSION

■ Look at several different samples of igneous rock. Decide which are intrusive and which are extrusive. Some igneous rocks look like sponges. They have many holes or pores in them, like the extrusive rock in Figure 14.8a. Using your knowledge of how igneous rock is formed, try to explain this appearance.

In places, streams of hot magma may slowly push their way farther upwards through the crust. Eventually, just like water leaving a hose, the liquid, or molten, rock breaks through onto the Earth's surface (Figure 14.6). The molten rock flowing on the Earth's surface is called **lava**. Clouds of gases and water vapour also escape from the red-hot lava. When the lava cools and hardens, it is called **extrusive rock** (Figure 14.7). A type of extrusive rock common in British Columbia is called basalt (Figure 14.8a).

How do we know that igneous rock was formed in these ways? Some evidence comes from looking at lava flows today in places like Hawaii. You can actually watch lava from volcanoes cool into rock.

Over 200 years ago, scientists were curious about this process and tried to make igneous rock. They collected different rock samples, melted them in the laboratory, then allowed the molten rock to cool and become solid again. The scientists obtained glassy minerals or mineral crystals, which differed in appearance depending on how fast each mineral cooled.

FIGURE 14.8

(a) Basalt was lava that cooled on the Earth's surface. Why do you think there are tiny holes in this rock? Some of them are filled with white minerals.

(b) Obsidian is an igneous rock that is actually shiny black glass. Obsidian is lava that cooled so quickly that there wasn't enough time for crystals to form. Where would lava cool quickly?

ACTIVITY 14D / IGNEOUS INQUIRY

In this experiment, you will observe how the size of a crystal depends on how fast a hot solution cools. Even though a hot solution is not the same as magma, the relationship between crystal size and speed of cooling is the same.

CAUTION!

- **Do not touch copper sulphate. If any gets on your hands, wash them thoroughly.**

MATERIALS

safety goggles
apron
three test tubes
three adhesive labels or masking tape
test tube rack
25 mL graduated cylinder
three 250 mL beakers
scoop
copper sulphate powder (blue)
balance
hotplate
stirring rod
tongs or heatproof gloves
crushed ice
hand lens

PROCEDURE

1. Copy Table 14.4 into your notebook. Read the procedure and predict what you might expect to find in the three test tubes after 24 h. Record your predictions in your table.

Test tube	Time	Your prediction		Actual observation	
		Crystal length	Description	Crystal length	Description
A					
B					

TABLE 14.4
Sample Data Table for Activity 14D

2. Put on your safety goggles and apron.
3. Label three test tubes A, B, and C. Write your name on each label and then place the test tubes in the rack.
4. Measure 25 mL of water and pour it into a beaker.
5. Measure 20 g of the copper sulphate powder and add it to the beaker. Gently heat the solution while stirring (Figure 14.9).
6. When most of the copper sulphate has dissolved, pick up the beaker with the heatproof gloves or tongs. Carefully pour equal amounts of the solution into each of the three test tubes. Be careful not to pour any undissolved solids into the test tubes.
7. Place test tube A into a beaker of crushed ice. Place test tubes B and C into a beaker of warm water (Figure 14.9). Leave test tubes A and B for 24 h. Examine test tube C after 12 h.
8. To observe the crystals, tilt each test tube slightly. Use a hand lens to examine the crystals more closely. Complete your table and sketch the shape of the crystals.

CAUTION!

- **Do not let the solution boil.**

DISCUSSION

1. Why did you wear safety goggles during the procedure?
2. How did the rate of cooling affect the size of the crystals?
3. Would you expect to find larger crystals in extrusive rock or intrusive rock? Give reasons for your answer. ❖

DID YOU KNOW

- The blue copper sulphate that you have used in the activities in this book also occurs in nature. It is the mineral chalcanthite and is formed through chemical weathering of other copper minerals. It is mined only in the desert of Chile. Why do you suppose it is found there?

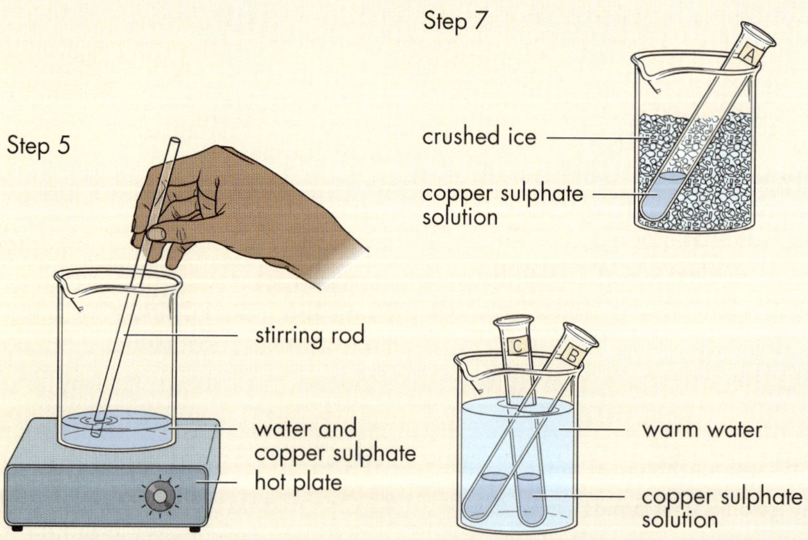

FIGURE 14.9 ▶
Mix the copper sulphate solution in Step 5, and place the test tubes into beakers in Step 7.

SEDIMENTARY ROCK — "LAYER UPON LAYER"

Have you ever looked at a cliff face in a hillside or road cut and seen rock stacked in layers like a pile of sandwiches (Figure 14.10)? If you look closely at a sample of layered rock, you may observe that it seems to be made from grains of rock material closely packed and cemented together. The grains may be smaller than sand or larger than pebbles. This kind of rock is called **sedimentary** rock.

Within the Earth's crust, there is far less sedimentary rock than igneous rock. However, sedimentary rock makes up about three-quarters of the rock found at the Earth's surface.

This family of rock begins its life at the Earth's surface. When bare rock is exposed on the Earth's surface, it is broken up into smaller pieces in many ways. These small fragments of rock are moved from one place to another. You can see this happening in a muddy stream or river, or in a dust storm (Figure 14.11). Over time, huge quantities of material, called **sediment**, are carried from the land into lakes and oceans, where they eventually settle to the bottom.

FIGURE 14.10
The layered appearance of these sedimentary rocks is a clue to how they were formed. What can you infer about the ages of the layers?

DID YOU KNOW

■ Every week, millions of tonnes of sediment are carried by the Fraser River past New Westminster, B.C. Most of this sediment is deposited where the river meets the sea. The sediment that builds up in these areas today will become the sedimentary rock of the future.

FIGURE 14.11 ◀
How could blowing dust and sand grains eventually become part of a sedimentary rock formation?

How do all these piled-up sediments become rock? First, they are squeezed together by the mass of the sediment on top of them. This process is similar to the way fresh snow turns from loose, fluffy flakes into a solid when you stand on it. In some rocks, the particles are further cemented together by chemicals that act like glue. The layers are produced when sediment of different sizes settle on top of each other. Later, if the layers of sediments are buried deeply, the resulting layers of rock are called **beds**.

The appearance and properties of a sedimentary rock can tell you what the original sediment was like (Figure 14.12). For example, sedimentary rocks called **mudstone** and **shale** are formed from fine grains of clay or mud. These rocks are weak and crumble easily. A harder, rougher rock called **sandstone** is formed from particles of sand, mostly made of quartz. Rounded pebbles and small stones cemented together form a type of sedimentary rock called **conglomerate**.

The size of the rock particles that rest on the bottom in a particular part of a river, lake, or ocean depends on the speed of water that carries them. For example, a narrow, swift-flowing mountain stream on a steep slope can move large rocks. But a wide, slow-flowing river on a flat plain will carry only the finest clay particles. By studying the layers of sediments in different places today, geologists can understand what conditions were like in the past.

(a) (b) (c)

FIGURE 14.12
Different types of sedimentary rock: (a) shale, (b) coarse sandstone, and (c) conglomerate. The appearance of the rocks depends on the size and colour of the original sediment. Can you find sedimentary rocks near your school?

ACTIVITY 14E / SETTLING SEDIMENTS

In this activity, you will observe how sediment of different sizes settles into layers.

MATERIALS

Part I
safety goggles
apron
large clear glass jar (2 L or more) with screw cap
water
mixture of clay, very fine sand, sand, and fine gravel (about 1 L in volume)

PART I Settling Sediments

PROCEDURE

1. Put on your safety goggles and apron.
2. Fill the jar about three-quarters full with water.
3. Pour the mixture of sediments into the jar.
4. Cap the jar tightly and shake it *very gently* until all the sediment is moving about.
5. Set the jar down and observe the sediments settling.
6. Draw a neat diagram that shows the different layers made up of the different-sized particles.
7. Describe the particle sizes in each layer.

MATERIALS

Part II
hand lens
ruler
sedimentary rock samples

DISCUSSION

1. Which size of sediment settled to the bottom of the jar first?
2. Which size of sediment settled last or floated in the water during your period of observation?
3. Based on your observations, suggest how this arrangement of sediments might occur in nature.

PART II Settled Sediments

PROCEDURE

1. Examine the sedimentary rock samples with a hand lens. In a data table, record the particle size, then give the geological name of each sample.

FIGURE 14.13
How were these patterns in the sedimentary rock formed?

(a) ripple pattern

(b) regular-shaped cracks

DISCUSSION

1. What do you see in the samples of sedimentary rock that suggests to you that the original sediment was deposited under water?
2. Can you think of another way to build up layers of sediment?
3. Examine Figure 14.13. Observe the features in each rock sample. What do you think conditions were like when the features were made? ❖

METAMORPHIC ROCK — "CHANGING FORM"

Around the year 1900, geologists walking along a sedimentary rock bed in Scotland noticed that the appearance of the rock changed from one end of the bed to the other. At one end, the bed was fine-grained, sedimentary shale. At the other end, however, the bed was made of another type of rock called slate. **Slate** is harder and more brittle than shale. It may contain different minerals than shale does. Slate also splits very easily into sheets. Because the slate was in the same bed as the shale, the geologists inferred that the slate had been formed from shale. Slate is an example of the third family of rock, called **metamorphic** rock.

Metamorphic rock is formed below the Earth's surface when rocks change their characteristics. This may happen in several ways. For example, when rock becomes buried to great depths, it is subjected to increased temperature and pressure. Or when magma moves through the crust, neighbouring rocks are heated and squeezed (Figure 14.14). When this happens, the rocks may become changed and new minerals may be formed.

Some metamorphic rock has been altered so much that it no longer resembles the original rock or parent rock. Some minerals, such as talc, are found only in metamorphic rock.

Often, however, geologists can trace the relationship between a metamorphic rock and its parent rock. For example, marble is a metamorphic rock formed from the sedimentary rock called limestone.

Although they look different from one another, both rocks have some characteristics that are the same. Both rocks are made of the mineral calcite (calcium carbonate) and have a hardness of 3.

Quartzite is a metamorphic rock formed from sandstone. If you drop a piece of sandstone, the rock will usually break along cracks *between* the grains of sand. If you drop a piece of quartzite, it will break *through* the grains. This is because the sand grains became closely bonded together during the changes that produced the metamorphic rock.

FIGURE 14.14 ▶
Metamorphic rock may be formed when hot magma moving through the Earth's crust heats and squeezes into the surrounding layers of sedimentary rock.

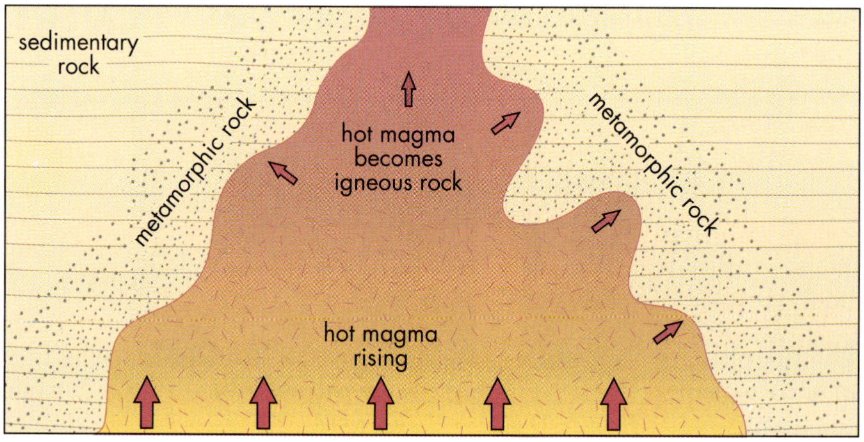

ACTIVITY 14F / THE BIG SQUEEZE

In this activity, you will observe some of the differences between metamorphic rocks and the parent rocks from which they were formed (Figure 14.15).

MATERIALS

safety goggles
apron
labelled rock samples:
- slate, mudstone
- quartzite, sandstone
- gneiss, granite
- marble, limestone
- schist

hand lens (10x)
Mohs hardness scale set of minerals (or substitutes: nail, penny, sandpaper)

(a)

(b)

FIGURE 14.15
Granite (a), an igneous rock, can be changed into gneiss (b), a metamorphic rock.

EXTENSION

■ You can make a model of metamorphic rock using two colours of modelling clay. Use one colour of clay to make a ball about the size of an apple. This ball represents the parent rock. From the second colour of clay, make six marble-sized balls. These represent minerals. Carefully insert the "minerals" into the "rock." Place the "rock" on a sheet of paper on the floor and lay a board over it. Push or stand on the board. Note what happened to the "minerals." Compare your model with the samples of schist and gneiss.

PROCEDURE

1. Draw a data table. Record the mineral in the left-hand column. Label other columns for each mineral property: colour, lustre, hardness, and crystal shape.
2. Put on your safety goggles and apron.
3. Use your hand lens to look at each rock sample. For each mineral, record colour, lustre, hardness, and crystal shape. Use the nail and the other Mohs set of minerals or substitutes to determine hardness.
4. Compare the samples in each of the four pairs listed under "Materials." Record the differences between the rocks in each pair.
5. Compare samples of gneiss and schist. Try to identify the minerals in each.

DISCUSSION

1. What conditions do you think produced the differences you observed in step 4? Give a reason for your answer.
2. How are the gneiss and schist different from the other metamorphic rocks you examined?
3. What does the difference between gneiss and schist tell you about the amount of change each rock has experienced? ❖

THE ROCK CYCLE

Rocks are made of minerals. Each mineral forms at certain temperatures and pressures. But rocks stay the same only in the environment where they are formed. If the environment of the rock changes, the rock (and the minerals) may also change. For example, if a rock is buried deeply enough in the Earth it may become hot enough to melt into magma. If the magma later cools, it will become igneous rock.

If an igneous rock becomes exposed at the Earth's surface, it will break down into small fragments. Eventually these fragments may be transported by wind or by a river. When the river reaches the ocean, the fragments sink to the ocean floor to form a deposit of different layers of sediment. Eventually the layers may be buried and squeezed to become sedimentary rock. If the sedimentary rock is buried at deeper levels, it may be heated and become metamorphic rock or magma.

In this way, over long periods of time, one kind of rock may change to another. Each family of rocks is linked to the others through this **rock cycle**. A diagram of the rock cycle summarizes all the processes of rock formation that you have learned about (Figure 14.16).

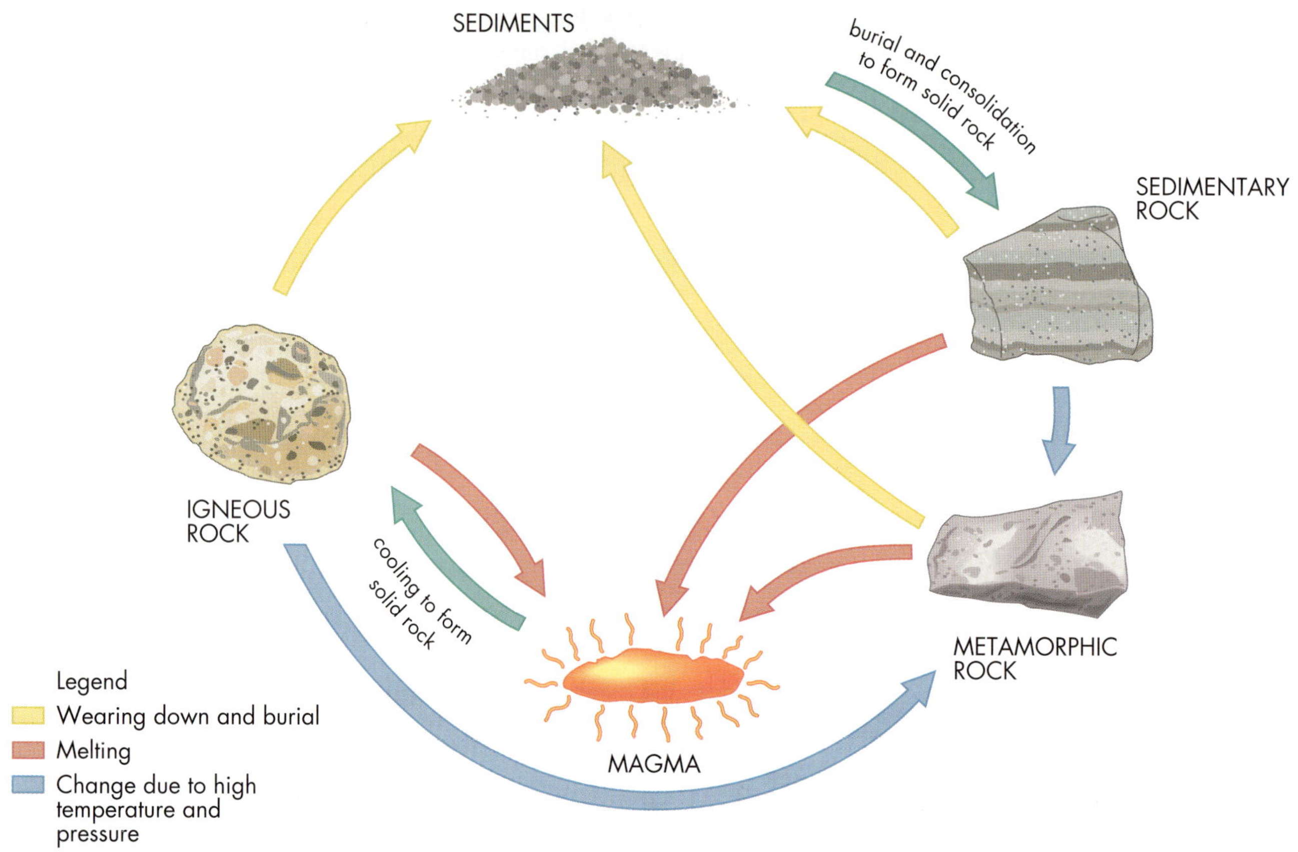

FIGURE 14.16
The rock cycle

► REVIEW 14.2

1. Each of the following terms is the correct answer to a question. Write a suitable question to match each answer:
   (a) lava
   (b) magma
   (c) intrusive rock
   (d) extrusive rock
2. What is the relationship between the size of mineral crystals in an igneous rock and the length of time it took the rock to form?
3. Explain why sedimentary rock often appears in horizontal layers.
4. Which family of rock is formed as a result of:
   (a) breaking up of other rocks on the Earth's surface??
   (b) pressure and heat?
   (c) melting and cooling?
5. Why is the changing of rock in one family into rock of a different family called a rock cycle? (Hint: What does "cycle" mean?)

CHAPTER REVIEW

KEY IDEAS

- Rocks are made of one or more minerals. Minerals are pure, solid materials that come from the Earth.
- Minerals may be identified by several properties, including colour, hardness, lustre, streak, magnetism, crystal shape, and cleavage.
- Rocks are classified into three major families. The families are igneous, sedimentary, and metamorphic.
- Igneous rocks are formed by the cooling of molten rock material. Intrusive rock is formed when magma cools beneath the Earth's surface. Extrusive rock is formed when lava cools on the Earth's surface.
- Sedimentary rock is formed when rock fragments pile up in layers. When these layers are buried, they become solid rock.
- Metamorphic rock is formed when any rock is buried and changed by great heat or pressure.
- Rock in any family may change into rock of another family. This change is part of a rock cycle.

VOCABULARY

geologist
mineral
rock
colour
hardness
Mohs hardness scale
lustre
streak
magnetism
fluorescence
crystal
cleavage
fracture
crust
igneous
magma
intrusive rock
lava
extrusive rock
sedimentary
sediment
beds
mudstone
shale
sandstone
conglomerate
slate
metamorphic
quartzite
rock cycle

V1. Write the word "rock" in the centre of a sheet of paper. Make a mind map by joining "rock" with words from the vocabulary list. Use as many words as you can. Use other ideas you have learned too.

V2. Match each of the descriptions below to a term from the vocabulary list.

(a) You can make a substitute for this using things such as a pencil, a copper coin, and sandpaper.

(b) You can use ultraviolet light to detect this mineral property.

(c) "Metallic," "glassy," and "waxy" are examples of this term.

(d) Molten rock flowing on the Earth's surface.

(e) Sedimentary rock made up of pebbles and small stones.

CONNECTIONS

C1. How can you tell whether a rock cliff beside a highway is made of igneous rock or sedimentary rock?

C2. What evidence would you look for to find out about volcanic eruptions in British Columbia in the past?

C3. Why do you think intrusive rock cools so slowly?

C4. Obsidian is a hard, glassy rock with smooth, shiny surfaces. Pumice is a soft, spongy rock with many small holes in it. Sometimes it floats on water. Both are igneous rocks formed during volcanic eruptions. Why do you think they look so different from one another?

C5. Make a sketch of three layers or beds of sedimentary rock formed by the following events:

(a) The bottom layer is made of sediment deposited near the mouth of a fast-flowing river.

(b) On top of it is a bed that was deposited when the river became shallower and slower.

(c) The upper layer was deposited after the mouth of the river was submerged under several metres of sea water.

C6. Pretend that you are the quartz crystal that you find in an igneous rock during a hike in the Coast Mountains. Write a short story to describe what might happen to you in the future as the rock you are in is changed through the rock cycle, first into sedimentary rock, then into metamorphic rock, and finally back to igneous rock.

EXPLORATIONS

E1. Find out what minerals are mined in British Columbia. Report to the class on the variety of minerals mined, their uses, and where they are found.

E2. Begin your own collection of minerals and rocks. A good way to start is by looking for samples on weekends and during your holidays. You can also buy or trade samples through mineral clubs, and shops that sell jewellery, rocks, and crystals. Look also for scraps from building-stone suppliers.

E3. Look at a geological map of an area near you and plan a route that would take you through as many different types of rocks as possible during a morning or afternoon drive. Sketch your route on a sheet of paper and label where different rocks or geological points of interest may be found along the route.

E4. The properties of compounds that you studied in Chapter 6 can also be used to identify minerals. List them. Find another property to help separate metallic minerals and non-metallic minerals into two groups. (Hint: You can try this blindfolded.)

E5. Interview a jeweller or museum expert and ask to see examples of minerals that are gemstones. Choose the one you like best. Find out why it is considered valuable. Ask about any problems in caring for it. Present your findings to your class. As a class, discuss the physical characteristics that make a mineral a gemstone.

E6. From your study of matter in Chapter 6, classify the following earth materials: granite, a sandy beach, galena, conglomerate, fossil shells, and diamonds. (Hint: first separate the materials into two categories: mixtures and pure substances.)

REFLECTIONS

R1. Look back at the notes you made in Activity 14A. Have your ideas about rocks changed since you began this chapter? Record any interesting facts you have learned or any questions you still have about rocks and minerals.

R2. To many people, finding out that rocks can change from one type to another is a surprise. Write a short poem that describes your ideas about rocks changing over long periods of time.

CHAPTER 15

EARTH'S CHANGING SURFACE

Turtle Mountain is located in the Rocky Mountains, near the British Columbia-Alberta border. Today, the mountain looks different from the way it did a hundred years ago. Early in the morning of April 29, 1903, a huge chunk of the mountain slid into the valley below. With a roar that was heard more than 150 km away, millions of tonnes of rock demolished part of the town of Frank, Alberta, then swept across the valley and up the other side. It was all over in less than two minutes. The landslide carried off a piece of the mountain over a kilometre wide and nearly 200 m thick.

Fortunately, such violent changes to the landscape do not happen often. We do not expect to see mountains and valleys change their appearance overnight. However, smaller changes in our surroundings occur every day. Over hundreds of millions of years, these small daily changes can affect the land far more than an event like the Frank landslide. In this chapter, you will investigate some ways that the land around us changes. You will examine evidence that everyday events can eventually wear away mountains, fill in valleys, change the direction of rivers, and even change the shape of continents and oceans.

ACTIVITY 15A / WHAT CHANGES TO THE LAND SURFACE DO YOU KNOW ABOUT?

The land in your neighbourhood does not stay exactly the same. Natural events and human activities bring about changes. Land may be overgrown by weeds and bushes, or cleared for roadways, new buildings, or power lines. Floods cover some land areas. In other places, ponds and marshes are drained.

PART I Observing Change

Think about the land in your neighbourhood. In your learning journal, list ways in which the land around you has changed or might change. Beside each item, record what brought about the change. Was it humans, other organisms, weather, or a combination of these? If it is weather, add more information, such as "wind" or "rain."

PART II Causes of Change

After you have completed Part I, answer these questions. What are the most common causes of change to the land in your neighbourhood? Do you think these are also the most common causes of change to the land in other parts of British Columbia? Explain why or why not. ❖

FIGURE 15.1
This old gravestone is starting to show wear. Compare it with a new one to see how rock weathers over the years.

■ 15.1 WEATHERING

An old cemetery can be an interesting place to visit. There, you can see how small, slow changes make a big difference after many years. Almost two hundred years ago, the gravestone in Figure 15.1 was polished and new. Today, the surface of the stone has tiny holes and chips have fallen from the edges. Later, the writing will be worn away. Eventually, the stone will crumble apart and disappear into the soil.

Weathering is the process that slowly breaks the gravestone into smaller pieces. Weathering is the breakdown of earth materials wherever they are found, in any part of the landscape. The **landscape** is all the features on the Earth's surface that you may see around you, such as mountains, valleys, streams, stream banks, and caves. The landscape also includes features that have been modified or created by people, such as a lake formed by damming a river.

The term "weathering" indicates that the changes in the landscape are brought about by the weather. Weather includes changing temperature, wind, rainfall, snowfall, and humidity (the amount of moisture in the air). Weathering slowly breaks down all materials in contact with the air, including boulders and rocks, and human-made structures such as roads and buildings.

Weathering occurs on the surface of a rock. If a large rock is broken up into smaller pieces, more surfaces are exposed to weathering. All these surfaces together make up the **surface area** — the total area of all the surfaces of all the pieces of the broken rock. A rock broken into many pieces has a much larger surface area than the original rock, and weathering breaks it down even faster (Figure 15.2).

There are three kinds of weathering: mechanical, chemical, and biological.

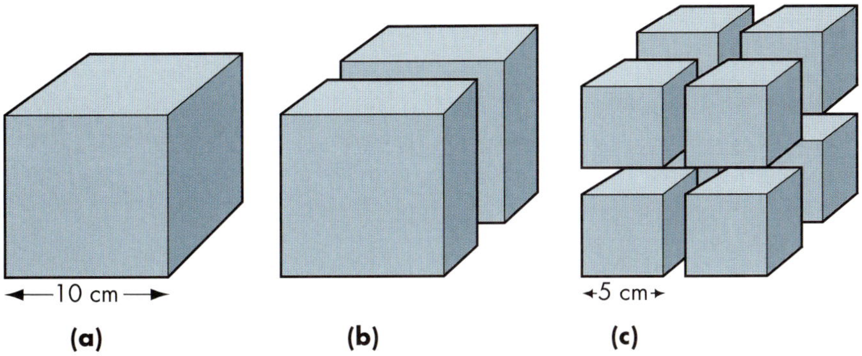

FIGURE 15.2
When rocks are broken into smaller pieces, their surface area is increased, even though the volume remains the same.

EXTENSION

■ Examine Figure 15.2 again. The rock in (a) has a volume of 1000 cm^3. It has six sides or surfaces, each one 10 cm x 10 cm = 100 cm^2. So the surface area of the rock is 600 cm^2 (six sides of 100 cm^2 each). In (b), the rock is cut in half. The volume is the same as in (a), but the surface area has increased. Calculate the total surface area of the shapes in (b). In (c), there are eight cubes. Their total volume is still 1000 cm^3. Calculate their total surface area.

ACTIVITY 15B / HOW DOES ICE WEATHER ROCK?

In this activity, you will observe the effect of freezing on water and relate this process to weathering in rock.

MATERIALS

masking tape
plastic well slide
dropper
glass slide
two elastic bands
water

PROCEDURE

1. Using the dropper, fill the well in the plastic slide with water.
2. Carefully place the glass slide on top of the plastic slide and hold the two slides together with elastic bands.
3. Write your name on a piece of masking tape and place it on the slides.
4. Place the slides in a freezer until the water has frozen (about 30 min).
5. Examine the slides and record your observations. Draw a picture of the slides in your notebook.

DISCUSSION

1. What happens when the water freezes?
2. From your observations in this experiment, suggest what might happen if rainwater flows into cracks in a rock and later freezes. ❖

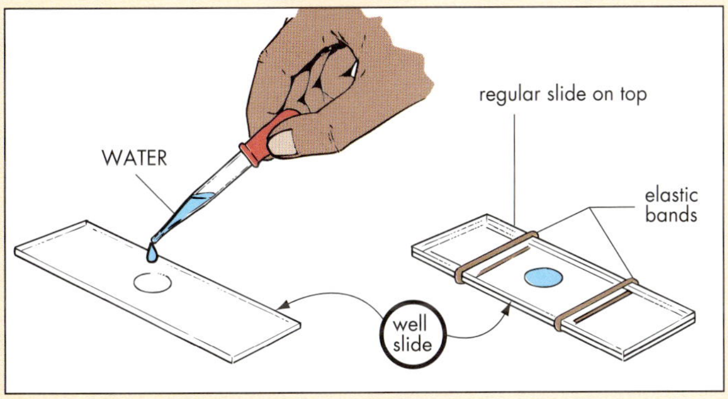

FIGURE 15.3 ◄
How to prepare the glass slide for Activity 15B

FIGURE 15.4
In cold climates, cracks in rock are commonly widened by ice wedging. If there is a rock cut near your home, examine it in the winter for pieces of rock broken off by ice.

MECHANICAL WEATHERING

Mechanical weathering breaks rock into smaller pieces. In Canada, mechanical weathering commonly occurs after water runs into cracks in rocks, then freezes. Unlike most materials, water expands (increases in volume) when it freezes.

Have you ever noticed how the ice cubes that form in a freezer bulge up from the top of the tray? In a similar way, water that freezes in a crack will form ice that bulges or expands. The expanding ice pushes with tremendous pressure against the walls of the crack. Acting like a wedge, the increasing pressure can suddenly split a rock in two (Figure 15.4). This process is called **ice wedging**.

In dry areas such as deserts, mechanical weathering may be caused by the wind. Gusts of wind that blow loose sand and small pieces of rock against a rock surface have the same effect as rubbing the surface with sandpaper. The rock surface gradually wears away into smaller fragments or grains of rock.

CHEMICAL WEATHERING

Chemical weathering occurs when chemicals in rain, snow, and air break down minerals in rock. Usually, mechanical and chemical weathering take place together.

ACTIVITY 15C / AN EXAMPLE OF CHEMICAL WEATHERING: HOW DOES ACID WEATHER ROCK?

In this activity, you will observe the effect of a weak acid on different types of rock.

CAUTION!

- **When handling acids, observe safety rules. Wash any spills immediately with plenty of water. Inform your teacher about spills.**

MATERIALS

safety goggles
apron
four test tubes
test tube rack
crushed limestone
granite chips
sand
carbonic acid (contains dissolved carbon dioxide gas)
distilled (very pure) water
pH paper or blue litmus paper

PROCEDURE

1. Copy Table 15.1 into your notebook.
2. Put on your safety goggles and apron.
3. Number the test tubes 1, 2, 3, and 4. Put a small amount of crushed limestone into test tubes 1 and 2, granite in test tube 3, and sand in test tube 4. Test tube 1 will be a control.
4. Add just enough carbonic acid to cover each of the three rock samples

in test tubes 2, 3, and 4 (Figure 15.5). (No acid will be added to test tube 1.) Observe and record what happens in each test tube.

5. Add just enough distilled water to test tube 1 (the control tube of limestone) to cover the rock sample. Record your observations.

6. Test the liquid in each tube with a piece of blue litmus paper. The litmus paper will turn pink if it contacts any acid. Record your results in the table.

FIGURE 15.5
Add just enough carbonic acid to test tubes 2, 3, and 4.

DISCUSSION

1. From your observations, which rock in the activity is most affected by acid?
2. What do you think happened to the rock affected by acid?
3. Suggest where a similar effect on rocks might occur in nature. (Hint: Some streams and rivers contain very weak acids.) ❖

TABLE 15.1 ▶
Sample Data Table for Activity 15C

Test tube #	Contents	Result of adding acid	Colour of litmus paper
1	Limestone	(control)	
2	Limestone		
3	Granite		
4	Sand		

WEATHERING AND CAVES

One of the most interesting results of chemical weathering is the formation of caves (Figure 15.6). These are underground spaces in the rock that have been hollowed out by chemical weathering and flowing water. Caves are most common in limestone rock. As you may have discovered in Activity 15C, limestone dissolves in a weak acid solution. In nature, carbon dioxide gas in the air dissolves in rainwater to form a weak acid (carbonic acid). When rainwater trickles over the surface of limestone and drains into cracks in the limestone, the weak acid dissolves some of the rock. Holes form in the rock. Over time, they grow larger and may connect to form spectacular underground tunnels and caverns. In British Columbia, there are small caves on Vancouver Island and in Glacier National Park. There is also a large cave near Mt. Robson. However, most of British Columbia has not been well explored for caves.

Chemical weathering affects different minerals in different ways. For example, the weak acid in rainwater slowly changes feldspar, a hard mineral, into softer clay. Clay is an important part of many soils. Another example: rock salt (the mineral halite) dissolves easily in rainwater. The solution of salt in water eventually washes from the land into the sea, giving oceans their salty flavour. Some minerals are not affected much by weathering. For example, grains of quartz do not

DID YOU KNOW

■ One of the longest caves in Canada is the Castleguard Cave near the British Columbia-Alberta border in Banff National Park. It is estimated to be 18 km long.

EXTENSION

■ Find out how the icicle-like spikes of rock called stalagmites and stalactites are formed inside limestone caves.

DID YOU KNOW

■ When astronauts first brought moon rocks back to Earth, they sealed the rocks in plastic to prevent chemical weathering from the Earth's atmosphere.

change as the rock around them crumbles. For this reason, quartz is the commonest mineral found in small grains of rock or sand.

Air is as important as water in chemical weathering. For example, oxygen gas in the air combines with iron in certain minerals in rocks to form rust (iron oxides). The reddish-brown iron oxide is the same compound you see on a rusty car. In parts of the world where iron minerals are common, the rocks, soil, and dust have a rust-red colour (Figure 15.7).

FIGURE 15.6
Spikes of calcium carbonate, called stalactites, hang from the roof of a cave that was formed when limestone dissolved in rainwater. How were the stalactites formed?

FIGURE 15.7
The red colour in these rocks and soils from Prince Edward Island is due to iron oxides that are produced by chemical weathering.

DID YOU KNOW

■ The stone steps of some historic buildings in Europe have been damaged by the acid in soft drinks, spilled on the steps by visitors.

WEATHERING AND POLLUTION

Human activities that pollute the air have increased the speed of chemical weathering. Smokestacks, fires, and your family automobile all produce waste gases. Some waste gases combine with moisture in the air to form strong acids such as sulphuric acid and nitric acid. These acids fall to the earth as **acid rain**. Because winds can blow waste gases hundreds of kilometres through the air, acid rain may fall far away from the sources of pollution.

Chemical weathering from acid rain has damaged many ancient stone buildings around the world. Chemical weathering affects structures made of limestone or marble most severely. Photographs of old buildings, statues, and gravestones show that air pollution has caused much chemical weathering over the past hundred years in some areas. More damage has occurred in the past hundred years than in hundreds or even thousands of previous years (Figure 15.8). Some polluting gases in the air may also contribute to global warming. Since the rate of chemical reactions increases with temperature, the result will be a further speed-up of chemical weathering.

FIGURE 15.8 ◀
Many famous stone sculptures, such as the Sphinx near Cairo, Egypt, are being damaged by chemical weathering. In your community, compare an old building with a newer one. Is there evidence of chemical weathering?

ACTIVITY 15D / HOW DO PLANTS WEATHER ROCK?

Can growing organisms affect the way rocks are weathered?

MATERIALS

bean seeds
dust mask
safety goggles
apron
small dish (such as empty plastic margarine container)
plaster of paris (Polyfilla)
water
stir stick

PROCEDURE

1. Soak the bean seeds overnight in water.
2. Put on your dust mask, safety goggles, and apron.
3. Half-fill the container with plaster of paris. Slowly add water and stir until all the powder is wet. The mixture will be like thick mud.
4. Push the seeds about 1 cm below the surface of the plaster. Place the container where it can remain undisturbed for a week.
5. Observe the contents of your container during the next week. Record your observations in your notebook.

DISCUSSION

1. Describe the changes you observed in
   (a) the plaster, (b) the seeds.
2. Suggest how plants might help to weather rock in nature. ❖

BIOLOGICAL WEATHERING

So far, you have learned about mechanical weathering and chemical weathering. When living things assist both these processes, the weathering is called **biological weathering**. For example, plant seeds or roots may grow in tiny cracks in the rock. As the plant grows bigger, it may force the crack apart (Figure 15.9). Burrowing animals move loose rock and expose new rock surfaces to air and water. Rotting vegetation and animal feces and urine contain acids that speed up chemical weathering.

FIGURE 15.9
Tree roots growing in cracks in the rock. As the roots thicken, they wedge the rock apart. How can this process speed up mechanical weathering?

FIGURE 15.10
A cross-section of soil. How could you estimate the amount of humus in a sample of soil?

FROM ROCK TO SOIL

Imagine a land surface consisting of bare rock. How much food could you grow? Would there be any forests or prairies? Without soil, there would be few plants of any kind. And without plants for food and shelter, there would be few animals.

On land, soil is a link between the non-living world of rock and the living world of organisms. If you look closely at a sample of soil, you may see that it consists mainly of grains of weathered rock, such as clay and sand. Added to these is decaying plant and animal matter, called **humus**. Together, these materials hold the food and water that plants need to grow. Figure 15.10 illustrates how soil builds up gradually from weathered rock, over hundreds or thousands of years.

ACTIVITY 15E / A CLOSE LOOK AT SOIL

In this activity, you will examine a sample of soil to see what it is made of.

MATERIALS

gloves
spade
old newspaper
ruler
notebook
hand lens

PROCEDURE

1. Find a suitable area of open land.
2. Put on your gloves and carefully dig out a section of soil about 30 cm deep. Lay the soil sample flat on the newspaper.
3. Examine the section of soil from the top (land surface) to the bottom. Use a hand lens to examine individual soil particles more closely.
4. Sketch the appearance of the soil section. If you notice any layers in the soil, measure their depth and record this on your sketch. Describe the features of the soil, such as its colour, texture, and particle size.

DISCUSSION

1. What materials did you find in the soil? Are there any rock fragments in the soil? If so, where do you think they come from?
2. How would you explain any differences in the content of soil near the surface of the land and soil several centimetres below the surface? ❖

► REVIEW 15.1

1. Name three types of weathering.
2. Name two important results of weathering.
3. Decide what kind of weathering produces the following:
   (a) a rusting automobile
   (b) holes in a statue
   (c) cracks in a sidewalk
4. Name two human activities that may increase the rate of weathering in rocks or stones. Describe the effect of each.
5. Why is soil important for plant growth?
6. Why are caves more common in limestone rock than in sandstone?
7. Do you think that natural weathering affects rocks more than human activities do? List reasons for your answer.
8. Why are gravestones, old statues, and old stone buildings particularly useful for illustrating weathering?

15.2 MOVING EARTH: EROSION AND THE LANDSCAPE

The landslide described at the beginning of this chapter might not have happened if the rock had not been weathered. Weathering helped break up the solid rock face of the mountainside. The process that brought the boulders and rocks crashing down is **erosion**. Erosion is the movement of weathered rock material from one place to another.

Like the landslide, erosion may be sudden, or it may take place slowly, over hundreds or thousands of years. Erosion can be the movement of grains of sand or the movement of gigantic boulders weighing hundreds

DID YOU KNOW

In 1965, 10 million cubic metres of rock broke free from Johnson Peak, along the Hope-Princeton Highway. Four travellers were buried instantly in the landslide. It took 21 days to clear the 2 km stretch of the highway. Are there any landslides or rockslides in your area?

FIGURE 15.11
The Fraser Canyon on the Fraser River. What do you think this area looked like when the canyon was just beginning to be formed?

of tonnes. And erosion can move rock materials any distance from a few metres to hundreds of kilometres. **Deposition** occurs when the eroded rock material stops moving and settles on the Earth's surface. When the movement stops, the eroded material is called a **deposit**.

In a landslide, erosion is caused by the pull of gravity. On the Earth, gravity is a force that pulls objects downward. Other important causes of erosion are moving water, wind, and moving ice. Each kind of erosion produces different kinds of deposits.

MOVING WATER

The Fraser Canyon is several hundred metres deep (Figure 15.11). Looking down at the river today, it is difficult to believe that there was a time when the Fraser Canyon was not here. But if you look carefully into the swift, tumbling currents, you may see the evidence of the canyon's past. Like any powerful flow of water, the Fraser River carries pieces of broken rock, sand, gravel, and mud. Little by little, over many years, a large river can move billions of tonnes of rock from the land it crosses. As it does so, it cuts slowly into the land and makes a deeper and deeper valley. How quickly a river erodes its valley depends on how steeply the river valley descends, the amount of water in the river, the speed of the water, and the types of rock in the valley.

ACTIVITY 15F / MAKING A MODEL RIVER (TEACHER DEMONSTRATION)

Your teacher will demonstrate this activity with the help of several students. In this activity, you will observe the effect of flowing water on different-sized fragments of rock.

MATERIALS

safety goggles
apron
stream table
rock fragments of different sizes:
clay (very small), sand (small), and pebbles (medium)
fragments of the mineral pyrite
rubber tubing (attached to tap)
bucket

PROCEDURE

1. Put on your safety goggles and apron.
2. With your teacher's assistance, set up a stream table as shown in Figure 15.12.
3. Pour the mixed rock and mineral fragments into the top half of the sloping stream table, to a depth of 3 to 4 cm.
4. Add water to the lower half of the stream table to represent a lake.
5. Place the tubing at the top end of the stream table and slowly turn on the tap until you have a gentle, steady flow of water. Observe what the moving water does to the different rock materials. Record your observations.
6. Predict what faster-moving water will do to each of the three rock materials and to the pyrite. Make a sketch and description in your notebook to illustrate your prediction.
7. *Very gradually* increase the water flow to medium speed. Record your observations.
8. Predict what will happen if you tilt the stream table to a steeper angle. Record your prediction.

FIGURE 15.12 ▶
How to build and use a stream table

EXTENSION

■ In many famous diamond localities on the Earth, diamonds are found in stream gravels. In these places you can pan for diamonds. Find out what properties of diamonds make this possible. Where are the most famous localities? Choose one of the following famous diamonds and trace its history back to where it was found: Kohinoor, Regent, Orloff, Victoria, Tiffany, Hope, Cullinan, Jonker, or Vargas.

9. Reduce the water flow to slow speed. Raise the top end of the stream table a few centimetres. Record your observations.

DISCUSSION

1. What happened to each size of fragment when the water was flowing slowly?
2. What happened to each size of fragment when the water was flowing more rapidly?
3. (a) Describe what happens to the stream of water where it joins the "lake" at the lower end of the stream table.
   (b) What happens to the fragments here?
4. (a) What effect does the speed of the water have on erosion?
   (b) How does the size of fragments affect this process?
5. What happened to the materials when you increased the slope of the stream table?
6. If a river valley is eroding rapidly, what features do you expect to see?
7. Which is heavier, a piece of pyrite or a pebble of the same size?
8. A particle of gold weighs over three times as much as a particle of pyrite of the same size. Where would you look for gold in your stream table? Where would you look for gold in a real river? ❖

RIVER VALLEYS

Moving water continually picks up rock fragments in one place and deposits them in another. As it does so, the moving water changes the shape of its valley. By studying the size and shape of a river valley, you can find out about the river's age.

THE BIG PICTURE — REMOTE SENSING SATELLITES

Suppose you are an engineer and want to construct a highway. It would help to look down at the Earth from above. Then you could see where the best places are to build the highway, and where to find the nearest gravel deposits for the road bed.

Or suppose you are a scientist looking at the environmental changes taking place all over the world. Are deserts getting larger? Are forests disappearing? Are cities expanding? Are wetland areas shrinking? You need to know what the Earth's surface is like now. And you need a record of the changes from year to year.

Manicouagan meteor crater in Quebec is 70 km in diameter and over 200 million years old. The circular crater lake is black and its beaches are pink. Forests are shades of green and yellow green. What do you think happened in the reddish area on the left side of the photograph?

The solution to all these problems could be in remote sensing satellites. Hundreds of kilometres up in space, satellites circle the earth. They carry equipment, called sensors, that gathers information about the Earth's surface and sends it down to ground stations. In Canada there are ground stations in Prince Albert, Saskatchewan, and Gatineau, Quebec.

Computers use this information to produce an image, like a photograph, that suits a user's needs. Images can be changed so that certain features on the ground show up more clearly. For example, colours may be changed so that a certain kind of tree can be distinguished from another. Certain areas can be increased in size so that they can be studied in more detail.

The first remote sensing satellite (Landsat) was launched by the United States in 1972. Since then, many more have been placed in orbit around the Earth. The sensors on French SPOT satellites can be pointed a little to one side or the other of the satellite's track. This means the same area of land can be viewed from two different angles. Using these two images, the computer can create a three-dimensional view of an area.

RADARSAT, Canada's first such satellite, was scheduled for launch in 1994. It will use radar to scan the earth's surface. This will allow the satellite to gather information day or night, and through clouds. Imagine how useful it could be for monitoring the movement of sea ice so that ships can avoid icebergs.

What other uses are there for satellite imagery?

Rivers usually begin as streams, starting from a small spring or lake. The young river is usually narrow, fast-flowing, and straight. It cuts downward into the land, forming a narrow valley with steep sides.

As one stream joins another, the river grows larger. It erodes rocks and soil along its edge to widen the valley. Rocks on the sides of the valley become weathered and tumble down the slopes. As a result, the older river valley becomes **V-shaped** (Figure 15.13).

On the way to the sea, many rivers cross flat areas, or plains, near the coast. Here, rivers are wide and slow-flowing. They may wind in loops across the flat land (Figure 15.14). Since the river is slow-moving, the heavier sediment is deposited on the river bed or river banks. At this stage, the river flows in a very wide, shallow valley. When heavy rains or melting snow bring more water, the river may rise, burst over its banks, and flood onto the flat areas nearby (Figure 15.15).

FIGURE 15.13
A V-shaped valley eroded into the landscape by a river. How does this valley compare with the canyon in Figure 15.11?

FIGURE 15.14
This river winds across the floodplain in loops called meanders. Do you think the lake in the foreground was once part of the river? Explain why or why not.

FIGURE 15.15
When a river overflows its banks and causes a flood, there is a danger to crops, livestock, buildings, and people who live on the floodplain. This photograph was taken in the Fraser Valley in 1948.

FLOODS AND FLOODPLAINS

The flat land beside a river that is covered by water during flooding is known as a **floodplain**. The brown, cloudy flood water contains fine eroded material. After the flood water drains away, the fine mud is deposited and helps build up a rich soil. Because of this, the floodplains of some large rivers around the world, such as the Nile, Mississippi, and Fraser, have become important agricultural areas. People try to control floods in these regions by building dams and raised banks, or **dikes**, along the river. In years of high rainfall, however, floods may break through the dikes and drown farmers' fields. Floods may also wash away bridges and roadways and damage houses and other buildings.

ACTIVITY 15G / FLOODS ALONG THE FRASER

GROUP ACTIVITY G — CROSS-CURRICULAR C

Floods may occur beside the Fraser River between Hope and the coast. For example, in spring 1948, snow melted rapidly in the mountains and the river flooded quickly. About one-tenth of the farmland was flooded by June (Figure 15.16). Two thousand homes were damaged by the floods. The total cost of the disaster was estimated to be over $20 million. In this activity, you will consider the most suitable uses of the land in this area of British Columbia.

PROCEDURE

1. Study the map in Figure 15.16.
2. In your notebook, list the communities that are affected by flooding.

DISCUSSION

1. What do you think were the main occupations of people living in the flooded communities in 1948?
2. Why do you think the communities are located where they are?
3. Suppose you worked for the local government in one of the flooded areas in 1948. Some years after the flood, a local resident applied for a permit to build a house on the floodplain. List arguments for why you would have (a) approved or (b) refused a permit.
4. Suggest what people could do to protect themselves and their houses and land from floods if they built on a floodplain.
5. Using your knowledge of erosion and deposition, what do you think is the most suitable use for the land in the Fraser River floodplain?
6. Discuss in your class how the use of the floodplain has changed since 1948. ❖

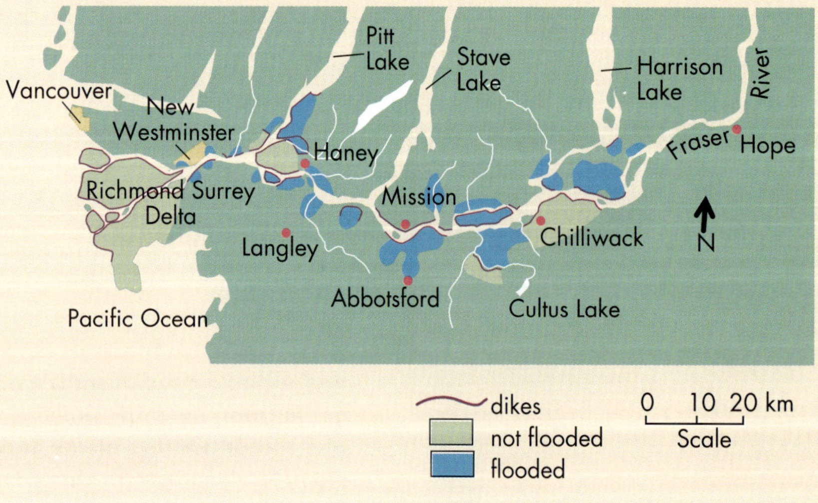

FIGURE 15.16 ◀ ***A map of the lower Fraser River valley showing the land that was flooded during the 1948 flood***

DELTAS

What happens when a river runs into a lake or sea? It is here that the flow of water suddenly slows down. As a result, much of the sediment in the water is deposited on the bottom of the lake or sea. As the sediment builds up, it causes the river to fan out over a broad area, often shaped like a giant triangle (Figure 15.17). These areas are called **deltas**, named after the shape of the Greek letter *delta* (Δ). At a delta, the river often breaks into a number of smaller channels, separated by islands of sediment. As time goes by, a large river extends its delta farther and farther out into the ocean.

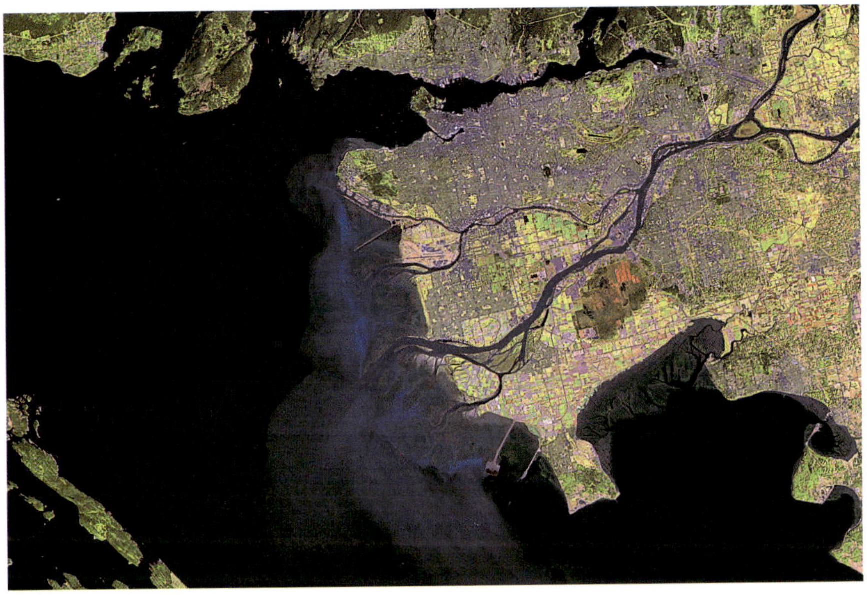

FIGURE 15.17
This satellite photograph shows the Fraser River delta in southern B.C. What do you think is causing the wispy blue colour around the delta?

DID YOU KNOW

■ The huge Mississippi River dumps over 500 million tonnes of sediment onto its delta every year. Over millions of years, the river has built up deposits as much as 9 km deep. Much of the state of Louisiana is built on sediment deposited by the Mississippi.

EXTENSION

■ Select a major river from this list: Nile, Mississippi, Rhine, Yangtze, Murray, Ganges, and Paraná. Conduct library research: (a) Find out how the use of the floodplain has changed over the centuries. (b) Make a poster to present your findings to the class. (c) Pretend that no one lives on the floodplain today. What do you think would be the best use for it?

LANDSCAPES SHAPED BY WIND

A blowing wind or air current is like a river of air. Like a river, an air current can carry particles of rock material with it. The size of particles that can be moved depends on the speed of the wind. Hurricanes, which blow at speeds over 120 km/h, can even move boulders through the air! Usually, however, the wind erodes small particles such as dust and fine sand, and leaves larger particles behind (Figure 15.18).

Wind erosion is most common in dry climates and in flat, open areas. During the 1930s, wind erosion became a tremendous problem on the North American prairies. Farmers had ploughed up huge areas of grassland to grow crops of grain. But after a crop of grain was harvested, bare soil was left exposed to the wind. In years with little rainfall, the soil dried out. Loose particles were carried through the air

DID YOU KNOW

■ Ten thousand years ago, the end of the Fraser River delta was in the New Westminster area, 30 km east of where it is today.

FIGURE 15.18
This severe dust storm in southern Alberta moved many tonnes of topsoil. What kind of damage could such a storm do to the soil layers? (You may want to refer to Figure 15.10.)

with every gust of wind. Fine dust rose high into the air. The dust was sometimes blown thousands of kilometres away. During the worst years of the dust storms, dust from the North American prairies could be seen in the skies halfway across the Atlantic Ocean.

Particles in the air are deposited when the wind speed drops. On some beaches and deserts, winds pick up and deposit dry, loose sand to form regular piles of sand, or **dunes** (Figure 15.19). If the wind usually blows from one direction, dunes may move slowly across the landscape. The wind rolls the sand grains up the side of the dune (Figure 15.20). As the grains go over the top of the dune they drop down the sheltered side to the bottom of the dune. The dune keeps its general shape, but creeps slowly overland in the direction of the wind.

FIGURE 15.19
Sand dunes are formed by the wind on deserts and beaches.

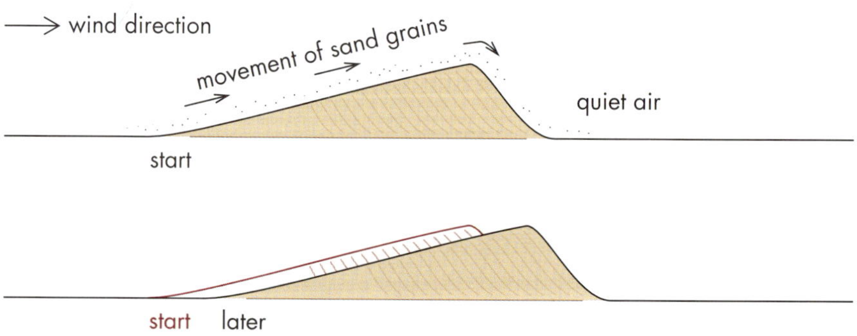

FIGURE 15.20
How dunes move

ACTIVITY 15H / WIND AT WORK

In this activity, you will consider the effect of wind erosion on different landscapes.

PROCEDURE

Examine the photographs in Figure 15.21.

DISCUSSION

1. Which beach do you think could be most easily eroded by wind? Why?
2. How could heavy rainfall affect wind erosion of the beach in your answer to question 1? Explain.
3. What reduces the wind erosion on the other two beaches?
4. Using your knowledge of sand dunes, suggest how the snowdrift in Figure 15.21d was formed. In which direction is the wind most likely blowing?
5. Think of an area in your neighbourhood where wind erosion might occur. Describe the area and explain why you chose it. ❖

FIGURE 15.21
Three kinds of beaches: (a) pebble, (b) sand, and (c) sand dunes with grass, and (d) a snowdrift

(a) Large pebble

(b) Fine sand

(c) Sand with vegetation

(d) Snowdrift

► REVIEW 15.2

1. Define erosion.
2. What is the difference between erosion and weathering?
3. Name three causes of erosion. Choose one of them and explain how it produces a particular change in the landscape.
4. Choose an example of weathering or erosion. Explain how your example affects human activities.
5. The map in Figure 15.16 shows the location of dikes along the Fraser River. Find out how dikes are built and describe why they are used.
6. How do you suppose Delta, B.C., got its name? Explain.

■ 15.3 GLACIATION AND THE LANDSCAPE

In the far north and south of our planet, and on high mountain peaks, there are regions so cold that much of the snow never melts. Every winter, new snow falls on top of snow that remains from previous years. As the piles of snow become deeper, the enormous weight of the snow on top gradually changes the lower layers into ice. After a long time, the growing mass of snow and ice causes the bottom of the ice to bulge and spread, the way pancake batter spreads over a pan when you pour more batter on top (Figure 15.22). These thick, slow-moving sheets of ice are called **glaciers** (Figure 15.23).

FIGURE 15.22
Like pancake batter, glaciers spread outward because of the increasing mass in the middle.

Along with running water and moving air, glaciers are an important cause of erosion. The largest glaciers in the world today are called **ice sheets**. They are thick, dome-shaped sheets of ice that cover most of

FIGURE 15.23
Glaciers are found only on high mountain ranges and in the polar regions. Here the Athabasca Glacier flows out of the Columbia Icefield on the British Columbia-Alberta border.

Greenland and Antarctica. In Greenland, ice covers all the land except a narrow strip around the coast. The Antarctic ice sheet is half the size of Canada and is over 4 km thick at its centre. It contains 90 per cent of all the ice in the world today. Even so, there are rocky areas and a few volcanoes on the edge of Antarctica, and some high mountain ranges poke through the ice sheet.

Hundreds of smaller glaciers are found in mountainous valleys around the world, including Canada. They are known as **alpine** (or mountain) **glaciers**. They begin in the permanent snowfields that build up on the tops of high mountains. When the layers of snow and ice reach a certain thickness, gravity causes the glacier to move slowly into valleys that lead down the mountainside (Figure 15.24). Alpine glaciers form "rivers" of blue-green ice up to 300 metres thick. They are usually a few kilometres wide, and may be up to 120 km long. The best known glaciers in western Canada are found in the Columbia Icefield on the British Columbia-Alberta border.

DID YOU KNOW

■ Glaciers normally move very slowly, at speeds of a few metres per year. Under certain conditions, however, they may flow much more quickly. The Steele Glacier, one of several fast-moving glaciers in the St. Elias Mountains of British Columbia and Yukon, once moved almost 10 km in a single year. It was nicknamed "the galloping glacier."

FIGURE 15.24
How glaciers are formed in a mountainous region

Snow builds up year after year. The bottom layer turns to ice.

As snow is added at the top, the ice below begins to spread out and flow downhill. Gravity pulls the glacier downhill.

Smaller mountain glaciers move downhill and join to form larger valley glaciers.

GLACIERS ADVANCE AND RETREAT

When glacier ice builds up faster than it melts away, the glacier slowly creeps down a valley. The glacier is said to move forward, or **advance**. Eventually, the glacier advances to a region where the climate is warmer and snow may melt faster. If the rate of melting is the same as the rate at which the ice builds up, the glacier will stop advancing at this point (Figure 15.25). Suppose that after a few years the climate gets cooler. The snow and ice build up faster than they melt, and the glacier will once again advance. Now suppose that temperatures get warmer. This will increase the amount of melting, and the glacier will shrink back or **retreat**.

FIGURE 15.25
How glaciers advance and retreat

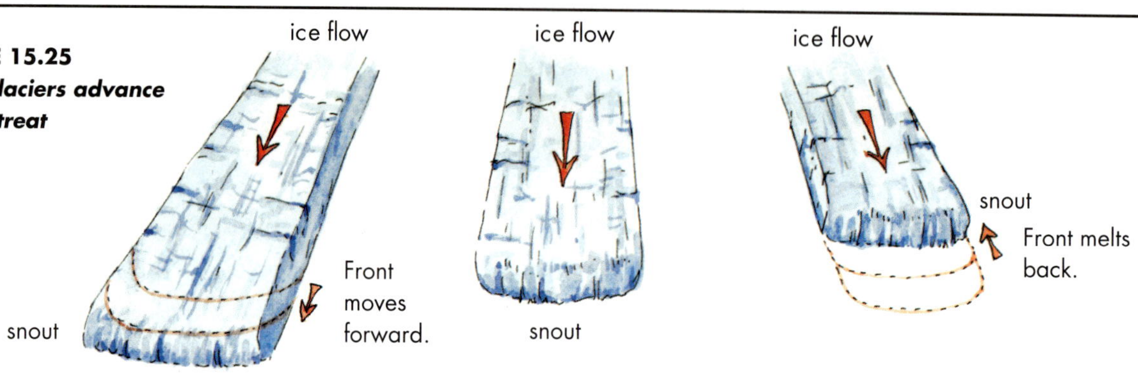

ADVANCE ***If rate of melt is slower than rate of accumulation, then glacier advances (gets larger).***

STATIONARY ***If rate of melt is equal to rate of accumulation, then glacier remains stationary (stays the same size).***

RETREAT ***If rate of melt is faster than rate of accumulation, then glacier retreats (gets smaller).***

ACTIVITY 15I / THE GREAT "ICE-SCAPE" (TEACHER DEMONSTRATION)

In this activity, you will observe what happens to rock fragments in ice as the ice melts. From your observations, you will predict what effect glaciers might have on the landscape.

MATERIALS

safety goggles
apron
loaf pan or similar-size container
sand
gravel
large pebbles
water
stream table
hair dryer

PROCEDURE

1. Put on your safety goggles and apron.
2. The loaf pan is to be filled with a mixture of sand, gravel, and pebbles. Water is added to cover the rock fragments (Figure 15.26). Then the container is placed in a freezer until the water has frozen.
3. Your teacher will set up the stream table with a layer of sand 3 to 4 cm deep (see Activity 15F). The table must have a steep slope.
4. An ice block is placed in the sand at the top of the slope.
5. Your teacher will use the hair dryer to speed up the melting of the ice. Observe and record what happens to the sand around the ice block as the ice melts.
6. Observe and record what happens to the rock materials embedded in the ice.

DISCUSSION

FIGURE 15.26 ▶
Making a "glacier"

1. What effect did water flowing from the melting ice have on the sand in the stream table?
2. What happened to each size of rock fragment in the ice as the ice melted?
3. Imagine an alpine glacier with large boulders and gravel frozen into it. What features in the landscape might be made if the glacier moves 10 km down a valley and then melts? Describe features made by
(a) the glacier ice,
(b) the rock embedded in the moving ice,
(c) the rock fragments after the ice melts,
(d) the water after the ice melts. ❖

THE PUZZLE OF THE BOULDERS

Until the 1830s, people thought that glaciers could exist only in the regions where they were found at that time. In 1837, a young Swiss scientist named Louis Agassiz was puzzled by some of the features he saw while hiking in the mountains in Europe. Agassiz and his friends noticed rock that was polished smooth, but marked by deep grooves. They saw valleys with rounded U-shapes. There were hills made of piled-up gravel. In places, they found huge boulders made of rock that was different from the rock in the surrounding area (Figure 15.27).

FIGURE 15.27
How did these giant boulders come to be standing among rocks of a different type?

Agassiz climbed higher to study alpine glaciers. He saw large deposits of gravel in the high valleys. He thought that the glaciers had advanced and then retreated, leaving the gravel behind. When he compared the features he saw in the high valleys with the features in the valleys far below the glaciers, he had no doubts. He came to the amazing conclusion that thick ice sheets had once filled the quiet green valleys of central Europe!

Over 150 years have passed since Agassiz shocked the scientific world with his discoveries. During that time, studies of landscapes around the world have shown that ice sheets and glaciers have advanced and retreated across much of Europe and North America — not just once, but several times in the past. During these times, ice sheets covered almost all of Canada, including British Columbia (Figure 15.28). The periods when ice sheets and glaciers covered large areas of Europe and North America are known as **ice ages**.

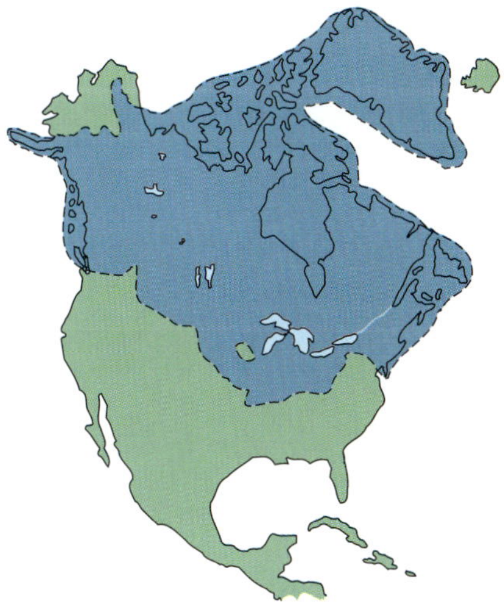

FIGURE 15.28
The blue shaded area on the map shows where ice sheets and glaciers covered the land during the last ice age, about 18 000 years ago. The glaciers left evidence that you can see today in the rocks and landscape of these areas.

CANADA'S ARCTIC ICE ISLAND

Imagine yourself in Canada's Arctic, where huge glaciers still cover the land as they covered most of Canada during the ice ages. In 1982, a billion-tonne slab of ice broke off from Canada's most northerly land — Ellesmere Island. It started floating southwest, a gigantic 8 km x 4 km ice island, as tall as a 14-storey building (although most of it was under water).

This was the home of Canada's Ice Island Research Station. The Canadian government built huts, scientific laboratories, radio communications centres, and a runway for aircraft on the island.

The ice island made an ideal research base because it moved around for free. Normally it is expensive to move a camp and scientific equipment from place to place. The island also plowed through ice-clogged seas to places that you cannot reach even with an ice-breaker.

Yet there are problems with working on a drifting slab of ice. One challenge is to know exactly where you are. Satellites and computers helped pinpoint the island's location. Its route depended on tides, winds, and ocean currents. "Unfortunately, we can't stick a sail or a motor on the island and drive it," said Bonni Hrycyk, Acting Director of the Polar Continental Shelf Project.

The weather is another challenge. Blizzards covered the buildings with snowdrifts. Mechanics had to repair helicopters at −45°C. Scientists packed hot water bottles around important equipment that should not get too cold.

The scientists are drilling a hole through the ice.

When summer arrived, the ice started to melt. There were puddles everywhere, and the buildings were surrounded by long moats of water. The runway melted.

Despite the tough living conditions, scientists working on the ice island gathered valuable information about the geology of the Arctic. They drilled holes through the ice and set off explosives, recording the sound waves that bounced off the ocean floor. They dropped heavy equipment 430 metres to the sea floor, and brought back samples of mud. They learned about the sea floor — the type of rock there, the structure of the layers, and the possibility of oil or gas deposits. As the ice island drifted, they had new areas to explore.

Scientists were hoping the ice island would circle around the Arctic Ocean for decades. They were disappointed when, in 1990, the island took a wrong turn down a channel and started heading inland. In spring 1992, the ice island unexpectedly began to break up. Huge icebergs were all that were left, and scientists had to abandon the ice island.

Some scientists think that the ice island was a place of incredible beauty, and they loved working there. Others found it uncomfortable and isolated. How do you think you would feel about working on an ice island?

The journey of Canada's Ice Island

ACTIVITY 15J / FINDING OUT ABOUT THE ICE AGE

In the next sections, you will learn about many of the features in the landscape caused by glaciers. You can see these features as you travel around British Columbia, other parts of Canada, and other places in the world. As you read the sections, think about the answers to the following questions:

What features are produced by glaciers in the mountains?

What features are produced by glaciers on the coast?

What features produced by glaciers do you see where you live? ❖

EFFECTS OF ICE SHEETS AND GLACIERS ON THE LANDSCAPE

Evidence indicates that the last ice age ended in most parts of Canada about 10 000 years ago. However, the effects of this past can still be seen on the landscape in many areas today. As rivers of ice moved down mountainsides, they deepened and widened their valleys. Sharp ridges of rock were worn away by the moving ice sheets, and the sides and floors of the valleys were dug out and eroded, forming **U-shaped valleys** with smooth, rounded bottoms and steep sides (Figure 15.29).

FIGURE 15.29 ▶
A glacier once moved along this valley in northern B.C., eroding the sides and bottom, leaving a U-shaped profile. How does this valley compare with the valley in Figure 15.13 and the canyon in Figure 15.11?

FIGURE 15.30
These scratch marks (striations) in the rock were carved by rock fragments carried in a glacier. The scratches indicate the direction of the glacier's movement.

Like rivers, glaciers pick up and carry loose rock material in their path. When sand and gravel are frozen in ice at the bottom of a glacier, they rub over the bare rock beneath the glacier. This rubbing produces a smooth, polished surface, as if the rock had been rubbed by a giant with a huge piece of sandpaper. In places, chunks of hard rock frozen in the edge of the moving glacier can scratch deep grooves if there is softer rock beneath. The long, parallel scratches left behind are called **striations** (Figure 15.30). In British Columbia, look for them especially on hillsides of igneous rock.

Along some coastlines, U-shaped valleys that were eroded by glaciers became filled with sea water after the glaciers retreated. The results are long, narrow inlets of the sea called **fiords** (Figure 15.31). Because glaciers often erode deep valleys, many fiords are hundreds of metres deep. The scoured sides of the glaciated valley give fiords spectacular walls that rise steeply far above the water. Howe Sound and Knight Inlet are examples of the many fiords found along the coastline of British Columbia.

FIGURE 15.31 ◀
A B.C. fiord, created by a retreating glacier.

GLACIAL DEPOSITS

When a glacier melts, it leaves behind the rock debris that was frozen in it. A large pile of mixed rock debris left by a melting glacier is called a **moraine**. Melting occurs most rapidly at the lowest end of a glacier, where the climate is warmer. The result is that rock debris is left piled up across a valley where the end of the glacier used to be. A moraine such as this marks the farthest point that the glacier had reached (Figure 15.32). Other moraines are left along the sides of the retreating glacier .

FIGURE 15.32
This moraine was deposited by an alpine glacier. Where do you think the rocks came from?

Individual boulders left behind by melting glaciers are called **erratics**. They have this name because they often seem out of place. (*Erro* is a Latin word, meaning "stray.") For example, you might find a granite boulder the size of a garage, sitting in a farmer's field far from any granite bedrock. The answer to the puzzle of such huge boulders is now clear (Figure 15.27). These boulders were picked up from their original site as a glacier moved over them. They were later deposited as erratics many kilometres away when the glacier melted. Mineral deposits have been located by tracing erratics containing ore minerals to their source many kilometres away.

DID YOU KNOW

■ In hot, dry parts of the world, such as Saudi Arabia and parts of California, people have proposed to supply water by towing giant icebergs from Antarctica. What do you think of this idea?

EFFECTS OF GLACIERS ON HUMAN ACTIVITIES

Moving glaciers during the past ice ages produced features of the landscape that are important to our lives today. When you drive on a road or travel by train, you can thank the glaciers. The sand and gravel used in road and rail construction are taken from huge deposits (glacial deposits) left when the ice melted (Figure 15.33).

Much of our farmland, too, was formed by glaciers. The rich soils were laid down when flowing water from the melting ice sheets picked up fine clay and silt particles from glacial deposits, then redeposited them over large areas farther south. These materials form gently rolling landscapes that produce ideal farmland.

On the prairies, the distant alpine glaciers of the Rocky Mountains are still very important to farmers. Some of the glacier ice melts every summer, supplying fresh water for the rivers during periods when there is little rain. Much of the water used for irrigation comes from melting glacier ice.

Fiords provide deepwater fishing close to the coast, as well as sheltered harbours for large ships. Fiords are also important tourist attractions on scenic cruises along the coasts of British Columbia and Alaska.

FIGURE 15.33 ▶ ***Huge deposits of sand and gravel were left by melting glaciers. This gravel pit is located near Coquitlam, B.C. What do people use these deposits for now?***

▶ REVIEW 15.3

1. What are the differences between an ice sheet and an alpine glacier?
2. Using sketches, explain how glaciers advance and retreat.
3. Give three examples of ways that glacial erosion (erosion due to the action of glaciers) affects human activities today.

4. On a camping trip, a friend tells you that the area you are in was once covered by glaciers. Name three bits of evidence that might have led your friend to this conclusion.

5. There are highways near the Pacific Ocean all the way from Mexico to Squamish. Why is there no coastal highway from Squamish to Prince Rupert?

6. Suggest one way that the huge "white rock" on the ocean beach at White Rock, B.C., could have arrived there.

CHAPTER REVIEW

KEY IDEAS

- Rock is broken down into small fragments or pieces by the process of weathering.
- Weathering of material on the Earth's surface can occur by mechanical, chemical, or biological means.
- The results of weathering include the production of soil from small fragments of weathered rock and the formation of caves.
- Air pollution has increased the rate of chemical weathering of natural formations and structures made by humans.
- Weathered materials are moved from one place to another by erosion. When the weathered material stops moving and settles on the Earth's surface, it forms a deposit.
- The main causes of erosion are gravity, flowing water, wind, and moving ice sheets and glaciers.
- Erosion and deposition slowly change the landscape over time, producing features such as valleys, deltas, dunes, fiords, moraines, and erratics.
- Weathering and erosion have shaped the landscapes we see today, affecting many human activities such as construction, farming, fishing, and tourism.

VOCABULARY

weathering
landscape
surface area
mechanical weathering
ice wedging
chemical weathering
acid rain
biological weathering
humus
erosion
deposition
deposit
V-shaped valley
floodplain
dike
delta
dune
glacier
ice sheet
alpine glacier
advance
retreat
ice age
U-shaped valley
striation
fiord
moraine
erratic

V1. Construct a mind map using the words in the vocabulary list.

V2. Prepare a geology quiz by writing down five questions that you can answer by using a term in the vocabulary list. Swap your quiz with a partner, then answer your partner's questions.

CONNECTIONS

C1. Why is mechanical weathering more likely to occur in winter?

C2. Describe how caves are formed by chemical weathering.

C3. How does pollution affect weathering? Give an example.

C4. Explain what is meant by biological weathering, using an anthill, a tree root, or an animal burrow as an example.

C5. "Without weathering we could not grow food, because without weathering there would be no soil." Do you agree or disagree with this statement? Give reasons.

C6. "Weathering must take place before erosion can occur." Is this statement true? Use examples to support your answer.

C7. Describe two different ways that people affect erosion. Use examples from your local area if possible.

C8. Suppose you were travelling in the mountains near Cranbrook, Kamloops, or Telegraph Creek, B.C. How would you tell the difference between a valley eroded by a river and a valley eroded by a glacier?

C9. List and describe three pieces of evidence that you could observe to help you decide if an area had once been covered by glaciers.

C10. What human activities in your local area are affected by one or more of the processes of weathering and erosion described in this chapter? How does the process affect the human activity?

EXPLORATIONS

E1. Some deposits of gold in British Columbia are called "placer" deposits.
- (a) Find out how these deposits were produced.
- (b) Explain how an understanding of weathering and erosion might help you to find gold in these regions.
- (c) Find out how people pan for gold. Make a poster to present your findings to the class.

E2. Figure 15.34 shows the imprint of an astronaut's boot on the surface of the moon.
- (a) Use your knowledge of weathering and erosion to explain why you think this imprint might still be visible a hundred years from now.
- (b) Would a similar footprint on Earth last as long?
- (c) Do you think a similar footprint on Mars would last as long?

FIGURE 15.34
Footprint on the moon

E3. Investigate the cost to the provincial highway department of weathering and erosion on the highway from Vancouver to Whistler, B.C. You might want to consider landslides, flooding, frost damage, and gully erosion.

E4. Who should be responsible for the damage to buildings caused by flooding on a floodplain, as in the Chilliwack River flood in 1990? Would it be the responsibility of the building owners or the government? Debate this question in your class.

E5. Boats are exposed to air, water, and chemicals. Talk to boat owners or do library research to find out what effects weathering has on boats. What can boat builders and boat owners do to reduce these effects?

E6. With a partner, examine a map of the British Columbia coastline in your school atlas. Now take turns using the atlas. One person is to look at the maps of the northern hemisphere; the other will examine maps of the southern hemisphere.
- (a) List the regions where you think fiords are located. (Hint: Look at islands too.) Give reasons for your answer.
- (b) List the places where you think there will be fiords in the future. Give reasons for your answer.

REFLECTIONS

R1. Do you think today's weather might have an effect on your grandchildren?

R2. What kinds of weathering and erosion do you think occur on the other planets of the solar system?

CHAPTER 16

LIFE ON A CHANGING EARTH

Have you ever gone through your family photographs looking for pictures of yourself? In recent photos, you may look much the same as you do now. In photos taken a year or two ago, you probably look different. In photos taken several years ago, you may look so different that you hardly recognize yourself. The evidence in the photos shows how much you have changed over the years. But these changes happen so slowly that you do not notice them from one day to the next. In this chapter, you will investigate changes that occur even more slowly. They take place so gradually that you may not even notice them within your lifetime.

You might already have discovered an example of very slow change in Chapter 15. That chapter describes how a river continually erodes a valley. You can see the evidence of erosion in the mud carried along by the water. But you may not notice the valley getting wider or deeper. Changes such as this take hundreds or thousands of years. It is hard to believe that things like valleys and mountains are actually changing — until you examine the evidence in the rocks.

In this chapter, you will explore how living things such as animals and plants can also change over time. You will examine evidence that many forms of living things on Earth in the past were different from those you can see today. These changes in life forms have occurred on Earth in the past, and still continue today. You will learn how these slow changes have been recorded.

ACTIVITY 16A / MAKING TIME

How do you know that time goes by? The only way we know that time passes is by measuring changes in something. Some changes are rapid. You can measure them in seconds or minutes. Other changes take years. In your learning journal, list as many things as you can that change with time. When you have at least 10 things, combine your list with those of your classmates to produce a class list. Classify the class list into categories, or groups. Give each category a name. For each category, tell what units of time are required for change to occur. How might you measure time in units of (a) hours? (b) a thousand years? ❖

16.1 FOSSILS: LINKS WITH THE PAST

When a large new building is being constructed, people sometimes bury a sealed container, called a time capsule, in the foundation. The time capsule contains newspapers, photographs, coins, and other objects. Each

FIGURE 16.1
(a) Fossil fish from Green River, Wyoming. (b) Ammonites were floating sea shells. They no longer live on the Earth. These three specimens were found on Vancouver Island and the Gulf Islands, an area well known for its ammonite fossils. Is there a rocky area near your school where your class could look for fossils?

object will give information to people who may dig up the capsule in the future, long after the building has fallen into ruins. In a similar way, the fossils found in some rocks are like natural time capsules (Figure 16.1).

Fossils are the remains or evidence of living things from the past, including plants and animals. Fossils are clues to the history of life on Earth. By studying fossils, you can also learn about the environment on the Earth at the time the **organisms** (or living things) died. For example, you can tell if the climate in the past was warmer or colder, or wetter or drier than today. Scientists use fossils to find out how organisms have changed, and where different organisms once lived. Scientists can also use fossils to learn about the behaviour of organisms that lived hundreds of millions of years ago.

HOW FOSSILS ARE FORMED

Fossils are found in sedimentary rocks all over the world. But fossils represent only a tiny fraction of all the organisms that have ever lived. That is because very special conditions are needed before an organism can be preserved as a fossil. To become a fossil, an organism must be buried quickly, before it decays or is eaten. For this reason, the most common fossils are of organisms that lived in or near water. When they died, the organisms quickly sank into soft mud or sand, and were soon covered by more sediment.

After an organism has been buried, the next stage begins. If an organism is to be preserved as a fossil, the chemical conditions in its surroundings are important. Also, the organism must be buried and left undisturbed for a long enough time to change into a fossil. There are three main ways that fossils are formed. They are: preserved original materials, molds, and replacement fossils.

FOSSILS AS ORIGINAL MATERIALS

Most fossils are the preserved, or slightly altered, hard parts of the actual organism, such as teeth, bones, and shells. Soft parts of the body quickly break down, and are preserved only in very rare situations. (See Other Kinds of Fossils.) By piecing together a number of fossil bones, scientists can reconstruct an animal's skeleton. From the skeleton, they can infer what the living animal probably looked like.

FOSSILS AS MOLDS

Millions of years ago, a living dinosaur walked across some mud or wet sand and left a footprint. The footprint then became buried under more mud and sand. After a long time, the sediment hardened into rock, preserving the shape of the footprint. The result is a type of fossil called a **mold** (Figure 16.2).

Figure 16.2
Millions of years ago, a dinosaur walked over an area of mud. Then the mud hardened and was covered by sediment. These footprints were preserved as fossils.

A mold may also be formed after an organism dies and is buried in sediment. When the organism decomposes, it leaves a hollow space in the sediment the same shape as the organism. In this way, molds can preserve the outline of soft organisms such as worms, which do not have hard parts that can be preserved as original materials. Molds usually show an organism's outside appearance, but not what is inside its body.

Sometimes, sediment fills a mold and later hardens into rock. This produces a fossil replica that shows the shape of the structure that produced the mold.

ACTIVITY 16B / MAKING FOSSILS

CROSS • CURRICULAR

By making objects that look like fossils, you can answer the question: How are fossils formed in nature?

MATERIALS

safety goggles
plastic gloves
apron
dust masks
two shallow paper plates
mixing bowl
250 mL fine sand
125 mL cement
125 mL water
stirring rod or spoon
sugar cube
various hard objects, such as shells, coins, and keys
petroleum jelly
samples of fossils

CAUTION!

■ **Do not touch the cement powder with your bare hands. Cement contains lime, which can irritate your eyes and skin.**

PROCEDURE

1. Label the plates Plate 1 and Plate 2.
2. Put on your apron, dust mask, and gloves.
3. Pour the sand and cement into the mixing bowl (Figure 16.3).

FIGURE 16.3
Some of the steps to follow to make "fossils"

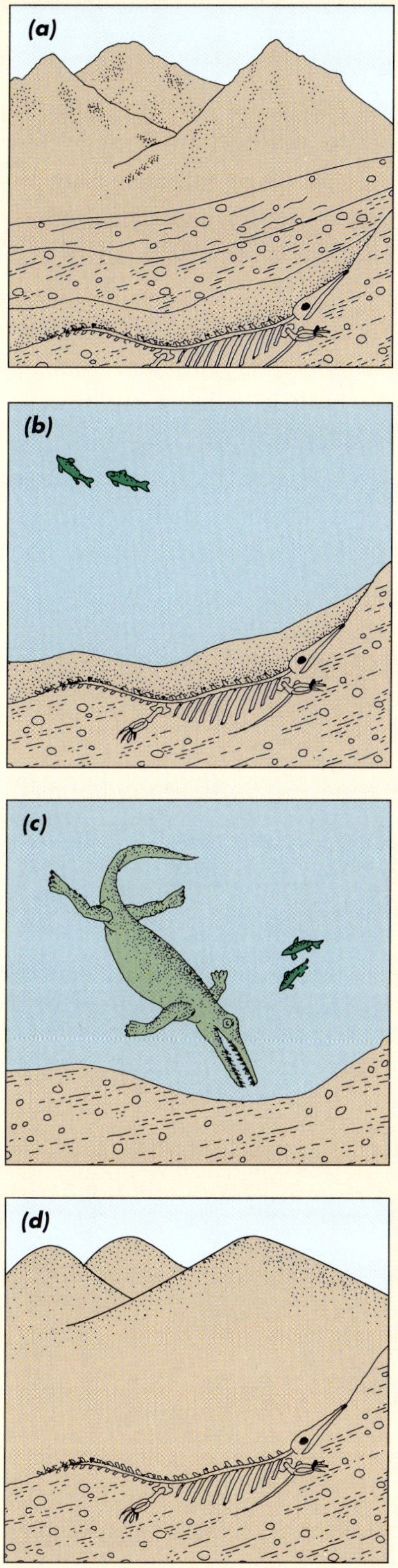

FIGURE 16.4
Illustrations for Discussion question 3

4. Slowly add water, stirring all the time, until you have a firm mixture.
5. Pour the mixture into both paper plates.
6. When the mixture begins to harden, push a sugar cube deep into the mixture in Plate 1, so that the cube is almost below the surface.
7. Lightly coat a small object, such as a shell or leaf, with petroleum jelly. Press the object into the surface of the mixture in Plate 2.
8. After the mixture in Plate 1 has hardened completely, dissolve the sugar cube by running hot water over it. Rinse out all the sugar. You are left only with a cement mold where the sugar cube used to be.
9. After the mixture in Plate 2 has hardened, remove the object you pressed into it. Use petroleum jelly to lightly coat the cement surface where the object was.
10. Prepare another mixture of sand, cement, and water. Pour some of this mixture into the mold in Plate 2 and leave it to harden.
11. Carefully remove the hardened object from the mold in Plate 2. You will have a cement copy of the original object.
12. Compare your manufactured "fossils" with the sample fossils provided by your teacher.

DISCUSSION

1. In your own words, describe what a mold is.
2. Describe how a mold fossil might form in nature.
3. Figure 16.4 shows four different stages in the formation of a fossil ichthyosaur. However, the four illustrations are not in the correct order.
   (a) Think about the sequence of events needed to form a fossil, then list the illustrations in that order.
   (b) Describe what each illustration shows.
4. Recall how each of the three families of rock are formed (Chapter 14). In which family of rock would you look for fossils? Explain your answer. ❖

REPLACEMENT FOSSILS

Parts of organisms such as bones, shells, and wood contain numerous small holes or pores. When organisms die and become buried, these pores may become filled with water and dissolved minerals from the surrounding sediment. After many years, the water may evaporate, or be forced out by the weight of more sediment on top. When this happens, the minerals stay behind in the pores. They form a hard, mineral framework throughout the remains of the organism. As parts of the plant or animal material dissolve or decompose bit by bit, they may also be replaced by minerals. The final result is called a **replacement fossil** because the organism has been completely replaced by minerals.

If the replacement mineral is a variety of quartz, the replacement fossil looks like a stone model of the original bone, shell, or piece of wood (Figure 16.5). These fossils are said to be **petrified fossils.** They may preserve very fine details of the original organism. There are also fossils made of carbon, like black charcoal or coal. The carbon is all that remains of the organic matter that was there. Fossil leaves and stems often occur in this form.

FIGURE 16.5 ▶ ***A petrified tree trunk lies exposed on the surface of the ground. What happened to this tree?***

DID YOU KNOW

■ One of the most important areas for fossils in the world is in Yoho National Park, on the eastern border of British Columbia. A small area of rock within the park, called the Burgess Shale, contains the fossils of soft-bodied animals buried by mud 530 million years ago. Some of the animals are unlike any in the world today, and have been found nowhere else.

OTHER KINDS OF FOSSILS

Fossils made of rock are not the only remains of organisms we have from the past. A few organisms have been preserved almost unchanged, like dill pickles in a jar, or like berries frozen in your freezer. This happens when organisms are trapped and preserved in a material that does not allow them to dissolve, decay, or turn to stone. For example, there is an area near downtown Los Angeles where prehistoric animals once became stuck in pools of natural tar (tar pits). The bones of these animals have been dug up after thousands of years, and are still made of the same materials found in the once-living animals. Similarly, insects trapped in the resin (sticky sap) from certain trees are completely preserved when the resin hardens and later becomes a transparent fossil material called **amber** (Figure 16.6).

FIGURE 16.6
This insect has been fossilized in amber.

Perhaps the most unusual fossils are those preserved in ice, such as the frozen mammoths discovered in Siberia and Alaska. Although the animals were buried in frozen soil more than 10 000 years ago, their skin and fur were in good condition, and undigested leaves were found in their stomachs. The flesh of these mammoths was also very well preserved. The explorers who first found a frozen mammoth fed some of the flesh to their sled dogs.

REVIEW 16.1

1. What is a fossil?
2. Name three different ways that fossils can be formed.
3. Would it be more difficult for you to find a fossil of a worm or a fossil of a snail? Explain your answer.
4. Why is it that only a very tiny percentage of organisms become fossils?
5. Why are fossils found in sedimentary rock but not in metamorphic rock? (Think about how the families of rock are formed.)

16.2 HISTORY IN STONE

Fossils show that many unfamiliar organisms once lived on Earth in the past. For example, the sea-living organisms called **ammonites** and **trilobites** are very common as fossils, but they do not live in the world today (Figures 16.1 and 16.7). Similarly, many places around the world contain the fossils of giant reptiles, or **dinosaurs**. These and other organisms that are no longer found anywhere on Earth are said to be **extinct**. But did trilobites and dinosaurs and other extinct organisms all live at the same time in the past? To answer this question, we must have a way of finding out the age of different fossils. You can do this from your knowledge of how sedimentary rock is formed.

FIGURE 16.7
Fossils such as this trilobite are valuable clues to the Earth's history. Most trilobites lived in the oceans some 300 to 500 million years ago.

Imagine a layer of sediment deposited by a river. Mixed among the sediments are the remains of dead animals and plants. Year by year, the dead organisms are covered by more layers of sediment. As time passes, other organisms are buried above the first ones. As this process continues, the layers of sediment and buried organisms pile up like a stack of old newspapers.

FIGURE 16.8
This formation is made of layers of sedimentary rock. If it contains fossils, where would the oldest ones be? Where would you find the newest fossils?

If you get a daily newspaper at home, you add another newspaper to the top of your pile every day. Where is the most recent newspaper in your pile? Where is the oldest? You could find out by sorting through the dates on each newspaper. But, unless someone has mixed the papers up, you already know that the most recent paper is on top of the pile and the oldest is at the bottom. Similarly, fossils found near the Earth's surface were probably formed more recently than those buried directly below them (Figure 16.8).

Recently formed fossils look similar to some organisms living today. For example, sabre-toothed tigers resemble the tigers of today. And woolly mammoths look like modern elephants. However, some of the older, more deeply buried fossils do not look much like any modern forms of life. From such clues, it is possible to piece together a history of life on Earth.

In the Grand Canyon, scientists can study a record of fossils going back several hundred million years (Figure 16.9). The fossils in the layers of sedimentary rock in the canyon walls are like a calendar in the rock. Reading from the bottom to the top, the fossils tell us about changes in life forms from the distant past to the present.

(a)

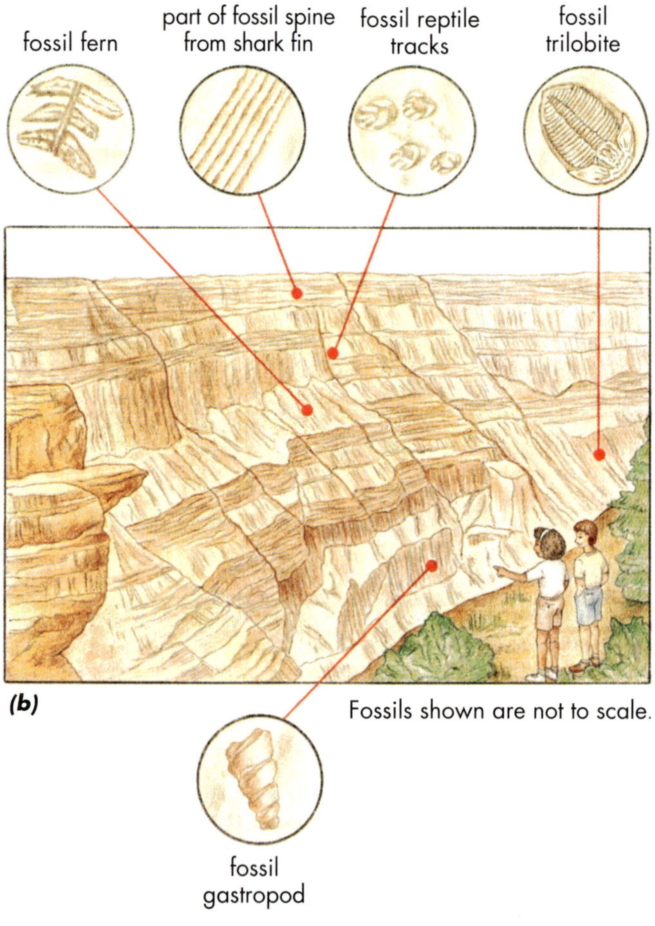

(b)

Fossils shown are not to scale.

FIGURE 16.9
Layers of rock (a) in the Grand Canyon hold fossils (b) of different organisms dating back more than 500 million years.

SCIENTIFIC ILLUSTRATOR

Vladimir Krb is a paleoartist (someone who draws illustrations of the past). He had this to say about his work.

Sometimes I wish I had a time machine. I could press a button and, pssssssschhhhhh, I would be back in the time of the dinosaurs. I would probably say, "Vladimir, how could you be so stupid! You got everything wrong!"

I paint pictures that show what the world might have been like 150 million years ago. I try to bring the past to life. Scientists are always finding new fossils, and discovering more about dinosaurs. That means I have more information and am less likely to make mistakes. Still, the window to the past is clouded.

When I was a boy in Czechoslovakia, I was fascinated by fossils. I imagined what these animals must have looked like long ago. I enjoyed both science and art, and I became an artist.

Canada has some of the best dinosaur fossils in the world. Much of my work has been done for the Royal Tyrrell Museum of Palaeontology in Alberta. I created the enormous, life-sized murals that hang in the museum.

I start a new dinosaur painting by reading everything ever published on that dinosaur. Then I see and touch as many bones as possible. I construct a scale model of the dinosaur in modelling clay, working out the shape of the skeleton and adding muscles where I think they might have been. I work closely with scientists to get as much accurate information as I can. Then I use my artistic imagination.

It's a bit like police work. When the police find a human skull, they can reconstruct a drawing of what the person probably looked like. They can do this because they've studied many human faces. We can't study real dinosaurs. So we sometimes make mistakes in the arrangement of the bones.

Scientists can suggest the texture of a dinosaur's skin by looking at fossils. I have to decide on the colour. I think most prehistoric animals blended in with their environments. Yet I suspect that some dinosaurs were more colourful than most pictures show.

When I paint, I also need to think about the landscape that the dinosaur lived in. What plants were growing there? Did it live in tropical forests or dry deserts? Also, what were the dinosaurs doing?

The painting must also tell a story, and be a work of art. I hope that my art excites people, especially children, and brings them to the world of science.

Picture a dinosaur in your mind. Where did you get your idea of what it would look like? How accurate is this dinosaur image likely to be?

Look carefully at Krb's illustration on this page. What things in the illustration are probably based on scientific information? What did he add to the painting from his artistic imagination?

MEASURING GEOLOGICAL TIME

Because the Earth is so old, geologists use a special time scale (or series of steps in time) to speak about events in the past. This **Geological Time Scale** is based on studies of fossils in sedimentary rock. It divides the history of the Earth into four large units called **eras** (Table 16.1). Unlike days or years, eras are not all the same length. Each era has a different name and different kinds of fossils. Using this scale, scientists can tell the age of a rock in any part of the world by the fossils it contains.

TABLE 16.1 ▶
Geological Time Scale

Era	Millions of years ago	Fossil record of major changes in life on Earth
Cenozoic Era	65 to present	First human-like fossils Increase in types of mammals Increase in flowering plants
Mesozoic Era	225 to 65	Dinosaurs increase, then disappear First flowering plants First birds and mammals
Paleozoic Era	570 to 225	First reptiles First large land animals (amphibians) Increase in types of fish First insects First large land plants First fish with jaws Numerous trilobites, shellfish, corals
Precambrian Era	4600 to 570	First soft-bodied animals First simple organisms (bacteria) Formation of the Earth

EXTENSION

■ Find out the origin of the words used to name each of the four eras in the Geological Time Scale. These meanings will help you remember the order of the eras.

The oldest era, named the **Precambrian Era**, stretches back to the origin of the Earth, about 4 600 000 000 (4.6 billion) years ago. Rock formed during this era has few fossils. Rock from the **Paleozoic Era** contains many more fossils, ranging from simple organisms such as sponges to the first amphibians, animals that could live both in water and on the land. Fossils of land plants, such as ferns, also first appeared during this era. The third era, the **Mesozoic Era**, is sometimes called the Age of Reptiles. Fossils of giant reptiles such as dinosaurs are buried in rocks of this era. The fourth era is called the **Cenozoic Era**, or "new life" era. We are living in this era. Fossils of ancient horses, elephants, and other familiar animals are found in these rocks. The most recently formed Cenozoic rocks hold the oldest fossils of prehistoric people and evidence of the last ice age.

WHAT IS "A LONG TIME"?

It is difficult to imagine the enormous periods of time that are measured on the Geological Time Scale (Table 16.1). The changes recorded by the fossils in each era took place over many millions of years. By comparison, a human lifetime is less than a hundred years. And the earliest cave paintings by prehistoric people were made about 30 000 years ago. To understand the difference between human history and the history of the Earth, it is helpful to make a model or chart showing these events on a single time scale.

ACTIVITY 16C / A MODEL OF GEOLOGICAL TIME

GROUP ACTIVITY

CROSS-CURRICULAR

In this activity, you will draw a time chart. You will compare the length of human history with the history of the dinosaurs and other events on Earth.

MATERIALS

5 m of adding machine tape
masking tape
tape measure or ruler
pen

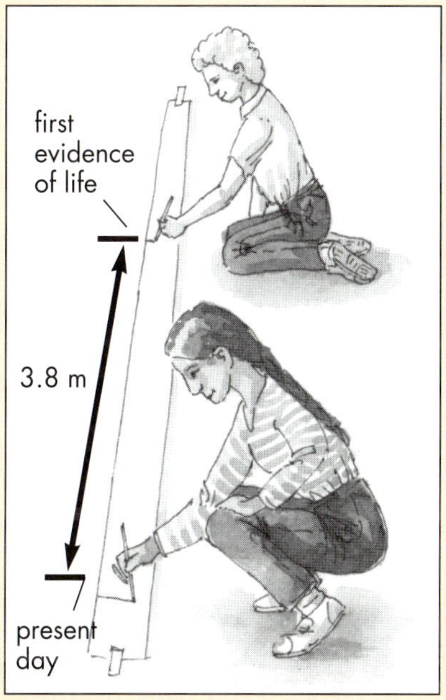

FIGURE 16.10
Making a time line

PROCEDURE

1. In your notebook, make two columns. Label one "Event A (B, C, etc.)" and the other "Distance along the paper tape."
2. Roll out 5 m of adding machine tape in a convenient place on the floor. Pull each end tight, and tape it down.
3. Draw a line at one end of the adding machine tape and label it "Present day."
4. Each metre on your tape is equal to 1 billion years of time. Using this scale, plot the information in Table 16.2 onto your tape. For example, draw a line 3.8 m from the line representing "Present day." Label this line "First evidence of life." The length 3.8 m represents 3800 million years. Your class may also want to research other important events in the Earth's history, including human history, and add them to your model.

Event	Number of years ago
A. Great pyramids of Egypt built	4 500
B. Last ice sheets cover most of Canada	11 000
C. Earliest humans	2 000 000
D. Extinction of dinosaurs	65 000 000
E. Earliest evidence of birds	150 000 000
F. Earliest evidence of mammals	190 000 000
G. First dinosaurs	225 000 000
H. First land animals	350 000 000
I. First land plants	430 000 000
J. Earliest fish	500 000 000
K. First fossils of many-celled organisms	700 000 000
L. First evidence of life	3 800 000 000
M. Formation of Earth's crust	4 600 000 000

TABLE 16.2 ***Events in the Earth's History***

EXTENSION

- Describe another way of illustrating and comparing the lengths of time of different events in the Earth's history.

DISCUSSION

1. Compare the length of time of human history with
   (a) the length of time that dinosaurs lived on Earth,
   (b) the age of the Earth.
2. What do you think is important about the comparisons in question 1?
3. (a) When did the first land plants appear on Earth?
   (b) When did the first land animals appear?
4. Do you think the events in question 3 could have happened in the reverse order? Explain your answer. ❖

► REVIEW 16.2

1. What are the large divisions of geological time called? Name each of them.
2. In terms of geological time, have humans been living on the Earth for
   (a) a fairly long time?
   (b) a fairly short time?
   (c) an extremely short time?
   Explain your answer.
3. "To dig down into the ground is to dig back in time." Explain the meaning of this phrase. (Hint: How are fossils formed in sedimentary rock?)
4. What evidence do we have that different types of organisms lived at different times in the past?
5. Using the first letter of each era, make up a phrase that will help you remember the names and order of the four eras in the Geological Time Scale.

■ 16.3 THE DIVERSITY OF LIFE

People who study fossils need an eye for detail and a good imagination. From pieces of skeleton, leaf, or shell that have changed into rock, they are able to reconstruct organisms that no one has ever seen alive. The study of fossils is called **paleontology**. Paleontologists do more than put the fossil bones of dinosaurs back together. They also use their observations to develop explanations — that is, they infer. From fossil remains, they may infer where different animals of the past lived, how they moved, what they ate, and many other details of their lives.

It is possible to infer what organisms of the past were like by comparing them with similar organisms living today. For example, you may never have seen the particular type of animal shown in Figure 16.12. However, you can infer from its fins and streamlined shape that it lives in water. The large, sharp teeth tell you that it is probably a meat-eater. The size of its eyes suggests that it might have good vision. These characteristics are examples of **adaptations**. All organisms have adaptations that allow them to live in a particular environment. Adaptations help organisms to survive in various ways — by helping them obtain food and energy, protect themselves, and reproduce.

DID YOU KNOW

■ Scientists have identified and named over 2 million different species of organisms living today, and another 250 000 have been found as fossils. Some scientists estimate there may be as many as 30 million living species of organisms not yet discovered. Most of them live in tropical forests.

FIGURE 16.11 ◀
Preparing a dinosaur bone for removal. Paleontologists study fossils to reconstruct the lives and environment of the animals that made them.

FIGURE 16.12 ◀
What clues in the appearance of this animal tell you about its environment and way of life?

ACTIVITY 16D / ADAPTATIONS FOR SURVIVAL

In this activity you will study some prehistoric organisms and re-create their lives.

1. Study the drawings of prehistoric organisms in Figure 16.13.
2. For each organism, list features that you think are adaptations.
3. Say how each item in your list might have helped the organism move, feed, or protect itself from enemies.
4. Describe the type of environment where each organism probably lived.

➡

EXTENSION

- Invent your own animal or plant. First, think of a particular environment. Then sketch an imaginary organism that might live in that environment. Add notes to your drawing to explain the adaptations that help your organism survive in its environment.

FIGURE 16.13
Prehistoric organisms

(a)

❖

VARIETY, PAST AND PRESENT

When you begin to study living things, the large variety of different species of organisms may seem confusing. A **species** is a number of similar organisms that can breed with one another to produce offspring (young). For example, a rabbit can breed with another rabbit, but not with a different species, such as a hare.

To help study them, you can sort or classify species into groups by using differences in their appearance. All species in each group will have characteristics in common. For example, scientists classify the species of plants that have needle-shaped leaves and cones into a group named conifers, or cone-producing trees. Fir, cedar, and pine are all examples of conifers. The thousands of different species of animals that have feathers, wings, and beaks are all classified as birds (Figure 16.14). A paleontologist who finds the fossil of an extinct animal that has feathers, wings, and a beak may therefore classify the animal as a bird (Figure 16.15).

FIGURE 16.15
From the fossil remains (a), scientists have reconstructed a prehistoric bird (b). The fossil bird is called Archaeopteryx, and was the same size as the modern crow. Judging by (b), do you think it could fly?

(a)

(b)

FIGURE 16.14
All these animals have feathers and are classified as birds. Do all of them fly?

EXTENSION

■ Study Figure 16.16. Describe any general patterns that you can see in the history of life on Earth. For example, has the overall variety of species increased or decreased? What other patterns can you discover?

Suppose you were to look at the fossils in different layers of rock — for example, in the Grand Canyon. You would find that the oldest rock near the bottom of the canyon has different fossils than rock near the top. This evidence suggests that different groups of organisms first appeared on Earth at different times. For example, rock that is 500 million years old may have fossils of fish, but no one has ever found fossils of reptiles or birds in rock that old (Table 16.2). Therefore, scientists infer that fish lived on Earth before reptiles or birds. Similarly, reptiles appeared on Earth before birds.

Fossils also show that the variety of species in each group of organisms has changed during the Earth's history. For example, there were more different species of reptiles alive in the past than there are today. On the other hand, few fossils of birds have been found. So, scientists infer that there were fewer species of birds living in the past than there are today.

Many organisms, such as sponges, first appeared millions of years ago and are still found today. Others, like the trilobites, are extinct. The changes over time in the variety of groups of organisms can be summarized on a chart (Figure 16.16).

ACTIVITY 16E / FIELD TRIPS TO THE PAST

Imagine that you have a time machine. You want to travel to the past to see and record what life was like in different eras. The data that you collect are displayed in a chart like that in Figure 16.16. Use this chart to answer the following questions. Now, set your time dial and fasten your safety belt. First stop — the Paleozoic Era.

STOP 1. Log Date: 450 million years ago

1. To study most of these organisms, which would be more useful: hiking boots or diving gear?
2. List the groups of organisms you observe that are now extinct.
3. List the groups of organisms that you can still see today.
4. Name the groups of organisms that have been on Earth for the longest time.

STOP 2. Log Date: 200 million years ago

5. Which era are you now in?
6. What new groups of organisms have appeared since your last stop in your time machine?
7. What adaptations might you observe on this stop that were not present on your last stop?
8. Which of the following trees might you see: flowering cherry, pine, fir, maple?
9. Are there more or fewer groups of organisms living now than on your last stop?

STOP 3. Log Date: 50 million years ago

10. Which era are you in now?
11. Which groups of organisms have become extinct since your last stop?
12. What new groups have appeared?
13. What new adaptations might you observe? ❖

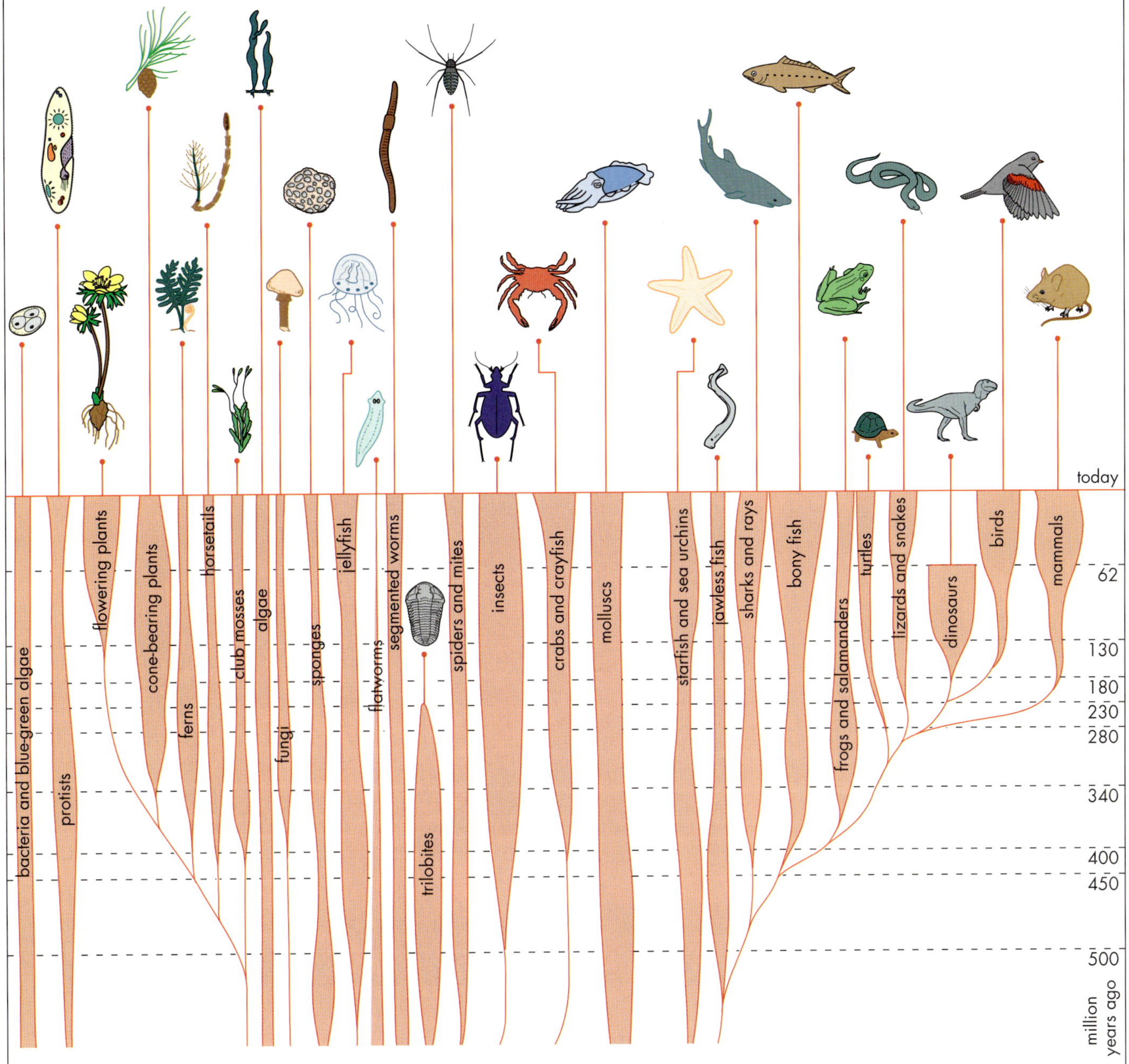

FIGURE 16.16

A chart such as this one allows you to compare the varieties of living things at different times in the past.

LIFE EXPANDS INTO NEW ENVIRONMENTS

Today, you can find organisms living in seas and lakes, in valleys and on mountaintops, and flying through the air. It was not always like that. The history of life shows that organisms with adaptations for living in these different environments first appeared on Earth in a particular order.

All the oldest known fossils are of organisms that lived only in water. Fossils of organisms that could live on land did not appear until much later — about 400 to 500 million years ago. The fossils of the earliest amphibians and land plants are found in rocks that used to be near the water's edge (Figure 16.17). Millions of years later, animals and plants had adaptations that prevented them from drying out. These adaptations allowed them to live far from water. Even later, species with wings appeared, such as flying insects, reptiles, birds, and bats. Wings are adaptations that allow these animals to travel through the air.

FIGURE 16.17
Toads and salamanders must live near water, because they lay their eggs in water or damp places. Are they fully adapted to living on land?

LIFE INCREASES IN DIVERSITY

Because the earliest forms of life lived in fewer different environments, there were fewer different species in the past than there are today. For example, all the earliest species lived only in the oceans, not on land. New adaptations allowed different organisms to survive in more places in the oceans, in lakes and rivers, and on the land. **Diversity** is this growth in the number of different species.

Organisms themselves also produced more environments. For example, before there was any plant life on land, there were no forests or animals that live in forests. After forests developed, the trees provided food and habitats for more species.

Human activities are rapidly decreasing the diversity of species on Earth today. People are destroying environments for organisms by polluting air and water, cutting and burning forests, damming rivers, draining swamps and marshes, and using more land for housing or farmland. These activities have caused many species to become extinct during this century, and many more are in danger of extinction.

LIFE CHANGES

A journey through time shows that life is always changing. Some groups of organisms have changed rapidly, whereas others have changed slowly. For example, some ants living today look much like the fossils of ants that lived 100 million years ago, when dinosaurs were walking the Earth. Some new species have appeared, and many other species have become extinct. Species that have become extinct have never reappeared.

LIFE INCREASES IN COMPLEXITY

Organisms with few different body parts, such as sponges, corals, and seaweeds, are considered to be simple organisms. Those with more different body parts, like insects, birds, and flowering plants, are called complex organisms. Complex organisms appeared later in the history of life than simple ones. The earliest forms of life, which lived in water, were all simple (Figure 16.18). Later, complex organisms such as fish appeared. New species with adaptations for living on land were more complex still.

EXTENSION

- Find out what species of animals or plants used to live in British Columbia, but were made extinct by people. Which human activities made them extinct? Which species of organisms in British Columbia are in danger of extinction today? Why?

FIGURE 16.18
The oldest fossils are of simple organisms, like these layered algae called stromatolites. They existed as far back as 3.5 billion years ago. This specimen is a polished cross-section.

HORSES THROUGH HISTORY

You have discovered that new species have appeared on Earth throughout the history of life. But how do new species develop? A well-known example will help you to understand. Paleontologists have found out the probable steps that led to the appearance of the horses we see today. They have done this by studying and comparing the fossils of many different horse-like animals that lived in the past (Figure 16.19).

One of the oldest horse-like animals lived about 55 million years ago. Its scientific name is *Hyracotherium* (hi-rack-o-thair-ee-um). It was about the size of a large dog and had four toes on each foot. During the time when *Hyracotherium* was alive, wet tropical forests covered much of the Earth. The animal's large feet were probably an adaptation that kept it from sinking into the soft ground. This small horse also had short teeth with bumpy surfaces. They would be suitable for grinding the leaves of the tropical plants.

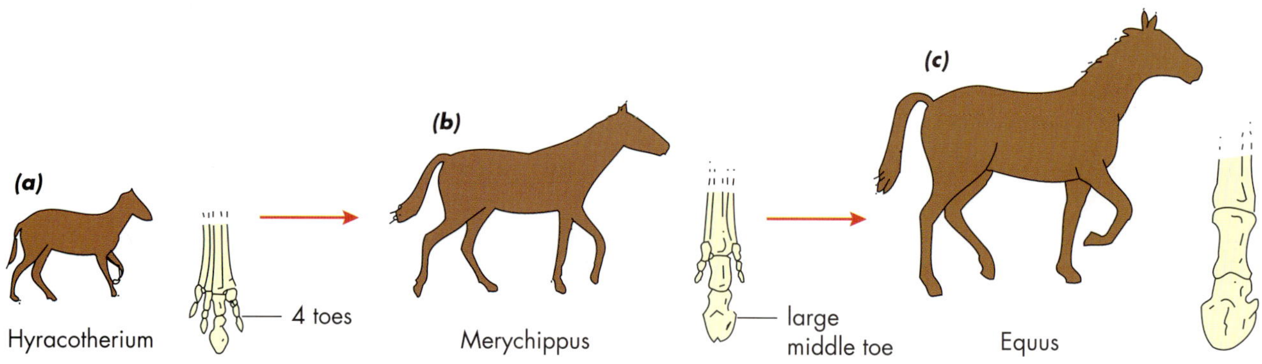

Figure 16.19
(a) **Hyracotherium** ***lived in forests about 55 million years ago. It stood only 30 cm tall.***
(b) **Merychippus** ***was a larger, swifter horse that lived on the prairie.***
(c) **Equus*****, the modern horse, first appeared about 4 million years ago. It has long legs for galloping.***

Over the next 20 million years, the climate on Earth grew drier. Scientists infer this from changes in the types of fossils in the sedimentary rocks. Many forests in North America died out. The forests were replaced by grasslands, which grow well in dry areas. *Hyracotherium* became extinct. In rocks from this period, scientists found fossils of larger horses, such as *Merychippus* (merry-chip-puss). *Merychippus* had longer legs, ending with a large central toe. This leg structure allowed it to run quickly over the hard, grass-covered plains. *Merychippus* also had bigger teeth, suitable for chewing coarse grasses. The change in the teeth produced a change in the shape of the head.

By 4 million years ago, *Merychippus* had become extinct. Fossils of a modern type of horse, named *Equus* (ek-wus) first appear in the sedimentary rocks from that time. *Equus* had only one large toe, or hoof, on each foot and looked like a large pony. It also had large teeth, adapted for grinding and chewing grass. The horses, donkeys, and zebras living today developed from *Equus*.

The fossils of these horses show changes that occurred in their feet, teeth, and size during the past 55 million years. The changes were probably adaptations to a changing environment. Gradually, *Hyracotherium* changed into a number of different, though similar, species. The process by which a new species develops from an earlier species is called **evolution**. One species is said to evolve into another. You will discover more evidence for evolution in the next section.

► REVIEW 16.3

1. What is meant by the term "extinct"?
2. Name two groups of animals that are extinct.
3. Give two examples each of adaptations for
   (a) feeding,
   (b) movement,
   (c) protection.
4. Describe the environment in which the earliest forms of life probably lived.
5. Name two adaptations that allowed later forms of life to live in different environments.
6. Describe three differences between horses that lived 55 million years ago and horses that live today.
7. How is each difference in the horses in question 6 related to a different environment?

16.4 HOW ORGANISMS CHANGE OVER TIME

In the last chapter, you learned that rocks and even entire landscapes have been slowly changed by processes such as weathering and erosion. The discovery of fossils showed that species of organisms have also changed throughout the Earth's history. This discovery led some people to suggest how organisms might change. A possible explanation about how something happens is called a hypothesis. A hypothesis includes a statement that can be tested by observations and experiments. If all the evidence supports a hypothesis, then the hypothesis may be called a theory. A theory explains a large number of different observations and allows accurate predictions based on them.

LAMARCKISM: A HYPOTHESIS THAT FAILED

In the 1700s, a French biologist named Jean Baptiste de Lamarck made a hypothesis about how organisms evolve. He suggested that organisms could gradually change their appearance through exercise and experience. He used giraffes as an example. He observed that the long necks of giraffes are an adaptation for feeding on leaves near the tops of trees. But how did giraffes develop their long necks?

FIGURE 16.20
The long neck of the giraffe allows it to reach leaves on high branches. How do you think the giraffes got their long necks?

Lamarck proposed that earlier, shorter-necked species of giraffes regularly stretched their necks to reach higher leaves. Lamarck thought that the exercise produced longer necks. He also thought that baby giraffes would inherit the longer necks of their parents (Figure 16.20). **Inherit** means to pass on a characteristic by birth. For example, you inherited your eye colour from your parents or grandparents.

The problem with Lamarck's hypothesis is that no one has ever observed such changes in nature or by experiment. You do not inherit the bodily characteristics that your parents develop through exercise. The son or daughter of a weightlifter is not born with larger muscles.

Another problem is that organisms are not able to control most of their adaptations. For example, the snowshoe hare in Figure 16.21 is hidden from its predators by the white colour of its fur. But it is hard to imagine how the ancestors of these rabbits could have practised becoming white!

FIGURE 16.21 ▶
Lamarck's hypothesis does not explain how this hare could develop its white camouflage. Like those of many northern animals, the hare's coat turns white in winter.

THE THEORY OF NATURAL SELECTION

Two Englishmen, Charles Darwin and Alfred Russel Wallace, proposed another hypothesis to explain how species change (Figure 16.22). However, Darwin was the first one to write about his hypothesis, which he called **natural selection**. He explained natural selection in his famous book the *Origin of Species*, published in 1859. Darwin supported his hypothesis with a huge amount of evidence. And much more evidence has been discovered since he wrote his book. His ideas are known today as Darwin's theory of natural selection, or simply "the theory of evolution."

Both Darwin and Wallace studied living organisms and fossils in different parts of the world. They developed the same hypothesis independently of one another. The key observations that led to their hypothesis are:

- Each organism in a species is slightly different from the others.
- Each organism can pass on characteristics to its offspring by reproducing.
- Not all organisms survive to reproduce.

You can easily make the first two observations for yourself. Start by looking around your classroom. You will see that no two students look exactly alike (unless there are identical twins in your class!). The same is true for all other species of organisms. Although all mosquitoes may at first look the same to you, they are not. Some are larger, some grow faster, some have a quicker speed of reaction, and so on.

Like every other student in your class, you inherited many of your characteristics from your parents — for example, the shape of your ears. Inherited characteristics are called **traits**. Human traits include the colour of your eyes, hair, and skin. Many different combinations of traits are possible. You can see that children of the same parents are slightly different from each other and from their parents. For example, you may have brown eyes whereas your sister or brother might have blue eyes (Figure 16. 23).

FIGURE 16.22
As a young man, Charles Darwin was hired as a ship's naturalist on a voyage of exploration around the world. His observations of landscapes, fossils, plants, and animals formed the basis of his theory.

FIGURE 16.23 ◀
These two boys are brothers, yet their faces are quite different. The next time you are in a family group, look closely at the members. Can you see any family resemblances between parents and children, or between brothers and sisters?

Darwin realized that some traits might give an organism a better chance of surviving and reproducing in a particular environment. For example, a thicker coat of hair will help an animal to survive in a cold environment. Suddenly standing still may help an animal avoid being seen by a predator. Whatever the reason, only the organisms that survive and reproduce pass on their traits to their offspring, the next **generation**. Those organisms without helpful traits are less likely to survive, and will gradually disappear from the species.

Particular traits may only be helpful in a particular environment. If the environment changes, a different set of traits may be needed to survive. For example, if the climate becomes drier, plants with short roots may not be able to obtain enough water to survive. Plants with long roots will have an advantage. So the drier environment "selects" the plants with long roots. They are the organisms best able to survive and reproduce in these particular conditions. That is why the theory is named "natural selection." As the environment changes, so do the organisms that are able to live in it.

ACTIVITY 16F / A MATTER OF LIFE OR DEATH

GROUP ACTIVITY

How might a predator change the adaptation of its prey? This activity is a model. It will show how variation in colour (a trait) affects the likelihood of an organism being caught by a predator. The colour that helps an individual organism to survive will be the most commonly found colour in the species.

MATERIALS

large sheet of white or black paper (about 1 m^2)
50 black paper squares (about 2 cm^2)
50 white paper squares (the same size)
drinking straws
bowl
timing device

PROCEDURE

1. Your teacher will divide your class into groups of about five students. Half the groups will use a large sheet of black paper and half will use a large sheet of white paper. All groups will have squares of both colours.
2. In your notebook, prepare a chart similar to Table 16.3. At the top, record the colour of your large sheet of paper.
3. Read steps 4 to 11. Predict whether there are likely to be more white moths or more black moths at the end of your experiment. Record your prediction.
4. Place the large sheet of paper on a table. This sheet represents the surface of a tree trunk.

Colour of large sheet of paper: ____________________

	No. of white moths at start	No. of black moths at start	No. of white moths at end	No. of black moths at end	No. of white moths x 2	No. of black moths x 2
1st generation	50	50				
2nd generation						
3rd generation						
4th generation						

TABLE 16.3 ***Sample Data Table for Activity 16F***

FIGURE 16.24
A "bird" hunting "moths"

5. Scatter 25 white squares and 25 black squares on the large sheet. The squares represent moths: half are white and half are black. Make sure the squares are separated so that one does not lie on top of another.
6. In your group, choose one student to represent a bird that feeds on moths. Choose another student to act as timekeeper (Figure 16.24). The "bird" must pick up "moths" by sucking on one end of the straw, and continue to use the straw to transfer the "moth" to the bowl. Practise this technique a few times before going to the next step.
7. At a signal from the timekeeper, the bird begins to catch moths as quickly as possible, continuing to do so until the timekeeper signals that 30 s have passed.
8. Now count the number of white moths and the number of black moths that remain on the large sheet. Record these numbers in the first row of your table.
9. The surviving moths now have to "reproduce." To do this, simply double the number of moths by adding one square for each square of the same colour remaining on the large sheet. For example, if you have 10 white squares and 20 black squares left at the end of step 7, add another 10 white squares and 20 black squares to the large sheet. Record the new totals at the end of the first row of your table.
10. The squares now on your sheet represent the next generation of moths. Record the numbers of each colour at the start of the second row of your table. (They will be the same numbers you just recorded at the end of the first row).
11. Repeat steps 6 to 9 for four more "generations" of moths. For each generation, have a different student play the part of the bird (using a new straw each time).
12. Average your group's final results and the results of other groups that used a sheet (tree trunk) of the same colour.
13. Collect the class results and compare them.

DISCUSSION

1. At the beginning of the experiment, the population consisted of 50 per cent black moths and 50 per cent white moths. How has the percentage changed after five generations for moths living

   (a) against the white background? (b) against the black background?
2. Compare this result with your prediction. If your prediction is different, give reasons why.
3. Was either colour of moth completely safe from the bird?
4. After several more generations, what might happen to the population of moths living

   (a) against the white background? (b) against the black background?
5. Suppose a predator hunts moths using its sense of smell, rather than sight. What might happen to the original moth population if it were hunted by this predator?
6. This activity is a model of what happens in nature. What factors are not considered? How might they affect the results? ❖

FIGURE 16.25
Against a dark tree trunk, a dark moth is camouflaged and a light moth stands out. Against a light-coloured trunk, the opposite is true. What would happen to the number of each kind of moth if local factories stopped polluting?

THE CASE OF THE PEPPERED MOTH

The last activity was a model based on real-life observations of a species of moth that lives in England. Before 1848, all the peppered moths seen in England had light-coloured wings. However, after 1848, people began to notice a dark-coloured form of the moth. The dark moths were most common near factories that were being built in some cities. By 1898, dark moths outnumbered the light-coloured moths in some of the industrial areas by as many as 99 to 1.

Biologists looked for an explanation for this change. They soon noticed that the tree trunks near the factories had been darkened by air pollution. In the countryside, most tree trunks were still covered with light-coloured lichens. An ecologist named H.D.B. Kettlewell suggested a hypothesis. He proposed that the change in the moth population had come about because dark-coloured moths were best adapted to the environment near the factories. He thought that the dark moths had a better chance of surviving because birds that eat moths would find it harder to see them against the dark trunks (Figure 16.25). In contrast, the birds would easily pick out the light-coloured moths against the darker trunks and eat them.

To test his idea, Kettlewell released equal numbers of light and dark-coloured moths in two different areas. One area had light tree trunks and the other had dark tree trunks. Later, he recaptured moths in both areas. He counted and compared the number of light to dark individuals. His results showed that the chances of survival were best for dark moths in areas with dark trunks, and for light moths in areas with light trunks (see Table 16.4). Kettlewell wanted to confirm that birds rely on their sense of vision to hunt moths. So he filmed them hunting. In some cases, birds passed right over a moth that was camouflaged against its background.

		White moths	Black moths
Unpolluted wood (light trees)	Released	496	473
	Recaptured	62	30
	% recaptured	12.5	6.3
Polluted wood (dark trees)	Released	137	447
	Recaptured	18	123
	% recaptured	13.1	27.5

TABLE 16.4 ***Kettlewell's Results***

THE SURVIVAL OF THE FITTEST

The result of natural selection in Darwin's theory has sometimes been called "survival of the fittest." Many people wrongly take this to mean that only the biggest and strongest individuals survive. However, "fittest" in this phrase means "those organisms that are best fitted to their environment." The fittest individuals may be smaller or bigger, or slower or quicker, than others. They may have any combination of traits that give them an advantage in a particular environment.

ACTIVITY 16G / HOW GIRAFFES GOT THEIR LONG NECKS

FIGURE 16.26
Use these illustrations to explain the theory of natural selection in Activity 16G.

The three drawings in Figure 16.26 show how giraffes may have evolved longer necks through the process of natural selection. In your notebook, write captions for each drawing to explain how natural selection takes place. ❖

(a) *(b)* *(c)*

THE APPEARANCE OF NEW SPECIES

You have seen that new adaptations can alter the appearance of a species such as the peppered moth. Can these new adaptations eventually produce new species?

In nature, organisms do not have the same chance of breeding with all other members of their species. They may not live in the same area. Organisms usually live in groups, called **populations**. Different populations of a species may have no contact with one another. For example, pigeons living in downtown Vancouver are unlikely to meet and breed with pigeons living in Lillooet, 160 km to the north, even though both populations belong to the same species and have a similar appearance and behaviour.

Now suppose that, after a long time, the environments of Vancouver and Lillooet become different. The climate of Lillooet may become much colder. Or the food supply or the predators in Vancouver may change. Through natural selection, the pigeons in each place may develop different adaptations to their particular environment. Slowly, the two populations of pigeons may become less and less alike. After a long time, the pigeons from Lillooet and Vancouver may become so different that they would no longer be able to breed, even if they were brought together in the same place. They would look and behave differently from one another. When this happens, the two populations have evolved into two different species.

ACTIVITY 16H / TWO SPECIES FROM ONE

How can the theory of natural selection explain the increase in numbers of species shown by the fossil record?

The three illustrations (Figure 16.27) show changes in a lake environment over thousands of years. Study the illustrations carefully. Write a description to fit each picture. Your description should explain the changes that appear to be taking place among the fish that live in the lake.

DISCUSSION

1. Describe the changes you see in each picture.
2. What different traits are shown by the two populations of fish?
3. How can these traits be interpreted as adaptations to different environments?
4. Suppose the water level in the lake rose once more, allowing the two populations of fish to mix again. What factors might prevent fish in the two populations from breeding together? ❖

FIGURE 16.27
Illustrations for Activity 16H

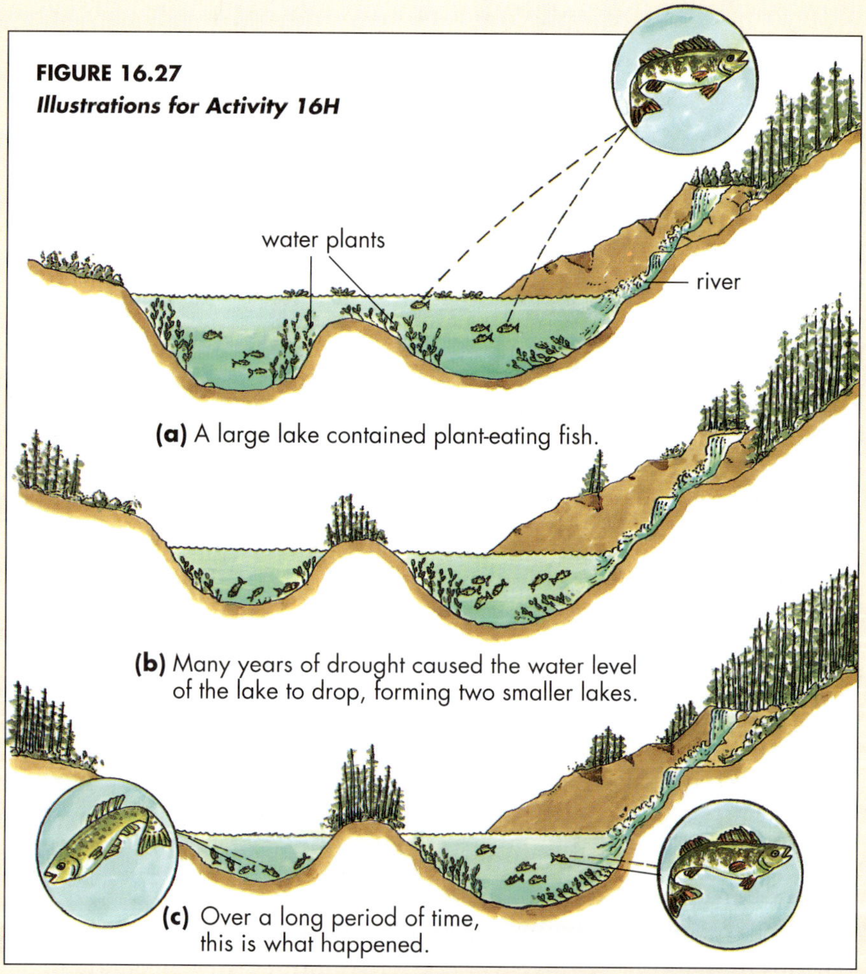

(a) A large lake contained plant-eating fish.

(b) Many years of drought caused the water level of the lake to drop, forming two smaller lakes.

(c) Over a long period of time, this is what happened.

► REVIEW 16.4

1. "Giraffes have long necks because they stretch for food. This characteristic is passed on to their offspring." Is this statement an example of Lamarck's hypothesis or Darwin's theory of evolution?
2. Give two reasons that explain why most scientists today do not accept Lamarck's hypothesis.
3. What three observations led to Darwin's theory of natural selection?
4. What is a trait?
5. Name three human traits.
6. Give an example of how a change in the environment might help some members of a population survive better than others (for example, a change in the climate or in the number of predators).

CHAPTER REVIEW

KEY IDEAS

- Organisms that lived on Earth in the past have been preserved as fossils.
- Fossils show that life has changed throughout the Earth's history. Many organisms that lived in the past are now extinct. And many organisms living today have not been found as fossils.
- Fossils found in layers of sedimentary rock can be used to place the layers in a division of the Geological Time Scale. The time scale is divided into four major eras. Each era lasts millions of years.
- The fossils found in each level of sedimentary rock differ from those found above and below it. Each layer is generally older than the layer immediately above it.
- Each species of organism has adaptations to a particular environment. Adaptations seen in fossils tell scientists about the environment and the way of life of extinct species.
- A study of fossils shows that life has increased in diversity and complexity throughout the Earth's history. Living things have also developed adaptations to new environments, such as land and air.
- Evolution is the process or way that species change and develop adaptations to different environments. Darwin's theory of natural selection explains how evolution may occur.

VOCABULARY

fossil
organism
mold
replacement fossil
petrified fossil
amber
ammonite
trilobite
dinosaur
extinct
Geological Time Scale
eras
Precambrian Era
Paleozoic Era
Mesozoic Era
Cenozoic Era
paleontology
adaptation
species
diversity
evolution
inherit
natural selection
trait
generation
population

V1. On a sheet of paper, draw a mind map using as many words from the vocabulary list as you can.

V2. Select the terms from the vocabulary list that best fit the following spaces:

(a) A dinosaur footprint is an example of a __________.

(b) All organisms have __________ for a particular environment.

(c) We are living in the __________ Era.

(d) Darwin's __________ of __________ explains how __________ may occur.

(e) A species that no longer lives on Earth is __________ .

CONNECTIONS

C1. Millions of years ago, a fish died and sank to the bottom of a lake. Last year, a rock collector found a piece of rock and saw the fish's shape and scales clearly in it. Describe how these details might have been preserved in the rock.

C2. George and Maria visited the Grand Canyon in Arizona during their holiday. "It's amazing. This whole area was once under water," said Maria. Describe two pieces of evidence that might have led her to this conclusion.

C3. Your younger brother has just been reading about dinosaurs. He says to you: "I bet the cavemen found dinosaurs really scary." What evidence can you use to explain to him that dinosaurs and people were not on Earth at the same time?

C4. "To really understand geology, you must have a different sense of time." What do you think is meant by this statement?

C5. Name some adaptations that help each of the following species live in their environments: sockeye salmon, Douglas fir, skunk, grizzly bear, earthworm.

C6. How did Darwin's ideas about evolution differ from those of Lamarck?

C7. Using an example of your own, describe how a predator might produce a change in the adaptation of its prey.

C8. Why do you think that many species of animals living on islands are found nowhere else in the world but on their island?

C9. Explain why evolution could not occur if all members of a species were exactly the same.

EXPLORATIONS

E1. (a) In this chapter, fossils were compared with time capsules. Use your library to find out about the time capsule placed on the *Voyager* spacecraft. When was this spacecraft launched? Where is it today? What was in its time capsule? Why do you think these items were chosen?

(b) Prepare a list, or an actual collection, of things you would put in a time capsule. Give reasons for your choices. Where would you put your time capsule?

E2. Fossils indicate that the last trilobites were crawling along the sea floor about 230 million years ago. At the same time, the number of crustaceans (for example, shrimps, lobsters, and crabs) began to increase. Find out about the lives of these animals. How might an increase in the numbers of crustaceans be linked to the extinction of trilobites?

E3. Why do you suppose many geologists believe we are living at a time when another ice age could develop?

E4. A human body melted out of the glacier ice in the European Alps in 1991. Do you think this is an example of a fossil? Why or why not?

REFLECTIONS

R1. The natural world is slowly and endlessly changing. Landscapes change and species of organisms change. These processes have gone on since the time the Earth first formed, and still go on today. Write a short story or a poem to describe the idea that changes in any part of the world always lead to changes in other parts.

R2. Do you think fossils are being formed today? Describe why or why not.

CHAPTER 17

WEATHER

It is a sunny day, but on the radio the weather forecaster says that tomorrow will bring rain. You cannot see any clouds in the sky, so how does the forecaster know what the weather will be like?

The weather is the local condition of the air. The weather includes sunshine, rain, snow, and wind. It differs from one part of the province to another, and from one day to the next. Understanding the weather and being able to predict changes in weather are important to everyone. For example, a rainstorm may wash out a picnic or baseball game that you were planning. A heavy snowfall means you must allow extra time to travel to and from school. Dry weather for a whole summer may spoil a farmer's crops and increase the price of food in the stores.

In this chapter, you will study some of the things that produce weather. You will discover how factors such as temperature, humidity, and winds affect each other. You will build devices to measure certain weather conditions and use these measurements to make simple predictions. You can already make one prediction that is certain to be correct. Simply say: "Today's weather will change sooner or later."

ACTIVITY 17A / THE WEATHER AND YOU

How does the weather affect your activities? In your learning journal, list several things that you have done over the last two weeks that depended on the weather. Other than listening to weather forecasts, do you know any ways to predict changes in the weather? If so, write them down. Share your ideas with your classmates. ❖

DID YOU KNOW

■ Our atmosphere is made up mostly of two gases: nitrogen (78 per cent of the atmosphere) and oxygen (21 per cent of the atmosphere). What other gases do you know that make up the remaining 1 per cent of the atmosphere?

■ 17.1 THE AIR AROUND YOU

If you lived on the moon, you would not need an umbrella, or rubber boots, or a jacket to keep out the wind and rain. The moon does not have weather as the Earth does. One important reason for this difference is that the Earth is surrounded by a layer of air, or atmosphere, but the moon has no **atmosphere**. The Earth's atmosphere extends upward for about 500 km. It is prevented from escaping into space by the pull of the Earth's gravity. Our ever-changing weather is produced by changes in the temperature, humidity (amount of moisture), and movement of air in the atmosphere.

The air around you is a mixture of invisible gases. Because we cannot see the gases in the air, it is easy to think of air as "nothing." But if you have ever been on an aircraft when it flies through some "bumpy air" or turbulence, you know that air may have a powerful force. (A force is a push or a pull.) Air turbulence makes an airplane suddenly drop downward or rise up with a shudder. The force that air exerts on a surface is known as **air pressure**. As you will discover later, air pressure plays an important part in the weather.

ACTIVITY 17B / AN INVISIBLE FORCE

In these experiments, you will observe the pushing force of air.

MATERIALS

safety goggles
apron
drinking glass filled to the brim with water
piece of stiff cardboard, slightly larger than the rim of the glass
metal bowl or container
empty pop can
tongs
hotplate

FIGURE 17.1
Will the cardboard stay on the glass of water, or will you get splashed?

CAUTION!

- **Be careful when working with boiling water and steam.**

PART I Observing the Force of Air

PROCEDURE

1. Place the cardboard carefully on the rim of the filled glass. Make sure there is no air trapped between the cardboard and the water.
2. Hold the cardboard tightly against the glass with one hand and turn the glass upside down over a bowl (Figure 17.1).
3. Predict what will happen when you remove your hand from the cardboard. Take your hand away from the cardboard. Observe and record what happens.
4. In your notebook, draw and label a diagram that illustrates your results.
5. Suggest what might happen if the glass was only half full of water. Repeat the experiment with the glass half full. Record your results.

DISCUSSION

1. How would you explain the result you observed when the glass was full of water? (Hint: Read the sentence below the title of this activity.)
2. How would you explain the result when the glass was half-full?

PART II Another Demonstration of Air Pressure

PROCEDURE

1. Put on your safety goggles and apron.
2. Half-fill a container with cold water.
3. Pour just enough water into an empty pop can to cover the bottom.
4. Place the can of water on a hotplate and heat the water until you see steam coming from the opening of the can (Figure 17.2).
5. When the can is full of steam, carefully pick up the can with the tongs (Figure 17.2).
6. Over the container of cold water, quickly turn the can upside down. Place the can upside down into the cold water, making sure that the open end of the can is below the surface of the water. Record your observations.

DISCUSSION

1. What effect did the water in the container have on the steam inside the can?
2. Suggest how the cooling of the steam inside the can might have changed the air pressure inside the can.
3. Explain your observations in terms of differences in air pressure on the inside and outside of the can. ❖

FIGURE 17.2 ◀
Using steam to find out about air pressure

DID YOU KNOW

■ You can feel the air pressure on your body change when you ride up or down an elevator in a tall building. As you ride up, the air pressure decreases. Air spaces inside your ears expand in the lower pressure, and you experience a pushing feeling against the inside of your eardrums.

AIR PRESSURE

As you move around or sit in the classroom, you are living under a thick blanket of air. Hold out your hand, palm upward, and imagine that you are supporting a column of air that extends all the way from the surface of your palm up to the outer limits of the atmosphere. The push of this air on your hand — and on everything else around you — produces air pressure. The height of the air column is greatest when you are standing on the Earth's surface at sea level. Therefore, air pressure is greatest at sea level. The higher up you go, the less atmosphere there is above you, and the lower the air pressure becomes (Figure 17.3). At a height of 5951 m on the top of Mt. Logan in the Yukon Territory — Canada's highest mountain — the air pressure is only about half as great as it is at sea level.

Air pressure does not change only with height above the Earth's surface. The air pressure in any place, such as your schoolyard, may also change from one hour to the next as air moves about. Changes in air pressure are important because they help people to predict changes in the weather. Increasing air pressure usually means good weather is on the way. If the air pressure is decreasing, watch out for rain showers.

Scientists measure air pressure using instruments called **barometers**. There are several types of barometers. One of the earliest barometers invented measures the ability of air pressure to support a column of liq-

FIGURE 17.3 ◀
At the top of a mountain there are fewer air molecules than at sea level. There are also fewer molecules above the mountain, so the air pressure is lower. In May, 1994 some Canadians tried to climb Mount Everest without using extra oxygen. Why was this a dangerous thing to attempt?

uid, usually mercury (Figure 17.4). The greater the air pressure, the higher the column of liquid in the tube. When the liquid in the tube stops moving, the pressure at the bottom of the liquid column is equal to the air pressure outside the tube.

Another type of barometer, which does not use liquid, is called an **aneroid barometer**. "Aneroid" comes from the Greek terms *a* (without) and *neron* (water). These barometers are smaller and more convenient, and avoid the risk of messy and dangerous spills. But they are less accurate. Aneroid barometers record differences in pressure between the inside and outside of a sealed container (Figure 17.5).

FIGURE 17.5
An aneroid barometer has a sealed container from which some of the air has been removed. As the air pressure changes, the top of the container moves in and out. An indicator needle is attached to the top of the container.

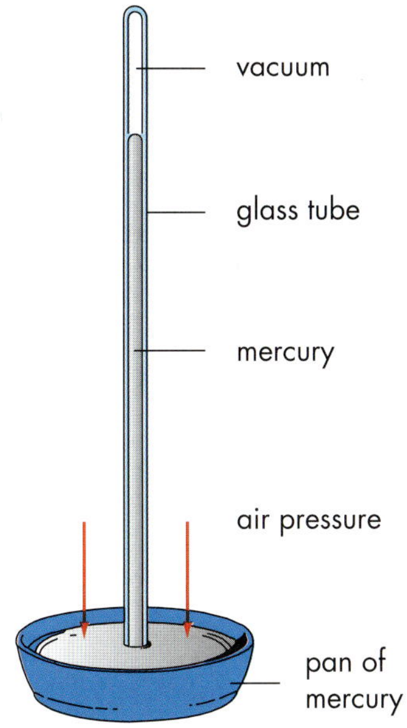

FIGURE 17.4
A simple barometer. Air pressure on the surface of the mercury in the pan pushes mercury up the tube. The top of the mercury column rises or falls as the air pressure changes. What is a vacuum? Why must you have a vacuum instead of air in the top part of the barometer?

ACTIVITY 17C / HOW AN ANEROID BAROMETER WORKS (TEACHER DEMONSTRATION)

In this activity, you will be able to find out how changes in air pressure are measured by an aneroid barometer.

MATERIALS

scissors
two balloons
small baby food bottle
large, wide-mouthed jar
two elastic bands
tape or glue
flat toothpick

PROCEDURE

1. Cut the top from one of the balloons.
2. Stretch the bottom of the balloon tightly across the open top of the small bottle and hold it in place with an elastic band.
3. Tape or glue one end of the toothpick to the centre of the rubber sheet.
4. Place the small bottle inside the large jar (Figure 17.6).
5. Cut the bottom from the second balloon.
6. Tie the neck of the balloon, and stretch the balloon over the mouth of the large jar. Hold the balloon in place with an elastic band.

FIGURE 17.6
Changing the air pressure in the jar

7. The small bottle is your aneroid barometer. What does the air in the large jar represent? Pull up and push down on the balloon stretched across the large jar, as shown in Figure 17.6. Observe any movement of the toothpick pointer. Record your observations in your notebook.

DISCUSSION

1. Sketch the apparatus used in this experiment, showing the toothpick pointer in the horizontal position.

2. When the balloon on the large jar is pushed down, does the air pressure inside the jar increase or decrease?

3. When air pressure inside the large jar increases, are the air molecules in the jar squeezed closer together or spread farther apart?

4. Would an increase in air pressure inside the large jar make the pointer on the small bottle move up or down?

5. When the balloon on the large jar is pulled up, what happens to
(a) air pressure inside the large jar?
(b) the spacing of the air molecules inside the large jar?
(c) the pointer on the small bottle?

6. Explain your answer to question 5c, referring to differences in air pressure on the inside and outside of the small bottle. ❖

AIR PRESSURE AND TEMPERATURE

You may have seen a weather map like the one in Figure 17.7. The map shows large areas where the air pressure is low (L) and other areas where the air pressure is high (H). Areas of low and high air pressure may move from day to day, bringing changes in the weather.

The most rapid changes in air pressure take place when a volume of air, or air mass, rises or sinks in the atmosphere. As an air mass sinks toward the ground, the air pressure increases. Also, the air molecules are squeezed more closely together (Figure 17.3). This squeezing together makes the air warmer.

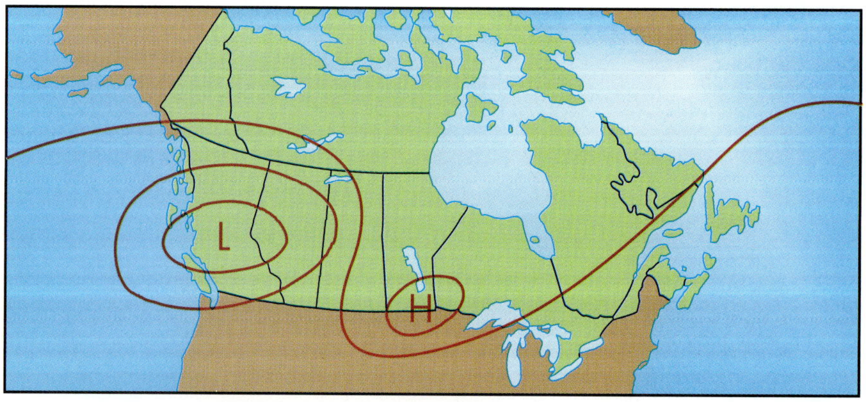

FIGURE 17.7 ▶
On this weather map, a low pressure system (L) is centred over British Columbia and a high pressure system (H) is over southern Manitoba. What weather would you expect in each of these places?

ACTIVITY 17D / A WARM SQUEEZE

In this activity, you will observe how increasing air pressure affects temperature.

MATERIALS

bicycle tire inner tube
bicycle pump

PROCEDURE

1. Inflate the tire with the hand pump (Figure 17.8).
2. Feel the temperature of several parts of the pump and the tire. Record your observations in your notebook.
3. Draw a diagram of the fully inflated inner tube. On your diagram, draw air molecules as dots, comparing how closely packed the air molecules are inside the inner tube compared with air molecules outside the tube.
4. Open the valve of the inner tube. Draw a diagram to show the direction of movement of the air inside and outside the tube.

FIGURE 17.8 ▶
Inflating the tire with a bicycle pump

DISCUSSION

1. When is air pressure inside the tube greatest? Explain how you know.
2. How is air pressure related to air temperature?
3. How is air pressure related to air movement? ❖

▶ REVIEW 17.1

1. Name two characteristics of the atmosphere.
2. Describe a way of measuring air pressure.
3. Suppose that you take a liquid barometer to the bottom of a deep mine. What would happen to the reading on the barometer? Why?
4. How does air pressure affect temperature?
5. Why do you think the moon has no atmosphere?

■ 17.2 TEMPERATURE AND WEATHER

The temperature in British Columbia may vary greatly from one place to another. Furthermore, the temperatures in the province are usually lower than in places farther south, such as southern California and Mexico. Why do temperatures on Earth vary in this way? There are many factors that affect temperature, including the amount of land and water in a region, and the angle of the sun's rays when they reach the Earth's surface.

THE GREENHOUSE EFFECT

Step outside, feel the temperature, and then imagine what it would have been like 18 000 years ago. That was the time of the last great ice age. Brrrrr. Now go back many million years, to the time of the dinosaurs. The Earth's surface was hotter then than it is now.

The Earth's climate has varied greatly. Scientists think that we are living in an unusual, pleasantly warm period of time between ice ages. If the change in climate followed the usual pattern, we might expect the Earth's surface to gradually cool again over the next 90 000 years.

Yet most scientists predict the opposite. They predict a warming trend. The reason is that human beings are now changing the world's climate. The atmosphere around our planet forms a natural blanket. Gases in the atmosphere trap heat and prevent it from escaping. Visit a greenhouse on a cold day and you can experience this yourself. The air trapped inside is warmer than the air outside. Without the natural "greenhouse" of the atmosphere, the Earth's surface would be like that of the moon — far too cold or far too hot. Yet too much greenhouse effect is also bad.

Over the past 100 years, people have pumped billions of tonnes of carbon dioxide and other gases into the atmosphere. Carbon dioxide increases the atmosphere's ability to act like a blanket and trap heat.

Scientists do not know exactly what the greenhouse effect will mean for us and for future generations. Some possible results of the greenhouse effect:

- As temperatures rise, the ice caps in the Arctic and Antarctic regions could melt. The result would be that the oceans could rise by one or more metres. Low-lying areas, including coastal cities, could be flooded.
- In many areas of the world, a hotter climate would bring drought. Forestry and farming would suffer.
- Although animals can migrate hundreds of miles to find climates they can live in, other species of life would face extinction. Trees, for instance, reproduce by dropping seeds. They cannot move fast enough to escape the change in climate.

The extra carbon dioxide comes mainly from burning fossil fuels — coal, oil, and natural gas. Think how important fossil fuels are to your way of life. We use fossil fuels to drive automobiles, heat houses, run factories, and produce electricity. To reduce the amount of carbon dioxide in the atmosphere, we need to use less of the fossil fuels and use them more effectively. And we need to switch to renewable fuels such as solar power.

Are you ready to make changes to your way of life? Do you think others are willing? We have a choice as to whether we speed up this warming trend, or slow it down.

ACTIVITY 17E / LOOKING FOR HOT SPOTS

Why are some parts of the Earth's surface warmer than others? This activity illustrates two factors that affect air temperature.

MATERIALS

safety goggles
apron
three plastic Petri dishes
water (at room temperature)
white sand
black sand or charcoal
timer or stopwatch
three thermometers
heat lamp with support stand
strip of construction paper (5 cm x 25 cm)
candle or dental wax

CAUTION!

- **Turn off the heat lamp if the liquid in any of the thermometers approaches the top of the thermometer.**

PART I Heating Different Materials

PROCEDURE

1. Copy Table 17.1 into your notebook.
2. Put on your safety goggles and apron.
3. Fill one dish with water at room temperature. Fill the second dish with white sand, and the third dish with black sand or charcoal.
4. Carefully hold a thermometer in each dish, with the bulb of the thermometer covered by the water or sand (Figure 17.9). After a minute, note the temperature on each thermometer. Record these values in your table.
5. Predict what the temperature in each of the three dishes will be after heating them for 5 min. Record your predictions in your table.
6. Place all three dishes under the heat lamp. Turn on the heat lamp for 5 min.
7. After 5 min, read the actual temperature in each dish and record the temperatures in your table.
8. Turn off the heat lamp. Predict what the temperature in each of the three dishes will be after 5 min of cooling. Record your predictions in your table.
9. Wait 5 min, then read and record the actual temperatures in your table.

TABLE 17.1 ▶
Sample Data Table for Activity 17E, Part I

Contents of dish	Temperature				
	Starting	After heating 5 min		After cooling 5 min	
		Prediction	Actual	Prediction	Actual
Water					
White sand					
Black sand					

FIGURE 17.9 ▶
Find out the temperature of different materials in Activity 17E, Part I.

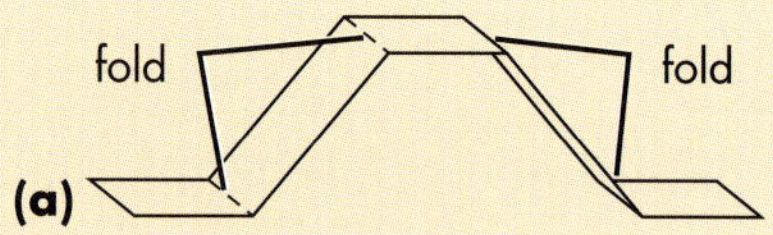

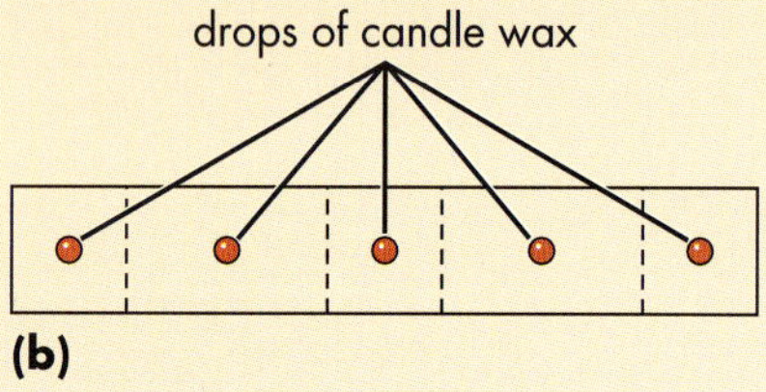

FIGURE 17.10
Apparatus for Activity 17E, Part II

DISCUSSION

1. After 5 min of heating, which material increased in temperature
   (a) the most?
   (b) the least?
2. After 5 min of cooling, which material lost heat
   (a) most rapidly?
   (b) most slowly?
3. From your results, and from your knowledge of heat transfer (Chapter 10), think about the temperatures you would expect to record at the end of a sunny day on
   (a) a large lake,
   (b) a bare, ploughed field of dark soil,
   (c) a beach of white sand.
   List these three areas in order from the warmest to the coolest. Explain your reasoning.
4. Which of the areas in question 3 do you think would cool down fastest at night? Which would cool slowest?

PART II Heating Different Areas of the Earth

PROCEDURE

1. Fold the paper strip as shown in Figure 17.10a.
2. Flatten the paper strip and place drops of candle wax of equal size in the positions shown in Figure 17.10b.
3. After the drops of wax have solidified, refold the paper strip and place it directly under the heat lamp.
4. Predict which wax drops will melt first and which will melt last.
5. Carefully observe the wax drops and record the order in which they melt.

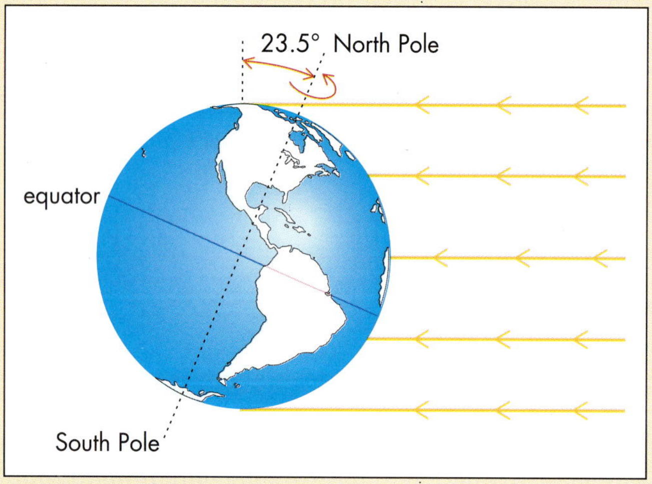

FIGURE 17.11
Equal amounts of energy from the sun heat different parts of the Earth's surface, depending on the angle at which the sun's rays strike the Earth. What season is it in the southern hemisphere?

DISCUSSION

1. What was the position of the drop that melted
   (a) first?
   (b) second?
   (c) third?
2. What do you think affects the amount of heat on a wax drop most:
   (a) its distance from the lamp?
   (b) whether the heat reaches the area directly or at a slanting angle?
   Explain your answer.
3. Study Figure 17.11, which shows how the sun's rays reach the Earth. From what you see in this figure, and from the results of this experiment, why do you think the sun's thermal energy received near the equator is greater than that received at the poles? ❖

HEAT AND WINDS

The sun's rays do not heat the air directly as they pass through it to reach the Earth's surface. First, the rays heat the land and water. Then the surface of the Earth warms the air above it by convection. (Refer to Chapter 10 for the different processes of transferring heat.) Areas of warm air rise, producing convection currents. The rising warm air, in turn, leads to horizontal movements of air, or winds.

ACTIVITY 17F / HEAT AND AIR MOVEMENT

In this activity, you will explore the relationship between temperature and air movement.

PROCEDURE

1. Study the apparatus shown in Figure 17.12.
2. Sketch the apparatus. On your sketch, label the areas where you would expect the air to be hot and the areas where the air is cool.
3. Label where you would expect air pressure to be highest and lowest.
4. Add arrows to indicate the direction of air movement.

DISCUSSION

1. Describe the path of the air movement in the apparatus.
2. Explain this movement, referring to changes in the temperature of the air at each step. ❖

FIGURE 17.12 ◀
Find out about air movement by using a convection box in Activity 17F.

SEA BREEZES

On hot, sunny days, the land near the ocean warms up more quickly than does the water in the ocean. As the warm air above the land rises, it is replaced by the cooler air from above the water. This movement of air produces a cool "sea breeze," blowing from the water onto the land during the day (Figure 17.13). At night, the reverse takes place. The land cools more rapidly than the water. Warm air over the water rises and is replaced by the cooler air from above the land. This air movement produces a land breeze that blows from land to water during the night. The next time you visit a beach on a hot, sunny day, remember to notice the direction of the breeze.

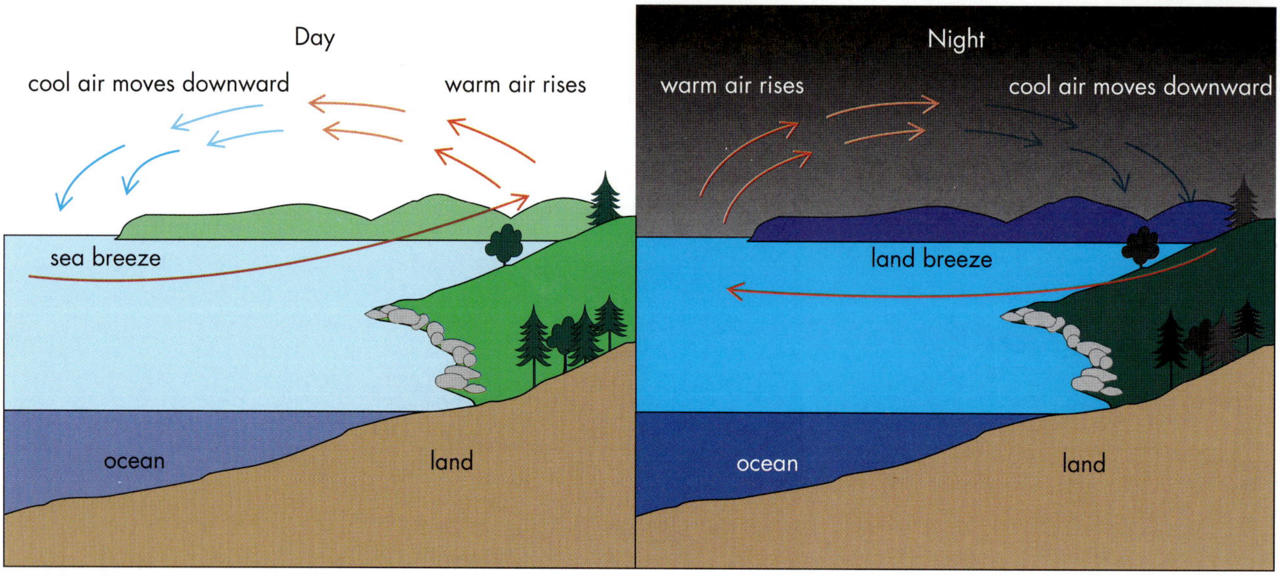

Figure 17.13
Differences in temperature between the land and the water produce breezes. Would you also get a sea breeze off a large lake? Off a small lake?

WINDS AROUND THE WORLD

The differences in temperature that produce breezes along the coast also help to produce air movements on a much larger scale around the world. Warm air rises over the equator, and cooler air sinks over the poles. Cold, dense polar air moves toward the equator close to the Earth's surface while, at the same time, warm tropical air moves toward the poles. Because the tropical air is less dense, it moves above the cold air.

Air movements are not that simple, however. Because the Earth is turning, winds do not blow straight north or south (Figure 17.14).

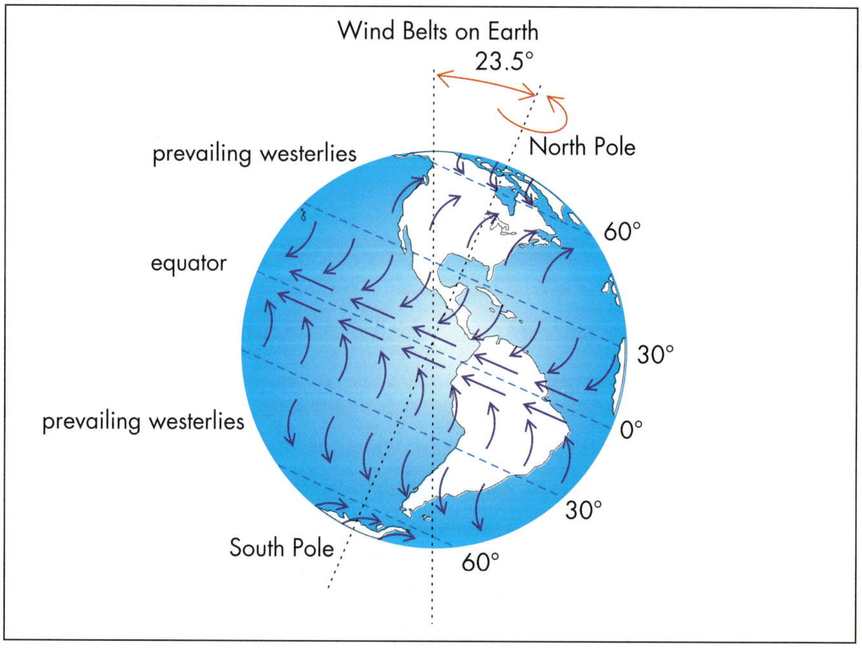

FIGURE 17.14
Prevailing winds around the world. Can you explain why they move in set directions?

In Canada, this means that our winds blow mainly from the west. These westerly winds are called the **prevailing winds**.

Within the prevailing wind system, wind speed and temperature are also affected by the location of the oceans and by features on land, such as deserts and mountain ranges. For example, the mountain ranges along the coast of British Columbia cause westerly winds from the ocean to rise. This produces cool, wet weather on the west side of the mountains and drier weather on the east side of the mountains. In the following section, you will discover the role of water in air, and how water affects weather.

WINDS AND OCEAN CURRENTS

If you blow on a bowl of hot soup, the force of your moving breath along the surface of the soup produces ripples. Similarly, the blowing of prevailing winds over the oceans results in the movements of great masses of sea water, called **ocean currents**. The pattern of ocean currents around the world is the same as the pattern of prevailing winds.

Ocean currents affect the air above them, and the weather, in many ways. Air flowing over a cold ocean current will become cooler, bringing a cold day. Air flowing over a warm current will become warmer, bringing a warm day. A warm ocean current flowing from the equator helps keep the weather mild in regions of land near the coast far to the north. For example, the Queen Charlotte Islands have a mild climate even though they are as far north as Hudson Bay. One of the most important ways in which the ocean affects the weather, however, is by providing moisture for the atmosphere.

EXTENSION

■ To illustrate how the spinning of the Earth affects wind direction, you need a circle of paper, a pencil, and a partner. Have your partner hold the paper circle flat on a table top. Hold the tip of the pencil at the centre of the circle. Now, slowly try to draw a pencil line straight toward yourself, while at the same time your partner turns the paper circle slowly clockwise. Repeat the experiment, turning the paper circle in the opposite direction. Examine a globe of the Earth and explain how the Earth's movement affects winds blowing from the equator to the poles.

REVIEW 17.2

1. Give two reasons why temperatures on Earth vary from one place to another.

2. (a) What causes the Earth's surface to become warmer?
(b) What effect does an increase in the temperature of the ground have on the air above it?

3. Why do air currents not blow straight north or south?

4. Describe two ways that the atmosphere and the oceans affect each other.

5. What effect do the Coast Mountains have on the weather in British Columbia?

17.3 WATER AND WEATHER

The atmosphere always holds a certain amount of water, as an invisible gas called water vapour. You may sometimes become aware of this on days when the air feels damp. The measure of the water vapour in the air is known as **humidity**.

The actual amount of humidity is always changing. The warmer the weather, the more water vapour the air is able to hold. However, although warm air can hold more water vapour than cold air, warm air does not always have a high humidity. Humidity depends on the availability of water as well as on temperature. A region near a large lake or an ocean is likely to be more humid than a desert, even when the air in the desert is warmer. Because of this, weather forecasters usually speak of the **relative humidity** of the air. Relative humidity is the actual amount of water vapour in the air compared with the total amount of water vapour that the air could hold at that temperature. Relative humidity is written as a per cent. For example, at a relative humidity of 50 per cent, the air is holding half the amount of water vapour that it is able to. Air that has 100 per cent relative humidity is said to be **saturated**. That means the air cannot hold any more water vapour.

Relative humidity affects your comfort. On a hot day, people usually sweat easily. Sweat is a salty fluid produced by the body as a way of cooling itself. If it is a hot, dry day, the sweat dries quickly, making your body cooler. If the air is humid, however, sweat evaporates more slowly. This makes you feel clammy. Differences in the humidity of the air produce differences in how fast sweat evaporates from your skin, or how fast any moisture evaporates from any surface. Weather forecasters use this fact to measure relative humidity.

ACTIVITY 17G / USING WET- AND DRY-BULB THERMOMETERS

By comparing the difference in temperature between a dry-bulb and wet-bulb thermometer, you can estimate the relative humidity of the air.

MATERIALS

two thermometers
small piece of cotton or muslin cloth
Petri dish
water
small rubber band

PROCEDURE

1. Place the two thermometers side by side. The temperatures on the two thermometers should be the same. Record the temperature in a data table in your notebook.
2. Soak the cloth in water at room temperature. Wrap the cloth around the bulb of one thermometer and hold it in place with the rubber band. After 5 min, record the readings on the two thermometers (Figure 17.15).
3. Set up the pair of thermometers outside where they will not be disturbed for several days. Make sure the cloth is kept moist. In your data table, record the temperatures on both thermometers on days with different weather conditions.

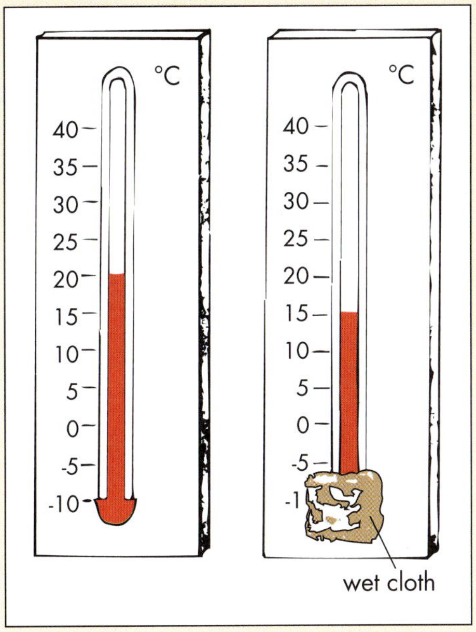

4. Make a graph to compare the different temperature readings on the two thermometers on different days.

DISCUSSION

1. What effect does moisture evaporating from the cloth have on the temperature reading?
2. Would you expect moisture to evaporate from the cloth more rapidly on days with a high humidity or a low humidity?
3. Would you expect the difference in temperature on the two thermometers to be greatest when the air is more humid or less humid? ❖

FIGURE 17.15 ◀ ***Wet- and dry-bulb thermometers set up for Activity 17C***

CLOUDS AND RAIN

After you take a hot shower or bath, you may notice that the bathroom mirror is covered with tiny droplets of water. The water droplets form when the humid air touches the cool mirror surface, loses heat, and condenses. You may see the same effect outdoors on a cool, clear, summer morning, when grass blades are covered with tiny drops of condensed water vapour called **dew**.

Whenever humid air grows cooler, it reaches a temperature — called the **dew point** — when it is holding all the water vapour it can. When the temperature drops farther below the dew point, some of the water vapour condenses to produce water drops. That is what produces water on your bathroom mirror after you have a hot shower, and dew on the grass on a cold morning. The same process also causes clouds to form in the sky (Figure 17.16).

You often see fluffy white clouds on sunny days. They float high above you on a current of warm air. The clouds are made of fine water drops or, if it is cold enough, ice crystals. The base of the cloud marks the height where the temperature of the air has cooled to the dew point. That is where invisible water vapour in the air begins to turn into visible moisture. It is the visible moisture that you see as a cloud.

The fine droplets of water in a cloud are much smaller than raindrops, and can be kept suspended in the sky by the rising air from below. If the air grows cooler, the water drops in the clouds may turn into tiny ice crystals. More cold water then collects and freezes onto the surface of the ice crystals, forming larger drops. When the mixture of ice and water grows too heavy to be supported by rising air currents, rain, hail, or snow begins to fall.

DID YOU KNOW

■ A single small cloud may hold over 1000 t of water.

FIGURE 17.16
Clouds help you predict the weather. What weather do you expect when you see towering, grey clouds? Small, white, fluffy clouds?

THE WATER CYCLE

After the clouds have dropped their rain and the skies have cleared, would you say to yourself: "Now there is no water vapour in the air and it will never rain again"? Fortunately, the movement of water from the atmosphere to the land is not a one-way trip. Moisture returns from the Earth's surface back into the atmosphere by evaporation, forming an endless **water cycle** (Figure 17.17).

FIGURE 17.17
The water cycle is powered by the energy of the sun. In what ways is the water cycle important to life on land?

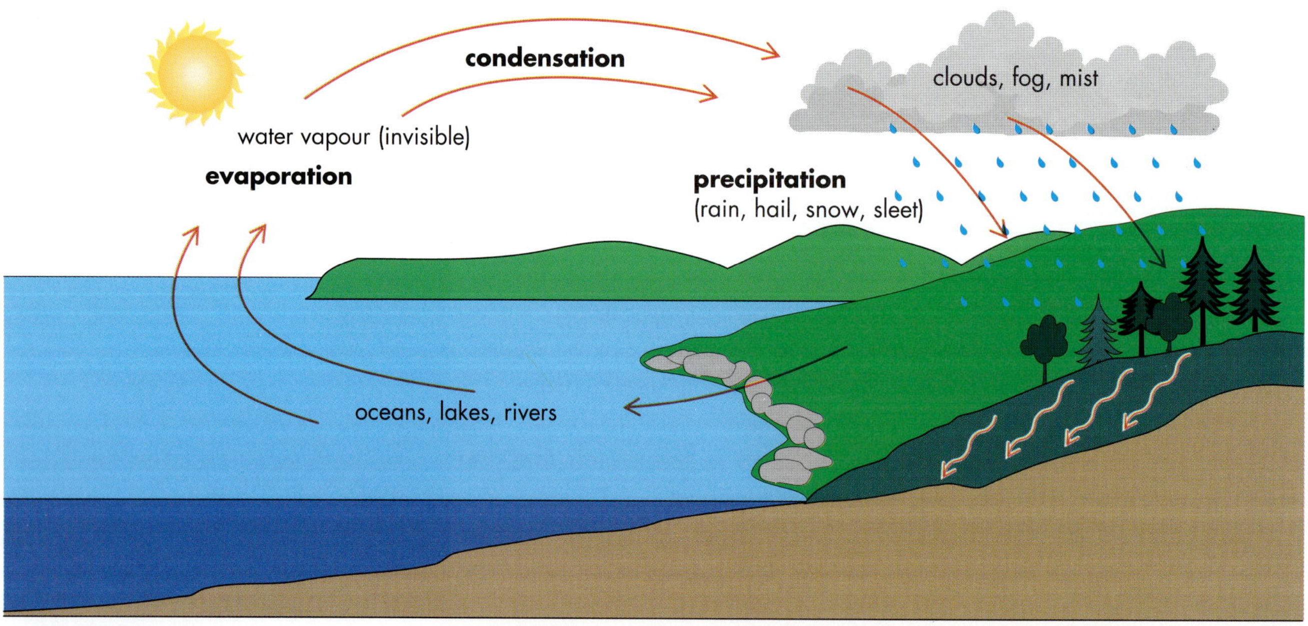

The energy for moving water through the water cycle comes from the sun. The sun's heat evaporates water from the surface of oceans, lakes, and the land. Winds pick up more water as they blow across open oceans. (Recall that winds are formed by rising air warmed indirectly by the sun). Additional small amounts of water vapour are put into the atmosphere from the breathing of plants and animals, and from burning fuels. Water that is removed from the Earth in these ways is eventually replaced by rainfall, which fills the lakes and swells the rivers that run into the oceans.

REVIEW 17.3

1. Describe how you can estimate the relative humidity of the air.
2. How do clouds form?
3. What is needed to make rain fall from clouds?
4. Why do water droplets form on the outside of a glass of ice water on a summer's day?
5. Suggest why there is no dew on the ground after a windy night.
6. Is this statement true? "Last year's snow can be this year's rain." Why?

17.4 FORECASTING THE WEATHER

Knowing how different kinds of weather are produced can help you tell what the weather is going to be like in the next day or so. The first step in weather forecasting is to record your observations of local weather conditions. Changes in temperature, wind direction, humidity, air pressure, and cloud formation are all useful clues to what the next few hours or days will bring.

FIGURE 17.18 *"Frankly, I don't like the look of the weather. . ."*

ACTIVITY 17H / WEATHER WATCH

GROUP ACTIVITY

This is a class activity. Your class will work in groups to record measurements of the weather and keep track of changes. You will also compare your measurements with those given in the daily weather reports produced by Environment Canada.

MATERIALS

thermometer
barometer
wind vane
other weather-recording apparatus, as available
daily weather reports from the newspaper

PROCEDURE

1. Each group will take measurements each day for 3 or 4 d. All the data will be recorded on class charts. The measurements you can record include temperature, air pressure, wind speed and direction, cloud cover, rainfall, and humidity.
2. From the daily newspaper, cut out weather data for your area each day, including the weather forecasts. Add these data to your charts.
3. When you have collected enough data, make graphs to show changes in the weather from day to day.
4. Examine the chart and graphs for patterns of change and discuss your results in class.

DISCUSSION

1. List the factors associated with
   (a) dry, sunny weather,
   (b) cool, wet weather.
2. What measurements would you use for predicting tomorrow's weather?
3. Suggest how a change in one of your measurements is related to a change that you saw afterwards in the weather.
4. How accurate were the weather forecasts in your newspaper?
5. Predict tomorrow's weather. ❖

EXTENSION

■ Contact the Atmospheric Environment Service in your area. Ask for any weather information booklets that can be sent free to you. How did meteorologists locate areas of low and high pressure before satellites were used?

IMPROVING PREDICTIONS

You can usually forecast that rain is moving into your neighbourhood when the air pressure falls. The falling pressure makes the air expand and cool, causing water to condense and clouds to form. Other signs of an approaching storm include stronger winds, lower temperatures, and increasing cloudiness. If the air pressure rises, it means that good weather is on the way. The atmosphere in your neighbourhood is warming up. The warmer air turns clouds back to water vapour, and the skies clear up.

Because high and low pressure areas are always moving, observations made in one place can only give advance notice of the weather a few hours ahead. To keep track of weather changes across the country, the Government of Canada operates many weather stations in every province. The observers at each station send their data several times a day to a central computer. Computers use the information to make weather maps. Scientists who study the weather, called **meteorologists**, use these maps to prepare a **weather forecast**, or prediction for the next few hours or days.

The biggest help to weather forecasting today comes from photographs and information provided by satellites many kilometres above the Earth (Figure 17.19). Satellite photographs actually show us the clouds as they move over the continent, allowing forecasts of the weather to be made days in advance. So you can get your weather forecast from the radio or newspaper, or predict for yourself based on winds, clouds, and other signs.

FIGURE 17.19

A satellite photograph showing clouds moving around the Earth. The white spot over Florida is a hurricane. What do you think the weather was like on Vancouver Island the day after this photograph was taken?

REVIEW 17.4

1. Name two different weather conditions and describe how each can help you predict the weather over the next few hours.
2. List three instruments used to measure various weather conditions. What does each instrument record?
3. What do the letters "H" and "L" mean on a weather map?
4. If your barometer shows the air pressure is rising, would you expect good or bad weather to follow? Why?
5. How do weather satellites help meteorologists make weather forecasts?

CHAPTER REVIEW

KEY IDEAS

- Weather is produced by changes in the temperature, humidity, and movement of air in the atmosphere.
- Air pressure is greatest at sea level and decreases as you get higher. An increase in air pressure leads to an increase in temperature.
- Air pressure is measured by a barometer. Changes in air pressure help us predict changes in the weather.
- The temperature of the Earth is affected by the amount of land or water in a region and the angle of the sun's rays when they reach the surface.
- The Earth's surface heats the air above it during the day, causing the air to rise. In turn, rising air currents produce winds.
- Patterns of wind movement around the world are caused by the rising of warm air at the equator and the sinking of cold air at the poles. The direction of the prevailing winds is also affected by the rotation, or turning, of the Earth.
- Wind blowing over the ocean produces ocean currents. Warm and cold ocean currents affect the weather of the land near the ocean.
- The humidity of the air depends on the air temperature and the closeness of a land region to an ocean or large lake.
- Clouds form when humid air cools to its dew point and the moisture in the air condenses. When the water or ice droplets in a cloud grow to a certain size, they fall as precipitation.
- Water continually evaporates from the Earth's surface into the atmosphere and falls from the atmosphere as precipitation, producing an endless water cycle.

VOCABULARY

atmosphere
air pressure
barometer
aneroid barometer
prevailing wind
ocean current
humidity
relative humidity
saturated
dew
dew point
water cycle
meteorologist
weather forecast

V1. Draw a mind map. Beginning with the word "atmosphere," use terms from the vocabulary list, or any other terms that you know.

V2. Prepare a short quiz, choosing five terms from the vocabulary list as answers. When you have written five questions, swap your quiz with a partner. Answer one another's questions, using the correct terms from the list.

CONNECTIONS

C1. How can air pressure be measured? List at least two ways and describe each.

C2. What happens to the gas molecules in a helium-filled balloon as it rises into the sky? Would you inflate a balloon to its maximum capacity with helium gas before releasing it? Explain why or why not. What will eventually happen to the balloon?

C3. How do changes in air temperature cause winds to form?

C4. (a) What effect does temperature have on the amount of water vapour in the air?
(b) What other factor affects the amount of water vapour in the air?

C5. List some weather observations that you could easily make in school that are most likely to be associated with
(a) cold, wet weather,
(b) warm, sunny weather.

C6. Why do most storms that bring rainy weather to British Columbia come from the west?

C7. Why are some parts of the world warmer than others? Suggest several reasons.

C8. It is a warm summer day on the west coast of British Columbia.
(a) In which direction is the wind most likely to blow?

(b) When are winds likely to be strongest?
(c) Why is there often no wind early in the morning?

C9. Think of some people for whom accurate weather forecasts are very important and explain why these people need good weather reports.

EXPLORATIONS

E1. Find out about violent weather conditions such as tornadoes and hurricanes. Do such storms ever occur in Canada? What causes them, and what signs would warn you of their approach?

E2. Consult a reference to find out how clouds are classified. Based on what you have learned, classify the cloud types shown in Figure 17.20. What sort of weather would you associate with each type of cloud?

E3. Interview someone whose job depends on the weather — for example, an airplane pilot or a ship's captain. Find out what weather information they need to carry out their work safely.

E4. There are many popular sayings about the weather. For example: "Red sky at night, sailors' delight. Red sky in the morning, sailors take warning." Find out and write down other sayings about the weather. Why do you think many of these old expressions come from sailors or farmers? Give evidence that might support some of these sayings.

E5. Weather maps usually show a lot more than high and low pressure areas. Find out about the following features:
(a) isobars,
(b) isotherms,
(c) cold front,
(d) warm front.
Make a poster to show how each term is displayed on a weather map and record what each term means.

E6. The type of weather in an area is closely connected with the type of plants that grow there. Make a map of British Columbia, showing
(a) the major types of vegetation growing in different regions,
(b) the type of weather in each region.

E7. Make some weather-recording instruments of your own and set up a meteorological station at your home or school. Keep records of the weather for a period of time and display your results on a chart.

REFLECTIONS

R1. In what ways have your ideas about the weather changed since you began studying this chapter?

(a) *(b)* *(c)*

FIGURE 17.20
Three types of clouds. What is each type called by meteorologists?

UNDERSTANDING ECOLOGY

Suppose you are standing on the floor of a forest in British Columbia. Trees tower above you and soil stretches below. The longer you stand listening and looking, the more you notice: drifting clouds, trickling water, rustling leaves, scurrying animals, and buzzing insects. Living and non-living things are all around you.

As the living things in the forest around you grow, build homes, eat or are eaten, they pass materials and energy from one place to another. Like the different parts of a huge machine, living and non-living things act together as a single system. No part of this system can be altered without affecting other parts.

Even standing on the forest floor, you are affecting your surroundings in small ways. Certain insects are attracted by your colourful clothing, some birds are frightened into the treetops, and your feet and your shadow block the sunlight from reaching small plants. Many human activities affect the natural world in much larger ways. Sometimes humans poison animals that cause damage to crops, pets, and human property. Sometimes they cut down forests in order to produce paper, build houses, or make playing fields.

In this unit, you will learn more about the ways plants and animals interact with each other and with the non-living parts of their environment. What role do humans play in this system? You will also consider the problems caused when certain plant and animal populations threaten human well-being. And in this unit, you will learn about the ways humans have altered forests like the one in this photograph. How are trees removed from forests? How are forests managed?

UNIT 6

CHAPTER 18

YOU AND THE ENVIRONMENT

These students from a school outdoor club are hiking and camping far from home for three days and two nights. The club members have all planned their adventure carefully. What supplies do you think they needed to bring along in order to survive? What living and non-living things from the wilderness environment might they use?

The outdoor club's rule is, "Take nothing but photographs and leave nothing but footprints." Do you think anyone could follow this rule perfectly? How do you think the hikers might affect the area where they hike and camp? How might the trip also affect them? After the students leave each campsite, how will the area and the students be different?

Because people are living creatures, we are also part of the natural world, whether we are hiking in a forest or walking to school. Sometimes when we are in our comfortable homes or classrooms, we do not realize that we are affecting our surroundings and that they are affecting us.

In this chapter, you will investigate some of the ways that all living things interact with their surroundings. By learning how plants and animals depend on one another, you will be able to understand more about the living world of which you are a part.

ACTIVITY 18A / YOUR ENVIRONMENT

In the centre of a large sheet of paper, write "the environment around my school." Beginning with these words, construct a mind map to show some of the important living and non-living things that are connected with you and your school environment. ❖

18.1 EARTH'S ECOSYSTEMS

The word **environment** is usually used to describe all the living and non-living things that surround and influence a living thing. The study of how Earth's living and non-living parts affect each other is called **ecology**. This word comes from two Greek words: *oikos* (home) and *logos* (to study). The non-living or **abiotic** parts of the environment include such things as water, soil, sunlight, and air. The living or **biotic** parts of the environment consist of animals and plants.

The planet Earth is home to millions of different kinds of living things called **organisms**. A huge number of these living things are so small that they can only be seen with the help of a microscope. These very tiny organisms are called **micro-organisms** (Figure 18.1).

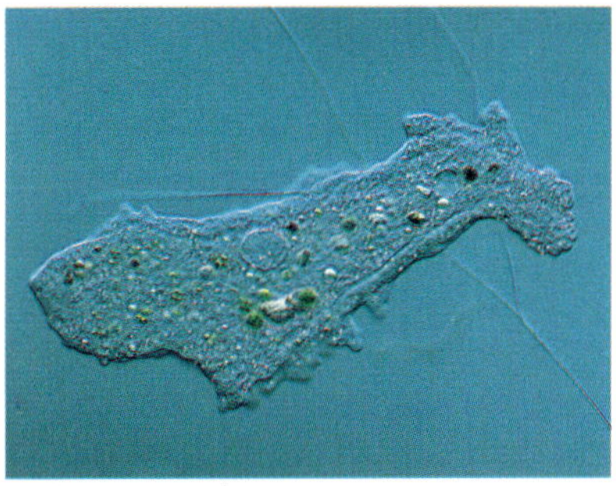

(a) An amoeba

(b) Rod-shaped bacteria

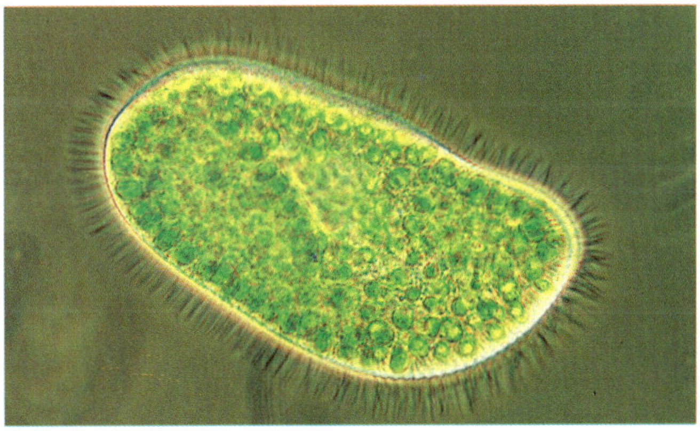

(c) A paramecium

FIGURE 18.1
Micro-organisms are so small that they can be studied only through a microscope, yet they play very important roles in maintaining life on Earth.

You already know many ways in which different parts of the environment act on each other or **interact**. These relationships between parts of the environment are called **interactions**. For instance, when rain washes away soil on a trail, that is an interaction between two abiotic parts of the environment. When a camper steps on a plant while collecting firewood, that is an interaction between two biotic parts of the environment. When you take a breath of air, that is an interaction between a biotic part and an abiotic part of the environment. Figure 18.2 shows some parts of the environment of a buttercup growing in a field.

FIGURE 18.2
The environment can be divided into abiotic and biotic parts. Think of your environment at home. What are the biotic parts? The abiotic parts?

The entire system formed by the interaction of the different parts of the environment is called an **ecosystem**. Scientists who study these interactions are called **ecologists**. Because their work involves every part of the environment, ecologists use knowledge from many branches of science. Chemistry, mathematics, geology, physics, biology, and even astronomy help ecologists understand the interactions that affect life on our planet.

ACTIVITY 18B / WHAT IS IN YOUR SCHOOLYARD?

GROUP ACTIVITY · CROSS-CURRICULAR

In this group activity, you will study your schoolyard environment (Figure 18.3) and consider how the biotic and abiotic parts affect each other.

MATERIALS

notebook
paper or cardboard
pen or pencil
hand lens
field guides

PROCEDURE

1. Before going outside to observe, work with your group to make a list of all the different types of organisms you think you could find around your school buildings. Be prepared to discuss this list with the whole class.
2. Work with your classmates to draw a large outline map on a piece of paper or cardboard, showing possible study areas. Label some important features such as buildings, soccer fields, fences, etc. Draw an arrow pointing north.
3. As a class, decide what symbols you will use to show different organisms on a map. For example, you might use green lines for trees, brown dots for insects, and blue circles for birds. Make a legend in the lower right-hand corner of your map. Copy this legend into your notebook.

FIGURE 18.3
If you look closely, you can find living things in many places, even where you don't expect to find them!

4. Follow your teacher's instructions about cutting this large map into "jigsaw" sections for the different small groups to explore. Later your class will reassemble the pieces to make a large, complete map.
5. Carefully study your group's map before you proceed outside. Review any outside safety procedures with your teacher.
6. Take your map, hand lens, notebook, and field guides and go to your group's study area. Walk around your area and take note of different places to search for organisms, such as an area under a tree, an area with water, or an area beside a wall.
7. While outside, record in your notebook all the abiotic factors you can observe. For example, is it shady or sunny? Warm or cool? Damp or dry? Is the soil sandy or clay-like? Is the ground level or hilly? On your map, use your class symbols to indicate all the kinds of organisms you can find in 10 to 15 minutes. On your map, show areas where plants are much smaller or much larger than in other areas. (Note: Do not pick or break any plants or damage flowerbeds. If you turn over a rock or log to see what is underneath, be sure to replace it carefully before you leave.)
8. When you have completed your section of the map, return to class and work with the other groups to tape the pieces back together to make one map that shows all the discoveries made by your class. Study the finished large map. In your notebook, make a table listing the location of all of the organisms that your class has mapped.

EXTENSION

■ Name a kind of wild plant that is found in your community but is missing from your schoolyard. Why do you think it does not live there? What changes would you need to make in your schoolyard environment before this plant could live there? Would you want to live with a large number of these plants? Which plant would you not choose to attract to your schoolyard?

DISCUSSION

1. On the large map, find areas where no plants or animals were observed. What could be a reason no living things were observed?
2. What living things did you find that you did not expect? What was the most common organism and what was the least common organism?
3. Briefly describe how one of the abiotic factors you observed might affect
   (a) a plant,
   (b) an animal.
   For example, does the plant or animal need a particular amount of light or moisture?
4. How might one of the animals you found affect one of the plants?
5. How might one of the plants affect one of the animals?
6. Explain why you might get different results in your survey if you did it
   (a) at night,
   (b) during winter,
   (c) during summer holidays.
7. Make a sketch map in which you redesign your schoolyard so that a greater variety of living things can share the area with you. For example, you might add a pond, certain trees, local shrubs, or flowers. Include a legend for your map.
8. In your learning journal, describe what you have learned about your schoolyard environment. ❖

FROM BIOSPHERE TO MICRO-ENVIRONMENT

An organism's home is the place where it lives. But where exactly does an organism's home begin and end? For example, is a slug's home the forest, or only the few square metres under a fallen tree where the slug spends most of its time? One answer is that both places are its home. In the same way, your home includes not only your house or apartment, but your community, your province, and the whole country of Canada (Figure 18.4). You live in all these places, as the address in the figure shows. Each line of the address describes just a part of the line that follows it.

In the study of ecology, you can draw many imaginary boundaries in the environment. You can choose to study any part of your surroundings, from the environment in a small puddle of water to the environment of the entire planet. Each smaller environment affects, and is affected by, the larger environments.

FIGURE 18.4 ▶
Where do you live?

The largest ecosystem that ecologists study is called the **biosphere** (Figure 18.5). It includes all the places on our planet where organisms can survive—from the ocean depths to high in the atmosphere, and from the poles to the equator. You can think of the biosphere as a layer of life covering the entire planet. All parts of this huge ecosystem are connected by currents of air and water, and by the movements of organisms.

Within the biosphere, different areas of our planet have different climates. Areas near the equator are generally hotter than those near the poles. Regions of land near oceans, such as the coastal area of British Columbia, usually have wetter climates than regions toward the centre of continents, such as the Okanagan. In different climates and soils, different types of plants tend to grow. For example, bunch grass, sagebrush, and Ponderosa pine grow in some dry regions of the British Columbia interior, whereas hemlock and salmonberry grow in wetter coastal areas. These different kinds of plants provide food for different kinds of animals—California bighorn sheep in some interior

DID YOU KNOW

■ Plant seeds may be carried by birds from one continent to another. The seeds stick to mud on the feet of migrating birds, or are carried inside the bird's stomach. Some seeds cannot grow unless they first pass through a bird or animal's stomach. How would this help both the bird and the plant?

(a) (b) (c) (d)

FIGURE 18.5

The Earth's biosphere (a) contains many ecosystems (b). Within each ecosystem are many habitats (c). Each habitat contains smaller micro-environments (d). Choose an animal that lives wild in your community (don't forget the insects!). What is its habitat?

areas and Columbia blacktailed deer in some coastal forests. The result is patterns of different ecosystems with their own particular climate, plants, and animals.

Within each large ecosystem, there are many different places in which organisms may live. Each different location, such as a pond, a forest, or a field, is called a **habitat**. In an organism's "address," a habitat is like the home town—the place where the organism spends most of its time. The size of an organism's habitat depends on the size and needs of the organism. For example, a wolf's habitat may include hundreds of square kilometres of forest. A spider's habitat may be a single bush or tree. A micro-organism may spend its entire life in a spoonful of soil.

EXTENSION

- In general, the climate gets colder and drier as you move from the equator toward the North and South Poles. The climate also changes as you climb a mountain from the base to the top. Find out how abiotic conditions change with altitude (height). What effect do you think altitude might have on the vegetation growing up the side of a mountain?
- In a suitable area near your school or home, measure differences in temperature in different micro-environments. For example, compare the temperature within different parts of a rotting tree stump.

Each habitat may include many smaller areas, or **micro-environments**, which have their own abiotic conditions (Figure 18.6). For example, in a forest habitat, an area beneath a fallen tree will be cooler, darker, and damper than other parts of the forest. Some organisms may be able to live only in these smaller parts of a habitat.

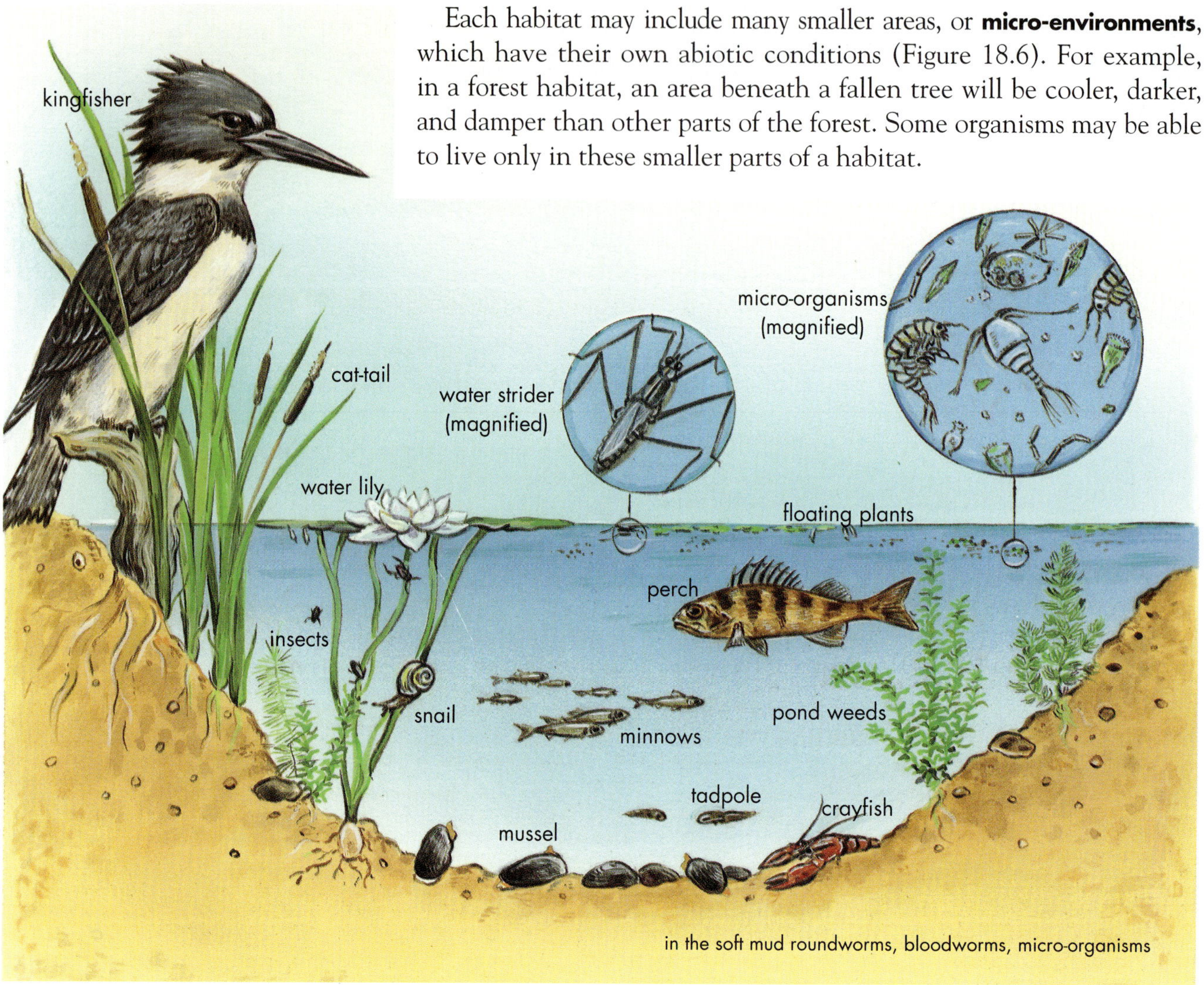

FIGURE 18.6
A pond habitat may be divided into several smaller micro-environments. How many micro-environments are there in this pond?

▶ REVIEW 18.1

1. List two examples of the abiotic parts of a forest environment and three examples of the biotic parts.

2. What abiotic factors might affect the survival of a group of pine trees growing near the edge of a rock cliff overlooking the Pacific Ocean?

3. List some of the
(a) abiotic parts of your environment and
(b) biotic parts of your environment that you have interacted with today. Describe each interaction.

4. Explain the term "micro-environment" by describing a micro-environment near your home. Name an animal that might live there.

5. Suppose a treed area in your community was cleared of underbrush. Suggest several changes in the area's ecosystem that might result.

18.2 OBTAINING ENERGY AND NUTRIENTS

Organisms need more than a suitable climate and habitat. They also need energy in order to carry out their activities. Organisms get their energy from food. But different organisms obtain food from their environment in very different ways (Figure 18.7).

Green plants, water plants called algae, and some micro-organisms can make their own food using materials from the abiotic environment alone. For example, green plants use water and carbon dioxide gas, plus the energy of sunlight, to produce sugar. You may have studied this process, called photosynthesis, in Chapter 9.

$$\text{water} + \text{carbon dioxide} \xrightarrow{\text{sunlight}} \text{sugar} + \text{oxygen}$$

FIGURE 18.7
How does each of these organisms obtain its food?

Because green plants can produce their own food in this way, ecologists call them **producers**. They form a very important link between the abiotic and the biotic environment.

Animals and most micro-organisms can obtain their energy only from consuming (eating) living things or the products of living things. Because of this, ecologists call them **consumers**. Consumers may be further grouped by the type of organisms they usually eat. Plant eaters, such as deer and rabbits, are called **primary consumers** or herbivores because they feed directly on producers. Meat eaters, such as wolves, frogs, and spiders, get most of their energy by eating other consumers. Animals that feed upon consumers are called **secondary consumers** or carnivores. Animals that kill and eat other animals are also called predators. The animals that they eat are called prey.

A few types of animals feed on secondary consumers—for example, hawks that eat snakes that eat frogs. These animals are called top predators or **higher order consumers**. Although these ways of

DID YOU KNOW

- Animals that are both primary and secondary consumers are called omnivores. People, bears, and rats are omnivores. How would it help an animal to be able to eat both plants and animals?

grouping consumers are useful for studying ecosystems, not all organisms fit exactly into one group or another. For example, there are organisms that eat plants *and* animals.

FOOD CHAINS AND FOOD WEBS

What happens when you eat an orange, or when a frog eats a worm, or when a grasshopper eats a leaf? When any organism eats, materials and energy pass from one organism to another. (Most of the energy that flows from one organism to another is given up or lost to the surrounding environment in the form of heat.) Organisms joined by this transfer of energy become part of a **food chain**. Each organism in the chain depends on the organism before it in the chain for its food. The next time you eat a meal of fish and chips, think of the tiny plants and animals in the ocean (plankton). There would be no fish for you to eat if it were not for the plankton that are eaten up by the smaller fish in the food chain.

Figure 18.8 shows how energy moves through one food chain on land and through a different food chain in a pond or lake. Notice that both food chains begin with energy from sunlight. The sun's energy is used by producers to produce plant sugars. The sugars then provide energy for consumers. All consumers depend on producers—either directly if they eat producers, or indirectly if they eat animals that eat producers.

Most organisms are part of more than one food chain. For example, the mouse in Figure 18.9 might eat several different types of seeds, fruits, and plants. The mouse may then be eaten by an owl or a fox or a snake. For this reason, the individual food chains in an ecosystem are linked together and are called **food webs**.

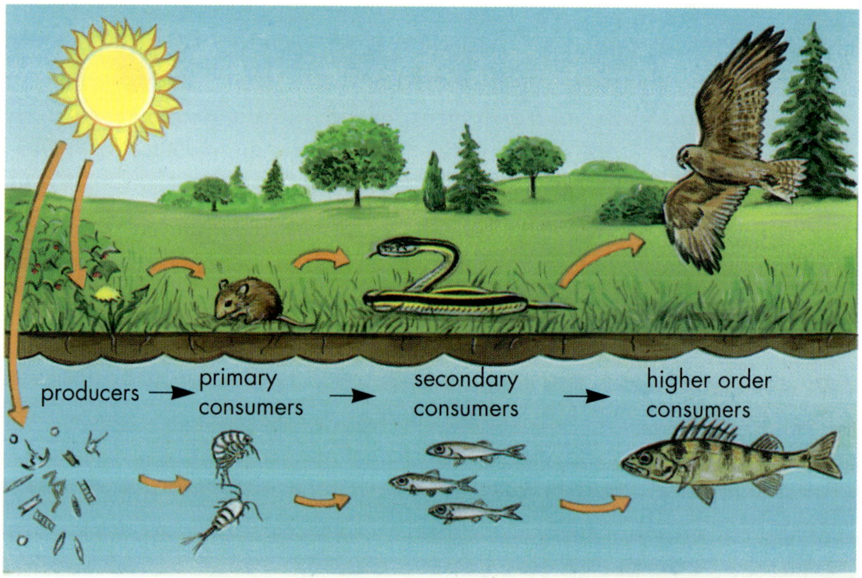

FIGURE 18.8 ▶
The flow of energy through two different food chains. The arrows show the direction of the energy flow. What is the original source of energy for each food chain?

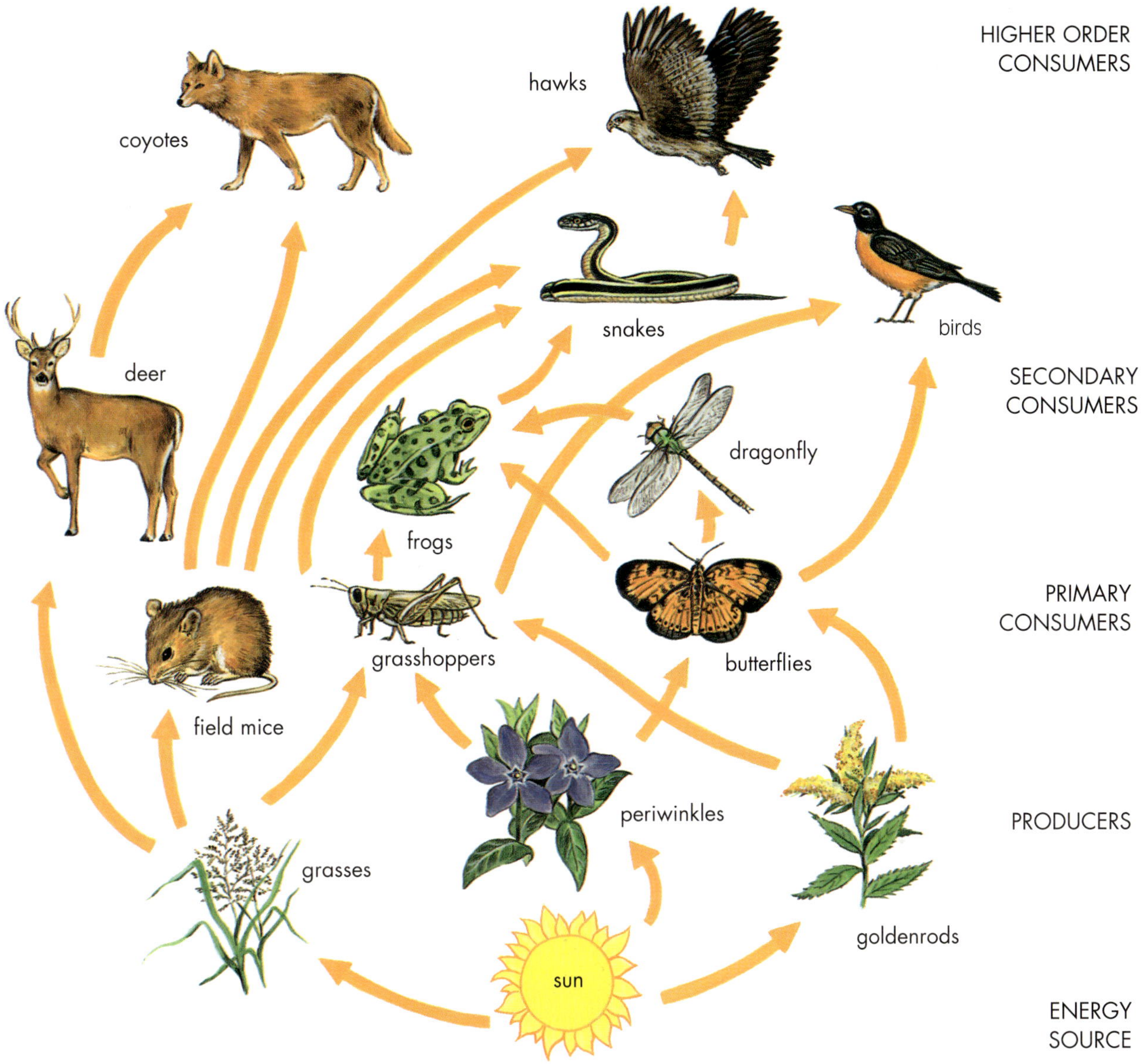

FIGURE 18.9

Food webs are made up of many food chains. If you wanted to add mosquitoes to this food web, where would you draw them?

ACTIVITY 18C / EAT AND BE EATEN

GROUP ACTIVITY

This group activity will help you understand how organisms are linked together in food webs (Figure 18.10).

MATERIALS

- scissors
- pictures of animals and plants
- paper
- coloured pens or pencils
- glue or tape ➡

FIGURE 18.10
Constructing food webs

PROCEDURE

1. Cut out the set of pictures of animals and plants provided by your teacher.
2. With two or three classmates, divide the organisms into groups: producers, primary consumers, secondary consumers, and higher order consumers. Mark all the pictures, using a different colour or symbol for each group. For example, you could use P for producers, PC for primary consumers, SC for secondary consumers, and HOC for higher order consumers.
3. Arrange the pictures on a large sheet of paper to make a food web. When you and your group members are satisfied with the arrangement of organisms, glue or tape the pictures to the paper.
4. Draw connecting arrows between the organisms in your food web to show how energy moves through the web.
5. Give your food web a name, such as "A Lake Food Web."
6. Use your completed food web to answer the questions that follow.

DISCUSSION

1. In a real food web, which group would have the most individuals in it: producers, primary consumers, secondary consumers, or higher order consumers? Arrange the groups from largest to smallest. Use examples from your food web to explain why you decided on this order.
2. Give examples of two other organisms that could be added to your food web. In your notebook, draw food chains to show how they would link to some of the organisms that are already in your web.
3. Predict what might happen to some of the organisms in your food web if you remove
   (a) one of the producers,
   (b) one of the primary consumers,
   (c) one of the secondary consumers,
   (d) one of the higher order consumers. ❖

NUTRIENT CYCLES

So far, you have considered food only as a source of energy. But organisms need **nutrients** as well as energy. Nutrients are chemical substances that organisms must have in order to live. Plants take up the nutrients they need from soil or water, and animals get nutrients from their food. Nitrogen is an example of a nutrient needed by plants and animals.

Nutrients and energy are different. Energy is always entering the biosphere as sunlight and leaving the biosphere as heat, while nutrients can only be found on the Earth itself. In order to supply the needs of organisms year after year, nutrients must be recycled and reused (Figure 18.11).

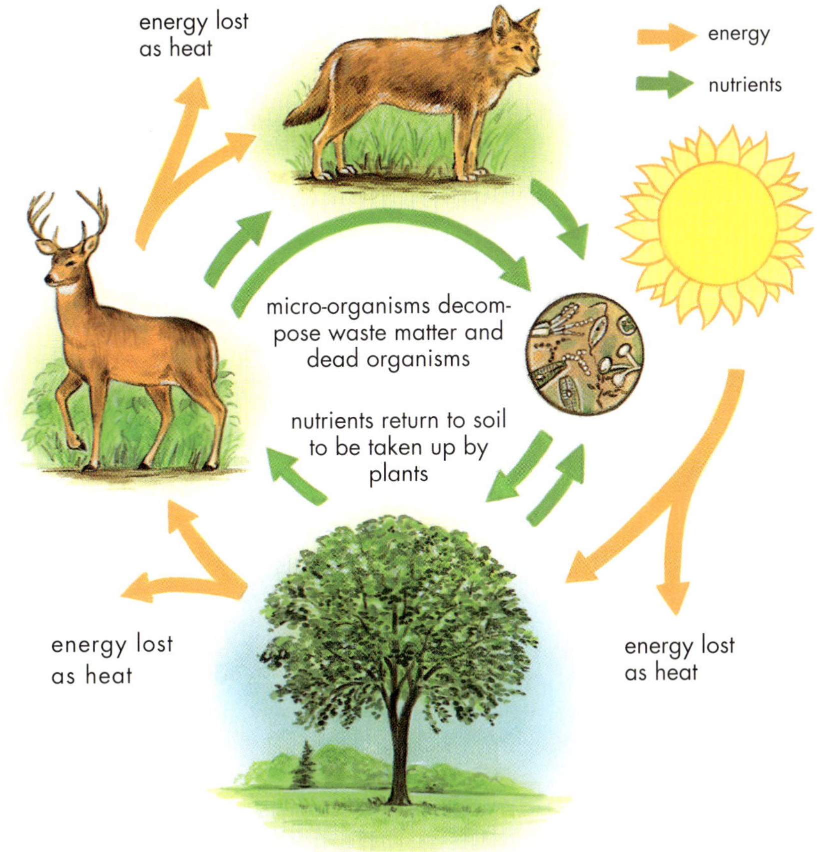

FIGURE 18.11
The sun's energy flows into ecosystems and spreads out through the different levels. Most of the energy that flows from one organism to another is "lost" as heat and is given up to the surrounding environment. Nutrients behave differently. Nutrients are recycled over and over within the biosphere.

Nutrients are often recycled through another sort of food chain—a food chain of decay. This chain is made up of organisms that feed on waste matter and things that are already dead. Such organisms are called **decomposers** (Figure 18.12). Bacteria (singular: bacterium) and fungi (singular: fungus) are some examples of decomposers. Bacteria are simple micro-organisms. Fungi include such organisms as mushrooms and molds. These and other decomposers break down (decompose) the bodies of dead animals and plants into smaller particles. This process releases nutrients into the soil, water, and air, where they can be taken in by producers to be used again. In this way, the nutrients in the biosphere move back and forth between the biotic and the abiotic environment.

FIGURE 18.12
Decomposers, such as fungi, break down dead organisms and waste matter and release their nutrients. What other examples of decomposers can you think of?

ACTIVITY 18D / JOURNEY OF A NUTRIENT

CROSS-CURRICULAR

In this activity, you will trace the path of a nutrient through an ecosystem.

PROCEDURE

Write a story describing the journey of a nutrient. (You might look at Figure 18.13 for some ideas.) Use some of the terms and information you have learned in this chapter to create a nutrient "adventure."

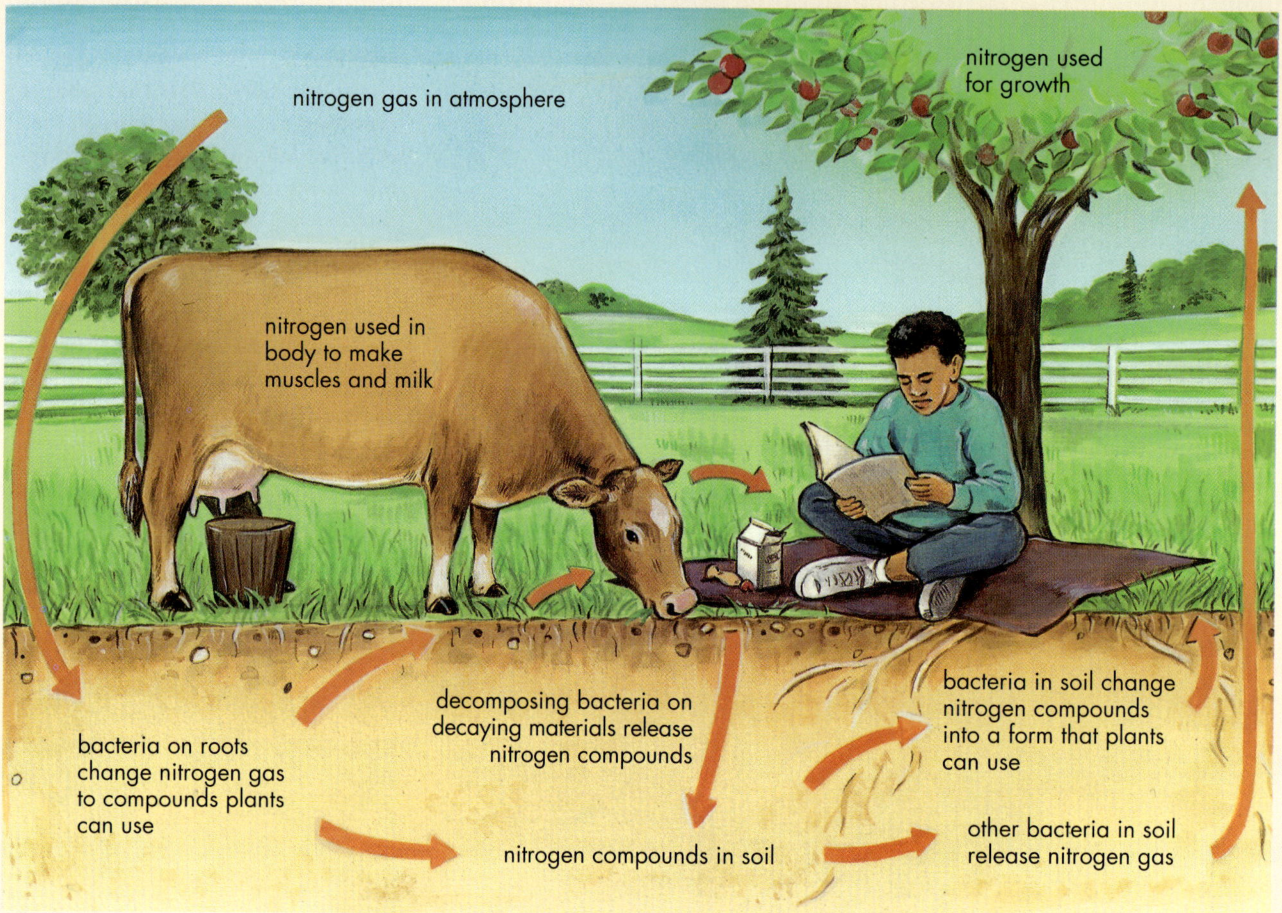

FIGURE 18.13

Nitrogen is a nutrient that moves through the ecosystem. We need nitrogen for our muscles and many other body parts. Although we are surrounded by nitrogen in the air, we cannot use it just by breathing. We need to eat food containing nitrogen compounds to get the nutrient into our bodies. ❖

▶ REVIEW 18.2

1. Give an example of a producer, a primary consumer, a secondary consumer, and a higher order consumer. Explain the role of each in a food chain.

2. Draw a food web that includes all the following organisms: mouse, dandelion, wheat, frog, grasshopper, hawk, house cat, sparrow, rattlesnake.

3. What is a nutrient?

4. In what ways are nutrients different from energy?

5. Give an example of an organism that is a decomposer, and describe what it does.

6. Name two places where you would expect to find a lot of decomposers, and explain why you think they would be there.

7. All the life on Earth can trace the energy it uses to the same source. What is that source? Sketch two possible paths that energy might take from this source to your body.

18.3 RELATIONSHIPS BETWEEN LIVING THINGS

Organisms are rarely found alone in nature. They are usually found together with other organisms of the same kind or **species**. For instance, Canada geese are usually found in a flock.

Depending on their size and the way they live, anywhere from two to hundreds of thousands of individuals of a particular species may live together in a particular area at a particular time. Because of this, ecologists often study an entire group of a species. This entire group is called a **population**.

Populations of different species living in the same habitat form a **community**. For example, a forest community might include populations of deer, wolves, squirrels, mosquitoes, mushrooms, ferns, mosses, cedars, maples, owls, woodpeckers, and many other species. The community of organisms along with the abiotic environment make up the ecosystem (Figure 18.14).

individual

population

community

ecosystem

FIGURE 18.14
The different levels of organization from individuals to the ecosystem. What population, community, and ecosystem do you belong to?

KINDS OF RELATIONSHIPS

You can get a better understanding of communities by studying the relationships between the different organisms in a community. There are many possible kinds of relationships between living things. In some cases, two different organisms benefit from the relationship between them. For instance, certain bacteria find a warm home with a steady food supply in the stomach of herbivores like deer. In return, the bacteria help digest the tough plant food that the deer consume. In another type of relationship, one community member benefits and the other is harmed, such as when a predator eats its prey (for example, a cougar eats a deer). Sometimes, one organism is helped by the presence of the other, but the other is neither harmed nor helped. An example of this is a robin living in the tree. The robin is helped because the tree provides it with a place for a nest, but the tree is probably not affected.

ACTIVITY 18E / THINKING ABOUT RELATIONSHIPS

GROUP ACTIVITY

In this group activity you will think about the possible ways that plants and animals might affect each other and you will use some symbols to record these interactions.

PROCEDURE

1. Copy Table 18.1 into your notebook.
2. In the square joining each pair of community members, describe the interaction by using a pair of symbols. Use a positive sign (+) to stand for a benefit, a minus sign (–) for a harmful effect, and a zero (0) for an interaction that is neither helpful nor harmful.

	bunch grass	mice	grass-hoppers	rattle-snakes	hawks	deer-flies	song-birds	white-tailed deer
bunch grass								
mice								
grasshoppers								
rattlesnakes								
hawks								
deerflies								
songbirds								
white-tailed deer								

TABLE 18.1
A Relationship Grid

If both organisms benefit, fill the square with (+,+).

If one organism benefits and the other is harmed, use (+,–).

If one benefits and the other is neither harmed nor helped, use (+,0).

For example, if you think that bunch grass would be harmed by deer feeding on it, you would write the relationship in this square as (–,+).

3. Discuss your ideas with other members of your group, then decide what you think each relationship might be. Complete the number of rows assigned by your teacher.

DISCUSSION

1. Examine the findings of other groups.
(a) Do most of your classmates agree about the symbols that should go into each square?
(b) Do you think that scientists always agree when describing relationships? Explain.

2. Make a list of (+,–) relationships that you can think of.

3. If all the snakes in an area were removed, what could happen to
(a) the mouse population?
(b) the bunch grass population?
(c) the deer population?

4. Some people refer to the total system of all of these relationships in ecosystems as "the balance of nature." Do you think that all these relationships are in a state of balance? Explain. ❖

NUMBERS OF LIVING THINGS

There are many reasons why people may want to know the numbers of animals or plants in an area. For example, a forester may need to know how many trees of a certain species are in a forest. A biologist may need to know the population of ducks in a marsh. A fruit-grower may want to know if the population of insect pests in an orchard is getting larger. How could the forester or biologist or fruit-grower determine these numbers?

Because it is usually difficult or impossible to count all the individual organisms in a large area, especially if the organisms move around, ecologists have developed many methods to help them estimate the sizes of different populations. One of these methods involves running lines of string through an area. At regular spaces along each line, you count every plant that touches or is close to the line. This is called the **line transect** method of estimating populations.

ACTIVITY 18F / TAGS AND STRINGS

GROUP ACTIVITY

In this field trip activity, you will use the line transect method to estimate plant populations.

MATERIALS

string, 30 m, wound
compass
surveyor tape (two or more colours)
coloured pencils
notebook
whistles (one per person)
field guides

PROCEDURE

1. As a class, select a treed area that appears to have an interesting variety of plant species. Review safety procedures before your group proceeds outside.
2. As a class, decide the general direction that you will be following into the forest. Tie one end of the 30 m string to a tree. Mark the tree with surveyor tape. You may need to use a longer string in more open forests. Hold the spool and let the string unwind as you walk from tree to tree following a compass line (Figure 18.15). Do not worry if your line is not exactly straight. Take care not to trample ferns and other small plants.
3. When you come to the end of your string, walk back along the marked line. Tag the line with surveyor tape each time a tree or shrub touches the line. You may tag the line with different colours to show different species.

FIGURE 18.15 ▶
Plants growing along a line transect are marked on the line using pieces of surveyor tape.

FIGURE 18.16
Leaf rubbings. Above each rubbing, keep score of the number of times that the species touched the line.

4. Pick a leaf or cluster of needles from every tree that touches the line. If the lowest branches are beyond your reach, sketch a leaf instead of picking it, or try to find a leaf of the same species that you can reach. Collect or sketch each type of leaf and try to group them. Use a coloured pencil and make a rubbing of each kind of leaf (Figure 18.16).
5. Use the samples and field guides to identify each species.
6. Note how many individual plants of each species touch your transect line.
7. Collect the surveyor tape and wind up your transect strings.

DISCUSSION

1. Arrange the samples or rubbings of the species that touched your line transect from most common to least common. How do your results differ from those of other students in the classroom?
2. What abiotic factors do you think might favour the most common species?
3. Communities are often named after their most common plant species. Decide on a name for the community that you have just studied.
4. How could a road be used as a line transect? How far away from the road do you think you should go to sample the populations? Explain your answers. ❖

FIGURE 18.17
How many birds are in the flock in this photograph? Count the number in each square and then total these numbers.

ESTIMATING ANIMAL POPULATIONS

Unlike plants, most animals do not stay in one place all the time. This makes it more difficult for ecologists to estimate the size of animal populations. One technique used for animals that gather in large flocks or herds involves photography. A researcher takes a photograph of the flock, then counts the animals in the photograph. For example, herds of seals and caribou may be photographed from an aircraft, and flocks of birds can be photographed as they fly overhead. To make the counting easier, a grid of squares is drawn on the photograph. The number of animals in each square is counted and recorded separately, then added up. You can use this technique to count the number of birds in the flock shown in Figure 18.17.

THE TRANSFER OF ENERGY THROUGH COMMUNITIES

You have learned that energy is transferred from one organism to another along food chains. Diagrams of food chains and food webs show how organisms interact. But diagrams of food chains and webs cannot show the numbers of organisms at each link or the amount of energy that is being transferred from one organism to another. To show such relationships, ecologists use a diagram called an **ecological pyramid**.

You can see from Figure 18.18 that an ecological pyramid has a broad base and a small top. This is because there are usually more organisms at the producer level (the base) than at the consumer levels. The reason is that not all the energy contained in an animal's food is used for its growth and reproduction. In fact, usually only about 10 per cent of the energy present is used. The rest is lost as heat. Because of this, a mouse must eat many seeds, a snake must eat many mice, and a hawk must eat many snakes.

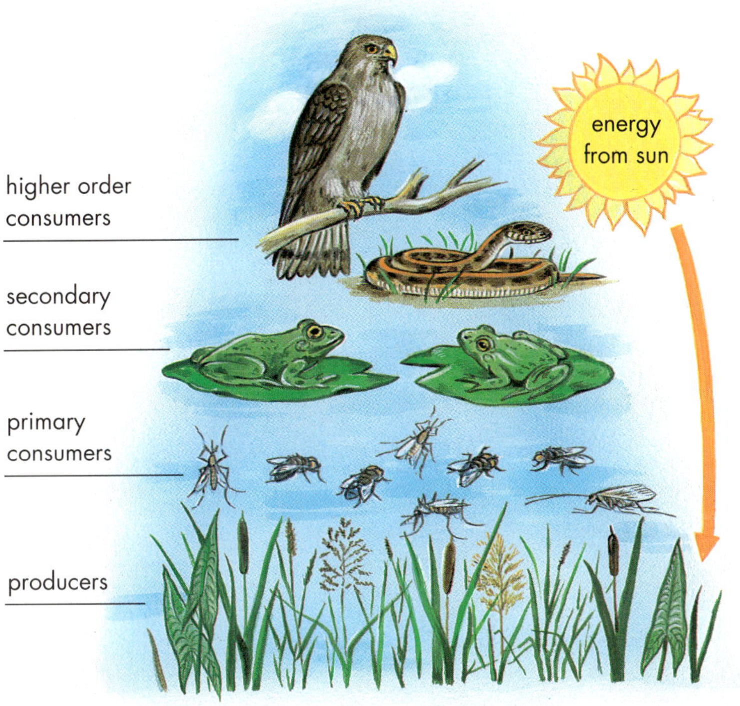

Figure 18.18 **◀**
An ecological pyramid. The mass of all the organisms at the top of an ecological pyramid is always much less than the mass of those at the bottom, because only a small part of the stored energy is passed from each level to the one above. Does this mean that the number of organisms at each level of a pyramid is always less than the number of organisms in the level below?

▶ REVIEW 18.3

1. Write out the sentence below in your notebook, inserting the words "population," "community," and "ecosystem" in the correct blank spaces.
   A ______ of wolves living in the tundra ______ of the far north is part of a ______ that includes caribou and willow trees.
2. Name three things that could affect the number of mice living in a barn. Include at least one biotic factor and one abiotic factor.
3. Suppose you are on a hike and you see a flock of sparrows feeding on bushes beside a road. What could you do to estimate
   (a) the population of sparrows?
   (b) the population of bushes?
4. Why might you see large flocks of pigeons or ducks in a habitat, but rarely see large numbers of eagles? Where do you think each would fit in an ecological pyramid?

18.4 HUMAN ACTIVITIES AND THE ENVIRONMENT

Together, all the activities and relationships that a species has in an ecosystem is called its **niche**. A niche can be thought of as the organism's role or "job" in its ecosystem. The different niches in an ecosystem may be compared to the different jobs that people have in a city. For example, some people drive buses, some manage banks, and some work in hospitals. Everybody in the community depends on everybody else in some way. Suppose all the nurses in your community disappeared. You would eventually be affected. Similarly, removing any species from an ecosystem may have far-reaching effects. For example, removing coyotes from the food web discussed earlier (page 452) can eventually affect such different organisms as mice, grasses, and snakes (Figure 18.19).

FIGURE 18.19
Coyotes, mice, grasses, and snakes always have different niches within their ecosystem. Each species affects the other. What would happen to the mice, grasses, and snakes if coyotes were removed from the ecosystem?

Every species has its own niche, and no two niches in a community are exactly the same. However, different organisms may have a similar niche in different ecosystems. For example, deer in North America and kangaroos in Australia have similar roles as herbivores even though they are very different-looking animals.

DISAPPEARING AND ENDANGERED SPECIES

By changing the environment to meet the needs of our rapidly growing human population, humans are affecting many different species. Human activities such as land clearing, hunting, farming, and fishing all alter the environment. Human attempts to control the numbers of certain species have sometimes had unexpected results. For instance, people have often tried to increase the populations of game animals, such as quail, deer, and fish, by killing their predators—hawks, wolves, and seals. In some cases, this has actually led to decreased numbers of the game animals. Killing hawks, for example, helps increase the populations of the hawks' other prey such as rats and squirrels. These animals, in turn, feed on the eggs and chicks of the ground-nesting quail, reducing the quail population.

When a species dies out and disappears from the biosphere forever, it is said to have become **extinct**. When we study fossils, we discover that extinctions have happened in the past because of events such as climate change and perhaps even the impact of huge meteors. In more recent times, human activities alone have caused species to become extinct or disappear from an area. When people cause oil spills, drain wetlands, cut down forests, dam rivers, and build cities and highways, they also change habitats. Many organisms that lived in the area before it was changed cannot live there afterwards because there is no longer any suitable food or shelter for them.

The disappearance of certain habitats and species may eventually alter the environment in some areas of the world so that humans can no longer live there. The American ecologist Paul Ehrlich once compared the Earth's ecosystems to an airplane. The organisms in an ecosystem are like the bolts that hold an airplane's parts together and allow it to function. What happens to an airplane if the bolts start to pop out? A few may not be missed, because the plane is made with extra bolts for strength and safety. After a certain point, however, the loss of even one more bolt could lead to a serious accident. Similarly, in an ecosystem, the loss of several species could eventually lead to a badly damaged environment in which most organisms could no longer survive.

EXTENSION

- For hundreds of years, the native people living on the land now called British Columbia have obtained food by hunting, fishing, and gathering. Find out about the hunting, fishing, or food-gathering traditions of native peoples in your area. What tools and techniques were used? How did native people regard fish and animals? Were any ceremonies held before or after food was obtained? Prepare an illustrated report of your findings.
- Find out about an organization or corporation that is doing something to help save endangered species of animals and plants. Produce a poster that explains what the organization does. Make up a slogan to use on your poster.

ACTIVITY 18G / GOING, GOING, GONE!

CROSS-CURRICULAR

In this activity, you will report on an endangered species of plant or animal.

PROCEDURE

1. Your teacher will provide you with a list of plants and animals that have either disappeared from areas where they were once common, or that seem to be disappearing because of human activities. Select a species to study. ➡

2. Use reference books and information from newspapers and magazines to find out more about the species you have chosen. Try to answer the following questions:
   - What is the species' habitat?
   - What niche in its ecosystem does the species occupy?
   - Is the species endangered in one area only or is it in danger worldwide?
   - How do we know that the species is endangered?
   - How might the disappearance of this species affect other organisms, including humans?
   - How might humans change what we are doing so that we can ensure the survival of the endangered species? How might these changes affect society?
3. Prepare a talk or a written report about the species you have chosen. Try to present your information in a fresh, creative way. For example, your talk or report might include an "interview" with an ecologist or an organism "representing" the species.
4. Illustrate your talk or report with photos and drawings of the species and a map showing where it is found. ❖

DID YOU KNOW

- About one-third of the people on the planet were born in the last 15 years.

YOU CAN MAKE A DIFFERENCE

People, like all other living things, depend on the environment for food, shelter, air, and water. Our environment also supplies all the materials we need to make the products we use. As we obtain the things we need and want, we change the environment in various ways. Sometimes these ways result in pollution or other damage to the land, water, and air. Because our world population is growing rapidly, we are putting more and more pressure on habitats that once supported many other living things.

Activities that harm the environment may seem to be part of our way of life, but they do not have to be. Many people use more energy and water than they really need and throw harmful materials such as antifreeze, paints, and old batteries into the garbage. We can all switch off lights when we leave rooms, turn off the water while we brush our teeth, and find out how to dispose of harmful waste materials safely. In other words, we can make a difference if we each decide to act a little more responsibly toward our environment (Figure 18.20). What could you do to help?

Knowing how the parts of an ecosystem are connected helps you understand how your actions may affect the environment. For example, you probably use many different kinds of paper products—notebooks, newspapers, magazines, shopping bags, tissues, envelopes, computer paper. Do you throw away paper products that can be recycled or reused? Doing this harms the environment in at least two ways.

- Paper is usually made from living things—trees. The demand for more paper means we must continue to cut trees at a rapid rate. As you will learn in Chapter 20, we are now cutting trees down faster than we are regrowing them.

FIGURE 18.20
Individuals can help to restore their environment in many ways.

- Throwing away reusable waste results in pollution or in loss of valuable land, whether your community's garbage is buried or burned.

There are several actions you can take.

- You can *refuse* to buy unnecessary paper products or products with too much packaging.
- You can *reduce* your use of paper products.
- You can *reuse* paper whenever possible.
- You can *recycle* paper whenever possible and buy products made from recycled paper (Figure 18.21).
- You can *write* to encourage companies and government departments to follow these "four R's" (Refuse, Reduce, Reuse, Recycle).

All these actions can help conserve resources and energy, reduce pollution, and slow down habitat destruction.

FIGURE 18.21
Recycling allows us to use the same resources several times.

JEFF GIBBS

South Moresby, one of the Queen Charlotte Islands

Jeff Gibbs, founder of an environmental group for young people, believes that individuals can make a difference. As a teenager, Gibbs took a trip with friends to South Moresby Island—one of the Queen Charlotte Islands off the northwest coast of British Columbia. After seeing South Moresby, Gibbs became concerned about the logging of old growth forests there. When he returned to school, he and his friends formed the TREE Club (Teenagers' Response to Endangered Ecosystems). The club members talked about the need to preserve South Moresby Island as a unique ecosystem. They held slide shows and sponsored petitions.

After finishing secondary school, Gibbs spent two more years working to preserve South Moresby. During this time he lived among the Haida people on the Queen Charlotte Islands, which they call Haida Gwaii or "Islands of the People." He learned about the customs and history of the Haida and about the environmental importance of Haida Gwaii—islands that are home to eight species of mammals found nowhere else in the world. Through the efforts of the Haida, Gibbs, and many others, the southern part of Haida Gwaii eventually became the South Moresby National Park Reserve.

Then Gibbs became concerned about the Amazon River area in South America. While attending the University of British Columbia, Gibbs joined an expedition to the rain forest of Brazil. There he attended a meeting of 26 Indian tribes. The tribes were working together against plans to build a hundred hydro-electric dams that would have flooded an area the size of France.

When Gibbs returned from South America, he prepared a slide show about Brazil for his university friends. Soon he was asked to give the show to schools all over British Columbia and across Canada. This experience eventually led to the founding of the Environmental Youth Alliance, or EYA.

Today, the EYA is a growing network of Canadian secondary school environmental clubs. One of EYA's projects is to preserve the variety of plant and animal species in all regions of Canada. The EYA hopes to have at least 12 per cent of each region protected as wilderness parks or reserves by 2000.

Jeff Gibbs is often asked how young people can do something about environmental issues. He says, "First, become involved now! Join or start an environmental club in your school and become part of the EYA network. Second, always think about helping your environment, whether you are at home, at school, or at work. Third, carry your awareness into whatever career you choose."

Is there land near your community that you would like to see protected? What is the land used for now? How would protecting this land affect you and other members of your community?

ACTIVITY 18H / PLANNING A PROJECT

GROUP ACTIVITY

In this activity, you will plan an environment restoration project for your area. Your entire class may work together to develop the plan or several groups may work on a number of smaller projects.

Many projects are possible. For example, does your school waste materials or energy? Are there plans for changes in your community that you feel strongly about and would like to support or oppose? Are there areas where you could create nature walks or place signs to educate people about their environment? Are there parks, ponds, or other green spaces nearby that need improving? Does the neighbourhood around the school need cleaning up?

PROCEDURE

1. As a class, make a list of ideas for possible local projects. Write down everyone's ideas.
2. After you have made the list, consult reference books and officials for your community. For example, if you are thinking about cleaning up a creek, you may ask a Fish and Wildlife officer whether certain items should be removed. Sometimes, thrown-away items can become good fish habitat. You may find it useful to develop a checklist for assessing the environmental "health" of an area.
3. From the class list, pick one or more practical projects. In groups, gather information about your project(s) from as many sources as you can.
4. Create a brief statement about the goal of your project. Prepare a list of the materials you need and the steps you will follow to achieve this goal. Develop a schedule or flow chart for the different parts of the project. Decide which members of the group would be best suited for certain tasks. (Note: If you decide to carry out your plan, follow your teacher's instructions. Often permission must be obtained from authorities. A well-researched plan is the first step in obtaining approval.)

DISCUSSION

1. What effects could your project have on
   (a) people? (b) other organisms? (c) the abiotic environment?
2. In what way do you think your project might improve the use of land or water in your community?
3. If an area such as a well-groomed lawn looks attractive, does that mean that it is good habitat for a variety of different living things? Explain your answer.
4. If you were trying to gain community support for a project, whom would you contact?
5. Describe a land or water use conflict in your area (or somewhere else in British Columbia) that has been resolved. What caused the conflict? What methods were used to resolve the conflict? ❖

REVIEW 18.4

1. What is the difference between a habitat and a niche?
2. Explain how several species can be affected when one species becomes extinct.
3. Give an example of a way in which a human activity affects (a) the abiotic environment, (b) the biotic environment.
4. Describe a change you could make in your habits that would help rather than harm the environment.
5. "In nature, everything is somehow connected to everything else." Give an example that illustrates the meaning of this statement.

CHAPTER REVIEW

KEY IDEAS

- The environment may be divided into living (biotic) and non-living (abiotic) parts. Interactions among these parts make up an ecosystem.
- Within the biosphere, there are many large ecosystems. Within these ecosystems, there are many different habitats. Within each habitat, there are very small areas with their own abiotic conditions and organisms. These smaller areas are called micro-environments.
- The original source of energy in all ecosystems is the sun.
- Organisms that obtain energy from the abiotic environment are called producers. Organisms that obtain energy from the biotic environment are called consumers.
- Energy flows through an ecosystem, and some is lost as heat when one organism feeds on another.
- Organisms are joined together in food chains and food webs.
- Nutrients are chemical substances that organisms need to live. Nutrients are recycled within ecosystems when decomposers break down dead organisms and waste matter.
- Usually there are more producers in an ecosystem than consumers. A way of illustrating this idea is called an ecological pyramid.
- An organism's niche is the role it plays within an ecosystem.
- Human activities can produce changes in ecosystems that affect many organisms, including other humans. Each of us can help make the world a healthier and safer place to live by avoiding activities that harm the environment.

VOCABULARY

environment
ecology
abiotic
biotic
organism
micro-organism
interact
interaction
ecosystem
ecologist
biosphere
habitat
micro-environment
producer
consumer
primary consumer
secondary consumer
higher order consumer
food chain
food web
nutrient
decomposer
species
population
community
line transect
ecological pyramid
niche
extinct

V1. Use the terms from the vocabulary list to create a mind map. Put "ecology" at the centre of your map. Add other ideas from your class discussions, or from your activities and reading. Remember that you should connect any two parts of your mind map with lines and words describing how they are linked.

V2. Choose a term from the vocabulary list and write a question to which your term is the answer. Do the same for two more terms. Exchange your list of three questions with a partner and write the correct answers to each other's questions.

CONNECTIONS

C1. Ferns, shrubs, trees, slugs, sap-sucking insects, birds, garter snakes, and people are all part of a forest ecosystem. From this list, identify the
(a) producers,
(b) primary consumers,
(c) secondary consumers.
Draw an example of a food web with some of these organisms in it.

C2. Describe an example of each of the following:
(a) community
(b) niche
(c) ecosystem
(d) habitat

C3. Imagine you have a sealed jar of water containing some water plants, small plant-eating fish, and water snails (Figure 18.22). Each of the organisms depends on others in the jar. Describe the niche of
(a) the water plants,
(b) the fish,
(c) the water snails.

FIGURE 18.22
A self-contained sealed mini-ecosystem. (See question C4.)

C4. Explain what might happen in the ecosystem shown in Figure 18.22 if
(a) the fish population increases,
(b) all the water snails die,
(c) the jar is kept in the dark.

C5. Draw an ecological pyramid for the mini-ecosystem in Figure 18.22. Based on what you have learned about the shape of the pyramid, how many of each organism would you recommend?

C6. List the following in order from largest to smallest: micro-environment, biosphere, habitat.

C7. Name one abiotic factor that you think is important in each of the following:
(a) a desert
(b) a pond
(c) a forest
Choose one of these habitats and describe how a change in the abiotic factor you named might affect different organisms in the community.

C8. Suggest at least one ecological result of the activities described below.
(a) You build a nesting box for birds in your schoolyard.
(b) You replace the bushes in your front yard with a lawn.
(c) Your local government drains a lake and uses the site to bury garbage.

C9. What might you do to increase the number of fish in a nearby river?

EXPLORATIONS

E1. Plan and build a habitat for birds in your schoolyard, home, or neighbourhood. First, consider what species of birds live in your area and what they eat. Find out what plants provide food or shelter for birds. Build a different habitat (for example, a butterfly garden) if there is a large population of cats in your area. Cats are a major predator of songbirds.

E2. Prepare a report on recycling programs used in your area. What materials are recycled, and what are the recycled materials used for? Suggest how the programs could be improved.

E3. Organize a local litter clean-up project or "Pride Day" for your school.

E4. Start a composting program at home. Find information about composting and build a compost box for your family.

E5. Create a photo report showing some of the different habitats in your area. List some of the organisms that live in each habitat. You may include habitats that have been improved or spoiled by people, as well as more natural areas.

E6. In section 18.4, you read about a scientist who compared an ecosystem to an airplane. Write a paragraph that develops and explains your own comparison. Begin by completing this sentence: "An ecosystem is like a ________ because ________ ."

REFLECTIONS

R1. People concerned about the environment often use the phrase "Think globally, act locally." Consider this term, then say how you think activities in your neighbourhood could help solve worldwide environmental problems.

R2. Look through your notebook and reread any parts of your learning journal written while studying this chapter. What did you think you could do to help the environment before studying this chapter? What do you think now?

CHAPTER 19

PESTS AND THE ENVIRONMENT

Imagine that you have been away on vacation for most of the summer. When you get home, you run to the apple tree in your yard, planning to bite into a juicy apple. To your surprise, most of the apples are gone and the tree is badly damaged. A neighbour tells you that several deer have been visiting your garden over the summer. How would you feel? Normally you like deer, but they have never caused any problems before. You are disappointed at missing your snack, but imagine how you might feel if you owned hundreds of fruit trees and you had to make your living by selling the apples. What would you do to save your fruit trees?

In this chapter, you will think about our relationships with other organisms that sometimes cause problems for us. You will discover why certain organisms are viewed as pests and you will examine one of our biggest challenges in pest control—limiting the destruction done by pests without causing harm to other parts of the environment.

ACTIVITY 19A / WHAT IS A PEST?

What does the word "pest" mean to you? Write your own definition, then list some examples. Include pests that you might find around your home. Explain what makes each organism you name a pest. ❖

19.1 PEST ECOLOGY

We often refer to the organisms that interfere with us, or with other species that are important to us, as **pests**. In our list of pests, we include all those organisms that damage crops, forests, and property, or cause diseases in humans, farm animals, or pets. In other words, we define pests by what they *do* to us, not by what they *are* or what their niche is in an ecosystem. Whether or not we define an organism as a pest is also determined by the organism's population size. Hundreds of slugs in a forest are not thought to be pests, but several slugs eating lettuce in a vegetable garden are thought of as pests. To put it another way, when there are too many of any type of organism in a place where people do not want them, we think of the organism as a pest.

Many types of living things, from micro-organisms to animals and plants, can become pests. Some pests can cause direct harm to people. This group includes some poisonous animals and plants, and organisms that carry or cause diseases that can hurt humans. Other pests damage buildings, property, and stored food. Examples in this group include termites, rats, and pigeons. Some pests, such as ticks, fleas, horseflies, and locoweed, harm our farm animals and pets. The biggest group of pests, however, causes damage to crops and includes certain insects, plants, fungi, birds, and mammals. Every year, billions of pests worldwide destroy over one-third of the food we produce for ourselves and our animals.

ACTIVITY 19B / INVENT A PEST

CROSS-CURRICULAR

In this activity, you will describe some of the important characteristics of pest organisms.

PROCEDURE

Using your knowledge of what pests do, invent a pest that might live in or around your community. It may be any type of plant or animal. Decide upon a name for your pest. Draw a picture of your pest and colour it, or make a model of your pest. Write a brief description. Your description should answer the following questions:

(a) What is the habitat of your pest?
(b) How big is it?
(c) How does it move from place to place? ➡

(d) What does it feed on?
(e) How does it feed?
(f) Do any consumers feed on your pest? If so, what are they?
(g) How quickly does it grow and reproduce?
(h) What abiotic conditions does your pest need?
(i) What does this plant or animal do that makes us call it a pest?

DISCUSSION

1. Sketch a food web that includes your pest and at least two other organisms that live in your pest's habitat.
2. Explain how your pest might sometimes benefit
   (a) the abiotic environment,
   (b) the biotic environment,
   (c) humans.
3. What might happen to your pest if it had
   (a) more food?
   (b) fewer consumers?
   (c) fewer animals or plants competing for the same food or space? ❖

EXTENSION

■ Collect some weeds and dry their seeds in paper bags. Examine the different seeds under a hand lens or microscope. Try to learn how these seeds travel, what numbers are produced by each plant, and why the plant is so successful.

PLANT PESTS

When plants become pests, we call them weeds. Many unwanted plant species grow in farmers' fields, managed forests, gardens, or waterways. These unwanted plants compete for space, light, water, and nutrients with other plants we are trying to grow. In gardens, weeds can stop vegetables and flowers from growing. In ditches, streams, and lakes, large weed populations can stop water from flowing (Figure 19.1). Worldwide there are about 30 000 different kinds of weeds that cause problems for people.

Weeds are hard to get rid of for several reasons. Most weeds grow and reproduce rapidly—either by producing hundreds of seeds from each plant, or by developing new plants from parts of their stems or roots. Their seeds may also remain in the soil for years, and sprout when growing conditions are right. Many weeds grow best in open, sunny places such as fields.

FIGURE 19.1 ▶
Weeds such as Eurasian water milfoil can infest healthy lakes and interfere with the other organisms that normally live there. These weeds may spread from one lake to another on boat propellers.

ANIMAL PESTS

There are many different kinds of animal pests, including insects, fish, birds, and mammals (Figure 19.2). Many animal pests are primary consumers that feed on crops, trees, and stored grains, fruit, and vegetables. Animal pests are usually at the base of the ecological pyramid you studied in Chapter 18 and normally have large populations. Most individual animal pests are small in size and can reproduce rapidly. A single pair of mice, for example, can produce up to 100 offspring each year. Table 19.1 lists a few of the animal pests found in Canada.

Many of the best-known animal pests are insects. Although there are over 1 million different species of insects on our planet, most are harmless and many are helpful to humans. About 10 000 of these species (only 1 per cent) cause problems for humans and only about 100 species seriously damage crops.

EXTENSION

- Find out more about one of the pests listed in Table 19.1 (or another pest found elsewhere in the world) and write a brief report about it.

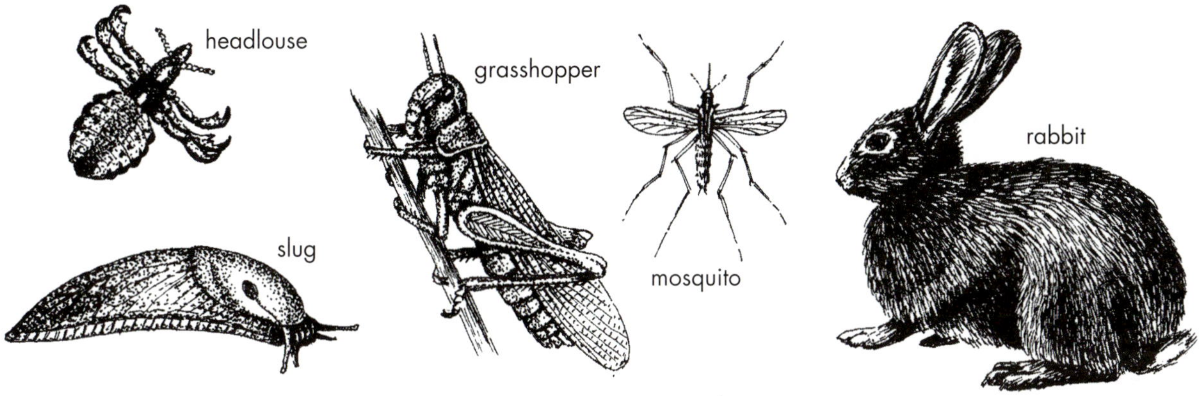

FIGURE 19.2 ***Some animal pests found in Canada. Can you think of others to add to the list in Table 19.1?***

Pest	Where found	What they do
Aphids	Gardens, orchards	Suck plant sap
Bark beetles	Forests	Bore through tree bark
Clothes moths	Stored clothing	Eat fabrics containing wool or fur
Flour beetles	Food warehouses	Damage stored food
Grasshoppers	Farmland	Eat plant leaves and stems
Hard-mouthed termite	Buildings	Eat dry wood in buildings and other structures
Head lice	Humans	Take small amounts of blood, cause itching
Ticks	Deer, cattle	Suck blood, may carry disease
Zebra mussels	Streams, lakes	Clog waterways
Lampreys	Oceans, lakes	Damage or kill fish
Pigeons	Cities	May cause disease
Deer	Tree farms	Damage young saplings
Rabbits	Farmland	Eat various crops
Fleas	Dogs and cats	Bite pets and people
Mosquitoes	Near standing water	Bite, may cause disease
Flies	Common	Some kinds bite, may cause disease
Slugs	Gardens, orchards	Eat leaves, fruit

TABLE 19.1 ***Some Animal Pests Found in Canada***

FIGURE 19.3
Weeds spread when human activities create good conditions for them to grow and reproduce. In some municipalities, property owners must control certain weeds. Does your municipality have such a bylaw? What weeds does it prohibit?

HOW ORGANISMS BECOME PESTS

Populations of most organisms normally remain at steady levels when left undisturbed. In any ecosystem, the numbers of each species of organism are limited by things such as growing space, food supply, weather conditions, diseases, and consumers. Rapid increases in the number of pests are called pest outbreaks. Pest outbreaks often happen when the ecosystem is disturbed or changed in some way. Very often these disturbances are the result of human activities.

Sometimes humans provide pest organisms with extra space or food or cause the pests' competitors or enemies to disappear. When these things happen, the population of a pest can grow very quickly. For example, you learned that most weed species are plants that grow well in open, sunny areas (Figure 19.3). These weed species grew on Earth long before there were humans, living in exposed places such as sand dunes, sea cliffs, river banks, and mountain slopes. When people clear forests for houses and roadways, they create more bare, open areas that are similar to the weeds' natural habitat. When people plant large areas with a single crop, they provide more food for certain insect pests. And when people drain ponds and cut bushes, they remove the shelter and living space used by many birds, spiders, snakes, frogs, and other animals that feed on insect pests. With fewer predators, the pests rapidly increase in numbers.

DID YOU KNOW

■ Sixty per cent of the weeds in Europe and 32 per cent of the weeds in Africa originally came from North America. Nearly half the major kinds of insect pests in North America came from other parts of the world.

PEST INVASIONS

Some species become pests when they are moved from their original ecosystem to another, whether by accident or on purpose. When a plant called St. John's wort was brought from the Mediterranean to British Columbia's dry interior, it soon became a pest. The plant was able to spread quickly on land that had been cleared of vegetation by grazing cattle (Figure 19.4). When cattle started to eat St. John's wort, there were problems: the plant contains a poison that affects breeds of cattle with light-coloured skins, so many animals became sick or sunburned. In central and western British Columbia, the weed is now nearly under control, but in some areas, St. John's wort is still a serious problem.

Sometimes pest organisms "hitchhike" into an area on plants, fruit, or other materials (Figure 19.5). Weed seeds often travel on clothing, shoes, animals, or vehicles without our noticing. Hitchhiking pests can easily hide in shipments of goods from other parts of the world. In the early 1900s, Dutch elm disease arrived in North America. The disease is caused by a fungus, which is carried into elm trees by the elm bark beetle. Both the beetle and the fungus were brought to North America in a shipment of logs. Since the disease arrived, it has spread across the continent, killing nearly all of Canada's elm trees. In British Columbia,

FIGURE 19.4
St. John's wort was moved to British Columbia from its original ecosystem. Ranchers call it a weed and a pest because it spreads quickly and can poison cattle.

FIGURE 19.5
Posters at airports, harbours, and border crossings explain the risks of accidentally bringing pests into the country.

foresters are now very worried that a recently arrived form of the gypsy moth could have a similar effect. Ships in Vancouver's harbour have been found to contain eggs from the Asian gypsy moth, which normally lives in Eurasia. Without any natural enemies to control them, these moths could cause serious damage to North American forests.

ACTIVITY 19C / CONTROLLING PESTS

GROUP ACTIVITY · CROSS-CURRICULAR

In this group activity, you will consider different methods of controlling a pest.

PROCEDURE

Imagine that you and members of your group are employees of a pest control company. You have been asked to get rid of some kind of pest in a neighbourhood, such as flies, cockroaches, wasps, rats, or starlings. Decide on a pest and think of at least two different methods of control you might use. Prepare a report describing the methods that you could use and explain the advantages and disadvantages of each method. Be prepared to present your report to the class. ❖

REVIEW 19.1

1. List three different ways in which pests cause problems for people. Give an example of each type of damage and name a pest that causes it.
2. Give two ways a weed differs from other plants. How does each characteristic make the weed difficult to control?
3. Name two characteristics of an animal pest. How does each characteristic make the pest difficult to control?

4. Choose two of the following animals: coyotes, seals, deer, wolves, wasps, flies, mosquitoes, cats, dogs. Give an example of the way each animal
   (a) helps people or our environment,
   (b) causes problems for people or harm to our environment.
5. "Any organism could become a pest." Do you agree or disagree with this statement? Give reasons for your answer.
6. Describe one way a pest problem might be created by human activities and one way a pest problem might be avoided.
7. Do you think people could stop new pests from being introduced to a country? Explain your answer.

19.2 CONTROLLING PESTS WITH CHEMICALS

Pest control refers to the many different methods used to control populations of pest organisms. The method chosen depends on the type of pest, where the pests are found, and even the time of year. Insect pests are particularly difficult to control because they are so small and numerous. Unlike birds and mammals, insects cannot be shot, scared away, stopped by fences, or easily trapped. Similarly, it takes a lot of time and effort to remove weeds from an area, and it is almost impossible to keep their seeds from spreading. Because of these difficulties, most insect pests and weeds today are managed by chemicals.

The substances used to destroy plant or animal pests are called **pesticides** (Figure 19.6). The ending "cide" comes from the Latin word meaning "to kill." All pesticides are **toxic** (poisonous) to some extent.

FIGURE 19.6
Chemical pest control is commonly used on insects and weeds. How are these workers protecting themselves from the toxic pesticides?

MEASURING TOXICITY

Toxicity is the degree to which a substance causes harm. Almost any substance can be toxic if you take in or are exposed to enough of it. Table salt, for example, has low toxicity. But if you ate enough of it at one time, even table salt could make you sick or prove **lethal**—lead to death.

The toxic effect of pesticides is measured in a number of ways. One way is called the **LD-50**, which means "the dose that will kill 50 per cent of a population of a particular organism." If a pesticide has a low LD-50 number (e.g., 500 or less), it is very poisonous. If a pesticide has a high LD-50 number (e.g., 100 000 or more) it has very low toxicity. However, having a high LD-50 number does not mean that a pesticide may not cause some other dangerous effects at a later time.

THE HISTORY OF PESTICIDES

More than 5000 pesticide products are now sold in Canada alone. About 200 different toxic chemicals are used in these products. Fifty years ago, only about 30 different chemicals were used. But chemical pest controls are not new. Early Chinese civilizations used chemicals taken from plants to control pest insects. Over 2000 years ago, the ancient Romans burned the yellow chemical sulphur to keep insect pests from their stored grains. On the British Columbia coast, native people used chemicals from plants to drive away mosquitoes and lice. In medieval Europe, people poisoned flies using the chemicals found in a type of mushroom.

By the early 1900s, two main groups of pesticides were widely used. One group was obtained from certain plants, such as chrysanthemums and tobacco. The second group was made from mineral ores, such as copper, lead, mercury, and iron. (You may have learned about some of these minerals in Unit V.)

In the 1940s, scientists started developing a third group of pesticides. Chemicals found in petroleum were used for most of these new pesticides. Many of these human-made or **synthetic** pesticides were very effective at quickly killing many different kinds of pests. Soon the synthetic pesticides almost completely replaced the older plant and mineral pesticides, and were used in great quantities around the world.

DID YOU KNOW

■ During the late 1980s, over 650 000 tonnes of pesticides were used each year in North America. Almost three-quarters of these were herbicides, and one-quarter were insecticides. Most of the insecticides were used on just three crops: corn, cotton, and soybeans. Can you think of a reason for this?

CLASSIFYING PESTICIDES

Pesticides are classified in several different ways. One way to classify them is by their **target**—the kind of pests they are intended to control. For example, **insecticides** are designed to kill insects, **herbicides** kill plants, **fungicides** stop fungi from growing, and **rodenticides** are aimed at rodents, such as rats, mice, and squirrels.

FIGURE 19.7 ▶
An orchard worker checks the trees for pest damage. Some fruit growers don't use pesticides unless there is a lot of damage. When orchards are sprayed, do you think residual or non-residual pesticides should be used? Explain why.

Pesticides may also be classified as liquids, powders, or pellets. Some are sprayed directly onto the pest, and others are applied to the crop or whatever the pest attacks.

Another way to classify pesticides is by the length of time they remain toxic. This is important when considering the problem of harm to species other than the pests. **Residual** pesticides may keep their toxic effects for many years after the pesticide has been applied. **Non-residual** pesticides quickly lose their toxic effect, usually within a week or two.

PESTICIDES AND HUMAN HEALTH

For centuries, pesticides have helped improve human health by killing organisms that cause disease and destroy crops. Many studies show that pesticides protect crops and thus increase the amount of food farmers can produce (Figure 19.8). But our health can be threatened by pesticides as well.

Pesticides are designed to damage or kill living things. Because of this, many pesticides can also harm people if they are not handled carefully (Figure 19.9). Pesticides can enter our bodies through our skin, or by being swallowed, or by being breathed into our lungs. Accidents can happen while pesticides are being mixed or used (Figure 19.10), and while they are being transported or stored. People can also come in contact with pesticides by touching sprayed surfaces or by eating food that contains pesticides.

The effect of pesticide poisoning depends on the type of pesticide, how much is taken, and the person's health. Pesticide poisoning can cause a mild headache, make you very sick, or lead to death. Many pesticides stay in the body for long periods of time.

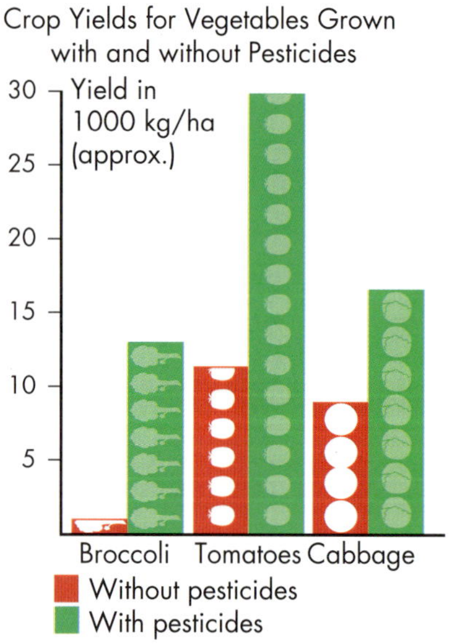

FIGURE 19.8
In this study, the yield of broccoli, tomato, and cabbage crops increased when the plants were treated with pesticides.

(a)

	LD-50 rating	Eye protection needed	Possible effects
 DANGER POISON	oral < 500 dermal 1000	Yes	Fatal and irreversible
 WARNING POISON	oral 500–1000 dermal 1000–2000	Yes	Non-fatal, but irreversible
 CAUTION POISON	oral 1000–25000 dermal 2000–5000	Suggested	Non-fatal, reversible

(b)

FIGURE 19.9
(a) One or more of these symbols appear on every pesticide label. The picture shows the type of hazard. The frame shows the degree of hazard. If you have household pesticides at home, check the labels. What warning symbols do you find?
(b) The three kinds of poison symbols that can appear on pesticide labels indicate how dangerous the product is and what precautions are needed. What do "oral" and "dermal" mean?

FIGURE 19.10
Treat pesticides with respect. This home gardener is dressed so that she does not breathe or touch the pesticide spray she is using. What precautions should she take after she finishes spraying?

Even small amounts of some pesticides taken into your body over time may build up and harm your kidney, liver, or other body parts and cause problems for unborn babies.

SAFETY FIRST

Anyone who uses a pesticide should know what chemicals are in it, and how, when, and where to use it safely. In Canada, this information is given on the product label, which must be attached to every package or container of pesticide sold (Figure 19.11). Each bit of information on the label helps you answer questions about using the product.

Only part of the product in the pesticide container is the **active ingredient**—the chemical that affects the target pest. The rest of the contents are materials added to increase the pesticide's effectiveness

(a) → **BRAND X**

(b) → **PRESSURIZED INSECT SPRAY**

For ornamentals, flowers, and around homes

(c) → Domestic

(d) → Warning

Poison **Flammable** **Explosive**

(e) → **Read the label before using**

Reg. No. 13287 PCP ACT

(f) → Guarantee: diazinon 0.5%

Net Content: 310g

Manufactured by

ABC Pesticides

123 Factory Road

Busytown

(g) → **DIRECTIONS FOR USE**

Remove the protective cap. Do not point the valve opening to the face. Press down on valve tip, spray with a slow sweeping motion. Do not spray when temperature is over 25°C.

LIMITATIONS

1 For outdoor use only.

2 Do not use on certain ferns, poinsettias, hibiscus, papaya, pilea, gardenia, orchids.

3 Do not use as a space spray.

ORNAMENTALS To control ants, aphids, flea beetles, leafhoppers, mites, tent caterpillars, white flies: Spray 45 cm away from foliage with slow sweeping motion, to upper and lower surfaces. Spot treat larger plants to control localized infestations.

ARBORVITAE To control leafminers and scale insects (crawlers), spray when insects first appear. Repeat as necessary.

APPLE, CHERRY, PEAR To control aphids, fruit tree leafrollers, leafhoppers, mealy bugs, mites, and scale insects (crawlers): Spray at the rate of 1 m^2 per 10 seconds. Do not use within 14 days on apple or pear; within 10 days on cherry—before harvest.

(h) → **PRECAUTIONS** KEEP OUT OF REACH OF CHILDREN.

Do not use in presence of open flame or spark. Avoid inhaling. Avoid contact with skin and eyes. May be absorbed through the skin. Avoid contamination of food and drinking water.

(i) → Do not burn or puncture container. Bury empty container.

(j) → **FIRST AID** In case of accident, call a doctor.

(k) → **TOXICOLOGICAL INFORMATION** Diazinon is a cholinesterase inhibitor. Atropine is antidotal.

Seller's guarantee shall be limited to the terms set out on the label and subject thereto, the buyer assumes the risk to persons or property arising from the use or handling of this product and accepts the product on that condition.

or make it easier to use. They may include substances that help the pesticide spread out evenly, stick to surfaces, or penetrate the pest's body.

All people using pesticides, whether around the home or on a farm, need to follow basic safety rules (Figure 19.12). Pesticides are poisons and must be stored and moved safely, as well as used safely. Pesticides should be transported in the locked trunk of a car or in the back of a covered truck. The containers should always be kept tightly sealed and stored well away from food, clothing, and people. Pesticides should be kept in a locked shed outside your home. They should always be kept in their original containers; pesticides should never be poured into unmarked jars or boxes. Pesticide containers should be disposed of properly after use. Pesticides should not be thrown into the regular garbage or dumped down the drains.

FIGURE 19.11
This label gives important information about a pesticide product:
(a) ***Trade name***
(b) ***Formulation (This refers to the form the pesticide takes—spray, liquid, or powder.)***
(c) ***Use classification (Pesticides are classified according to how they may be used and who may use them. Domestic pesticides may be used by adults at home. Commercial and Restricted pesticides are for trained and licensed adults who work on farms, orchards, and forests, and in industries.)***
(d) ***Hazard symbols (See Figure 19.9 also.)***
(e) ***Registration number (All pesticides must be registered by Agriculture Canada before they can be legally sold. PCP is an abbreviation for "Pest Control Product.")***
(f) ***Guarantee (The percentage tells how much of the product's total mass is made up of the active ingredient.)***
(g) ***Where, how, and when to use the product and what pests are affected***
(h) ***Precautions***
(i) ***Disposal method***
(j) ***First aid***
(k) ***Toxicological (poison) information (This includes information that medical staff need to know when treating accidentally poisoned persons.)***

Safety Rules for Using Pesticides

1. Choose the right pesticide.
2. Read labels carefully. Follow directions strictly.
3. Store pesticides safely where children and pets are not likely to find them.
4. Do not mix pesticides in a closed space. Never mix two pesticides together unless you know it is safe to do so.
5. Do not spray on windy days.
6. Do not spray insecticides until after sunset—a time when bees will have reduced their activities.
7. Tell your neighbours where and when you plan to use pesticides.
8. Wear protective clothing when using pesticides (see Figure 19.10).
9. Wear a mask when spraying to avoid inhaling the pesticide.
10. Shower or bathe after spraying and immediately wash all clothing and gloves that were worn while spraying.
11. Never allow pesticides to touch your bare skin. If your skin does come into contact with pesticides, wash the affected area immediately with water.
12. Do not eat or drink while applying sprays.
13. Do not reuse pesticide containers.
14. Never dump pesticides down the drain. Dispose of empty containers by following the instructions on the label or by wrapping the containers in newspaper and placing them in a sealed garbage bag.
15. To dispose of partly used containers of pesticides, call your municipal government and ask for the location of a community depot for hazardous wastes.

FIGURE 19.12 ***Always follow safety rules when using pesticides.***

CROSS-CURRICULAR

ACTIVITY 19D / DESIGN A PESTICIDE LABEL

In this activity, you will create a label for an imaginary pesticide.

PROCEDURE

Use the pest you invented in Activity 19B or invent another pest for this activity. Imagine that you have now developed a pesticide to kill this pest. Study the pesticide label and caption in Figure 19.11. Design a label like it for your new imaginary pesticide. Be sure to include all the information a pesticide user would need, including the safety rules shown in Figure 19.12.

DISCUSSION

1. How does your pesticide attack your pest?
2. How long does the pesticide remain toxic?
3. Are any other plants or animals likely to be affected by your pesticide?
4. Before you are allowed to sell your product, you will need to prove certain things to government officials. What do you think are the two most important things you will need to prove? ❖

▶ REVIEW 19.2

1. Which pesticide would have the least risk, a pesticide with a low LD-50 or a pesticide with a high LD-50? Explain your answer.
2. What do you think is meant by "The dosage makes the poison"?
3. What were pesticides in the past made from?
4. What are most pesticides used today made from?
5. What are the following pesticides used for: fungicide, rodenticide, insecticide, herbicide?
6. What is the difference between residual and non-residual pesticides?
7. Why do pesticides contain materials other than the chemical that affects the pest?
8. Name three ways pesticides might get into the body.
9. Suggest one advantage and one disadvantage of storing and using pesticides sold in the form of
   (a) liquid,
   (b) powder.
10. What precautions should you take when storing pesticides?
11. What should you do when disposing of unused pesticides or pesticide containers? What should you not do?

Paul Müller

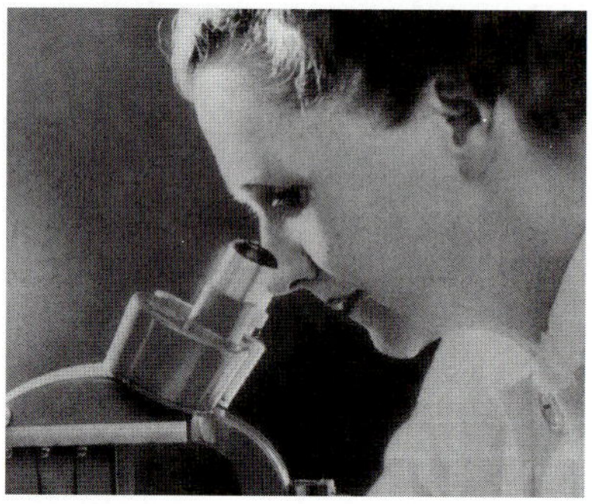

Rachel Carson

FIGURE 19.13
Swiss chemist Paul Müller won the Nobel Prize for discovering the toxic effects of DDT. Later, American biologist and writer Rachel Carson wrote about DDT in her book* Silent Spring. *Carson presented evidence that the pesticide caused serious damage to many species of wildlife.

19.3 PROBLEMS WITH PESTICIDES: THE DDT STORY

Pesticides can be both helpful and harmful, as is shown by the story of a pesticide called DDT (Figure 19.13). DDT was the first in a series of powerful synthetic pesticides developed after 1940.

DDT reduced the pest damage to fruit, corn, and grain. It also controlled several deadly diseases spread by body lice, fleas, and mosquitoes. Within 20 years, DDT had saved the lives of many millions of people around the world by killing the species of mosquito that helps spread malaria, a disease common in Africa and Asia. The insects that caused bubonic plague, typhus, and yellow fever were also soon under control.

But heavy use of DDT over large areas eventually caused problems in ecosystems. DDT not only killed insect pests, it killed many other organisms. Before long, dead birds, fish, frogs, and other animals were found in areas that had been sprayed. Their bodies contained high levels of DDT. Many harmless or useful insects, such as honeybees and butterflies, started to disappear from sprayed areas. As well, this pesticide remained in the environment for a long time. Each spraying added to the amount of DDT left in the soil or water from the spraying before. Gradually the total amount of pesticide in the environment built up. In some heavily sprayed orchards, for example, DDT was still found in the soil 10 years after spraying stopped.

DDT AND FOOD CHAINS

DDT did not stay only in the areas where it was used. Small amounts of DDT were found in the bodies of organisms in ecosystems around the world. This poisonous chemical had travelled throughout the biosphere. One of the ways in which the pesticide moved was from organism to organism through the connecting links of food chains.

DDT does not pass out of an organism's body like other waste products or poisonous substances. Instead, DDT is stored in the body. This means that an organism that frequently takes in small amounts of DDT can end up with much larger amounts in its body.

The DDT that animals cannot get rid of passes into the bodies of the animals that eat them. So, for example, if a robin eats five insects that contain DDT, the bird's body will contain five times as much pesticide as each insect's body. If a hawk then eats two robins, it will have 10 times as much pesticide in its body as each insect (Figure 19.14). In this way, the bodies of animals at the top of food chains can collect and store toxic substances found in their environment.

DDT affected the ability of some female birds of prey, such as hawks, eagles, and osprey, to produce normal eggshells. Many of their eggs had thin shells that broke in the nest (Figure 19.15). Other birds with this pesticide in their bodies had slow rates of growth, or were less able to survive cold weather. These effects led to alarming declines in the populations of some species of birds.

Because of scientific evidence and demands from the public for action, the use of DDT was restricted in Canada after 1969.

FIGURE 19.14
Predators at the top of the food web, such as this bald eagle, consume and store certain pesticides when they eat other organisms.

EXTENSION

■ Use your library and other resources to find out more about DDT. Where in the world is DDT still used? Why is it still used? In what ways is DDT similar to or different from modern pesticides? Prepare a report on your findings. List the advantages of using DDT. List the disadvantages. Based on this information, would you ever recommend using DDT to control pests? Why or why not?

FIGURE 19.15 ◀
This peregrine falcon has already lost one of her eggs. The picture was taken in 1969, the year the use of DDT was restricted in Canada. The population of most of the affected birds has increased since DDT was restricted.

DID YOU KNOW

■ By the mid-1980s, over 420 species of insects, 150 species of bacteria and fungi, and 50 species of plants had developed resistance to at least one type of pesticide.

OTHER PROBLEMS WITH PESTICIDES

Strange as it may seem, one result of the use of DDT and other pesticides has been an increase in the numbers of many pests. In part, this happens because many pest populations are controlled to some extent by their predators. Because pesticides often kill a pest's predators as well as the pest itself, more pests ultimately survive.

Another problem is that some insect species become **resistant** to pesticides over time. A resistant pest is one that is no longer killed by pesticides. It may be able to survive by having a slightly thicker skin that prevents the pesticide from getting into its body. Or it may be able to break down the poison inside its body into non-poisonous chemicals.

Pests can inherit resistance from their parents, just as you have inherited certain characteristics such as your height or hair colour. As a result, resistant pests can become very common in a short period of time.

ACTIVITY 19E / LEARNING FROM OUR MISTAKES

In this activity, you will analyse some records of fish and birds killed by pesticides in British Columbia.

PROCEDURE

Study Table 19.2, which lists numbers of non-target animals that were reported killed by pesticides in British Columbia between 1975 and 1985. Use this information and your knowledge of pesticides and ecology to answer the questions that follow.

Year	Program	Location	Reported deaths	Species killed
1975	Lake treatment Mosquito control Garbage dump	Sardis Delta Victoria	Many 100+ —	Trout, catfish Stickleback fish Seagulls
1977	Agriculture Agriculture	Victoria Delta	16 150	Ducks Ducks
1979	Agriculture Agriculture	Summerland Steveston	500 150	Brook trout Ducks
1982	Agriculture Landscaping	Aldergrove Richmond	13 27	Canada Geese Small birds
1984	Wood preservation	Surrey	10 000	Salmon, trout
1985	Wood preservation Wood preservation	Brunette R. Duncan Bay	2 000+ 100	Salmon Salmon
Source: B.C. Ministry of the Environment				

TABLE 19.2
Examples of Fish and Birds Accidentally Killed by Pesticides in British Columbia

DISCUSSION

1. What types of animals were most commonly killed, according to the table?
2. Do you think these data record all the animals harmed by pesticides between 1975 and 1985? Explain your answer.
3. (a) Which of the deaths recorded in the table do you think were a result of the build-up of pesticides in the food chain?
   (b) Which deaths do you think were caused by accidents such as spills of pesticides? Give a reason for your answer.

EXTENSION

■ Liquid pesticides are commonly painted on lumber to keep insects and fungi from destroying the wood. Describe what precautions you would take when applying these pesticides to prevent them from (a) spreading elsewhere in the environment and (b) harming the person who is applying them.

4. According to the table, which two human activities that involve pesticides have had the greatest effect on animals?
5. Look at the data for 1984 and 1985. How do you think pesticides used for wood preservation ended up killing fish?
6. Rapid, large-scale kills of organisms that are not the target pest are usually noticed by newspaper and television reporters. What less dramatic effects from the dangerous use of pesticides might go unnoticed?
7. What penalties do you think should be given to people who use pesticides in a dangerous way? Whom should you tell if you think someone is using pesticides in a dangerous way? ❖

THE SEARCH FOR NEW SOLUTIONS

The problems caused by DDT and other early synthetic pesticides made it clear that pests cannot be controlled by a single "miracle" pesticide. The problem is not just in using chemical pesticides to control pests. The problem is in using pesticides that

- kill a wide range of organisms,
- stay in the environment,
- are used frequently, regularly, and in large quantities,
- are stored in the bodies of organisms, and
- remain toxic long after they have completed their purpose of killing pests.

Learning from these mistakes, scientists are now carrying out research to develop pesticides that:

- kill only the target pests and few or no other organisms,
- can be used in combination with other chemicals to avoid developing resistant pests,
- break down quickly into harmless products,
- are effective in small quantities,
- are applied only when needed, and
- are not stored in the body of an organism.

More importantly, the DDT story has taught people that it is necessary to study the ecosystems and niches of pests before trying to control them. With a better understanding of ecosystems, scientists have begun to think about alternatives to pesticides. They have developed an approach called **integrated pest control (IPC)**, which uses a combination of chemical controls together with other techniques. Rather than using only one solution—pesticides, IPC uses different solutions for different situations. You will learn more about some of these methods in the next section.

DID YOU KNOW

■ The use of pesticides has been increasing each year. In 1987, the total worldwide use of pesticides was about 1800 million tonnes. Even though North Americans are using 10 times more chemicals than they did 50 years ago, pest damage to crops has doubled.

REVIEW 19.3

1. Name two helpful effects of DDT and two harmful effects.
2. If a forest were sprayed with a pesticide, which animal would you expect to have more pesticide in its body—a mouse or an owl? Explain your answer.
3. How might a pesticide reduce the numbers of an organism that is not the target pest, apart from killing it?
4. What is a resistant pest?
5. Why do you think the DDT story is told in many books on pesticides?
6. What do researchers want pesticides to be able to do today?
7. What does "integrated pest control" mean?

DID YOU KNOW

■ In Singapore, it is against the law to leave any uncovered containers outside where they can collect rainwater. This includes discarded pop bottles, cans, jars, and tires. This law has helped control mosquitoes, which breed in puddles of water.

■ 19.4 ALTERNATIVES TO PESTICIDES

Why do people sweep and vacuum their homes? Why do they make sure that food is always stored in sealed containers and that kitchen scraps are not left uncovered? Apart from keeping a home tidy, these are ways of preventing pests. Pests such as fleas and carpet beetles thrive in the dust that collects on floors and furniture. Cockroaches, flies, and mice are attracted by exposed food. By removing the food or shelter that they like, you can sometimes control animal pests before they become a problem (Figure 19.16).

FIGURE 19.16

Flies, ants, fleas, and weeds do well when they have plenty of nutrients and space. What can you do to help prevent the spread of pests without using pesticides?

In a similar way, you can work to prevent weeds and animal pests from becoming a problem in your garden. Regularly digging the soil prevents weeds from growing. Encouraging predators such as frogs helps lower the number of insect pests. Planting shady bushes will keep sun-loving weeds away. Clearing away piles of leaves and branches removes places where pests can shelter. Removing diseased or insect-covered plants stops pests from spreading. Covering garbage removes places where pests such as flies can breed. Turning over the soil in your garden before winter helps kill weeds by exposing their roots to frost or drying out. As with human health, prevention is better than cure.

FIGURE 19.17
One of the first biological pest controls was the cat. But cats catch more than just mice. What other animals are killed by domestic cats?

USING OTHER LIVING THINGS TO CONTROL PESTS

More than 3500 years ago, the Egyptians encouraged cats to live with them. The cats helped to keep rats and mice from damaging stored grain. The use of cats to catch pests is an example of **biological pest control** (Figure 19.17). This term describes methods of pest control that use living organisms such as predatory animals or disease-causing bacteria.

There are many examples of biological pest control in Canada today. Throughout Canada, a species of bacteria called *Bacillus thuringiensis kurstaki* or Btk is sprayed into forests to control pests such as spruce budworm and pine sawfly, both of which damage trees by eating the needles and buds. The bacteria cause a fatal disease in the insect pests but are not known to harm mammals, birds, fish, or plants.

ADVANTAGES AND DISADVANTAGES OF BIOLOGICAL PEST CONTROL

Biological pest control has several advantages over chemical pest control. It does not cause pollution. If managed carefully, it does not harm other organisms. It can be cheaper than chemicals, and there is little risk of resistance developing in pests. Once the predators or diseases have done their job, the populations of the pest and their enemies usually remain in balance for many years. A disadvantage is that it sometimes takes many years to carry out the research and testing needed to find a good biological control. Also, different biological pest controls are needed for different pests.

Although biological pest control has been used on several hundred species of pests worldwide, this method also has its risks. If the ecosystem is not studied carefully before a living control is introduced, the control itself may cause damage. This happened in Puerto Rico during the 1880s. At that time, mongooses were released to control rats

DID YOU KNOW

- Many birds eat insect pests, and some birds eat only insects. A Purple Martin can devour 10 000 mosquitoes a day, wrens can eat 500 caterpillars and ground insects, and a woodpecker can consume hundreds of bark-infesting beetles and larvae. By protecting the habitat of songbirds, we are also helping to control pests.

(Figure 19.18). At first, the mongooses killed many rats. But the rats soon learned to escape the mongoose predators by climbing trees. The mongooses then turned to other prey, killing chickens, songbirds, lizards, and snakes, while the rats took the eggs and chicks of wild birds. Because snakes also eat rats, the mongooses were now helping the rats rather than controlling them! Furthermore, the lizards eaten by mongooses were predators of the larvae of June beetles, a pest of crops. Instead of having only a rat problem, the Puerto Ricans soon had a problem with rats, mongooses, June beetles, and other insect pests.

EXTENSION

■ Many plants in British Columbia have been used in the past to control pests. For example, the Shuswap people boiled sagebrush leaves to make an insect repellent. Find out more about how native people used plants to control pests. Use library materials or interview a native elder in your area who knows about local plants. Create a display using drawings, photographs, and labels.

FIGURE 19.18 ▶
The mongoose is a cat-sized predator.

USING CHEMICALS FROM PLANTS AND ANIMALS

For millions of years, plants have produced their own chemical defences against the insects that feed on them. As you learned earlier, some of the first pesticides were made from plants. The painted daisy, for example, was used to make an insecticide called pyrethrum. Tobacco was the source of another natural poison—nicotine. This extremely toxic substance is still used in insecticides today.

While some plants contain very poisonous substances, others simply taste bitter, so the pest stops feeding. Some plants have a strong odour that keeps pests away. Others have chemicals that slow down or speed up the pest's growth, or make the pest unable to reproduce. Scientists are studying some of these plant chemicals and are now making some of them in the laboratory.

Another group of chemicals useful for controlling pests may come from pests themselves. For example, many insects produce chemicals that attract insects of the opposite sex for mating. By placing samples of these attracting chemicals in traps at the right time, people can catch large numbers of insect pests. Once caught, they cannot mate and so do not produce more pest offspring. Using these attracting substances, together with newer, safer chemical pesticides and biological controls, we should be able to control pests more effectively and cause less harm to the environment.

DID YOU KNOW

■ The chemicals in plants also have medical uses. A chemical found in British Columbia's western yew trees has been used to fight cancer. Chemicals found in St. John's wort and in marigolds also show promise as disease fighters. There are thousands of plants with chemicals that have not yet been investigated. A plant growing in the disappearing tropical rain forests may be the source of a valuable medicine.

FIGHTING INSECTS WITH INSECTS

On a farm just north of Victoria, British Columbia, Don Elliott raises hundreds of millions of insects and other tiny predators in several large greenhouses. He sends these insects to farmers and gardeners across Canada who want to solve pest problems using biological control. Elliott's company is one of the largest breeders of insect predators in North America.

This tiny orange predatory mite is attacking a spider mite.

The biggest users of Elliott's predators are farmers who grow vegetables in greenhouses. Other customers include the Vancouver Aquarium, Butchart Gardens, and shopping malls and office buildings where there are many indoor plants.

Pests such as spider mites and whitefly can cause serious damage to greenhouse crops of tomatoes, cucumbers, and peppers. These pests are a particular problem because they are resistant to chemical pesticides. To combat the spider mite—which is not an insect, but a relative of the spider—Elliott breeds another type of mite that eats it. Each shiny orange predator can eat up to 20 spider mites in a day. The predators reproduce twice as fast as their prey. They can develop from eggs to adults in only one week, and rapidly build up in numbers. Before long, the large numbers of hungry predators consume nearly all of the pests.

"Educating growers to use predators is very important," says Elliott, who used to teach secondary school biology in British Columbia. "When people start using insects for biological control of pests, they gain a better understanding of pest problems. They usually don't go back to using chemicals." To teach his customers about pests, Elliott gives them a magnifying lens so they can look closely at the pests, and tells them to watch their crops closely for the early signs of a pest invasion. The sooner a problem is identified, the more effective the biological control.

Growers receive the predators in small containers, and distribute them evenly over their plants. Within a few weeks, the predators spread throughout the crop and consume the pests. The total cost of using this method is similar to or less than the cost of using chemical pesticides. And because the crop plants are not damaged by chemicals, they produce more vegetables. As a result of this success, over three-quarters of cucumber and tomato greenhouses in Canada now use biological pest control.

Don Elliott's insect predators are used to control pests that attack plants in shopping malls and office buildings. Why might mall and building managers prefer biological pest control to chemical pest control?

ACTIVITY 19F / PESTICIDES FROM PLANTS

This activity will help you learn about some of the plants that produce their own pesticides.

PROCEDURE

Table 19.3 lists the effects of some natural pesticides found in different plants. Study the table, then answer the questions that follow.

Plant	Effect of plant chemical on feeding animals
Painted daisy	Acts on the nervous system
Tobacco	Causes breathing difficulty and paralysis
Tomato (leaves)	Stops protein digestion
Potato (parts)	Stops protein digestion
Deadly nightshade	Stops protein digestion
Milkweed	Acts on the heart
Castor bean	Clumps red blood cells
White poppy	Stuns insects and grazing animals
Morning glory (seeds)	Affects the brain
Wild cabbage	Burns the tongue
Foxglove	Interferes with the beating of the heart
Rhubarb (leaves)	Attacks kidneys and the nervous system
Water hemlock	Attacks nervous system
Certain mushrooms	Attack the heart, brain, or kidneys
Hot peppers	Burn digestive tract and tongue

TABLE 19.3
Some Common Plants and Their Poisons

DISCUSSION

1. Some plants contain parts that can be eaten as well as parts that are poisonous. Which plants listed in the table are common food plants for people? Which parts of these plants are safe to eat?
2. How does having poisonous leaves or seeds help a plant to survive?
3. Why should you never eat mushrooms that you pick in the wild without first getting expert identification of the species?
4. How could knowing about the poisons found in plants help a home gardener or farmer in planning where to plant?
5. Could any of the foods that you eat contain very small amounts of poisons? Explain your answer.
6. Some gardeners experiment with their own pesticides, using natural substances.
   (a) Which of the plants in Table 19.3 do you think might be safe for a gardener to grind up and spray on insect pests?
   (b) Which might be too dangerous?
7. Just because a chemical comes from a plant or animal, does that mean it is always safer than a human-made chemical? Explain your answer. ❖

REVIEW 19.4

1. Describe three ways of controlling pests without using either chemicals or natural enemies.
2. "When dealing with pests, prevention is better than cure." Explain what this statement means and say whether you agree with it.
3. Define "biological pest control" and give two examples.
4. Compare biological pest control and chemical pest control. Make a chart of advantages and disadvantages for each method.
5. Some people argue that natural toxic substances found in some foods are similar to tiny amounts of synthetic pesticides sometimes found in food. Do you agree? Explain.

CHAPTER REVIEW

KEY IDEAS

- Pests are organisms that damage crops, forests, and property, or cause diseases in humans, other animals, or plants. Plant pests are usually called weeds.
- Most animal pests are small and reproduce rapidly. They can live in a wide range of habitats. For these reasons, animal pests are often difficult to control.
- Pest problems are often created when human activities change ecosystems. These changes may provide more food, space, or shelter for pest organisms, or may remove pests' predators from a food chain. Pest problems are also created when organisms are moved from one area to another.
- Pests may be controlled by toxic chemicals and other substances, called pesticides. Early synthetic pesticides such as DDT produced many serious environmental problems.
- Integrated pest control (IPC) may be the most effective approach to pest control today. IPC is based on our knowledge of ecology and uses a variety of methods.
- Careful maintenance of homes, gardens, farms, and managed forests can prevent organisms from becoming pests.
- Biological pest control methods use organisms such as predators or disease-causing bacteria to control pests.
- Plants contain many chemicals. Some of these are natural pesticides. Some of these chemicals may also help us fight diseases.

VOCABULARY

pest
pest control
pesticide
toxic
lethal
LD-50
synthetic
target
insecticide
herbicide
fungicide
rodenticide
residual
non-residual
active ingredient
resistant
integrated pest control (IPC)
biological pest control

V1. Create a mind map using words from the vocabulary list. Use the chapter title, or another phrase or word from the list, for the centre of your map.

V2. Design a crossword puzzle using at least 10 words from the vocabulary list. Include a clue for each word that appears in your puzzle.

CONNECTIONS

C1. Describe some of the dangers of moving a species from one area to another where it was not previously found.

C2. What are some disadvantages of using predators to control insect populations? What are some advantages?

C3. During the 1800s, rabbits from Britain were brought to Australia, where rabbits had never lived before. Within 50 years, rabbits had spread across the entire country. Suggest two different methods you might use to control the numbers of rabbits.

C4. Imagine that you are carrying out research to develop a "perfect" pesticide. Consider what you want the pesticide to do. Describe your pesticide. Could such a pesticide really be produced? Explain why or why not.

C5. (a) Why do you think some people use pesticides in their homes and gardens rather than other methods of pest control?
(b) What suggestions would you offer to encourage people to reduce or eliminate their use of pesticides?

C6. Your friend says, "What good are mosquitoes? We'd be better off if they were all wiped out." Use information from Chapter 18 and this chapter to respond to this statement.

C7. Why is it a good idea for people who live near lakes to build bird houses for swallows around their home?

C8. What are some of the health risks faced by people who frequently handle pesticides? How can these risks be reduced?

C9. Some people compare pesticide use to the use of medicines. How are pesticides and medicines similar and how are they different?

C10. In Chapter 18, you learned about ecosystems. What information from Chapter 18 helped you understand why dealing with pests is often not as easy as it seems?

EXPLORATIONS

E1. Which would you choose: a perfect apple that was produced with chemical pesticides or a more expensive apple with a few marks that was produced at an orchard that does not use chemicals? One reason for the increasing use of pesticides is that many people in North America today expect fruits and vegetables in the stores to look perfect. Conduct a survey in your school or neighbourhood. Find out if people would buy fruits and vegetables that do not look perfect if it meant that pesticide use could be reduced. Think of two to four questions you could ask. Create a data table to record your results.

E2. An insect called the spruce budworm has been a serious forest pest in eastern Canada for many years. Find out how this insect, or any other important forest pest, causes problems in the forests of British Columbia. What methods of pest control are used against these forest pests? Write a report or make a presentation that describes your findings, and include your sources of information.

E3. Find out how researchers test the safety of new pesticides, by writing to one of the following: the B.C. Ministry of Environment, Agriculture Canada, Environment Canada, or a company that produces pesticides (their address will be on the pesticide label). Do you think testing should be done by the pesticide manufacturers, private companies, or government scientists? Give reasons for your answer.

E4. List the foods that you eat during one day. Draw a food web showing some of the plants and animals that provide your food. Can you see any risks to your health from pesticides in these foods building up in your body? Suggest why you are or are not concerned.

E5. In Sri Lanka, there were 2 million cases of malaria in the mid-1950s. Officials began to use DDT to kill the malaria-causing mosquitoes, and by 1963 there were only 17 cases. In 1964, when spraying was stopped, the malaria rate began to soar again, reaching 2 million cases within five years. If you were a Sri Lankan health officer, what would you do? Write a report outlining the action you would take and why.

E6. How are pests controlled in your neighbourhood? Find out what methods and safety procedures are used by talking to local government or school board employees or other adults. Design a brochure that describes local pests and the methods used to control them.

E7. Prepare to take part in a debate based on the following statement: "Humans are becoming pests to themselves and to the Earth's ecosystems."

REFLECTIONS

R1. How have your ideas about pests changed since reading this chapter? Make a chart to show how your ideas have changed. Divide a page of your notebook in two. Title the left-hand column "What I used to think" and the right-hand column "What I think now." Write down all the changes you can think of.

R2. What did you learn that surprised you about pests or the methods used to control them?

CHAPTER 20

FORESTRY AND THE ENVIRONMENT

All Canadians regularly use things made from trees: pencils, paper, envelopes, wooden chairs, soap, and hockey sticks, to name just a few. Think about how many forest products you have used today. To make these products, trees had to be cut down. Every year in Canada, the total area of forest we cut adds up to an area about one-third the size of Vancouver Island. Most areas of forest that have been logged will eventually grow trees again, but it can take dozens of years before the trees are mature enough to log. Because of this, many Canadians worry that we are cutting our forests faster than we are regrowing them.

Most of the trees being cut in British Columbia today are from forests that have never been logged before. What will happen to the supply of wood products once these original forests are gone? What effects do logging activities have on plants and animals that live in the forests, and on the soil, rivers, and streams? How does logging affect other activities in the forest, such as hiking and fishing? How does logging affect lands that are important to native peoples? How important is logging to everyone's way of life? What are "good" logging practices? You will consider some of these questions in this chapter.

ACTIVITY 20A / WHAT ARE FORESTS AND WHY ARE THEY VALUABLE?

With the members of your group, discuss the question: "What is a forest?" Use a large sheet of paper to record everyone's ideas. Next, write in your notebook, "A forest is like a ________ because ________." Complete the sentence and share your comparisons with other class members. Finally, list reasons why a forest is valuable to

(a) you,
(b) people in your community,
(c) other organisms,
(d) the ecosystem. ❖

■ 20.1 WHY PEOPLE VALUE FORESTS

People everywhere need forests (Figure 20.1). Forests play an important part in the cycling of water and gases in the atmosphere. Millions of species of organisms live in forests. And people all over the world live in homes made of wood and use many different wood products.

Forests are important to many of the world's people for cultural reasons, as well. The Haida people, for example, spend a large portion of their time on the land, hunting, fishing, and gathering food. These activities and the land itself have inspired many songs, dances, and stories. The land has also provided materials for canoes, artwork, and totem poles.

Forests are valued for many different reasons and provide many different things: water, habitat, food, money, jobs, products, songs, and artwork. Because of this and because people can have a major effect on forests, it is important to learn about forests and how we use them.

FIGURE 20.1
Around the world, forests provide us with food, water, shelter, and many other things.

PRODUCTS FROM THE FOREST

Canada is a major producer of forest products. Many of our businesses and much of our day-to-day living depends upon products we make from trees. The cardboard box that holds your breakfast cereal, the wooden tables in your school, and the book you are now reading all came from the forest. These are just a few of the things that started out as trees (Figure 20.2). Sales of newsprint, material for making paper, and lumber bring Canada billions of dollars each year, and our forest products industry provides work for thousands of people.

The forest products industry can be divided into two major manufacturing groups: lumber, and pulp and paper. The lumber group produces such things as different sizes of lumber, plywood, particle board, cedar shingles, and chipboard. Some of the mills that produce lumber products are small businesses with fewer than a dozen employees. Others are large operations with hundreds of employees who produce a variety of products. British Columbia mills produce over 60 per cent of Canada's lumber products.

The pulp and paper part of the forest products industry changes trees into material that can be made into many kinds of paper. The mills where this happens are large, multimillion dollar operations (Figure 20.3). **Pulp** is usually made in these mills by grinding up wood, adding water and chemicals, then cooking the mixture. Repeated washings remove the cooking liquids, leaving raw pulp. About one-third of the pulp produced in Canada is sold to other countries; the rest is made into paper or paperboard.

Most paper is fairly easy to make. When pulp is strained through a wire mesh screen, a thin layer of thread-like parts, or fibres, is left. These fibres are tangled tightly together. When the layer of fibres is pressed and dried, it forms a sheet of paper.

FIGURE 20.2
Some products made from wood

DID YOU KNOW

■ Canada supplies one-third of the world's pulp and paper needs and one-fifth of the world's other wood products.

FIGURE 20.3
A pulp and paper mill in Port Mellon, British Columbia. Find out how mills are changing to meet new laws about water pollution.

ACTIVITY 20B / MAKING PAPER

In this activity, you will work with a partner to make different types of paper.

MATERIALS

safety goggles
apron
samples of scrap paper (newsprint, tissue, magazine pages, envelopes, etc.)
electric blender
large container such as a mixing bowl
stirring rod
wire or nylon mesh screen attached to frame (about 15 cm x 15 cm)
paper towel
iron

PROCEDURE

1. Put on your safety goggles and apron before starting to make paper.
2. Half fill the blender with warm water. Tear up paper scraps into small pieces and add them to the blender. Do not fill more than half full or the blender may clog. Blend until you have a soupy suspension of paper fibres. To obtain more pulp, repeat this procedure, using small quantities each time.
3. Pour the pulp into the large container and stir it around until the fibres are spread throughout the liquid.
4. Dip the mesh screen below the surface of the pulp mixture. Holding the screen horizontally, move it rapidly from side to side a few times to get an even spread of fibres onto the mesh. Carefully lift the screen out of the pulp, keeping it horizontal, and hold it over the bowl until the liquid has finished dripping from it.
5. Quickly turn the screen upside down onto a paper towel. The layer of matted fibres should drop from the mesh. If it does not, leave it until it has dried out a little more, or tap the back of the mesh gently.
6. Cover the layer of fibres with another paper towel to absorb more moisture.
7. When your new sheet of paper is nearly dry, sandwich it between two fresh sheets of paper towel and iron it with a warm (not hot) iron, or leave it to dry.
8. Compare your paper with samples made by other students.

EXTENSION

■ Carry out library research or contact a pulp and paper mill to find out how paper is made in a modern plant. What bleaching process is used? What procedures are involved in making paper? What kind of waste products do mills produce? How do these waste products affect the environment? How have newer pulp mill designs tried to solve environmental problems? Make a flow chart to describe the paper-making process and present your findings to the class.

9. Carry out another paper-making experiment. Make pulp as described above, but add different ingredients to your pulp, such as flower petals, lint from your clothes dryer, shredded apple slices, or grass. Describe how each ingredient influences the characteristics of your paper.

DISCUSSION

1. Why are goggles and aprons needed for this activity?
2. In your own words, explain what paper is.
3. Describe the sheet of paper you made.
4. Suggest how you might change one of the characteristics of your paper (such as colour, texture, or strength) when making another sheet.
5. Describe the kind of paper you would get from a mixture that had a larger content of cloth.
6. Find out how paper pulp can be made from rice straw. ❖

USING FOREST RESOURCES

As well as being major producers of forest products, Canadians are major consumers. Although Canada has a small population, our country is the world's second largest user of forest products. Our demand for these products has a large impact on our forests. One way to reduce this impact is for everyone—producers and consumers—to avoid waste.

At one time, wood chips and scraps produced in sawmills used to be thrown out or burned. This meant thousands of tonnes of waste. Today, the products we need are obtained from fewer trees by avoiding waste.

People who buy and use forest products can also avoid waste. In Chapter 18, you may have discussed ways that you and the people in your community can waste less. These ways include refusing unnecessary packaging, reducing the amount of paper you use, reusing some paper products, and recycling.

HOW FOREST LAND IS CONTROLLED

In British Columbia, about 95 per cent of the forest and rangeland (land where cattle graze) is owned by the public. This land is managed for the public by the provincial government's Ministry of Forests. The Ministry gives licences to private forest companies to cut the trees and oversees the way provincial forests are logged. Many people work for the Ministry, including **foresters**—people who are trained to care for forests and who use science to recommend how to use forests.

DID YOU KNOW

■ It takes about 8 ha of forest to make enough paper for one day's edition of a major Canadian newspaper.

EXTENSION

■ Find out about forest land arrangements by contacting a registered professional forester (RPF) or writing to the Ministry of Forests. For what period of time are different kinds of licences granted? What must companies do to keep their licences? Who makes sure that the companies do what is required? Contact a forest company and a group of native people in your community to compare their ideas about these arrangements. Design a poster that shows what you have learned about the different arrangements for forest land use.

In British Columbia, the most common arrangement between forest companies and the government is called a **Forest Licence**. A Forest Licence is not for any particular location, but gives cutting rights for a certain amount of wood. The trees needed for this wood may be growing in different places.

Another forest use arrangement in British Columbia involves a **Tree Farm Licence**. Unlike a Forest Licence, a Tree Farm Licence (TFL) gives cutting rights in one particular part of the provincial forest. About 10 per cent of British Columbia's forests are managed by holders of TFLs.

A large portion of the land now being managed by the Ministry of Forests is the subject of disputes between the federal government and native First Nations governments. The question of who should control these areas will be discussed over the next few years by native peoples and the governments of British Columbia and Canada. While very little forest land is now controlled by native people, more land may come under native control in the future.

CONFLICTS OVER FORESTS

No doubt you have read or seen reports of disagreement or conflict over the use of forests in British Columbia (Figure 20.4). Often the conflict is between forest companies and **environmentalists**. Environmentalists are any members of society concerned about protecting the environment. To make their views known, groups of

FIGURE 20.4 ▶
These people want to see some changes in the way a forest is being used. Do you feel most forests in B.C. are used wisely?

environmentalists may print newsletters or brochures, talk to reporters, hold meetings, distribute posters, or even block roads. Sometimes environmentalists have been arrested for taking certain actions, such as stopping loggers from entering a forest they have permission to log. Sometimes forest companies and various groups have taken their disagreements over forest use to a court of law.

A list of the people concerned about British Columbia's forests would be a very long one and would include many clubs, associations, companies, and organizations. Some of the groups that care about British Columbia's forests are unions representing forest workers, hunting and fishing clubs, groups of native people, community councils, forest companies, and environmental organizations.

Because British Columbia is home to more than 3 million people with different thoughts, beliefs, and values, conflict cannot be avoided. However, with study and discussion, many conflicts can be resolved. You will learn more about resolving conflicts at the end of this chapter.

EXTENSION

■ Many people call themselves environmentalists. Complete a survey of members of your class or community. Ask at least six people to define the words "environmentalist," "activist," and "preservationist." Use a data table to record and compare the definitions. What can you conclude from your survey?

► REVIEW 20.1

1. List reasons that forests are important.
2. List at least 10 forest products used in your school.
3. What are the two main manufacturing groups in the forest products industry?
4. How is pulp different from paper?
5. Since paper comes from trees, which can be planted and grown over and over again, why should we bother to recycle paper?
6. Explain the difference between a Tree Farm Licence and a Forest Licence.
7. Describe a recent unresolved conflict over forest use in your area. How do you think it might be resolved?

■ 20.2 LOGGING FORESTS

The chain-saw sputters, then stops. With ear-piercing cracks, a massive tree leans from the cuts at its base and topples with a thundering crash to the forest floor (Figure 20.5).

Many people think of these sounds and sights when they hear the term **logging**, a process that involves cutting down trees, sawing them into logs, and moving logs out of the forest. The cutting down or **felling** of trees (called "falling" by many forest workers) is exciting and dangerous. It is only one of the many steps needed to get from a living tree to a forest product such as lumber or plywood.

FIGURE 20.5
High-tech comes to the forest. Smaller trees can be felled with special equipment.

CLASSIFYING TREES

The trees logged in Canada may be divided into two main groups: those with cones and needles or scale-like leaves, and those with broad leaves. The trees with cones and needles or scales are called **coniferous** trees or conifers. The trees with broad leaves that drop off in the fall are called **deciduous** trees. Deciduous trees are also called **hardwoods**, whereas conifers are called **softwoods** (Figure 20.6). British Columbia is the major source of softwoods in Canada (Figure 20.7). About 99 per cent of the trees harvested in British Columbia are softwoods.

FIGURE 20.6
Needle, scale, and leaf arrangements can be used to identify species of different softwoods and hardwoods.

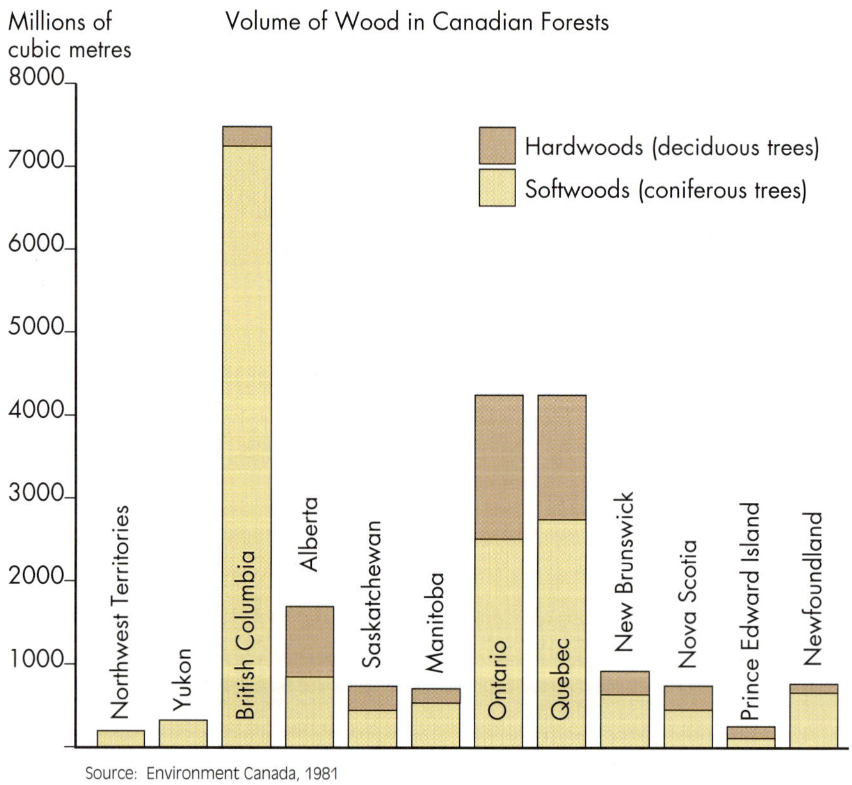

FIGURE 20.7 ▶
No other province or territory produces as much softwood as British Columbia does. Which province produces the most hardwood?

ACTIVITY 20C / IDENTIFYING LOCAL CONIFERS

GROUP ACTIVITY

In this activity, you will find out which trees make up the forest nearest to you.

MATERIALS

8 to 12 numbered clippings, 1 from each type of wild coniferous tree in your area
copy of a Family Tree Key to Conifers

PROCEDURE

1. List the names of all the wild trees that you can recall.
2. Copy Table 20.1 into your notebook. (The first two entries are samples.) Make as many rows in your table as you have clippings.
3. Study each sample. Sketch the needles or scales of each conifer, or make a rubbing of each sample.
4. Make up a name for each species based on what you observe.
5. Classify the specimens by placing them in groups that are similar.
6. Use the Family Tree Key to identify each specimen. Note the uses of each tree as well.
7. Compare your classification groups and identifications with other students. Take turns quizzing the members of your group to see if you can remember the names. How many samples can you recognize and remember?

Local Coniferous Trees			
Specimen No.	**Made-up name**	**Common name (from Key)**	**Uses/Comments**
1.	"Christmas trees with hanging-down cones"	Douglas fir	Used for inside construction
2.	"Snakeskin tree"	Western red cedar	Used for outside construction Makes attractive walls
3.			

TABLE 20.1 ***Sample Data Table for Activity 20C***

DISCUSSION

1. How many trees named in your Family Tree Key were found in your area? Which of these trees are the most common in your area?
2. Are there any trees in your area that are important to the forest industry? What kinds of forest products are made from these trees?
3. Conifers are divided into groups by features. For example, some have needles while others have scales like snakeskin. Look at the Family Tree Key and list some of the other features used to divide conifers into groups.
4. Do you think the Family Tree Key could have been organized another way? Explain.
5. How many trees from your area could you identify before you started this activity? How many can you identify now? ❖

FINDING OUT WHAT IS IN A FOREST

Proper planning of forest use depends on answering many questions, including the following: How large is the area covered by forest? How much wood from each kind of tree is in the forest? Should this forest be logged? How fast would new trees grow to replace the trees that are cut down? What effects would removing the trees have on other plants

EXTENSION

■ Use reference books to find out what native people called trees and other plants in your area. Find out how trees and plants were used by native people.

DID YOU KNOW

■ The tree we call Douglas fir was first thought to be a member of the pine family. Later, a Scottish scientist named David Douglas recognized that the tree was an unknown species and gave it its present scientific name, *Pseudotsuga menziesii* (false hemlock). In Douglas's honour, this tree is now commonly called Douglas fir, but for centuries before, the tree was known as *Kwek-welh-à'y* (the real tree) by Squamish people. Today, Douglas fir is prized because it is extremely strong, holds nails, and does not warp. Do you think "the real tree" was a good name?

and animals in the area? To answer these and other questions, the area to be logged is mapped and studied (Figure 20.8).

The information obtained from studying an area of forest is called a forest inventory. A forest **inventory** identifies the kinds of trees growing in an area and the number and size of the trees. A complete inventory includes information about the streams and rivers running through the forest, the species of fish in them, and the populations of animals and plants that live in the forest. The inventory may also describe other possible or established uses for the land in the area—recreation, preservation, mining, and farming.

Preparing forest inventories takes a lot of time and effort. Part of the problem is the large size and the remote location of many forested areas. Another challenge comes when putting together information about forests that has been collected by different groups. Forestry data are collected by the B.C. ministries of Forests, Parks, Environment, and Crown Lands, and the federal departments Forestry Canada, Environment Canada, and Fisheries and Oceans Canada. Forest companies and environmental organizations also collect their own information. For many years, people have been collecting different data in different ways. Today, people are trying to measure the same things using similar methods so that pieces of the forest inventory "puzzle" can be put together.

Surveys of Canada's forests show that not all forests are suitable for logging. In fact, only about half the total forested land in Canada can provide trees that are large enough and close enough to mills and markets to make cutting them worthwhile. Much of the remaining forest is difficult or impossible to reach by roads or rivers or is in northern areas or at high altitudes where trees grow slowly.

(a)

(b)

FIGURE 20.8
(a) Foresters use instruments to measure the height, diameter, and age of trees. What is this forester measuring? (b) Surveys taken from aircraft and satellites help foresters count trees.

Some forests may also be unsuitable for logging because they contain rare habitat for plants and animals or are important places for recreation. These and other reasons may be more important than the money that can be made from using the wood.

GETTING READY TO LOG

After forest inventories have been obtained, foresters prepare detailed management and logging plans. These plans show what will be done for the next five years, including where and when logging will take place. These plans also describe the way trees will be cut and moved out of the forest and how roads will be built (Figure 20.9).

Because trees may take many years to mature, long-term plans are made as well. Various government departments examine the plans, and the public is given a chance to study them too. After a plan has been approved, the area of forest may be logged.

FIGURE 20.9
Roads are built into forests to move people and equipment in and logs out.

LOGGING METHODS

There are two main methods used to log trees. **Clearcutting** is by far the most common logging method (Figure 20.10). As the name suggests, all the trees in an area are cut and removed at the same time, leaving large, clear openings in the forest. Because powerful machines can be used to cut and remove trees, forest companies find that clearcutting is the least expensive logging method, especially in coastal forests. However, clearcutting does completely clear areas and can allow soil to wash away. Replanting after clearcutting usually requires the use of fertilizers and herbicides.

When a clearcut area is reforested, the trees that grow in the area will be the same age, and sometimes may all be of the same species. Individual clearcuts in British Columbia have ranged in size from about 40 ha (hectares) to 700 ha (7 km^2). Now most clearcuts are limited to 40 ha—about as big as 40 football fields.

In **selection logging**, a selection of trees is cut and removed from the forest while other trees are left standing (Figure 20.10). Some large, desirable trees are cut and removed along with damaged or diseased and less desirable trees. Most of the work is done with hand-held chain-saws. Since people are needed to do work that machines can do more quickly and cheaply, this method costs more than clearcutting. However, replanting an area logged by selection methods may cost less than replanting a clearcut. Because the logged area is not cleared, the soil is protected. The trees that remain can drop seed on the ground, so new trees may grow. Fewer people may be needed to fertilize and replant the land.

DID YOU KNOW

■ Clearcut areas in Sweden average 10 ha in size. The average clearcut in Finland is 2 ha. In 1991, the B.C. Ministry of Forests recommended that most clearcuts in the province be limited to about 40 ha.

(a)

(b)

FIGURE 20.10
(a) A clearcut area
(b) An area logged by selection

When selection logging is used, trees of different ages and species can continue to grow side by side. In 1989, about 9 per cent of the forested land in British Columbia was being logged using selection methods.

Because clearcutting has an obvious effect on the appearance of the landscape, everyone has an opinion about it. The debate about clearcutting is an example of the conflict over forest use that was described earlier. Some people say there are many arguments in favour of clearcutting. They say clearcutting creates areas that are easily replanted and maintained (see Figure 20.11). Other people say there are many arguments against clearcutting. They say clearcutting may lead to the destruction of micro-organisms in the soil—something future trees depend on (see Figure 20.11).

FIGURE 20.11
(a) Clearcut lands have produced successful forests. This new forest is on Vancouver Island.
(b) Clearcutting on steep slopes can cause serious soil erosion.

(a)

(b)

People who argue for or against clearcutting have raised questions that everyone in society can think about. For example, should clearcutting be allowed in some forests but not in others? Should parts of a forest damaged by pests be clearcut? What will happen to forest workers and the forest industry if clearcutting is stopped completely? What will happen to the forest ecosystem if clearcutting continues? Are there other methods we could or should be using to log forests?

ACTIVITY 20D / COMPARING LOGGING METHODS

GROUP ACTIVITY

This group activity will allow you to find out more about logging methods by interviewing a knowledgeable member of your community.

PROCEDURE

1. Your teacher will help your group and other groups in the class contact someone to interview. You might interview one of the following people: a forester, an environmentalist, an ecologist, a mill worker, a logger, a forest company operations manager, a B.C. Ministry of Forests employee, a local politician.
2. Work with the members of your group to prepare a list of questions about logging methods. Include the following questions in your list:
   - What does the term "clearcutting" mean to you?
   - What does the term "selection logging" mean to you?
   - How do you think different logging methods affect
     (a) the soil and water in the forest?
     (b) the plants and animals in the forest?
   - Do you think there are forests where
     (a) selection logging methods cannot be used?
     (b) clearcutting methods cannot be used?
   - What do you think are the advantages and disadvantages of
     (a) clearcutting?
     (b) selection logging?
3. Use your list of questions to conduct an interview.
4. Record the answers to your questions on a chart that can become part of a class display.
5. Study the class display of charts and compare the answers given by the different people interviewed.

DISCUSSION

1. Did the different people interviewed by you and your classmates define the two main logging methods in the same way?
2. Did the people interviewed agree or disagree about the ways different logging methods affect the forest?
3. Did the people interviewed agree or disagree about the advantages and disadvantages of different logging methods?
4. What else would you like to find out about different logging methods? ❖

TURNING LOGS INTO FOREST PRODUCTS

Once trees are felled, branches are cut off (limbed) and the trunks are cut into smaller lengths (bucked). The logs are then taken (skidded) to a central loading place, called a yard. In the yard, all logs are stamped with an identification code. Logs may then be transported from the yard to a mill by truck or train, or by log boom down rivers, lakes, or along the sea coast (Figure 20.12). Once at a lumber mill, the logs are measured and their value is calculated.

Logs delivered to mills are sorted by species, grade (quality), and size. Logs with few knots from certain tree species may be peeled into thin layers to make products such as plywood. Medium-size logs are cut into lumber for construction. Lumber can be used for many purposes (Figure 20.13). Smaller logs may be cut up for lumber or chipped into pulp for making paper. The chips, bark, and sawdust that are left behind after sawing operations also have uses. They may be used for pulp, particle board, or chipboard, or they can be burned to produce heat energy or electricity for the mill.

(a)

(b)

(c)

FIGURE 20.12
(a) The branches are cut from a felled tree. Then, (b) the trunk is bucked into shorter lengths. Some logs are trucked, and others are transported by water to the mill (c).

FIGURE 20.13 ◀
Wood is used to make many different things. Can you identify which wood was used to make the wooden items in your classroom?

ACTIVITY 20E / A FOREST, PAST AND FUTURE

In this field trip activity, you will look for clues to past logging activities and try to discover evidence to predict the future of a forest.

MATERIALS

compass
measuring tape or metre stick
paper
crayons
hand lens
bug boxes with lids

FIGURE 20.14
Before 1950, loggers used long flexible planks of wood (springboards), inserted near the base of a large tree, to stand on while sawing or chopping. How do loggers fell large trees now?

PROCEDURE

1. Your teacher will review safety and other procedures before your trip to a park or logged-over area begins.
2. In the forest study area, locate a tree stump and measure its height and diameter. Record the data in your notebook. Later, you can share this information with your classmates by adding it to a class data table.
3. Count the total number of cut stumps in an area 25 m x 25 m. Record this number in your notebook.
4. Locate a fairly new stump with clear rings. Place a sheet of paper on the cut surface of a fresh stump and make a rubbing to show the tree rings. Count the number of rings to determine the age of the tree when it was cut.
5. Look for signs of springboard cuts in very old stumps (see Figure 20.14).
6. Look for evidence to determine if the tree was felled by chain-saws, hand-held saws, axes, or a modern type of mechanical faller. Describe your observations in your notebook.
7. Look for signs on stumps, such as the two saw cuts (the undercut and main cut), or other clues in the ground to show the direction in which the tree fell. In what direction was the tree probably dragged away?
8. Find an old stump or log that has organisms living on its outer surface. Examine and sketch some of the fungi and plants that are growing on the stump. These may include mushrooms, mosses, ferns, salal, huckleberry, and small tree seedlings. Record and sketch any animals that you find, such as beetles, ants, and centipedes. (Note: Do not tear apart or damage the stump. After finishing your observations, return any organisms to the place you found them.)
9. Use your Family Tree Key from Activity 20C to identify the most common species of
   (a) large standing trees,
   (b) young trees (3 m or less in height).

DISCUSSION

1. Create a class data table. Use your class table to find
   (a) the diameter of the widest stump measured in the area,
   (b) the diameter of the thinnest stump,
   (c) the height of the tallest stump,
   (d) the height of the shortest stump,
   (e) the age of the oldest stump measured by your class,
   (f) the age of the youngest stump.
2. In mountainous areas, a lot of cutting is done during winter. How would the height of stumps tell you when cutting took place? ➡

EXTENSION

■ Often the history of a logging operation is not written down, but you can still find out about it by talking and listening to the older men and women who lived in the area long ago. Try to locate and interview someone who knows about logging in the past. Share the results of your research with your class.

3. Do you think the area you studied was clearcut, or was selection logging used? Explain your answer.
4. Describe what you might see if you were able to return to this forest in 50 years. Describe the evidence you used to make your prediction.
5. Suggest how the logging of this area might have affected large grazing animals such as moose or elk. Do you think there are more or fewer of these animals in the area now?
6. Suggest how the logging of this area might have affected soil micro-organisms. Do you think there are more or fewer micro-organisms in the area now?
7. Estimate the number of trees removed by logging from the 25 m x 25 m area. How could you calculate the total volume of wood removed in these trees? What is the value of the trees if the wood was sold at \$70 for each m^3? ❖

▶ REVIEW 20.2

1. What different kinds of information might be found in a forest inventory?
2. Name two differences between a coniferous tree and a deciduous tree.
3. List three different softwood species and their special characteristics and uses.
4. Why must forest companies allow the public to see their management plans? Who checks to see that these plans are acceptable?
5. Describe the two main methods used to log trees.
6. Describe what happens to a log from the time it is felled to the time it is made into lumber or pulp and paper.

■ 20.3 MANAGING THE FORESTS

Like fish and fresh water, trees are considered to be a **renewable resource**. Forests can be logged over and over again because more trees can be grown on the same land. However, the ability of a logged area to grow enough wood to meet the needs of people far into the future depends on careful **forest management**. Forest management begins with preparing forest inventories and deciding which forests should be logged and which should not. Planning, road building, cutting trees, preparing sites, replanting, and maintaining forests are also part of forest management.

One hundred years ago, the timber taken by loggers was replaced by the natural growth of forest trees. Most people thought that there was an unlimited supply of trees and did not think of planting them. Today, there are more people using more wood and paper products than ever before. To meet this growing demand, large areas of forest are cut each year. In some places, trees are now being removed from the forest at a faster rate than they are growing back. As a result, both the total amount of forest and the supply of wood that can be harvested in Canada have been shrinking.

To protect both forests and jobs, many people believe we need to find alternatives to the forest management practices common in British Columbia over the last 30 years. They believe the way we make and use wood products must change and that large-scale logging operations must be replaced by small-scale operations. This new approach to forest management is sometimes called **holistic forestry**. "Holistic" refers to the importance of the relationship between parts and wholes. In holistic forestry, people are seen as part of the forest ecosystem.

EXTENSION

- Find out more about holistic or "new" forestry. Invite a forester or an instructor from a college or university to speak about the subject. Prepare a list of questions for the speaker. Include questions about the lifestyle changes that holistic forestry might require. Summarize the speaker's explanation of holistic forestry and its possible effect on society in a report.

PLANTING TREES AND MAINTAINING FORESTS

The planning and work done to plant and care for forest trees is known as **silviculture**. This term comes from the Latin word meaning "forest" (*silva*). Silviculture includes such activities as site preparation, planting seedlings, caring for stands of young trees, and controlling forest pests (Figure 20.15).

Although foresters knew as early as 1930 about the problems caused by non-reforested lands, little was done to help new trees grow in logged areas before the 1960s. By the late 1970s, forest companies and the B.C. Forest Service were doing much more. Some type of site preparation was carried out on nearly half of Canada's logged areas. By the late 1980s, almost half of the country's logged areas were being planted after logging. Herbicides and brush control were used to control weeds. These activities all helped tree seedlings survive and grow.

Foresters today recommend planting the species of tree that is best suited to each habitat and climate. Over a dozen species of trees are commonly planted in British Columbia, including white spruce, lodge-

(a) *(b)*

FIGURE 20.15
(a) Rakes and chains are sometimes pulled over a logged area to break up the litter of chips and branches left over from logging. This is called site preparation. It helps prepare the ground for new tree growth.
(b) Thinning helps trees grow faster by giving each tree more light and space. Without thinning, a reforested area may develop into a stand of small trees growing too close together.

pole pine, and Douglas fir. But planting and seeding are not the only ways a new forest grows. Natural growth occurs when seeds are left on the ground after logging, when seeds fall to the ground from trees that are left, or when animals carry seeds to a logged site. About half of logged areas are left to reforest naturally.

Although planting helps most forests grow back, in some places many young trees do not survive. In the past, about one-quarter of the areas that were planted or seeded did not develop into productive forests. Today, we know that certain slopes cannot be reforested and certain soils cannot grow a new crop of trees easily. Foresters are continuing to learn why some areas are difficult to replant.

EXTENSION

■ Do some research on British Columbia's Allowable Annual Cut (AAC). Has it been increased or reduced recently? Write two paragraphs: one explaining what the AAC is today and another explaining what this might mean to your community.

SUSTAINED YIELD

A major goal of forest management is to match the amount of wood harvested with the amount of wood grown from new trees. When harvests of wood are produced over many years and the forest ecosystem is healthy, we call this **sustained yield** management. "Sustained" means steady or unchanging, and "yield" is an amount produced. To get an idea of what is meant by a sustained yield, study Figure 20.16.

A forest ecosystem is much more complicated than the greenhouse in Figure 20.16, but the same rules of sustained yield can be used. In order for a forest to provide a steady supply of wood, the amount of wood harvested must be matched with the amount of wood grown. Although trees may live for several hundred years and grow throughout their lives, their rate of growth changes. Most species grow most rapidly during their first 80 years (Figure 20.17). After that, their growth slows down. In managed forests, a tree is felled as soon as its period of rapid growth is finished. By planting a new tree to replace it, foresters can grow wood faster on that piece of land than by allowing the same tree to continue growing for another 80 years or more. Some foresters say, though, that we should be leaving certain species of tree to grow longer in order to have better quality wood and a healthier forest ecosystem.

Since trees can only be harvested once or twice every hundred years, planning for sustained yield is a challenge. A lot can happen while the new trees grow. Many events—from fires and pest damage to bad weather and changes in the price of wood—can interfere with plans made for the forest.

The total amount of wood that can be cut each year for an area is called the **Allowable Annual Cut** (AAC). The AAC is much like the fraction of radishes that can be harvested at one time for sustained yield in Figure 20.16. Cutting more now must result in cutting less later.

FIGURE 20.16

Imagine that you are starting a business growing radishes. You have a large greenhouse where radishes can grow all year round. Each crop of radishes takes three weeks to produce—from planting the seeds to harvesting. But your customers want a steady supply of radishes every week, and your employees want steady work year-round. You can meet these goals by dividing your greenhouse into three units of equal size. By planting and harvesting a portion of your greenhouse area as shown here, you can have a steady supply of radishes.

EXTENSION

- How would you change the sustained yield operation shown in Figure 20.16 if (a) pests damaged one planting of your crop? (b) you had to reduce your growing area by one-third? (c) a disease killed the kind of radish you had been using? (d) radishes were being produced much more cheaply throughout the year in California?

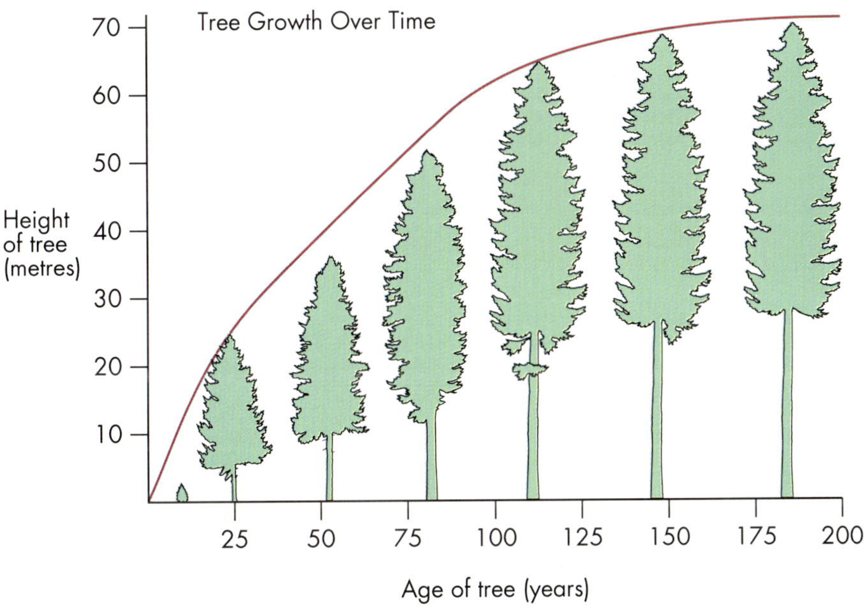

FIGURE 20.17

Trees grow most rapidly during their first 80 years of life. Do all trees grow at the same rate? Do trees die of old age?

FORESTER

Mary Thomas is a forester and vice-president of the Intertribal Forestry Association of British Columbia. Here is what she says about her career:

Mary Thomas

When I graduated from secondary school, I did not know what I wanted to do. Then my band, the Canim Lake Indian Band, decided to introduce an integrated resource management plan for band lands. This meant preparing an inventory of the area's forest resources. I was given a job collecting data for the inventory.

It was interesting work, but I soon realized that I needed more education if I was going to make forestry my career. I travelled to the Buckinghamshire College of Higher Education in England, where I studied and earned a degree in timber technology and management.

When I returned from England, I worked with several bands on the management of their forest resources. I also became involved with the Intertribal Forestry Association of B.C. The association actively promotes opportunities in forestry for native people. Members try to find ways to use forests while recognizing the cultural and heritage values of the land and providing employment for many native people. The association favours an approach where a band-operated company cuts trees down, saws the logs into lumber, and then cares for logged areas. An example of this approach is the Tanizul Timber Company in Fort St. James. The company employs up to 50 band members to log its own Tree Farm Licence, process the logs in its own sawmill, and then replant the area.

My position as vice-president of the Intertribal Forestry Association has involved me in many projects. I have served on a committee dealing with changes needed to give native people control of the development and use of the resources on their lands. I have also been a member of a group studying the relationship of native people, forest companies, and the British Columbia government. This group has been trying to increase opportunities for native management of forest resources.

One project I really enjoyed was the preparation of an educational video about forestry careers and opportunities for young native people. I hope this video will help other young people find the same rewards and satisfaction that I have found in my career.

Mary Thomas mentions an "inventory" of forest resources. Besides trees, what forest resources might an inventory include? How might logging affect these resources?

GROUP ACTIVITY · CROSS-CURRICULAR

ACTIVITY 20F / A PAPER FOREST: MANAGING FOR SUSTAINED YIELD

In this group activity, you will consider some of the problems of managing a forest for sustained yield.

MATERIALS

paper or cardboard (1 m^2)
coloured pencils, felt pens, or pastels

PROCEDURE

1. Suppose that you and your group members are licensed to manage an imaginary logging operation in an area of forest measuring 50 km x 50 km. Start by mapping the forest on your large sheet of paper. Write the name of your company at the top of the map. Add a scale (1 cm = 0.5 km).
2. Use a black pencil crayon, felt pen, or pastel to draw two or three low mountains with valleys between them.
3. Use blue to show rivers and creeks in the valleys. Add five or six lakes and some swampy wetlands. One of your larger lakes has a healthy trout population that spawns in the rivers and creeks. Draw some boats in the lake.
4. Use dark green dots to mark Douglas fir trees scattered on hilltops and some valleys. Use lighter green to mark hemlock trees scattered among the Douglas fir. Use lime-green to mark cedar near wetter lands.
5. Use purple to mark logging roads and bridges constructed through the area.
6. Use red to mark a small area where you were able to put out a forest fire.
7. Use orange to mark an old clearcut area near the edge of your forest lands 5 cm x 5 cm.
8. Draw a compass arrow pointing north on one corner of your map.
9. Draw a log sorting area, your logging camp, and the main road or railroad used to transport logs out of the area.
10. You know that it takes about 80 years before a tree is ready to cut, and that there may be unexpected problems. You decide that you can log an area of forest measuring 5 km x 5 km each year and have a sustained yield. Use brown to sketch five squares measuring 10 cm x 10 cm to show where you would cut trees during your first five years of operation.

DISCUSSION

1. How did you decide where your roads should and should not go?
2. Suppose the roads cost you $10 000 per kilometre to build. How much did you spend on roads?
3. If it takes 60 to 80 years for most of your trees to be ready for cutting, what fraction of your trees should you cut down each year?
4. Describe how the following events might affect your logging operation and what you could do about them. Say who you think should pay to solve each problem and why.
   (a) A fire caused by lightning burns some of your forest area.
   (b) Two years of dry weather slow the growth of young trees to half their normal rate.
   (c) A fishing lodge is built nearby. The tourists staying at the lodge catch trout that spawn in shallow river beds running through a stand of valuable Douglas fir in your forest. ➡

(d) Because of an increase in house building, the need for lumber increases rapidly. However, you expect this increased need will only last for two or three years.
(e) A severe pest outbreak is killing mature trees in one area of your forest.
(f) Heavy rains stop logging activities during one season. The rain causes mudslides on logging roads and some mud enters the trout-spawning streams.
(g) A rare species of bird is discovered nesting in a small area of the forest. The government bans logging in this area.
(h) The government makes a 2 km x 2 km area near the large lake into a park.
(i) A clearcut area logged years ago by another company was not properly replanted.

5. Describe three more situations that could affect your cutting plans. ❖

FIGURE 20.18
Trees attacked by mountain pine beetles may weaken or die. What is done to control this pest?

WILL WE RUN OUT OF TREES?

In some areas, too much logging (overcutting) and too little successful replanting are not the only problems facing Canada's forest managers. Every year, huge areas of forest are destroyed by fires and pests (Figures 20.18 and 20.19). And despite planting, seeding, and natural regrowth, parts of Canada's logged areas have not grown back into productive forest. As a result, the difference between the area of forest lost in Canada and the area of forest regrown is becoming greater each year (Figure 20.20).

Forest researchers working for the governments of British Columbia and Canada think that we may not produce enough wood to meet the demand in the future. Already, most of the best-quality trees in areas close to paper mills have been logged.

FIGURE 20.19
There are about 10 000 forest fires in Canada each year. Most of these fires are caused by people.

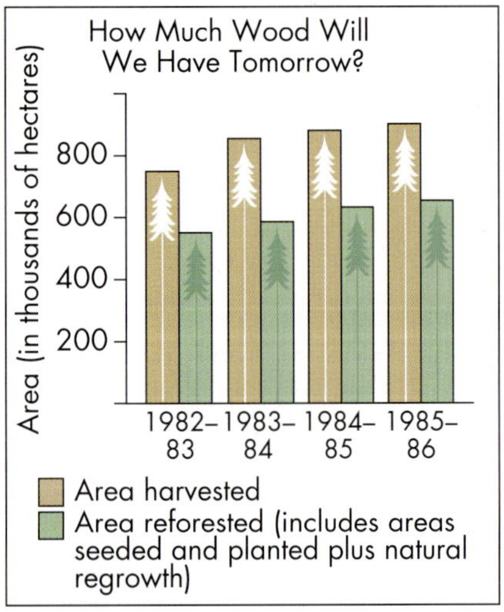

FIGURE 20.20
There is a difference between the area of forest harvested in Canada each year and the area that is reforested each year.

In British Columbia, most of the trees now being cut come from forests that have been developing for thousands of years. Forests that have never been logged before and have trees that are at least 150 years old are called **old growth forests**. Once they have been logged, the old growth forests are gradually replaced by new forests, called **second growth forests** (Figure 20.21). As the old growth forests are logged, the amount of wood being harvested in British Columbia will decrease.

Many foresters believe that we must either plant more trees or harvest fewer trees. If we harvest fewer trees, some wood and paper products may become more expensive, people will lose their jobs as forest companies and mills close, and many communities in Canada will suffer. Yet many people feel that we have to experience this short-term "pain" for long-term "gain." Some people believe that we can harvest fewer trees and still keep people working by developing local industries that make finished wood products such as fine furniture.

FIGURE 20.21
(a) Old growth forest.
(b) Second growth forest. Large areas of British Columbia's old growth forest are being replaced by younger second growth forest. What are some of the differences between old growth forests and second growth forests?

(a)

(b)

REVIEW 20.3

1. Explain the meaning of "renewable resources." Give an example of a renewable resource in your area.
2. Other than logging, what can reduce the size of a forest?
3. What is "holistic forestry"?
4. Describe three silviculture activities.
5. (a) What is sustained yield management?
   (b) Are Canada's forests now being managed for sustained yield? Explain your answer.
6. What might lead to a change in the Allowable Annual Cut (AAC) in an area?
7. (a) What is old growth forest?
   (b) How does a second growth forest differ from an old growth forest?
8. List all the major activities that make up modern forest management.

COMPUTER APPLICATION

STUDYING FORESTS BY SATELLITE

Each year, a group of science students at Sir Alexander MacKenzie Secondary School in Bella Coola, British Columbia have an opportunity to use their science and computer skills. Near the end of the school term they take part in a project called "Remote Sensing and the Environment" under the direction of Karl Osmers, an instructor at North Island College. One day a week, the students do field work and investigate the effects of logging on the environment around Bella Coola, a small community about halfway up the coast of British Columbia.

The students study changes that have occurred in the area, using aerial photographs and satellite images provided by the B.C. Ministry of Forests. These photographs and images show big changes in an area, such as clearings made by logging and forest fires, as well as smaller changes, such as new roads or bridges and buildings.

The students feed the images into a computer with a colour monitor. The images are then examined using different kinds of software and are printed out using a colour laser printer. In 1991, students studied the changes that had occurred because of clearcut logging on the Saloompt River system, an important salmon-spawning area. First they used the computer to study the images and to locate places where logging might be expected to cause soil erosion and damage streams. Then they went to these locations and inspected the streams. They used a piece of equipment called a turbidimeter to measure the turbidity or dirt content of water samples from each location. Turbidity is important because when it increases, a stream becomes unsuitable for salmon to spawn.

The students found that in areas where slash (branches and other waste left after logging) covered the ground, the soil was held in place and erosion did not occur. However, in an area where a forest fire had destroyed the slash, the topsoil was washed away by rain and melting snow and the streams were full of dirt. The students also looked at the effect of logging roads and found that properly built roads reduced erosion considerably.

Students using a turbidimeter to test water from a stream.

Finally, the students wrote reports on the project and their reports appeared in the local newspaper. As a result of the project, some students found summer jobs. One student was hired at a nearby fish hatchery and another was hired to work with computer systems like the ones used in the school project.

Have you ever seen an aerial or satellite photograph of the area where you live? What features were you able to find? How might an aerial or satellite photograph be used by someone making plans for a forest?

20.4 MAKING DECISIONS ABOUT FOREST USE

In Activity 20A, you were asked to list reasons why a forest is valuable. You may have listed some ecological reasons. Forests protect soil, store water, and provide habitat for wild animals and plants. You may have recorded some of the many products we get from forests. And your list might have included recreational activities (Figure 20.22).

Different people value forests for many different reasons. Because of this, forest users sometimes come into conflict with one another. For example, large numbers of campers in a forest may damage plants and scare away some of the wildlife that others want to photograph. Loggers may want to cut trees near a stream that fish biologists say needs shade for spawning trout. People who manage forests have to consider everyone's concerns, society's needs, and the health of the forest ecosystem when making their management plans.

EXTENSION

- Find out some of the reasons why many tropical forests are being logged and the reasons why people oppose the logging. Compare the arguments in the debate over tropical forests with debates over Canada's forests. How are the problems similar and how are they different?

FIGURE 20.22
Every year, millions of people visit British Columbia to camp, fish, hike, and watch wildlife. Contact a local tourist office. Ask how many people visited your area and where they came from.

MULTIPLE USE MANAGEMENT

Science can help us make decisions regarding forest use by answering questions about how various activities may affect the forest. For example, scientific studies can show how logging may affect populations of forest organisms or the water that is stored in a forest. This kind of information is important when deciding how to manage a forest for a particular goal. But many conflicts over forest use arise because different people have different goals. A logging company's goal may be to

FIGURE 20.23
Scientific studies are needed to determine the effects of logging on the populations of different animal species in a forest. Clearcutting, for example, increases the population of some large animals.

have a sustained yield of wood, while the goal of a hunting guide may be to increase the forest's populations of elk and deer (Figure 20.23). Other groups may want to preserve areas of forest for their beauty or to protect animals and plants.

A method that tries to consider different goals of forest users is called **multiple use management**. The aim of this kind of management is to supply wood while helping other forest users achieve their goals. One way to practise multiple use management is to set aside different parts of the forest for different uses. In this way, each forest area is managed for one main use only, but a balance of uses is maintained over a large area as a whole. Another way to practise multiple use management is to allow different groups to use the same forest area. For example, several groups of forest users can take advantage of managed forests. The thinning done in second growth forests increases the production of wood, creates space that provides more grasses and shrubs for forest animals such as deer, and opens up trails and roads to people for hiking, fishing, and camping. But in some cases, using the forest in one way means that it cannot be used in others. For example, an area that has been clearcut is usually unsuitable for tourists, hikers, and some forest animals for many years. And an area that has been preserved for wildlife cannot be used for logging and some forms of recreation.

A problem with all methods of multiple use management involves deciding how much of the forest should be given for each use. Often, forests that are most wanted for logging—areas with big trees that are easy to reach—are also the forests most wanted for recreation or for preservation. It is not possible to satisfy all forest users all the time.

ACTIVITY 20G / RESOLVING CONFLICTS

GROUP ACTIVITY G

CROSS • CURRICULAR C

In this role-playing activity, you will consider the ways that different users of the forest may be in conflict with one another. You will also try to resolve the conflicts

PROCEDURE

1. Suppose the government is considering how to manage an old growth forest somewhere in British Columbia. The government has asked many groups how they want to use this forest. Your teacher will help you choose a group and will provide some background information.

Forest User Groups

- Forest Workers Union (represents people who log in the forest and work in lumber mills for Bestwood Lumber)
- Wilderness Holidays Company (gives tours of the forest to many people)
- Citizens for the Environment (interested in preserving areas of old growth forest and protecting wildlife)
- Mountain Trout Fishing Club (members fish in rivers and lakes in the forest)

- Blue Lake Tribal Council (represents native people who have a burial site in the forest and who want to regain control of land they have lived on for hundreds of years)
- foresters and executives of Bestwood Lumber Company (interested in obtaining a TFL for this area)
- Forestville Business Association (interested in creating jobs for community members who want to work in the forests and in the manufacture of forest products)

2. With the group that you join, hold a meeting in one part of the classroom. Complete the following tasks:
   (a) Discuss how your group thinks the forest should be used.
   (b) Discuss what other groups might want.
   (c) Identify possible areas of disagreement.
   (d) Identify possible areas of agreement.
   (e) Develop reasons why your group's uses might be more important than other groups' uses.
   (f) Design a poster that outlines what your group thinks should be done.
   (g) Design a logo (symbol) for your group and its outlook.
   (h) Decide how your group will present their ideas to influence the whole "community" (your entire class).
3. Present your ideas to the "community," then listen to the other groups.
4. Take part in a class discussion at the end of the presentations. Try to find a solution that everyone can agree on.

DISCUSSION

1. Summarize each group's presentation. Did any of the presentations cause you to change your mind? Explain.
2. Was your class able to find a solution that most groups could support? Explain.
3. Is your class's solution something that your group could live with? Explain.
4. Does your class's solution meet as many of the different groups' goals as possible? Make suggestions for groups that were unhappy with the class's solution.
5. What else could you do to help each person understand the views of other groups? ❖

REVIEW 20.4

1. Name three different groups that use forest resources. Explain why the forest is important to each of these groups.
2. Explain what is usually meant by "multiple use management."
3. Give an example of a way in which one group of forest users may disagree with another group.
4. In what ways is a role-playing activity different from a real conflict?
5. How might conflicts over forest use be resolved? Do you think that all conflicts are solvable? Explain.

CHAPTER REVIEW

KEY IDEAS

- Forests are valuable for many reasons. They provide Canadians with many products and jobs. They are sources of fresh water and home to many plants and animals. They are also valued for cultural reasons.
- The two main divisions of the forest products industry are lumber, and pulp and paper.
- The B.C. Ministry of Forests gives companies the right to manage and use public forests in the form of Forest Licences or Tree Farm Licences (TFLs).
- Because people value forests for different reasons, deciding how to manage forests has led to conflict in British Columbia.
- Trees are classified as hardwoods or softwoods. Most trees in British Columbia are softwoods.
- The most common method of cutting trees is clearcutting. Another method is selection logging.
- Trees are called a renewable resource because most forest land can grow more trees after a forest is logged.
- Forest management includes preparing inventories, planning, building roads, felling trees, preparing sites, replanting, and maintaining new forests.
- When the rate of logging is the same or less than the rate of tree growth, forests can supply a sustained yield of wood.
- Old growth forests are forests that have never been logged. They contain trees that are over 150 years old. The forests that grow after old growth are called second growth.
- Multiple use management tries to allow for as many different uses for a forest area as possible.

VOCABULARY

pulp
forester
Forest Licence
Tree Farm Licence (TFL)
environmentalist
logging
felling
coniferous
deciduous
hardwood
softwood
inventory
clearcutting
selection logging
renewable resource
forest management
holistic forestry
silviculture
sustained yield
Allowable Annual Cut (AAC)
old growth forest
second growth forest
multiple use management

V1. Create a mind map using words from the vocabulary list and other words that you learned while studying this chapter. Use the chapter title or another key phrase or word for the centre of your map.

V2. Match each of the descriptions below to a term in the vocabulary list:
(a) tree with cones
(b) cutting trees
(c) trees used to make fine furniture and veneers
(d) tree planting is an example of this
(e) forest that grows after an old growth forest is logged

CONNECTIONS

C1. Why are forest inventories important? Why are complete forest inventories difficult to obtain?

C2. List 10 forest products used by your family. Note whether each product comes from a hardwood or softwood tree. Say whether you could replace any of these products with something not made of wood.

C3. Compare two different logging methods.

C4. Explain why Canada's forests are getting smaller.

C5. Prepare a two-column data table. Under "How Resources Are Wasted," list examples of ways forest resources are wasted by (a) people in forest industries and (b) consumers of forest products. Under "How We Can Reduce Waste," suggest ways that each type of waste can be reduced or eliminated.

C6. Give an example of sustained yield.

C7. Name two different groups of forest users who might disagree about how to manage a forest. Explain why they disagree.

EXPLORATIONS

E1. Write a report about an industry near you that depends on the forest. How important is this industry to your community? Explain what might happen to this industry in the next 20 years and why.

E2. Design an experiment that could help you answer the following question: "Are computers increasing or reducing the amount of paper my school uses?"

E3. Arrange a field trip to a logging camp, sawmill, or paper mill, or have a forest company representative visit your school to talk about the company's work. Prepare questions before the field trip or the visit.

E4. Make a presentation to the class about a day in the life of one of the following:
(a) a registered professional forester (RPF) who works for a forest company
(b) a feller
(c) a logging-truck driver
(d) a sawmill manager
(e) a tree planter
(f) a lumber scaler
(g) a biologist who works for the Ministry of Forests
(h) a forest ecologist who works for a university

E5. Interview someone who organizes vacations for people who want to visit the forest—hikers, campers, birdwatchers, or hunters. Ask how this person feels about the relationship between the vacation industry and the logging industry. Prepare a report about your interview.

E6. Contact an environmental organization, a group of native people, and a forest company that is concerned about an area of forest. Find out what each group thinks should be done to manage the area. Design a poster describing the groups' ideas.

E7. Survey some people in your community to find out how they feel about forestry practices. In a study in the early 1990s, members of the public said they were concerned about the following (listed in order of importance): clearcutting, not enough reforestation, too much logging, preserving old growth, mill pollution, and slash burning. Use these and other topics to complete your survey.

FIGURE 20.24
A logger working in B.C.'s old growth forest

E8. What do you think when words like "protester," "preservationist," and "environmental activist" are used? What do your classmates think? Discuss the way these words are used in news reports.

REFLECTIONS

R1. If you became Minister of Forests in this province, what, if anything, would change?

R2. Reread any of the sections in your learning journal written while studying Chapter 20.
(a) What have you learned about forests?
(b) What have you learned about your use of forest products?
(c) How have your ideas about forests changed?

Appendix A

SI UNITS OF MEASUREMENT

The International System of Units—the metric system—is usually referred to as the SI. SI comes from the French name *Le Système internationale d'unités*.

Table A.1 shows some common SI and non-SI units. It includes all the units used in this book. Sometimes units are combined to measure other quantities. For example, speed can be measured in kilometres per hour (km/h).

Table A.2 shows the most commonly used SI prefixes. You can see that all the prefixes are related to each other by multiples of 10. The SI prefixes may be combined with the base units in Table A.1—for example, centimetre (cm), kilogram (kg), millilitre (mL).

TABLE A.1 ***Some Common Symbols, Units, and Quantities***

Symbol	Unit	Quantity
a	year	time
d	day	time
g	gram	mass
h	hour	time
ha	hectare	area
L	litre	volume
m	metre	length
min	minute	time
s	second	time
t	tonne, metric ton	mass
°C	degree Celsius	temperature

Note: one tonne (1 t) = one megagram (1 Mg)
one hectare (1 ha) = one square hectometre (1 hm^2)

TABLE A.2 ***SI Prefixes***

Prefix	Symbol	Factor by which the base unit is multiplied	Example
mega	M	10^6 = 1 000 000	10^6 m = 1 Mm
kilo	k	10^3 = 1 000	10^3 m = 1 km
hecto	h	10^2 = 100	
deca	da	10^1 = 10	
		10^0 = 1	10^0 m = 1m
deci	d	10^{-1} = 0.1	
centi	c	10^{-2} = 0.01	10^{-2} m = 1 cm
milli	m	10^{-3} = 0.001	10^{-3} m = 1 mm
micro	μ	10^{-6} = 0.000 001	10^{-6} m = 1 μm

Appendix B

DRUGS THAT AFFECT THE NERVOUS SYSTEM

TABLE B.1 ***Major Drug Groups***

Type of Drug	Examples	Medical Uses in Canada	Some Short-term Effects	Some Long-term Effects
Stimulants	Cocaine	Used very rarely as an anaesthetic.	Alertness, rapid heartbeat and breathing, increased body temperature. Large doses can cause violent behaviour, twitching, lack of co-ordination, seizures, vomiting, even death.	Restlessness, inability to sleep, weight loss, strokes.
	Caffeine	An ingredient in pain relievers, cold medicines, and diet pills.	Increased blood pressure and body temperature; lack of hunger; increased rate at which body functions occur. Large doses can cause headache, nervousness.	Inability to sleep, depression, long-lasting stomach upset.
	Amphetamines	First developed to treat depression and weight problems; now have little medical use.	Increased alertness and energy; rapid heart rate and breathing; sweating; dryness of mouth; overall sense of feeling "good." Large doses produce irregular heartbeat, seizures, violent behaviour, fever; death can result.	Mental illness, kidney damage, lung problems. Because some amphetamines are injected, illegal users face danger of AIDS and other diseases from unsterilized needles.
	Nicotine	None	Increased heart rate, lowered skin temperature, decreased hunger.	Increased rate of cancer and lung disease.
Depressants **1.** Painkillers	Opium	None	Inability to feel pain and hunger; a feeling of pleasure; stomach upset; sweating; itchy skin; slowed breathing. Large doses cause skin to become cold; breathing may slow so much that user dies.	Moodiness, severe constipation, lung problems, liver and brain damage. Because these drugs are often injected, there is a danger of AIDS and other diseases from unsterilized needles.
	Codeine	Eases coughs, headaches		
	Morphine	Pain control		
	Heroin	None		
2. Sedative-hypnotics	Barbiturates	Previously used to treat sleeplessness, tension, anxiety; now only limited use as anaesthetic.	Nervous system slowed; reflexes and breathing slowed. Small doses relieve anxiety, tension. Large doses cause staggering, slurred speech, impaired thinking, even death.	Liver damage, long-lasting headache, slurred speech, poor vision, depression.
	Non-barbiturates	Limited use for treatment of tension, anxiety.		

Type of Drug	Examples	Medical Uses in Canada	Some Short-term Effects	Some Long-term Effects
2. Sedative-hypnotics (cont.)	Alcohol	Not commonly used for any medical purpose.	Reduced tension. Small doses cause relaxation, sleepiness, dizziness, feelings of "happiness" and recklessness. Larger doses produce slurred speech, staggering, blurred vision. Very large doses can cause death by blocking the brain's control of breathing.	Liver and brain damage, heart disease, certain types of cancer.
3. Tranquillizers	Brand names such as Valium and Librium	Used to treat anxiety, to relax muscles, to produce calm without sleepiness.	Relaxation of muscles, reduced co-ordination and alertness, a feeling of calm. Side effects such as skin rashes, stomach upset, and dizziness are possible.	Sometimes increased aggressiveness.
Hallucinogens	LSD	None	Hallucinations, extreme mood swings (e.g., from joy to terror), confusion, loss of memory.	Depression, decreased interest in usual activities.
	PCP	None	Hallucinations; difficulty in concentrating and communicating. Users may become terrified, happy, aggressive, or quiet. Too large a dose can cause death.	Long-lasting speech problems, depression, mental illness.
	Mescaline or peyote	None	Hallucinations, memory loss, loss of concentration, fever, dry skin, vomiting, stomach upset, slowing of heart rate, confusion.	Unknown

TABLE B.2 ***Inhalants***

Type of Inhalant	Examples	Medical Uses in Canada	Some Short-term Effects	Some Long-term Effects
1. Solvents	Glues, gasoline, polish remover, paint thinner, typewriter correction fluid	None	Light-headedness; fantasies; slowing of heart rate, breathing, and other body functions. If user passes out with plastic bag over head, death may result.	Forgetfulness, inability to think, weight loss, thirst, kidney and liver damage, depression.
2. Aerosols	Cooking oil, hair spray, deodorant in spray cans	None		
3. Inhaled medicines	Various nasal (nose) sprays and inhalers	To improve breathing by unclogging nose or	Breathing passages cleared, reduced production of mucus, inflammation (swelling) of breathing passages soothed, relaxed muscles around airways allow airways to open.	Trembling, irregular heartbeat, dry mouth, blurred vision, headaches If used too much, may cause clogged nose when use is stopped.

Appendix C

TABLE OF PROPERTIES

NOTE: In the "Comments" column, common names of substances are enclosed in parentheses.
M.P. = melting point
B.P. = boiling point

Name	Symbol or formula	M.P. (°C)	B.P. (°C)	Density (g/cm^3 or g/mL)	Appearance (at room temperature)	Comments
Elements						
aluminum	Al	660	2467	2.7	shiny white solid	Soft metal with relatively low density; used to make kitchen utensils and bodies of airplanes.
bromine	Br_2	–7.2	58.8	3.12	red-brown liquid	Liquid causes severe chemical burns; vapour harmful to lungs; used to make certain pain-relieving drugs.
carbon (diamond)	C	3500	3930	3.51	colourless solid crystals	Hardest known material; gemstone; used for drilling through rock.
carbon (graphite)	C	3500	3930	2.25	grey-black solid	Very soft; used as lubricant.
chlorine	Cl_2	–101.6	–34.6	denser than air	green gas	Poisonous; used to kill harmful organisms in water.
chromium	Cr	1857	2672	7.2	shiny silvery solid	Very hard metal; used to make stainless steel.
copper	Cu	1084	2567	8.95	shiny reddish solid	Soft metal; good conductor of heat, electricity.
gold	Au	1063	2808	19.3	shiny yellow solid	Very soft metal; highly resistant to tarnishing.
hydrogen	H_2	–259	–253	much less dense than air	colourless gas	Highly flammable; liquid hydrogen is used as rocket fuel.
iodine	I	114	184	4.95	grey, solid crystals	Crystals sublime readily to form poisonous violet vapour.
iron	Fe	1535	2750	7.86	shiny grey solid	Hard metal; strong but brittle; rusts readily.
lead	Pb	327.4	1740	11.34	shiny blue-grey solid	Soft metal; forms poisonous compounds.
mercury	Hg	–38.9	356.6	13.6	shiny silvery liquid	Only liquid metal; forms poisonous compounds.

Name	Symbol or formula	M.P. (°C)	B.P. (°C)	Density (g/cm^3 or g/mL)	Appearance (at room temperature)	Comments
Elements						
nitrogen	N_2	–209.9	–195.8	has similar density to that of air	colourless gas	Will not burn or support burning; makes up 4/5 of air.
oxygen	O_2	–218	–183	slightly denser than air	colourless gas	Must be present for burning to take place; makes up 1/5 of air.
silver	Ag	960.8	2212	10.5	shiny white solid	Soft metal; used in jewellery, photography.
sulphur	S	112.8	444.6	2.07	yellow solid	(Brimstone) Used to make dyes, pesticides, and other chemicals.
tin	Sn	231.9	2270	7.31	shiny grey or white solid	Soft metal; rust-resistant.
zinc	Zn	419	907	7.13	shiny blue-white solid	Used in galvanized iron and steel to prevent corrosion.
Compounds						
aluminum chlorohydrate	$Al_2(OH)_5Cl$	—	—	—	white solid	Used in antiperspirants.
aluminum potassium sulphate	$K_2SO_4 \bullet Al_2 (SO_4)3 \bullet 24H_2O$	decomposes at 64.5°C	—	1.75	white solid	(Alum) Used as an astringent.
calcium carbonate	$CaCO_3$	decomposes at 825°C	—	2.93	white to grey solid	(Limestone) Main ingredient in chalk, marble, cement; used as building stone.
calcium hydroxide	$Ca(OH)_2$	decomposes at 522°C	—	2.24	white solid	(Slaked lime or lime) Used to mark lines on playing fields.
copper sulphate	$CuSO_4 \bullet 5H_2O$	decomposes at 150°C	—	2.28	blue solid crystals	(Bluestone) Used in pesticides.
anhydrous copper sulphate	$CuSO_4$	805	decomposes before it boils	3.6	powdery white solid	Turns blue in contact with water.
ethanol	C_2H_5OH	–114.5	78.4	0.79	colourless liquid	(Ethyl alcohol) Used as solvent or fuel; found in wine.
galena	PbS	1114	—	7.4–7.6	bright metallic solid	Soft metallic mineral; source of lead.
glucose	$C_6H_{12}O_6$	146	decomposes before it boils	1.54	white solid	A simple sugar; human body converts most sugars and starches to glucose.
glycerin(e)	$C_3H_8O_3$	18.2	—	1.26	thick, colourless liquid	(Glycerol) Used in antifreeze, hand lotion, plastics.

Name	Symbol or formula	M.P. (°C)	B.P. (°C)	Density (g/cm^3 or g/mL)	Appearance (at room temperature)	Comments
Compounds						
hydrogen peroxide	H_2O_2	–0.4	150.2	1.45	colourless liquid	Thick and syrupy when pure; usually sold as a water solution.
magnetite	Fe_3O_4	1594	—	5.18	shiny metallic black solid	Strongly magnetic hard mineral.
methanol	CH_3OH	–97	64.5	0.79	colourless liquid	(Methyl alcohol or wood alcohol) Poisonous if taken internally.
naphthalene	$C_{10}H_8$	80.2	218	1.15	white solid	Poisonous; sublimes readily; vapour has strong, penetrating odour; used as moth repellant.
potassium nitrate	KNO_3	334.3	decomposes at 400°C	2.11	white solid	Used for pickling meat and in explosives.
propanol	C_3H_7OH	–89.5	82.4	0.79	colourless liquid	(Isopropanol, rubbing alcohol)
pyrite	FeS_2	1194	—	5.02	brassy yellow solid	(Fool's gold) Mineral.
sodium chloride	NaCl	801	1465	2.16	white solid	(Table salt or salt)
sodium hydrogen carbonate	$NaHCO_3$	decomposes at 270°C; does not melt	—	2.20	white solid	(Baking soda) Used to make baking powder.
sodium hydroxide	NaOH	322	1557	2.13	white solid	(Lye) Causes severe burns.
sucrose	$C_{12}H_{22}O_{11}$	170	decomposes at 186°C	1.59	white solid	(Table sugar or sugar) Made from sugar cane or sugar beets.
water	H_2O	0	100	1	colourless liquid	Good solvent for non-greasy matter.
Solutions						
hydrochloric acid	HCl	varies	varies	varies	colourless liquid	Fuming, corrosive acid, a solution of hydrogen chloride in water; properties vary according to concentration.
sulphuric acid	H_2SO_4	varies with amount of water present	varies	varies	colourless liquid	Corrosive acid; causes severe burns; there is a violent reaction if water is added to it; properties depend on concentration.

GLOSSARY

A

abiotic: Non-living parts of the environment, such as air, water, and rocks.

absolute zero: The lowest temperature possible. It occurs when particles reach their lowest level of energy. Absolute zero is -273° on the Celsius scale and 0 on the Kelvin scale.

accelerated aging: A way of testing how long a product will last by giving it extra-hard use over a short period of time.

acid rain: Rainfall that contains small amounts of sulphuric or nitric acid, formed by contact between polluting gases and moisture in the atmosphere.

acoustics: The study of sound.

active ingredient: The chemical in a pesticide that affects the target pest.

adaptation: Any characteristic that helps organisms to survive in their particular environment.

addiction: The repeated use of a drug that the user finds difficult to stop.

advance: In geology, the forward movement of the front edge of a glacier.

aerosol: In terms of drugs, an aerosol is an inhalant that comes in a spray can. For example, cooking oil that comes in a spray can, hair spray, and spray paint can be aerosol drugs.

air pressure: The pressure caused by the weight of the air or atmosphere.

Allowable Annual Cut (AAC): The total amount of wood that may be cut in an area in one year.

alloy: A solidified solution of two or more metals. For example, brass is a solidified solution of copper and zinc.

amber: Fossilized tree resin. Small organisms are often trapped and preserved in amber.

ammonite: A type of extinct sea shell.

amphetamine: A type of stimulant drug.

amplitude: The farthest distance that a particle moves from its rest position in a wave or a vibration.

anaesthetic: A drug that reduces a person's ability to sense pain.

analysing: Examining carefully.

aneroid barometer: A barometer that measures air pressure directly.

antibiotic: A drug that kills or slows the growth of some types of micro-organisms such as bacteria.

association nerve cell: A nerve cell that carries nerve impulses between sensory nerve cells and motor nerve cells. Association nerve cells also interpret stimuli.

atmosphere: The layer of air surrounding the Earth.

atom: The smallest particle of an element.

audible: Describes a sound that you can hear.

axis: An imaginary line around which an object spins. The Earth's axis is tilted on an angle of 23½°.

B

barbiturate: Any one of a group of very addictive sedative-hypnotic drugs. In the past, barbiturates were commonly prescribed to help people feel relaxed or to help them sleep.

barometer: An instrument for measuring air pressure.

beds: The different layers in sedimentary rock.

biological pest control: Methods of pest control that use living organisms, such as predators or disease-causing bacteria.

biological weathering: The breaking down of rock by living things. For example, tree roots growing into cracks can eventually split apart rock.

biosphere: All places on Earth where living things may be found.

biotic: Living parts of the environment, including animals, plants, and micro-organisms.

boiling point: The temperature at which a liquid pure substance bubbles and changes rapidly to a gas.

brain: The large mass of nerve cells and supporting cells that is located inside your skull at the top of your spinal cord. It is the "main computer" of your nervous system, controlling most of your body's activities.

C

caloric theory: An 18th-century theory that suggested that heat was a fluid, called caloric, that flowed from hot objects into cold ones.

cell: One of the tiny sub-units that make up all living things.

Celsius scale: A temperature scale in which pure water freezes at 0° and boils at 100°.

Cenozoic Era: The present era of geological time. It began 65 million years ago.

cerebellum: The part of your brain that helps you keep your balance and perform voluntary actions in a co-ordinated way.

cerebrum: The part of your brain that is responsible for learning and thinking and for deciding what voluntary actions you should perform.

chemical change: A change in matter that produces one or more new substances. The new substances have properties that are different from the properties of the starting substance or substances.

chemical energy: The form of energy stored in matter.

chemical weathering: A process in which chemicals in the rain, snow, and air cause permanent changes in the minerals in rock.

chlorophyll: A chemical that enables green plants to capture the sun's energy and transform it into chemical energy.

classify: To group together objects or living things according to the ways they are alike.

clearcutting: A logging method in which all the trees in an area are cut at one time.

cleavage: In certain minerals, the property of splitting along smooth, flat surfaces. The way mica splits is an example of cleavage.

colloid: A suspension in which the clusters of particles do not dissolve but are too small to settle. For example, fog is a suspension of tiny water droplets in air.

colour: A property that is sometimes used to identify minerals.

community: Different species of organisms (plants, animals, and micro-organisms) living together in the same habitat.

compacted: Describes a solid layer of sedimentary rock formed by the squeezing and pressing together of particles of sediment.

compound: A pure substance that is made up of two or more elements combined together.

compression: In sound waves, the part of the wave where the particles of the medium are pressed closer together.

compressional wave: A sound wave; called a compressional wave because it is made up of compressions and rarefactions.

concave: Curved inwards. A term used to describe mirrors that are curved inwards, and lenses that are thinner at the centre than at the edges.

concentrated: Containing a great deal of dissolved solute.

condensation: Change of state from a gas to a liquid.

conduction: The transfer of heat in a solid by the collision of particles.

conductor: A substance, such as steel, that conducts heat well.

cones: Cone-shaped sensory receptors found in your eye. Cones, which work best in bright light, allow people to see colours. There are three different types of cones; each type is stimulated by a different colour (red, green, or blue.)

conglomerate: Sedimentary rock formed from pebbles and small stones.

coniferous: Used to describe trees with cones and needles or scale-like leaves.

consumer (biological): An organism that obtains its energy and nutrients by consuming other organisms.

consumer survey: A questionnaire asking consumers what they think about a product or service.

contraction: The decrease in volume of a substance that results when the particles in the substance move closer together.

control: The part of an experiment in which conditions do not change.

controlled experiment: An experiment in which only one variable is changed at a time, while all the other possible variables remain the same.

convection: The transfer of heat in fluids (liquids and gases) by the movement of particles from one part of the fluid to another.

convection current (geological): A stream of warm air that rises from the ground.

convection current (physical): Moving stream or current that forms in a fluid when it is heated.

convex: Curved outwards. A term used to describe mirrors that are curved outwards, and lenses that are thicker at the centre than at the edges.

crust: The layer of rock that forms the hard surface of our planet. It is usually from 5 km to 50 km thick.

crystal: A mineral or other substance that occurs in a well-defined shape.

crystallize: To form crystals.

cycle: A series of actions repeated in the same order every time.

D

data: Information.

day: The amount of time (24 hours) that the Earth takes to complete one rotation.

day and night cycle: The repetition of daylight followed by darkness. This cycle is caused by the Earth's rotation on its axis.

deciduous: Used to describe trees with leaves that drop off in the fall.

decomposer: An organism that feeds on waste and dead organisms.

delta: The deposit of sediment where a river flows into a lake or sea.

density: The amount of matter in a certain volume of a substance. The density of a sample of a solid, liquid, or gas is calculated by dividing the mass by the volume.

deposit: The build-up of sediment in one place.

deposition: Occurs when eroded material, such as mud, sand, gravel, and boulders, stops moving and settles on the Earth's surface.

depressant: A drug that slows down the activity of the nervous system, and thus slows down the rate of many body activities. For example, depressants can slow down breathing rate and reflexes.

detect: Sense, or become aware of, or "pick up." When a sensory receptor detects a stimulus, it becomes aware of that stimulus.

dew: The tiny drops of water that condense on solid objects.

dew point: The temperature at which the air is holding all the water vapour it can. It is the temperature at which dew begins to form.

diffusion: The gradual mixing of substances that occurs without stirring.

dike: A wall built to raise a bank and help prevent flooding of a body of water.

dilute: Containing only a little dissolved solute.

dinosaur: An extinct reptile of the Mesozoic Era. The word "dinosaur" comes from the Greek words meaning "terrible lizard."

direct measurement: A way of measuring using only the measuring device and the object you are measuring.

disease: A condition in which any structure or part of an organism does not function correctly. Diseases have many causes, including birth defects, poor diet, infections, and poisons in the environment. The terms "illness," "condition," and "disorder" are sometimes used instead of "disease."

displacement of water: A type of indirect measurement in which you measure a volume of water and then place the object to be measured in the water. You measure the volume of liquid again and subtract the original volume of the water. The difference is equal to the volume of the object.

dissolve: To completely mix the particles of two or more substances, forming a solution.

distillate: The liquid that is recovered during distillation.

distillation: A method of separating the parts of a solution and recovering both the solute and the solvent.

diversity: The way species evolve into new species when living in new environments.

dose: The amount or quantity of a drug that a person takes.

drug: A substance (other than food, water, or oxygen) which, when taken into your body, can affect how your body works.

drug abuse: Any use of a drug that causes a problem (other than the side effects of medicine). Drug abuse can result in physical, social, and legal problems.

drug dependence: Another term for addiction. Drug dependence can be either physical or psychological.

drug effect: A change in your body caused by taking a drug.

dune: A pile of sand deposited by winds.

E

echo: Reflected sound waves.

eclipse: An event that occurs when one object in space blocks the light rays from the sun to another object.

ecological pyramid: A diagram with a broad base and small top, used to illustrate relationships between an organism's population size and its place in a food chain.

ecologist: A scientist who studies ecology.

ecology: The study of how Earth's living and non-living parts interact.

ecosystem: The system formed by interactions among living and non-living parts of the environment.

effector: The body part that responds to a stimulus. Most effectors are either muscles or glands.

elastic energy: The energy stored in an object whose shape is changed by stretching (pulling apart), compressing (pushing together), or twisting.

electrical energy: The energy of moving electrical particles.

element: A pure substance that cannot be broken down into any other pure substances.

emulsifier: A substance added to a mixture to prevent the parts of the mixture from separating.

emulsion: a suspension of one liquid in another liquid that has been treated to keep it from separating. For example, homogenized milk is an emulsion of fat droplets in the watery part of the milk.

energy: The ability to make things move.

energy source: The substance or object that provides input energy. All energy transformations start with an energy source.

energy transformation: The change from one form of energy to another. Energy cannot be used without these energy transformations.

environment: All the living and non-living things that surround and influence an organism.

environmentalist: A person concerned about protecting the environment.

era: One of the four periods of time on the Geological Time Scale, measured in many millions of years. Each era is a different length of time.

erosion: The movement of rock material from one place to another. Erosion can be caused by gravity, running water, waves, wind, or moving ice.

erratic: A large boulder left stranded by a melting glacier.

estimate: To roughly determine the measurement or nature of something.

evaporation: Change of state from a liquid to a gas.

evolution: The process by which new species develop from older species.

expansion: The increase in the volume of a substance that results when the particles in the substance move farther apart.

experiment: A series of activities that help solve a problem or find an answer to a question.

extinct: Refers to a species that has completely disappeared from the Earth.

extrusive rock: Igneous rock formed by the cooling and hardening of lava on the Earth's surface.

F

family: Class of rocks based on the way they were formed.

felling: Cutting down trees.

fever: A body temperature that is higher than normal.

fibre: A thin, hairlike strand of material that can be woven into cloth.

field test: A test of a product in which people use the product and then tell researchers whether they liked it.

filter: A device that allows smaller particles to pass through but holds back larger ones.

filtrate: The part of a mixture that passes through a filter.

filtration: A method of separating the parts of mixtures based on the size of the pieces. For example, mud can be separated from water by filtration.

fiord: Long, narrow, deep bay of the sea bordered by cliffs. Fiords are U-shaped valleys formed by glaciers and later filled by the sea.

flood plain: The flat land beside a river that is covered by water during flooding, when the river overflows its banks.

fluid: A state of matter (liquid or gas) in which the particles are free to flow from place to place.

fluorescence: Describes the change in colour that some minerals show when illuminated by ultraviolet light.

focus: The place where light rays come together to a single point.

food chain: A series of organisms, each of which relies for its food on the organism before it in the chain.

food web: Food chains linked together within a particular ecosystem.

Forest Licence: A licence from the British Columbia government that gives a company permission to cut a certain amount of wood.

forest management: Managing a forested area to produce wood. Management includes finding out which organisms live in the area, planning, road building, deciding which logging methods to use, and replanting.

forester: A person trained to care for and decide how to use forests.

fossil: The remains of a living thing from the past. Fossils are usually preserved in rock.

freezing: Change of state from a liquid to a solid.

freezing point: The temperature at which a pure substance changes from a liquid to a solid. The freezing point of a substance is the same temperature as its melting point.

frequency: The number of times an event, such as clapping or vibrations, occurs in a given length of time. Usually the length of time is one second.

function: Purpose or job. For example, the function of your eyelids is to protect your eyes.

fungicide: A pesticide used to control mushrooms, mould, and other fungi.

G

gas: A state of matter that has a fixed mass but does not have a fixed volume or a fixed shape. A gas takes the shape of the container in which it is placed and always fills the container.

generation: A group of organisms having the same parents.

Geological Time Scale: A time scale covering the millions of years of the Earth's existence.

geologist: A scientist who studies rocks and the Earth's history.

glacier: A thick mass of moving ice.

gland: A body part that makes and releases one or more of the many chemicals your body needs in order to work properly.

gravitational energy: The energy that an object has when it is above the surface of the Earth. Any object that can drop, roll, or slide down has gravitational energy.

H

habitat: A part of the ecosystem, such as a pond or forest, where a particular organism spends most of its time.

hallucinogen: Any of the drugs that cause people to see or hear things that are not really there. In other words, users of these drugs have hallucinations.

hardness: In a mineral, the property of being able to scratch another mineral. It is used to identify minerals.

hardwood: A deciduous tree.

heat: The energy transferred from an object at a higher temperature to an object at a lower temperature. Also, the energy transferred along a conductor.

thermal energy: The total energy of all the particles in an object. The greater the movement of the particles, the more thermal energy the object has.

heat stroke: A condition caused by your body's becoming overheated. It causes high fever, and may cause convulsions, fainting, and even death.

heat transfer: The transfer of energy from particles of greater average energy to particles of lower average energy.

herbicide: A pesticide used to control weeds.

hertz: The unit for measuring frequency. One vibration in one second is called one hertz (Hz).

higher order consumer: An animal that feeds on secondary consumers.

holistic forestry: A kind of forest management concerned with the whole forest, not only the production of wood.

humidity: The amount of water vapour in the atmosphere.

humus: Decaying plant and animal matter that is found in the soil.

hypothermia: Describes the condition when your body temperature drops below normal. It is caused by the loss of too much thermal energy from your body.

hypothesis: A possible explanation of how something happens in nature.

I

ice age: One of the periods of time during the Earth's history when ice sheets covered large areas the size of continents.

ice sheet: A huge, domed glacier. Today the Earth's largest ice sheets are in Greenland and Antarctica.

ice wedging: A process of physical weathering. Water freezes in cracks in the rock. As the water freezes and expands as ice, the rock splits apart.

igneous rock: Rock formed by the cooling and hardening of molten rock, either lava or magma.

image: What you see when something looks like an object but is not the object itself. A photograph is an example of an image.

inaudible: Describes sounds that are too low, too high, or too faint for you to hear.

incident ray: The ray of light travelling from a light source to a mirror's surface. Also, the light ray that passes through an object or a substance and hits the surface of a different object or substance.

indirect measurement: A way of measuring in which you first measure the mass or volume of a container and then place the material to be measured in the container. You measure the mass or volume of the container again and subtract the original measurement. The difference is equal to the mass or volume of the material you are measuring.

infer: To develop explanations from observations.

inference: An explanation that results from an observation.

infrasonic: The frequencies of sound waves below our normal range of hearing.

inhalant: A drug that is taken into the body by being breathed in (inhaled) or sniffed.

inherit: To receive a characteristic from parents (or ancestors) by birth. For example, eye colour is inherited.

injection: The use of a syringe (a thin hollow needle with a pump attached) to put a liquid drug into the body.

inner ear: The innermost section of your ear. It includes the cochlea, which is a fluid-filled structure containing the ear's sound receptors.

input energy: The starting energy in any energy transformation.

insecticide: A pesticide used to control insects.

insoluble: Unable to be dissolved.

insulation: The use of insulators.

insulator: A substance that prevents or slows down the transfer of heat.

integrated pest control (IPC): A way to control pests that uses a combination of chemicals and non-chemical methods.

intended effect: In terms of drugs, the intended effect is the effect the drug is expected or designed to have on the body. For example, the intended effect of a drug used to relieve headaches is a decrease in head pain.

interact: To affect one another.

interaction: Action on one another.

internal sensory receptor: A sensory receptor that detects stimuli inside your body. For example, some internal sensory receptors detect the presence of certain chemicals, whereas others detect how far your muscles have stretched.

interpret (biological): In terms of nerve functions, "interpret" means that a nerve impulse either is passed on along the nerve cell into the next nerve cell (or effector) or is not passed along.

interpreting: Explaining the meaning of anything you have observed.

intrusive rock: Igneous rock formed beneath the Earth's surface. It is formed by the cooling and hardening of magma.

inventory: A survey that lists what is in a forest, including the numbers and types of trees, rivers, animals, and other plants.

issue: A topic about which people have different points of view.

K

Kelvin scale: A temperature scale on which the zero mark is at absolute zero and the space between the degrees is the same size as that on the Celsius scale.

kinetic energy: The energy of anything in motion.

kinetic molecular theory: A theory that explains the behaviour of matter. This theory suggests that all matter consists of very small particles in constant motion.

L

landscape: All the physical features of the Earth's surface.

lava: Molten rock that flows onto the Earth's surface.

LD-50: The dose of a pesticide that will kill 50 per cent of a population of a particular organism.

leeward: The side of an object that is sheltered from the wind.

lens: A transparent object that can refract light rays. Lenses are usually made from plastic or glass and have at least one curved surface.

lethal: Leading to death.

light energy: The form of energy that you can see.

line transect: A method of estimating the size of an animal or a plant population. The method involves counting how many individuals touch or are close to a straight line that runs through an area.

liquid: A state of matter that has a fixed mass and volume but does not have a fixed shape. A liquid takes the shape of the container in which it is placed.

logging: A process that includes cutting trees, sawing them into logs, and moving the logs out of the forest.

long-term effect: In terms of drugs, a long-term effect lasts for a long time after a drug is used. Long-term effects usually occur only if a person uses too much of a drug or uses it for too long a period of time.

lunar eclipse: An eclipse of the moon, which occurs when the Earth is directly between the sun and the moon. During a lunar eclipse, the Earth casts a shadow on part of the moon.

lustre: A property of minerals. It describes how the surface of a mineral reflects light.

M

magma: Molten rock formed deep below the Earth's surface.

magnetic energy: The form of energy that causes some kinds of metal to attract (pull together) or repel (push apart) some metal objects. (Also known as magnetism.)

magnetism: The property of a mineral that attracts a magnet or compass needle.

mass: The amount of matter in an object. Mass is usually measured in milligrams, grams, kilograms, or tonnes.

matter: Anything that has mass and volume.

measure: To find exact information about characteristics such as height, length, mass, or temperature.

mechanical energy: The energy in any set of moving parts.

mechanical mixture: A mixture in which two or more parts can be seen with the unaided eye.

mechanical weathering: A process that breaks down rock into smaller pieces. Ice wedging is an example of mechanical weathering.

medicine: A drug used to prevent or treat illness, pain, or discomfort.

medium: The material that carries or transmits sound energy.

medulla oblongata: The part of your brain that controls internal body functions such as breathing and digesting food. The medulla oblongata makes sure that these activities occur automatically so that you do not have to think about them.

melting: Change of state from a solid to a liquid.

melting point: Temperature at which a pure substance changes from solid to liquid (same temperature as the substance's freezing point).

meniscus: The curved surface of liquid where it touches the side of its container.

Mesozoic Era: Geological time that occurred from 225 to 65 million years ago. It is sometimes called "The Age of Reptiles."

metamorphic rock: Rock formed below the Earth's surface when heat and pressure cause existing rocks to change their characteristics.

meteorologist: A scientist who studies the weather.

micro-environment: A small part of a habitat with its own distinct abiotic conditions; for example, the area under a rock.

micro-organism: A tiny living thing that can only be seen with the help of a microscope—for example, bacteria and single-celled algae.

middle ear: The middle section of your ear, located inside your head between the eardrum and the inner ear. It contains three tiny bones: the hammer, the anvil, and the stirrup.

mineral: A pure, naturally occurring substance found in the Earth's crust.

mirror: Any surface that reflects light so that it produces a visible image.

mixture: Matter that has two or more kinds of particles and thus may have different properties in different samples. There are three kinds of mixtures: mechanical mixtures, suspensions, and solutions.

model: An object, a design, or an idea that helps you to understand something that you cannot observe directly.

Mohs hardness scale: A number scale of 10 minerals. A mineral with a higher number can scratch a mineral with a lower number. For example, a diamond (10) can scratch talc (1).

mold: A type of fossil that is formed when the shape of an organism is preserved in mud or sand. Later the mud and sand hardens into rock.

molecule: A particle made up of two or more atoms joined together.

month: The amount of time it takes for the moon to revolve once around the Earth.

moraine: A large pile of rock left by a melting glacier, at the end of the glacier or on the walls of the valley.

motor nerve cell: A nerve cell that carries nerve impulses to effectors (usually muscles or glands), causing them to respond to stimuli.

mountain glacier (or alpine glacier): A glacier formed in a cold, high mountain valley. Mountain glaciers are found in many parts of the world.

mudstone: Sedimentary rock formed from compacted mud.

multiple use management: Managing an area, such as a forest, for several different uses. An example is allowing logging and recreation in the same forest.

N

natural fibre: A fibre made from animal or plant material.

natural selection: The theory of how new species develop from older species, first proposed by Charles Darwin.

negative effect: In terms of drugs, a negative effect causes some type of harm or damage to people who use the drug. Drugs with negative effects may damage organs or kill brain cells, for example.

nerve: A bundle of nerve cells.

nerve cell: A type of cell that carries messages (nerve impulses) from one part of your body to another.

nerve impulse: A message, or electrical signal, that travels from one end of a nerve cell to the other end after the nerve cell has been stimulated.

nervous system: The body system that co-ordinates all of your body's activities. It is made up of billions of nerve cells, as well as other cells that support the nerve cells and help them do their work.

neuron: A nerve cell.

niche: The role of an organism in the environment, including its relationships with other species.

noise: Any unwanted sound.

non-barbiturate: Any of the group of sedative-hypnotic drugs that have the same effects as barbiturate drugs, but are less addictive.

non-residual: Used to describe a pesticide that loses its toxic effect soon after it is applied.

normal body temperature: Your body's usual temperature (37°C).

nuclear energy: The energy stored in the central part of an atom (the nucleus).

nutrient: A chemical substance that an organism needs in order to survive.

O

observe: To watch, or to examine carefully by using your five senses.

ocean current: A great mass of seawater that moves in the same direction.

old growth forest: A forest that has not been logged and has trees 150 years old or older.

opaque: Describes substances that do not allow any light to pass through them.

organ: A body part that performs a particular task or tasks. For example, the heart is an organ that pumps blood, and the lungs are organs that help you breathe.

organism: A living thing.

organizing: Putting observations and data together so that they can be discussed with others and more easily understood.

oscilloscope: An electronic device (similar to a television) that can be used to display sounds on a screen.

outer ear: The outermost section of your ear. It includes the structure located on the side of your head, the auditory canal, and the eardrum.

output energy: The energy that results from an energy transformation.

over-the-counter drug: A drug that can be purchased without a prescription.

P

paleontology: The study of life in the past through the use of fossils.

Paleozoic Era: Occurred from 570 to 225 million years ago. Rocks from this era contain fossils of sponges, amphibians, and land plants.

parent rock: The rock from which a particular type of metamorphic rock was produced.

particle model: A model that suggests that matter is made up of tiny particles. This model explains the properties of solids, liquids, and gases.

penumbra: The part of a shadow where only some of the light rays have been blocked.

personal care product: A product that you use to clean your body or to make yourself look or smell good.

pest: An organism that harms humans, property, or domestic plants and animals.

pest control: Methods used to reduce populations of pests.

pesticide: A substance used to control plant or animal pests.

pharmacist: A person who has been trained to understand drugs and their effects and who is permitted to fill drug prescriptions.

photosynthesis: The process in which plants transform light energy into chemical energy.

physical change: A change in matter in which no new substance is produced.

physical dependence: A type of drug dependence in which a person's body has become so used to the presence of a drug that the body must have the drug in order to work properly.

pitch: Describes the highness and lowness of sounds.

population: A group of individuals of the same species living in the same area.

positive effect: In terms of drugs, a positive effect is helpful to people that use the drug. Drugs with positive effects may improve a person's health or reduce pain, for example.

potential energy: Stored energy.

Precambrian Era: The oldest era of geological time, beginning 4.6 billion years ago when the Earth was formed, and lasting until 570 million years ago.

predict: To use observations made in the past to describe what you think might happen.

premarket testing: A series of tests that is conducted before a drug (or other product) is sold. Premarket testing is done on drugs to make sure that they are not harmful as well as to determine what dose of the drug is needed.

prescription: A note, written by a doctor, that allows a person to obtain a certain amount of a controlled drug at a pharmacy.

prescription drug: A drug for which a person needs a doctor's prescription.

prevailing wind: Wind that usually blows in one direction.

primary consumer: An organism that feeds on producers.

prism: A transparent object that can separate light into its spectrum of colour.

process: A series of actions carried out in a specific order.

process skill: A procedure, such as observing or measuring, that is used in scientific research.

producer: An organism that produces its own food from abiotic materials, usually by photosynthesis.

property: A characteristic used to describe matter. Colour, hardness, and freezing point are some examples of properties.

psychological dependence: A type of drug dependence in which a person has a strong emotional need for a drug and may feel lost or desperate without it.

pulp: Ground-up wood fibres combined with water and chemicals.

pure substance: A substance that has the same properties in any sample you choose. There are two kinds of pure substances: elements and compounds.

Q

qualitative properties: Properties that describe matter without using numbers.

quantitative properties: Properties that describe matter using numbers.

quartzite: A metamorphic rock made from sandstone.

R

radiant energy: Energy transferred by radiation. Light energy is a form of radiant energy.

radiation: A method of energy transfer that does not require particles.

random sampling (or **spot testing**): Carrying out a test on an item that has been selected at random from many similar items.

rarefaction: In sound waves, the part of the wave where the particles of the medium are farther apart.

rays: Lines of light energy that radiate from a source.

reaction (biological): An action that follows detection of a stimulus. Reactions, which can be reflex or voluntary actions, are also called responses.

reaction time: The length of time it takes you to respond to a stimulus.

receiver: The object that receives sound energy that comes from a source and travels through a medium.

reflected ray: The ray of light that leaves a mirror's surface.

reflection: A visible image in a mirror. The change in direction of a light ray when it strikes the surface of a mirror.

reflex action: A predictable action that occurs immediately and automatically in response to a stimulus.

reflex arc: The pathway followed by the nerve impulses that produce a reflex action. Most reflex arcs have five parts: a sensory receptor, a sensory nerve cell, an association nerve cell, a motor nerve cell, and an effector.

refracted ray: A light ray that bends as it passes from one substance into another.

refraction: The change in direction of a light ray as it passes from one substance to another.

relative humidity: The amount of water vapour in the air compared with the total amount of water vapour that the air could hold at that temperature. It is written as a per cent.

renewable resource: A resource that can replace itself over time. Two examples are fish and trees.

replacement fossil: Formed when all or part of a dead organism is replaced by minerals.

residual: Used to describe a pesticide that keeps its toxic effect for a long period after it is applied.

residue: Something that remains. In distillation, the residue is the material that remains in the original container. In filtration, the residue is the part of the mixture that is held back by a filter.

resistant: Used to describe a pest that is not killed by pesticides.

response (biological): An action that occurs because a particular stimulus has been detected by sensory receptors. The response, which follows the stimulus, is sometimes called a reaction to the stimulus.

retreat: In geology, the backward movement of the front edge of a shrinking glacier.

revolution: The movement of an object in a path around another object. The Earth revolves around the sun, and the moon revolves around the Earth.

rock: Earth materials made up of one or more minerals.

rock cycle: The ways igneous, sedimentary, and metamorphic rocks change from one to the other.

rodenticide: A pesticide used to control rats, mice, and other rodents.

rods: Rod-shaped sensory receptors found in your eyes. Rods work best in dim light.

rotation: The spinning of an object on its axis. The Earth rotates completely once every 24 hours.

S

sandstone: A sedimentary rock formed from particles of sand that are cemented together.

saturated (weather): Describes air with 100 per cent relative humidity. Saturated air cannot hold any more moisture.

saturated (chemical): Containing as much solute as can be held at that temperature; said of a solution.

science: Both a body of knowledge and a process for gaining more knowledge about the world in which we live.

second growth forest: A forest that grows after an original old-growth forest has been logged.

second-hand smoke: Unfiltered smoke from the burning end of a cigarette, cigar, or pipe, which enters the environment when a person smokes.

secondary consumer: An organism that feeds on primary consumers.

sedative-hypnotic: A type of depressant drug that causes a person to feel sleepy as well as relaxed and calm.

sediment: Fragments of eroded rock, including clay, mud, sand, gravel, and boulders.

sedimentary rock: Rock formed by the breaking down, deposition, and compaction of sediments.

selection logging: A logging method in which some trees in an area are cut and others are left standing.

sensory nerve cell: A nerve cell that carries nerve impulses from sensory receptors into other parts of the nervous system, where these impulses will be interpreted.

sensory organ: A body part that contains many sensory receptors. For example, your eyes and ears are sensory organs.

sensory receptor: A body part that is specialized to detect stimuli. A sensory receptor is usually a single nerve cell.

shadow: The dark area behind an object, created when the object blocks the light rays from a light source.

shale: Sedimentary rock formed from compacted clay.

short-term effect: In terms of drugs, a short-term effect occurs soon after the drug is taken and lasts for a short time only.

side effect: Any effect on the body caused by a drug other than the drug's intended effect. Side effects are often negative.

sidestream smoke: Another term for second-hand smoke.

silviculture: Planting and caring for forest trees.

slate: Metamorphic rock formed from shale.

society: A group of individuals who must work together.

softwood: A coniferous tree.

solar eclipse: An eclipse of the sun, which occurs when the moon is directly between the sun and the Earth. During a solar eclipse, the moon casts a shadow on part of the Earth.

solar energy: The general term for the forms of energy that we receive from the sun.

solar system: The sun and all the objects that travel around it, including the planets, the moons that travel around some of the planets, comets, meteors, and asteroids.

solid: A state of matter that has a fixed mass, volume, and shape.

soluble: Able to be dissolved.

solute: The material that is dissolved in a solution. For example, in a solution of sugar and water, sugar is the solute.

solution: A mixture that appears to be all one substance.

solvent: The material in which a solute dissolves to produce a solution. For example, in a solution of sugar and water, water is the solvent. In terms of drugs, a solvent is an inhalant such as nail polish remover or paint thinner.

sonar: A word formed from the phrase "Sound Navigation and Ranging." It is the use of high-frequency sound waves to detect objects (such as fish) below the surface of the water.

sound energy: The form of energy that you can hear. It travels as vibrations through materials and through air.

species: Refers to organisms of the same kind that can breed with one another, or reproduce.

spinal cord: The long bundle of nerves and nerve cells that runs from the base of your brain down to your lower back.

spine: The long tube of bones running down your back. The spine surrounds and protects the spinal cord.

spectrum: The colours in white light. A spectrum can be produced using a prism. It may also be seen as a rainbow.

spot testing (or **random sampling):** Carrying out a test on an item that has been selected at random from many similar items.

steroid: A type of drug usually taken to increase a person's muscle growth. Steroids can also have harmful side effects, such as a decrease in bone growth and injury to various body organs.

states of matter: Solid, liquid, and gas.

stimulant: A drug that speeds up the activity of the nervous system and thus of other body systems. Stimulants can increase heart rate and breathing rate, for example.

stimulate: In terms of the nervous system, "to stimulate" means to cause a nerve impulse to begin travelling along a nerve cell.

stimulus (plural: stimuli): A change in the environment that a sensory receptor is able to detect. For example, a sound loud enough to be heard is a stimulus for the sensory receptors in your ear.

streak: Describes the colour of the powdery mark that some minerals make when they are scratched against a hard surface.

striations: Long parallel scratches made on rock by boulders that are carried along by moving glaciers.

structure: The parts of something and the way those parts are arranged.

sublimation: Change of state from a gas directly to a solid or from a solid directly to a gas. No liquid is formed during this process.

summer and winter cycle: The repetition of the four seasons (spring, summer, fall, winter). This cycle is caused by the tilt of the Earth's axis combined with the Earth's motion around the sun.

surface area: The surface of a grain of sand or other sediment that is exposed to weathering.

surfactant: The cleaning agent in soap.

suspension: A cloudy mixture that consists of clumps of a solid or droplets of liquid scattered throughout the mixture. The parts of a suspension will separate if it is left to stand.

sustained yield: The production of materials such as wood over a long period of time without causing harm to the ecosystem.

synthetic: Made by humans.

synthetic fibre: A fibre that is made from materials developed by chemists.

T

target: In pest control, the organism that the control method is aimed at and intends to reduce.

taste buds: Sensory receptors located on your tongue. They detect the presence of different types of chemicals on your tongue.

technology: The use of scientific knowledge to solve a problem.

temperature: A way of expressing how hot or how cold something is. Temperature is a measure of the average energy of all the particles in an object.

theory: A well-accepted hypothesis that is supported by repeated observations and experiments. A theory makes predictions that can be tested.

thermometer: An instrument that is used to measure temperature.

tides: The regular rise and fall in the water level in bodies of water on the Earth. Tides are caused by the pull of gravity from the moon and the sun.

tolerance: In terms of drugs, tolerance is a condition in which a drug has less effect when it is used repeatedly. A person who has a tolerance to a drug feels the drug's effects less and less each time he or she uses the drug.

toxic: Poisonous.

trait: An inherited characteristic.

tranquillizer: A type of depressant drug that can cause a person to feel calm and relaxed without feeling sleepy.

translucent: Describes substances that allow some light to pass through but do not allow you to see clearly through them.

transparent: Describes substances that allow light rays to pass through them. Transparent substances may be colourless or coloured.

Tree Farm Licence (TFL): A licence from the British Columbia government that gives a company permission to cut trees in a particular area of the provincial forest.

trilobite: A type of extinct undersea organism. Today trilobites are known only as fossils.

U

U-shaped valley: A valley formed when a moving glacier digs out and erodes the sides of a valley into a smooth, rounded shape. Fiords are U-shaped valleys that are occupied by the ocean.

ultrasonic: The frequencies of sound waves above our normal hearing range (above 20 000 Hz).

umbra: The part of a shadow where all the light rays have been blocked. It is the darkest part of the shadow.

V

V-shaped valley: A valley formed when a river cuts a channel in the Earth's surface.

vaccine: A drug that causes the body to build up its own internal protection against a particular disease.

variable: A factor that changes in an experiment.

vibrations: The back-and-forth movements of an object.

volume (physical): The amount of space that matter occupies. Volume is usually measured in millilitres or litres.

volume (sound): The loudness of a sound. Volume is determined by the amplitude of the sound wave. The greater the amplitude of the wave, the louder the sound.

voluntary action: A response that you can control. Voluntary actions, which you must think about before doing, are controlled by your brain.

W

wavelength: The distance between two waves. The length of compressional waves is measured from the middle of one compression to the middle of the next one. For transverse waves, the wavelength can be measured from the highest point of one wave to the highest point of the next wave.

water cycle: The continuous movement of water from the Earth's surface into the atmosphere and back again.

weather forecast: A prediction of the weather in an area over the next few hours or days. Weather forecasts are based on measurements and satellite photographs.

weathering: The processes that slowly break down rocks into smaller pieces.

windward: The side of an object that faces the wind.

withdrawal reaction: The reaction suffered by a person who is addicted to a drug after the person stops taking it. The withdrawal reaction may be slight (for example, a headache), or the reaction may result in serious illness or death.

Y

year: The amount of time required for the Earth to revolve once around the sun.

INDEX

PHOTO CREDITS

Front Matter xiii Al Harvey; xv Brian Milne/First Light.

Unit Openers: Unit 1 Al Harvey; Unit 2 Al Harvey; Unit 3 Al Harvey; Unit 4 Earth Satellite Corporation/Science Photo Library; Unit 5 Ron Watts/First Light; Unit 6 Trevor Bonderud/First Light.

Sidebars: Science In Our World COMSTOCK/W. Marin Jr.; Computer Application COMSTOCK/W. Marin Jr.; Profile Comstock; Career Comstock.

Chapter One: Opener Michael Newman/Photo Edit; 1.1 David Keevil; Science In Our World B.C. Tourism; 1.13 David Keevil; 1.14 Al Harvey.

Chapter 2: Opener Max Schneider/The Image Bank; 2.10a Jeremy Jones; 2.10b Ron Watts/First Light; 2.10c Energy Mines and Resources Canada; Career Greg Kinch; 2.11 Al Harvey; 2.12 HMS Images/The Image Bank; Computer Application Peter Booth; 2.14 David Keevil; 2.15 David Keevil; 2.16 David Keevil; 2.18 David Keevil; 2.20 Ken Sherman/First Light; 2.21 David Keevil; 2.26 Thomas Bowman/Photo Edit; 2.27 Michael Newman/Photo Edit; 2.30 Kjell B. Sandved; 2.34 Lou Jones/The Image Bank.

Chapter 3: Opener Patti McConville/ The Image Bank; 3.1a Grafton M. Smith/The Image Bank; 3.1b Michael Skott/The Image Bank; 3.2 David Keevil; 3.3 Nancy Flood; 3.4 David Keevil; 3.10 Man In Motion World Tour Society; 3.12 Gord Fong/ Cedarbrae High School; 3.13a Nancy Flood; 3.13b Tony Freeman/ Photo Edit; 3.13c David Young Wolff/ Photo Edit; 3.15 Heinz Fischer/The Image Bank; Profile Greg Kinch; 3.18 Canadian Amateur Hockey Association; 3.19 Tim Beddow/Science Photo Library.

Chapter 4: Opener Tim Beddow/ Science Photo Library; 4.1a Hattie Young/Science Photo Library; 4.1b Alan Marsh/First Light; 4.2 Canada Wide Feature Service; Science In Our World A. Sirulnikoff/First Light; 4.4a Phil Jude/Science Photo Library; 4.4b Ontario Ministry of Agriculture and Rural Affairs; 4.5 Jim Selby/Science Photo Library; 4.7 Judy Nisenholt/Asia Access; Profile Dr. F. Kelsey; 4.10 D & J Heaton/Science Photo Library; 4.12 Steven Mangold/First Light; 4.13 Metropolitan Toronto Police; 4.15 David Keevil; 4.16a,b James Stevenson/Science Photo Library; 4.17 The Image Bank; 4.18 John Durham/Science Photo Library; 4.19 David Keevil; 4.20 Canadian Sports Images.

Chapter 5: Opener Lawrence Migdale/Tony Stone; Profile Greg Kinch; 5.11 David Keevil; 5.12 David Keevil; 5.13 David Keevil; 5.20 Alvin Upitis/The Image Bank; 5.21 Amy Etra/Photo Edit; 5.22 Pekka Parviainen/Science Photo Library; 5.24 Hank deLespinasse/The Image Bank; 5.25a Dr. Dennis Kunkel/First Light; 5.25b Fred Ward/First Light; 5.25c David Leah/Science Photo Library; 5.25d Dr. Dennis Kunkel/First Light; 5.27 David Keevil; 5.28 David Keevil.

Chapter 6: Opener David Keevil; 6.1 David Keevil; 6.5 Nelson Max; 6.6a,b,c David Keevil; 6.7 David Keevil; 6.8 Terje Rakke/The Image Bank; 6.11 David Keevil; 6.18 Energy Mines and Resources Canada; Computer Application Greg Kinch; 6.23 David Keevil; 6.24 David Keevil; 6.28 David Keevil; 6.30a Obremski/The Image Bank; 6.30b Alan Marsh/The Image Bank; 6.30c Energy Mines and Resources Canada; 6.30d World Gold Council.

Chapter 7: Opener David Keevil; 7.2 Al Harvey; 7.5a David Brownell/The Image Bank; 7.5b Steve Chenn/First Light; 7.7 David Keevil; 7.9 David Keevil; 7.10 Alan Sirulnikoff/First Light; 7.11 Cradoc Bagshaw/First Light; 7.12a Manfred Kage/First Light; 7.12b Dr. Jeremy Burgess/Science Photo Library; 7.12c Arnold Fisher/Science Photo Library; 7.12d Dr. Jeremy Burgess/Science Photo Library; 7.19 Ontario Agricultural Museum; 7.20 Bridge Maintenance Department, Ontario Ministry of Transportation; 7.21 Greg Stott/Masterfile; 7.22 Ron Watts/First Light; 7.23 Paul Morrison, Viewpoints West.

Chapter 8: Opener 1 Al Harvey; 2 First Light; 3 Robert Copeland/First Light; 4 Benjamin Rondel/First Light; 8.1 Comnet/First Light; 8.2 Wiley file photo; 8.5 The Public Archives of Canada; 8.6a U.S. Department of Agriculture; 8.6b Image Finders; 8.6c Ken Rogers/First Light; 8.6d John Burbridge/Science Photo Library; 8.8a,b University of Guelph; 8.9a,b Wiley file photo; 8.10 Dominion Textiles; 8.12 Al Harvey; 8.16 Ikea Canada; 8.17 Crane Canada Inc.; 8.19 David Keevil; Career Wiley file photo.

Chapter 9: Opener David Keevil; 9.3a Canadian Sports Images; 9.3b Thomas Kitchin/First Light; 9.3c Whitney Lane/The Image Bank; 9.3d Stephen Homer/First Light; 9.8 David Keevil; 9.9 Peter Miller/The Image Bank; Career P. Marra; 9.12 Wiley file photo; 9.13 Energy Mines and Resources; 9.14 Wiley file photo.

Chapter 10: Opener Benn Mitchell/ The Image Bank; 10.1 David Keevil; 10.7 David Keevil; 10.8 David Keevil; 10.9 David Keevil; 10.10 David Keevil; 10.11 David Keevil; 10.12 David Keevil; 10.18 David Keevil; 10.19 David Keevil; 10.22 W. Vliegenthart; 10.23a Pat Morrow/First Light; 10.23b Thomas Kitchin/First Light; 10.23c Ken Straiton/First Light; 10.23d David Keevil; 10.24a,b Ontario Ministry of Energy; 10.26a,c,d Wiley file photos; 10.26b Climatizer Insulation; Computer Application Wiley file photos; 10.28 Canapress; 10.30 Geoff Williams & Howard Metcalf/Science Photo Library; 10.31 Wiley file photo; Profile Wiley file photo.

Chapter 11: Opener Al Harvey; 11.1 David Keevil; 11.3 John Sanford/ Science Photo Library; 11.7 Tony Freeman/Photo Edit; 11.8 Wiley file photo; 11.12 David Keevil; Career Mitchell Funk/The Image Bank; 11.13 Tony Freeman/Photo Edit; 11.15 David Keevil; 11.20 David Keevil; 11.23 David Keevil; 11.27 David Keevil.

Chapter12: Opener Trevor Bonderud/First Light; 12.1 David Keevil; 12.3 Lou Jones/The Image Bank; 12.4 David Keevil; 12.5 David Keevil; 12.6 David Keevil; 12.7 Barry Dursley/First Light; 12.8 David Keevil; 12.9 David Keevil; 12.10 David Keevil; 12.11 Martin Dohrn/Science Photo Library; Science In Our World The Twelfth Fret Guitarist's Pro Shop; 12.15 David Keevil; 12.16 David Keevil; 12.19 Custom Medical Stock Photo; 12.20 CNRI/Science Photo Library; 12.21a Michel Tcherevkoff; 12.21b Tony Freeman/Photo Edit; 12.22 David Keevil; 12.23 Tony Freeman/Photo Edit.

Chapter 13: Opener 1 John Sanford/ Science Photo Library; 2 Dr. Fred Espenak/Science Photo Library; 13.5 Lick Obervatory Photographs; 13.16 John Sanford/Science Photo Library; 13.18 Wiley file photos; 13.24 Rev. Ronald Royer/Science Photo Library; 13.25 John Sanford/Science Photo Library; 13.28 NASA/Science Photo Library; Science In Our World Rev. Ronald Royer/Science Photo Library; 13.13 Lorenz Denney/Science Photo Library.

Chapter 14: Opener David Keevil; 14.1 David Keevil; 14.2 David Keevil; 14.3 David Keevil; 14.4 J. Nagel; Career Wiley file photo; 14.5a Sinclair Stammers/Science Photo Library; 14.5b Martin Land/Science Photo Library; 14.5c Kaj Svensson,Viewpoints West; 14.5d Roberto De Gugliemo/Science Photo Library; 14.6 A. Penner; 14.8 Wiley file photo; 14.10 A. Penner; 14.11 A. Penner; 14.12 V. Wilkinson/Valan Photos; 14.12b J.R. Page/Valan Photos; 14.12c Wiley file photo; 14.13a G. Birchall; 14.13b Wiley file photo; 14.15a A. Penner; 14.15b Charles R. Belinky/Photo Researchers.

Chapter 15: Opener Glenbow Archives; 15.1 Ken Straiton/First Light; 15.4 Eric Grace; 15.6 Virginia Division of Tourism; 15.7 Bob Semple; 15.8 Richard Wormser/First Light; 15.9 Janet Dwyer/First Light; 15.10 Wiley file photo; 15.11 Ted Russell/The Image Bank; Computer Application Canada Centre For Remote Sensing, Natural Resources Canada; 15.13 Geographical Visual Aids; 15.14 Cliff Wallis; 15.15 Wiley file photo; 15.17 Canada Remote Sensing; 15.18 Wiley file photo; 15.19 Al Harvey; 15.21a Geographical Visual Aids; 15.21b Geographical Visual Aids; 15.21c John Sylvester/First Light; 15.21d Al Harvey; 15.23 Wiley file photo; 15.27 Geographical Visual Aids; Science In Our World Polar Continental Shelf Project; 15.29 J. Ricker; 15.30 Geographical Visual Aids; 15.31 Alan Sirulnikoff/First Light; 15.32 Geographical Visual Aids; 15.33 W. Durward; 15.34 NASA.

Chapter 16: Opener David Young Wolff/Photo Edit; 16.1a,b Wiley file photo; 16.2 Royal Ontario Museum; 16.5 Geographical Visual Aids; 16.6 Alfred Pasieka/Science Photo Library; 16.7 Dr. Gerald Newlands; 16.8 J. Ramey/The Image Bank; Career Vladirmir Krb; 16.11 Imperial Oil Limited; 16.15 James L. Amos/Photo Researchers; 16.17a Paul Franklin/ Oxford Scientific Films;16.17b James H. Carmichael, Jr./The Image Bank; 16.18 J. Nagel; 16.20 Guido A. Rossi/The Image Bank; 16.21 Thomas Kitchin/First Light; 16.23 Warren Morgan/First Light; 16.24 David Keevil.

Chapter 17: Opener Al Harvey; 17.5 Thermor Ltd.; Science In Our World Agriculture Canada; 17.9 David Keevil; 17.16 Dave Reede/First Light; 17.19 Hasler & Pierce, NASA GSFC/Science Photo Library; 17.20a Thomas Kitchin/First Light; 17.20b Al Harvey; 17.20c Pekka Parvianen/Science Photo Library.

Chapter 18: Opener Jose Carrillo/ Photo Edit; 18a Andrew Syred/Science Photo Library; 18b Dr. Tony Brain & David Parker/Science Photo Library; 18c Sinclair Stammers/ Science Photo Library; 18.3 David Keevil; 18.5a WSI/Science Photo Library; 18.5b Robert Semeniuk/First Light; 18.5c Geographical Visual Aids; 18.5d Jim Zuckerman/First Light; 18.7a Bob Semple; 18.7b Alvis Upitis/The Image Bank; 18.7c Victoria Hurst/First Light; 18.10 David Keevil; 18.12 Al Harvey; 18.15 David Keevil; 18.17 Joe Van Os/The Image Bank; 18.20 Steven McBrady/Photo Edit; 18.21 David Keevil; Profile Trevor Bonderud/First Light.

Chapter 19: Opener Thomas Kitchin/ First Light; 19.1 B.C. Environment; 19.3 Al Harvey; 19.4 Michael P. Gadomski/Photo Researchers; 19.5 Reproduced from Agriculture Canada poster "Don't Bring it Back"/"N'En Rapportex Pas", 1986, by permission of the Minister Supply and Services Canada, 1994; 19.6a Al Harvey; 19.6b Steve Strickland/First Light; 19.7 Al Harvey; 19.13a,b Bettman Archives; 19.14 Thomas Kitchin/First Light; 19.15 R. Wayne Nelson; 19.17 Julie Habel/First Light; Science In Our World Martin Dohrn/Science Photo Library.

Chapter 20: Opener David Seawell/First Light; 20.1a U.S. Department of Agriculture; 20.1b Thomas Kitchin/First Light; 20.1c Paul Crum/Photo Researchers; 20.3 Pacific Forestry Centre; 20.4 M. Van Man, Vancouver Sun; 20.5 Ontario Ministry of Natural Resources; 20.8a Al Harvey; 20.8b Canada Centre For Remote Sensing, Natural Resources Canada; 20.9 Western Canada Wilderness Committee; 20.10a Al Harvey; 20.10b B.C. Ministry of Forests; 20.11a David Nunuk/First Light; 20.11b W. Dumont; 20.12a Jeff Smith/The Image Bank; 20.12b Warren Morgan/First Light; 20.12c Grant V. Faint/The Image Bank; 20.13 Pacific Foresty Centre; 20.14 Wiley file photo; 20.15a Al Harvey; 20.15b Pacific Forestry Centre; Career Betty Price; 20.19 Wiley file photo; 20.21a Brian Milne/First Light; 20.21b Anne Rippy/The Image Bank; Computer Application B.C. Ministry of Forests; 20.22a Michael Newman/Photo Edit; 20.22b Patrick Morrow/First Light; 20.23 Steve Short/First Light; 20.24 Thomas Kitchin/First Light.